1995

James F. Dows

The New Testament and Psalms

THE EDITORS

VICTOR ROLAND GOLD

THOMAS L. HOYT, JR.   SHARON H. RINGE

SUSAN BROOKS THISTLETHWAITE

BURTON H. THROCKMORTON, JR.

BARBARA A. WITHERS

The New Testament and Psalms

An Inclusive Version

New York   Oxford

OXFORD UNIVERSITY PRESS

OXFORD UNIVERSITY PRESS

Oxford   New York
Athens   Auckland   Bangkok   Bombay   Calcutta
Cape Town   Dar es Salaam   Delhi   Florence   Hong Kong
Istanbul   Karachi   Kuala Lumpur   Madras   Madrid
Melbourne   Mexico City   Nairobi   Paris
Singapore   Taipei   Tokyo   Toronto

and associated companies in
Berlin   Ibadan

9 8 7 6 5 4 3 2 1

Printed in the United States of America

Printed on recycled paper

Contents

Abbreviations

The following abbreviations are used for the books of the Bible:

Mt	Matthew	Eph	Ephesians	Heb	Hebrews
Mk	Mark	Phil	Philippians	Jas	James
Lk	Luke	Col	Colossians	1 Pet	1 Peter
Jn	John	1 Thess	1 Thessalonians	2 Pet	2 Peter
Acts	Acts of the Apostles	2 Thess	2 Thessalonians	1 Jn	1 John
Rom	Romans	1 Tim	1 Timothy	2 Jn	2 John
1 Cor	1 Corinthians	2 Tim	2 Timothy	3 Jn	3 John
2 Cor	2 Corinthians	Titus	Titus	Jude	Jude
Gal	Galatians	Philem	Philemon	Rev	Revelation
		Ps(s)	Psalm(s)		

In the notes to the Psalms the following abbreviations are used:

Ch, chs	Chapter, chapters
Cn	Correction; made where the text has suffered in transmission and the versions provide no satisfactory restoration but where the Standard Bible Committee agrees with the judgment of competent scholars as to the most probable reconstruction of the original text.
Gk	Septuagint, Greek version of the Old Testament
Heb	Hebrew of the consonantal Masoretic Text of the Old Testament
Ms(s)	Manuscript(s)
MT	The Hebrew of the pointed Masoretic Text of the Old Testament
Q Ms(s)	Manuscript(s) found at Qumran by the Dead Sea
Syr	Syriac Version of the Old Testament
Tg	Targum
Vg	Vulgate, Latin Version of the Old Testament

General Introduction

Why Another Version of the Bible?

"Why do we need so many versions of the Bible?" people often ask whenever a new one is introduced. The answer is twofold.

First, we need new versions because the languages into which the Bible is rendered (hundreds worldwide) are themselves changing. New words and expressions come into use and older expressions fall out of use, seem tired and trite, or do not convey much meaning at all. Do we ask "whither" we are going, or claim that we are going "thither"? No, we ask "where" and go "there." Christians in every culture around the world want to hear their Bible in the language of their time, speaking specifically to them, as well it should.

Second, the languages in which the Bible was originally written are the subject of scholarly study. New manuscripts are discovered that are older and more reliable, and new investigations into the meanings of words reveal that more accurate renderings are possible. Thoughtful Christians everywhere want the fruit of this scholarship reflected in the Bible versions they use.

Changes in the English Language

The English language has changed in recent years in many ways, and one important change has been in the direction of greater specificity with regard to gender. We see this in simple ways all around us. We now have "firefighters" instead of "firemen," we are asked to contribute to "the policeperson's ball," and even Star Trek now boldly goes "where *no one* has gone before." This language is more specific because it is not just men who fight fires, defend us from crime, or travel to distant planets. Replays of the moon landing now seem very dated in their reference to "one small step for man, one giant leap for mankind." Men and women have both explored space, men and women have both died in the exploration of space, and our language needs to specify this.

But it is not only with regard to gender where English has developed greater specificity. People who have disabilities are no longer referred to as "the blind" or "the lame," but as "people who are blind" or "those who are lame." They are people first and they have disabilities second. Racial sensitivity has increased, too, during this time, as there has been a greater awareness of how language and race are related (is it really only the beige crayon that is "flesh-colored"?).

This new, inclusive version of the Bible not only reflects the newest scholarly work on the most reliable manuscripts available, it also reflects and *attempts to anticipate* developments in the English language with regard to specificity about a number of issues such as gender, race, and physical disability. Bibles are widely read and therefore can serve to influence the development of important changes in language. Martin Luther's translation of the Bible into the German spoken by the common people in his country is an example of this. Luther's translation helped to develop and unify German as not only a spoken, but also a written language.

The Interpretive Character of this Version

Any effort to express in one language a text that was written in another inevitably involves some interpretation. In the case of technical writing translated from one modern language to another closely related one, the interpretation is usually minimal; but in the case of an ancient text such as the Bible, efforts to render it in a modern language involve considerable interpretation.

This introduction is intended to inform the reader about the interpretive character of the text. Attention should be paid to the kinds of adaptations in language that have been made in order to express the intent of the text in the most inclusive way possible. In addition, readers should note that since this version is an adaptation of the New Revised Standard Version Bible text, anyone wondering about changes made in a particular passage has readily available a comparison text that will show exactly what the editors have done.

Every adaptation is discussed in this introduction, along with the reasons for it. The whole volume thus serves as a teaching tool for understanding the tasks involved in rendering an ancient text into a modern idiom.

The Inclusive Character of this Version

When we render the Bible into English with attention to greater specificity with regard to gender, race, physical ability and other such concerns, we are aiming at producing a specific version of the biblical text: an inclusive version.

This version has undertaken the effort to *replace or rephrase all gender-specific language not referring to particular historical individuals, all pejorative references to race, color, or religion, and all identifications of persons by their physical disability alone, by means of paraphrase, alternative renderings, and other acceptable means of conforming the language of the work to an inclusive idea.*

The members of the editorial board came together in the Fall of 1990 to undertake a rendition of the whole New Testament and the Psalms that was inclusive with regard to gender, race, religion, or physical condition, but yet that did not violate the meaning of the gospel. The editors were committed to accelerating changes in English usage toward inclusiveness in a holistic sense. The result is another step in the continuing process of rendering Scripture in language that reflects our best understanding of the nature of God, of the humanity and divinity of Jesus Christ, and of the wholeness of human beings.

While part of the authority for this version comes from the fact that English itself is changing and this must be reflected in our renderings of the Bible text, part of the authority for this project comes from within the Scriptures themselves. Human beings are created in the image of God—both male and female. This means that every human being, a woman or a man, a boy or a girl, is equally precious to God and should be treated accordingly by every other person. Thus, the equal value of all people, both genders, every race, religion, and physical condition, is premised by these central biblical concerns.

Additional authority for this version comes from the function of the Bible itself. The Bible is the book of the community of faith, an inclusive community in which there is "no longer Jew or Greek, . . . enslaved or free, . . . male and female, for all of you are one in Christ Jesus" (Gal 3.28). This inclusive community looks to its Scriptures for guidance and authority in how to form community; the way community is formed ultimately influences how the Scriptures themselves are read. Thus, the language of Scripture reflects the community and the community is shaped by language. When we make our churches accessible to persons with disabilities, when we struggle against the pervasive racism and violence of our societies, when all persons, women, men, children, the elderly, are treated equally and nonviolently, we are forming the Body of Christ. This task of becoming Christians is aided by the clarity with which our Scripture calls us to be whole, well, and one.

This version, therefore, will be particularly useful in the context of the church's liturgy, where inclusivity is of major importance. When the church gathers for the worship of God, it should be faithful to its gospel and recognize, in the language it uses, the equality of all people before God. This version of the New Testament and Psalms will assure that all readings from those Scriptures will facilitate that end. This version also lends itself well to use in private Bible reading and devotions.

Bible Translation and Metaphor

Words can seem simple: this is a chair, this is a table. Actually, the way meaning is communicated in language is very complex. Take a commonly used expression: "Life is just a bowl of cherries." Now, if we don't think about it too much, that phrase is not especially puzzling. There seem to be ways in which life is like a bowl of cherries. If there weren't, the metaphor would convey no meaning. Yet it's hard to say exactly why life is like a bowl of cherries. There are obviously ways in which life is not like a bowl of cherries. The phrase, "Life is just a bowl of cherries," is a metaphor. A metaphor is a figure of speech used to extend meaning through the comparison of things that are dissimilar. The power of metaphor comes from the creative tension between the fact that there *is* a likeness between the metaphor and the idea it seeks to communicate, but that there also *is not* a likeness between them.

Biblical language is filled with metaphors. The famous Christian writer John Bunyan observed in *Pilgrim's Progress*, "Were not God's laws, God's gospel laws, in types, images, and metaphors?" One of the reasons "God's gospel laws" use metaphorical language, that is, use expressions that talk about "this" in order to say "that," is because the Bible is about complex issues: What is central to human life? What is God like? What is evil? How are we to be the church? Biblical language is rich and complex language.

It can be hard to recognize some biblical images as metaphors because we have become so accustomed to them. Obviously, Jesus is not a lamb, even though the New Testament refers to Jesus as "the Lamb of God" (Jn 1.29,36). The practice of the sacrifice of lambs at the Passover conveys the meaning of "likeness" to Jesus; the fact that Jesus is a human being and not an actual lamb conveys the "unlikeness."

Another metaphor to which we have become accustomed is God as Father. When we say that God is Father, we are saying that God is like a human father in the kinds of qualities good fathers have, like love and concern. But obviously, God is also not like every human father, since some do not always show love and concern, and, even more profoundly, God is not a finite being, like human fathers. So there are many ways in which God is *not like* a human father. The power of the metaphor comes from both the *likeness* and the *unlikeness*. But if we try to cast any biblical metaphor in stone and say that, for example, God is literally a father, we lose the power of communication which makes us *think*, How is God like a father? How is God much more than a father?

We have based much of this inclusive version on this insight into the nature of metaphor. When we have crafted new metaphors, such as Father-Mother, we have done so to make the reader think about what is being read and to experience the power of metaphor to make us ask, How is this the same? and, How is this different?

The New Revised Standard Version and this Inclusive Version

This new, inclusive version, an independent project not sponsored by the National Council of the Churches of Christ in the U.S.A., has used the New Revised Standard Version Bible as the starting point. The NRSV, based on the latest biblical scholarship available, has gone a long way toward greater specificity in regard to human gender. This version, however, goes beyond the NRSV to include people of every race, people of every class, people with disabilities—so that all may hear the New Testament and Psalms speaking directly to them. Also, this version, in contrast to the NRSV, uses inclusive metaphors for God. The major ways in which this rewording has been accomplished will be described below. Briefer discussions of the various books that required renderings applicable only, or mostly, to them, follow the explanation of general principles.

Masculine Pronouns

In the original languages of the biblical writings, Hebrew and Greek, all pronouns referring to God must be masculine because both languages have grammatical gender, and the words for God in both languages are masculine. In this way, Greek and Hebrew are like such modern languages as French and Spanish. In these languages, for example, the words for table—*la table* and *la mesa*—are feminine, and, as such, require feminine pronouns. Obviously, though, a table would not be referred to as "she" in English. In languages where nouns have grammatical gender, that gender does not necessarily have anything to do with biological gender, but in English, the gender of nouns and pronouns indicates only *biological* gender—that is, masculine gender refers only to males ("he," "his," "him"), feminine gender refers only to females ("she" and "her"), and everything that is not male or female is neuter. This can confuse the reader of an English translation of Scripture who may think that when God is referred to as "he," it is also said that God is a male being.

Because the church does not assume that God is a male being, or, indeed, that God has a sex, in this version God is never referred to by a masculine pronoun, or by any pronoun at all. This has been accomplished either by saying "God," or by using another expression for "God," rather than by using a pronoun, or by changing the syntax of a sentence so as to avoid using a pronoun—for example, replacing "he said" by a participle, "saying."

Also in this version, while we very frequently retain the masculine pronoun for the historical person Jesus, we have avoided using a pronoun for either the pre-existent or the post-crucifixion Jesus. If God the "Father" does not have a sex, then neither does the "Son."

"Father" for God

The metaphor "Father," used for God, occurs in every book of the New Testament except its shortest work, 3 John. It is used for God over one hundred times in the Gospel of John alone. It is, of course, a male metaphor, and leads those who read it repeatedly to think of God as a male being. It is also a highly personal metaphor, connoting family intimacy, authority, care, and protection. By repetition, however, all metaphors tend to lose their metaphorical meaning, and begin to be understood as propositions, as literal statements. This has happened in the church with the New Testament metaphor, "Father." By speaking to God, and by referring to God again and again, as "Father," one may begin to think of God, literally, as a "Father," hence also as a male being; and those for whom the word "father" has negative, rather than positive connotations, have great difficulty with that metaphor for God—do not want either to use it, or to hear it used.

Occasionally in the Bible, however, God is thought of on the analogy of a mother, and as the church does not believe that God is literally a father, and understands "Father" to be a metaphor, the metaphor "Father" is rendered in this version by a new metaphor, "Father-Mother." This new metaphor is not even understandable as a literal statement and can be understood only in a metaphorical way. One cannot be literally a "Father-Mother," so the metaphor allows the mind to oscillate between the picture of God as "Father" and the picture of God as "Mother," the mind attributing both fatherly and motherly attributes to God.

Because in a number of instances, especially in the Fourth Gospel, "Father" has lost its metaphorical force and is used occasionally as a synonym for God, in this version the Greek *pater* is often rendered "God." In three Johannine contexts, however, it is rendered "Father-Mother": when preceded by a pronominal adjective ("my," "your," etc.), when used in conjunction with "Child," and in Jesus' prayer to God.

"Lord" for God or Christ

The word "Lord" is used to designate either God or Jesus Christ in every book of the New Testament except Titus and the three Johannine letters. It is also frequently used in the Psalms either to address God or to refer to God. Because the word "Lord" is believed by some to be male-oriented, but by others to be gender neutral, similar to the way in which "God" is usually understood, this version retains "Lord" in some instances, but makes a substitution for it in others. In the case of the Psalms, "Lord" is sometimes retained as the divine name; frequently, however, "God," or an alternative word or expression referring to God, is substituted, and occasionally the syntax is altered so that the name can be dropped with no substitute needed.

The Greek word *kyrios*, translated "Lord" in English, has a number of meanings in the New Testament, other than the divine name. For example, it can mean "owner"—of a vineyard, or of a colt; and that meaning easily passed over into that of "lord" or "master," one who has control of something—of life, of one's own body, of a person who is enslaved. *Kyrios* is also used as a term of address to someone in a higher position than the speaker, and sometimes is the equivalent of "sir." In the New Testament there are also references to the *kyrios* of the harvest, or the *kyrios* of the sabbath.

In the Septuagint (the Greek version of the Hebrew Scriptures), *kyrios* is one of the two most commonly used words to speak about God—the other is *theos* (God). The early church continued to use both words for God—*kyrios* and *theos*; and the former was used also to refer to Christ. The result is that *kyrios* in the New Testament is a word used for both God and Christ, and it is sometimes difficult, if not impossible, to tell to which it refers.

In this New Testament "Lord" is retained in every instance in which the antecedent is ambiguous, being either God or Christ; it is also retained in phrases such as "the Lord Jesus" or "the Lord Jesus Christ." Where the antecedent of "Lord" is clearly God, "God" is often substituted for "Lord"; where the antecedent is the historical Jesus, "Jesus" is often substituted; and where the antecedent is clearly the risen Christ, "Christ" is often substituted. The result is that references to "Lord" in this version are considerably diminished. On occasion, also, when Jesus is being addressed, it is difficult to know whether the meaning is "Lord" or simply "Sir."

"Child" for "Son"

In most books of the New Testament Jesus is referred to, sometimes very frequently, as "Son," and "Son" also occurs in various combinations: Son of God, Son of Man, Son of the Blessed One, Son of the Most High, Son of David, and so on. When in the Gospels the historical person, Jesus, is referred to as "son," the word is retained. But when Jesus is called "Son of God" or "Son of the Blessed One," and the maleness of the historical person Jesus is not relevant, but the "Son's" intimate relation to the "Father" is being spoken about (see Mt 11.25–27), the formal equivalent "Child" is used for "Son," and gender-specific pronouns referring to the "Child" are avoided. Thus readers are enabled to identify themselves with Jesus' *humanity*.

If the fact that Jesus was a man, and not a woman, has no christological significance in the New Testament, then neither does the fact that Jesus was a *son* and not a *daughter*. If Jesus is identified as "Son," believers of both sexes become "sons" of God, but if Jesus is called "Child," believers of both sexes can understand themselves as "children of God."

The title "Son of David," used frequently in the Gospels for Jesus, is retained.

"The Human One" for "The Son of Man"

The title for Jesus, "the Son of Man," is found frequently in the Gospels and almost nowhere else in the New Testament. With a single exception only Jesus uses the term, and always, in Gospel contexts, to refer to himself. The title has a complex history, but it is not possible to show that the use of the term in Judaism has influenced its widespread use in early Christianity. The Greek term, whose literal translation is "the Son of the Man," is clearly enigmatic, but in the Gospels it takes on its meanings from the contexts in which it is used. The term may easily be misunderstood, however, as referring to a male offspring, "the son" of another male being, "the man"; hence this version uses "the Human One" as a formal equivalent to "the Son of Man." "The Human One" is clearly a title of a non-androcentric form, and is also open to the many nuances of interpretation that are possible in the original Greek term. No gender is ascribed to the term.

"Dominion" for "Kingdom"

"Kingdom of God" is a term that appears in almost every book of the New Testament, but particularly in the synoptic Gospels, and on the lips of Jesus. It was presumably the focus of Jesus' preaching. This version speaks of the "dominion" rather than the "kingdom" of God. There are two reasons for this.

1. The Greek work *basileia*, usually translated "kingdom" in English, has two different meanings—"rule" or "reign" *and* "realm"—that is, the exercise of authority ("rule") and the place where the authority is exercised ("realm"). In contemporary usage, however, "kingdom" means only realm, and not rule; but "dominion" means both the exercise of authority (one has dominion over) and the place where authority is exercised (one may enter a dominion). So "dominion" is a more accurate rendering of *basileia* than "kingdom" is.

2. In the second place "dominion" is preferable to "kingdom" because of the latter's blatantly androcentric and patriarchal character, though, of course, it is also recognized that etymologically "dominion" is a male-oriented word.

"King" as Metaphor for God

Occasionally in the New Testament, and more frequently in the Psalms, "King" is used as a metaphor for God. This version substitutes either "Ruler" or "Sovereign" for "King" when it refers to God. "King" is retained, however, in references to Jesus as "King of the Jews" or "King of Israel." Generally, when the Greek or Hebrew word has a human referent, it is rendered "ruler." In the case of specific historical kings, however, the title "king" is retained, as well as in parables about kings.

The Gender of the Devil, Satan, and Angels

The images of the devil and Satan are represented exclusively as masculine in the NRSV, and only masculine pronouns are used to refer to them. In the Greek language both words (the "devil" and "Satan") are masculine, so only masculine pronouns can be used to speak about them in the Greek New Testament. In this version, however, neither the devil nor Satan is identified by gender. For example, in Mt 4.9,10 the NRSV twice refers to the devil by masculine pronouns. In this version both pronouns are eliminated. In this version Mt 12.26 reads, "If Satan casts out Satan, Satan is divided; how then will Satan's dominion stand?" Here three masculine pronouns referring to Satan have been dropped.

We have a similar situation with the Greek word for "angel," which is also masculine in gender; and in English translations only masculine pronouns are used to refer to angels. By using nouns to replace pronouns, no gender is attributed to angels in this version.

Dark, Darken, Darkness

The words "dark," "darken" and "darkness" occur in many of the Psalms and throughout most books of the New Testament. They are often used in a straightforward way to identify qualities of color, or the absence of light. For example, in Ps 18.28, "my God lights up my darkness," and in Ps 104.20, "You make darkness, and it is night, when all the animals of the forest come creeping out," the word "darkness" is used in a neutral, non-pejorative sense, and is retained in this version.

However, very frequently in both the Psalms and the New Testament the word "darkness" is used as a metaphor, connoting such negative qualities as ignorance, dishonesty, evil, sin, and what is shady or sinister. These negative connotations of the metaphor "dark" or "darkness" become associated with dark-skinned people, who, as a result, have been called "darkies." And at the opposite end of the spectrum, "whiteness" becomes associated with purity, with "darkness" connoting what is tainted or impure.

For this reason, when "darkness" or a variation of the word appears in the New Testament or Psalms as a metaphor that carries with it the negative connotations discussed above, we have substituted another word. For example, Ps 107.10 in the NRSV reads, "Some sat in darkness and in gloom, prisoners in misery and in irons" has been altered to read, "some sat in captivity and in gloom, prisoners in misery and in irons." This rendering is allowed because vv 10–16 of the psalm describe the plight of captives who have been released from prison. The version does not in any way distort the text—in fact, it tends to clarify it—but it avoids using the word "darkness," associated with dark-skinned people, as a synonym for "gloom," "misery," and "irons." Likewise, in the New Testament, the NRSV of Eph 5.11 reads, "take no part in the unfruitful works of darkness." Here the "unfruitful works of darkness" are the opposite of "all that is good and right and true" that has been spoken of in v 9; hence this version has reworded the text so that it speaks of the "unfruitful works of the night," changing the metaphor from "darkness" to "night," without in any way altering the intent of the passage. Throughout this version the root "dark," used as a negative metaphor, is altered in several different ways.

Synoptic Gospels
Addition Of Women's Names

Women's names have been added to those of men when the origin or generation of a people is under discussion. The addition of such names is consistent with the biblical tradition where, for example, Sarah's name is added to Abraham's in dealing with Israel's progenitors (see, for instance, Isa 51.2; Heb 11.11). In the genealogy that begins the Gospel of Matthew, women's names, where they are known, have been supplied—for example, in this version Mt 1.6 is rendered, "David and Bathsheba, the wife of Uriah, were the parents of Solomon," whereas the NRSV says that "David was the father of Solomon by the wife of Uriah." This version also changes the Greek way of speaking of husbands as "begetting by their wives," which is also the way that genealogies are usually worded in English translations. The NRSV of Mt 1.3 says that "Judah [was] the father of Perez and Zerah by Tamar"; this version says that "Judah and Tamar [were] the parents of Perez and Zerah," thus putting the woman on a par with the man.

"Master" In The Gospel Of Luke

Six times in Luke Jesus is addressed by the Greek word *epistata*, five of those times by disciples (see Lk 5.5; 8.24,45; 9.33,49; 17.13). That word is always translated "Master" in the NRSV. In the Latin Vulgate the word is regularly translated by a Latin word meaning "teacher" or "instructor." Three of the passages in which the word occurs in Luke are based on passages in the Gospel of Mark where Mark's word is either *didaskale* (teacher) or *rabbi* ("my lord" or "teacher"). In this version *epistata* is regularly rendered as "Teacher."

Conditions Of People Characterizing Their Identities

Very often, especially in the Gospels and particularly in Matthew, Mark, and Luke, adjectives are used to describe people's conditions: they are "deaf," or "blind," or "lame." When in English translation those adjectives are used as nouns, they tend to characterize such people's whole identities, as though nothing else could be said about them. If one speaks of a "person who is lame," other characteristics of the person are not being ignored; but if one speaks of "the lame," the impression is given that lameness is the main characteristic, or the only significant characteristic, of such people.

In reading the Gospels in English, one finds many such nouns. For example, the NRSV of Mt 11.5 reads: "the blind receive their sight, the lame walk, the lepers are cleansed, the deaf hear, ... and the poor have good news brought to them." Such a translation divides people into categories, and assumes that to describe their conditions is to identify them completely. Of course, this is not true. And it is interesting to note that in the original Greek text of Mt 11.5 six *adjectives* are used (not nouns), each adjective requiring in English the noun "people" to be supplied. The Greek speaks of blind people, lame or crippled people, leprous people, deaf people, dead people, and poor people. Greek can *only* speak of "leprous people"—there is no Greek word corresponding to the English "leper," just as there is no Greek word corresponding to the English "demoniac" (Greek speaks of "people possessed by a demon") and there is no Greek word corresponding to the English "paralytic" (Greek speaks of "people who are lame or paralyzed").

Following the idiom of New Testament Greek, this version does not identify people by their conditions, but uses the adjectives that are found in the

Greek original. Matthew 11.5 is rendered, "those who are blind receive their sight, those who are lame walk, the people with leprosy are cleansed, those who are deaf hear, ... and those who are poor have good news brought to them."

"Slaves" Or "Enslaved People"

Just as this version speaks of "blind people" and "people with leprosy" instead of "the blind" and "lepers," following the Greek idiom, so it also refers to "enslaved people" instead of "slaves." If one uses the word "slave," one speaks not of a condition of a human being who also has other conditions, but one speaks of a human being's full identity, as though everything important had been said about a person who is identified as a "slave." But the term "enslaved person" says only that a person about whom many different things might be said is, among other things, enslaved. So this version uses the latter term.

As examples of changes made in this version, we may look at the parable of the Wicked Tenants (Mt 21.33–46) where, instead of the landowner sending "his slaves" to the tenants (NRSV of Mt 21.34), the landowner sends "those enslaved to him"; and in this version, the centurion has "a person who is enslaved to him," rather than "a slave" (Lk 7.2).

The Gospel of John and the Johannine Letters
"The Jews" In John

The term "the Jews" is used frequently in the Gospel of John, and in two different ways: (1) It is used in a straightforward, historical way to refer to the ethnic people, of whom Jesus was one. (2) It is used to connote unbelieving people or hostile groups. A good case can be made for the argument that "the Jews" in John is often a code-word for religious people (including Christians) who misunderstand the identity of the One who comes from God and is returning to God. "The Jews" are religious people who miss the revelation.

In this version when "the Jews" is used to refer to the ethnic people, it remains unchanged. When it is used to refer to unbelieving people, it is rendered "the religious authorities," or simply the "leaders" or "authorities," in order to minimize what could be perceived as a warrant for anti-Jewish bias.

Jesus As The "Son"

In the Gospel of John, preeminently, Jesus is the "Son," without any modifiers. Only twice in the synoptics (Mk 13.32; Mt 11.27=Lk 10.22), once in Paul (1 Cor 15.28), and five times in Hebrews (1.2,8; 3.6; 5.8; 7.28) does the term "the Son" occur, but it appears twenty-four times in the Johannine literature. Paul's usual expression is "his [God's] Son." Thus Jesus as *the* Son is a major theme of Johannine theology and christology, being used to designate the deeper and mysterious dimensions of Jesus' work on earth.

A "son" is a male offspring, and the historical person Jesus was, of course, a man. But that Jesus was a male person was not thought in the early church to have christological significance, or significance for salvation. It was not Jesus' maleness that was believed to save males, but Jesus' humanness that was believed to save human beings. As was said by many theologians in the early church, what was not assumed (by Jesus) was not saved. When Jesus is called "Son of God," it is not Jesus' masculinity that is being designated, but Jesus' relation to God, "the Father." As Gregory of Nazianzus wrote in the fourth century: "Father is not a name either of an essence or of an action, . . . but it is the name of the relation in which the Father stands to the Son, and the Son to the Father" (*The Third Theological Oration* 15).

If the fact that Jesus was a "son" and not a "daughter" has no theological significance, then we are justified in rendering the Greek *huios* (usually "son") as "Child" or "Child of God" instead of "Son" when it occurs in a christological sense. In this version gender-specific pronouns are not used when referring to the "Child," thus enabling all readers to identify themselves with Jesus' *humanity*. When Jesus is identified as "Son," believers, as heirs, become "sons"; but when Jesus is identified as "Child," believers become "children of God"—both women and men.

The Pauline Letters

Most of the changes in the Pauline letters are made either with respect to masculine pronouns referring to God or Christ, or with respect to Paul's many uses of the metaphors "Father," "Son," and "Lord." As we have done in the New Testament generally, so in the Pauline letters we substitute the antecedents, "God" or "Christ" for masculine pronouns, or we change the syntax and drop the pronoun. For example, in Rom 8.11 of the NRSV "he who raised Christ from the dead" becomes in this version "the one who raised Christ from the dead"; in Rom 6.10 "the death he died" becomes "the death Christ died"; in Rom 1.9 "his Son" becomes "God's Child."

With regard to the metaphors "Father," "Son," and "the Lord," we usually substitute "Father-Mother" for "Father," and the "Child" for the "Son." Where "Lord" is ambiguous, it is retained in Paul's letters, as elsewhere in the New Testament. For example, in Rom 10.13 Paul writes, "Everyone who calls on the name of the Lord shall be saved." It cannot be said with assurance that Paul is referring either to God exclusively, or to Christ exclusively. In favor of a reference to God, who cannot be excluded entirely as an antecedent, is the fact that Paul is quoting Joel 2.32, where "the Lord" is obviously a reference to God. But Paul, like other early Christian writers, often takes words from the Hebrew Scriptures and applies them to Christ, as he does in this passage, in which he goes on to talk about the one who has been proclaimed—that is, of course, Christ. So we have here a double reference, and only the word "Lord" allows that. The word "Lord" can be used as a bridge word that may refer to both God and Christ.

But if it is clear that when Paul writes "Lord" he is referring to God, we exchange "God" for "the Lord"—for example, at 1 Cor 3.20. Here Paul is quoting Ps 94.11 that refers to "the Lord," who is, of course, "God"; and in the context of 1 Cor 3.19–20 Paul is dealing with the wisdom and foolishness of *God*, so "the Lord," not only in the psalm but also in Paul's letter, is "God."

Second, if it is clear that when Paul writes "Lord" he is referring to "Christ," we exchange "Christ" for "Lord." For example, at 1 Cor 6.14, where NRSV reads, "God raised the Lord," this version reads "God raised Christ," because it is obvious that by "the Lord" Paul is referring here to Christ and not to God.

"Circumcision" And "Uncircumcision" And Related Terms

The term "circumcision" in the Bible refers both to a physical characteristic that can only apply to males and to a moral or spiritual character that can apply to both men and women. It is also used, as in the post-Pauline passage at Eph 2.11, as a near-synonym for "the Jews," just as "the uncircumcision" means "non-Jews."

Because the image is so deeply embedded in Paul's thought, we have generally left the term unchanged even when it could be taken to apply to both men and women in a spiritual sense. In several instances, however, we have changed "the uncircumcision" to "those outside the law" and "the circumcision" to "those under the law" (see Gal 2.7,8).

The Post-Pauline Letters
Colossians, Ephesians, 1 and 2 Timothy, Titus, 1 and 2 Peter, Jude

These letters contain lists of obligations and responsibilities of various members of households, particularly those pertaining to the relations of wives to their husbands and enslaved people to their masters. The early church took over from Hellenistic Judaism a scheme of ethical instruction that had come down from the popular philosophy of the ancient world. It reiterated those instructions intact, occasionally adding to them some elements derived from the Christian faith.

The instructions include exhortations to wives to be "subject" or "submissive" to their husbands, or to "accept the authority" of their husbands (Eph 5.22; Col 3.18; Titus 2.5; 1 Pet 3.1, as translated in NRSV). The same Greek verb, *hypotasso*, lies behind all the above passages, though it is translated in different ways in the NRSV. The verb means "to be subject or subordinate to," "to obey," as it is often translated; but it also occurs in the sense of voluntarily yielding oneself to another in love. That is clearly its meaning, for example, in 1 Cor 16.16 where Paul urges Christians in Corinth to "put themselves at the service of" (NRSV) people such as the members of the household of Stephanas, and of "everyone who works and toils with them." The verb that NRSV translates "put themselves at the service of" is *hypotasso*, and the same verb occurs in a similar sense also in Eph 5.21, though NRSV does not recognize that meaning in the Ephesians passage. But plainly *hypotasso* does not always mean "to be subject to," or "to obey."

It is in light of this second meaning of *hypotasso* that the same meaning is given it here in Colossians, Ephesians, Titus, and 1 Peter in passages where the verb is used to describe the proper relationship of wives to their husbands. In this version the verb is rendered "be committed to." So, for example, Col 3.18 becomes "Wives, be committed to your husbands" (see also Eph 5.22; Titus 2.5; 1 Pet 3.1,5). In order to reflect the somewhat different situation of enslaved persons, *hypotasso* in Titus 2.9 is rendered "Tell those who are enslaved to accept the authority of those who enslave them" (see also 1 Pet 2.18).

Against the obvious intention of the authors of these New Testament books, the above passages are all too frequently used to justify men's abuse of women, and they have also been used to justify the condition of slavery. It is in light of the misuse of such biblical passages, based on traditional translations, that they have been rendered here differently, but in a way allowed by the original Greek.

Colossians and Ephesians also exhort children to "obey" (NRSV) their parents (Col 3.20; Eph 6.1), and "slaves" to "obey" (NRSV) their "masters" (Col 3.22; Eph 6.5). The Greek verb that the NRSV translates "obey" is *hypakouo*, which also has the meaning of "hearing sympathetically," or "listening to," or "heeding." In this version it is rendered "heed" in the above passages: "Children, heed your parents" (Col 3.20; Eph 6.1); "You who are enslaved, heed your earthly masters" (Col 3.22; Eph 6.5). Once again, the rendition here is different from what one usually finds, but it is entirely permitted by the original Greek words.

The Letter to the Hebrews

This version incorporates the usual changes in the text of the letter to the Hebrews, but Hebrews also contains a passage in which the change that has been made deserves some discussion. In the twelfth chapter of Hebrews the author talks about the *paideia* (verb *paideuo*) of God. What is the meaning of that Greek word?

The Revised Standard Version and the New Revised Standard Version translate the word as "discipline," both the noun and the verb: "Endure trials for the sake of *discipline*. God is treating you as children; for what child is there whom a parent does not *discipline*?" (Heb 12.7, NRSV). Earlier translations spoke of "chastening." The King James of Heb 12.7 is: "If ye endure chastening, God dealeth with you as with sons; for what son is he whom the father chasteneth not?" "Chasten" is not a word that is used often these days, but "discipline" has to be very carefully defined if it is to represent accurately the intent of the author. Unfortunately, a parent's right to "discipline" children too easily becomes in our day justification for unmitigated abuse. Because this passage in Hebrews is sometimes misused to justify such abuse, this version renders the Greek word differently.

The New Revised Standard Version also translates the noun *paideia* (or the verb) differently in other contexts. For example, in Acts 7.22 it is translated "instructed"; in Acts 22.3 "educated"; in 1 Tim. 1.20 "learn"; in 2 Tim. 2.25

"correcting"; in 2 Tim. 3.16 and Titus 2.12 "training." The Greek word has a number of shades of meaning, many of them used in the NRSV, and therefore this version of Hebrews 12 renders the Greek by "guide" and "guidance."

The Revelation to John

The author of the Revelation to John employed many vivid images and strands of mythical folklore in telling his cosmic story. This version faithfully represents those images and does not disguise them by concealing gender. In Rev 12.1–6, for example, there is no attempt to obscure the gender of the cosmic woman "clothed with the sun, with the moon under her feet," nor to mask the point that she gives birth to a "son, a male child," spoken of centuries earlier in the second psalm.

As is the case with the images of the devil, Satan, and angels, found in other New Testament writings, none of them is identified in the Revelation to John with a gender. But the Revelation to John also uses other images that are largely, if not entirely, distinctive to it—the dragon, "that ancient serpent," two beasts, and the Lamb as an image for Christ. No gender is ascribed to any of these images in this version.

The Psalms

The book of the Psalms is the best-known and most-used of all of the books of the Hebrew Scriptures. It is used in public worship and private devotion. It is certainly to be included among the masterpieces of world literature. It is the only book of the Bible whose entire content is addressed to God. We have attended closely to these considerations as we have rephrased the Psalms in inclusive language.

"Lord" in the Psalms

The two most common names for God in the Hebrew Bible are *Yahweh* and *Elohim*. While they are in a way synonymous (see p. xii), *Elohim* is always translated as "God," and *Yahweh* as "Lord," in the NRSV. *Yahweh* does not properly mean Lord; "the one who causes to come into existence" or a similar phrase would be more accurate. Lord is a convention adopted by the Jews probably in order to avoid pronouncing the divine name, which they regarded as sacred. It represents the Hebrew *Adonai*, and was translated as *kyrios* in the ancient Greek version, or Septuagint (see p. xiii). This inclusive version usually uses "God" for *Yahweh* and "God" for *Elohim*.

On occasion, *Yahweh* is rendered as "Creator"—probably closer to the original meaning of the name. "Most High" is a term often used for God. Where it seemed appropriate, "Most High" has been used for *Yahweh* (as in Pss 20.7; 33.12; 56.10). Similar considerations resulted in the use of "the Holy One" (Ps 106.48).

When the psalmist speaks of God's concern for the poor and needy, and of God's coming to their rescue and delivering them with power, we have generally used "LORD," as in Pss 35.9,10; 70.1; 86.1,17; 147.6. In many modern versions, the exultant *Hallelujah!* has been translated as "Praise the LORD!" While this is certainly a correct translation, we have retained "Hallelujah!" in many instances, and have rendered it as "Praise GOD!" in other places. "Hallelujah!" is used in Psalms where it has been traditional, especially in that category of Psalms known as "*Hallel* (Praise) Psalms."

Other Terms

As noted on p. xiv, when God is referred to as "king," either "sovereign," as in Pss 5.2; 44.9, or "ruler," 24.7ff., is used. When the term "king" refers to a human ruler, we have sometimes kept "king," as in Pss 45.1,5; 72.10f.; 89.27. In other places we have used "ruler," as in Pss 21.1; 48.4. The term "kingdom" has been replaced by "dominion" as discussed above (p. xiv); see, for instance, Pss 22.28; 103.19; 145.11ff.

In current usage, the word "fear" suggests fright, even terror. Except in rare instances, this is not the intention of the phrases "to fear God" or "the fear of God." The word "fear" has been replaced by "to revere," as in Pss 22.25; 61.5; 128.1, or "reverence," as in Pss 19.9; 36.1; 111.10, or "to be in awe," as in Pss 40.3; 60.4; 119.38.

The term "right hand" used of God is, of course, a metaphor. It is not to be interpreted literally. The church does not teach that God, literally, has a back and front side, or a right and left side, or hands. In the Bible the metaphor "right hand" has at least two connotations.

It speaks of power. When Moses and the Israelites "sang this song to God": "Your right hand, O God, glorious in power—your right hand, O God, shattered the enemy" (Ex 15.1,6), the significance of the "right hand" of God is clear. The same connotation is exhibited also in Ps 63.8, "Your right hand upholds me." The psalmist is praising God for God's "power and glory" that sustain life (see v 2). Where the "right hand" of God points to the power or might of God, as often in the Psalms, "mighty" or "powerful" hand of God is frequently substituted for "right" hand.

There are also, however, passages where the "right hand" connotes proximity or nearness. When, for example, we read: "I keep God always before me; because God is at my right hand, I shall not be moved" (Ps 16.8), the point is surely that God is beside me, very near, so I am safe. Hence, in some passages, in the interest of clarification, the metaphor "at the right hand" has been rendered "beside" or "near."

When, however, "right" is not used figuratively, but literally, it is not altered.

May this volume provide direction and sustenance to those who long for justice, and who believe that the gospel, as represented in the canon, provides a way, and does not disappoint.

The Editors

The New Testament

≋ ≋ ≋ ≋ ≋ ≋ ≋ ≋ ≋ ≋ ≋ ≋ ≋ ≋

The Gospel According to Matthew

The Genealogy of Jesus the Messiah

1 An account of the genealogy[a] of Jesus the Messiah,[b] the son of David, the son of Abraham.

2 Abraham and Sarah were the parents of Isaac, and Isaac and Rebekah the parents of Jacob, and Jacob and Leah the parents of Judah and his brothers, 3 and Judah and Tamar the parents of Perez and Zerah, and Perez the father of Hezron, and Hezron the father of Aram, 4 and Aram of Aminadab, and Aminadab of Nahshon, and Nahshon of Salmon; 5 and Salmon and Rahab were the parents of Boaz, and Boaz and Ruth the parents of Obed, and Obed was the father of Jesse, 6 and Jesse was the father of King David.

And David and Bathsheba, the wife of Uriah, were the parents of Solomon, 7 and Solomon was the father of Rehoboam, and Rehoboam the father of Abijah, and Abijah of Asaph,[c] 8 and Asaph[c] of Jehoshaphat, and Jehoshaphat of Joram, and Joram of Uzziah; 9 and Uzziah was the father of Jotham, and Jotham of Ahaz, and Ahaz of Hezekiah; 10 and Hezekiah was the father of Manasseh, and Manasseh of Amos,[d] and Amos[d] of Josiah; 11 and Josiah was the father of Jechoniah and his brothers, at the time of the deportation to Babylon.

12 And after the deportation to Babylon: Jechoniah was the father of Salathiel, and Salathiel of Zerubbabel, 13 and Zerubbabel of Abiud, and Abiud of Eliakim, and Eliakim of Azor; 14 and Azor was the father of Zadok, and Zadok of Achim, and Achim of Eliud, 15 and Eliud of Eleazar, and Eleazar of Matthan, and Matthan of Jacob; 16 and Jacob was the father of Joseph the husband of Mary, of whom Jesus was born, who is called the Messiah.[e]

17 So all the generations from Abraham to David are fourteen generations;

---

a Or *birth*   b Or *Jesus Christ*   c Other ancient authorities read *Asa*
d Other ancient authorities read *Amon*   e Or *the Christ*

and from David to the deportation to Babylon, fourteen generations; and from the deportation to Babylon to the Messiah,[f] fourteen generations.

The Birth of Jesus the Messiah

18 Now the birth of Jesus the Messiah[g] took place in this way. When his mother Mary had been engaged to Joseph, but before they lived together, she was found to be with child from the Holy Spirit. [19]Her husband Joseph, being a righteous man and unwilling to expose Mary to public disgrace, planned to dismiss her quietly. [20]But just when he had resolved to do this, an angel of God appeared to him in a dream and said, "Joseph, son of David, do not be afraid to marry her, for the child conceived in her is from the Holy Spirit. [21]She will bear a child whom you will name Jesus, for that child will save the people from their sins." [22]All this took place to fulfill what had been spoken by God through the prophet:

23   "A virgin shall conceive and bear a son,
            and they shall name him Emmanuel,"

which means, "God is with us." [24]When Joseph awoke from sleep, he did as the angel of God commanded, and married her, [25]but he had no marital relations with Mary until she had borne a child;[h] and Joseph named the child Jesus.

The Visit of the Magi

2 In the time of King Herod, after Jesus was born in Bethlehem of Judea, magi[i] from the East came to Jerusalem, [2]asking, "Where is the child who has been born king of the Jews? For we observed his star at its rising,[j] and have come to pay him homage." [3]When King Herod heard this, he was frightened, and all Jerusalem with him; [4]and calling together all the chief priests and scribes of the people, Herod inquired of them where the Messiah[f] was to be born. [5]They told him, "In Bethlehem of Judea; for so it has been written by the prophet:

6   'And you, Bethlehem, in the land of Judah,
            are by no means least among the rulers of Judah;
        for from you shall come a ruler
            who is to shepherd[k] my people Israel.' "

7 Then Herod secretly called for the magi[i] and learned from them the exact time when the star had appeared. [8]Then he sent them to Bethlehem, saying, "Go and search diligently for the child; and when you have found him, bring me word so that I may also go and pay him homage." [9]When they had heard the king, they set out; and there, ahead of them, went the star that they

---

f Or *the Christ*   g Or *Jesus Christ*   h Other ancient authorities read *her firstborn child*
i Or *astrologers*   j Or *in the East*   k Or *rule*

had seen at its rising,ˡ until it stopped over the place where the child was. [10]When they saw that the star had stopped,ᵐ they were overwhelmed with joy. [11]On entering the house, they saw the child with Mary his mother; and they knelt down and paid him homage. Then, opening their treasure chests, the magi offered the child gifts of gold, frankincense, and myrrh. [12]And having been warned in a dream not to return to Herod, they left for their own country by another road.

The Escape to Egypt

13 Now after the magi had left, an angel of God appeared to Joseph in a dream and said, "Get up, take the child and his mother, and flee to Egypt, and remain there until I tell you; for Herod is about to search for the child, to destroy him." [14]Then Joseph got up, took the child and his mother by night, and went to Egypt, [15]and remained there until the death of Herod. This was to fulfill what God had spoken through the prophet, "Out of Egypt I have called my child."

The Massacre of the Infants

16 When Herod saw that he had been tricked by the magi,ⁿ he was infuriated, and he sent and killed all the children in and around Bethlehem who were two years old or under, according to the time that he had learned from the magi.ⁿ [17]Then was fulfilled what had been spoken through the prophet Jeremiah:

18
> "A voice was heard in Ramah,
> wailing and loud lamentation,
> Rachel weeping for her children;
> she refused to be consoled, because they are no
> more."

The Return from Egypt

19 When Herod died, an angel of God suddenly appeared in a dream to Joseph in Egypt and said, [20]"Get up, take the child and his mother, and go to the land of Israel, for those who were seeking the child's life are dead." [21]Then Joseph got up, took the child and his mother, and went to the land of Israel. [22]But when he heard that Archelaus was ruling over Judea in place of his father Herod, Joseph was afraid to go there. And after being warned in a dream, he went away to the district of Galilee. [23]There Joseph made his home in a town called Nazareth, so that what had been spoken through the prophets might be fulfilled, "He will be called a Nazorean."

---

l Or *in the East*   m Gk *saw the star*   n Or *astrologers*

The Proclamation of John the Baptist

3 In those days John the Baptist appeared in the wilderness of Judea,
proclaiming, 2 "Repent, for the dominion of heaven has come near."[o] 3 This
is the one of whom the prophet Isaiah spoke when he said,

> "The voice of one crying out in the wilderness:
> 'Prepare the way of the Lord,
> make the paths of the Lord straight.' "

4 Now John wore clothing of camel's hair with a leather belt around his waist,
and his food was locusts and wild honey. 5 Then the people of Jerusalem and all
Judea were going out to him, and all the region along the Jordan, 6 and they
were baptized by him in the river Jordan, confessing their sins.
7 But when John saw many Pharisees and Sadducees coming for baptism,
he said to them, "You brood of vipers! Who warned you to flee from the
wrath to come? 8 Bear fruit worthy of repentance. 9 Do not presume to say to
yourselves, 'We have Abraham and Sarah as our ancestors'; for I tell you, God
is able from these stones to raise up children to them. 10 Even now the ax is
lying at the root of the trees; every tree therefore that does not bear good fruit
is cut down and thrown into the fire.
11 "I baptize you with[p] water for repentance, but one who is more
powerful than I is coming after me, whose sandals I am not worthy to carry.
That one will baptize you with[p] the Holy Spirit and fire. 12 With winnowing
fork in hand, the one who is coming will clear the threshing floor and will
gather the wheat into the granary, but will burn the chaff with unquenchable
fire."

The Baptism of Jesus

13 Then Jesus came from Galilee to John at the Jordan, to be baptized by him.
14 John would have prevented him, saying, "I need to be baptized by you, and
do you come to me?" 15 But Jesus answered him, "Let it be so now; for it is
proper for us in this way to fulfill all righteousness." Then John consented.
16 And when Jesus had been baptized, just as he came up from the water,
suddenly the heavens were opened to him and he saw the Spirit of God
descending like a dove and alighting on him. 17 And a voice from heaven said,
"This is my Child, the Beloved,[q] with whom I am well pleased."

The Temptation of Jesus

4 Then Jesus was led up by the Spirit into the wilderness to be tempted by
the devil. 2 He fasted forty days and forty nights, and afterward he was
famished. 3 The tempter came and said to Jesus, "If you are the Child of God,

---

o Or *is at hand* p Or *in* q Or *my beloved Child*

command these stones to become loaves of bread." 4But Jesus answered, "It is written,

> 'One does not live by bread alone,
>> but by every word that comes from the mouth of
>> God.' "

5 Then the devil took Jesus to the holy city and placed him on the pinnacle of the temple, 6saying, "If you are the Child of God, throw yourself down; for it is written,

> 'God will command the angels concerning you,'
>> and 'On their hands they will bear you up,
>> so that you will not dash your foot against a stone.' "

7Jesus said to the devil, "Again it is written, 'Do not put the Sovereign your God to the test.' "

8 Again, the devil took Jesus to a very high mountain and showed him all the nations of the world and their splendor; 9and said, "All these I will give you, if you will fall down and worship me." 10Jesus replied, "Away with you, Satan! for it is written,

> 'Worship the Sovereign your God,
>> and serve only God.' "

11Then the devil left Jesus, and suddenly angels came and served him.

Jesus Begins His Ministry in Galilee

12 Now when Jesus heard that John had been arrested, he withdrew to Galilee. 13He left Nazareth and made his home in Capernaum by the sea, in the territory of Zebulun and Naphtali, 14so that what had been spoken through the prophet Isaiah might be fulfilled:

15   "Land of Zebulun, land of Naphtali,
          on the road by the sea, across the Jordan, Galilee of
            the Gentiles—
16   the people who sat without light
          have seen a great light,
        and for those who sat in the region and shadow of
            death
          light has dawned."

17From that time Jesus began to proclaim, "Repent, for the dominion of heaven has come near."ʳ

---

r Or *is at hand*

Jesus Calls the First Disciples

18 Then walking by the Sea of Galilee, Jesus saw two brothers, Simon, who is called Peter, and Andrew his brother, casting a net into the sea—for they were fishers. ¹⁹And Jesus said to them, "Follow me, and I will make you fish for people." ²⁰Immediately they left their nets and followed Jesus. ²¹As he went from there, he saw two other brothers, James son of Zebedee and his brother John, in the boat with their father Zebedee, mending their nets, and he called them. ²²Immediately they left the boat and their father, and followed Jesus.

Jesus Heals Many People

23 Jesus went throughout Galilee, teaching in their synagogues and proclaiming the good news[s] of the dominion of heaven and curing every disease and every sickness among the people. ²⁴So Jesus' fame spread throughout all Syria, and they brought to him all those who were sick, those who were afflicted with various diseases and pains, people with demons and epilepsy, people who were paralyzed, and Jesus cured them. ²⁵And great crowds followed him from Galilee, the Decapolis, Jerusalem, Judea, and from beyond the Jordan.

The Beatitudes

5 When Jesus saw the crowds, he went up the mountain; and after he sat down, the disciples came to him. ²Then Jesus began to speak, and taught them, saying:

3 "Blessed are the poor in spirit, for theirs is the dominion of heaven.

4 "Blessed are those who mourn, for they will be comforted.

5 "Blessed are the meek, for they will inherit the earth.

6 "Blessed are those who hunger and thirst for righteousness, for they will be filled.

7 "Blessed are the merciful, for they will receive mercy.

8 "Blessed are the pure in heart, for they will see God.

9 "Blessed are the peacemakers, for they will be called children of God.

10 "Blessed are those who are persecuted for righteousness' sake, for theirs is the dominion of heaven.

11 "Blessed are you when people revile you and persecute you and utter all kinds of evil against you falsely[t] on my account. ¹²Rejoice and be glad, for your reward is great in heaven, for in the same way they persecuted the prophets who were before you.

Salt and Light

13 "You are the salt of the earth; but if salt has lost its taste, how can its saltiness be restored? It is no longer good for anything, but is thrown out and trampled under foot.

---

s Gk *gospel*   t Other ancient authorities lack *falsely*

14 "You are the light of the world. A city built on a hill cannot be hid. [15]No one after lighting a lamp puts it under the bushel basket, but on the lampstand, and it gives light to all in the house. [16]In the same way, let your light shine before others, so that they may see your good works and give glory to your Father-Mother in heaven.

The Law and the Prophets

17 "Do not think that I have come to abolish the law or the prophets; I have come not to abolish but to fulfill. [18]For truly I tell you, until heaven and earth pass away, not one letter,[u] not one stroke of a letter, will pass from the law until all is accomplished. [19]Therefore, whoever breaks[v] one of the least of these commandments, and teaches others to do the same, will be called least in the dominion of heaven; but whoever does them and teaches them will be called great in the dominion of heaven. [20]For I tell you, unless your righteousness exceeds that of the scribes and Pharisees, you will never enter the dominion of heaven.

Concerning Anger

21 "You have heard that it was said to those of ancient times, 'You shall not murder'; and 'whoever murders shall be liable to judgment.' [22]But I say to you that if you are angry with a brother or sister,[w] you will be liable to judgment; and if you insult[x] a brother or sister, you will be liable to the council; and if you say, 'You fool,' you will be liable to the hell[y] of fire. [23]So when you are offering your gift at the altar, if you remember that your sister or brother has something against you, [24]leave your gift there before the altar and go; first be reconciled to your sister or brother, and then come and offer your gift. [25]Come to terms quickly with your accuser while you are on the way to court,[z] or your accuser may hand you over to the judge, and the judge to the guard, and you will be thrown into prison. [26]Truly I tell you, you will never get out until you have paid the last penny.

Concerning Adultery

27 "You have heard that it was said, 'You shall not commit adultery.' [28]But I say to you that any one of you who looks at another lustfully has already committed adultery in your heart. [29]If your right eye causes you to sin, tear it out and throw it away; it is better for you to lose one of your members than for your whole body to be thrown into hell.[y] [30]And if your right hand causes you to sin, cut it off and throw it away; it is better for you to lose one of your members than for your whole body to go into hell.[y]

---

u Gk *one iota*   v Or *annuls*   w Other ancient authorities add *without cause*
x Gk *say Raca to* (an obscure term of abuse)   y Gk *Gehenna*   z Gk lacks *to court*

Concerning Divorce

31 "It was also said, 'Whoever divorces his wife, let him give her a certificate of divorce.' 32 But I say to you that anyone who divorces his wife, except on the ground of unchastity, causes her to commit adultery; and whoever marries a divorced woman commits adultery.

Concerning Oaths

33 "Again, you have heard that it was said to those of ancient times, 'You shall not swear falsely, but carry out the vows you have made to God.' 34 But I say to you, Do not swear at all, either by heaven, for it is the throne of God, 35 or by the earth, for it is God's footstool, or by Jerusalem, for it is the city of the great King. 36 And do not swear by your head, for you cannot make one hair white or black. 37 Let your word be 'Yes, Yes' or 'No, No'; anything more than this comes from the evil one.ᵃ

Concerning Retaliation

38 "You have heard that it was said, 'An eye for an eye and a tooth for a tooth.' 39 But I say to you, Do not resist an evildoer. But if anyone strikes you on the right cheek, turn the other also; 40 and if anyone wants to sue you and take your coat, give your cloak as well; 41 and if anyone forces you to go one mile, go also the second mile. 42 Give to everyone who begs from you, and do not refuse anyone who wants to borrow from you.

Love for Enemies

43 "You have heard that it was said, 'You shall love your neighbor and hate your enemy.' 44 But I say to you, Love your enemies and pray for those who persecute you, 45 so that you may be children of your Father-Mother in heaven; for God makes the sun rise on the evil and on the good, and sends rain on the righteous and on the unrighteous. 46 For if you love those who love you, what reward do you have? Do not even the tax collectors do the same? 47 And if you greet only your sisters and brothers, what more are you doing than others? Do not even the Gentiles do the same? 48 Be perfect, therefore, as God, your heavenly Father-Mother, is perfect.

Concerning Almsgiving

6 "Beware of practicing your piety before others in order to be seen by them; for then you have no reward from God in heaven.

2 "So whenever you give alms, do not sound a trumpet before you, as the hypocrites do in the synagogues and in the streets, so that they may be praised by others. Truly I tell you, they have received their reward. 3 But when you give alms, do not let your left hand know what your right hand is doing, 4 so

---

a Or *evil*

that your alms may be done in secret; and your Father-Mother who sees in secret will reward you.[b]

Concerning Prayer

5 "And whenever you pray, do not be like the hypocrites; for they love to stand and pray in the synagogues and at the street corners, so that they may be seen by others. Truly I tell you, they have received their reward. 6 But whenever you pray, go into your room and shut the door and pray to your Father-Mother who is in secret; and your Father-Mother who sees in secret will reward you.[b]

7 "When you are praying, do not heap up empty phrases as the Gentiles do; for they think that they will be heard because of their many words. 8 Do not be like them, for your Father-Mother knows what you need before you ask.

9 "Pray then in this way:

> Our Father-Mother in heaven,
>   hallowed be your name.
10 Your dominion come.
> Your will be done,
>   on earth as it is in heaven.
11 Give us this day our daily bread.[c]
12 And forgive us our debts,
>   as we also have forgiven our debtors.
13 And do not bring us to the time of trial,[d]
>   but rescue us from the evil one.[e]

14 For if you forgive others their trespasses, your heavenly Father-Mother will also forgive you; 15 but if you do not forgive others, neither will your Father-Mother forgive your trespasses.

Concerning Fasting

16 "And whenever you fast, do not look dismal, like the hypocrites, for they disfigure their faces so as to show others that they are fasting. Truly I tell you, they have received their reward. 17 But when you fast, put oil on your head and wash your face, 18 so that your fasting may be seen not by others but by your Father-Mother who is in secret; and your Father-Mother who sees in secret will reward you.[b]

---

b Other ancient authorities add *openly*   c Or *our bread for tomorrow*
d Or *us into temptation*
e Or *from evil.* Other ancient authorities add, in some form, *For the dominion and the power and the glory are yours forever. Amen.*

Concerning Treasures

19 "Do not store up for yourselves treasures on earth, where moth and rust[f] consume and where thieves break in and steal; [20]but store up for yourselves treasures in heaven, where neither moth nor rust[f] consumes and where thieves do not break in and steal. [21]For where your treasure is, there your heart will be also.

The Healthy Eye

22 "The eye is the lamp of the body. So, if your eye is healthy, your whole body will be full of light; [23]but if your eye is unhealthy, your whole body will be deprived of light. If then the light in you is extinguished, it will be like midnight!

Serving Two Masters

24 "No one can serve two masters; for a person who is enslaved will either hate the one and love the other, or be devoted to the one and despise the other. You cannot serve God and wealth.[g]

Do Not Worry

25 "Therefore I tell you, do not worry about your life, what you will eat or what you will drink,[h] or about your body, what you will wear. Is not life more than food, and the body more than clothing? [26]Look at the birds of the air; they neither sow nor reap nor gather into barns, and yet your heavenly Father-Mother feeds them. Are you not of more value than they? [27]And can any of you by worrying add a single hour to your span of life?[i] [28]And why do you worry about clothing? Consider the lilies of the field, how they grow; they neither toil nor spin, [29]yet I tell you, even Solomon in all his glory was not clothed like one of these. [30]But if God so clothes the grass of the field, which is alive today and tomorrow is thrown into the oven, will God not much more clothe you—you of little faith? [31]Therefore do not worry, saying, 'What will we eat?' or 'What will we drink?' or 'What will we wear?' [32]For it is the Gentiles who strive for all these things; and indeed God, your heavenly Father-Mother, knows that you need all these things. [33]But strive first for the dominion of God[j] and God's[k] righteousness, and all these things will be given to you as well.

34 "So do not worry about tomorrow, for tomorrow will bring worries of its own. Today's trouble is enough for today.

---

f Gk *eating*   g Gk *mammon*   h Other ancient authorities lack *or what you will drink*
i Or *add one cubit to your height*   j Other ancient authorities lack *of God*   k Or *its*

Judging Others

7 "Do not judge, so that you may not be judged. ²For with the judgment you make you will be judged, and the measure you give will be the measure you get. ³Why do you see the speck in your neighbor's eye, but do not notice the log in your own eye? ⁴Or how can you say to your neighbor, 'Let me take the speck out of your eye,' while the log is in your own eye? ⁵You hypocrite, first take the log out of your own eye, and then you will see clearly to take the speck out of your neighbor's eye.

Profaning the Holy

6 "Do not give what is holy to dogs; and do not throw your pearls before swine, or they will trample them under foot and turn and maul you.

Ask, Search, Knock

7 "Ask, and it will be given you; search, and you will find; knock, and the door will be opened for you. ⁸For everyone who asks receives, and everyone who searches finds, and for everyone who knocks, the door will be opened. ⁹Is there anyone among you who, if your child asks for bread, will give a stone? ¹⁰Or if the child asks for a fish, will give a snake? ¹¹If you then, who are evil, know how to give good gifts to your children, how much more will your Father-Mother in heaven give good things to those who ask!

The Golden Rule

12 "In everything do to others as you would have them do to you; for this is the law and the prophets.

The Narrow Gate

13 "Enter through the narrow gate; for the gate is wide and the road is easy[1] that leads to destruction, and there are many who take it. ¹⁴For the gate is narrow and the road is hard that leads to life, and there are few who find it.

A Tree and Its Fruit

15 "Beware of false prophets, who come to you in sheep's clothing but inwardly are ravenous wolves. ¹⁶You will know them by their fruits. Are grapes gathered from thorns, or figs from thistles? ¹⁷In the same way, every good tree bears good fruit, but the bad tree bears bad fruit. ¹⁸A good tree cannot bear bad fruit, nor can a bad tree bear good fruit. ¹⁹Every tree that does not bear good fruit is cut down and thrown into the fire. ²⁰Thus you will know them by their fruits.

---

[1] Other ancient authorities read *for the road is wide and easy*

Concerning Self-Deception

21 "Not everyone who says to me, 'Lord, Lord,' will enter the dominion of heaven, but only the one who does the will of my Father-Mother in heaven. 22 On that day many will say to me, 'Lord, Lord, did we not prophesy in your name, and cast out demons in your name, and do many deeds of power in your name?' 23 Then I will declare to them, 'I never knew you; go away from me, you evildoers.'

Hearers and Doers

24 "Everyone then who hears these words of mine and acts on them will be like someone wise enough to build a house on rock. 25 The rain fell, the floods came, and the winds blew and beat on that house, but it did not fall, because it had been founded on rock. 26 And everyone who hears these words of mine and does not act on them will be like the foolish person who built a house on sand. 27 The rain fell, and the floods came, and the winds blew and beat against that house, and it fell—and great was its fall!"

28 Now when Jesus had finished saying these things, the crowds were astounded at his teaching, 29 for Jesus taught them as one having authority, and not as their scribes.

Jesus Cleanses a Person with Leprosy

8 When Jesus had come down from the mountain, great crowds followed him; 2 and there was a person with leprosy[m] who came up and knelt before him, saying, "Lord, if you choose, you can make me clean." 3 Jesus stretched out his hand and touched the person, saying, "I do choose. Be made clean!" Immediately the leprosy[m] was cleansed. 4 Then Jesus said to the person who had been cleansed, "See that you say nothing to anyone; but go, show yourself to the priest, and offer the gift that Moses commanded, as a testimony to them."

Jesus Heals a Centurion's Servant

5 When Jesus entered Capernaum, a centurion came and appealed to him 6 saying, "Lord, my servant is lying at home paralyzed, in terrible distress." 7 And Jesus responded, "I will come and cure your servant." 8 The centurion answered, "Lord, I am not worthy to have you come under my roof; but only speak the word, and my servant will be healed. 9 For I too am a man under authority, with soldiers under me; and I say to one, 'Go,' and he goes, and to another, 'Come,' and he comes, and to someone who is enslaved to me, 'Do this,' and it is done." 10 Jesus having heard this, was amazed and said to those who followed, "Truly I tell you, in no one[n] in Israel have I found such faith. 11 I tell you, many will come from east and west and will eat with Abraham and

---

m The term *leprosy* can refer to several diseases
n Other ancient authorities read *Truly I tell you, not even*

Isaac and Jacob in the dominion of heaven, 12 while the heirs of the dominion will be thrown into the outer regions, where there will be weeping and gnashing of teeth." 13 And to the centurion Jesus said, "Go; let it be done for you according to your faith." And the servant was healed in that hour.

Jesus Heals Many at Peter's House

14 When Jesus entered Peter's house, he saw Peter's mother-in-law lying in bed with a fever; 15 Jesus touched her hand, and the fever left her, and she got up and began to serve Jesus. 16 That evening they brought to him many who were possessed with demons; and he cast out the spirits with a word, and cured all who were sick. 17 This was to fulfill what had been spoken through the prophet Isaiah, "This one took our infirmities and bore our diseases."

Would-Be Followers of Jesus

18 Now when Jesus saw great crowds around him, he gave orders to go over to the other side. 19 A scribe then approached and said, "Teacher, I will follow you wherever you go." 20 And Jesus said to him, "Foxes have holes, and birds of the air have nests; but the Human One has nowhere to lie down and sleep." 21 Another of the disciples said to him, "Lord, first let me go and bury my father." 22 But Jesus replied, "Follow me, and let the dead bury their own dead."

Jesus Stills the Storm

23 And when Jesus got into the boat, the disciples followed. 24 A windstorm arose on the sea, so great that the boat was being swamped by the waves; but Jesus was asleep. 25 And the disciples went and woke him up, saying, "Lord, save us! We are perishing!" 26 And Jesus answered, "Why are you afraid, you of little faith?" Then Jesus got up and rebuked the winds and the sea; and there was a dead calm. 27 They were amazed, saying, "What sort of person is this, that even the winds and the sea obey?"

Jesus Heals Two People Possessed by Demons

28 When Jesus came to the other side, to the country of the Gadarenes,° two people possessed by demons came out of the tombs and met him. They were so fierce that no one could pass that way. 29 Suddenly they shouted, "What have you to do with us, Child of God? Have you come here to torment us before the time?" 30 Now a large herd of swine was feeding at some distance from them. 31 The demons begged Jesus, "If you cast us out, send us into the herd of swine." 32 And he said to them, "Go!" So they came out and entered the swine; and suddenly, the whole herd rushed down the steep bank into the sea and perished in the water. 33 The swineherds ran off, and on going into the town, they told the whole story about what had happened to the people who had been possessed by demons. 34 Then the whole town came out to meet Jesus; and

---

o Other ancient authorities read *Gergesenes*; others, *Gerasenes*

13

9 when they saw him, they begged him to leave their neighborhood. 1 And
after getting into a boat Jesus crossed the sea and came to his own town.

Jesus Heals a Person Who Was Paralyzed

2 And just then some people were carrying a person who was paralyzed and
lying on a bed. Then seeing their faith, Jesus said to the one who was
paralyzed, "Take heart, my child; your sins are forgiven." 3 Then some of the
scribes said to themselves, "This person is blaspheming." 4 But Jesus, perceiving
their thoughts, said, "Why do you think evil in your hearts? 5 For which is
easier, to say, 'Your sins are forgiven,' or to say, 'Stand up and walk'? 6 But so
that you may know that the Human One has authority on earth to forgive
sins"—Jesus then said to the one who was paralyzed—"Stand up, take your
bed, and go to your home." 7 And the one who had been paralyzed stood up
and went home. 8 When the crowds saw it, they were filled with awe, and they
glorified God, who had given such authority to human beings.

The Call of Matthew

9 As Jesus was walking along, he saw a man called Matthew sitting at the tax
booth, and said to him, "Follow me." And Matthew got up and followed Jesus.
10 And as Jesus sat at dinner[p] in the house, many tax collectors and
people called sinners came and were sitting[q] with Jesus and the disciples.
11 When the Pharisees saw this, they said to the disciples, "Why does your
teacher eat with tax collectors and sinners?" 12 But hearing this, Jesus said,
"Those who are well have no need of a physician, but those who are sick. 13 Go
and learn what this means, 'I desire mercy, not sacrifice.' For I have come to
call not the righteous but sinners."

The Question about Fasting

14 Then the disciples of John came to Jesus, saying, "Why do we and the
Pharisees fast often,[r] but your disciples do not fast?" 15 And Jesus responded,
"The wedding guests cannot mourn as long as the bridegroom is with them, can
they? The days will come when the bridegroom is taken away from them, and
then they will fast. 16 No one sews a piece of unshrunk cloth on an old cloak,
for the patch pulls away from the cloak, and a worse tear is made. 17 Neither is
new wine put into old wineskins; otherwise, the skins burst, and the wine is
spilled, and the skins are destroyed; but new wine is put into fresh wineskins,
and so both are preserved."

A Girl Restored to Life and a Woman Healed

18 While Jesus was saying these things to them, suddenly a leader of the
synagogue[s] came in and knelt before him, saying, "My daughter has just died;

---

p Gk *reclined* q Gk *were reclining* r Other ancient authorities lack *often*
s Gk lacks *of the synagogue*

but come and lay your hand on her, and she will live." [19]And Jesus got up and followed him, with the disciples. [20]Then suddenly a woman who had been suffering from hemorrhages for twelve years came up behind Jesus and touched the fringe of his cloak, [21]for she said to herself, "If I only touch his cloak, I will be made well." [22]Jesus turned, and seeing her, said, "Take heart, daughter; your faith has made you well." And instantly the woman was made well. [23]When Jesus came to the leader's house and saw the flute players and the crowd making a commotion, [24]he said, "Go away; for the girl is not dead but sleeping." And the people began to laugh. [25]But when the crowd had been put outside, Jesus went in and took the girl by the hand, and she got up. [26]And the report of this spread throughout the district.

Jesus Heals Two Blind People

27 As Jesus went on from there, two people who were blind followed him, crying loudly, "Have mercy on us, Son of David!" [28]When Jesus entered the house, the two came to him; and Jesus said to them, "Do you believe that I am able to do this?" They said, "Yes, Lord." [29]Then Jesus touched their eyes and said, "According to your faith let it be done to you." [30]And their eyes were opened. Then Jesus sternly ordered them, "See that no one knows of this." [31]But they went away and spread the news about Jesus throughout that district.

Jesus Heals a Person Who Was Mute

32 After they had gone away, a person who was possessed by a demon and could not speak was brought to Jesus. [33]And when the demon had been cast out, the one who had been mute spoke; and the crowds were amazed and said, "Never has anything like this been seen in Israel." [34]But the Pharisees said, "By the ruler of the demons this one casts out the demons."[t]

The Harvest Is Great, the Laborers Few

35 Then Jesus went about all the cities and villages, teaching in their synagogues, and proclaiming the good news of the dominion, and curing every disease and every sickness. [36]When Jesus saw the crowds, he had compassion for them, because they were harassed and helpless, like sheep without a shepherd. [37]Then he said to the disciples, "The harvest is plentiful, but the laborers are few; [38]therefore ask the Lord of the harvest to send out laborers into the harvest."

The Twelve Apostles

10 Then Jesus summoned his twelve disciples and gave them authority over unclean spirits, to cast them out, and to cure every disease and every sickness. [2]These are the names of the twelve apostles: first, Simon, also known as Peter, and his brother Andrew; James son of Zebedee, and his brother John;

---

t Other ancient authorities lack this verse

³Philip and Bartholomew; Thomas and Matthew the tax collector; James son of Alphaeus, and Thaddaeus;ᵘ ⁴Simon the Cananaean, and Judas Iscariot, the one who betrayed Jesus.

The Mission of the Twelve

5 These twelve Jesus sent out with the following instructions: "Go nowhere among the Gentiles, and enter no town of the Samaritans, ⁶but go rather to the lost sheep of the house of Israel. ⁷As you go, proclaim the good news, 'The dominion of heaven has come near.'ᵛ ⁸Cure those who are sick, raise those who are dead, cleanse those with leprosy,ʷ cast out demons. You received without payment; give without payment. ⁹Take no gold, or silver, or copper in your belts, ¹⁰no bag for your journey, or two tunics, or sandals, or a staff; for laborers deserve their food. ¹¹Whatever town or village you enter, find out who in it is worthy, and stay there until you leave. ¹²As you enter the house, greet it. ¹³If the house is worthy, let your peace come upon it; but if it is not worthy, let your peace return to you. ¹⁴If anyone will not welcome you or listen to your words, shake off the dust from your feet as you leave that house or town. ¹⁵Truly I tell you, it will be more tolerable for the land of Sodom and Gomorrah on the day of judgment than for that town.

Coming Persecutions

16 "See, I am sending you out like sheep into the midst of wolves; so be wise as serpents and innocent as doves. ¹⁷Beware of them, for they will hand you over to councils and flog you in their synagogues; ¹⁸and you will be dragged before governors and rulers because of me, as a testimony to them and the Gentiles. ¹⁹When they hand you over, do not worry about how you are to speak or what you are to say; for what you are to say will be given to you at that time; ²⁰for it is not you who speak, but the Spirit of God speaking through you. ²¹A brother will betray a brother to death; in the same way, a sister will betray a sister, and a parent a child, and children will rise against parents and have them put to death; ²²and you will be hated by all because of my name. But the one who endures to the end will be saved. ²³When they persecute you in one town, flee to the next; for truly I tell you, you will not have gone through all the towns of Israel before the Human One comes.

24 "A disciple is not above the teacher, nor is one who is enslaved above the master; ²⁵it is enough for the disciple to be like the teacher, and the enslaved one like the master. If they have called the householder Beelzebul, how much more will they malign those of his household!

---

u Other ancient authorities read *Lebbaeus*, or *Lebbaeus called Thaddaeus*   v Or *is at hand*
w The term *leprosy* can refer to several diseases

Whom to Fear

26 "So have no fear of them; for nothing is covered up that will not be uncovered, and nothing secret that will not become known. [27] What I say to you under cover of night, tell in the daylight; and what you hear whispered, proclaim from the housetops. [28] Do not fear those who kill the body but cannot kill the soul; rather fear the one who can destroy both soul and body in hell.[x] [29] Are not two sparrows sold for a penny? Yet not one of them will fall to the ground apart from your Father-Mother. [30] And even the hairs of your head are all counted. [31] So do not be afraid; you are of more value than many sparrows.

32 "Everyone therefore who acknowledges me before others, I also will acknowledge before my Father-Mother in heaven; [33] but whoever denies me before others, I also will deny before my Father-Mother in heaven.

Not Peace, but a Sword

34 "Do not think that I have come to bring peace to the earth; I have not come to bring peace, but a sword.

35   For I have come to set a man against his father,
        and a daughter against her mother,
        and a daughter-in-law against her mother-in-law;
36   and one's foes will be members of one's own household.

[37] Whoever loves father or mother more than me is not worthy of me; and whoever loves son or daughter more than me is not worthy of me; [38] and whoever does not take up the cross and follow me is not worthy of me. [39] Those who find their life will lose it, and those who lose their life for my sake will find it.

Rewards

40 "Whoever welcomes you welcomes me, and whoever welcomes me welcomes the one who sent me. [41] Whoever welcomes a prophet in the name of a prophet will receive a prophet's reward; and whoever welcomes a righteous person in the name of a righteous person will receive the reward of the righteous; [42] and whoever gives even a cup of cold water to one of these little ones in the name of a disciple—truly I tell you, none of these will lose their reward."

---

x Gk *Gehenna*

11 Now when Jesus had finished instructing the twelve disciples, he went on from there to teach and proclaim his message in their cities.

Messengers from John the Baptist

2 When John heard in prison what the Messiah[y] was doing, he sent word by his[z] disciples 3 and said to Jesus, "Are you the one who is to come, or are we to wait for another?" 4 Jesus answered them, "Go and tell John what you hear and see: 5 those who are blind receive their sight, those who are lame walk, the people with leprosy[a] are cleansed, those who are deaf hear, the dead are raised, and those who are poor have good news brought to them. 6 And blessed is anyone who takes no offense at me."

Jesus Praises John the Baptist

7 As they went away, Jesus began to speak to the crowds about John: "What did you go out into the wilderness to look at? A reed shaken by the wind? 8 What then did you go out to see? Someone[b] dressed in soft robes? Look, those who wear soft robes are in royal palaces. 9 What then did you go out to see? A prophet?[c] Yes, I tell you, and more than a prophet. 10 This is the one about whom it is written,

> 'See, I am sending my messenger ahead of you,
>   who will prepare your way before you.'

11 Truly I tell you, among those born of women no one has arisen greater than John the Baptist; yet the least in the dominion of heaven is greater than he. 12 From the days of John the Baptist until now the dominion of heaven has suffered violence,[d] and the violent take it by force. 13 For all the prophets and the law prophesied until John came; 14 and if you are willing to accept it, he is Elijah who is to come. 15 Let everyone pay attention!

16 "But to what will I compare this generation? It is like children sitting in the marketplaces and calling to one another,

17
> 'We played the flute for you, and you did not dance;
>   we wailed, and you did not mourn.'

18 For John came neither eating nor drinking, and they say, 'He has a demon'; 19 the Human One came eating and drinking, and they say, 'Look, a glutton and a drunkard, a friend of tax collectors and sinners!' Yet wisdom is vindicated by her deeds."[e]

---

y Or *the Christ*   z Other ancient authorities read *two of his*
a The term *leprosy* can refer to several diseases
b Or *Why then did you go out? To see someone*
c Other ancient authorities read *Why then did you go out? To see a prophet?*
d Or *has been coming violently*   e Other ancient authorities read *children*

Woes to Unrepentant Cities

20 Then Jesus began to reproach the cities in which most of his deeds of power had been done, because they did not repent. 21 "Woe to you, Chorazin! Woe to you, Bethsaida! For if the deeds of power done in you had been done in Tyre and Sidon, they would have repented long ago in sackcloth and ashes. 22 But I tell you, on the day of judgment it will be more tolerable for Tyre and Sidon than for you. 23 And you, Capernaum,

> will you be exalted to heaven?
> No, you will be brought down to Hades.

For if the deeds of power done in you had been done in Sodom, it would have remained until this day. 24 But I tell you that on the day of judgment it will be more tolerable for the land of Sodom than for you."

Jesus Thanks His Father-Mother

25 At that time Jesus said, "I thank[f] you, Father-Mother, God of heaven and earth, because you have hidden these things from the wise and the intelligent and have revealed them to infants; 26 yes, O God, for such was your gracious will.[g] 27 All things have been handed over to me by my Father-Mother; and no one knows the Child except the Father-Mother, and no one knows the Father-Mother except the Child and anyone to whom the Child chooses to reveal God.

28 "Come to me, all you that are weary and are carrying heavy burdens, and I will give you rest. 29 Take my yoke upon you, and learn from me; for I am gentle and humble in heart, and you will find rest for your souls. 30 For my yoke is easy, and my burden is light."

Plucking Grain on the Sabbath

12 At that time Jesus went through the grainfields on the sabbath; the disciples were hungry, and they began to pluck heads of grain and to eat. 2 When the Pharisees saw it, they said to Jesus, "Look, your disciples are doing what is not lawful to do on the sabbath." 3 He said to them, "Have you not read what David did when he and his companions were hungry? 4 He entered the house of God and ate the bread of the Presence, which it was not lawful for him or his companions to eat, but only for the priests. 5 Or have you not read in the law that on the sabbath the priests in the temple break the sabbath and yet are guiltless? 6 I tell you, something greater than the temple is here. 7 But if you had known what this means, 'I desire mercy and not sacrifice,' you would not have condemned the guiltless. 8 For the Human One is lord of the sabbath."

---

f Or *praise*   g Or *for so it was well-pleasing in your sight*

The Person with a Withered Hand

9 Jesus left that place and entered their synagogue; 10a person was there with a withered hand, and the Pharisees asked him, "Is it lawful to heal on the sabbath?" so that they might accuse him. 11Jesus said to them, "Suppose one of you has only one sheep and it falls into a pit on the sabbath; will you not lay hold of it and lift it out? 12How much more valuable is a human being than a sheep! So it is lawful to do good on the sabbath." 13Then Jesus said to the the one with the withered hand, "Stretch out your hand." The person stretched it out, and it was restored, as sound as the other. 14But the Pharisees went out and conspired against Jesus, how to destroy him.

God's Chosen Servant

15 Jesus, aware of this, departed. Many crowdsh followed, and Jesus healed all of them, 16and ordered them not to make him known. 17This was to fulfill what had been spoken through the prophet Isaiah:

18   "Here is my servant, whom I have chosen,
           my beloved, with whom my soul is well pleased.
        I will put my Spirit upon my servant,
           who will proclaim justice to the Gentiles.
19   My servant will not wrangle or cry aloud,
           nor be heard in the streets.
20   My servant will not break a bruised reed
           or quench a smoldering wick
        until justice is brought to victory.
21   And in the servant's name the Gentiles will hope."

Jesus and Beelzebul

22 Then they brought to Jesus a person possessed by a demon, who was blind and mute; and Jesus cured the person, so that the one who had been mute could both speak and see. 23All the crowds were amazed and said, "Can this be the Son of David?" 24But when the Pharisees heard it, they said, "It is only by Beelzebul, the ruler of the demons, that this person casts out the demons." 25Jesus knew what the Pharisees were thinking and said to them, "Every dominion divided against itself is laid waste, and no city or house divided against itself will stand. 26If Satan casts out Satan, Satan is divided; how then will Satan's dominion stand? 27If I cast out demons by Beelzebul, by whom do your own exorcistsi cast them out? Therefore they will be your judges. 28But if it is by the Spirit of God that I cast out demons, then the dominion of God has come to you. 29Or how can one enter a house whose owner is strong and plunder the property that belongs to the strong person, without first tying up

---

h Other ancient authorities lack *crowds*   i Gk *sons*

the owner? Then indeed the house can be plundered. 30 Whoever is not with me is against me, and whoever does not gather with me scatters. 31 Therefore I tell you, people will be forgiven for every sin and blasphemy, but blasphemy against the Spirit will not be forgiven. 32 Whoever speaks a word against the Human One will be forgiven, but whoever speaks against the Holy Spirit will not be forgiven, either in this age or in the age to come.

A Tree and Its Fruit

33 "Either make the tree good, and its fruit good; or make the tree bad, and its fruit bad; for the tree is known by its fruit. 34 You brood of vipers! How can you speak good things, when you are evil? For out of the abundance of the heart the mouth speaks. 35 The good person brings good things out of a good treasure, and the evil person brings evil things out of an evil treasure. 36 I tell you, on the day of judgment you will have to give an account for every careless word you utter; 37 for by your words you will be justified, and by your words you will be condemned."

The Sign of Jonah

38 Then some of the scribes and Pharisees said to Jesus, "Teacher, we wish to see a sign from you." 39 But he answered them, "An evil and adulterous generation asks for a sign, but no sign will be given to it except the sign of the prophet Jonah. 40 For just as Jonah was three days and three nights in the belly of the sea monster, so for three days and three nights the Human One will be in the heart of the earth. 41 The people of Nineveh will rise up at the judgment with this generation and condemn it, because they repented at the proclamation of Jonah, and see, something greater than Jonah is here! 42 The queen of the South will rise up at the judgment with this generation and condemn it, because she came from the ends of the earth to listen to the wisdom of Solomon, and see, something greater than Solomon is here!

The Return of the Unclean Spirit

43 "When the unclean spirit has gone out of a person, it wanders through waterless regions looking for a resting place, but it finds none. 44 Then it says, 'I will return to my house from which I came.' When it comes, it finds it empty, swept, and put in order. 45 Then it goes and brings along seven other spirits more evil than itself, and they enter and live there; and the last state of that person is worse than the first. So will it be also with this evil generation."

The True Kindred of Jesus

46 While Jesus was still speaking to the crowds, his mother and brothers were standing outside, wanting to speak to him. 47 Someone told him, "Look, your mother and your brothers are standing outside, wanting to speak to you."j

---

j Other ancient authorities lack verse 47

48 But to the one who had told him this, Jesus replied, "Who is my mother, and who are my brothers?" 49 And pointing to the disciples, Jesus said, "Here are my mother and my brothers! 50 For whoever does the will of my Father-Mother in heaven is my brother and sister and mother."

The Parable of the Sower

13 That same day Jesus went out of the house and sat beside the sea. 2 Such great crowds gathered around him that he got into a boat and sat there, while the whole crowd stood on the beach. 3 And Jesus told them many things in parables, saying: "Listen! A sower went out to sow. 4 And as the seeds were scattered, some fell on the path, and the birds came and ate them up. 5 Other seeds fell on rocky ground, where they did not have much soil, and they sprang up quickly, since they had no depth of soil. 6 But when the sun rose, they were scorched; and since they had no root, they withered away. 7 Other seeds fell among thorns, and the thorns grew up and choked them. 8 Other seeds fell on good soil and brought forth grain, some a hundredfold, some sixty, some thirty. 9 Let everyone pay attention!"

The Purpose of the Parables

10 Then the disciples came and asked Jesus, "Why do you speak to them in parables?" 11 He answered, "To you it has been given to know the secrets[k] of the dominion of heaven, but to them it has not been given. 12 For to those who have, more will be given, and they will have an abundance; but from those who have nothing, even what they have will be taken away. 13 The reason I speak to them in parables is that 'seeing they do not perceive, and hearing they do not listen, nor do they understand.' 14 With them indeed is fulfilled the prophecy of Isaiah that says:

> 'You will indeed listen, but never understand,
>   and you will indeed look, but never perceive.
> 15 For this people's heart has grown dull,
>   and their ears are hard of hearing,
>   and they have shut their eyes;
>   so that they might not look with their eyes,
>   and listen with their ears,
>   and understand with their heart and turn—
>   and I would heal them.'

16 But blessed are your eyes, for they see, and your ears, for they hear. 17 Truly I tell you, many prophets and righteous people longed to see what you see, but did not see it, and to hear what you hear, but did not hear it.

---

k Or *mysteries*

The Parable of the Sower Explained

18 "Hear then the parable of the sower. 19 When anyone hears the word of the dominion and does not understand it, the evil one comes and snatches away what is sown in the heart; this is what was sown on the path. 20 As for what was sown on rocky ground, this is the one who hears the word and immediately receives it with joy; 21 yet such a person has no root, but endures only for a while, and when trouble or persecution arises on account of the word, that person immediately falls away.[l] 22 As for what was sown among thorns, this is the one who hears the word, but the cares of the world and the lure of wealth choke the word, and it yields nothing. 23 But as for what was sown on good soil, this is the one who hears the word and understands it, who indeed bears fruit and yields, in one case a hundredfold, in another sixty, and in another thirty."

The Parable of Weeds among the Wheat

24 Jesus put before them another parable: "The dominion of heaven may be compared to someone who sowed good seed in the field; 25 but while everybody was asleep, an enemy came and sowed weeds among the wheat, and then went away. 26 So when the plants came up and bore grain, then the weeds appeared as well. 27 And the ones enslaved to the householder came and said, 'Did you not sow good seed in your field? Where, then, did these weeds come from?' 28 The householder answered, 'An enemy has done this.' They responded, 'Then do you want us to go and gather them?' 29 But the householder replied, 'No; for in gathering the weeds you would uproot the wheat along with them. 30 Let both of them grow together until the harvest; and at harvest time I will tell the reapers, Collect the weeds first and bind them in bundles to be burned, but gather the wheat into my barn.' "

The Parable of the Mustard Seed

31 Jesus put before them another parable: "The dominion of heaven is like a mustard seed that someone took and sowed in the field; 32 it is the smallest of all the seeds, but when it has grown it is the greatest of shrubs and becomes a tree, so that the birds of the air come and make nests in its branches."

The Parable of the Yeast

33 Jesus told them another parable: "The dominion of heaven is like yeast that a woman took and mixed in with[m] three measures of flour until all of it was leavened."

---

l Gk *stumbles*　　m Gk *hid in*

Jesus' Use of Parables

34 Jesus told the crowds all these things in parables; without a parable he told them nothing. 35 This was to fulfill what had been spoken through the prophet:[n]

> "I will open my mouth to speak in parables;
> I will proclaim what has been hidden from the
>   foundation of the world."[o]

Jesus Explains the Parable of the Weeds

36 Then Jesus left the crowds and went into the house. And the disciples approached, saying, "Explain to us the parable of the weeds of the field." 37 Jesus answered, "The one who sows the good seed is the Human One; 38 the field is the world, and the good seed are the children of the dominion of heaven; the weeds are the children of the evil one, 39 and the enemy who sowed them is the devil; the harvest is the end of the age, and the reapers are angels. 40 Just as the weeds are collected and burned up with fire, so will it be at the end of the age. 41 The Human One will send angels, and they will collect out of the world all causes of sin and all evildoers, 42 and throw them into the furnace of fire, where there will be weeping and gnashing of teeth. 43 Then the righteous will shine like the sun in the dominion of their God. Let everyone pay attention!

Three Parables

44 "The dominion of heaven is like treasure hidden in a field, which someone found and hid; then with joy the finder goes and sells everything and buys that field.

45 "Again, the dominion of heaven is like a merchant in search of fine pearls, who 46 finding one pearl of great value, went and sold everything and bought it.

47 "Again, the dominion of heaven is like a net that was thrown into the sea and caught fish of every kind; 48 when it was full, they drew it ashore, sat down, and put the good into baskets but threw out the bad. 49 So it will be at the end of the age. The angels will come out and separate the evil from the righteous 50 and throw them into the furnace of fire, where there will be weeping and gnashing of teeth.

Treasures New and Old

51 "Have you understood all this?" They answered, "Yes." 52 And Jesus said to them, "Therefore every scribe who has been trained for the dominion of heaven

---

n Other ancient authorities read *the prophet Isaiah*
o Other ancient authorities lack *of the world*

is like a householder who brings out of the treasury what is new and what is old." 53 When Jesus had finished these parables, he left that place.

The Rejection of Jesus at Nazareth

54 Jesus came to his hometown and began to teach the people in their synagogue, so that they were astounded and said, "Where did this man get this wisdom and these deeds of power? 55 Is not this the carpenter's son? Is not his mother called Mary? And are not his brothers James and Joseph and Simon and Judas? 56 And are not all his sisters with us? Where then did this man get all this?" 57 And they took offense at Jesus. But Jesus said to them, "Prophets are not without honor except in their own country and in their own house." 58 And he did not do many deeds of power there, because of their unbelief.

The Death of John the Baptist

14 At that time Herod the ruler[p] heard reports about Jesus; 2 and he said to his servants, "This is John the Baptist; he has been raised from the dead, and for this reason these powers are at work in him." 3 For Herod had arrested John, bound him, and put him in prison on account of Herodias, his brother Philip's wife,[q] 4 because John had been telling Herod, "It is not lawful for you to have her." 5 Though Herod wanted to put John to death, he feared the crowd, because they regarded John as a prophet. 6 But when Herod's birthday came, the daughter of Herodias danced before the company, and she pleased Herod 7 so much that he promised on oath to grant her whatever she might ask. 8 Prompted by her mother, she said, "Give me the head of John the Baptist here on a platter." 9 The king was grieved, yet out of regard for his oaths and for the guests, he commanded it to be given; 10 he sent and had John beheaded in the prison. 11 The head was brought on a platter and given to the daughter, who brought it to her mother. 12 John's disciples came and took the body and buried it; then they went and told Jesus.

Feeding the Five Thousand

13 Having heard this, Jesus withdrew from there in a boat to a deserted place by himself. But when the crowds heard it, they followed him on foot from the towns. 14 Going ashore, Jesus saw a great crowd, and had compassion for them and cured their sick. 15 When it was evening, the disciples came to Jesus and said, "This is a deserted place, and the hour is now late; send the crowds away so that they may go into the villages and buy food for themselves." 16 Jesus said to them, "They need not go away; you give them something to eat." 17 They replied, "We have nothing here but five loaves and two fish." 18 And he said, "Bring them here to me." 19 Then he ordered the crowds to sit down on the grass. Taking the five loaves and the two fish, Jesus looked up to heaven, and blessed and broke the loaves, and gave them to the disciples, and the disciples

---

p Gk *tetrarch*   q Other ancient authorities read *his brother's wife*

gave them to the crowds. 20 And all ate and were filled; and they took up what was left over of the broken pieces, twelve baskets full. 21 And those who ate were about five thousand men, besides women and children.

Jesus Walks on the Water

22 Immediately Jesus made the disciples get into the boat and go on ahead to the other side, while he dismissed the crowds. 23 And after dismissing the crowds, Jesus went up the mountain by himself to pray. When evening came, he was there alone, 24 but by this time the boat, battered by the waves, was far from the land,ʳ for the wind was against them. 25 And early in the morning he came walking toward the disciples on the sea. 26 But when they saw Jesus walking on the sea, they were terrified, saying, "It is a ghost!" And they cried out in fear. 27 But immediately Jesus spoke to them and said, "Take heart, it is I; do not be afraid."

28 Peter answered, "Lord, if it is you, command me to come to you on the water." 29 Jesus said, "Come." So Peter got out of the boat, started walking on the water, and came toward Jesus. 30 But when Peter noticed the strong wind,ˢ he became frightened, and beginning to sink, he cried out, "Lord, save me!" 31 Jesus immediately reached out and caught Peter, saying to him, "You of little faith, why did you doubt?" 32 When they got into the boat, the wind ceased. 33 And those in the boat worshiped Jesus, saying, "Truly you are the Child of God."

Jesus Heals in Gennesaret

34 When they had crossed over, they came to land at Gennesaret. 35 After the people of that place recognized Jesus, they sent word throughout the region and brought all who were sick to him, 36 and begged him that they might touch even the fringe of his cloak; and all who touched it were healed.

The Tradition of the Elders

15 Then Pharisees and scribes came to Jesus from Jerusalem and said, 2 "Why do your disciples break the tradition of the elders? For they do not wash their hands before they eat." 3 Jesus answered, "And why do you break the commandment of God for the sake of your tradition? 4 For God said,ᵗ 'Honor your father and your mother,' and, 'Whoever speaks evil of father or mother must surely die.' 5 But you say that whoever tells father or mother, 'Whatever support you might have had from me is given to God,'ᵘ then that person need not honor father or mother. 6 So, for the sake of your tradition, you make void the wordᵛ of God. 7 You hypocrites! Isaiah prophesied rightly about you when he said:

---

r Other ancient authorities read *was out on the sea*
s Other ancient authorities read *the wind*   t Other ancient authorities read *commanded, saying*
u Or *is an offering*   v Other ancient authorities read *law*; others, *commandment*

26

8   'This people honors me with their lips,
           but their hearts are far from me;
9   in vain do they worship me,
           teaching human precepts as doctrines.' "

Things That Defile

10 Then Jesus called the crowd to him and said to them, "Listen and understand: 11 it is not what goes into the mouth that defiles a person, but it is what comes out of the mouth that defiles." 12 Then the disciples approached and said to Jesus, "Do you know that the Pharisees took offense when they heard what you said?" 13 He answered, "Every plant that God, my heavenly Father-Mother, has not planted will be uprooted. 14 Let them alone; they are blind guides of people who are blind.ʷ And if one blind person guides another, both will fall into a pit." 15 But Peter said to Jesus, "Explain this parable to us." 16 Then Jesus said, "Are you also still without understanding? 17 Do you not see that whatever goes into the mouth enters the stomach and goes out into the sewer? 18 But what comes out of the mouth proceeds from the heart, and this is what defiles. 19 For out of the heart come evil intentions, murder, adultery, fornication, theft, false witness, slander. 20 These are what defile a person, but to eat with unwashed hands does not defile."

The Canaanite Woman's Faith

21 Jesus left that place and went away to the district of Tyre and Sidon. 22 Just then a Canaanite woman from that region came out and started shouting, "Have mercy on me, Lord, Son of David; my daughter is tormented by a demon." 23 But Jesus did not answer her at all. And the disciples came and urged him, saying, "Send her away, for she keeps shouting after us." 24 He answered, "I was sent only to the lost sheep of the house of Israel." 25 But she came and knelt before Jesus, saying, "Lord, help me." 26 He answered, "It is not fair to take the children's food and throw it to the dogs." 27 She said, "Yes, Lord, yet even the dogs eat the crumbs that fall from their owners' table." 28 Then Jesus answered her, "Woman, great is your faith! Let it be done for you as you wish." And her daughter was healed instantly.

Jesus Cures Many People

29 After leaving that place, Jesus passed along the Sea of Galilee, and he went up the mountain, where he sat down. 30 Great crowds came up, bringing with them those who were lame and maimed, those who were blind, those who could not speak, and many others. They put them at Jesus' feet, and he cured them, 31 so that the crowd was amazed when they saw those who had been mute speaking, those who had been maimed whole, those who had been lame

---

w Other ancient authorities lack *of people who are blind*

walking, and those who had been blind seeing. And they praised the God of Israel.

Feeding the Four Thousand

32 Then Jesus called the disciples to him and said, "I have compassion for the crowd, because they have been with me now for three days and have nothing to eat; and I do not want to send them away hungry, for they might faint on the way." 33 The disciples said to Jesus, "Where are we to get enough bread in the desert to feed so great a crowd?" 34 Jesus asked them, "How many loaves have you?" They said, "Seven, and a few small fish." 35 Then ordering the crowd to sit down on the ground, 36 Jesus took the seven loaves and the fish; and after giving thanks, Jesus broke them and gave them to the disciples, and the disciples gave them to the crowds. 37 And all of them ate and were filled; and they took up the broken pieces left over, seven baskets full. 38 Those who had eaten were four thousand men, besides women and children. 39 After sending away the crowds, Jesus got into the boat and went to the region of Magadan.[x]

The Demand for a Sign

16 The Pharisees and Sadducees came, and to test Jesus they asked him to show them a sign from heaven. 2 He answered them, "When it is evening, you say, 'It will be fair weather, for the sky is red.' 3 And in the morning, 'It will be stormy today, for the sky is red and threatening.' You know how to interpret the appearance of the sky, but you cannot interpret the signs of the times.[y] 4 An evil and adulterous generation asks for a sign, but no sign will be given to it except the sign of Jonah." Then he left them and went away.

The Yeast of the Pharisees and Sadducees

5 When the disciples reached the other side, they had forgotten to bring any bread. 6 Jesus said to them, "Watch out, and beware of the yeast of the Pharisees and Sadducees." 7 They said to one another, "It is because we have brought no bread." 8 And becoming aware of it, Jesus said, "You of little faith, why are you talking about having no bread? 9 Do you still not perceive? Do you not remember the five loaves for the five thousand, and how many baskets you gathered? 10 Or the seven loaves for the four thousand, and how many baskets you gathered? 11 How could you fail to perceive that I was not speaking about bread? Beware of the yeast of the Pharisees and Sadducees!" 12 Then they understood that Jesus had not told them to beware of the yeast of bread, but of the teaching of the Pharisees and Sadducees.

---

x Other ancient authorities read *Magdala* or *Magdalan*
y Other ancient authorities lack 2*When it is . . . of the times*

Peter's Declaration about Jesus

13 Now when Jesus came into the district of Caesarea Philippi, he asked the disciples, "Who do people say that the Human One is?" [14] And they said, "Some say John the Baptist, but others Elijah, and still others Jeremiah or one of the prophets." [15] Jesus said to them, "But who do you say that I am?" [16] Simon Peter answered, "You are the Messiah,[z] the Child of the living God." [17] And Jesus answered, "Blessed are you, Simon son of Jonah! For flesh and blood has not revealed this to you, but my Father-Mother in heaven. [18] And I tell you, you are Peter,[a] and on this rock[b] I will build my church, and the gates of Hades will not prevail against it. [19] I will give you the keys of the dominion of heaven, and whatever you bind on earth will be bound in heaven, and whatever you loose on earth will be loosed in heaven." [20] Then Jesus sternly ordered the disciples not to say to anyone, "Jesus is the Messiah."[z]

Jesus Foretells His Death and Resurrection

21 From that time on, Jesus began to show the disciples that he must go to Jerusalem and undergo great suffering at the hands of the elders and chief priests and scribes, and be killed, and on the third day be raised. [22] And Peter took Jesus aside and began to rebuke him, saying, "God forbid it, Lord! This must never happen to you." [23] But Jesus turned and said to Peter, "Get behind me, Satan! You are a stumbling block to me; for you are setting your mind not on divine things but on human things."

The Cross and Discipleship

24 Then Jesus told the disciples, "If any want to become my followers, let them deny themselves and take up their cross and follow me. [25] For those who want to save their life will lose it, and those who lose their life for my sake will find it. [26] For what will it profit them if they gain the whole world but forfeit their life? Or what will they give in return for their life?

27 "For the Human One is to come with the angels in the glory of God, and then will repay everyone for what has been done. [28] Truly I tell you, there are some standing here who will not taste death before they see the Human One coming in power and glory."

The Transfiguration

17 Six days later, Jesus took with him Peter and James and his brother John and led them up a high mountain, by themselves. [2] And Jesus was transfigured before them, with his face shining like the sun, and with clothes of dazzling white. [3] Suddenly there appeared to them Moses and Elijah, talking with Jesus. [4] Then Peter said to Jesus, "Lord, it is good for us to be here; if you

---

z Or *the Christ*   a Gk *Petros*   b Gk *petra*

wish, I^c will make three dwellings^d here, one for you, one for Moses, and one for Elijah." ⁵While Peter was still speaking, suddenly a bright cloud overshadowed them, and from the cloud a voice said, "This is my Child, the Beloved,^e with whom I am well pleased; to this one you shall listen!" ⁶When the disciples heard this, they fell to the ground and were overcome by fear. ⁷But Jesus came and touched them, saying, "Get up and do not be afraid." ⁸And when they looked up, they saw no one except Jesus, alone.

The Coming of Elijah

9 As they were coming down the mountain, Jesus ordered them, "Tell no one about the vision until after the Human One has been raised from the dead." ¹⁰And the disciples asked Jesus, "Why, then, do the scribes say that Elijah must come first?" ¹¹Jesus replied, "Elijah is indeed coming and will restore all things; ¹²but I tell you that Elijah has already come, and they did not recognize him, but they did to him whatever they pleased. So also the Human One is about to suffer at their hands." ¹³Then the disciples understood that Jesus was speaking to them about John the Baptist.

Jesus Heals a Child with Epilepsy

14 When they came to the crowd, someone came and knelt before Jesus, ¹⁵and said, "Lord, have mercy on my son, for he has epilepsy and he suffers terribly; he often falls into the fire and often into the water. ¹⁶And I brought him to your disciples, but they could not cure him." ¹⁷Jesus answered, "You faithless and perverse generation, how much longer must I be with you? How much longer must I put up with you? Bring the child here to me." ¹⁸And Jesus rebuked the demon, and the demon came out of the child, who was cured instantly. ¹⁹Then the disciples came to Jesus privately and said, "Why could we not cast it out?" ²⁰Jesus said to them, "Because of your little faith. For truly I tell you, if you have faith the size of a^f mustard seed, you will say to this mountain, 'Move from here to there,' and it will move; and nothing will be impossible for you."^g

Jesus Again Foretells His Death and Resurrection

22 As they were gathering^h in Galilee, Jesus said to them, "The Human One is going to be betrayed into human hands, ²³and will be killed by them, and will be raised on the third day." And they were greatly distressed.

---

c Other ancient authorities read *we*   d Or *tents*   e Or *my beloved Child*
f Gk *faith as a grain of*
g Other ancient authorities add verse 21, *But this kind does not come out except by prayer and fasting*   h Other ancient authorities read *living*

Jesus and the Temple Tax

24 When they reached Capernaum, the collectors of the temple tax came to Peter and said, "Does your teacher not pay the temple tax?" 25 Peter said, "Yes, he does." And when Peter came home, Jesus spoke of it first, asking, "What do you think, Simon? From whom do rulers of the earth take toll or tribute? From their children or from others?" 26 When Peter said, "From others," Jesus said to him, "Then the children are free. 27 However, so that we do not give offense to them, go to the sea and cast a hook; take the first fish that comes up; and when you open its mouth, you will find a coin; take that and give it to them for you and me."

True Greatness

18 At that time the disciples came to Jesus and asked, "Who is the greatest in the dominion of heaven?" 2 Jesus called a child, whom he put among them, 3 and said, "Truly I tell you, unless you change and become like children, you will never enter the dominion of heaven. 4 Whoever becomes humble like this child is the greatest in the dominion of heaven. 5 Whoever welcomes one such child in my name welcomes me.

Temptations to Sin

6 "If any of you put a stumbling block before one of these little ones who believe in me, it would be better for you if a great millstone were fastened around your neck and you were drowned in the depth of the sea. 7 Woe to the world because of stumbling blocks! Occasions for stumbling are bound to come, but woe to the one by whom the stumbling block comes!

8 "If your hand or your foot causes you to stumble, cut it off and throw it away; it is better for you to enter life maimed or lame than to have two hands or two feet and to be thrown into the eternal fire. 9 And if your eye causes you to stumble, tear it out and throw it away; it is better for you to enter life with one eye than to have two eyes and to be thrown into the hell[i] of fire.

The Parable of the Lost Sheep

10 "Take care that you do not despise one of these little ones; for, I tell you, in heaven their angels continually see the face of my Father-Mother in heaven.[j] 12 What do you think? If a shepherd has a hundred sheep, and one of them has gone astray, does the shepherd not leave the ninety-nine on the mountains and go in search of the one that went astray? 13 And if it is found, truly I tell you, the shepherd rejoices over it more than over the ninety-nine that never went

---

i Gk *Gehenna*
j Other ancient authorities add verse 11, *For the Human One came to save the lost*

astray. [14]So it is not the will of your[k] Father-Mother in heaven that one of these little ones should be lost.

Reproving Another Who Sins

15 "If another member of the church sins against you,[l] go and point out the fault when the two of you are alone. If the member listens to you, you have regained that one. [16]But if you are not listened to, take one or two others along with you, so that every word may be confirmed by the evidence of two or three witnesses. [17]If the member refuses to listen to them, tell it to the church; and if the offender refuses to listen even to the church, let such a one be to you as a Gentile and a tax collector. [18]Truly I tell you, whatever you bind on earth will be bound in heaven, and whatever you loose on earth will be loosed in heaven. [19]Again, truly I tell you, if two of you agree on earth about anything you ask, it will be done for you by my Father-Mother in heaven. [20]For where two or three are gathered in my name, I am there among them."

Forgiveness

21 Then Peter came and said to Jesus, "Lord, if another member of the church sins against me, how often should I forgive? As many as seven times?" [22]Jesus replied, "Not seven times, but, I tell you, seventy-seven[m] times.

The Parable of the Unforgiving Servant

23 "For this reason the dominion of heaven may be compared to a king who wished to settle accounts with those enslaved to him. [24]When the king began the reckoning, one of the enslaved persons was brought in owing more than a lifetime's wages; [25]and, as he could not pay, the king ordered him to be sold, together with his wife and children and all his possessions, and payment to be made. [26]So he fell on his knees before the king, saying, 'Have patience with me, and I will pay you everything.' [27]And out of pity for him the king released him and forgave the debt. [28]But that same person, going out, came upon another enslaved person, who owed him a few months' wages; and seizing the latter by the throat, he said, 'Pay what you owe.' [29]Then the latter fell down, pleading, 'Have patience with me, and I will pay you.' [30]But he refused, and went and threw his debtor into prison until the debt would be paid. [31]When the other enslaved people saw what had happened, they were greatly distressed, and they went and reported to the king all that had taken place. [32]Then the king summoned the one he had released and said, 'You wicked person! I forgave you all that debt because you pleaded with me. [33]Should you not have had mercy on your own debtor, as I had mercy on you?' [34]And in anger the king handed him over to be tortured until he would pay his entire debt. [35]So my heavenly

---

k Other ancient authorities read *my*   l Other ancient authorities lack *against you*
m Or *seventy times seven*

Father-Mother will also do to every one of you, if you do not forgive your brother or sister from your heart."

Teaching about Divorce

19 Having finished saying these things, Jesus left Galilee and went to the region of Judea beyond the Jordan. [2] Large crowds followed, and Jesus cured them there.

[3] Some Pharisees came to Jesus, and to test him they asked, "Is it lawful for a man to divorce his wife for any cause?" [4] Jesus answered, "Have you not read that the one who made them at the beginning 'made them male and female,' [5] and said, 'For this reason a man shall leave his father and mother and be joined to his wife, and the two shall become one flesh'? [6] So they are no longer two, but one flesh. Therefore what God has joined together, let no one separate." [7] The Pharisees said to Jesus, "Why then did Moses command us to give a certificate of dismissal and to divorce her?" [8] Jesus said to them, "It was because you were so hard-hearted that Moses allowed you to divorce your wives, but from the beginning it was not so. [9] And I say to you, whoever divorces his wife, except for unchastity, and marries another commits adultery."[n]

[10] Jesus' disciples said to him, "If such is the case of a man with his wife, it is better not to marry." [11] But he said to them, "Not everyone can accept this teaching, but only those to whom it is given. [12] For there are eunuchs who have been so from birth, and there are eunuchs who have been made eunuchs by others, and there are eunuchs who have made themselves eunuchs for the sake of the dominion of heaven. Let anyone accept this who can."

Jesus Blesses Little Children

[13] Then little children were being brought to Jesus in order that he might lay his hands on them and pray. The disciples spoke sternly to those who brought them; [14] but Jesus said, "Let the little children come to me, and do not stop them; for it is to such as these that the dominion of heaven belongs." [15] And Jesus laid his hands on them and went on his way.

A Question about Eternal Life

[16] Then someone came to Jesus and said, "Teacher, what good deed must I do to have eternal life?" [17] And Jesus answered, "Why do you ask me about what is good? There is only one who is good. If you wish to enter into life, keep the commandments." [18] The questioner said to Jesus, "Which ones?" And Jesus replied, "You shall not murder; You shall not commit adultery; You shall not steal; You shall not bear false witness; [19] Honor your father and mother; also,

---

n Other ancient authorities read *except on the ground of unchastity, causes her to commit adultery*; others add at the end of the verse *and he who marries a divorced woman commits adultery*

You shall love your neighbor as yourself." 20The young person said to Jesus, "I have kept all these;° what do I still lack?" 21Jesus answered, "If you wish to be perfect, go, sell your possessions, and give the money^p to those who are poor, and you will have treasure in heaven; then come, follow me." 22Having heard this word, the questioner went away grieving, for that person had many possessions.

23 Then Jesus said to the disciples, "Truly I tell you, it will be hard for a rich person to enter the dominion of heaven. 24Again I tell you, it is easier for a camel to go through the eye of a needle than for someone who is rich to enter the dominion of God." 25When the disciples heard this, they were greatly astounded and said, "Then who can be saved?" 26But Jesus looked at them and said, "For mortals it is impossible, but for God all things are possible."

27 Then Peter said in reply, "Look, we have left everything and followed you. What then will we have?" 28Jesus said to them, "Truly I tell you, at the renewal of all things, when the Human One is seated on the throne of glory, you who have followed me will also sit on twelve thrones, judging the twelve tribes of Israel. 29And everyone who has left houses or brothers or sisters or father or mother or children or fields, for my name's sake, will receive a hundredfold,^{q} and will inherit eternal life. 30But many who are first will be last, and the last will be first.

The Laborers in the Vineyard

20 "For the dominion of heaven is like a landowner who went out early in the morning to hire laborers for the vineyard. 2After agreeing with the laborers for the usual daily wage, the landowner sent them into the vineyard. 3Going out about nine o'clock, the landowner saw others standing idle in the marketplace, 4and said to them, 'You also go into the vineyard, and I will pay you whatever is right.' So they went. 5Going out again about noon and about three o'clock, the landowner did the same. 6And about five o'clock the landowner went out and found others standing around, and said to them, 'Why are you standing here idle all day?' 7They replied, 'Because no one has hired us.' The landowner said to them, 'You also go into the vineyard.' 8When evening came, the owner of the vineyard said to the manager, 'Call the laborers and give them their pay, beginning with the last and then going to the first.' 9When those hired about five o'clock came, each of them received the usual daily wage. 10Now when the first came, they thought they would receive more; but each of them also received the usual daily wage. 11And when they received it, they grumbled against the landowner, 12saying, 'These last worked only one hour, and you have made them equal to us who have borne the burden of the day and the scorching heat.' 13But the landowner replied to one of them, 'Friend, I am doing you no wrong; did you not agree with me for the usual

---

o Other ancient authorities add *from my youth*   p Gk lacks *the money*
q Other ancient authorities read *manifold*

daily wage? ¹⁴Take what belongs to you and go; I choose to give to this last the same as I give to you. ¹⁵Am I not allowed to do what I choose with what belongs to me? Or are you envious because I am generous?' ¹⁶So the last will be first, and the first will be last."ʳ

A Third Time Jesus Foretells His Death and Resurrection

17 While Jesus was going up to Jerusalem, he took the twelve disciples aside by themselves, and said to them on the way, ¹⁸"See, we are going up to Jerusalem, and the Human One will be handed over to the chief priests and scribes, and will be condemned to death by them, ¹⁹and handed over to the Gentiles to be mocked and flogged and crucified, and on the third day will be raised."

The Request of the Mother of James and John

20 Then the mother of the sons of Zebedee came to Jesus with her sons, and kneeling before him, she asked a favor. ²¹And Jesus said to her, "What do you want?" She replied, "Declare that these two sons of mine will sit, one at your right hand and one at your left, in your dominion." ²²But Jesus answered, "You do not know what you are asking. Are you able to drink the cup that I am about to drink?"ˢ They said to Jesus, "We are able." ²³He said to them, "You will indeed drink my cup, but to sit at my right hand and at my left, this is not mine to grant, but it is for those for whom it has been prepared by God."

24 When the ten heard it, they were angry with the two brothers. ²⁵But Jesus called them to him and said, "You know that the rulers of the Gentiles lord it over them, and their great ones are tyrants over them. ²⁶It will not be so among you; but whoever wishes to be great among you must minister to you, ²⁷and whoever wishes to be first among you must be your servant; ²⁸just as the Human One came not to be served but to serve, and to give up life as a ransom for many."

Jesus Heals Two People Who Were Blind

29 As they were leaving Jericho, a large crowd followed. ³⁰Two people who were blind were sitting by the roadside. When they heard that Jesus was passing by, they shouted, "Haveᵗ mercy on us, Son of David!" ³¹The crowd sternly ordered them to be quiet; but they shouted even more loudly, "Have mercy on us, Lord, Son of David!" ³²Jesus stood still and called them, saying, "What do you want me to do for you?" ³³They answered, "Lord, let our eyes be opened." ³⁴Moved with compassion, Jesus touched their eyes. Immediately they regained their sight and followed Jesus.

---

r Other ancient authorities add *for many are called but few are chosen*
s Other ancient authorities add *or to be baptized with the baptism that I am baptized with?*
t Other ancient authorities prefix *Lord*

Jesus' Triumphal Entry into Jerusalem

21 When they had come near Jerusalem and had reached Bethphage, at the Mount of Olives, Jesus sent two disciples, ²saying to them, "Go into the village ahead of you, and immediately you will find a donkey tied, and a colt with it; untie them and bring them to me. ³If anyone says anything to you, just say this, 'The Lord needs them and will send them back immediately.'ᵘ" ⁴This took place to fulfill what had been spoken through the prophet, saying,

> 5   "Tell this to Zion,
>   Your king is coming to you,
>   humble, and mounted on a donkey,
>   and on a colt, the foal of a donkey."

⁶The disciples went and did as Jesus had directed them; ⁷they brought the donkey and the colt, and put their cloaks on them, and Jesus sat on them. ⁸A very large crowdᵛ spread their cloaks on the road, and others cut branches from the trees and spread them on the road. ⁹The crowds that went ahead of Jesus and that followed were shouting,

> "Hosanna to the Son of David!
> Blessed is the one who comes in the name of God!
> Hosanna in the highest heaven!"

¹⁰When Jesus entered Jerusalem, the whole city was in turmoil, asking, "Who is this?" ¹¹The crowds were saying, "This is the prophet Jesus from Nazareth in Galilee."

Jesus Protests in the Temple

12 Then Jesus entered the templeʷ and drove out all who were selling and buying in the temple, and he overturned the tables of the money changers and the seats of those who sold doves. ¹³Jesus said to them, "It is written,

> 'My house shall be called a house of prayer';
>   but you are making it a den of robbers."

14 Those who were blind and lame came to Jesus in the temple and were healed. ¹⁵But when the chief priests and the scribes saw the amazing things that he did, and heardˣ the children crying out in the temple, "Hosanna to the Son of David," they became angry ¹⁶and said to Jesus, "Do you hear what these are saying?" Jesus said to them, "Yes; have you never read,

> 'Out of the mouths of infants and nursing babies
>   you have prepared praise for yourself'?"

---

u Or 'The Lord needs them. And the Lord will send them immediately.'
v Or Most of the crowd   w Other ancient authorities add of God   x Gk lacks heard

17 Jesus left them, went out of the city to Bethany, and spent the night there.

Jesus Curses the Fig Tree

18 In the morning, when Jesus returned to the city, he was hungry. 19 And seeing a fig tree by the side of the road, he went to it and found nothing at all on it but leaves. Then Jesus said to it, "May no fruit ever come from you again!" And the fig tree withered at once. 20 When the disciples saw it, they were amazed, saying, "How did the fig tree wither at once?" 21 Jesus answered them, "Truly I tell you, if you have faith and do not doubt, not only will you do what has been done to the fig tree, but even if you say to this mountain, 'Be lifted up and thrown into the sea,' it will be done. 22 Whatever you ask for in prayer with faith, you will receive."

Jesus' Authority Is Questioned

23 When Jesus entered the temple, the chief priests and the elders of the people came up as he was teaching, and said, "By what authority are you doing these things, and who gave you this authority?" 24 Jesus said to them, "I will also ask you one question; if you tell me the answer, then I will also tell you by what authority I do these things. 25 Did the baptism of John come from heaven, or was it of human origin?" And they argued with one another, "If we say, 'From heaven,' he will say to us, 'Why then did you not believe him?' 26 But if we say, 'Of human origin,' we are afraid of the crowd; for all regard John as a prophet." 27 So they answered Jesus, "We do not know." And he said to them, "Neither will I tell you by what authority I am doing these things.

The Parable of the Two Sons

28 "What do you think? A man had two sons; he went to the first and said, 'Son, go and work in the vineyard today.' 29 He answered, 'I will not'; but later he changed his mind and went. 30 The father went to the second and said the same; and he answered, 'I go, sir'; but he did not go. 31 Which of the two did the will of his father?" They said, "The first." Jesus said to them, "Truly I tell you, the tax collectors and the prostitutes are going into the dominion of God ahead of you. 32 For John came to you in the way of righteousness and you did not believe him, but the tax collectors and the prostitutes believed him; and even after you saw it, you did not change your minds and believe him.

The Parable of the Wicked Tenants

33 "Listen to another parable. There was a landowner who planted a vineyard, put a fence around it, dug a winepress in it, and built a watchtower. Then the owner leased it to tenants and went to another country. 34 When the harvest time had come, the owner sent to the tenants some of those enslaved to him in order to collect the produce. 35 But the tenants seized them and beat one, killed another, and stoned another. 36 Again the landowner sent others, more than the first; and they treated them in the same way. 37 Finally the landowner sent his

child to them, saying, 'They will respect my child.' 38 But when the tenants saw the owner's child, they said to themselves, 'This is the heir; come, let us kill this one too and get the inheritance.' 39 So they seized and threw the heir out of the vineyard, and then killed the heir. 40 Now when the owner of the vineyard comes, what will be done to those tenants?" 41 Those who heard the parable said, "The owner will put those wretches to a miserable death, and lease the vineyard to other tenants who will give him the produce at the harvest time."

42 Jesus said to them, "Have you never read in the scriptures:

> 'The stone that the builders rejected
>   has become the cornerstone;[y]
> this was God's doing,
>   and it is amazing in our eyes'?

43 Therefore I tell you, the dominion of God will be taken away from you and given to a people that produces the fruits of the dominion.[z] 44 The one who falls on this stone will be broken to pieces; and it will crush anyone on whom it falls."[a]

45 When the chief priests and the Pharisees heard Jesus' parables, they realized that he was speaking about them. 46 They wanted to arrest him, but they feared the crowds, because they regarded Jesus as a prophet.

The Parable of the Wedding Banquet

22 Once more Jesus spoke to them in parables, saying: 2 "The dominion of heaven may be compared to a king who gave a wedding banquet for his son. 3 He sent those enslaved to him to call those who had been invited to the wedding banquet, but they would not come. 4 Again he sent others, saying, 'Tell those who have been invited: Look, I have prepared my dinner, my oxen and my fat calves have been slaughtered, and everything is ready; come to the wedding banquet.' 5 But they made light of it and went away, one to farm, another to business, 6 while the rest seized those he had sent, mistreated them, and killed them. 7 The king was enraged. He sent his troops, destroyed those murderers, and burned their city. 8 Then he said to those who were enslaved, 'The wedding is ready, but those invited were not worthy. 9 Go therefore into the main streets, and invite everyone you find to the wedding banquet.' 10 They went out into the streets and gathered all whom they found, both good and bad; so the wedding hall was filled with guests.

11 "But when the king came in to see the guests, he noticed someone there who was not wearing a wedding robe, 12 and the king said, 'Friend, how did you get in here without a wedding robe?' And the guest was speechless. 13 Then the king said to the attendants, 'Let the guest be bound hand and foot, and thrown into the outer regions, where there will be weeping and gnashing of teeth.' 14 For many are called, but few are chosen."

---

y Or *keystone*   z Gk *the fruits of it*   a Other ancient authorities lack verse 44

The Question about Paying Taxes

15 Then the Pharisees went and plotted to entrap Jesus in what he said. ¹⁶So they sent their disciples to him, along with the Herodians, saying, "Teacher, we know that you are sincere, and teach the way of God in accordance with truth, and show deference to no one; for you do not regard people with partiality. ¹⁷Tell us, then, what you think. Is it lawful to pay taxes to the emperor, or not?" ¹⁸But Jesus, aware of their malice, said, "Why are you putting me to the test, you hypocrites? ¹⁹Show me the coin used for the tax." And they brought him a coin. ²⁰Then Jesus said to them, "Whose head is this, and whose title?" ²¹They answered, "The emperor's." Then Jesus said to them, "Give therefore to the emperor the things that are the emperor's, and to God the things that are God's." ²²When they heard this, they were amazed; and they left Jesus and went away.

The Question about the Resurrection

23 The same day some Sadducees came to Jesus, saying there is no resurrection;ᵇ and they asked him a question, saying, ²⁴"Teacher, Moses said, 'If a man dies childless, his brother shall marry the widow, and raise up children for his brother.' ²⁵Now there were seven brothers among us; the first married, and died childless, leaving the widow to his brother. ²⁶The second did the same, so also the third, down to the seventh. ²⁷Last of all, the woman herself died. ²⁸In the resurrection, then, whose wife of the seven will she be? For all of them had married her."

29 Jesus answered them, "You are wrong, because you know neither the scriptures nor the power of God. ³⁰For in the resurrection they neither marry nor are given in marriage, but are like angelsᶜ in heaven. ³¹And as for the resurrection of the dead, have you not read what was said to you by God, ³²'I am the God of Abraham, the God of Isaac, and the God of Jacob'? God is God not of the dead, but of the living." ³³And when the crowd heard it, they were astounded at his teaching.

The Greatest Commandment

34 When the Pharisees heard that Jesus had silenced the Sadducees, they gathered together, ³⁵and one of them, a lawyer, asked Jesus a question as a test. ³⁶"Teacher, which commandment in the law is the greatest?" ³⁷Jesus said to him, " 'You shall love the Sovereign your God with all your heart, and with all your soul, and with all your mind.' ³⁸This is the greatest and first commandment. ³⁹And a second is like it: 'You shall love your neighbor as yourself.' ⁴⁰On these two commandments hang all the law and the prophets."

---

b Other ancient authorities read *who say that there is no resurrection*
c Other ancient authorities add *of God*

A Question about the Messiah

41 Now while the Pharisees were gathered together, Jesus asked them this question: 42"What do you think of the Messiah?d Whose descendant is the Messiah?" They said to him, "David's." 43Jesus said to them, "How is it then that David by the Spirite calls the Messiah Lord, saying,

44   'God said to my Lord,
             "Sit at my side,
                 until I put your enemies under your feet" '?

45If David thus calls the Messiah Lord, how can the Messiah be David's descendant?" 46No one was able to give Jesus an answer, nor from that day did anyone dare to ask any more questions.

Jesus Denounces Scribes and Pharisees

23 Then Jesus said to the crowds and to the disciples, 2"The scribes and the Pharisees sit on Moses' seat; 3therefore, do whatever they teach you and follow it; but do not do as they do, for they do not practice what they teach. 4They tie up heavy burdens, hard to bear,f and lay them on the shoulders of others; but they themselves are unwilling to lift a finger to move them. 5They do all their deeds to be seen by others; for they make their phylacteries broad and their fringes long. 6They love to have the place of honor at banquets and the best seats in the synagogues, 7and to be greeted with respect in the marketplaces, and to have people call them rabbi. 8But you are not to be called rabbi, for you have one teacher, and you are all students. 9And call no one on earth by the title 'father,' for you have only one who deserves such a title, your Father-Mother—the one in heaven. 10Nor are you to be called instructors, for you have one instructor, the Messiah.g 11The greatest among you will be your servant. 12All who exalt themselves will be humbled, and all who humble themselves will be exalted.

13 "But woe to you, scribes and Pharisees, hypocrites! For you lock people out of the dominion of heaven. For you do not go in yourselves, and when others are going in, you stop them.h 15Woe to you, scribes and Pharisees, hypocrites! For you cross sea and land to make a single convert, and you make the new convert twice as much a child of helli as yourselves.

16 "Woe to you, stupid guides, who say, 'Whoever swears by the sanctuary is bound by nothing, but whoever swears by the gold of the sanctuary is bound by the oath.' 17You fools! For which is greater, the gold or the

---

d Or Christ   e Gk in spirit   f Other ancient authorities lack hard to bear
g Or the Christ
h Other authorities add here (or after verse 12) verse 14, Woe to you, scribes and Pharisees, hypocrites! For you devour widows' houses and for the sake of appearance you make long prayers; therefore you will receive the greater condemnation   i Gk Gehenna

sanctuary that has made the gold sacred? 18 And you say, 'Whoever swears by the altar is bound by nothing, but whoever swears by the gift that is on the altar is bound by the oath.' 19 How stupid you are! For which is greater, the gift or the altar that makes the gift sacred? 20 So whoever swears by the altar, swears by it and by everything on it; 21 and whoever swears by the sanctuary, swears by it and by the one who dwells in it; 22 and whoever swears by heaven, swears by the throne of God and by the one who is seated upon it.

23 "Woe to you, scribes and Pharisees, hypocrites! For you tithe mint, dill, and cummin, and have neglected the weightier matters of the law: justice and mercy and faith. It is these you ought to have practiced without neglecting the others. 24 You stupid guides! You strain out a gnat but swallow a camel!

25 "Woe to you, scribes and Pharisees, hypocrites! For you clean the outside of the cup and of the plate, but inside they are full of greed and self-indulgence. 26 You stupid Pharisee! First clean the inside of the cup,[j] so that the outside also may become clean.

27 "Woe to you, scribes and Pharisees, hypocrites! For you are like whitewashed tombs, which on the outside look beautiful, but inside they are full of the bones of the dead and of all kinds of filth. 28 So you also on the outside look righteous to others, but inside you are full of hypocrisy and lawlessness.

29 "Woe to you, scribes and Pharisees, hypocrites! For you build the tombs of the prophets and decorate the graves of the righteous, 30 and you say, 'If we had lived in the days of our ancestors, we would not have taken part with them in shedding the blood of the prophets.' 31 Thus you testify against yourselves that you are descendants of those who murdered the prophets. 32 Fill up, then, the measure of your ancestors. 33 You snakes, you brood of vipers! How can you escape being sentenced to hell?[k] 34 Therefore I send you prophets, sages, and scribes, some of whom you will kill and crucify, and some you will flog in your synagogues and pursue from town to town, 35 so that upon you may come all the righteous blood shed on earth, from the blood of righteous Abel to the blood of Zechariah son of Barachiah, whom you murdered between the sanctuary and the altar. 36 Truly I tell you, all this will come upon this generation.

The Lament over Jerusalem

37 "Jerusalem, Jerusalem, the city that kills the prophets and stones those who are sent to it! How often have I desired to gather your children together as a hen gathers her brood under her wings, and you were not willing! 38 See, your house is left to you, desolate.[l] 39 For I tell you, you will not see me again until you say, 'Blessed is the one who comes in the name of the Lord.' "

---

j Other ancient authorities add *and of the plate*   k Gk *Gehenna*
l Other ancient authorities lack *desolate*

The Destruction of the Temple Foretold

24 As Jesus came out of the temple and was going away, the disciples came to point out to him the buildings of the temple. [2] Then he asked them, "You see all these, do you not? Truly I tell you, not one stone will be left here upon another; all will be thrown down."

3 When Jesus was sitting on the Mount of Olives, the disciples came to him privately, saying, "Tell us, when will this be, and what will be the sign of your coming and of the end of the age?" [4] Jesus answered them, "Beware that no one leads you astray. [5] For many will come in my name, saying, 'I am the Messiah!'[m] and they will lead many astray. [6] And you will hear of wars and rumors of wars; see that you are not alarmed; for this must take place, but the end is not yet. [7] For nation will rise against nation, and kingdom against kingdom, and there will be famines[n] and earthquakes in various places: [8] all this is but the beginning of the birth pangs.

Persecution Foretold

9 "Then they will hand you over to be tortured and will put you to death, and you will be hated by all nations because of my name. [10] Then many will fall away,[o] and they will betray one another and hate one another. [11] And many false prophets will arise and lead many astray. [12] And because of the increase of lawlessness, the love of many will grow cold. [13] But the one who endures to the end will be saved. [14] And this good news[p] of the dominion will be proclaimed throughout the world, as a testimony to all the nations; and then the end will come.

The Desolating Sacrilege

15 "So when you see the desolating sacrilege standing in the holy place, as was spoken of by the prophet Daniel (let the reader understand), [16] then those in Judea must flee to the mountains; [17] the one on the housetop must not go down to take what is in the house; [18] the one in the field must not turn back to get a coat. [19] Woe to the women who are pregnant and to those who are nursing infants in those days! [20] Pray that your flight may not be in winter or on a sabbath. [21] For at that time there will be great suffering, such as has not been from the beginning of the world until now, no, and never will be. [22] And if those days had not been cut short, no one would be saved; but for the sake of the elect those days will be cut short. [23] Then if anyone says to you, 'Look! Here is the Messiah!'[m] or 'There is the Messiah!'—do not believe it. [24] For false messiahs[q] and false prophets will appear and produce great signs and omens, to lead astray, if possible, even the elect. [25] Take note, I have told you beforehand. [26] So, if they say to you, 'Look! The Messiah[m] is in the wilderness,' do not go

---

m Or *the Christ*　　n Other ancient authorities add *and pestilences*　　o Or *stumble*
p Or *gospel*　　q Or *christs*

out. If they say, 'Look! The Messiah[r] is in the inner rooms,' do not believe it. [27] For as the lightning comes from the east and flashes as far as the west, so will be the coming of the Human One. [28] Wherever the corpse is, there the vultures will gather.

The Coming of the Human One

29 "Immediately after the suffering of those days

> the sun will be extinguished,
> and the moon will not give its light;
> the stars will fall from heaven,
> and the powers of the heavens will be shaken.

[30] Then the sign of the Human One will appear in heaven, and then all the tribes of the earth will mourn, and they will see 'the Human One coming on the clouds of heaven' with power and great glory. [31] And that one will send out angels with a loud trumpet call, and they will gather the elect from the four winds, from one end of heaven to the other.

The Lesson of the Fig Tree

32 "From the fig tree learn its lesson: as soon as its branch becomes tender and puts forth its leaves, you know that summer is near. [33] So also, when you see all these things, you know that the Human One[s] is near, at the very gates. [34] Truly I tell you, this generation will not pass away until all these things have taken place. [35] Heaven and earth will pass away, but my words will not pass away.

The Necessity for Watchfulness

36 "But about that day and hour no one knows, neither the angels of heaven, nor the Child,[t] but the Father-Mother only. [37] For as the days of Noah were, so will be the coming of the Human One. [38] For as in those days before the flood they were eating and drinking, marrying and giving in marriage, until the day Noah entered the ark, [39] and they knew nothing until the flood came and swept them all away, so too will be the coming of the Human One. [40] Then two will be in the field; one will be taken and one will be left. [41] Two women will be grinding meal together; one will be taken and one will be left. [42] Keep awake therefore, for you do not know on what day[u] your Lord is coming. [43] But understand this: if the owner of the house had known in what part of the night the thief was coming, the owner would have stayed awake and would not have let the house be broken into. [44] Therefore you also must be ready, for the Human One is coming at an unexpected hour.

---

r Or *the Christ*   s Or *it*   t Other ancient authorities lack *nor the Child*
u Other ancient authorities read *at what hour*

Faithfulness and Watchfulness

45 "Who then is the faithful and wise enslaved person, whom the master has put in charge of the household, to give the others[v] their allowance of food at the proper time? [46]Blessed is that person whom the master will find at work when he arrives. [47]Truly I tell you, he will put that person in charge of all his possessions. [48]But if that wicked person thinks, 'My master is delayed,' [49]and begins to beat other workers, and eats and drinks with drunkards, [50]the master of that person will come on an unexpected day and at an unknown hour, [51]and will cut the wicked person in pieces[w] and put that one with the hypocrites, where there will be weeping and gnashing of teeth.

The Parable of the Ten Bridesmaids

25 "Then the dominion of heaven will be like this. Ten bridesmaids[x] took their lamps and went to meet the bridegroom.[y] [2]Five of them were foolish, and five were wise. [3]When the foolish took their lamps, they took no oil with them; [4]but the wise took flasks of oil with their lamps. [5]As the bridegroom was delayed, all of them became drowsy and slept. [6]But at midnight there was a shout, 'Look! Here is the bridegroom! Come out to meet him.' [7]Then all those bridesmaids[x] got up and trimmed their lamps. [8]The foolish said to the wise, 'Give us some of your oil, for our lamps are going out.' [9]But the wise replied, 'No! there will not be enough for you and for us; you had better go to the dealers and buy some for yourselves.' [10]And while they went to buy it, the bridegroom came, and those who were ready went with him into the wedding banquet; and the door was shut. [11]Later the other bridesmaids[x] came also, saying, 'Lord, lord, open to us.' [12]But the bridegroom replied, 'Truly I tell you, I do not know you.' [13]Keep awake therefore, for you know neither the day nor the hour.[z]

The Parable of the "Talents"

14 "For it is as if someone, going on a journey, summoned servants to him and entrusted his property to them, [15]giving to one servant five talents,[a] to another two, to another one, to each according to their ability; and then went away. [16]The one who had received the five talents went off at once and traded with them, and made five more talents. [17]In the same way, the one who had the two talents made two more talents. [18]But the one who had received the one talent went off and dug a hole in the ground and hid the money. [19]After a long time the master of those servants came and settled accounts. [20]Then the one who had received the five talents came forward, bringing five more talents, saying,

---

v Gk to give them   w Or cut the wicked person off   x Gk virgins
y Other ancient authorities add and the bride
z Other ancient authorities add in which the Human One is coming
a A talent was worth more than fifteen years' wages of a laborer

'Master, you handed over to me five talents; see, I have made five more talents.' 21 The master said, 'Well done, good and trustworthy servant; you have been trustworthy in a few things, I will put you in charge of many things; enter into the joy of your master.' 22 And the one with the two talents also came forward, saying, 'Master, you handed over to me two talents; see, I have made two more talents.' 23 The master replied, 'Well done, good and trustworthy servant; you have been trustworthy in a few things, I will put you in charge of many things; enter into the joy of your master.' 24 Then the one who had received the one talent also came forward, saying, 'Master, I knew that you were a harsh person, reaping where you did not sow, and gathering where you did not scatter seed; 25 so I was afraid, and I went and hid your talent in the ground. Here you have what is yours.' 26 But the master replied, 'You wicked and lazy servant! You knew, did you, that I reap where I did not sow, and gather where I did not scatter? 27 Then you ought to have invested my money with the bankers, and on my return I would have received what was my own with interest. 28 So take back the talent, and give it to the one with the ten talents. 29 For to all those who have, more will be given, and they will have an abundance; but from those who have nothing, even what they have will be taken away. 30 Cast this worthless servant into the outer regions, where there will be weeping and gnashing of teeth.'

The Judgment of the Nations

31 "When the Human One comes in glory with all the angels, then that one will sit on the throne of glory. 32 All the nations will be gathered before the Human One, who will separate people one from another as a shepherd separates the sheep from the goats, 33 putting the sheep on the right hand and the goats at the left. 34 Then the ruler will say to those on the right hand, 'Come, you that are blessed by my Father-Mother, inherit the dominion prepared for you from the foundation of the world; 35 for I was hungry and you gave me food, I was thirsty and you gave me something to drink, I was a stranger and you welcomed me, 36 I was naked and you gave me clothing, I was sick and you took care of me, I was in prison and you visited me.' 37 Then the righteous will answer, 'Lord, when was it that we saw you hungry and gave you food, or thirsty and gave you something to drink? 38 And when was it that we saw you a stranger and welcomed you, or naked and gave you clothing? 39 And when was it that we saw you sick or in prison and visited you?' 40 And the ruler will answer them, 'Truly I tell you, just as you did it to one of the least of these who are members of my family, you did it to me.' 41 Then the ruler will say to those at the left hand, 'You that are accursed, depart from me into the eternal fire prepared for the devil and the devil's angels; 42 for I was hungry and you gave me no food, I was thirsty and you gave me nothing to drink, 43 I was a stranger and you did not welcome me, naked and you did not give me clothing, sick and in prison and you did not visit me.' 44 Then they also will answer, 'Lord, when was it that we saw you hungry or thirsty or a

stranger or naked or sick or in prison, and did not take care of you?' [45]Then the ruler will answer them, 'Truly I tell you, just as you did not do it to one of the least of these, you did not do it to me.' [46]And these will go away into eternal punishment, but the righteous into eternal life."

The Plot to Kill Jesus

26 When Jesus had finished saying all these things, he said to the disciples, [2]"You know that after two days the Passover is coming, and the Human One will be handed over to be crucified."

[3] Then the chief priests and the elders of the people gathered in the palace of the high priest, who was called Caiaphas, [4]and they conspired to arrest Jesus by stealth and kill him. [5]But they said, "Not during the festival, or there may be a riot among the people."

The Anointing at Bethany

[6] Now while Jesus was at Bethany in the house of Simon, who had leprosy,[b] [7]a woman came to him with an alabaster jar of very costly ointment, and she poured it on Jesus' head as he sat at the table. [8]But when the disciples saw it, they were angry and said, "Why this waste? [9]For this ointment could have been sold for a large sum, and the money given to those who are poor." [10]But Jesus, aware of this, said to them, "Why do you trouble the woman? She has performed a good service for me. [11]For you always have with you those who are poor, but you will not always have me. [12]By pouring this ointment on my body she has prepared me for burial. [13]Truly I tell you, wherever this good news[c] is proclaimed in the whole world, what she has done will be told in remembrance of her."

Judas Agrees to Betray Jesus

[14] Then one of the twelve, who was called Judas Iscariot, went to the chief priests [15]and said, "What will you give me if I betray Jesus to you?" They paid him thirty pieces of silver. [16]And from that moment Judas began to look for an opportunity to betray Jesus.

The Passover with the Disciples

[17] On the first day of Unleavened Bread the disciples came to Jesus, saying, "Where do you want us to make the preparations for you to eat the Passover?" [18]Jesus said, "Go into the city to a certain man, and say to him, 'The Teacher says, My time is near; I will keep the Passover at your house with my disciples.' " [19]So the disciples did as Jesus had directed them, and they prepared the Passover meal.

---

b The term *leprosy* can refer to several diseases   c Or *gospel*

20 When it was evening, Jesus sat at the table with the twelve;[d] 21 and while they were eating, he said, "Truly I tell you, one of you will betray me." 22 And they became greatly distressed and began to say to Jesus one after another, "Surely not I, Lord?" 23 He answered, "The one who has dipped his hand into the bowl with me will betray me. 24 The Human One goes as it is written, but woe to that person by whom the Human One is betrayed! It would have been better for that one not to have been born." 25 Judas, who betrayed Jesus, said, "Surely not I, Rabbi?" He replied, "You have said so."

26 While they were eating Jesus took a loaf of bread, blessed and broke it, and gave it to the disciples, saying, "Take, eat; this is my body." 27 Then taking a cup, and after giving thanks, Jesus gave it to them, saying, "Drink from it, all of you; 28 for this is my blood of the[e] covenant, which is poured out for many for the forgiveness of sins. 29 I tell you, I will never again drink of this fruit of the vine until that day when I drink it new with you in the dominion of God."

30 When they had sung the hymn, they went out to the Mount of Olives.

Jesus Predicts Peter's Denial

31 Then Jesus said to them, "You will all become deserters because of me this night; for it is written,

> 'I will strike the shepherd,
> and the sheep of the flock will be scattered.'

32 But after I am raised up, I will go ahead of you to Galilee." 33 Peter said to Jesus, "Though all become deserters because of you, I will never desert you." 34 Jesus said to him, "Truly I tell you, this very night, before the cock crows, you will deny me three times." 35 Peter replied, "Even though I must die with you, I will not deny you." And so said all the disciples.

Jesus Prays in Gethsemane

36 Then Jesus went with the disciples to a place called Gethsemane, and said to them, "Sit here while I go over there and pray." 37 He took with him Peter and the two sons of Zebedee, and began to be grieved and agitated. 38 Then Jesus said to them, "I am deeply grieved, even to death; remain here, and stay awake with me." 39 And going a little farther, he fell to the ground and prayed, "God, my Father-Mother, if it is possible, let this cup pass from me; yet not what I want but what you want." 40 Then Jesus came to the disciples and found them sleeping, and said to Peter, "So, could you not stay awake with me one hour? 41 Stay awake and pray that you may not come into the time of trial;[f] the spirit indeed is willing, but the flesh is weak." 42 Again Jesus went away for the second time and prayed, "My Father-Mother, if this cannot pass unless I drink it, your will be done." 43 Again he came and found them sleeping, for their eyes

---

d Other ancient authorities add *disciples*   e Other ancient authorities add *new*
f Or *into temptation*

were heavy. ⁴⁴So leaving them again, Jesus went away and prayed for the third time, saying the same words. ⁴⁵Then Jesus came to the disciples and said to them, "Are you still sleeping and taking your rest? See, the hour is at hand, and the Human One is betrayed into the hands of sinners. ⁴⁶Get up, let us be going. See, my betrayer is at hand."

The Betrayal and Arrest of Jesus

47 While Jesus was still speaking, Judas, one of the twelve, arrived; with him was a large crowd with swords and clubs, from the chief priests and the elders of the people. ⁴⁸Now the betrayer had given them a sign, saying, "The one I will kiss is the person; arrest him." ⁴⁹At once Judas came up to Jesus and said, "Greetings, Rabbi!" and kissed him. ⁵⁰Jesus said to him, "Friend, do what you are here to do." Then they came and laid hands on Jesus and arrested him. ⁵¹Suddenly, one of those with Jesus put his hand on his sword, drew it, and struck the servant of the high priest, cutting off his ear. ⁵²Then Jesus said to him, "Put your sword back into its place; for all who take the sword will perish by the sword. ⁵³Do you think that I cannot appeal to my Father-Mother, who will at once send me more than twelve legions of angels? ⁵⁴But how then would the scriptures be fulfilled, which say it must happen in this way?" ⁵⁵At that hour Jesus said to the crowds, "Have you come out with swords and clubs to arrest me as though I were a bandit? Day after day I sat in the temple teaching, and you did not arrest me. ⁵⁶But all this has taken place, so that the scriptures of the prophets may be fulfilled." Then all the disciples deserted him and fled.

Jesus before the Council

57 Those who had arrested Jesus took him to Caiaphas the high priest, in whose house the scribes and the elders had gathered. ⁵⁸But Peter was following him at a distance, as far as the courtyard of the high priest; and going inside, he sat with the guards in order to see how this would end. ⁵⁹Now the chief priests and the whole council were looking for false testimony against Jesus so that they might put him to death, ⁶⁰but they found none, though many false witnesses came forward. At last two came forward ⁶¹and said, "This fellow said, 'I am able to destroy the temple of God and to build it in three days.'" ⁶²The high priest stood up and said, "Have you no answer? What is it that they testify against you?" ⁶³But Jesus was silent. Then the high priest said to him, "I put you under oath before the living God, tell us if you are the Messiah,ᵍ the Child of God." ⁶⁴Jesus said to him, "You have said so. But I tell you,

> From now on you will see the Human One
>   seated at the side of the Power
>   and coming on the clouds of heaven."

g Or *Christ*

⁶⁵Then the high priest tore his clothes and said, "He has blasphemed! Why do we still need witnesses? You have now heard his blasphemy. ⁶⁶What is your verdict?" They answered, "He deserves death." ⁶⁷Then they spat in Jesus' face and struck him; and some slapped him, ⁶⁸saying, "Prophesy to us, you Messiah!ʰ Who is it that struck you?"

Peter Denies Jesus

69 Now Peter was sitting outside in the courtyard. A womanservant came up and said, "You also were with Jesus the Galilean." ⁷⁰But Peter denied it before all of them, saying, "I do not know what you are talking about." ⁷¹When he went out to the porch, another womanservant saw him, and she said to the bystanders, "This man was with Jesus of Nazareth."ⁱ ⁷²Again Peter denied it with an oath, "I do not know the man." ⁷³After a little while the bystanders came up and said to Peter, "Certainly you are also one of them, for your accent betrays you." ⁷⁴Then Peter began to curse, and he swore an oath, "I do not know the man!" At that moment the cock crowed. ⁷⁵Then Peter remembered what Jesus had said: "Before the cock crows, you will deny me three times." And Peter went out and wept bitterly.

Jesus before Pilate

27 When morning came, all the chief priests and the elders of the people conferred together against Jesus in order to bring about his death. ²They bound him, led him away, and handed him over to Pilate the governor.

The Suicide of Judas

3 When Judas, the betrayer, saw that Jesus was condemned, he repented and brought back the thirty pieces of silver to the chief priests and the elders. ⁴Judas said, "I have sinned by betraying innocentʲ blood." But they said, "What is that to us? See to it yourself." ⁵Throwing down the pieces of silver in the temple, Judas departed; and he went and hanged himself. ⁶But the chief priests, taking the pieces of silver, said, "It is not lawful to put them into the treasury, since they are blood money." ⁷After conferring together, they used them to buy the potter's field as a place to bury foreigners. ⁸For this reason that field has been called the Field of Blood to this day. ⁹Then was fulfilled what had been spoken through the prophet Jeremiah,ᵏ "And they tookˡ the thirty pieces of silver, the price of the one on whom a price had been set,ᵐ on whom some of the people of Israel had set a price, ¹⁰and they gaveⁿ them for the potter's field, as God commanded me."

---

h Or *Christ*   i Gk *the Nazorean*   j Other ancient authorities read *righteous*
k Other ancient authorities read *Zechariah* or *Isaiah*   l Or *I took*
m Or *the price of the precious One*   n Other ancient authorities read *I gave*

Pilate Questions Jesus

11 Now Jesus stood before the governor; and the governor asked him, “Are
you the King of the Jews?” Jesus said, “You say so.” 12 But when accused by
the chief priests and elders, Jesus did not answer. 13 Then Pilate said to him,
“Do you not hear how many accusations they make against you?” 14 But Jesus
gave Pilate no answer, not even to a single charge, so that the governor was
greatly amazed.

Pilate Hands Jesus Over to Be Crucified

15 Now at the festival the governor was accustomed to release a prisoner for
the crowd, anyone whom they wanted. 16 At that time they had a notorious
prisoner, called Jesus[o] Barabbas. 17 So after they had gathered, Pilate said to
them, “Whom do you want me to release for you, Jesus[o] Barabbas or Jesus
who is called the Messiah?”[p] 18 For Pilate realized that it was out of jealousy
that they had handed over Jesus. 19 While Pilate was sitting on the judgment
seat, his wife sent word, “Have nothing to do with that innocent man, for
today I have suffered a great deal because of a dream about him.” 20 Now the
chief priests and the elders persuaded the crowds to ask for Barabbas and to
have Jesus killed. 21 The governor again said to them, “Which of the two do you
want me to release for you?” And they said, “Barabbas.” 22 Pilate said to them,
“Then what should I do with Jesus who is called the Messiah?”[p] All of them
said, “Let him be crucified!” 23 Then Pilate asked, “Why, what evil has he
done?” But they shouted all the more, “Let him be crucified!”

24 So when Pilate saw that he could do nothing, but rather that a riot was
beginning, he took some water and washed his hands before the crowd, saying,
“I am innocent of this blood;[q] see to it yourselves.” 25 Then the people as a
whole answered, “His blood be on us and on our children!” 26 So Pilate released
Barabbas for them; and after flogging Jesus, he handed him over to be crucified.

The Soldiers Mock Jesus

27 Then the soldiers of the governor took Jesus into the governor’s headquarters,[r] and they gathered the whole cohort around him. 28 They stripped Jesus
and put a scarlet robe on him, 29 and after twisting some thorns into a crown,
they put it on his head. They put a reed in his hand, and, kneeling down, they
mocked Jesus, saying, “Hail, King of the Jews!” 30 They spat on Jesus, and took
the reed and struck him on the head. 31 After mocking Jesus, they stripped him
of the robe and put his own clothes on him. Then they led Jesus away to be
crucified.

---

o Other ancient authorities lack *Jesus* p Or *the Christ*

q Other ancient authorities read *this righteous blood*, or *this righteous one’s blood*

r Gk *the praetorium*

The Crucifixion of Jesus

32 As they went out, they came upon a man from Cyrene named Simon; they compelled this man to carry Jesus' cross. 33 And when they came to a place called Golgotha (which means Place of a Skull), 34 they offered Jesus wine to drink, mixed with gall; but after tasting it, he would not drink it. 35 And when they had crucified him, they divided his clothes among themselves by casting lots;^s 36 then they sat down there and kept watch over him. 37 Over Jesus' head they put the charge against him, which read, "This is Jesus, the King of the Jews."

38 Then two bandits were crucified with him, one on the right and one on the left. 39 Those who passed by derided^t him, shaking their heads 40 and saying, "You who would destroy the temple and build it in three days, save yourself! If you are the Child of God, come down from the cross." 41 In the same way the chief priests also, along with the scribes and elders, were mocking Jesus, saying, 42 "This one saved others, but cannot save himself.^u He is the King of Israel; let him come down from the cross now, and we will believe in him. 43 He trusts in God; let God deliver him now, if God wants to; for he said, 'I am the Child of God.' " 44 The bandits who were crucified with Jesus also taunted him in the same way.

The Death of Jesus

45 From noon on, night came over the whole land^v until three in the afternoon. 46 And about three o'clock Jesus cried with a loud voice, "Eli, Eli, lema sabachthani?" that is, "My God, my God, why have you forsaken me?" 47 When some of the bystanders heard it, they said, "This man is calling for Elijah." 48 At once one of them ran and got a sponge, filled it with sour wine, put it on a stick, and gave it to Jesus to drink. 49 But the others said, "Wait, let us see whether Elijah will come to save him."^w 50 Then Jesus cried again with a loud voice and died.^x 51 At that moment the curtain of the temple was torn in two, from top to bottom. The earth shook, and the rocks were split. 52 The tombs also were opened, and many bodies of the saints who had fallen asleep were raised. 53 After Jesus' resurrection they came out of the tombs and entered the holy city and appeared to many. 54 Now when the centurion and those with him, who were keeping watch over Jesus, saw the earthquake and what took place, they were terrified and said, "Truly this was the Child of God!"^y

55 Many women were also there, looking on from a distance; they had followed Jesus from Galilee and had provided for him. 56 Among them were

---

s Other ancient authorities add *in order that what had been spoken through the prophet might be fulfilled, "They divided my clothes among themselves, and for my clothing they cast lots."*
t Or *blasphemed*   u Or *is he unable to save himself?*   v Or *earth*
w Other ancient authorities add *And another took a spear and pierced his side, and out came water and blood*   x Or *gave up the spirit*   y Or *a child of God*

Mary Magdalene, and Mary the mother of James and Joseph, and the mother of the sons of Zebedee.

The Burial of Jesus

57 When it was evening, there came a rich man from Arimathea, named Joseph, who was also a disciple of Jesus. [58]He went to Pilate and asked for the body of Jesus; then Pilate ordered it to be given to him. [59]So Joseph took the body and wrapped it in a clean linen cloth [60]and laid it in his own new tomb, which he had hewn in the rock. Joseph then rolled a great stone to the door of the tomb and went away. [61]Mary Magdalene and the other Mary were there, sitting opposite the tomb.

The Guard at the Tomb

62 The next day, that is, after the day of Preparation, the chief priests and the Pharisees gathered before Pilate [63]and said, "Sir, we remember what that impostor said while still alive, 'After three days I will rise again.' [64]Therefore command the tomb to be made secure until the third day; otherwise the disciples may go and steal the body, and tell the people, 'Jesus has been raised from the dead,' and the last deception would be worse than the first." [65]Pilate said to them, "You have a guard[z] of soldiers; go, make it as secure as you can."[a] [66]So they went with the guard and made the tomb secure by sealing the stone.

The Resurrection of Jesus

28 After the sabbath, as the first day of the week was dawning, Mary Magdalene and the other Mary went to see the tomb. [2]And suddenly there was a great earthquake; for an angel of God, descending from heaven, came and rolled back the stone and sat on it. [3]The angel's appearance was like lightning, and its clothing white as snow. [4]For fear of the angel the guards shook and became like dead people. [5]But the angel said to the women, "Do not be afraid; I know that you are looking for Jesus who was crucified. [6]Jesus is not here, but has been raised, as he said. Come, see the place where Jesus[b] lay. [7]Then go quickly and tell the disciples, 'Jesus has been raised from the dead,[c] and even now is going ahead of you to Galilee; there you will see Jesus.' This is my message for you." [8]So they left the tomb quickly with fear and great joy, and ran to tell the disciples. [9]Suddenly Jesus met them and said, "Greetings!" And they came up, took hold of Jesus' feet, and worshiped Jesus. [10]Then Jesus said to them, "Do not be afraid; go and tell my sisters and brothers to go to Galilee; there they will see me."

---

z Or *Take a guard*   a Gk *you know how*   b Other ancient authorities read *the Lord*
c Other ancient authorities lack *from the dead*

The Report of the Guard

11 While they were going, some of the guard went into the city and told the chief priests everything that had happened. 12 After the priests had assembled with the elders, they devised a plan to give a large sum of money to the soldiers, 13 telling them, "You must say, 'Jesus' disciples came by night and stole Jesus away while we were asleep.' 14 If this comes to the governor's ears, we will satisfy him and keep you out of trouble." 15 So they took the money and did as they were directed. And this story is still told among the Jews to this day.

The Commissioning of the Disciples

16 Now the eleven disciples went to Galilee, to the mountain to which Jesus had directed them. 17 When they saw Jesus, they worshiped Jesus; but some doubted. 18 And Jesus came and said to them, "All authority in heaven and on earth has been given to me. 19 Go therefore and make disciples of all nations, baptizing them in the name of the Father-Mother and of the beloved Child and of the Holy Spirit, 20 and teaching them to obey everything that I have commanded you. And remember, I am with you always, to the end of the age."d

---

d Other ancient authorities add *Amen*

The Gospel According to Mark

The Proclamation of John the Baptist

1 The beginning of the good news[a] of Jesus Christ, the Child of God.[b] 2 As it is written in the prophet Isaiah,[c]

> "See, I am sending my messenger ahead of you,[d]
> who will prepare your way;
> 3 the voice of one crying out in the wilderness:
> 'Prepare the way of the Lord,
> make the paths of the Lord straight,' "

4 John the baptizer appeared[e] in the wilderness, proclaiming a baptism of repentance for the forgiveness of sins. 5 And people from the whole Judean countryside and all the people of Jerusalem were going out to him, and were baptized by him in the river Jordan, confessing their sins. 6 Now John was clothed with camel's hair, with a leather belt around his waist, and he ate locusts and wild honey. 7 He proclaimed, "The one who is more powerful than I is coming after me, the thong of whose sandals I am not worthy to untie. 8 I have baptized you with[f] water; but that one will baptize you with[f] the Holy Spirit."

The Baptism of Jesus

9 In those days Jesus came from Nazareth of Galilee and was baptized by John in the Jordan. 10 Just as Jesus was coming up out of the water, he saw the heavens torn apart and the Spirit descending to him like a dove. 11 And a voice

---

a Or *gospel*   b Other ancient authorities lack *the Child of God*
c Other ancient authorities read *in the prophets*   d Gk *before your face*
e Other ancient authorities read *John was baptizing*   f Or *in*

came from heaven, "You are my Child, the Beloved;[g] with you I am well pleased."

The Temptation of Jesus

12 And the Spirit immediately drove Jesus out into the wilderness. [13] Jesus was in the wilderness forty days, tempted by Satan, and was with the wild beasts, and the angels served him.

The Beginning of the Galilean Ministry

14 Now after John was arrested, Jesus came to Galilee, proclaiming the good news[h] of God,[i] [15] and saying, "The time is fulfilled, and the dominion of God has come near;[j] repent, and believe in the good news."[h]

Jesus Calls the First Disciples

16 Walking along the Sea of Galilee, Jesus saw Simon and his brother Andrew casting a net into the sea—for they were fishers. [17] And Jesus said to them, "Follow me and I will make you fish for people." [18] And immediately they left their nets and followed him. [19] And going on a little farther, Jesus saw James son of Zebedee and his brother John, who were in their boat mending the nets. [20] Immediately he called them; and they left their father Zebedee in the boat with the hired help, and followed him.

The Person with an Unclean Spirit

21 They went into Capernaum; and immediately on the sabbath, Jesus entered the synagogue and taught. [22] They were astounded at Jesus' teaching, for he taught them as one having authority, and not as the scribes. [23] Just then there was in their synagogue a person with an unclean spirit [24] who cried out, "What have you to do with us, Jesus of Nazareth? Have you come to destroy us? I know who you are, the Holy One of God." [25] But Jesus rebuked the spirit, saying, "Be silent, and come out!" [26] And the unclean spirit, convulsing the person and crying with a loud voice, came out. [27] They were all amazed, and they kept on asking one another, "What is this? A new teaching—with authority! He[k] commands even the unclean spirits, and they obey." [28] At once Jesus' fame began to spread throughout the surrounding region of Galilee.

Jesus Heals Many at Simon's House

29 As soon as they[l] left the synagogue, they entered the house of Simon and Andrew, with James and John. [30] Now Simon's mother-in-law was in bed with a fever, and they told Jesus about her at once. [31] He came and took her by the hand and lifted her up. Then the fever left her, and she began to serve them.

---

g Or *my beloved Child*   h Or *gospel*   i Other ancient authorities read *of the dominion*
j Or *is at hand*   k Or *A new teaching! With authority he*
l Other ancient authorities read *he*

32 That evening, at sundown, they brought to Jesus all who were sick or possessed with demons. 33 And the whole city was gathered around the door. 34 And Jesus cured many who were sick with various diseases, and cast out many demons and would not permit the demons to speak, because they knew him.

A Preaching Tour in Galilee

35 In the morning, while it was still very dark, Jesus got up and went out to a deserted place, and there he prayed. 36 And Simon and his companions hunted for Jesus. 37 When they found him, they said, "Everyone is searching for you." 38 He answered, "Let us go on to the neighboring towns, so that I may proclaim the message there also; for that is what I came out to do." 39 And he went throughout Galilee, proclaiming the message in their synagogues and casting out demons.

Jesus Cleanses a Person with Leprosy

40 A person with leprosy[m] came and knelt down and, begging Jesus, said, "If you choose, you can make me clean." 41 Moved with pity,[n] Jesus reached out and touched the person, and said, "I do choose. Be made clean!" 42 Immediately the leprosy[m] went away, and the person was made clean. 43 After a stern warning Jesus sent away the person who had been healed, 44 saying, "See that you say nothing to anyone; but go, show yourself to the priest, and offer for your cleansing what Moses commanded, as a testimony to them." 45 But the one who had been healed went out and began to proclaim it freely, and to spread the word, so that Jesus could no longer go into a town openly, but stayed out in the country; and people came to him from every quarter.

Jesus Heals a Person Who Was Paralyzed

2 When Jesus returned to Capernaum after some days, it was reported that he was at home. 2 So many gathered around that there was no longer room for them, not even in front of the door; and he was speaking the word to them. 3 Then some people[o] came, bringing a person who was paralyzed, carried by four of them. 4 And when they could not bring the person to Jesus because of the crowd, they removed the roof above him; and after having dug through it, they let down the mat on which the person lay. 5 When Jesus saw their faith, he said to the one who was paralyzed, "My child, your sins are forgiven." 6 Now some of the scribes were sitting there, questioning in their hearts, 7 "Why does this fellow speak in this way? It is blasphemy! Who can forgive sins but God alone?" 8 At once Jesus perceived in his spirit that they were discussing these questions among themselves, and said to them, "Why do you raise such questions in your hearts? 9 Which is easier, to say to the one who is paralyzed,

---

m The term *leprosy* can refer to several diseases   n Other ancient authorities read *anger*
o Gk *they*

'Your sins are forgiven,' or to say, 'Stand up and take your mat and walk'?
[10] But so that you may know that the Human One has authority on earth to
forgive sins"—Jesus said to the one who was paralyzed— [11] "I say to you,
stand up, take your mat, and go to your home." [12] And the one who had been
paralyzed stood up, and immediately took the mat and went out before all of
them; so that they were all amazed and glorified God, saying, "We have never
seen anything like this!"

Jesus Calls Levi

13 Jesus went out again beside the sea, and with the whole crowd gathered
around, he taught them. [14] While walking along, Jesus saw Levi son of Alphaeus
sitting at the tax booth, and he said to him, "Follow me." And Levi got up and
followed Jesus.

15 And as Jesus sat at dinner[p] in Levi's house, many tax collectors and
people called sinners were also sitting[q] with Jesus and the disciples—for there
were many who followed him. [16] When the scribes of[r] the Pharisees saw that
Jesus was eating with sinners and tax collectors, they said to the disciples, "Why
does he eat[s] with tax collectors and sinners?" [17] When Jesus heard this, he said
to them, "Those who are well have no need of a physician, but those who are
sick; I have come to call not the righteous but sinners."

The Question about Fasting

18 Now John's disciples and the Pharisees were fasting; and people[t] came and
said to Jesus, "Why do John's disciples and the disciples of the Pharisees fast,
but your disciples do not fast?" [19] Jesus said to them, "The wedding guests
cannot fast while the bridegroom is with them, can they? As long as they have
the bridegroom with them, they cannot fast. [20] The days will come when the
bridegroom is taken away from them, and then they will fast on that day.

21 "No one sews a piece of unshrunk cloth on an old cloak; otherwise, the
patch pulls away from it, the new from the old, and a worse tear is made.
[22] And no one puts new wine into old wineskins; otherwise, the wine will burst
the skins, and the wine is lost, and so are the skins; but one puts new wine
into fresh wineskins."[u]

Pronouncement about the Sabbath

23 One sabbath Jesus was going through the grainfields; and as they made their
way the disciples began to pluck heads of grain. [24] The Pharisees said to him,
"Look, why are they doing what is not lawful on the sabbath?" [25] And he said
to them, "Have you never read what David did when he and his companions
were hungry and in need of food? [26] He entered the house of God, when

---

p Gk *reclined*   q Gk *reclining*   r Other ancient authorities read *and*
s Other ancient authorities add *and drink*   t Gk *they*
u Other ancient authorities lack *but one puts new wine into fresh wineskins*

Abiathar was high priest, and ate the bread of the Presence, which it is not lawful for any but the priests to eat, and he gave some to his companions." 27Then Jesus said to them, "The sabbath was made for humankind, and not humankind for the sabbath; 28so the Human One is lord even of the sabbath."

The Person with a Withered Hand

3 Again Jesus entered the synagogue, and a person was there who had a withered hand. 2They watched to see whether Jesus would heal on the sabbath, so that they might accuse him. 3And Jesus said to the one who had the withered hand, "Come forward." 4Then Jesus said to them, "Is it lawful to do good or to do harm on the sabbath, to save life or to kill?" But they were silent. 5Looking around at them with anger, grieved at their hardness of heart, Jesus said to the person, "Stretch out your hand." The one with the withered hand stretched it out, and it was restored. 6The Pharisees went out and immediately conspired with the Herodians against Jesus, how to destroy him.

A Multitude at the Seaside

7 Jesus departed with the disciples to the sea, and a great multitude from Galilee followed; 8hearing all that Jesus was doing, they came to him in great numbers from Judea, Jerusalem, Idumea, beyond the Jordan, and the region around Tyre and Sidon. 9Jesus told the disciples to have a boat ready for him because of the crowd, so that they would not crush him; 10for Jesus had cured many, so that all who had diseases pressed upon him to touch him. 11Whenever the unclean spirits saw Jesus, they fell down before him and shouted, "You are the Child of God!" 12But Jesus sternly ordered them not to make him known.

Jesus Appoints the Twelve Apostles

13 Jesus went up the mountain and called those whom he wanted, and they came to him. 14And he appointed twelve, whom he also named apostles,ᵛ to be with him, and to be sent out to proclaim the message, 15and to have authority to cast out demons. 16So Jesus appointed the twelve:ʷ Simon (to whom he gave the name Peter); 17James son of Zebedee and John the brother of James (to whom he gave the name Boanerges, that is, Sons of Thunder); 18and Andrew, and Philip, and Bartholomew, and Matthew, and Thomas, and James son of Alphaeus, and Thaddaeus, and Simon the Cananaean, 19and Judas Iscariot, who betrayed him.

Jesus and Beelzebul

Then Jesus went home; 20and the crowd came together again, so that they could not even eat. 21When Jesus' family heard it, they went out to restrain him, for people were saying, "Jesus has gone out of his mind." 22And the scribes who

---

v Other ancient authorities lack *whom he also named apostles*
w Other ancient authorities lack *So Jesus appointed the twelve*

came down from Jerusalem said, "He has Beelzebul, and by the ruler of the demons he casts out demons." 23 And Jesus called them to him, and spoke to them in parables, "How can Satan cast out Satan? 24 If a dominion is divided against itself, that dominion cannot stand. 25 And if a house is divided against itself, that house will not be able to stand. 26 And if Satan has risen up against Satan and is divided, Satan cannot stand, but is coming to an end. 27 But no one can enter a house whose owner is strong and plunder the property without first tying up the owner; then indeed the house can be plundered.

28 "Truly I tell you, people will be forgiven for their sins and whatever blasphemies they utter; 29 but whoever blasphemes against the Holy Spirit can never have forgiveness, but is guilty of an eternal sin"— 30 for they had said, "Jesus has an unclean spirit."

The True Kindred of Jesus

31 Then Jesus' mother and brothers came; and standing outside, they sent to him and called him. 32 A crowd was sitting around Jesus; and they said, "Your mother and your brothers and sisters^x are outside, asking for you." 33 And he replied, "Who are my mother and my brothers?" 34 And looking at those who sat around him, he said, "Here are my mother and my brothers! 35 Whoever does the will of God is my brother and sister and mother."

The Parable of the Sower

4 Again Jesus began to teach beside the sea. Such a very large crowd gathered around that he got into a boat on the sea and sat there, while the whole crowd was beside the sea on the land. 2 Jesus began to teach them many things in parables, and while teaching, said to them: 3 "Listen! A sower went out to sow. 4 As the seed was being scattered, some fell on the path, and the birds came and ate it up. 5 Other seed fell on rocky ground, where it did not have much soil, and it sprang up quickly, since it had no depth of soil. 6 And when the sun rose, it was scorched; and since it had no root, it withered away. 7 Other seed fell among thorns, and the thorns grew up and choked it, and it yielded no grain. 8 Other seed fell into good soil and brought forth grain, growing up and increasing and yielding thirty and sixty and a hundredfold." 9 And Jesus said, "Let everyone pay attention!"

The Purpose of the Parables

10 When Jesus was alone, those who were there, along with the twelve, asked about the parables. 11 And he said to them, "To you has been given the secret^y of the dominion of God, but for those outside, everything comes in parables; 12 in order that

'they may indeed look, but not perceive,

---

x Other ancient authorities lack *and sisters*   y Or *mystery*

and may indeed listen, but not understand;
so that they may not turn again and be forgiven.' "

The Parable of the Sower Explained

13 And Jesus said to them, "Do you not understand this parable? Then how will you understand all the parables? 14 The sower sows the word. 15 These are the ones on the path where the word is sown: when they hear, Satan immediately comes and takes away the word that is sown in them. 16 And these are the ones sown on rocky ground: when they hear the word, they immediately receive it with joy. 17 But they have no root, and endure only for a while; then, when trouble or persecution arises on account of the word, immediately they fall away.ᶻ 18 And others are those sown among the thorns: these are the ones who hear the word, 19 but the cares of the world, and the lure of wealth, and the desire for other things come in and choke the word, and it yields nothing. 20 And these are the ones sown on the good soil: they hear the word and accept it and bear fruit, thirty and sixty and a hundredfold."

A Lamp under a Bushel Basket

21 Jesus said to them, "Is a lamp brought in to be put under the bushel basket, or under the bed, and not on the lampstand? 22 For there is nothing hidden, except to be disclosed; nor is anything secret, except to come to light. 23 Let anyone with ears to hear listen!" 24 And Jesus said to them, "Pay attention to what you hear; the measure you give will be the measure you get, and still more will be given you. 25 For to those who have, more will be given; and from those who have nothing, even what they have will be taken away."

The Parable of the Growing Seed

26 Jesus also said, "The dominion of God is as if a farmer would scatter seed on the ground, 27 and would sleep and rise night and day, and the seed would sprout and grow, without the farmer's knowing how. 28 The earth produces of itself, first the stalk, then the head, then the full grain in the head. 29 But when the grain is ripe, at once the farmer goes in with a sickle, because the harvest has come."

The Parable of the Mustard Seed

30 Jesus also said, "With what can we compare the dominion of God, or what parable will we use for it? 31 It is like a mustard seed, which, when sown upon the ground, is the smallest of all the seeds on earth; 32 yet when it is sown it grows up and becomes the greatest of all shrubs, and puts forth large branches, so that the birds of the air can make nests in its shade."

---

z Or *stumble*

Jesus' Use of Parables

33 With many such parables Jesus spoke the word to them, as they were able to hear it; 34 he did not speak to them except in parables, but he explained everything in private to the disciples.

Jesus Stills a Storm

35 On that day, when evening had come, Jesus said to the disciples, "Let us go across to the other side." 36 And leaving the crowd behind, they took him with them in the boat, just as he was. Other boats were there. 37 A great windstorm arose, and the waves beat into the boat, so that the boat was already being swamped. 38 The disciples woke Jesus, who was asleep on a cushion in the stern, and they said, "Teacher, do you not care that we are perishing?" 39 Jesus woke up and rebuked the wind, and said to the sea, "Peace! Be still!" Then the wind ceased, and there was a dead calm. 40 Jesus said to them, "Why are you afraid? Have you still no faith?" 41 And they were filled with great awe and said to one another, "Who then is this, whom even the wind and the sea obey?"

Jesus Heals a Person Possessed by Demons

5 They came to the other side of the sea, to the country of the Gerasenes.[a] 2 And when Jesus had stepped out of the boat, immediately a man out of the tombs with an unclean spirit met him. 3 The one with an unclean spirit lived among the tombs; and no one could restrain him any more, even with a chain; 4 for he had often been restrained with shackles and chains, but the chains he wrenched apart, and the shackles he broke in pieces; and no one had the strength to subdue him. 5 Night and day among the tombs and on the mountains he was always howling and bruising himself with stones. 6 When he saw Jesus from a distance, he ran and bowed down before him; 7 and he shouted at the top of his voice, "What have you to do with me, Jesus, Child of the Most High God? I adjure you by God, do not torment me." 8 For Jesus had said to him, "Come out of the man, you unclean spirit!" 9 Then Jesus asked, "What is your name?" He replied, "My name is Legion; for we are many." 10 He begged Jesus earnestly not to send them out of the country. 11 Now there on the hillside a great herd of swine was feeding; 12 and the unclean spirits begged him, "Send us into the swine; let us enter them." 13 So Jesus gave them permission. And the unclean spirits came out and entered the swine; and the herd, numbering about two thousand, rushed down the steep bank into the sea, and were drowned in the sea.

14 The swineherds ran off and told it in the city and in the country. Then people came to see what it was that had happened. 15 They came to Jesus and saw the one who had been possessed by demons sitting there, clothed and in his right mind, the very one who had had the legion; and they were afraid.

---

a Other ancient authorities read *Gergesenes*; others, *Gadarenes*

16 Those who had seen what had happened to the one who had been possessed, and to the swine, reported it. 17 Then they began to beg Jesus to leave their neighborhood. 18 As Jesus was getting into the boat, the one who had been possessed begged Jesus that he might be with him. 19 But Jesus refused, and said, "Go home to your friends, and tell them how much the Lord has done for you, and what mercy has been shown to you." 20 And the man went away and began to proclaim in the Decapolis how much Jesus had done for him; and everyone was amazed.

A Girl Restored to Life and a Woman Healed

21 When Jesus had crossed again in the boat[b] to the other side, a great crowd gathered around him; and he was by the sea. 22 Then one of the leaders of the synagogue named Jairus came and, when he saw Jesus, fell at his feet 23 and pleaded repeatedly, "My little daughter is at the point of death. Come and lay your hands on her, so that she may be made well, and live." 24 So Jesus went with him.

And a large crowd followed and pressed in on Jesus. 25 Now there was a woman who had been suffering from hemorrhages for twelve years. 26 She had endured much under many physicians, and had spent all that she had; and she was no better, but rather grew worse. 27 Having heard about Jesus, she came up in the crowd from behind, and touched Jesus' cloak, 28 for she said, "If I but touch Jesus' clothes, I will be made well." 29 Immediately her hemorrhage stopped; and she felt in her body that she was healed of her disease. 30 Immediately aware that power had gone forth from him, Jesus turned about in the crowd and said, "Who touched my clothes?" 31 And the disciples said, "You see the crowd pressing in on you; how can you say, 'Who touched me?' " 32 Jesus looked all around to see who had done it. 33 But the woman, knowing what had happened to her, came in fear and trembling, fell down before Jesus, and told the whole truth. 34 Jesus said to her, "Daughter, your faith has made you well; go in peace, and be healed of your disease."

35 While Jesus was still speaking, some people came from the leader's house to say, "Your daughter is dead. Why trouble the teacher any further?" 36 But overhearing[c] what they said, Jesus said to the leader of the synagogue, "Do not fear, only believe." 37 He allowed no one to follow him except Peter, James, and John, the brother of James. 38 When they came to the house of the leader of the synagogue, Jesus saw a commotion, people weeping and wailing loudly. 39 Having entered, Jesus said to them, "Why do you make a commotion and weep? The child is not dead but sleeping." 40 And they laughed at him. Then Jesus put them all outside, and took the child's father and mother and those who were with him, and went in where the child was. 41 Jesus took her by the hand and said to her, "Talitha cum," which means, "Little girl, get up!"

---

b Other ancient authorities lack *in the boat*
c Or *ignoring*; other ancient authorities read *hearing*

42 And immediately the girl got up and began to walk about (she was twelve years of age). At this they were overcome with amazement. 43 Jesus strictly ordered them that no one should know this, and told them to give her something to eat.

The Rejection of Jesus at Nazareth

6 Jesus left that place and came to his hometown, and the disciples followed him. 2 On the sabbath he began to teach in the synagogue, and many who heard him were astounded. They said, "Where did this man get all this? What is this wisdom that has been given to him? What deeds of power are being done by his hands! 3 Is not this the carpenter, the son of Mary[d] and brother of James and Joses and Judas and Simon, and are not his sisters here with us?" And they took offense[e] at him. 4 Then Jesus said to them, "Prophets are not without honor, except in their hometown, and among their own kin, and in their own house." 5 And Jesus could do no deed of power there, except to lay hands on a few sick people and cure them. 6 And he was amazed at their unbelief.

The Mission of the Twelve

Then Jesus went about among the villages teaching. 7 He called the twelve and began to send them out two by two, and gave them authority over the unclean spirits. 8 He ordered them to take nothing for their journey except a staff; no bread, no bag, no money in their belts; 9 but to wear sandals and not to put on two tunics. 10 Jesus said to them, "Wherever you enter a house, stay there until you leave the place. 11 If any place will not welcome you and they refuse to hear you, as you leave, shake off the dust that is on your feet as a testimony against them." 12 So they went out and proclaimed that all should repent. 13 They cast out many demons, and anointed with oil many who were sick and cured them.

The Death of John the Baptist

14 King Herod heard of it, for Jesus' name had become known. Some were[f] saying, "John the baptizer has been raised from the dead; and for this reason these powers are at work in Jesus." 15 But others said, "It is Elijah." And others said, "It is a prophet, like one of the prophets of old." 16 But when Herod heard of it, he said, "John, whom I beheaded, has been raised."

17 For Herod himself had sent men who arrested John, bound him, and put him in prison on account of Herodias, his brother Philip's wife, because Herod had married her. 18 For John had been telling Herod, "It is not lawful for you to have your brother's wife." 19 And Herodias had a grudge against John, and wanted to kill him. But she could not, 20 for Herod feared John,

---

d Other ancient authorities read *son of the carpenter and of Mary*   e Or *stumbled*
f Other ancient authorities read *He was*

knowing that he was a righteous and holy man, and Herod protected him. When Herod heard John, he was greatly perplexed;[g] and yet he liked to listen to John. 21 But an opportunity came when Herod on his birthday gave a banquet for his courtiers and officers and for the leaders of Galilee. 22 When his daughter Herodias[h] came in and danced, she pleased Herod and his guests; and the king said to his daughter, "Ask me for whatever you wish, and I will give it." 23 And Herod solemnly swore to her, "Whatever you ask me, I will give you, even half of my kingdom." 24 She went out and said to her mother, "What should I ask for?" Her mother replied, "The head of John the baptizer." 25 Immediately the daughter rushed back to the king and requested, "I want you to give me at once the head of John the Baptist on a platter." 26 The king was deeply grieved; yet out of regard for his oaths and for the guests, he did not want to refuse her. 27 Immediately the king sent a soldier of the guard with orders to bring John's head. He went and beheaded him in the prison, 28 brought his head on a platter, and gave it to his daughter. Then she gave it to her mother. 29 When John's disciples heard about it, they came and took his body, and laid it in a tomb.

Feeding the Five Thousand

30 The apostles gathered around Jesus, and told him all that they had done and taught. 31 He said to them, "Come away to a deserted place all by yourselves and rest a while." For many were coming and going, and they had no leisure even to eat. 32 And they went away in the boat to a deserted place by themselves. 33 Now many saw them going and recognized them, and they hurried there on foot from all the towns and arrived ahead of them. 34 Going ashore, Jesus saw a great crowd and had compassion for them, because they were like sheep without a shepherd; and Jesus began to teach them many things. 35 When it grew late, the disciples came to him and said, "This is a deserted place, and the hour is now very late; 36 send them away so that they may go into the surrounding country and villages and buy something for themselves to eat." 37 But Jesus answered them, "You give them something to eat." They said to him, "Are we to go and buy six months' wages worth of bread, and give it to them to eat?" 38 And Jesus answered, "How many loaves have you? Go and see." When they had found out, they said, "Five, and two fish." 39 Then Jesus ordered them to get all the people to sit down in groups on the green grass. 40 So they sat down in groups of hundreds and of fifties. 41 Taking the five loaves and the two fish, Jesus looked up to heaven, and blessed and broke the loaves, and gave them to the disciples to set before the people; and Jesus divided the two fish among them all. 42 And all ate and were filled; 43 and they took up twelve baskets full of broken pieces and of the fish. 44 Those who had eaten the loaves numbered five thousand men.

---

g Other ancient authorities read *he did many things*
h Other ancient authorities read *the daughter of Herodias herself*

Jesus Walks on the Water

45 Immediately Jesus made the disciples get into the boat and go on ahead to the other side, to Bethsaida, while he dismissed the crowd. 46 After saying farewell to them, he went up on the mountain to pray.

47 When evening came, the boat was out on the sea, and Jesus was alone on the land. 48 Seeing that they were straining at the oars against an adverse wind, Jesus came toward them early in the morning, walking on the sea. Jesus intended to pass them by. 49 But when they saw Jesus walking on the sea, they thought it was a ghost and cried out; 50 for they all saw Jesus and were terrified. But immediately Jesus spoke to them and said, "Take heart, it is I; do not be afraid." 51 Then Jesus got into the boat with them and the wind ceased. And they were utterly astounded, 52 for they did not understand about the loaves, but their hearts were hardened.

Healing in Gennesaret

53 When they had crossed over, they came to land at Gennesaret and moored the boat. 54 When they got out of the boat, people at once recognized Jesus, 55 and rushed about that whole region and began to bring those who were sick, on mats, to wherever they heard he was. 56 And wherever Jesus went, into villages or cities or farms, people laid those who were sick in the marketplaces and they begged to touch even the fringe of Jesus' cloak; and all who touched it were healed.   *

The Tradition of the Elders

7 Now when the Pharisees and some of the scribes who had come from Jerusalem gathered around Jesus, 2 they noticed that some of the disciples were eating with defiled hands, that is, without washing them. 3 (For the Pharisees, and all the Jews, do not eat unless they thoroughly wash their hands,[i] thus observing the tradition of the elders; 4 and they do not eat anything from the market unless they wash it;[j] and there are also many other traditions that they observe, the washing of cups, pots, and bronze kettles.[k]) 5 So the Pharisees and the scribes asked Jesus, "Why do your disciples not live[l] according to the tradition of the elders, but eat with defiled hands?" 6 Jesus said to them, "Isaiah prophesied rightly about you hypocrites, as it is written,

> 'This people honors me with their lips,
>   but their hearts are far from me;
> in vain do they worship me,
>   teaching human precepts as doctrines.'

7

---

i Meaning of Gk uncertain
j Other ancient authorities read *and when they come from the marketplace, they do not eat unless they purify themselves*   k Other ancient authorities add *and beds*   l Gk *walk*

8 You abandon the commandment of God and hold to human tradition."

9 Then Jesus said to them, "You have a fine way of rejecting the commandment of God in order to keep your tradition! 10 For Moses said, 'Honor your father and your mother'; and, 'Whoever speaks evil of father or mother must surely die.' 11 But you say that if anyone tells father or mother, 'Whatever support you might have had from me is Corban' (that is, an offering to God[m])— 12 then you no longer permit doing anything for a father or mother, 13 thus making void the word of God through your tradition that you have handed on. And you do many things like this."

Things that Defile

14 Then Jesus called the crowd again and said to them, "Listen to me, all of you, and understand: 15 there is nothing outside a person that by going in can defile, but the things that come out are what defile."[n]

17 When Jesus had left the crowd and entered the house, the disciples asked him about the parable. 18 He said to them, "Then do you also fail to understand? Do you not see that whatever goes into a person from outside cannot defile, 19 since it enters, not the heart but the stomach, and goes out into the sewer?" (Thus Jesus declared all foods clean.) 20 And he said, "It is what comes out of a person that defiles. 21 For it is from within, from the human heart, that evil intentions come: fornication, theft, murder, 22 adultery, avarice, wickedness, deceit, licentiousness, envy, slander, pride, folly. 23 All these evil things come from within, and they defile a person."

The Syrophoenician Woman's Faith

24 From there Jesus set out and went away to the region of Tyre.[o] Jesus entered a house and did not want anyone to know he was there, yet he could not escape notice. 25 But a woman whose little daughter had an unclean spirit immediately heard about Jesus, and she came and bowed down at his feet. 26 Now the woman was a Gentile, of Syrophoenician origin. She begged him to cast the demon out of her daughter. 27 Jesus said to her, "Let the children be fed first, for it is not fair to take the children's food and throw it to the dogs." 28 But she answered, "Lord,[p] even the dogs under the table eat the children's crumbs." 29 Then Jesus said to her, "For saying that, you may go—the demon has left your daughter." 30 So she went home, found the child lying on the bed, and the demon gone.

Jesus Cures a Person Who Was Deaf

31 Then Jesus returned from the region of Tyre, and went by way of Sidon toward the Sea of Galilee, in the region of the Decapolis. 32 They brought to

---

m Gk lacks *to God*
n Other ancient authorities add verse 16, *"Let anyone with ears to hear listen"*
o Other ancient authorities add *and Sidon*   p Other ancient authorities prefix *Yes*

him a person who was deaf and had a speech impediment, on whom they begged Jesus to lay his hands. ³³ Taking the person aside in private, away from the crowd, Jesus put his fingers into the person's ears, and spat and touched the person's tongue. ³⁴ Then looking up to heaven, Jesus sighed and said, "Ephphatha," that is, "Be opened." ³⁵ And immediately the ears were opened, the tongue was released, and the person spoke plainly. ³⁶ Then Jesus ordered them to tell no one; but the more he ordered them, the more zealously they proclaimed it. ³⁷ They were astounded beyond measure, saying, "Jesus has done everything well, even making those who are deaf to hear and those who are mute to speak."

Feeding the Four Thousand

8 In those days when there was again a great crowd without anything to eat, Jesus called the disciples and said to them, ² "I have compassion for the crowd, because they have been with me now for three days and have nothing to eat. ³ If I send them away hungry to their homes, they will faint on the way—and some of them have come from a great distance." ⁴ The disciples replied, "How can one feed these people with bread here in the desert?" ⁵ Jesus asked them, "How many loaves do you have?" They said, "Seven." ⁶ Then Jesus ordered the crowd to sit down on the ground, and having taken the seven loaves, and after giving thanks, Jesus broke them and gave them to the disciples to distribute; and they distributed them to the crowd. ⁷ They had also a few small fish; and after blessing them, Jesus ordered that these too should be distributed. ⁸ They ate and were filled; and they took up the broken pieces left over, seven baskets full. ⁹ Now there were about four thousand people. And Jesus sent them away. ¹⁰ And immediately he got into the boat with the disciples and went to the district of Dalmanutha.q

The Demand for a Sign

11 The Pharisees came and began to argue with Jesus, asking for a sign from heaven, to test Jesus. ¹² And sighing deeply in spirit, Jesus said, "Why does this generation ask for a sign? Truly I tell you, no sign will be given to this generation." ¹³ And Jesus left them, and getting into the boat again, went across to the other side.

The Yeast of the Pharisees and of Herod

14 Now the disciples had forgotten to bring any bread; and they had only one loaf with them in the boat. ¹⁵ And Jesus cautioned them, saying, "Watch out—beware of the yeast of the Pharisees and the yeast of Herod."r ¹⁶ They said to one another, "It is because we have no bread." ¹⁷ And becoming aware of it, Jesus said to them, "Why are you talking about having no bread? Do you

---

q Other ancient authorities read *Mageda* or *Magdala*
r Other ancient authorities read *the Herodians*

still not perceive or understand? Are your hearts hardened? [18]Are you able to see, and do not see? Are you able to hear, and do not hear? And do you not remember? [19]When I broke the five loaves for the five thousand, how many baskets full of broken pieces did you collect?" They answered, "Twelve." [20]"And the seven for the four thousand, how many baskets full of broken pieces did you collect?" And they said, "Seven." [21]Then Jesus said to them, "Do you not yet understand?"

Jesus Cures a Blind Man at Bethsaida

22 They came to Bethsaida. Some people[s] brought to Jesus a blind man whom they begged Jesus to touch. [23]Jesus took the man by the hand and led him out of the village; and when Jesus had put saliva on the man's eyes and laid hands on him, Jesus asked, "Can you see anything?" [24]And the man looked up and said, "I can see people, but they look like trees, walking." [25]Then Jesus laid his hands on the man's eyes again; and the man looked intently and his sight was restored, and he saw everything clearly. [26]Then Jesus sent him home, saying, "Do not even go into the village."[t]

Peter's Declaration about Jesus

27 Jesus went on with the disciples to the villages of Caesarea Philippi; and on the way he asked the disciples, "Who do people say that I am?" [28]And they answered him, "John the Baptist; and others, Elijah; and still others, one of the prophets." [29]Jesus asked them, "But who do you say that I am?" Peter answered, "You are the Messiah."[u] [30]And Jesus sternly ordered them not to tell anyone about him.

Jesus Foretells His Death and Resurrection

31 Then Jesus began to teach them that the Human One must undergo great suffering, and be rejected by the elders, the chief priests, and the scribes, and be killed, and after three days rise again. [32]He said all this quite openly. And Peter took him aside and began to rebuke him. [33]But turning and looking at the disciples, Jesus rebuked Peter and said, "Get behind me, Satan! For you are setting your mind not on divine things but on human things."

The Cross and Discipleship

34 Jesus called the crowd with the disciples, and said to them, "If any want to become my followers, let them deny themselves and take up their cross and follow me. [35]For those who want to save their life will lose it, and those who lose their life for my sake, and for the sake of the gospel,[v] will save it. [36]For what will it profit them to gain the whole world and forfeit their life? [37]Indeed, what can they give in return for their life? [38]Those who are ashamed of me and

---

s Gk *They*   t Other ancient authorities add *or tell anyone in the village*   u Or *the Christ*
v Other ancient authorities read *lose their life for the sake of the gospel*

of my words[w] in this adulterous and sinful generation, of them the Human One will also be ashamed when the Human One comes in the glory of God

9 with the holy angels." [1]And Jesus said to them, "Truly I tell you, there are some standing here who will not taste death until they see that the dominion of God has come with[x] power."

The Transfiguration

2 Six days later, Jesus took with him Peter and James and John and led them up a high mountain apart, by themselves. And Jesus was transfigured before them, [3]with clothes that became dazzling white, such as no one[y] on earth could bleach them. [4]And there appeared to them Elijah with Moses, who were talking with Jesus. [5]Then Peter said to Jesus, "Rabbi, it is good for us to be here; let us make three dwellings,[z] one for you, one for Moses, and one for Elijah." [6]Peter did not know what to say, for they were terrified. [7]Then a cloud overshadowed them, and from the cloud there came a voice, "This is my Child, the Beloved;[a] to this one you shall listen!" [8]Suddenly when they looked around, they saw no one with them any more, but only Jesus.

The Coming of Elijah

9 As they were coming down the mountain, Jesus ordered them to tell no one about what they had seen, until after the Human One had risen from the dead. [10]So they kept the matter to themselves, questioning what this rising from the dead could mean. [11]Then they asked Jesus, "Why do the scribes say that Elijah must come first?" [12]He said to them, "Elijah is indeed coming first to restore all things. How then is it written that the Human One is to go through many sufferings and be treated with contempt? [13]But I tell you that Elijah has come, and they did to him whatever they pleased, as it is written about him."

Jesus Heals a Child with a Spirit

14 When they came to the disciples, they saw a great crowd around them, and some scribes arguing with them. [15]When the whole crowd saw Jesus, they were immediately overcome with awe, and they ran forward to greet him. [16]Jesus asked them, "What are you arguing about with them?" [17]Someone from the crowd answered, "Teacher, I brought you my son; he has a spirit that makes him unable to speak; [18]and whenever it seizes him, it dashes him down; and he foams and grinds his teeth and becomes rigid; and I asked your disciples to cast it out, but they could not do so." [19]Jesus answered them, "You faithless generation, how much longer must I be among you? How much longer must I put up with you? Bring him to me." [20]And they brought the child to Jesus. When the spirit saw Jesus, immediately it convulsed the child, and he fell on the ground and rolled about, foaming at the mouth. [21]Jesus asked the father,

---

w Other ancient authorities read *and of mine*   x Or *in*   y Gk *no fuller*   z Or *tents*
a Or *my beloved Child*

"How long has this been happening to him?" And he said, "From childhood. 22 It has often cast him into the fire and into the water, to destroy him; but if you are able to do anything, have pity on us and help us." 23 Jesus said to him, "If you are able!—All things can be done for the one who believes." 24 Immediately the father of the child cried out,[b] "I believe; help my unbelief!" 25 When Jesus saw that a crowd came running together, he rebuked the unclean spirit, saying to it, "You spirit that keeps this child from speaking and hearing, I command you, come out of him, and never enter him again!" 26 After crying out and convulsing him terribly, it came out, and the child was like a corpse, so that most of them said, "He is dead." 27 But Jesus took him by the hand and lifted him up, and he was able to stand. 28 When Jesus had entered the house, the disciples asked privately, "Why could we not cast it out?" 29 Jesus said to them, "This kind can come out only through prayer."[c]

Jesus Again Foretells His Death and Resurrection

30 They went on from there and passed through Galilee. Jesus did not want anyone to know it; 31 for he was teaching the disciples, saying to them, "The Human One is to be betrayed into human hands and will be killed by them, and three days after being killed, the Human One will rise." 32 But they did not understand what Jesus was saying and were afraid to ask him.

True Greatness

33 Then they came to Capernaum; and when Jesus was in the house he asked the disciples, "What were you arguing about on the way?" 34 But they were silent, for on the way they had argued with one another who was the greatest. 35 Jesus sat down, called the twelve, and said to them, "Whoever wants to be first must be last of all and servant of all." 36 Then Jesus took a little child and put it among them; and taking it in his arms, he said to them, 37 "Whoever welcomes one such child in my name welcomes me, and whoever welcomes me welcomes not me but the one who sent me."

Another Exorcist

38 John said to him, "Teacher, we saw someone[d] casting out demons in your name, and we forbade it, because the one who did it was not following us." 39 But Jesus said, "Do not stop such a person; for no one who does a deed of power in my name will be able soon afterward to speak evil of me. 40 Whoever is not against us is for us. 41 For truly I tell you, whoever gives you a cup of water to drink because you bear the name of Christ will by no means lose the reward.

---

b Other ancient authorities add *with tears*   c Other ancient authorities add *and fasting*
d Other ancient authorities add *who does not follow us*

Temptations to Sin

42 "If any of you put a stumbling block before one of these little ones who believe in me,[e] it would be better for you if a great millstone were hung around your neck and you were thrown into the sea. 43 If your hand causes you to stumble, cut it off; it is better for you to enter life maimed than to have two hands and to go to hell,[f] to the unquenchable fire.[g] 45 And if your foot causes you to stumble, cut it off; it is better for you to enter life lame than to have two feet and to be thrown into hell.[f,g] 47 And if your eye causes you to stumble, tear it out; it is better for you to enter the dominion of God with one eye than to have two eyes and to be thrown into hell,[f] 48 where their worm never dies, and the fire is never quenched.

49 "For everyone will be salted with fire.[h] 50 Salt is good; but if salt has lost its saltiness, how can you season it?[i] Have salt in yourselves, and be at peace with one another."

Teaching about Divorce

10 Jesus left that place and went to the region of Judea and[j] beyond the Jordan. And crowds again gathered around him; and, as was Jesus' custom, he again taught them.

2 Some Pharisees came, and to test Jesus they asked, "Is it lawful for a man to divorce his wife?" 3 He answered them, "What did Moses command you?" 4 They said, "Moses allowed a man to write a certificate of dismissal and to divorce her." 5 But Jesus said to them, "Because of your hardness of heart he wrote this commandment for you. 6 But from the beginning of creation, 'God made them male and female.' 7 'For this reason a man shall leave his father and mother and be joined to his wife,[k] 8 and the two shall become one flesh.' So they are no longer two, but one flesh. 9 Therefore what God has joined together, let no one separate."

10 Then in the house the disciples asked him again about this matter. 11 Jesus said to them, "Whoever divorces his wife and marries another commits adultery against her; 12 and if she divorces her husband and marries another, she commits adultery."

Jesus Blesses Little Children

13 People were bringing little children to Jesus in order that he might touch them; and the disciples spoke sternly to them. 14 But when Jesus saw this, he was indignant and said to them, "Let the little children come to me; do not

---

e Other ancient authorities lack *in me*   f Gk *Gehenna*
g Verses 44 and 46 (which are identical with verse 48) are lacking in the best ancient authorities
h Other ancient authorities either add or substitute *and every sacrifice will be salted with salt*
i Or *how can you restore its saltiness?*   j Other ancient authorities lack *and*
k Other ancient authorities lack *and be joined to his wife*

stop them; for it is to such as these that the dominion of God belongs. 15 Truly I tell you, whoever does not receive the dominion of God as a little child will never enter it." 16 And Jesus took them up in his arms, laid his hands on them, and blessed them.

A Question about Eternal Life

17 As Jesus was setting out on a journey, some one ran up and knelt before him, and asked, "Good Teacher, what must I do to inherit eternal life?" 18 Jesus replied, "Why do you call me good? No one is good but God alone. 19 You know the commandments: 'You shall not murder; You shall not commit adultery; You shall not steal; You shall not bear false witness; You shall not defraud; Honor your father and mother.'" 20 The questioner said to Jesus, "Teacher, I have kept all these since my youth." 21 Jesus looked upon the questioner with love and said, "You lack one thing; go, sell what you own, and give the money[l] to the those who are poor, and you will have treasure in heaven; then come, follow me." 22 Having heard this, the person was shocked and went away grieving, for the questioner had many possessions.

23 Then Jesus looked around and said to the disciples, "How hard it will be for those who have wealth to enter the dominion of God!" 24 And the disciples were perplexed at these words. But Jesus said to them again, "Children, how hard it is[m] to enter the dominion of God! 25 It is easier for a camel to go through the eye of a needle than for someone who is rich to enter the dominion of God." 26 They were greatly astounded and said to one another,[n] "Then who can be saved?" 27 Jesus looked at them and said, "For mortals it is impossible, but not for God; for God all things are possible."

28 Peter began to say to him, "Look, we have left everything and followed you." 29 Jesus said, "Truly I tell you, there is no one who has left house or brothers or sisters or mother or father or children or fields, for my sake and for the sake of the good news,[o] 30 who will not receive a hundredfold now in this age—houses, brothers and sisters, mothers and children, and fields with persecutions—and in the age to come eternal life. 31 But many who are first will be last, and the last will be first."

A Third Time Jesus Foretells His Death and Resurrection

32 They were on the road, going up to Jerusalem, and Jesus was walking ahead of them; they were amazed, and those who followed were afraid. He took the twelve aside again and began to tell them what was to happen to him, 33 saying, "See, we are going up to Jerusalem, and the Human One will be handed over to the chief priests and the scribes, and condemned to death, and will be handed over to the Gentiles; 34 and the Human One will be mocked and spit upon, flogged, and killed, and after three days will rise."

---

l Gk lacks *the money*   m Other ancient authorities add *for those who trust in riches*
n Other ancient authorities read *to him*   o Or *gospel*

The Request of James and John

35 James and John, the sons of Zebedee, came forward and said to Jesus, "Teacher, we want you to do for us whatever we ask of you." ³⁶And Jesus replied, "What is it you want me to do for you?" ³⁷And they said to him, "Grant us to sit, one at your right hand and one at your left, in your glory." ³⁸But Jesus said to them, "You do not know what you are asking. Are you able to drink the cup that I drink, or be baptized with the baptism that I am baptized with?" ³⁹They replied, "We are able." Then Jesus said to them, "The cup that I drink you will drink; and with the baptism with which I am baptized, you will be baptized; ⁴⁰but to sit at my right hand or at my left is not mine to grant, but it is for those for whom it has been prepared."

41 When the ten heard this, they began to be angry with James and John. ⁴²So Jesus called them and said to them, "You know that among the Gentiles those whom they recognize as their rulers lord it over them, and their great ones are tyrants over them. ⁴³But it is not so among you; but whoever wishes to become great among you must minister to you, ⁴⁴and whoever wishes to be first among you will be servant of all. ⁴⁵For the Human One came not to be served but to serve, and to give up life as a ransom for many."

Jesus Heals Bartimaeus

46 They came to Jericho. As Jesus and the disciples and a large crowd were leaving Jericho, Bartimaeus, who was the son of Timaeus and who was blind, was sitting by the roadside begging. ⁴⁷Hearing that it was Jesus of Nazareth, Bartimaeus began to shout out and say, "Jesus, Son of David, have mercy on me!" ⁴⁸Many sternly ordered him to be quiet, but he cried out even more loudly, "Son of David, have mercy on me!" ⁴⁹Jesus stood still and said, "Call him here." And they called him, saying, "Take heart; get up, Jesus is calling you." ⁵⁰So throwing off his cloak, Bartimaeus sprang up and came to Jesus. ⁵¹Then Jesus said to him, "What do you want me to do for you?" The blind man replied, "My teacher,ᵖ let me see again." ⁵²Jesus said, "Go; your faith has made you well." Immediately Bartimaeus regained his sight and followed Jesus on the way.

Jesus' Entry into Jerusalem

11 When they were approaching Jerusalem, at Bethphage and Bethany, near the Mount of Olives, Jesus sent two of the disciples ²and said to them, "Go into the village ahead of you, and immediately as you enter it, you will find tied there a colt that has never been ridden; untie it and bring it. ³If anyone says to you, 'Why are you doing this?' just say this, 'The Lord needs it and will send it back here immediately.' " ⁴They went away and found a colt tied near a door, outside in the street. As they were untying it, ⁵some of the

---

p Aramaic *Rabbouni*

bystanders said to them, "What are you doing, untying the colt?" 6They told
them what Jesus had said; and they allowed them to take it. 7Then they
brought the colt to Jesus and threw their cloaks on it; and he sat on it. 8Many
people spread their cloaks on the road, and others spread leafy branches that
they had cut in the fields. 9Then those who went ahead and those who
followed were shouting,

"Hosanna!
 Blessed is the one who comes in the name of God!
10 Blessed is the coming dominion of our ancestor David!
Hosanna in the highest heaven!"

11 Then Jesus entered Jerusalem and went into the temple; and having
looked around at everything, as it was already late, he went out to Bethany
with the twelve.

Jesus Curses the Fig Tree

12 On the following day, when they came from Bethany, Jesus was hungry.
13Seeing in the distance a fig tree in leaf, Jesus went to see whether perhaps he
would find anything on it. Coming near to it, Jesus found nothing but leaves,
for it was not the season for figs. 14Jesus said to it, "May no one ever eat fruit
from you again." And the disciples heard it.

Jesus Protests in the Temple

15 Then they came to Jerusalem. And Jesus entered the temple and began to
drive out those who were selling and those who were buying in the temple, and
overturned the tables of the money changers and the seats of those who sold
doves; 16and Jesus would not allow anyone to carry anything through the
temple. 17Jesus was teaching and saying, "Is it not written,

'My house shall be called a house of prayer for all the
 nations'?
 But you have made it a den of robbers."

18And when the chief priests and the scribes heard it, they kept looking for a
way to kill him; for they were afraid of Jesus, because the whole crowd was
spellbound by his teaching. 19And when evening came, Jesus and the disciples[q]
went out of the city.

The Lesson from the Withered Fig Tree

20 In the morning as they passed by, they saw the fig tree withered away to its
roots. 21Then Peter remembered and said to Jesus, "Rabbi, look! The fig tree
that you cursed has withered." 22Jesus answered them, "Have[r] faith in God.
23Truly I tell you, if you say to this mountain, 'Be taken up and thrown into

---

q Gk *they*: other ancient authorities read *he* r Other ancient authorities read *"If you have*

the sea,' and if you do not doubt in your heart, but believe that what you say will come to pass, it will be done for you. 24 So I tell you, whatever you ask for in prayer, believe that you have received[s] it, and it will be yours.

25 "Whenever you stand praying, forgive, if you have anything against anyone; so that God your Father-Mother in heaven may also forgive you your trespasses."[t]

Jesus' Authority Is Questioned

27 Again they came to Jerusalem. As Jesus was walking in the temple, the chief priests, the scribes, and the elders came up 28 and said, "By what authority are you doing these things? Who gave you this authority to do them?" 29 Jesus said to them, "I will ask you one question; answer me, and I will tell you by what authority I do these things. 30 Did the baptism of John come from heaven, or was it of human origin? Answer me." 31 They argued with one another, "If we say, 'From heaven,' Jesus will say, 'Why then did you not believe him?' 32 But shall we say, 'Of human origin'?"—they were afraid of the crowd, for all regarded John as truly a prophet. 33 So they answered Jesus, "We do not know." And Jesus said to them, "Neither will I tell you by what authority I am doing these things."

The Parable of the Wicked Tenants

12 Then Jesus began to speak to them in parables. "A person planted a vineyard, put a fence around it, dug a pit for the winepress, and built a watchtower, and then leased it to tenants and went to another country. 2 When the season came, the owner sent to the tenants a person enslaved to him in order to collect from them his share of the produce of the vineyard. 3 But they seized, beat, and sent the owner's representative away empty-handed. 4 And again the owner sent another person to them; this one they beat over the head and insulted. 5 Then the owner sent another, and that one they killed. And so it was with many others; some they beat, and others they killed. 6 The owner had still one other, a beloved child. Finally the owner sent that child to them, saying, 'They will respect my child.' 7 But those tenants said to one another, 'This is the heir; come, let us kill this one too, and the inheritance will be ours.' 8 So they seized and killed the heir, and threw the body out of the vineyard. 9 What then will the owner of the vineyard do? The owner will come and destroy the tenants and give the vineyard to others. 10 Have you not read this scripture:

> 'The stone that the builders rejected
> has become the cornerstone;[u]

---

s Other ancient authorities read *are receiving*
t Other ancient authorities add verse 26, "*But if you do not forgive, neither will your Father-Mother in heaven forgive your trespasses.*"   u Or *keystone*

11   this was God's doing,
                and it is amazing in our eyes'?"

12 When they realized that Jesus had told this parable against them, they wanted to arrest him, but they feared the crowd. So they left him and went away.

The Question about Paying Taxes

13 Then they sent to Jesus some Pharisees and some Herodians to trap him in what he said. 14 And they came and said, "Teacher, we know that you are sincere, and show deference to no one; for you do not regard people with partiality, but teach the way of God in accordance with truth. Is it lawful to pay taxes to the emperor, or not? 15 Should we pay them, or should we not?" But knowing their hypocrisy, Jesus said to them, "Why are you putting me to the test? Bring me a coin and let me see it." 16 And they brought one. Then Jesus said to them, "Whose head is this, and whose title?" They answered, "The emperor's." 17 Jesus said to them, "Give to the emperor the things that are the emperor's, and to God the things that are God's." And they were utterly amazed at him.

The Question about the Resurrection

18 Some Sadducees, who say there is no resurrection, came up and asked Jesus a question, saying, 19 "Teacher, Moses wrote for us that if a man's brother dies, leaving a wife but no child, the man[v] shall marry the widow and raise up children for his brother. 20 There were seven brothers; the first married and, when he died, left no children; 21 and the second married her and died, leaving no children; and the third likewise; 22 none of the seven left children. Last of all the woman herself died. 23 In the resurrection[w] whose wife will she be? For the seven had married her."

24 Jesus said to them, "Is not this the reason you are wrong, that you know neither the scriptures nor the power of God? 25 For when they rise from the dead, they neither marry nor are given in marriage, but are like angels in heaven. 26 And as for the dead being raised, have you not read in the book of Moses, in the story about the bush, how God said to him, 'I am the God of Abraham, the God of Isaac, and the God of Jacob'? 27 God is God not of the dead, but of the living; you are quite wrong."

The First Commandment

28 One of the scribes came near and heard them disputing with one another, and seeing that Jesus answered them well, he asked, "Which commandment is the first of all?" 29 Jesus answered, "The first is, 'Hear, O Israel: the Sovereign our God, the Sovereign is one; 30 you shall love the Sovereign your God with

---

v Gk *his brother*   w Other ancient authorities add *when they rise*

all your heart, and with all your soul, and with all your mind, and with all your strength.' ³¹The second is this, 'You shall love your neighbor as yourself.' There is no other commandment greater than these." ³²Then the scribe said, "You are right, Teacher; you have truly said that 'God is one, and besides God there is no other'; ³³and 'to love God with all the heart, and with all the understanding, and with all the strength,' and 'to love one's neighbor as oneself,'—this is much more important than all whole burnt offerings and sacrifices." ³⁴When Jesus saw that the scribe answered wisely, he said, "You are not far from the dominion of God." After that no one dared to ask Jesus any question.

A Question about the Messiah

35 While Jesus was teaching in the temple, he said, "How can the scribes say that the Messiah[x] is the descendant of David? ³⁶David himself, by the Holy Spirit, declared,

> 'God said to my Lord,
> "Sit at my side,
>   until I put your enemies under your feet." '

³⁷David himself calls the Messiah Lord; so how can the Messiah be David's descendant?" And the large crowd was listening to Jesus with delight.

Jesus Denounces the Scribes

38 As Jesus taught, he said, "Beware of the scribes, who like to walk around in long robes, and to be greeted with respect in the marketplaces, ³⁹and to have the best seats in the synagogues and places of honor at banquets! ⁴⁰They devour widows' houses and for the sake of appearance say long prayers. They will receive the greater condemnation."

The Widow's Coins

41 Jesus sat down opposite the treasury, and watched the crowd putting money into the treasury. Many rich people put in large sums. ⁴²A widow who was poor came and put in two small copper coins, which are worth a penny. ⁴³Then Jesus called the disciples and said to them, "Truly I tell you, this widow has put in more than all those who are contributing to the treasury. ⁴⁴For all of them have contributed out of their abundance; but she out of her poverty has put in everything she had, all she had to live on."

---

x Or the Christ

The Destruction of the Temple Foretold

13 As Jesus came out of the temple, one of the disciples said to him, "Look, Teacher, what large stones and what large buildings!" [2] Then Jesus asked him, "Do you see these great buildings? Not one stone will be left here upon another; all will be thrown down."

3 When Jesus was sitting on the Mount of Olives opposite the temple, Peter, James, John, and Andrew asked him privately, [4] "Tell us, when will this be, and what will be the sign that all these things are about to be accomplished?" [5] Then Jesus began to say to them, "Beware that no one leads you astray. [6] Many will come in my name and say, 'I am the one!'[y] and they will lead many astray. [7] When you hear of wars and rumors of wars, do not be alarmed; this must take place, but the end is still to come. [8] For nation will rise against nation, and kingdom against kingdom; there will be earthquakes in various places; there will be famines. This is but the beginning of the birth pangs.

Persecution Foretold

9 "As for yourselves, beware; for they will hand you over to councils; and you will be beaten in synagogues; and you will stand before governors and rulers because of me, as a testimony to them. [10] And the good news[z] must first be proclaimed to all nations. [11] When they bring you to trial and hand you over, do not worry beforehand about what you are to say; but say whatever is given you at that time, for it is not you who speak, but the Holy Spirit. [12] A brother will betray a brother to death; in the same way, a sister will betray a sister, and a parent a child, and children will rise against parents and kill them; [13] and you will be hated by all because of my name. But the one who endures to the end will be saved.

The Desolating Sacrilege

14 "But when you see the desolating sacrilege set up where it ought not to be (let the reader understand), then those in Judea must flee to the mountains; [15] the one on the housetop must not go down or enter the house to take anything away; [16] the one in the field must not turn back to get a coat. [17] Woe to those who are pregnant and to those who are nursing infants in those days! [18] Pray that it may not be in winter. [19] For in those days there will be suffering, such as has not been from the beginning of the creation that God created until now, no, and never will be. [20] And if God had not cut short those days, no one would be saved; but for the sake of the elect, whom God chose, God has cut short those days. [21] And if anyone says to you at that time, 'Look! Here is the Messiah!'[a] or 'Look! There is the Messiah!'—do not believe it. [22] False messiahs[b] and false prophets will appear and produce signs and omens, to lead

---

y Gk *I am*   z Gk *gospel*   a Or *the Christ*   b Or *christs*

astray, if possible, the elect. 23 But be alert; I have already told you everything.

The Coming of the Human One

24 "But in those days, after that suffering,

> the sun will be extinguished,
> and the moon will not give its light,
25   and the stars will be falling from heaven,
> and the powers in the heavens will be shaken.

26 Then they will see 'the Human One coming in clouds' with great power and glory. 27 Then the Human One will send out the angels, and gather the elect from the four winds, from the ends of the earth to the ends of heaven.

The Lesson of the Fig Tree

28 "From the fig tree learn its lesson: as soon as its branch becomes tender and puts forth its leaves, you know that summer is near. 29 So also, when you see these things taking place, you know that the Human One[c] is near, at the very gates. 30 Truly I tell you, this generation will not pass away until all these things have taken place. 31 Heaven and earth will pass away, but my words will not pass away.

The Necessity for Watchfulness

32 "But about that day or hour no one knows, neither the angels in heaven, nor the Child, but only the Father-Mother. 33 Beware, keep alert;[d] for you do not know when the time will come. 34 It is like someone going on a journey, who when leaving home, puts in charge people who are enslaved, each with a particular task, and commands the doorkeeper to be on the watch. 35 Therefore, keep awake—for you do not know when the owner of the house will come, in the evening, or at midnight, or at cockcrow, or at dawn, 36 or else the owner may come suddenly and find you asleep. 37 And what I say to you I say to all: Keep awake."

The Plot to Kill Jesus

14 It was two days before the Passover and the festival of Unleavened Bread. The chief priests and the scribes were looking for a way to arrest Jesus by stealth and kill him; 2 for they said, "Not during the festival, or there may be a riot among the people."

The Anointing at Bethany

3 While Jesus was at Bethany sitting at the table in the house of Simon, who had leprosy,[e] a woman came with an alabaster jar of very costly ointment of

---

c Or it   d Other ancient authorities add *and pray*
e The term *leprosy* can refer to several diseases

nard, and she broke open the jar and poured the ointment on Jesus' head. ⁴But some were there who said to one another in anger, "Why was the ointment wasted in this way? ⁵For this ointment could have been sold for a year's wages, and the money given to the those who are poor." And they scolded her. ⁶But Jesus said, "Let her alone; why do you trouble her? She has performed a good service for me. ⁷For you always have with you those who are poor, and you show kindness to them whenever you wish; but you will not always have me. ⁸She has done what she could; she has anointed my body beforehand for its burial. ⁹Truly I tell you, wherever the good news[f] is proclaimed in the whole world, what she has done will be told in remembrance of her."

Judas Agrees to Betray Jesus

10 Then Judas Iscariot, who was one of the twelve, went to the chief priests in order to betray Jesus to them. ¹¹When they heard it, they were greatly pleased, and promised to give him money. So Judas began to look for an opportunity to betray Jesus.

The Passover with the Disciples

12 On the first day of Unleavened Bread, when the Passover lamb is sacrificed, the disciples said to Jesus, "Where do you want us to go and make the preparations for you to eat the Passover?" ¹³So Jesus sent two disciples, saying to them, "Go into the city, and a man carrying a jar of water will meet you; follow him, ¹⁴and wherever he enters, say to the owner of the house, 'The Teacher asks, Where is my guest room where I may eat the Passover with my disciples?' ¹⁵He will show you a large room upstairs, furnished and ready. Make preparations for us there." ¹⁶So the disciples set out and went to the city, and found everything as Jesus had told them; and they prepared the Passover meal.

17 When it was evening, Jesus came with the twelve. ¹⁸And when they had taken their places and were eating, Jesus said, "Truly I tell you, one of you will betray me, one who is eating with me." ¹⁹They began to be distressed and to say to Jesus one after another, "Surely, not I?" ²⁰Jesus said to them, "It is one of the twelve, one who is dipping bread[g] into the bowl[h] with me. ²¹For the Human One goes as it is written, but woe to that person by whom the Human One is betrayed! It would have been better for that one not to have been born."

22 While they were eating, Jesus took a loaf of bread, and after blessing it, broke it, gave it to them and said, "Take; this is my body." ²³Then Jesus took a cup, and after giving thanks, gave it to them, and all of them drank from it. ²⁴Jesus said to them, "This is my blood of the[i] covenant, which is poured out for many. ²⁵Truly I tell you, I will never again drink of the fruit of the vine until that day when I drink it new in the dominion of God."

---

f Or *gospel*   g Gk lacks *bread*   h Other ancient authorities read *same bowl*
i Other ancient authorities add *new*

Jesus Predicts Peter's Denial

26 When they had sung the hymn, they went out to the Mount of Olives.
27 And Jesus said to them, "You will all become deserters; for it is written,

> 'I will strike the shepherd,
>   and the sheep will be scattered.'

28 But after I am raised up, I will go before you to Galilee." 29 Peter said to
Jesus, "Even though all become deserters, I will not." 30 Jesus said to him,
"Truly I tell you, this day, this very night, before the cock crows twice, you
will deny me three times." 31 But Peter said vehemently, "Even though I must
die with you, I will not deny you." And all of them said the same.

Jesus Prays in Gethsemane

32 They went to a place called Gethsemane; and Jesus said to the disciples, "Sit
here while I pray." 33 And taking Peter and James and John, Jesus began to be
distressed and agitated. 34 And he said to them, "I am deeply grieved, even to
death; remain here, and keep awake." 35 And going a little farther, Jesus fell to
the ground and prayed that, if it were possible, the hour might pass from him.
36 He said, "Abba, Father-Mother, for you all things are possible; remove this
cup from me; yet, not what I want, but what you want." 37 Jesus came and
found them sleeping; and he said to Peter, "Simon, are you asleep? Could you
not keep awake one hour? 38 Keep awake and pray that you may not come into
the time of trial;ʲ the spirit indeed is willing, but the flesh is weak." 39 And
again Jesus went away and prayed, saying the same words. 40 And once more he
came and found them sleeping, for their eyes were very heavy; and they did not
know what to say to him. 41 Jesus came a third time and said to them, "Are
you still sleeping and taking your rest? Enough! The hour has come; the
Human One is betrayed into the hands of sinners. 42 Get up, let us be going.
See, my betrayer is at hand."

The Betrayal and Arrest of Jesus

43 Immediately, while Jesus was still speaking, Judas, one of the twelve, arrived;
and with him there was a crowd with swords and clubs, from the chief priests,
the scribes, and the elders. 44 Now the betrayer had given them a sign, saying,
"The one I will kiss is the person; arrest him and lead him away under guard."
45 So when Judas came, he went up to Jesus at once and said, "Rabbi!" and
kissed him. 46 Then they laid hands on Jesus and arrested him. 47 But one of
those who stood near drew his sword and struck the servant of the high priest,
cutting off his ear. 48 Then Jesus said to them, "Have you come out with swords
and clubs to arrest me as though I were a bandit? 49 Day after day I was with

---

j Or *into temptation*

you in the temple teaching, and you did not arrest me. But let the scriptures be fulfilled." ⁵⁰All of them deserted Jesus and fled.

51 A certain young man was following Jesus, wearing nothing but a linen cloth. They caught hold of him, ⁵²but he left the linen cloth and ran off naked.

Jesus before the Council

53 They took Jesus to the high priest; and all the chief priests, the elders, and the scribes were assembled. ⁵⁴Peter had followed Jesus at a distance, right into the courtyard of the high priest; and he was sitting with the guards, warming himself at the fire. ⁵⁵Now the chief priests and the whole council were looking for testimony against Jesus to put him to death; but they found none. ⁵⁶For many gave false testimony against Jesus, and their testimony did not agree. ⁵⁷Some stood up and gave false testimony, saying, ⁵⁸"We heard him say, 'I will destroy this temple that is made with hands, and in three days I will build another, not made with hands.' " ⁵⁹But even on this point their testimony did not agree. ⁶⁰Then the high priest stood up before them and asked Jesus, "Have you no answer? What is it that they testify against you?" ⁶¹But Jesus was silent and did not answer. Again the high priest asked Jesus, "Are you the Messiah,ᵏ the Child of the Blessed One?" ⁶²Jesus said, "I am; and

> 'you will see the Human One
> seated at the side of the Power,'
> and 'coming with the clouds of heaven.' "

⁶³Then the high priest tore his clothes and said, "Why do we still need witnesses? ⁶⁴You have heard his blasphemy! What is your decision?" All of them condemned Jesus as deserving death. ⁶⁵Some began to spit on Jesus, to blindfold him, and to strike him, saying, "Prophesy!" The guards also took Jesus and beat him.

Peter Denies Jesus

66 While Peter was below in the courtyard, one of the womanservants of the high priest came by. ⁶⁷When she saw Peter warming himself, she stared at him and said, "You also were with Jesus, the Nazarene." ⁶⁸But Peter denied it, saying, "I do not know or understand what you are talking about." And he went out into the forecourt.ˡ Then the cock crowed.ᵐ ⁶⁹And the womanservant, on seeing him, began again to say to the bystanders, "This is one of them." ⁷⁰But again Peter denied it. Then after a little while the bystanders again said to Peter, "Certainly you are one of them; for you are a Galilean." ⁷¹But he began to curse, and he swore an oath, "I do not know this person you are talking about." ⁷²At that moment the cock crowed for the second time. Then Peter remembered that Jesus had said to him, "Before the cock crows twice, you will deny me three times." And he broke down and wept.

---

k Or *the Christ*   l Or *gateway*   m Other ancient authorities lack *Then the cock crowed*

Pilate Questions Jesus

15 As soon as it was morning, the chief priests held a consultation with the elders and scribes and the whole council. They bound Jesus, led him away, and handed him over to Pilate. 2 Pilate asked Jesus, "Are you the King of the Jews?" Jesus answered, "You say so." 3 Then the chief priests accused Jesus of many things. 4 Pilate asked again, "Have you no answer? See how many charges they bring against you." 5 But Jesus made no further reply, so that Pilate was amazed.

Pilate Hands Jesus over to Be Crucified

6 Now at the festival Pilate used to release a prisoner for them, anyone for whom they asked. 7 Now a man called Barabbas was in prison with the rebels who had committed murder during the insurrection. 8 So the crowd came and began to ask Pilate to do for them according to his custom. 9 Then he answered them, "Do you want me to release for you the King of the Jews?" 10 For he realized that it was out of jealousy that the chief priests had handed Jesus over. 11 But the chief priests stirred up the crowd to have him release Barabbas for them instead. 12 Pilate spoke to them again, "Then what do you wish me to do[n] with the one you call[o] the King of the Jews?" 13 They shouted back, "Crucify him!" 14 Pilate asked them, "Why, what evil has he done?" But they shouted all the more, "Crucify him!" 15 So Pilate, wishing to satisfy the crowd, released Barabbas for them; and after flogging Jesus, he handed him over to be crucified.

The Soldiers Mock Jesus

16 Then the soldiers led Jesus into the courtyard of the palace (that is, the governor's headquarters[p]); and they called together the whole cohort. 17 And they clothed Jesus in purple; and after twisting some thorns into a crown, they put it on him. 18 And they began saluting Jesus, "Hail, King of the Jews!" 19 They struck Jesus' head with a reed, spat upon him, and knelt down in homage to him. 20 After mocking Jesus, they stripped him of the purple[q] and put his own clothes on him. Then they led Jesus out to be crucified.

The Crucifixion of Jesus

21 They compelled a passer-by, who was coming in from the country, to carry Jesus' cross; it was Simon of Cyrene, the father of Alexander and Rufus. 22 Then they brought Jesus to the place called Golgotha (which means the place of a skull). 23 And they offered Jesus wine mixed with myrrh; but he did not take it. 24 And they crucified Jesus, and divided his clothes among them, casting lots to decide what each should take.

---

n Other ancient authorities read *what should I do*
o Other ancient authorities lack *the one you call*   p Gk *the praetorium*
q The *purple* refers to a cloak or robe that symbolizes royalty

25 It was nine o'clock in the morning when they crucified Jesus. 26 The inscription of the charge against him read, "The King of the Jews." 27 And with Jesus they crucified two bandits, one on the right and one on the left.ʳ 29 Those who passed by der`ided`ˢ Jesus, shaking their heads and saying, "Aha! You who would destroy the temple and build it in three days, 30 save yourself, and come down from the cross!" 31 In the same way the chief priests, along with the scribes, were also mocking Jesus among themselves and saying, "He saved others, but cannot save himself. 32 Let the Messiah,ᵗ the King of Israel, come down from the cross now, so that we may see and believe." Those who were crucified with Jesus also taunted him.

The Death of Jesus

33 When it was noon, night fell over the whole landᵘ until three in the afternoon. 34 At three o'clock Jesus cried out with a loud voice, "Eloi, Eloi, lema sabachthani?" which means, "My God, my God, why have you forsaken me?"ᵛ 35 When some of the bystanders heard it, they said, "Listen, Jesus is calling for Elijah." 36 And someone ran, filled a sponge with sour wine, put it on a stick, and gave it to Jesus to drink, saying, "Wait, let us see whether Elijah will come to take Jesus down." 37 Then Jesus gave a loud cry, and died. 38 And the curtain of the temple was torn in two, from top to bottom. 39 Now when the centurion, who stood facing Jesus, saw that Jesusʷ had died in this way, he said, "Truly this was the Child of God!"ˣ

40 There were also women looking on from a distance; among them were Mary Magdalene, and Mary the mother of James the younger and of Joses, and Salome. 41 When Jesus was in Galilee, they used to follow and provide for him; and there were many other women who had come up with Jesus to Jerusalem.

The Burial of Jesus

42 When evening had come, and since it was the day of Preparation, that is, the day before the sabbath, 43 Joseph of Arimathea, a respected member of the council, who was also himself waiting expectantly for the dominion of God, went boldly to Pilate and asked for the body of Jesus. 44 Then Pilate wondered if Jesus were already dead; and summoning the centurion, he asked him whether Jesus had been dead for some time. 45 On learning from the centurion that Jesus was dead, Pilate granted the body to Joseph. 46 Then Joseph bought a linen cloth, and taking down the body, wrapped it in the linen cloth, and laid it in a tomb that had been hewn out of the rock. He then rolled a stone against the door of the tomb. 47 Mary Magdalene and Mary the mother of Joses saw where the body was laid.

---

r Other ancient authorities add verse 28, *And the scripture was fulfilled that says, "And he was counted among the lawless."*   s Or *blasphemed*   t Or *the Christ*   u Or *earth*
v Other ancient authorities read *made me a reproach*
w Other ancient authorities add *had cried out and*   x Or *a child of God*

The Resurrection of Jesus

16 When the sabbath was over, Mary Magdalene, and Mary the mother of James, and Salome bought spices, so that they might go and anoint Jesus. ²And very early on the first day of the week, when the sun had risen, they went to the tomb. ³They had been saying to one another, "Who will roll away the stone for us from the entrance to the tomb?" ⁴When they looked up, they saw that the stone, which was very large, had already been rolled back. ⁵As they entered the tomb, they saw someone, dressed in a white robe, sitting on the right side; and they were alarmed. ⁶But the person said to them, "Do not be alarmed; you are looking for Jesus of Nazareth, who was crucified. Jesus has been raised and is not here. Look, there is the place they laid the body. ⁷But go, tell the disciples and Peter that Jesus is going ahead of you to Galilee; there you will see Jesus, just as he told you." ⁸So they went out and fled from the tomb, for terror and amazement had seized them; and they said nothing to anyone, for they were afraid.ʸ

THE SHORTER ENDING OF MARK

⟦And all that had been commanded them they told briefly to those around Peter. And afterward that same Jesus sent out through them, from east to west, the sacred and imperishable proclamation of eternal salvation.ᶻ⟧

THE LONGER ENDING OF MARK

Jesus Appears to Mary Magdalene

9 ⟦Now having risen early on the first day of the week, Jesus appeared first to Mary Magdalene, from whom Jesus had cast out seven demons. ¹⁰She went out and told those who had been with Jesus, while they were mourning and weeping. ¹¹But when they heard that Jesus was alive and had been seen by her, they would not believe it.

Jesus Appears to Two Disciples

12 After this Jesus appeared in another form to two of them, as they were walking into the country. ¹³And they went back and told the rest, but they did not believe them.

---

y Some of the most ancient authorities bring the book to a close at the end of verse 8. One authority concludes the book with the shorter ending; others include the shorter ending and then continue with verses 9-20. In most authorities verses 9-20 follow immediately after verse 8, though in some of these authorities the passage is marked as being doubtful.

z Other ancient authorities add *Amen*

Jesus Commissions the Disciples

14 Later Jesus appeared to the eleven themselves as they were sitting at the table, and upbraided them for their lack of faith and stubbornness, because they had not believed those who saw Jesus after Jesus had risen.[a] 15 And Jesus said to them, "Go into all the world and proclaim the good news[b] to the whole creation. 16 The one who believes and is baptized will be saved; but the one who does not believe will be condemned. 17 And these signs will accompany those who believe: by using my name they will cast out demons; they will speak in new tongues; 18 they will pick up snakes in their hands,[c] and if they drink any deadly thing, it will not hurt them; they will lay their hands on those who are sick, and they will recover."

The Ascension of Jesus

19 So then the Lord Jesus, after speaking to them, was taken up into heaven and sat at the side of God. 20 And they went out and proclaimed the good news everywhere, while the Lord worked with them and confirmed the message by the signs that accompanied it.[d]

---

a Other ancient authorities add, in whole or in part, *And they excused themselves, saying, "This age of lawlessness and unbelief is under Satan, who does not allow the truth and power of God to prevail over the unclean things of the spirits. Therefore reveal your righteousness now"—thus they spoke to Christ. And Christ replied to them, "The term of years of Satan's power has been fulfilled, but other terrible things draw near. And for those who have sinned I was handed over to death, that they may return to the truth and sin no more, that they may inherit the spiritual and imperishable glory of righteousness that is in heaven."*   b Or *gospel*
c Other ancient authorities lack *in their hands*   d Other ancient authorities add *Amen*

The Gospel According to Luke

Dedication to Theophilus

1 Since many have undertaken to set down an orderly account of the events that have been fulfilled among us, ²just as they were handed on to us by those who from the beginning were eyewitnesses and servants of the word, ³I too decided, after investigating everything carefully from the very first,ᵃ to write an orderly account for you, most excellent Theophilus, ⁴so that you may know the truth concerning the things about which you have been instructed.

The Birth of John the Baptist Foretold

5 In the days of King Herod of Judea, there was a priest named Zechariah, who belonged to the priestly order of Abijah. His wife was a descendant of Aaron, and her name was Elizabeth. ⁶Both of them were righteous before God, living blamelessly according to all of God's commandments and regulations. ⁷But they had no children, because Elizabeth was infertile, and both were getting on in years.

8 Once when Zechariah was serving as priest before God and his section was on duty, ⁹he was chosen by lot, according to the custom of the priesthood, to enter the sanctuary of God and offer incense. ¹⁰Now at the time of the incense offering, the whole assembly of the people was praying outside. ¹¹Then there appeared to him an angel of God, standing at the right side of the altar of incense. ¹²When Zechariah saw the angel, he was terrified; and fear overwhelmed him. ¹³But the angel said to him, "Do not be afraid, Zechariah, for your prayer has been heard. Your wife Elizabeth will bear you a son, and you will name him John. ¹⁴You will have joy and gladness, and many will rejoice at his birth, ¹⁵for John will be great in the sight of God. He must never drink wine or strong drink; even before his birth he will be filled with the Holy

---

a Or *for a long time*

87

Spirit. [16]John will turn many of the people of Israel to the Sovereign their God. [17]With the spirit and power of Elijah John will go before the Lord, to turn the hearts of parents to their children, and the disobedient to the wisdom of the righteous, to make ready a people prepared for the Lord." [18]Zechariah said to the angel, "How will I know that this is so? For I am old and my wife is getting on in years." [19]The angel replied, "I am Gabriel. I stand in the presence of God, and I have been sent to speak to you and to bring you this good news. [20]But now, because you did not believe my words, which will be fulfilled in their time, you will become mute, unable to speak, until the day these things occur."

21 Meanwhile the people were waiting for Zechariah, and wondered at his delay in the sanctuary. [22]When he did come out, he could not speak to them, and they realized that he had seen a vision in the sanctuary. Zechariah kept motioning to them and remained unable to speak. [23]When his time of service was ended, he went to his home.

24 After those days his wife Elizabeth conceived, and for five months she remained in seclusion. She said, [25]"This is what God has done for me when God looked favorably on me and took away the disgrace I have endured among my people."

The Birth of Jesus Foretold

26 In the sixth month the angel Gabriel was sent by God to a town in Galilee called Nazareth, [27]to a virgin engaged to a man whose name was Joseph, of the house of David. The virgin's name was Mary. [28]And the angel came to her and said, "Greetings, favored one! God is with you."[b] [29]But she was much perplexed by the angel's words and pondered what sort of greeting this might be. [30]The angel said to her, "Do not be afraid, Mary, for you have found favor with God. [31]And now, you will conceive in your womb and bear a child, whom you will name Jesus. [32]This child will be great, and will be called the Child of the Most High, and on this child the Sovereign God will bestow the throne of David's lineage. [33]Jesus will reign over the house of Jacob forever, and of that reign there will be no end." [34]Mary said to the angel, "How can this be, since I am a virgin?"[c] [35]The angel said to her, "The Holy Spirit will come upon you, and the power of the Most High will overshadow you; therefore the child to be born[d] will be holy and will be called Child of God. [36]And now, your relative Elizabeth in her old age has also conceived a child; and this is the sixth month for her who was said to be infertile. [37]For nothing will be impossible with God." [38]Then Mary said, "Here am I, the servant of God; let it be with me according to your word." Then the angel departed from her.

---

b Other ancient authorities add *Blessed are you among women*   c Gk *I do not know a man*
d Other ancient authorities add *of you*

Mary Visits Elizabeth

39 In those days Mary set out and went with haste to a Judean town in the hill country, 40 where she entered the house of Zechariah and greeted Elizabeth. 41 When Elizabeth heard Mary's greeting, the child leaped in her womb. And Elizabeth was filled with the Holy Spirit 42 and exclaimed with a loud cry, "Blessed are you among women, and blessed is the fruit of your womb. 43 And why has this happened to me, that the mother of my Lord comes to me? 44 For as soon as I heard the sound of your greeting, the child in my womb leaped for joy. 45 And blessed is she who believed that there would be^e a fulfillment of what was spoken to her by God."

Mary's Song of Praise

46 And Mary^f said,

> "My soul magnifies the Most High,
47 >   and my spirit rejoices in God my Savior,
48 > who has looked with favor on the lowliness of God's
>   servant.
>   Surely, from now on all generations will call
>   me blessed;
49 > for the Mighty One has done great things for me,
>   and holy is God's name.
50 > God's mercy is for those who revere God
>   from generation to generation.
51 > God has shown strength with God's arm,
>   and has scattered the proud in the thoughts of their
>   hearts.
52 > God has brought down the powerful from their thrones,
>   and lifted up the lowly;
53 > God has filled the hungry with good things,
>   and sent the rich away empty.
54 > God has helped God's servant Israel,
>   in remembrance of God's mercy,
55 > according to the promise God made to our ancestors,
>   to Abraham and Sarah and to their descendants
>   forever."

56 And Mary remained with her about three months and then returned to her home.

---

e Or *believed, for there will be*   f Other ancient authorities read *Elizabeth*

The Birth of John the Baptist

57 Now the time came for Elizabeth to give birth, and she bore a son. 58 Her neighbors and relatives heard that God had shown great mercy to her, and they rejoiced with her.

59 On the eighth day they came to circumcise the child, and they were going to name him Zechariah after his father. 60 But his mother said, "No; he is to be called John." 61 They said to her, "None of your relatives has this name." 62 Then they began motioning to his father to find out what name he wanted to give him. 63 He asked for a writing tablet and wrote, "His name is John." And all of them were amazed. 64 Immediately Zechariah's mouth was opened and his tongue freed, and he began to speak, praising God. 65 Fear came over all their neighbors, and all these things were talked about throughout the entire hill country of Judea. 66 All who heard them pondered them and said, "What then will this child become?" For, indeed, the hand of God was with him.

Zechariah's Prophecy

67 Then his father Zechariah was filled with the Holy Spirit and spoke this prophecy:

68   "Blessed be the Sovereign God of Israel,
            who has looked favorably on God's people and
                redeemed them.
69   God has raised up a mighty savior[g] for us
            in the house of God's servant David,
70   as God spoke through the mouth of God's holy
                prophets from of old,
71   that we would be saved from our enemies and from
            the hand of all who hate us.
72   Thus God has shown the mercy promised to our
                ancestors,
            and has remembered God's holy covenant,
73   the oath that God swore to our ancestor Abraham,
            to grant us 74 that we, being rescued from the hands of
            our enemies,
            might serve God without fear, 75 in holiness and
                righteousness
            before God all our days.
76   And you, child, will be called the prophet of the Most
                High;
            for you will go before the Lord to prepare the ways
                of the Lord,

---

g Gk *a horn of salvation*

77 to give knowledge of salvation to the people
by the forgiveness of their sins.
78 By the tender mercy of our God,
the dawn from on high will break upon[h] us,
79 to give light to those who sit in the night and in the
shadow of death,
to guide our feet into the way of peace."

80 The child grew and became strong in spirit, and was in the wilderness until the day he appeared publicly to Israel.

The Birth of Jesus

2 In those days a decree went out from Emperor Augustus that all the world should be registered. ²This was the first registration and was taken while Quirinius was governor of Syria. ³All went to their own towns to be registered. ⁴Joseph also went from the town of Nazareth in Galilee to Judea, to the city of David called Bethlehem, because he was descended from the house and family of David. ⁵Joseph went to be registered with Mary, to whom he was engaged and who was expecting a child. ⁶While they were there, the time came for her to deliver her child. ⁷And she gave birth to her firstborn child whom she wrapped in bands of cloth and laid in a manger, because there was no place for them in the inn.

The Shepherds and the Angels

8 In that region there were shepherds living in the fields, keeping watch over their flock by night. ⁹Then an angel of God stood before them, and the glory of God shone around them, and they were terrified. ¹⁰But the angel said to them, "Do not be afraid; for see—I am bringing you good news of great joy for all the people: ¹¹to you is born this day in the city of David a Savior, who is the Messiah,[i] the Lord. ¹²This will be a sign for you: you will find a child wrapped in bands of cloth and lying in a manger." ¹³And suddenly there was with the angel a multitude of the heavenly host,[j] praising God and saying,

14 "Glory to God in the highest heaven,
and on earth peace among those with whom God is
pleased!"[k]

15 When the angels had left them and gone into heaven, the shepherds said to one another, "Let us go now to Bethlehem and see this thing that has taken place, which God has made known to us." ¹⁶So they went with haste and found Mary and Joseph, and the child lying in the manger. ¹⁷When they saw this, they made known what had been told them about this child; ¹⁸and all who

---

h Other ancient authorities read *has broken upon*   i Or *the Christ*   j Gk *army*
k Other ancient authorities read *peace, goodwill among people*

heard it were amazed at what the shepherds told them. [19] But Mary treasured all these words and pondered them in her heart. [20] The shepherds returned, glorifying and praising God for all they had heard and seen, as it had been told them.

Jesus Is Named

21 After eight days had passed, it was time to circumcise the child; he was called Jesus, the name given by the angel before he was conceived in the womb.

Jesus Is Presented in the Temple

22 When the time came for their purification according to the law of Moses, they brought Jesus up to Jerusalem to be presented to God [23] (as it is written in God's law, "Every firstborn male shall be designated as holy to God"), [24] and they offered a sacrifice according to what is stated in the law of God, "a pair of turtledoves or two young pigeons."

25 Now there was a man in Jerusalem whose name was Simeon,[l] who was righteous and devout, looking forward to the consolation of Israel; and the Holy Spirit rested on him. [26] It had been revealed to Simeon by the Holy Spirit that he would not see death before he had seen God's Messiah.[m] [27] Guided by the Spirit, Simeon[n] came into the temple; and when the parents brought in the child Jesus, to do for him what was customary under the law, [28] Simeon took the child in his arms and praised God, saying,

29   "Sovereign God, now you are dismissing your servant in
            peace,
          according to your word;
30   for my eyes have seen your salvation,
31   which you have prepared in the presence of all
            peoples,
32   a light for revelation to the Gentiles
          and for glory to your people Israel."

33 And Jesus' father and mother were amazed at what was being said about their child. [34] Then Simeon[l] blessed them and said to Mary, Jesus' mother, "This child is destined for the falling and the rising of many in Israel, and to be a sign that will be opposed [35] so that the inner thoughts of many will be revealed—and a sword will pierce your own soul too."

36 There was also a prophet, Anna[o] the daughter of Phanuel, of the tribe of Asher. She was of a great age, having lived with her husband seven years after her marriage, [37] then as a widow to the age of eighty-four. She never left the temple but worshiped there with fasting and prayer night and day. [38] At that moment she came, and began to praise God and to speak about the child to all who were looking for the redemption of Jerusalem.

---

l Gk *Symeon*   m Or *the Christ of God*   n Gk *In the Spirit, he*   o Gk *Hanna*

The Return to Nazareth

39 When they had finished everything required by the law of God, they
returned to Galilee, to their own town of Nazareth. 40 The child grew and
became strong, filled with wisdom; and the favor of God was upon him.

The Young Jesus in the Temple

41 Now every year Jesus' parents went to Jerusalem for the festival of the
Passover. 42 And when he was twelve years old, they went up as usual for the
festival. 43 When the festival was ended and they started to return, the young
Jesus stayed behind in Jerusalem, but his parents did not know it. 44 Assuming
that Jesus was in the group of travelers, they went a day's journey. Then they
started to look for him among their relatives and friends. 45 When they did not
find him, they returned to Jerusalem to search for him. 46 After three days they
found Jesus in the temple, sitting among the teachers, listening to them and
asking them questions. 47 And all who heard him were amazed at his understanding and his answers. 48 When his parents saw him they were astonished;
and his mother said to him, "Child, why have you treated us like this? Look,
your father and I have been searching for you in great anxiety." 49 Jesus said to
them, "Why were you searching for me? Did you not know that I must be in
the house of my Father-Mother?"[p] 50 But they did not understand what Jesus
said to them. 51 Then he went down with them and came to Nazareth, and was
obedient to them. His mother treasured all these things in her heart.

52 And Jesus increased in wisdom and in years,[q] and in divine and human
favor.

The Proclamation of John the Baptist

3 In the fifteenth year of the reign of Emperor Tiberius, when Pontius Pilate
was governor of Judea, and Herod was ruler[r] of Galilee, and his brother
Philip ruler[r] of the region of Ituraea and Trachonitis, and Lysanias ruler[r] of
Abilene, 2 during the high priesthood of Annas and Caiaphas, the word of God
came to John, son of Zechariah and Elizabeth, in the wilderness. 3 John went
into all the region around the Jordan, proclaiming a baptism of repentance for
the forgiveness of sins, 4 as it is written in the book of the words of the prophet
Isaiah,

> "The voice of one crying out in the wilderness:
> 'Prepare the way of the Lord,
>   make the paths of the Lord straight.
> 5 Every valley shall be filled,
>   and every mountain and hill shall be made low,
> and the crooked shall be made straight,

---

p Or *be about my Father-Mother's interests?* q Or *in stature* r Gk *tetrarch*

and the rough ways made smooth;

6   and all flesh shall see the salvation of God.' "

7 John said to the crowds that came out to be baptized by him, "You brood of vipers! Who warned you to flee from the wrath to come? 8 Bear fruits worthy of repentance. Do not begin to say to yourselves, 'We have Abraham and Sarah as our ancestors'; for I tell you, God is able from these stones to raise up children to them. 9 Even now the ax is lying at the root of the trees; every tree therefore that does not bear good fruit is cut down and thrown into the fire."

10 And the crowds asked John, "What then should we do?" 11 In reply he said to them, "Whoever has two coats must share with anyone who has none; and whoever has food must do likewise." 12 Even tax collectors came to be baptized, and they asked John, "Teacher, what should we do?" 13 He said to them, "Collect no more than the amount prescribed for you." 14 Soldiers also asked him, "And we, what should we do?" John said to them, "Do not extort money from anyone by threats or false accusation, and be satisfied with your wages."

15 As the people were filled with expectation, and all were questioning in their hearts concerning John, whether he might be the Messiah,ˢ 16 John answered all of them by saying, "I baptize you with water; but one who is more powerful than I is coming, the thong of whose sandals I am not worthy to untie. That one will baptize you withᵗ the Holy Spirit and fire. 17 With winnowing fork in hand, that one will clear the threshing floor and gather the wheat into the granary, but will burn the chaff with unquenchable fire."

18 So, with many other exhortations, John proclaimed the good news to the people. 19 But Herod the ruler,ᵘ who had been rebuked by John because of Herodias, the wife of Herod's brother, and because of all the evil things that Herod had done, 20 added to them all by shutting up John in prison.

The Baptism of Jesus

21 Now when all the people were baptized, and when Jesus also had been baptized and was praying, the heaven was opened, 22 and the Holy Spirit descended upon Jesus in bodily form like a dove. And a voice came from heaven, "You are my Child, the Beloved;ᵛ with you I am well pleased."ʷ

The Ancestors of Jesus

23 Jesus was about thirty years old when he began his work. He was the son (as was thought) of Joseph whose ancestors went back (in order) from Heli, 24 to Matthat, to Levi, to Melchi, to Jannai, to Joseph, 25 to Mattathias, to Amos, to Nahum, to Esli, to Naggai, 26 to Maath, to Mattathias, to Semein, to Josech,

---

s Or *the Christ*   t Or *in*   u Gk *tetrarch*   v Or *my beloved Child*
w Other ancient authorities read *You are my Child, today I have begotten you*

to Joda, 27to Joanan, to Rhesa, to Zerubbabel, to Shealtiel,ˣ to Neri, 28to Melchi, to Addi, to Cosam, to Elmadam, to Er, 29to Joshua, to Eliezer, to Jorim, to Matthat, to Levi, 30to Simeon, to Judah, to Joseph, to Jonam, to Eliakim, 31to Melea, to Menna, to Mattatha, to Nathan, to David, 32to Jesse, to Obed, to Boaz, to Sala,ʸ to Nahshon, 33to Amminadab, to Admin, to Arni,ᶻ to Hezron, to Perez, to Judah, 34to Jacob, to Isaac, to Abraham, to Terah, to Nahor, 35to Serug, to Reu, to Peleg, to Eber, to Shelah, 36to Cainan, to Arphaxad, to Shem, to Noah, to Lamech, 37to Methuselah, to Enoch, to Jared, to Mahalaleel, to Cainan, 38to Enos, to Seth, to Adam, who was son of God.

The Temptation of Jesus

4 Jesus, full of the Holy Spirit, returned from the Jordan and was led by the Spirit in the wilderness, 2where for forty days he was tempted by the devil. Jesus ate nothing at all during those days, and when they were over, he was famished. 3The devil said to Jesus, "If you are the Child of God, command this stone to become a loaf of bread." 4Jesus answered, "It is written, 'One does not live by bread alone.' "

5 Then the devil led Jesus up and showed him in an instant all the nations of the world. 6And the devil said, "To you I will give their glory and all this authority; for it has been given over to me, and I give it to anyone I please. 7If you, then, will worship me, it will all be yours." 8Jesus answered, "It is written,

'Worship the Sovereign your God,
    and serve God alone.' "

9 Then the devil took Jesus to Jerusalem, and placed him on the pinnacle of the temple, and said, "If you are the Child of God, throw yourself down from here, 10for it is written,

'God will command the angels concerning you,
    to protect you,'

11and

'On their hands they will bear you up,
    so that you will not dash your foot against a stone.' "

12Jesus answered, "It is said, 'Do not put the Sovereign your God to the test.' "
13Having finished every test, the devil departed from Jesus until an opportune time.

---

x Gk *Salathiel*   y Other ancient authorities read *Salmon*
z Other ancient authorities read *Amminadab, to Aram*; others vary widely

Jesus Begins His Ministry in Galilee

14 Then Jesus, filled with the power of the Spirit, returned to Galilee, and a report about him spread through all the surrounding country. 15 He began to teach in their synagogues and was praised by everyone.

The Rejection of Jesus at Nazareth

16 When Jesus came to Nazareth, where he had been brought up, he went to the synagogue on the sabbath day, as was his custom. He stood up to read, 17 and the scroll of the prophet Isaiah was given to him. Jesus unrolled the scroll and found the place where it was written:

18   "The Spirit of God is upon me,
                 who has anointed me
                      to bring good news to those who are poor,
                 who has sent me to proclaim release to those who are
                      captive
                 and recovery of sight to those who are blind,
                      to let those who are oppressed go free,
19   to proclaim the year of God's favor."

20 And Jesus rolled up the scroll, gave it back to the attendant, and sat down. The eyes of all in the synagogue were fixed on Jesus, 21 who began to say to them, "Today this scripture has been fulfilled in your hearing." 22 All spoke well of him and were amazed at the gracious words that came from his mouth. They said, "Is not this Joseph's son?" 23 Jesus said to them, "Doubtless you will quote to me this proverb, 'Healer, cure yourself!' And you will say, 'Do here also in your hometown the things that we have heard you did at Capernaum.' " 24 And Jesus said, "Truly I tell you, no prophet is accepted in the prophet's hometown. 25 But the truth is, there were many widows in Israel in the time of Elijah, when the heaven was shut up three years and six months, and there was a severe famine over all the land; 26 yet Elijah was sent to none of them except to a widow at Zarephath in Sidon. 27 There were also many people with leprosy[a] in Israel in the time of the prophet Elisha, and none of them was cleansed except Naaman the Syrian." 28 When they heard this, all in the synagogue were filled with rage. 29 They got up, drove Jesus out of the town, and led him to the brow of the hill on which their town was built, so that they might hurl him off the cliff. 30 But Jesus passed through the midst of them and went away.

The Person with an Unclean Spirit

31 Jesus went down to Capernaum, a city in Galilee, and was teaching them on the sabbath. 32 They were astounded at Jesus' teaching, because it was spoken with authority. 33 In the synagogue there was a person who had the spirit of an

---

a The term *leprosy* can refer to several diseases

unclean demon, who cried out with a loud voice, 34"Let us alone! What have you to do with us, Jesus of Nazareth? Have you come to destroy us? I know who you are, the Holy One of God." 35But Jesus rebuked the demon, saying, "Be silent, and come out!" After throwing the person down before them, the demon came out and the person was not harmed. 36They were all amazed and kept saying to one another, "What kind of utterance is this? For with authority and power Jesus commands the unclean spirits, and out they come!" 37And a report about Jesus began to reach every place in the region.

Healings at Simon's House

38 After leaving the synagogue Jesus entered Simon's house. Now Simon's mother-in-law was suffering from a high fever, and they asked Jesus about her. 39Then Jesus stood over her and rebuked the fever, and it left her. Immediately she got up and began to serve them.

40 As the sun was setting, all those who had any people who were sick with various kinds of diseases brought them to Jesus, who laid hands on each of them and cured them. 41Demons also came out of many, shouting, "You are the Child of God!" But Jesus rebuked them and would not allow them to speak, because they knew that he was the Messiah.b

Jesus Preaches in the Synagogues

42 At daybreak Jesus departed and went into a deserted place. And the crowds were looking for him; and when they reached him, they wanted to prevent him from leaving them. 43But Jesus said to them, "I must proclaim the good news of the dominion of God to the other cities also; for I was sent for this purpose." 44So he continued proclaiming the message in the synagogues of Judea.c

Jesus Calls the First Disciples

5 Once while Jesus was standing beside the lake of Gennesaret, and the crowd was pressing in on him to hear the word of God, 2he saw two boats there at the shore of the lake; the fishers had gone out of them and were washing their nets. 3Jesus got into one of the boats, the one belonging to Simon, and asked Simon to put out a little way from the shore. Then Jesus sat down and taught the crowds from the boat. 4When he had finished speaking, he said to Simon, "Put out into the deep water and let down your nets for a catch." 5Simon answered, "Teacher, we have worked all night long but have caught nothing. Yet if you say so, I will let down the nets." 6When they had done this, they caught so many fish that their nets were beginning to break. 7So they signaled their partners in the other boat to come and help them. And they came and filled both boats, so that they began to sink. 8But when Simon Peter saw it, he fell down at Jesus' knees, saying, "Go away from me, Lord, for I am

---

b Or the Christ   c Other ancient authorities read Galilee

a sinful person!" 9For he and all who were with him were amazed at the catch of fish that they had taken; 10and so also were James and John, sons of Zebedee, who were partners with Simon. Then Jesus said to Simon, "Do not be afraid; from now on you will be catching people." 11When they had brought their boats to shore, they left everything and followed Jesus.

Jesus Cleanses a Person with Leprosy

12 Once, when Jesus was in one of the cities, a person covered with leprosy[d] saw Jesus, bowed low before him, and begged, "Lord, if you choose, you can make me clean." 13Then Jesus stretched out his hand, touched the person, and said, "I do choose. Be made clean." Immediately the leprosy[d] went away. 14And Jesus ordered the person to tell no one. "Go," he said, "and show yourself to the priest, and, as Moses commanded, make an offering for your cleansing, for a testimony to them." 15But now more than ever the word about Jesus spread abroad; many crowds would gather to hear him and to be cured of their diseases. 16But he would withdraw to deserted places and pray.

Jesus Heals a Person Who Was Paralyzed

17 One day, while Jesus was teaching, Pharisees and teachers of the law were sitting near by (they had come from every village of Galilee and Judea and from Jerusalem); and the power of God was with Jesus to heal.[e] 18Just then some men came, carrying on a bed a person who was paralyzed, whom they were trying to bring in and lay before Jesus; 19but finding no way to bring the person in because of the crowd, they went up on the roof and lowered the one on the bed through the tiles into the middle of the crowd[f] in front of Jesus. 20Seeing their faith, Jesus said, "Friend, your sins are forgiven you." 21Then the scribes and the Pharisees began to question, "Who is this who is speaking blasphemies? Who can forgive sins but God alone?" 22Perceiving their questionings, Jesus answered them, "Why do you raise such questions in your hearts? 23Which is easier, to say, 'Your sins are forgiven you,' or to say, 'Stand up and walk'? 24But so that you may know that the Human One has authority on earth to forgive sins"—Jesus said to the one who was paralyzed—"I say to you, stand up and take your bed, and go to your home." 25Immediately the person stood up before them, took up the bed, and went home, glorifying God. 26Amazement seized all of them, and they glorified God and were filled with awe, saying, "We have seen strange things today."

Jesus Calls Levi

27 After this Jesus went out and saw a tax collector named Levi, sitting at the tax booth; and Jesus said to him, "Follow me." 28And Levi got up, left everything, and followed Jesus.

---

d The term *leprosy* can refer to several diseases
e Other ancient authorities read *was present to heal them*   f Gk *into the midst*

29 Then Levi gave a great banquet for Jesus in his house; and there was a large crowd of tax collectors and others sitting at the table[g] with them. [30]The Pharisees and their scribes were complaining to Jesus' disciples, saying, "Why do you eat and drink with tax collectors and sinners?" [31]Jesus answered, "Those who are well have no need of a physician, but those who are sick; [32]I have come to call not the righteous but sinners to repentance."

The Question about Fasting

33 Then they said to Jesus, "John's disciples, like the disciples of the Pharisees, frequently fast and pray, but your disciples eat and drink." [34]Jesus said to them, "You cannot make wedding guests fast while the bridegroom is with them, can you? [35]The days will come when the bridegroom will be taken away from them, and then they will fast in those days." [36]Jesus also told them a parable: "No one tears a piece from a new garment and sews it on an old garment; otherwise the new will be torn, and the piece from the new will not match the old. [37]And no one puts new wine into old wineskins; otherwise the new wine will burst the skins and will be spilled, and the skins will be destroyed. [38]But new wine must be put into fresh wineskins. [39]And no one after drinking old wine desires new wine, but says, 'The old is good.' "[h]

The Question about the Sabbath

6 One sabbath[i] while Jesus was going through the grainfields, the disciples plucked some heads of grain, rubbed them in their hands, and ate them. [2]But some of the Pharisees said, "Why are you doing what is not lawful[j] on the sabbath?" [3]Jesus answered, "Have you not read what David did when he and his companions were hungry? [4]He entered the house of God and took and ate the bread of the Presence, which it is not lawful for any but the priests to eat, and gave some to his companions?" [5]Then Jesus said to them, "The Human One is lord of the sabbath."

The Person with a Withered Hand

6 On another sabbath Jesus entered the synagogue and taught, and there was a person there whose right hand was withered. [7]The scribes and the Pharisees watched to see whether Jesus would cure on the sabbath, so that they might find an accusation against him. [8]Even though he knew what they were thinking, Jesus said to the one who had the withered hand, "Come and stand here." The person got up and stood there. [9]Then Jesus said to them, "I ask you, is it lawful to do good or to do harm on the sabbath, to save life or to destroy it?" [10]After looking around at all of them, Jesus said, "Stretch out your hand." The

g Gk *reclining*   h Other ancient authorities read *better*; others lack verse 39
i Other ancient authorities read *On the second first sabbath*
j Other ancient authorities add *to do*

person did so, and the hand was restored. ¹¹But they were filled with fury and discussed with one another what they might do to Jesus.

Jesus Chooses the Twelve Apostles

12 Now during those days Jesus went out to the mountain to pray; and he spent the night in prayer to God. ¹³And when day came, Jesus called the disciples and chose twelve of them, who were also named apostles: ¹⁴Simon, whom Jesus named Peter, and his brother Andrew, and James, and John, and Philip, and Bartholomew, ¹⁵and Matthew, and Thomas, and James son of Alphaeus, and Simon, who was called the Zealot, ¹⁶and Judas son of James, and Judas Iscariot, who became a traitor.

Jesus Teaches and Heals

17 Jesus came down with them and stood on a level place, with a great crowd of the disciples and a great multitude of people from all Judea, Jerusalem, and the coast of Tyre and Sidon. ¹⁸They had come to hear him and to be healed of their diseases; and those who were troubled with unclean spirits were cured. ¹⁹And all in the crowd were trying to touch Jesus, for power came out from him and healed all of them.

Blessings and Woes

20 Then Jesus looked up at the disciples and said:

> "Blessed are you who are poor,
>   for yours is the dominion of God.
21   "Blessed are you who are hungry now,
>   for you will be filled.
> "Blessed are you who weep now,
>   for you will laugh.

22 "Blessed are you when people hate you, and when they exclude you, revile you, and defame you^k on account of the Human One. ²³Rejoice in that day and leap for joy, for surely your reward is great in heaven; for that is what their ancestors did to the prophets.

24   "But woe to you who are rich,
>   for you have received your consolation.
25   "Woe to you who are full now,
>   for you will be hungry.
> "Woe to you who are laughing now,
>   for you will mourn and weep.

26 "Woe to you when all speak well of you, for that is what their ancestors did to the false prophets.

---

k Gk *cast out your name as evil*

Love for Enemies

27 "But I say to you that listen, Love your enemies, do good to those who hate you, 28bless those who curse you, pray for those who abuse you. 29If anyone strikes you on the cheek, offer the other also; and from anyone who takes away your coat do not withhold even your shirt. 30Give to everyone who begs from you; and if anyone takes away your goods, do not ask for them again. 31Do to others as you would have them do to you.

32 "If you love those who love you, what credit is that to you? For even those known as 'sinners'[l] love those who love them. 33If you do good to those who do good to you, what credit is that to you? For even sinners do the same. 34If you lend to those from whom you hope to receive, what credit is that to you? Even sinners lend to sinners, to receive as much again. 35But love your enemies, do good, and lend, expecting nothing in return.[m] Your reward will be great, and you will be children of the Most High; for God is kind to the ungrateful and the wicked. 36Be merciful, just as your Father-Mother is merciful.

Judging Others

37 "Do not judge, and you will not be judged; do not condemn, and you will not be condemned. Forgive, and you will be forgiven; 38give, and it will be given to you. A good measure, pressed down, shaken together, running over, will be put into your lap; for the measure you give will be the measure you get back."

39 Jesus also told them a parable: "Can one blind person guide another? Will not both fall into a pit? 40A disciple is not above the teacher, but everyone who is fully qualified will be like the teacher. 41Why do you see the speck in your neighbor's eye, but do not notice the log in your own eye? 42Or how can you say to your neighbor, 'Friend, let me take out the speck in your eye,' when you yourself do not see the log in your own eye? You hypocrite, first take the log out of your own eye, and then you will see clearly to take the speck out of your neighbor's eye.

A Tree and Its Fruit

43 "No good tree bears bad fruit, nor again does a bad tree bear good fruit; 44for each tree is known by its own fruit. Figs are not gathered from thorns, nor are grapes picked from a bramble bush. 45The good person out of the good treasure of the heart produces good, and the evil person out of evil treasure produces evil; for it is out of the abundance of the heart that the mouth speaks.

---

l The term *"sinners"* designated all those people unable or unwilling to follow all the teachings of the law.   m Other ancient authorities read *despairing of no one*

The Two Foundations

46 "Why do you call me 'Lord, Lord,' and do not do what I tell you? [47]I will show you what someone is like who comes to me, hears my words, and acts on them. [48]That one is like a person building a house, who dug deeply and laid the foundation on rock; when a flood arose, the river burst against that house but could not shake it, because it had been well built.[n] [49]But the one who hears and does not act is like a person who built a house on the ground without a foundation. When the river burst against it, immediately it fell, and great was the ruin of that house."

Jesus Heals a Centurion's Servant

7 After Jesus had finished all his sayings in the hearing of the people, he entered Capernaum. [2]A centurion there had a person enslaved to him whom he valued highly, who was ill and close to death. [3]Having heard about Jesus, the centurion sent some Jewish elders, asking Jesus to come and heal the one who was sick. [4]When they came to Jesus, they appealed to him earnestly, saying, "The centurion is worthy of having you do this for him, [5]for he loves our people and built our synagogue for us." [6]And Jesus went with them, but when he was not far from the house, the centurion sent friends to say to him, "Lord, do not trouble yourself, for I am not worthy to have you come under my roof; [7]therefore I did not presume to come to you. But only speak the word, and let my servant be healed. [8]For I also am a man set under authority, with soldiers under me; and I say to one, 'Go,' and he goes, and to another, 'Come,' and he comes, and to the one enslaved, 'Do this,' and it is done." [9]When Jesus heard this he was amazed at the centurion, and turned to the crowd that followed and said, "I tell you, not even in Israel have I found such faith." [10]When those who had been sent returned to the house, they found the one enslaved in good health.

Jesus Raises the Widow's Son at Nain

11 Soon afterward[o] Jesus went to a town called Nain, and the disciples and a large crowd went with him. [12]As he approached the gate of the town, a man who had died was being carried out. He was his mother's only son, and she was a widow; and with her was a large crowd from the town. [13]And seeing her, Jesus had compassion for her and said to her, "Do not weep." [14]Then he came forward and touched the bier, and the bearers stood still. And he said, "Young man, I say to you, rise!" [15]The dead man sat up and began to speak, and Jesus gave him to his mother. [16]Fear seized all of them; and they glorified God, saying, "A great prophet has risen among us!" and "God has looked favorably

---

n Other ancient authorities read *founded upon the rock*
o Other ancient authorities read *Next day*

on God's people!" [17]This word about Jesus spread throughout Judea and all the surrounding country.

Messengers from John the Baptist

18 The disciples of John reported all these things to him. So John summoned two of his disciples [19]and sent them to Jesus to ask, "Are you the one who is to come, or are we to wait for another?" [20]When they had come to Jesus, they said, "John the Baptist has sent us to you to ask, 'Are you the one who is to come, or are we to wait for another?' " [21]Jesus had just then cured many people of diseases, plagues, and evil spirits, and had given sight to many who were blind. [22]And he answered John's disciples, "Go and tell John what you have seen and heard: those who are blind receive their sight, those who are lame walk, those with leprosy[p] are cleansed, those who are deaf hear, the dead are raised, those who are poor have good news brought to them. [23]And blessed is anyone who takes no offense at me."

Jesus Praises John the Baptist

24 When John's messengers had gone, Jesus began to speak to the crowds about John: "What did you go out into the wilderness to look at? A reed shaken by the wind? [25]What then did you go out to see? Someone[q] dressed in soft robes? Look, those who put on fine clothing and live in luxury are in royal palaces. [26]What then did you go out to see? A prophet? Yes, I tell you, and more than a prophet. [27]This is the one about whom it is written,

> 'See, I am sending my messenger ahead of you,
>   who will prepare your way before you.'

[28]I tell you, among those born of women no one is greater than John; yet the least in the dominion of God is greater than John." [29](And all the people who heard this, including the tax collectors, acknowledged the justice of God,[r] because they had been baptized with John's baptism. [30]But by refusing to be baptized by John, the Pharisees and the lawyers rejected God's purpose for themselves.)

31 "To what then will I compare the people of this generation, and what are they like? [32]They are like children sitting in the marketplace and calling to one another,

> 'We played the flute for you, and you did not dance;
>   we wailed, and you did not weep.'

[33]For John the Baptist has come eating no bread and drinking no wine, and you say, 'He has a demon'; [34]the Human One has come eating and drinking,

---

p The term *leprosy* can refer to several diseases
q Or *Why then did you go out? To see someone*   r Or *praised God*

and you say, 'Look, a glutton and a drunkard, a friend of tax collectors and sinners!' 35 Nevertheless, wisdom is vindicated by all her children."

A Sinful Woman Forgiven

36 One of the Pharisees asked Jesus to eat with him, and he went into the Pharisee's house and took his place at the table. 37 And a woman in the city, who was a sinner, having learned that Jesus was eating in the Pharisee's house, brought an alabaster jar of ointment. 38 She stood behind Jesus at his feet, weeping, and began to bathe his feet with her tears and to dry them with her hair. Then she continued kissing his feet and anointing them with the ointment. 39 Now when the Pharisee who had invited him saw it, he said to himself, "If this man were a prophet, he would have known who and what kind of woman this is who is touching him—that she is a sinner." 40 Jesus spoke up and said to him, "Simon, I have something to say to you." "Teacher," Simon replied, "Speak." 41 "A certain creditor had two debtors; one owed more than a year's wages and the other less. 42 When they could not pay, he canceled the debts for both of them. Now which of them will love the creditor more?" 43 Simon answered, "I suppose the one for whom the creditor canceled the greater debt." And Jesus said to him, "You have judged rightly." 44 Then turning toward the woman, Jesus said to Simon, "Do you see this woman? I entered your house; you gave me no water for my feet, but she has bathed my feet with her tears and dried them with her hair. 45 You gave me no kiss, but from the time I came in she has not stopped kissing my feet. 46 You did not anoint my head with oil, but she has anointed my feet with ointment. 47 Therefore, I tell you, her sins, which were many, have been forgiven; hence she has shown great love. But the one to whom little is forgiven, loves little." 48 Then Jesus said to the woman, "Your sins are forgiven." 49 But those who were at the table with Jesus began to say among themselves, "Who is this who even forgives sins?" 50 And Jesus said to the woman, "Your faith has saved you; go in peace."

Some Women Accompany Jesus

8 Soon afterward Jesus went on through cities and villages, proclaiming and bringing the good news of the dominion of God. The twelve were with him, 2 as well as some women who had been cured of evil spirits and infirmities: Mary, called Magdalene, from whom seven demons had gone out, 3 and Joanna, the wife of Herod's steward Chuza, and Susanna, and many others, who provided for them[s] out of their resources.

The Parable of the Sower

4 When a great crowd gathered and people from town after town came to him, Jesus said in a parable: 5 "A sower went out to sow seed; and as the seed was being scattered, some fell on the path and was trampled on, and the birds of the

---

s Other ancient authorities read *him*

air ate it up. ⁶Some fell on the rock; and as it grew up, it withered for lack of moisture. ⁷Some fell among thorns, and the thorns grew with it and choked it. ⁸Some fell into good soil, and when it grew, it produced a hundredfold." Having said this, Jesus called out, "Let everyone pay attention!"

The Purpose of the Parables

9 Then the disciples asked Jesus what this parable meant. ¹⁰Jesus said, "To you it has been given to know the secrets[t] of the dominion of God; but to others I speak[u] in parables, so that

'looking they may not perceive,
    and listening they may not understand.'

The Parable of the Sower Explained

11 "Now the parable is this: The seed is the word of God. ¹²The ones on the path are those who have heard; then the devil comes and takes away the word from their hearts, so that they may not believe and be saved. ¹³The ones on the rock are those who, when they hear the word, receive it with joy. But these have no root; they believe only for a while and in a time of testing fall away. ¹⁴As for what fell among the thorns, these are the ones who hear; but as they go on their way, they are choked by the cares and riches and pleasures of life, and their fruit does not mature. ¹⁵But as for that in the good soil, these are the ones who, when they hear the word, hold it fast in an honest and good heart, and bear fruit with patient endurance.

A Lamp under a Jar

16 "No one after lighting a lamp hides it under a jar, or puts it under a bed, but puts it on a lampstand, so that those who enter may see the light. ¹⁷For nothing is hidden that will not be disclosed, nor is anything secret that will not become known and come to light. ¹⁸Then pay attention to how you listen; for to those who have, more will be given; and from those who do not have, even what they seem to have will be taken away."

The True Kindred of Jesus

19 Then Jesus' mother and brothers came to him, but they could not reach him because of the crowd. ²⁰And he was told, "Your mother and your brothers are standing outside, wanting to see you." ²¹But Jesus said to them, "My mother and my brothers are those who hear the word of God and do it."

Jesus Calms a Storm

22 One day Jesus got into a boat with the disciples and said to them, "Let us go across to the other side of the lake." So they put out, ²³and while they were

---

t Or mysteries   u Gk lacks I speak

sailing Jesus fell asleep. A windstorm swept down on the lake, and the boat was filling with water, and they were in danger. 24They went to him and woke him up, shouting, "Teacher, Teacher, we are perishing!" And Jesus woke up and rebuked the wind and the raging waves; they ceased, and there was a calm. 25Jesus said to them, "Where is your faith?" They were afraid and amazed, and said to one another, "Who then is this, who commands even the winds and the water, and they obey him?"

Jesus Heals a Person Possessed by Demons

26 Then they arrived at the country of the Gerasenes,ᵛ which is opposite Galilee. 27As Jesus stepped out on land, a man of the city who had demons met him. For a long time the man had wornʷ no clothes and did not live in a house but in the tombs. 28Seeing Jesus, the man fell down before him and shouted at the top of his voice, "What have you to do with me, Jesus, Child of the Most High God? I beg you, do not torment me"— 29for Jesus had commanded the unclean spirit to come out of the man. (For many times it had seized him; he was kept under guard and bound with chains and shackles, but he would break the bonds and be driven by the demon into the wilds.) 30Jesus then asked, "What is your name?" The reply came, "Legion"; for many demons had entered the man. 31They begged Jesus not to order them to go back into the abyss.

32 Now there on the hillside a large herd of swine was feeding; and the demons begged Jesus to let them enter these. So he gave them permission. 33Then the demons came out of the man and entered the swine, and the herd rushed down the steep bank into the lake and was drowned.

34 When the swineherds saw what had happened, they ran off and told it in the city and in the country. 35Then people came out to see what had happened, and when they came to Jesus, they found the man from whom the demons had gone, clothed and in his right mind, sitting at the feet of Jesus. And they were afraid. 36Those who had seen it told them how the one who had been possessed by demons had been healed. 37Then all the people of the surrounding country of the Gerasenesᵛ asked Jesus to leave them; for they were seized with great fear. So Jesus got into the boat and returned. 38The one from whom the demons had gone begged to be with Jesus; but Jesus sent him away, saying, 39"Return to your home, and declare how much God has done for you." So the man went away, proclaiming throughout the city how much Jesus had done for him.

---

v Other ancient authorities read *Gadarenes*; others, *Gergesenes*
w Other ancient authorities read *a man of the city who had had demons for a long time met him. He wore*

A Girl Restored to Life and a Woman Healed

40 Now when Jesus returned, the crowd welcomed him, for they were all waiting for him. ⁴¹Just then there came a man named Jairus, a leader of the synagogue. He fell at Jesus' feet and begged to come to his house, ⁴²for Jairus had an only daughter, about twelve years old, who was dying.

As Jesus went, the crowds pressed in on him. ⁴³Now there was a woman who had been suffering from hemorrhages for twelve years; and though she had spent all she had on ⋅physicians,ˣ no one could cure her. ⁴⁴She came up behind Jesus and touched the fringe of his clothes, and immediately her hemorrhage stopped. ⁴⁵Then Jesus asked, "Who touched me?" When all denied it, Peterʸ said, "Teacher, the crowds surround you and press in on you." ⁴⁶But Jesus said, "Someone touched me; for I noticed that power had gone out from me." ⁴⁷When the woman saw that she could not remain hidden, she came trembling; and falling down before Jesus, she declared in the presence of all the people why she had touched him, and how she had been immediately healed. ⁴⁸Jesus said to her, "Daughter, your faith has made you well; go in peace."

49 While Jesus was still speaking, someone came from the leader's house to say, "Your daughter is dead; do not trouble the teacher any longer." ⁵⁰When Jesus heard this, he replied, "Do not fear. Only believe, and she will be saved." ⁵¹When Jesus came to the house, he did not allow anyone to enter with him, except Peter, John, and James, and the child's father and mother. ⁵²They were all weeping and wailing for her; but Jesus said, "Do not weep; for she is not dead but sleeping." ⁵³And they laughed at him, knowing that she was dead. ⁵⁴But Jesus took her by the hand and called out, "Child, get up!" ⁵⁵Her spirit returned, and she got up at once. Then Jesus directed them to give her something to eat. ⁵⁶Her parents were astounded; but Jesus ordered them to tell no one what had happened.

The Mission of the Twelve

9 Then Jesus called the twelve together and gave them power and authority over all demons and to cure diseases, ²and he sent them out to proclaim the dominion of God and to heal. ³He said to them, "Take nothing for your journey, no staff, nor bag, nor bread, nor money—not even an extra tunic. ⁴Whatever house you enter, stay there, and leave from there. ⁵Wherever they do not welcome you, as you are leaving that town shake the dust off your feet as a testimony against them." ⁶They departed and went through the villages, bringing the good news and curing diseases everywhere.

---

x Other ancient authorities lack *and had spent all she had on physicians*
y Other ancient authorities add *and those who were with him*

Herod's Perplexity

7 Now Herod the ruler[z] heard about all that had taken place, and he was perplexed, because it was said by some that John had been raised from the dead, 8by some that Elijah had appeared, and by others that one of the ancient prophets had arisen. 9Herod said, "John I beheaded; but who is this about whom I hear such things?" And Herod tried to see Jesus.

Feeding the Five Thousand

10 On their return the apostles told Jesus all they had done. He took them with him and withdrew privately to a city called Bethsaida. 11When the crowds found out about it, they followed him; and Jesus welcomed them, and spoke to them about the dominion of God, and healed those who needed to be cured.

12 The day was drawing to a close, and the twelve came to Jesus and said, "Send the crowd away, so that they may go into the surrounding villages and countryside, to lodge and get provisions; for we are here in a deserted place." 13But he said to the twelve, "You give them something to eat." They said, "We have no more than five loaves and two fish—unless we are to go and buy food for all these people." 14For there were about five thousand men. And Jesus said to the disciples, "Make them sit down in groups of about fifty each." 15They did so and made them all sit down. 16And taking the five loaves and the two fish, Jesus looked up to heaven, and blessed and broke them, and gave them to the disciples to set before the crowd. 17And all ate and were filled. What was left over was gathered up, twelve baskets of broken pieces.

Peter's Declaration about Jesus

18 Once when Jesus was praying alone, with only the disciples near him, Jesus asked them, "Who do the crowds say that I am?" 19They answered, "John the Baptist; but others, Elijah; and still others, that one of the ancient prophets has arisen." 20Jesus said to them, "But who do you say that I am?" Peter answered, "The Messiah[a] of God."

Jesus Foretells His Death and Resurrection

21 Jesus sternly ordered and commanded them not to tell anyone, 22saying, "The Human One must undergo great suffering, and be rejected by the elders, chief priests, and scribes, and be killed, and on the third day be raised."

The Cross and Discipleship

23 Then Jesus said to them all, "If any want to become my followers, let them deny themselves and take up their cross daily and follow me. 24For those who want to save their life will lose it, and those who lose their life for my sake will save it. 25What does it profit them if they gain the whole world, but lose

---

z Gk *tetrarch*   a Or *The Christ*

or forfeit themselves? 26 Those who are ashamed of me and of my words, of them the Human One will be ashamed, when coming in glory and also in the glory of the Father-Mother and of the holy angels. 27 But truly I tell you, there are some standing here who will not taste death before they see the dominion of God."

The Transfiguration

28 Now about eight days after these sayings Jesus took Peter and John and James, and went up on the mountain to pray. 29 And while Jesus was praying, the appearance of his face changed, and his clothes became dazzling white. 30 Suddenly they saw two men, Moses and Elijah, talking to him. 31 They appeared in glory and were speaking of Jesus' departure, which he was about to accomplish at Jerusalem. 32 Now Peter and his companions were weighed down with sleep; but since they had stayed awake,[b] they saw Jesus' glory and the two men who stood with him. 33 Just as they were leaving Jesus, Peter said, "Teacher, it is good for us to be here; let us make three dwellings,[c] one for you, one for Moses, and one for Elijah"—not knowing what he said. 34 While Peter was saying this, a cloud came and overshadowed them; and they were terrified as they entered the cloud. 35 Then from the cloud came a voice that said, "This is my Child, my Chosen;[d] to this one you shall listen!" 36 When the voice had spoken, Jesus was found alone. And they kept silent and in those days told no one any of the things they had seen.

Jesus Heals a Child with a Demon

37 On the next day, when they had come down from the mountain, a great crowd met Jesus. 38 Just then a man from the crowd shouted, "Teacher, I beg you to look at my son; he is my only child. 39 Suddenly a spirit seizes him, and all at once he[e] shrieks. It convulses him until he foams at the mouth; it mauls him and will scarcely leave him. 40 I begged your disciples to cast it out, but they could not." 41 Jesus answered, "You faithless and perverse generation, how much longer must I be with you and bear with you? Bring your son here." 42 While he was coming, the demon dashed him to the ground in convulsions. But Jesus rebuked the unclean spirit, healed the child, and gave him back to his father. 43 And all were astounded at the greatness of God.

Jesus Again Foretells His Death

While everyone was amazed at all that he was doing, Jesus said to the disciples, 44 "Let these words sink into your ears: The Human One is going to be betrayed into human hands." 45 But they did not understand this saying; its meaning was concealed from them, so that they could not perceive it. And they were afraid to ask Jesus about this saying.

---

b Or *but when they were fully awake*   c Or *tents*
d Other ancient authorities read *my Beloved*   e Or *it*

True Greatness

46 An argument arose among them as to which one of them was the greatest.
47 But Jesus, aware of their inner thoughts, took a little child and put it by his side, 48 and said to them, "Whoever welcomes this child in my name welcomes me, and whoever welcomes me welcomes the one who sent me; for the least among all of you is the greatest."

Another Exorcist

49 John answered, "Teacher, we saw someone casting out demons in your name, and we forbade it, because that one does not follow with us." 50 But Jesus said to John, "Do not stop such a person; for whoever is not against you is for you."

A Samaritan Village Refuses to Receive Jesus

51 When the days drew near for Jesus to be taken up, he set his face to go to Jerusalem. 52 And Jesus sent messengers ahead of him. On their way they entered a village of the Samaritans to make ready for him; 53 but the people did not receive Jesus, because his face was set toward Jerusalem. 54 When the disciples James and John saw it, they said, "Lord, do you want us to command fire to come down from heaven and consume them?"[f] 55 But Jesus turned and rebuked them. 56 Then[g] they went on to another village.

Would-Be Followers of Jesus

57 As they were going along the road, someone said to Jesus, "I will follow you wherever you go." 58 And Jesus replied, "Foxes have holes, and birds of the air have nests; but the Human One has nowhere to lie down and sleep." 59 To another Jesus said, "Follow me." But that one said, "Lord, first let me go and bury my father." 60 But Jesus said, "Let the dead bury their own dead; but as for you, go and proclaim the dominion of God." 61 Another said, "I will follow you, Lord; but let me first say farewell to those at my home." 62 Jesus replied, "No one who puts a hand to the plow and looks back is fit for the dominion of God."

The Mission of the Seventy

10 After this the Lord appointed seventy[h] others and sent them on ahead in pairs to every town and place where he himself intended to go. 2 He said to them, "The harvest is plentiful, but the laborers are few; therefore ask the Lord of the harvest to send out laborers into the harvest. 3 Go on your

---

f Other ancient authorities add *as Elijah did*
g Other ancient authorities read *rebuked them, and said, "You do not know what spirit you are of, 56for the Human One has not come to destroy the lives of human beings but to save them."*
Then   h Other ancient authorities read *seventy-two*

way. See, I am sending you out like lambs into the midst of wolves. ⁴Carry no purse, no bag, no sandals; and greet no one on the road. ⁵Whatever house you enter, first say, 'Peace to this house!' ⁶And if anyone is there who shares in peace, your peace will rest on that person; but if not, it will return to you. ⁷Remain in the same house, eating and drinking whatever they provide, for the laborer deserves to be paid. Do not move about from house to house. ⁸Whenever you enter a town and its people welcome you, eat what is set before you; ⁹cure the sick who are there, and say to them, 'The dominion of God has come near to you.'ⁱ ¹⁰But whenever you enter a town and they do not welcome you, go out into its streets and say, ¹¹'Even the dust of your town that clings to our feet, we wipe off in protest against you. Yet know this: the dominion of God has come near.'ʲ ¹²I tell you, on that day it will be more tolerable for Sodom than for that town.

Woes to Unrepentant Cities

13 "Woe to you, Chorazin! Woe to you, Bethsaida! For if the deeds of power done in you had been done in Tyre and Sidon, they would have repented long ago, sitting in sackcloth and ashes. ¹⁴But at the judgment it will be more tolerable for Tyre and Sidon than for you. ¹⁵And you, Capernaum,

> will you be exalted to heaven?
> No, you will be brought down to Hades.

16 "Whoever listens to you listens to me, and whoever rejects you rejects me, and whoever rejects me rejects the one who sent me."

The Return of the Seventy

17 The seventyᵏ returned with joy, saying, "Lord, in your name even the demons submit to us!" ¹⁸Jesus said to them, "I watched Satan fall from heaven like a flash of lightning. ¹⁹See, I have given you authority to tread on snakes and scorpions, and over all the power of the enemy; and nothing will hurt you. ²⁰Nevertheless, do not rejoice at this, that the spirits submit to you, but rejoice that your names are written in heaven."

Jesus Rejoices

21 At that same hour Jesus rejoiced in the Holy Spiritˡ and said, "I thankᵐ you, Father-Mother, God of heaven and earth, because you have hidden these things from the wise and the intelligent and have revealed them to infants; yes, O God, for such was your gracious will.ⁿ ²²All things have been handed over to me by my Father-Mother; and no one knows who the Child is except the

---

i Or *is at hand for you*   j Or *is at hand*   k Other ancient authorities read *seventy-two*
l Other authorities read *in the spirit*   m Or *praise*
n Or *for so it was well-pleasing in your sight*

Father-Mother, or who the Father-Mother is except the Child and anyone to whom the Child chooses to reveal God."

23 Then turning to the disciples, Jesus said to them privately, "Blessed are the eyes that see what you see! 24For I tell you that many prophets and rulers desired to see what you see, but did not see it, and to hear what you hear, but did not hear it."

The Parable of the Good Samaritan

25 Just then a lawyer stood up to test Jesus. "Teacher," he said, "what must I do to inherit eternal life?" 26Jesus said to him, "What is written in the law? What do you read there?" 27The lawyer answered, "You shall love the Sovereign your God with all your heart, and with all your soul, and with all your strength, and with all your mind; and your neighbor as yourself." 28And Jesus said to him, "You have given the right answer; do this, and you will live."

29 But wanting to justify himself, the lawyer asked Jesus, "And who is my neighbor?" 30Jesus replied, "A man was going down from Jerusalem to Jericho, and fell into the hands of robbers, who stripped him, beat him, and went away, leaving him half dead. 31Now by chance a priest was going down that road; and when he saw him, he passed by on the other side. 32So likewise a Levite, when he came to the place and saw him, passed by on the other side. 33But a Samaritan while traveling came near him; and when he saw him, he was moved with pity. 34He went to him and bandaged his wounds, having poured oil and wine on them. Then the Samaritan put him on his own animal, brought him to an inn, and took care of him. 35The next day he took out some money, gave it to the innkeeper, and said, 'Take care of him; and when I come back, I will repay you whatever more you spend.' 36Which of these three, do you think, was a neighbor to the man who fell into the hands of the robbers?" 37The lawyer said, "The one who showed him mercy." Jesus said to him, "Go and do likewise."

Jesus Visits Martha and Mary

38 Now as they went on their way, Jesus entered a certain village, where a woman named Martha welcomed him into her home. 39She had a sister named Mary, who sat at the Lord's feet and listened to what he was saying. 40But Martha was distracted by her many tasks; so she came to him and asked, "Lord, do you not care that my sister has left me to do all the work by myself? Tell her then to help me." 41But the Lord answered her, "Martha, Martha, you are worried and distracted by many things; 42there is need of only one thing.° Mary has chosen the better part, which will not be taken away from her."

---

o Other ancient authorities read *few things are necessary, or only one*

Concerning Prayer

11 Jesus was praying in a certain place, and after he had finished, one of the disciples said to him, "Lord, teach us to pray, as John taught his disciples." 2Jesus said to them, "When you pray, say:

Father-Mother,[p] hallowed be your name.
May your dominion come.[q]
3 Give us each day our daily bread.[r]
4 And forgive us our sins,
for we ourselves forgive everyone indebted to us.
And do not bring us to the time of trial."[s]

5 And Jesus said to them, "Suppose one of you has a friend, and you go at midnight and say to him, 'Friend, lend me three loaves of bread; 6for a friend of mine has arrived, and I have nothing to serve.' 7And your friend answers from within, 'Do not bother me; the door has already been locked, and my children are with me in bed; I cannot get up and give you anything.' 8I tell you, even though your friend will not get up and give you anything because of being a friend, at least because of your persistence the friend will get up and give whatever is needed.

9 "So I say to you, Ask, and it will be given you; search, and you will find; knock, and the door will be opened for you. 10For everyone who asks receives, and everyone who searches finds, and for everyone who knocks, the door will be opened. 11Is there anyone among you who, if your child asks for[t] a fish, will give a snake instead of a fish? 12Or if the child asks for an egg, will give a scorpion? 13If you then, who are evil, know how to give good gifts to your children, how much more will the heavenly Father-Mother give the Holy Spirit[u] to those who ask!"

Jesus and Beelzebul

14 Now Jesus was casting out a demon that was mute; when the demon had gone out, the one who had been mute spoke, and the crowds were amazed. 15But some of them said, "He casts out demons by Beelzebul, the ruler of the demons." 16Others, as a test, kept demanding from Jesus a sign from heaven. 17But Jesus knew what they were thinking and said to them, "Every dominion divided against itself becomes a desert, and house falls on house. 18If Satan also is divided against Satan, how will Satan's dominion stand?—for you say that I

p Other ancient authorities read *Our Father-Mother in heaven*
q A few ancient authorities read *Your Holy Spirit come upon us and cleanse us.* Other ancient authorities add *Your will be done, on earth as in heaven* r Or *our bread for tomorrow*
s Or *us into temptation.* Other ancient authorities add *but rescue us from the evil one* (or *from evil*) t Other ancient authorities add *bread, will give a stone; or if your child asks for*
u Other ancient authorities read *the Father-Mother give the Holy Spirit from heaven*

cast out the demons by Beelzebul. 19Now if I cast out the demons by Beelzebul, by whom do your exorcists cast them out? Therefore they will be your judges. 20But if it is by the finger of God that I cast out the demons, then the dominion of God has come to you. 21When a strong people, fully armed, guard their castle, their property is safe. 22But when a stronger force attacks them and overpowers them, it takes away their armor in which they had trusted and divides their plunder. 23Whoever is not with me is against me, and whoever does not gather with me scatters.

The Return of the Unclean Spirit

24 "When the unclean spirit has gone out of a person, it wanders through waterless regions looking for a resting place, but not finding any, it says, 'I will return to my house from which I came.' 25When the unclean spirit comes, it finds the house swept and put in order. 26Then it goes and brings seven other spirits more evil than itself, and they enter and live there; and the last state of that person is worse than the first."

True Blessedness

27 While Jesus was saying this, a woman in the crowd raised her voice and said to him, "Blessed is the womb that bore you and the breasts that nursed you!" 28But Jesus said, "Blessed rather are those who hear the word of God and obey it!"

The Sign of Jonah

29 When the crowds were increasing, Jesus began to say, "This generation is an evil generation; it asks for a sign, but no sign will be given to it except the sign of Jonah. 30For just as Jonah became a sign to the people of Nineveh, so the Human One will be to this generation. 31The queen of the South will rise at the judgment with the people of this generation and condemn them, because she came from the ends of the earth to listen to the wisdom of Solomon, and see, something greater than Solomon is here! 32The people of Nineveh will rise up at the judgment with this generation and condemn it, because they repented at the proclamation of Jonah, and see, something greater than Jonah is here!

The Light of the Body

33 "No one after lighting a lamp puts it in a cellar,ᵛ but on the lampstand so that those who enter may see the light. 34Your eye is the lamp of your body. If your eye is healthy, your whole body is full of light; but if it is not healthy, your body is deprived of light. 35Therefore consider whether the light in you is not absent. 36If then your whole body is full of light, with no part of it

---

v Other ancient authorities add or under the bushel basket

deprived of light, it will be as full of light as when a lamp gives you light with its rays."

Jesus Denounces Pharisees and Lawyers

37 While Jesus was speaking, a Pharisee invited him to dinner; so Jesus went in and took his place at the table. 38 The Pharisee was amazed to see that Jesus did not first wash before dinner. 39 Then Jesus said to the Pharisee, "Now you Pharisees clean the outside of the cup and of the dish, but inside you are full of greed and wickedness. 40 You fools! Did not the one who made the outside make the inside also? 41 So give for alms those things that are within; and see, everything will be clean for you.

42 "But woe to you Pharisees! For you tithe mint and rue and herbs of all kinds, and neglect justice and the love of God; it is these you ought to have practiced, without neglecting the others. 43 Woe to you Pharisees! For you love to have the seat of honor in the synagogues and to be greeted with respect in the marketplaces. 44 Woe to you! For you are like unmarked graves, and people walk over them without realizing it."

45 One of the lawyers answered Jesus, "Teacher, when you say these things, you insult us too." 46 And Jesus said, "Woe also to you lawyers! For you load people with burdens hard to bear, and you yourselves do not lift a finger to ease them. 47 Woe to you! For you build the tombs of the prophets whom your ancestors killed. 48 So you are witnesses and approve of the deeds of your ancestors; for they killed them, and you build their tombs. 49 Therefore also the Wisdom of God said, 'I will send them prophets and apostles, some of whom they will kill and persecute,' 50 so that this generation may be charged with the blood of all the prophets shed since the foundation of the world, 51 from the blood of Abel to the blood of Zechariah, who perished between the altar and the sanctuary. Yes, I tell you, it will be charged against this generation. 52 Woe to you lawyers! For you have taken away the key of knowledge; you did not enter yourselves, and you hindered those who were entering."

53 When Jesus went outside, the scribes and the Pharisees began to be very hostile and to cross-examine him about many things, 54 lying in wait, to catch Jesus in something he might say.

A Warning against Hypocrisy

12 Meanwhile, when the crowd gathered by the thousands, so that they trampled on one another, Jesus began to speak first to the disciples, "Beware of the yeast of the Pharisees, that is, their hypocrisy. 2 Nothing is covered up that will not be uncovered, and nothing secret that will not become known. 3 Therefore whatever you have said under cover of night will be heard in the daylight, and what you have whispered behind closed doors will be proclaimed from the housetops.

Exhortation to Fearless Confession

4 "I tell you, my friends, do not fear those who kill the body, and after that can do nothing more. 5But I will warn you whom to fear: fear the one who, after killing someone, has authority^w to cast into hell.^{x} Yes, I tell you, fear that person! 6Are not five sparrows sold for two pennies? Yet not one of them is forgotten in God's sight. 7But even the hairs of your head are all counted. Do not be afraid; you are of more value than many sparrows.

8 "And I tell you, everyone who acknowledges me before others, the Human One also will acknowledge before the angels of God; 9but whoever denies me before others will be denied before the angels of God. 10And everyone who speaks a word against the Human One will be forgiven; but whoever blasphemes against the Holy Spirit will not be forgiven. 11When they bring you before the synagogues, the rulers, and the authorities, do not worry about how^y you are to defend yourselves or what you are to say; 12for the Holy Spirit will teach you at that very hour what you ought to say."

The Parable of the Rich Fool

13 Someone in the crowd said to Jesus, "Teacher, tell my brother to divide the family inheritance with me." 14But Jesus replied to him, "Friend, who set me to be a judge or arbitrator over you?" 15And Jesus said to them, "Take care! Be on your guard against all kinds of greed; for one's life does not consist in the abundance of possessions." 16Then Jesus told them a parable: "The land of a rich man produced abundantly. 17And he thought to himself, 'What should I do, for I have no place to store my crops?' 18Then the rich man said, 'I will do this: I will pull down my barns and build larger ones, and there I will store all my grain and my goods. 19And I will say to myself, 'Look you, you have ample goods laid up for many years; relax, eat, drink, be merry.' 20But God said to the rich man, 'You fool! This very night your life is being demanded of you. And the things you have prepared, whose will they be?' 21So it is with those who store up treasures for themselves but are not rich toward God."

Do Not Worry

22 Jesus said to the disciples, "Therefore I tell you, do not worry about your life, what you will eat, or about your body, what you will wear. 23For life is more than food, and the body more than clothing. 24Consider the ravens: they neither sow nor reap, they have neither storehouse nor barn, and yet God feeds them. Of how much more value are you than the birds! 25And can any of you by worrying add a single hour to your span of life? 26If then you are not able to do so small a thing as that, why do you worry about the rest? 27Consider the lilies, how they grow: they neither toil nor spin;^{z} yet I tell you, even

---

w Or *power*   x Gk *Gehenna*   y Other ancient authorities add *or what*
z Other ancient authorities read *Consider the lilies; they neither spin nor weave*

Solomon in all his glory was not clothed like one of these. 28 But if God so clothes the grass of the field, which is alive today and tomorrow is thrown into the oven, how much more will God clothe you—you of little faith! 29 And do not keep striving for what you are to eat and what you are to drink, and do not keep worrying. 30 For it is the nations of the world that strive after all these things, and your Father-Mother knows that you need them. 31 Instead, strive for God's dominion, and these things will be given to you as well.

32 "Do not be afraid, little flock, for it is God's good pleasure to give you the dominion. 33 Sell your possessions, and give alms. Make purses for yourselves that do not wear out, an unfailing treasure in heaven, where no thief comes near and no moth destroys. 34 For where your treasure is, there your heart will be also.

Watchful Servants

35 "Be dressed for action and have your lamps lit; 36 be like those who are waiting for the one who rules over them to return from the wedding banquet, so that they may open the door at once when the ruler comes and knocks. 37 Blessed are those servants who are found alert when the ruler comes; truly I tell you, the ruler will get ready, have them sit down to eat, and come and serve them. 38 If the ruler comes during the middle of the night, or near dawn, and finds them so, blessed are those servants.

39 "But know this: if the owner of the house had known at what hour the thief was coming, that owner[a] would not have let the house be broken into. 40 You also must be ready, for the Human One is coming at an unexpected hour."

Faithfulness and Watchfulness

41 Peter said, "Jesus, are you telling this parable for us or for everyone?" 42 And Jesus said, "Who then is the faithful and prudent manager whom the master will put in charge of those enslaved to him, to give them their allowance of food at the proper time? 43 Blessed is that manager whom the master will find at work when he arrives. 44 Truly I tell you, he will put that one in charge of all his possessions. 45 But if that manager thinks, 'My master is delayed in coming,' and begins to beat the other enslaved people, men and women, and to eat and drink and get drunk, 46 the manager's master will come on an unexpected day and at an unknown hour, and will cut the manager into pieces,[b] and put the manager with the unfaithful. 47 The manager who knew what the master wanted, but did not get ready or do what was wanted, will receive a severe beating. 48 But the one who did not know and did what deserved a beating will receive a light beating. From everyone to whom much has been given, much will be required; and from the one to whom much has been entrusted, even more will be demanded.

---

a Other ancient authorities add *would have watched and*   b Or *cut him off*

Jesus the Cause of Division

49 "I came to bring fire to the earth, and how I wish it were already kindled! 50 I have a baptism with which to be baptized, and what stress I am under until it is completed! 51 Do you think that I have come to bring peace to the earth? No, I tell you, but rather division! 52 From now on five in one household will be divided, three against two and two against three; 53 they will be divided:

> father against son
>   and son against father,
> mother against daughter
>   and daughter against mother,
> mother-in-law against her daughter-in-law
>   and daughter-in-law against mother-in-law."

Interpreting the Time

54 Jesus also said to the crowds, "When you see a cloud rising in the west, you immediately say, 'It is going to rain'; and so it happens. 55 And when you see the south wind blowing, you say, 'There will be scorching heat'; and it happens. 56 You hypocrites! You know how to interpret the appearance of earth and sky, but why do you not know how to interpret the present time?

Settling with Your Opponent

57 "And why do you not judge for yourselves what is right? 58 Thus, when you go with your accuser before a magistrate, on the way make an effort to settle the case,c or you may be dragged before the judge, and the judge hand you over to the officer, and the officer throw you in prison. 59 I tell you, you will never get out until you have paid the very last penny."

Repent or Perish

13 At that very time there were some present who told Jesus about the Galileans whose blood Pilate had mingled with their sacrifices. 2 Jesus asked them, "Do you think that because these Galileans suffered in this way they were worse sinners than all other Galileans? 3 No, I tell you; but unless you repent, you will all perish as they did. 4 Or those eighteen who were killed when the tower of Siloam fell on them—do you think that they were worse offenders than all the others living in Jerusalem? 5 No, I tell you; but unless you repent, you will all perish just as they did."

The Parable of the Barren Fig Tree

6 Then Jesus told this parable: "A man who had a fig tree planted in a vineyard came looking for fruit on it, and finding none, 7 said to the gardener,

---

c Gk *settle with your accuser*

'See here! For three years I have come looking for fruit on this fig tree, and still I find none. Cut it down! Why should it be wasting the soil?' 8The gardener replied, 'Sir, let it alone for one more year, until I dig around it and put manure on it. 9If it bears fruit next year, well and good; but if not, you can cut it down.' "

Jesus Heals a Woman Who Was Bent Over

10 Now Jesus was teaching in one of the synagogues on the sabbath. 11And just then there appeared a woman with a spirit that had crippled her for eighteen years. She was bent over and was quite unable to stand up straight. 12When Jesus saw her, he called her over and said, "Woman, you are set free from your ailment." 13When he laid his hands on her, immediately she stood up straight and began praising God. 14But the leader of the synagogue, indignant because Jesus had cured on the sabbath, kept saying to the crowd, "There are six days on which work ought to be done; come on those days and be cured, and not on the sabbath day." 15But Jesus answered, "You hypocrites! Does not each of you on the sabbath untie your ox or your donkey from the manger, and lead it away to give it water? 16And ought not this woman, a daughter of Abraham and Sarah whom Satan bound for eighteen long years, be set free from this bondage on the sabbath day?" 17When Jesus said this, all his opponents were put to shame; and the entire crowd was rejoicing at all the wonderful things that Jesus was doing.

The Parable of the Mustard Seed

18 Jesus said therefore, "What is the dominion of God like? And to what should I compare it? 19It is like a mustard seed that someone took and sowed in the garden; it grew and became a tree, and the birds of the air made nests in its branches."

The Parable of the Yeast

20 And again Jesus said, "To what should I compare the dominion of God? 21It is like yeast that a woman took and mixed in with^d three measures of flour until all of it was leavened."

The Narrow Door

22 Jesus went through one town and village after another, teaching as he made his way to Jerusalem. 23Someone asked Jesus, "Will only a few be saved?" Jesus said to them, 24"Strive to enter through the narrow door; for many, I tell you, will try to enter and will not be able. 25When once the owner of the house has got up and shut the door, and you begin to stand outside and to knock at the door, saying, 'Open to us,' then in reply the householder will say to you, 'I do not know where you come from.' 26Then you will begin to say, 'We ate and

---

d Gk *hid in*

drank with you, and you taught in our streets.' ²⁷But the householder will say, 'I do not know where you come from; go away from me, all you evildoers!' ²⁸There will be weeping and gnashing of teeth when you see Abraham and Isaac and Jacob and all the prophets in the dominion of God, and you yourselves thrown out. ²⁹Then people will come from east and west, from north and south, and will eat in the dominion of God. ³⁰Indeed, some are last who will be first, and some are first who will be last."

The Lament over Jerusalem

31 At that very hour some Pharisees came and said to Jesus, "Get away from here, for Herod wants to kill you." ³²Jesus said to them, "Go and tell that fox for me,ᵉ 'Listen, I am casting out demons and performing cures today and tomorrow, and on the third day I finish my work. ³³Yet today, tomorrow, and the next day I must be on my way, because it is impossible for a prophet to be killed outside of Jerusalem.' ³⁴Jerusalem, Jerusalem, the city that kills the prophets and stones those who are sent to it! How often have I desired to gather your children together as a hen gathers her brood under her wings, and you were not willing! ³⁵See, your house is left to you. And I tell you, you will not see me until the time comes whenᶠ you say, 'Blessed is the one who comes in the name of the Lord.' "

Jesus Heals on the Sabbath

14 On one occasion when Jesus was going to the house of a leader of the Pharisees to eat a meal on the sabbath, they were watching him closely. ²Just then, in front of him, there was a person who suffered with swelling. ³And Jesus asked the lawyers and Pharisees, "Is it lawful to cure people on the sabbath, or not?" ⁴But they were silent. So Jesus, having taken and healed the sufferer, sent the person away. ⁵Then Jesus said to them, "If one of you has a childᵍ or an ox that has fallen into a well, will you not immediately pull it out on a sabbath day?" ⁶And they could not reply to this.

Humility and Hospitality

7 Noticing how the guests chose the places of honor, Jesus told them a parable. ⁸"When you are invited by someone to a wedding banquet, do not sit down at the place of honor, in case someone more distinguished than you has been invited by your host; ⁹and the host who invited both of you may come and say to you, 'Give this person your place,' and then in disgrace you would start to take the lowest place. ¹⁰But when you are invited, go and sit down at the lowest place, so that upon your arrival, the host may say to you, 'Friend, move up higher'; then you will be honored in the presence of all who sit at the table

---

e Gk lacks *for me*   f Other ancient authorities lack *the time comes when*
g Other ancient authorities read *a donkey*

with you. [11]For all who exalt themselves will be humbled, and those who humble themselves will be exalted."

12 Jesus said also to the one who had invited him, "When you give a luncheon or a dinner, do not invite your friends or your sisters and brothers or your relatives or rich neighbors, in case they may invite you in return, and you would be repaid. [13]But when you give a banquet, invite those who are poor and maimed and lame and blind, [14]and you will be blessed, because they cannot repay you, for you will be repaid at the resurrection of the righteous."

The Parable of the Great Dinner

15 One of the dinner guests, on hearing this, said to Jesus, "Blessed is anyone who will eat bread in the dominion of God!" [16]Then Jesus said, "Someone gave a great dinner and invited many. [17]At the time for the dinner the host sent a servant to say to those who had been invited, 'Come; for everything is ready now.' [18]But they all alike began to make excuses. The first said, 'I have bought a piece of land, and I must go out and see it; please accept my regrets.' [19]Another said, 'I have bought five yoke of oxen, and I am going to try them out; please accept my regrets.' [20]Another said, 'I have just been married, and therefore I cannot come.' [21]So the servant returned and reported this to the householder. Then the owner of the house became angry and said to the servant, 'Go out at once into the streets and lanes of the town and bring in those who are poor and maimed and blind and lame.' [22]And the servant said, 'What you ordered has been done, and there is still room.' [23]Then the householder said to the servant, 'Go out into the roads and lanes, and compel people to come in, so that my house may be filled. [24]For I tell you,[h] none of those who were invited will taste my dinner.' "

The Cost of Discipleship

25 Now large crowds were traveling with Jesus; and he turned and said to them, [26]"Whoever comes to me and does not hate father and mother, wife and children, brothers and sisters, yes, and even life itself, cannot be my disciple. [27]Whoever does not carry the cross and follow me cannot be my disciple. [28]For which of you, intending to build a tower, does not first sit down and estimate the cost, to see whether there is enough to complete it? [29]Otherwise, when the foundation is laid and the tower cannot be finished, all who see it will begin to ridicule the builder, [30]saying, 'This person began to build and was not able to finish.' [31]Or what king, going out to wage war against another king, will not sit down first and consider whether he is able with ten thousand to oppose the one who comes against him with twenty thousand? [32]If not, then, while the other is still far away, he sends a delegation and asks for the terms of peace. [33]So therefore, none of you can become my disciple if you do not give up all your possessions.

---

h The Greek word for *you* here is plural

About Salt

34 "Salt is good; but if salt has lost its taste, how can its saltiness be restored?ⁱ ³⁵It is fit neither for the soil nor for the manure pile; they throw it away. Let everyone pay attention!"

The Parable of the Lost Sheep

15 Now all the tax collectors and sinners were coming near to listen to Jesus. ²And the Pharisees and the scribes were grumbling and saying, "This fellow welcomes sinners and eats with them."

3 So Jesus told them this parable: ⁴"Which one of you, having a hundred sheep and losing one of them, does not leave the ninety-nine in the wilderness and go after the one that is lost until it is found? ⁵And having found it, the shepherd lays it on his shoulders and rejoices. ⁶And returning home, the shepherd calls together friends and neighbors, saying to them, 'Rejoice with me, for I have found my sheep that was lost.' ⁷Just so, I tell you, there will be more joy in heaven over one sinner who repents than over ninety-nine righteous persons who need no repentance.

The Parable of the Lost Coin

8 "Or what woman having ten silver coins, if she loses one of them, does not light a lamp, sweep the house, and search carefully until she finds it? ⁹When she has found it, she calls together her friends and neighbors, saying, 'Rejoice with me, for I have found the coin that I had lost.' ¹⁰Just so, I tell you, there is joy in the presence of the angels of God over one sinner who repents."

The Parable of the Prodigal and His Brother

11 Then Jesus said, "There was a man who had two sons. ¹²The younger of them said to his father, 'Father, give me the share of the property that will belong to me.' So he divided his property between them. ¹³A few days later the younger son gathered all he had and traveled to a distant country, and there he squandered his property in dissolute living. ¹⁴When he had spent everything, a severe famine took place throughout that country, and he began to be in need. ¹⁵So he went and hired himself out to one of the citizens of that country, who sent him to his fields to feed the pigs. ¹⁶He would gladly have filled himself withʲ the pods that the pigs were eating; and no one gave him anything. ¹⁷But when he came to himself he said, 'How many of my father's hired hands have bread enough and to spare, but here I am dying of hunger! ¹⁸I will get up and go to my father, and I will say to him, "Father, I have sinned against heaven and before you; ¹⁹I am no longer worthy to be called your son; treat me like one of your hired hands." ' ²⁰So he set off and went to his father. But while he

---

i Or *how can it be used for seasoning?*
j Other ancient authorities read *filled his stomach with*

was still far off, his father saw him and was filled with compassion; he ran and put his arms around him and kissed him. 21 Then the son said to him, 'Father, I have sinned against heaven and before you; I am no longer worthy to be called your son.'ᵏ 22 But the father said to his servants, 'Quickly, bring out a robe—the best one—and put it on him; put a ring on his finger and sandals on his feet. 23 And get the fatted calf and kill it, and let us eat and celebrate; 24 for this son of mine was dead and is alive again; he was lost and is found!' And they began to celebrate.

25 "Now his elder son was in the field; and when he came and approached the house, he heard music and dancing. 26 He called one of the servants and asked what was going on. 27 The servant replied, 'Your brother has come, and your father has killed the fatted calf, because he has got him back safe and sound.' 28 Then the elder son became angry and refused to go in. His father came out and began to plead with him. 29 But he answered his father, 'Listen! For all these years I have been working for you like a person enslaved, and I have never disobeyed your command; yet you have never given me even a young goat so that I might celebrate with my friends. 30 But when this son of yours came back, who has devoured your property with prostitutes, you killed the fatted calf for him!' 31 Then the father said to him, 'Son, you are always with me, and all that is mine is yours. 32 But we had to celebrate and rejoice, because this brother of yours was dead and has come to life; he was lost and has been found.' "

The Parable of the Unjust Manager

16 Then Jesus said to the disciples, "Someone who was rich had a manager, and charges were brought that the manager was squandering the property. 2 So the rich person summoned the manager and said, 'What is this that I hear about you? Give me an accounting of your management, because you cannot be my manager any longer.' 3 Then the manager thought, 'What will I do, now that my master is taking the position away from me? I am not strong enough to dig, and I am ashamed to beg. 4 I have decided what to do so that, when I am dismissed as manager, people may welcome me into their homes.' 5 So, summoning the rich person's debtors one by one, the manager asked the first, 'How much do you owe my master?' 6 The debtor answered, 'A hundred jugs of olive oil.' The manager said, 'Take your bill, sit down quickly, and make it fifty.' 7 Then the manager asked another, 'And how much do you owe?' That debtor replied, 'A hundred containers of wheat.' The manager said, 'Take your bill and make it eighty.' 8 And the rich person commended the unjust manager for acting shrewdly; for the children of this age are more shrewd in dealing with their own generation than are the children of light. 9 And I tell

---

k Other ancient authorities add *treat me as one of your hired servants*

you, make friends for yourselves by means of unjust wealth[l] so that when it is gone, they may welcome you into the eternal homes.[m]

10 "Whoever is faithful in a very little is faithful also in much; and whoever is unjust in a very little is unjust also in much. [11]If then you have not been faithful with the unjust wealth,[l] who will entrust to you the true riches? [12]And if you have not been faithful with what belongs to another, who will give you what is your own? [13]No person who is enslaved can serve two masters at the same time; for such a person will either hate the one and love the other, or be devoted to the one and despise the other. You cannot serve God and wealth."[l]

The Law and the Dominion of God

14 The Pharisees, who were lovers of money, heard all this, and they ridiculed Jesus. [15]So Jesus said to them, "You are those who justify yourselves in the sight of others; but God knows your hearts; for what is prized by human beings is an abomination in the sight of God.

16 "The law and the prophets were in effect until John came; since then the good news of the dominion of God is proclaimed, and everyone tries to enter it by force.[n] [17]But it is easier for heaven and earth to pass away, than for one stroke of a letter in the law to be dropped.

18 "Anyone who divorces his wife and marries another commits adultery, and whoever marries a woman divorced from her husband commits adultery.

The Rich Man and Lazarus

19 "There was a rich man who was dressed in purple and fine linen and who feasted sumptuously every day. [20]And at the gate lay a poor man named Lazarus, covered with sores, [21]who longed to satisfy his hunger with what fell from the rich man's table; even the dogs would come and lick his sores. [22]The poor man died and was carried away by the angels to be with Abraham.[o] The rich man also died and was buried, [23]and being in torment in Hades, he looked up and saw Abraham far away with Lazarus by his side.[p] [24]The rich man called out, 'Father Abraham, have mercy on me, and send Lazarus to dip the tip of his finger in water and cool my tongue; for I am in agony in these flames.' [25]But Abraham said, 'Child, remember that during your lifetime you received your good things, and Lazarus in like manner evil things; but now he is comforted here, and you are in agony. [26]Besides all this, between you and us a great chasm has been fixed, so that those who might want to pass from here to you cannot do so, and no one can cross from there to us.' [27]The rich man said, 'Then, father, I beg you to send Lazarus to my parents' house— [28]for I have five brothers—that he may warn them, so that they will not also come into this place of torment.' [29]Abraham replied, 'They have Moses and the

---

l Gk mammon   m Gk tents   n Or everyone is strongly urged to enter it
o Gk to Abraham's bosom   p Gk in his bosom

prophets; they should listen to them.' 30The rich man said, 'No, father Abraham; but if someone goes to them from the dead, they will repent.' 31Abraham answered, 'If they do not listen to Moses and the prophets, neither will they be convinced even if someone rises from the dead.' "

Some Sayings of Jesus

17 Jesus said to the disciples, "Occasions for stumbling are bound to come, but woe to anyone by whom they come! 2It would be better for you if a millstone were hung around your neck and you were thrown into the sea than for you to cause one of these little ones to stumble. 3Be on your guard! If another disciple sins, you must rebuke the offender, and if there is repentance, you must forgive. 4And if the same person sins against you seven times a day, and turns back to you seven times and says, 'I repent,' you must forgive."

5 The apostles said to Jesus, "Increase our faith!" 6Jesus replied, "If you had faith the size of aq mustard seed, you could say to this mulberry tree, 'Be uprooted and planted in the sea,' and it would obey you.

7 "Who among you would say to someone enslaved to you who has just come in from plowing or tending sheep in the field, 'Come here at once and take your place at the table'? 8Would you not rather say, 'Prepare supper for me, put on your apron and serve me while I eat and drink; later you may eat and drink'? 9Do you thank that person for doing what was commanded? 10So you also, when you have done all that you were ordered to do, say, 'We are worthless; we have done only what we ought to have done!' "

Jesus Cleanses Ten People with Leprosy

11 On the way to Jerusalem Jesus was going through the region between Samaria and Galilee. 12As he entered a village, ten people with leprosyr approached. Keeping their distance, 13they called out, saying, "Jesus, Teacher, have mercy on us!" 14And seeing them, Jesus said to them, "Go and show yourselves to the priests." And as they went, they were made clean. 15Then one of them, seeing that he was healed, turned back, praising God with a loud voice. 16He prostrated himself at Jesus' feet and thanked him. Now that one was a Samaritan. 17Then Jesus asked, "Were not ten made clean? But the other nine, where are they? 18Was none of them found to return and give praise to God except this foreigner?" 19Then Jesus said to him, "Get up and go on your way; your faith has made you well."

The Coming of the Dominion of God

20 Once Jesus was asked by the Pharisees when the dominion of God was coming, and he answered, "The dominion of God is not coming with things

---

q Gk *faith as a grain of*　　r The term *leprosy* can refer to several diseases that can be observed; 21nor will they say, 'Look, here it is!' or 'There it is!' For, in fact, the dominion of God is among[s] you."

22 Then Jesus said to the disciples, "The days' are coming when you will long to see one of the days of the Human One, and you will not see it. 23They will say to you, 'Look there!' or 'Look here!' Do not go, do not set off in pursuit. 24For as the lightning flashes and lights up the sky from one side to the other, so will the Human One be in that day.[t] 25But first the Human One must endure much suffering and be rejected by this generation. 26Just as it was in the days of Noah, so too it will be in the days of the Human One. 27They were eating and drinking, and marrying and being given in marriage, until the day Noah entered the ark, and the flood came and destroyed all of them. 28Likewise, just as it was in the days of Lot: they were eating and drinking, buying and selling, planting and building, 29but on the day that Lot left Sodom, it rained fire and sulfur from heaven and destroyed all of them 30—it will be like that on the day that the Human One is revealed. 31On that day, anyone on the housetop who has belongings in the house must not come down to take them away; and likewise anyone in the field must not turn back. 32Remember Lot's wife. 33Those who try to make their life secure will lose it, but those who lose their life will keep it. 34I tell you, on that night there will be two in one bed; one will be taken and the other left. 35There will be two women grinding meal together; one will be taken and the other left."[u] 37Then they asked him, "Where, Lord?" Jesus said to them, "Where the corpse is, there the vultures will gather."

The Parable of the Widow and the Unjust Judge

18 Then Jesus told them a parable about their need to pray always and not to lose heart. 2He said, "In a certain city there was a judge who neither feared God nor had respect for people. 3In that city there was a widow who kept coming to the judge and saying, 'Grant me justice against my opponent.' 4For a while the judge refused, but later thought, 'Though I have no fear of God and no respect for anyone, 5yet because this widow keeps bothering me, I will grant her justice, so that she may not wear me out by continually coming.' "[v] 6And Jesus said, "Listen to what the unjust judge says. 7And will not God grant justice to the chosen ones who cry to God day and night? Will God delay long in helping them? 8I tell you, God will quickly grant justice to them. And yet, when the Human One comes, will the Human One find faith on earth?"

---

s Or *within*   t Other ancient authorities lack *in that day*
u Other ancient authorities add verse 36, *"Two will be in the field; one will be taken and the other left."*   v Or *so that she may not finally come and slap me in the face*

The Parable of the Pharisee and the Tax Collector

9 Jesus also told this parable to some who trusted in themselves that they were righteous and regarded others with contempt: 10 "Two people went up to the temple to pray, one a Pharisee and the other a tax collector. 11 The Pharisee, standing alone, was praying thus, 'God, I thank you that I am not like other people: thieves, rogues, adulterers, or even like this tax collector. 12 I fast twice a week; I give a tenth of all my income.' 13 But the tax collector, standing far off, would not even look up to heaven, but was grieving and saying, 'God, be merciful to me, a sinner!' 14 I tell you, this one went home justified rather than the other; for all who exalt themselves will be humbled, but all who humble themselves will be exalted."

Jesus Blesses Little Children

15 People were bringing even infants to Jesus that he might touch them; and when the disciples saw it, they sternly ordered them not to do it. 16 But Jesus called for the children and said, "Let the little children come to me, and do not stop them; for it is to such as these that the dominion of God belongs. 17 Truly I tell you, whoever does not receive the dominion of God as a little child will never enter it."

A Question about Eternal Life

18 A certain ruler asked Jesus, "Good Teacher, what must I do to inherit eternal life?" 19 Jesus answered, "Why do you call me good? No one is good but God alone. 20 You know the commandments: 'You shall not commit adultery; You shall not murder; You shall not steal; You shall not bear false witness; Honor your father and mother.' " 21 The ruler replied, "I have kept all these since my youth." 22 Hearing this, Jesus said to the ruler, "There is still one thing lacking. Sell all that you own and distribute the money^w to those who are poor, and you will have treasure in heaven; then come, follow me." 23 But having heard this, the ruler, who was very rich, became sad. 24 Jesus looked at the ruler and said, "How hard it is for those who have wealth to enter the dominion of God! 25 Indeed, it is easier for a camel to go through the eye of a needle than for someone who is rich to enter the dominion of God."

26 Those who heard it said, "Then who can be saved?" 27 Jesus replied, "What is impossible for mortals is possible for God."

28 Then Peter said, "Look, we have left our homes and followed you." 29 And Jesus said to them, "Truly I tell you, there is no one who has left house or wife or brothers or parents or children, for the sake of the dominion of God, 30 who will not get back very much more in this age, and in the age to come eternal life."

---

w Gk lacks *the money*

A Third Time Jesus Foretells His Death and Resurrection

31 Then Jesus took the twelve aside and said to them, "See, we are going up to Jerusalem, and everything that is written about the Human One by the prophets will be accomplished. 32For the Human One will be handed over to the Gentiles and will be mocked and insulted and spat upon; 33after being flogged and killed, on the third day the Human One will rise again." 34But they understood nothing about all these things; in fact, what Jesus said was hidden from them, and they did not grasp what was said.

Jesus Heals a Person Who Was Blind Near Jericho

35 As Jesus approached Jericho, a person who was blind was sitting by the roadside begging; 36and hearing a crowd going by, he asked what was happening. 37They said, "Jesus of Nazareth˟ is passing by." 38Then the person shouted, "Jesus, Son of David, have mercy on me!" 39Those who were in front sternly ordered him to be quiet; but he shouted even more loudly, "Son of David, have mercy on me!" 40Jesus stood still and ordered the person to be brought to him; and when he came near, Jesus asked, 41"What do you want me to do for you?" He said, "Lord, let me see again." 42Jesus answered, "Receive your sight; your faith has saved you." 43Immediately the person regained sight and followed Jesus, glorifying God; and all the people, when they saw it, praised God.

Jesus and Zacchaeus

19 Jesus entered Jericho and was passing through it. 2A man named Zacchaeus was there, a chief tax collector who was rich. 3He was trying to see who Jesus was, but on account of the crowd he could not, because he was short in stature. 4So Zacchaeus ran ahead and climbed a sycamore tree to see Jesus, who was going to pass that way. 5When Jesus came to the place, he looked up and said to him, "Zacchaeus, hurry and come down; for I must stay at your house today." 6So he hurried down and was happy to welcome Jesus. 7All who saw it began to grumble and said, "Jesus has gone to be the guest of one who is a sinner." 8Zacchaeus stood there and said to Jesus, "Look, half of my possessions I will give to those who are poor; and if I have defrauded anyone of anything, I will pay back four times as much." 9Then Jesus said to him, "Today salvation has come to this house, because he too is a son of Sarah and Abraham. 10For the Human One came to seek out and to save the lost."

The Parable of the Minas

11 As they were listening to this, Jesus went on to tell a parable, because he was near Jerusalem, and because they supposed that the dominion of God was to appear immediately. 12So Jesus said, "A nobleman went to a distant country

---

x Gk *the Nazorean*

to get royal power for himself and then return. 13Summoning ten servants, he gave them ten minas,y and said to them, 'Do business with these until I come back.' 14But the citizens of the country hated him and sent a delegation, saying, 'We do not want this person to rule over us.' 15Having returned and having received royal power, the nobleman ordered those servants to whom the money had been given to be summoned, to find out what they had gained by trading. 16The first came forward and said, 'Sir, your mina has made ten more minas.' 17The nobleman said, 'Well done, good servant! Because you have been trustworthy in a very small thing, take charge of ten cities.' 18Then the second came, saying, 'Sir, your mina has made five minas.' 19The nobleman replied, 'And you, rule over five cities.' 20Then the other came, saying, 'Sir, here is your mina. I wrapped it up in a piece of cloth, 21for I was afraid of you, because you are harsh; you take what you did not deposit, and reap what you did not sow.' 22The nobleman responded, 'I will judge you by your own words, you wicked servant! You knew, did you, that I was harsh, taking what I did not deposit and reaping what I did not sow? 23Why then did you not put my money into the bank? Then when I returned, I could have collected it with interest.' 24The nobleman said to the bystanders, 'Take the mina from this servant and give it to the one who has ten.' 25(And they said, 'Sir, that servant has ten minas!') 26'I tell you, to all those who have, more will be given; but from those who have nothing, even what they have will be taken away. 27But as for these enemies of mine who did not want me to rule over them—bring them here and slaughter them in my presence.' "

Jesus' Entry into Jerusalem

28 Having said this, Jesus went on ahead, going up to Jerusalem.

29 When Jesus had come near Bethphage and Bethany, at the place called the Mount of Olives, he sent two of the disciples, 30saying, "Go into the village ahead of you, and as you enter it you will find tied there a colt that has never been ridden. Untie it and bring it here. 31If anyone asks you, 'Why are you untying it?' just say this, 'The Lord needs it.' " 32So those who were sent departed and found it as Jesus had told them. 33As they were untying the colt, its owners asked them, "Why are you untying the colt?" 34They said, "The Lord needs it." 35Then they brought it to Jesus; and after throwing their cloaks on the colt, they set Jesus on it. 36As he rode along, people kept spreading their cloaks on the road. 37As Jesus was now approaching the path down from the Mount of Olives, the whole multitude of the disciples began to praise God joyfully with a loud voice for all the deeds of power that they had seen, 38saying,

> "Blessed is the king
>   who comes in the name of God!

---

y The mina was about three months' wages for a laborer

> Peace in heaven,
>> and glory in the highest heaven!"

39 Some of the Pharisees in the crowd said to Jesus, "Teacher, order your disciples to stop." 40 Jesus answered, "I tell you, if these were silent, the stones would shout out."

Jesus Weeps over Jerusalem

41 As Jesus came near and saw the city, he wept over it, 42 saying, "If you, even you, had only recognized on this day the things that make for peace! But now they are hidden from your eyes. 43 Indeed, the days will come upon you, when your enemies will set up ramparts around you and surround you, and hem you in on every side. 44 They will crush you to the ground, you and your children within you, and they will not leave within you one stone upon another; because you did not recognize the time of your visitation from God."z

Jesus Protests in the Temple

45 Then Jesus entered the temple and began to drive out those who were selling things there, 46 saying, "It is written,

> 'My house shall be a house of prayer';
>> but you have made it a den of robbers."

47 Every day Jesus was teaching in the temple. The chief priests, the scribes, and the leaders of the people kept looking for a way to kill him; 48 but they did not find anything they could do, for all the people were spellbound by what they heard.

Jesus' Authority Is Questioned

20 One day, as Jesus was teaching the people in the temple and telling the good news, the chief priests and the scribes came with the elders 2 and said, "Tell us, by what authority are you doing these things? Who is it who gave you this authority?" 3 Jesus answered them, "I will also ask you a question, and you tell me: 4 Did the baptism of John come from heaven, or was it of human origin?" 5 They discussed it with one another, saying, "If we say, 'From heaven,' Jesus will say, 'Why did you not believe John?' 6 But if we say, 'Of human origin,' all the people will stone us; for they are convinced that John was a prophet." 7 So they answered that they did not know where it came from. 8 Then Jesus said to them, "Neither will I tell you by what authority I am doing these things."

---

z Gk lacks *from God*

The Parable of the Wicked Tenants

9 Jesus began to tell the people this parable: "A person planted a vineyard, and leased it to tenants, and went to another country for a long time. 10When the season came, the owner sent to the tenants a person enslaved to him in order that they might give him his share of the produce of the vineyard; but the tenants beat and sent away empty-handed the owner's representative. 11Next the owner sent another; that one also they beat and insulted and sent away empty-handed. 12And the owner sent still a third; this one also they wounded and threw out. 13Then the owner of the vineyard said, 'What shall I do? I will send my beloved child; perhaps they will respect that one.' 14But when the tenants saw the child, they discussed it among themselves and said, 'This is the heir; let us kill the heir so that the inheritance may be ours.' 15So they threw the heir out of the vineyard, and they killed the heir. What then will the owner of the vineyard do to them? 16He will come and destroy those tenants and give the vineyard to others." When they heard this, they said, "Heaven forbid!" 17But Jesus looked at them and said, "What then does this text mean:

> 'The stone that the builders rejected
> has become the cornerstone'?[a]

18Everyone who falls on that stone will be broken to pieces; and it will crush anyone on whom it falls." 19When the scribes and chief priests realized that Jesus had told this parable against them, they wanted to lay hands on him at that very hour, but they feared the people.

The Question about Paying Taxes

20 So they watched Jesus and sent spies who pretended to be honest, in order to trap him by what he said, so as to hand Jesus over to the jurisdiction and authority of the governor. 21So they asked, "Teacher, we know that you are right in what you say and teach, and you show deference to no one, but teach the way of God in accordance with truth. 22Is it lawful for us to pay taxes to the emperor, or not?" 23But Jesus perceived their craftiness and said to them, 24"Show me a coin. Whose head and whose title does it bear?" They said, "The emperor's." 25Jesus said to them, "Then give to the emperor the things that are the emperor's, and to God the things that are God's." 26And they were not able in the presence of the people to entrap him by what he said; and being amazed by his answer, they became silent.

The Question about the Resurrection

27 Some Sadducees, those who say there is no resurrection, came to Jesus 28and asked a question, "Teacher, Moses wrote for us that if a man's brother dies, leaving a wife but no children, the man[b] shall marry the widow and raise up

---

a Or *keystone*   b Gk *his brother*

children for his brother. 29 Now there were seven brothers; the first married, and died childless; 30 then the second 31 and the third married her, and so in the same way all seven died childless. 32 Finally the woman also died. 33 In the resurrection, therefore, whose wife will the woman be? For the seven had married her."

34 Jesus said to them, "Those who belong to this age marry and are given in marriage; 35 but those who are considered worthy of a place in that age and in the resurrection from the dead neither marry nor are given in marriage. 36 Indeed they cannot die anymore, because they are like angels and are children of God, being children of the resurrection. 37 And even Moses showed the fact that the dead are raised, in the story about the bush, where Moses speaks of God as the God of Abraham, the God of Isaac, and the God of Jacob. 38 Now God is God not of the dead, but of the living; for to God all of them are alive." 39 Then some of the scribes answered, "Teacher, you have spoken well." 40 For they no longer dared to ask Jesus another question.

A Question about the Messiah

41 Then Jesus said to them, "How can they say that the Messiah[c] is David's descendant? 42 For David himself says in the book of Psalms,

'God said to my Lord,
"Sit at my side,
43   until I make your enemies your footstool." '

44 David thus calls the Messiah Lord; so how can the Messiah be David's descendant?"

Jesus Denounces the Scribes

45 In the hearing of all the people Jesus said to the disciples, 46 "Beware of the scribes, who like to walk around in long robes, and love to be greeted with respect in the marketplaces, and to have the best seats in the synagogues and places of honor at banquets. 47 They devour widows' houses and for the sake of appearance say long prayers. They will receive the greater condemnation."

The Widow's Coin

21 Jesus looked up and saw rich people putting their gifts into the treasury, 2 and also a widow, who was poor, putting in two small copper coins. 3 Jesus said, "Truly I tell you, this widow who is poor has put in more than all of them; 4 for all of them have contributed out of their abundance, but she out of her poverty has put in all she had to live on."

The Destruction of the Temple Foretold

5 When some were speaking about the temple, how it was adorned with beautiful stones and gifts dedicated to God, Jesus said, 6 "As for these things

---

c Or the Christ

that you see, the days will come when not one stone will be left upon another;
all will be thrown down."

Signs and Persecutions

7 They asked, "Teacher, when will this be, and what will be the sign that this
is about to take place?" 8 And Jesus said, "Beware that you are not led astray;
for many will come in my name and say, 'I am the one!'[d] and, 'The time is
near!'[e] Do not go after them.

9 "When you hear of wars and insurrections, do not be terrified; for these
things must take place first, but the end will not follow immediately." 10 Then
Jesus said to them, "Nation will rise against nation, and kingdom against
kingdom; 11 there will be great earthquakes, and in various places famines and
plagues; and there will be dreadful portents and great signs from heaven.

Persecutions Foretold

12 "But before all this occurs, they will arrest you and persecute you; they will
hand you over to synagogues and prisons, and you will be brought before
rulers and governors because of my name. 13 This will give you an opportunity
to testify. 14 So make up your minds not to prepare your defense in advance;
15 for I will give you words[f] and a wisdom that none of your opponents will
be able to withstand or contradict. 16 You will be betrayed even by parents and
brothers and sisters, by relatives and friends; and they will put some of you to
death. 17 You will be hated by all because of my name. 18 But not a hair of your
head will perish. 19 By your endurance you will gain your lives.

The Destruction of Jerusalem Foretold

20 "When you see Jerusalem surrounded by armies, then know that its
desolation has come near.[g] 21 Then those in Judea must flee to the mountains,
and those inside the city must leave it, and those out in the country must not
enter it; 22 for these are days of vengeance, as a fulfillment of all that is written.
23 Woe to those who are pregnant and to those who are nursing infants in those
days! For there will be great distress on the earth and wrath against this people;
24 they will fall by the edge of the sword and be taken away as captives among
all nations; and Jerusalem will be trampled on by the Gentiles, until the times
of the Gentiles are fulfilled.

The Coming of the Human One

25 "There will be signs in the sun, the moon, and the stars, and on the earth
distress among nations confused by the roaring of the sea and the waves.
26 People will faint from fear and foreboding of what is coming upon the world,
for the powers of the heavens will be shaken. 27 Then they will see 'the Human
One coming in a cloud' with power and great glory. 28 Now when these things

---

d Gk *I am* e Or *at hand* f Gk *a mouth* g Or *is at hand*

begin to take place, stand up and raise your heads, because your redemption is drawing near."

The Lesson of the Fig Tree

29 Then Jesus told them a parable: "Look at the fig tree and all the trees; 30 as soon as they sprout leaves you can see for yourselves and know that summer is already near. 31 So also, when you see these things taking place, you know that the dominion of God is near. 32 Truly I tell you, this generation will not pass away until all things have taken place. 33 Heaven and earth will pass away, but my words will not pass away.

Exhortation to Watch

34 "Be on guard so that your hearts are not weighed down with dissipation and drunkenness and the worries of this life, and that day catch you unexpectedly, 35 like a trap. For it will come upon all who live on the face of the whole earth. 36 Be alert at all times, praying that you may have the strength to escape all these things that will take place, and to stand before the Human One."

37 Every day Jesus was teaching in the temple, and at night he would go out and spend the night on the Mount of Olives, as it was called. 38 And all the people would get up early in the morning to listen to Jesus in the temple.

The Plot to Kill Jesus

22 Now the festival of Unleavened Bread, which is called the Passover, was near. 2 The chief priests and the scribes were looking for a way to put Jesus to death, for they were afraid of the people.

Judas Agrees to Betray Jesus

3 Then Satan entered into Judas called Iscariot, who was one of the twelve; 4 Judas went away and conferred with the chief priests and officers of the temple police about how he might betray Jesus to them. 5 They were greatly pleased and agreed to give Judas money. 6 So he consented and began to look for an opportunity to betray Jesus to them when no crowd was present.

The Passover with the Disciples

7 Then came the day of Unleavened Bread, on which the Passover lamb had to be sacrificed. 8 So Jesus sent Peter and John, saying, "Go and prepare the Passover meal for us that we may eat it." 9 They asked him, "Where do you want us to make preparations for it?" 10 "Listen," he said to them, "when you have entered the city, a man carrying a jar of water will meet you; follow him into the house he enters 11 and say to the owner of the house, 'The teacher asks you, "Where is the guest room, where I may eat the Passover with my disciples?" ' 12 The owner will show you a large room upstairs, already furnished. Make preparations for us there." 13 So they went and found everything as Jesus had told them; and they prepared the Passover meal.

14 When the hour came, Jesus took his place at the table, and the apostles with him. 15 Jesus said to them, "I have eagerly desired to eat this Passover with you before I suffer; 16 for I tell you, I will not eat it[h] until it is fulfilled in the dominion of God." 17 Then Jesus took a cup, and after giving thanks, said, "Take this and divide it among yourselves; 18 for I tell you that from now on I will not drink of the fruit of the vine until the dominion of God comes." 19 Then Jesus took a loaf of bread, and having given thanks, broke it and gave it to them, saying, "This is my body, which is given for you. Do this in remembrance of me." 20 And Jesus did the same with the cup after supper, saying, "This cup that is poured out for you is the new covenant in my blood.[i] 21 But see, the one who betrays me is with me, and his hand is on the table. 22 For the Human One is going as it has been determined, but woe to that person by whom the Human One is betrayed!" 23 Then they began to ask one another, which one of them it could be who would do this.

The Dispute about Greatness

24 A dispute also arose among them as to which one of them was to be regarded as the greatest. 25 But Jesus said to them, "The rulers of the Gentiles lord it over them; and those in authority over them are called benefactors. 26 But not so with you; rather the greatest among you must become like the youngest, and the leader like one who serves. 27 For who is greater, the one who is at the table or the one who serves? Is it not the one at the table? But I am among you as one who serves.

28 "You are those who have stood by me in my trials; 29 and I confer on you, just as my Father-Mother has conferred on me, a dominion, 30 so that you may eat and drink at my table in my dominion, and you will sit on thrones judging the twelve tribes of Israel.

Jesus Predicts Peter's Denial

31 "Simon, Simon, listen! Satan has demanded[j] to sift all of you like wheat, 32 but I have prayed for you that your own faith may not fail; and you, when once you have turned back, strengthen your brothers and sisters." 33 And Simon said to Jesus, "Lord, I am ready to go with you to prison and to death!" 34 Jesus said, "I tell you, Peter, the cock will not crow this day, until you have denied three times that you know me."

Purse, Bag, and Sword

35 Jesus said to them, "When I sent you out without a purse, bag, or sandals, did you lack anything?" They said, "No, not a thing." 36 He said to them, "But now, the one who has a purse must take it, and likewise a bag. And any one

---

h Other ancient authorities read *never eat it again*
i Other ancient authorities lack, in whole or in part, verses 19b-20 (*which is given ... in my blood*)   j Or *has obtained permission*

of you who has no sword must sell your cloak and buy one. 37 For I tell you, this scripture must be fulfilled in me, 'And he was counted among the lawless'; and indeed what is written about me is being fulfilled." 38 They said, "Lord, look, here are two swords." Jesus replied, "It is enough."

Jesus Prays on the Mount of Olives

39 Jesus came out and went, as was his custom, to the Mount of Olives; and the disciples followed him. 40 Having reached the place, he said to them, "Pray that you may not come into the time of trial."ᵏ 41 Then Jesus withdrew from them about a stone's throw, knelt down, and prayed, 42 "Father-Mother, if you are willing, remove this cup from me; yet, not my will but yours be done." ⟦43 Then an angel from heaven appeared and strengthened him. 44 In anguish Jesus prayed more earnestly, and his sweat became like great drops of blood falling down on the ground.⟧ˡ 45 When Jesus got up from prayer, he came to the disciples and found them sleeping because of grief, 46 and he said to them, "Why are you sleeping? Get up and pray that you may not come into the time of trial."ᵏ

The Betrayal and Arrest of Jesus

47 While Jesus was still speaking, suddenly a crowd came, and the one called Judas, one of the twelve, was leading them. Judas approached Jesus to kiss him; 48 but Jesus said, "Judas, is it with a kiss that you are betraying the Human One?" 49 When those who were around him saw what was coming, they asked, "Lord, should we strike with the sword?" 50 Then one of them struck the servant of the high priest and cut off his right ear. 51 But Jesus said, "No more of this!" And Jesus touched his ear and healed him. 52 Then Jesus said to the chief priests, the officers of the temple police, and the elders who had come for him, "Have you come out with swords and clubs as if I were a bandit? 53 When I was with you day after day in the temple, you did not lay hands on me. But this is your hour, and the power of evil!"

Peter Denies Jesus

54 Then they seized Jesus and led him away, bringing him into the high priest's house. But Peter was following at a distance. 55 When they had kindled a fire in the middle of the courtyard and sat down together, Peter sat among them. 56 Then a womanservant, seeing him in the firelight, stared at him and said, "This man also was with him." 57 But Peter denied it, saying, "Woman, I do not know him." 58 A little later someone else, on seeing him, said, "You also are one of them." But Peter said, "Man, I am not!" 59 Then about an hour later still another kept insisting, "Surely this man also was with him; for he is a Galilean." 60 But Peter said, "Man, I do not know what you are talking about!" At that moment, while he was still speaking, the cock crowed. 61 The Lord

---

k Or *into temptation*   l Other ancient authorities lack verses 43 and 44

turned and looked at Peter. Then Peter remembered the word that the Lord had said to him, "Before the cock crows today, you will deny me three times." [62] And Peter went out and wept bitterly.

The Mocking and Beating of Jesus

63 Now the men who were holding Jesus began to mock him and beat him; [64] they also blindfolded him and kept insisting, "Prophesy! Who is it that struck you?" [65] They kept heaping many other insults on him.

Jesus before the Council

66 When day came, the assembly of the elders of the people, both chief priests and scribes, gathered together, and they brought Jesus to their council. [67] They said, "If you are the Messiah,[m] tell us." Jesus replied, "If I tell you, you will not believe; [68] and if I question you, you will not answer. [69] But from now on the Human One will be seated at the side of the power of God." [70] All of them asked, "Are you, then, the Child of God?" Jesus said to them, "You say that I am." [71] Then they said, "What further testimony do we need? We have heard it ourselves from his own lips!"

Pilate Questions Jesus

23 Then the assembly rose as a body and brought Jesus before Pilate. [2] They began to accuse him, saying, "We found this man perverting our nation, forbidding us to pay taxes to the emperor, and saying that he himself is the Messiah, a king."[n] [3] Then Pilate asked Jesus, "Are you the king of the Jews?" Jesus answered, "You say so." [4] Then Pilate said to the chief priests and the crowds, "I find no basis for an accusation against this man." [5] But they were insistent and said, "He stirs up the people by teaching throughout all Judea, from Galilee where he began even to this place."

Jesus before Herod

6 When Pilate heard this, he asked whether the man was a Galilean. [7] And when he learned that he was under Herod's jurisdiction, Pilate sent Jesus off to Herod, who was himself in Jerusalem at that time. [8] When Herod saw Jesus, he was very glad, for he had been wanting to see him for a long time, because he had heard about him and was hoping to see him perform some sign. [9] Herod questioned Jesus at some length, but Jesus gave him no answer. [10] The chief priests and the scribes stood by, vehemently accusing Jesus. [11] Even Herod with his soldiers treated him with contempt and mocked him; then he put an elegant robe on him, and sent him back to Pilate. [12] That same day Herod and Pilate became friends with each other; before this they had been enemies.

---

m Or *the Christ*   n Or *is an anointed king*

Pilate Hands Jesus Over to be Crucified

13 Pilate then called together the chief priests, the leaders, and the people,
14 and said to them, "You brought me this man as one who was perverting the
people; and here I have examined him in your presence and have not found this
man guilty of any of your charges against him. 15 Neither has Herod, for he
sent Jesus back to us. Indeed, he has done nothing to deserve death. 16 I will
therefore have him flogged and release him."[o]

18 Then they all shouted out together, "Away with this man! Release
Barabbas for us!" 19 (This was someone who had been put in prison for an
insurrection that had taken place in the city, and for murder.) 20 Pilate, wanting
to release Jesus, addressed them again; 21 but they kept shouting, "Crucify,
crucify him!" 22 A third time Pilate said to them, "Why, what evil has he done?
I have found in him no ground for the sentence of death; I will therefore have
him flogged and then release him." 23 But they kept urgently demanding with
loud shouts that Jesus should be crucified; and their voices prevailed. 24 So Pilate
gave his verdict that their demand should be granted. 25 He released the one
they asked for, the one who had been put in prison for insurrection and
murder, and he handed Jesus over as they wished.

The Crucifixion of Jesus

26 As they led Jesus away, they seized someone named Simon of Cyrene, who
was coming from the country, and they laid the cross on him, and made him
carry it behind Jesus. 27 A great number of the people followed Jesus, and
among them were women who were beating their breasts and wailing for him.
28 But Jesus turned to them and said, "Daughters of Jerusalem, do not weep for
me, but weep for yourselves and for your children. 29 For the days are surely
coming when they will say, 'Blessed are the childless, and the wombs that never
bore, and the breasts that never nursed.' 30 Then they will begin to say to the
mountains, 'Fall on us'; and to the hills, 'Cover us.' 31 For if they do this when
the wood is green, what will happen when it is dry?"

32 Two others also, who were criminals, were led away to be put to death
with Jesus. 33 When they came to the place that is called The Skull, they
crucified Jesus there with the criminals, one on the right and one on the left.
⟦34 Then Jesus said, "Father-Mother, forgive them; for they do not know what
they are doing."⟧[p] And they cast lots to divide his clothing. 35 And the people
stood by, watching; but the leaders scoffed at Jesus, saying, "He saved others;
let him save himself if he is the Messiah[q] of God, the chosen one!" 36 The
soldiers also mocked Jesus, coming up and offering him sour wine, 37 and

---

o Here, or after verse 19, other ancient authorities add verse 17, *Now he was obliged to release someone for them at the festival*

p Other ancient authorities lack the sentence *Then Jesus . . . what they are doing*

q Or *the Christ*

saying, "If you are the King of the Jews, save yourself!" [38]There was also an inscription over him,[r] "This is the King of the Jews."

[39] One of the criminals who were hanged there kept deriding[s] Jesus and saying, "Are you not the Messiah?[t] Save yourself and us!" [40]But the other rebuked him, saying, "Do you not fear God, since you are under the same sentence of condemnation? [41]And we indeed have been condemned justly, for we are getting what we deserve for our deeds, but this man has done nothing wrong." [42]Then he said, "Jesus, remember me when you come into[u] your dominion." [43]Jesus replied, "Truly I tell you, today you will be with me in Paradise."

The Death of Jesus

[44] It was now about noon, and night fell over the whole land[v] until three in the afternoon, [45]while the sun's light failed;[w] and the curtain of the temple was torn in two. [46]Then Jesus, crying with a loud voice, said, "Father-Mother, into your hands I commend my spirit." Having said this, Jesus died. [47]When the centurion saw what had taken place, he praised God and said, "Certainly this man was innocent."[x] [48]And when all the crowds who had gathered there for this spectacle saw what had taken place, they returned home, beating their breasts. [49]But all Jesus' acquaintances, including the women who had followed him from Galilee, stood at a distance, watching these things.

The Burial of Jesus

[50] Now there was a good and righteous man named Joseph, who, though a member of the council, [51]had not agreed to their plan and action. He came from the Jewish town of Arimathea, and he was waiting expectantly for the dominion of God. [52]This man went to Pilate and asked for the body of Jesus. [53]Then Joseph took the body down, wrapped it in a linen cloth, and laid it in a rock-hewn tomb where no one had ever been laid. [54]It was the day of Preparation, and the sabbath was beginning.[y] [55]The women who had come with Jesus from Galilee followed, and they saw the tomb and how the body was laid. [56]Then they returned, and prepared spices and ointments.

On the sabbath they rested according to the commandment.

The Resurrection of Jesus

24 But on the first day of the week, at early dawn, the women came to the tomb, taking the spices that they had prepared. [2]They found the stone rolled away from the tomb, [3]but when they went in, they did not find the body.[z] [4]While they were perplexed about this, suddenly two people dressed in

---

r Other ancient authorities add *written in Greek and Latin and Hebrew* (that is, *Aramaic*)
s Or *blaspheming*   t Or *the Christ*   u Other ancient authorities read *in*   v Or *earth*
w Or *the sun was eclipsed*. Other ancient authorities read *the sun was darkened*
x Or *righteous*   y Gk *was dawning*   z Other ancient authorities add *of the Lord Jesus*

dazzling clothes stood beside them. [5] The women were terrified and bowed their faces to the ground, but the two said to them, "Why do you look for the living among the dead? Jesus is not here, but has risen.[a] [6] Remember how Jesus told you, while still in Galilee, [7] that the Human One must be handed over to sinners, and be crucified, and on the third day rise again." [8] Then the women remembered these words, [9] and returning from the tomb, they told all this to the eleven and to all the rest. [10] Now it was Mary Magdalene, Joanna, Mary the mother of James, and the other women with them who told this to the apostles. [11] But these words seemed to them an idle tale, and they did not believe the women. [12] But Peter got up and ran to the tomb; stooping and looking in, he saw the linen cloths by themselves; then he went home, amazed at what had happened.[b]

The Walk to Emmaus

13 Now on that same day two of them were going to a village called Emmaus, about seven miles from Jerusalem, [14] and talking with each other about all these things that had happened. [15] While they were talking and discussing, Jesus came near and went with them, [16] but their eyes were kept from recognizing Jesus. [17] And Jesus said to them, "What are you discussing with each other while you walk along?" They stood still, looking sad.[c] [18] Then one of them, whose name was Cleopas, answered, "Are you the only stranger in Jerusalem who does not know the things that have taken place there in these days?" [19] Jesus asked them, "What things?" They replied, "The things about Jesus of Nazareth,[d] who was a prophet mighty in deed and word before God and all the people, [20] and how our chief priests and leaders handed Jesus over to be condemned to death and they crucified Jesus. [21] But we had hoped that Jesus was the one to redeem Israel.[e] Yes, and besides all this, it is now the third day since these things took place. [22] Moreover, some women of our group astounded us. They were at the tomb early this morning, [23] and when they did not find Jesus' body there, they came back and told us that they had indeed seen a vision of angels who said that Jesus was alive. [24] Some of those who were with us went to the tomb and found it just as the women had said; but they did not see Jesus." [25] Then Jesus said to them, "Oh, how foolish you are, and how slow of heart to believe all that the prophets have declared! [26] Was it not necessary that the Messiah[f] should suffer these things and then be glorified?" [27] Then beginning with Moses and all the prophets, Jesus interpreted to them the things about the Messiah in all the scriptures.

28 As they came near the village to which they were going, Jesus walked

---

a Other ancient authorities lack *Jesus is not here, but has risen*
b Other ancient authorities lack verse 12
c Other ancient authorities read *walk along, looking sad?"*
d Other ancient authorities read *Jesus the Nazorean*   e Or *to set Israel free*
f Or *the Christ*

ahead, appearing to go farther. [29] But they urged, "Stay with us, because it is almost evening and the day is now nearly over." So Jesus went in to stay with them. [30] While at the table with them, Jesus took bread, blessed and broke it, and gave it to them. [31] Then their eyes were opened, and they recognized Jesus, who then vanished from their sight. [32] They said to each other, "Were not our hearts burning within us[g] while Jesus was talking to us on the road and opening the scriptures to us?" [33] That same hour they got up and returned to Jerusalem; and they found the eleven and their companions gathered together. [34] They were saying, "The Lord has risen indeed and has appeared to Simon!" [35] Then they told what had happened on the road, and how Jesus had been made known to them in the breaking of the bread.

Jesus Appears to the Disciples

36 While they were talking about this, Jesus stood among them and said to them, "Peace be with you."[h] [37] They were startled and terrified, and thought that they were seeing a ghost. [38] Jesus said to them, "Why are you frightened, and why do doubts arise in your hearts? [39] Look at my hands and my feet; see that it is I myself. Touch me and see; for a ghost does not have flesh and bones as you see that I have." [40] And having said this, Jesus showed them the hands and the feet.[i] [41] While in their joy they were disbelieving and still wondering, Jesus said to them, "Have you anything here to eat?" [42] They gave Jesus a piece of broiled fish, [43] and Jesus took it and ate in their presence.

44 Then Jesus said to them, "These are my words that I spoke to you while I was still with you—that everything written about me in the law of Moses, the prophets, and the psalms must be fulfilled." [45] Then Jesus opened their minds to understand the scriptures [46] and said to them, "Thus it is written, that the Messiah[j] is to suffer and to rise from the dead on the third day, [47] and that repentance and forgiveness of sins is to be proclaimed in the Messiah's name to all nations, beginning from Jerusalem. [48] You are witnesses[k] of these things. [49] And see, I am sending upon you what my Father-Mother promised; so stay here in the city until you have been clothed with power from on high."

The Ascension of Jesus

50 Then Jesus led them out as far as Bethany, and, with uplifted hands, Jesus blessed them. [51] While blessing them, Jesus withdrew from them and was carried up into heaven.[l] [52] And they worshiped Jesus, and[m] returned to Jerusalem with great joy; [53] and they were continually in the temple blessing God.[n]

---

g Other ancient authorities lack *within us*
h Other ancient authorities lack *and said to them, "Peace be with you."*
i Other ancient authorities lack verse 40   j Or *the Christ*
k Or *nations. Beginning from Jerusalem you are witnesses*
l Other ancient authorities lack *and was carried up into heaven*
m Other ancient authorities lack *worshiped Jesus, and*   n Other ancient authorities add *Amen*

⤳ ⤳ ⤳ ⤳ ⤳ ⤳ ⤳ ⤳ ⤳ ⤳ ⤳ ⤳ ⤳ ⤳ ⤳

The Gospel According to John

The Word Became Flesh

1 In the beginning was the Word, and the Word was with God, and the Word was God. ²The Word was in the beginning with God. ³All things came into being through the Word, and without the Word not one thing came into being. What has come into being ⁴in the Word was life,ᵃ and the life was the light of all people. ⁵The light shines in the deepest night, and the night did not overcome it.

6 There was a man sent from God, whose name was John. ⁷He came as a witness to testify to the light, so that all might believe through him. ⁸John was not the light, but came to testify to the light. ⁹The true light, which enlightens everyone, was coming into the world.ᵇ

10 The Word was in the world, and the world came into being through the Word; yet the world did not know the Word. ¹¹The Word came to what the Word had madeᶜ and the Word's own people did not accept the Word. ¹²But to all who received the Word, who believed in the name of the Word, power was given to become children of God, ¹³who were born, not of blood or of the will of the flesh or of human will, but of God.

14 And the Word became flesh and lived among us, and we have seen the Word's glory, the glory as of a parent's only child,ᵈ full of grace and truth. ¹⁵(John testified to the child and cried out, "This was the one of whom I said, 'The one who comes after me ranks ahead of me because that one was before me.' ") ¹⁶From the fullness of the Child we have all received, grace upon grace. ¹⁷The law indeed was given through Moses; grace and truth came through Jesus

---

a Or *3 through the Word. And without the Word not one thing came into being that has come into being. 4In the Word was life*
b Or *The Word was the true light that enlightens everyone coming into the world*
c Or *to the Word's own home*   d Or *the only Child of the Father-Mother*

Christ. [18] No one has ever seen God. It is God the only Child,[e] who is close to the bosom of the Father-Mother, who has made God known.

The Testimony of John the Baptist

[19] This is the testimony given by John when the Jews sent priests and Levites from Jerusalem to ask him, "Who are you?" [20] John confessed and did not deny it, but confessed, "I am not the Messiah."[f] [21] And they asked, "What then? Are you Elijah?" John said, "I am not." "Are you the prophet?" He answered, "No." [22] Then they said, "Who are you? Let us have an answer for those who sent us. What do you say about yourself?" [23] John said,

> "I am the voice of one crying out in the wilderness,
> 'Make straight the way of the Lord,' "

as the prophet Isaiah said.

[24] Now they had been sent from the Pharisees. [25] They asked John, "Why then are you baptizing if you are neither the Messiah,[f] nor Elijah, nor the prophet?" [26] John answered them, "I baptize with water. Among you stands one whom you do not know, [27] the one who is coming after me, the thong of whose sandal I am not worthy to untie." [28] This took place in Bethany across the Jordan where John was baptizing.

The Lamb of God

[29] The next day John saw Jesus coming toward him and declared, "Here is the Lamb of God who takes away the sin of the world! [30] This is the one of whom I said, 'After me comes someone who ranks ahead of me because that one was before me.' [31] I myself did not know who it was; but I came baptizing with water for this reason, that the one who was to come might be revealed to Israel." [32] And John testified, "I saw the Spirit descending from heaven like a dove, and it remained on Jesus. [33] I myself did not know who it was, but the one who sent me to baptize with water said to me, 'The person on whom you see the Spirit descend and remain is the one who baptizes with the Holy Spirit.' [34] And I myself have seen and have testified that this is the Child of God."[g]

The First Disciples of Jesus

[35] The next day John again was standing with two of his disciples, [36] and looking at Jesus walking by, he exclaimed, "Look, here is the Lamb of God!" [37] The two disciples heard John say this, and they followed Jesus. [38] Jesus turned, and saw them following, and said to them, "What are you looking for?" They said, "Rabbi" (which translated means Teacher), "where are you staying?" [39] He said to them, "Come and see." They came and saw where Jesus was staying, and they remained with him that day. It was about four o'clock in the

e Other ancient authorities read *It is an only Child, God,* or *It is the only Child*
f Or *the Christ*   g Other ancient authorities read *is God's chosen one*

afternoon. ⁴⁰One of the two who heard John speak and followed Jesus was Andrew, Simon Peter's brother. ⁴¹Andrew first found his brother Simon and said to him, "We have found the Messiah" (which is translated Anointedʰ). ⁴²Andrew brought Simon to Jesus, who looked at him and said, "You are Simon son of John. You are to be called Cephas" (which is translated Peterⁱ).

Jesus Calls Philip and Nathanael

43 The next day Jesus decided to go to Galilee. He found Philip and said to him, "Follow me." ⁴⁴Now Philip was from Bethsaida, the city of Andrew and Peter. ⁴⁵Philip found Nathanael and said to him, "We have found the one about whom Moses in the law and also the prophets wrote, Jesus son of Joseph from Nazareth." ⁴⁶Nathanael said to Philip, "Can anything good come out of Nazareth?" Philip replied, "Come and see." ⁴⁷When Jesus saw Nathanael coming toward him, he said, "Here is truly an Israelite in whom there is no deceit!" ⁴⁸Nathanael asked him, "Where did you get to know me?" Jesus answered, "I saw you under the fig tree before Philip called you." ⁴⁹Nathanael replied, "Rabbi, you are the Child of God! You are the King of Israel!" ⁵⁰Jesus answered, "Do you believe because I told you that I saw you under the fig tree? You will see greater things than these." ⁵¹And Jesus said to Nathanael, "Very truly, I tell you,ʲ you will see heaven opened and the angels of God ascending and descending upon the Human One."

The Wedding at Cana

2 On the third day there was a wedding in Cana of Galilee, and the mother of Jesus was there. ²Jesus and the disciples had also been invited to the wedding. ³When the wine gave out, the mother of Jesus said to him, "They have no wine." ⁴And Jesus said to her, "Woman, what concern is that to you and to me? My hour has not yet come." ⁵His mother said to the servants, "Do whatever he tells you." ⁶Now standing there were six stone water jars for the Jewish rites of purification, each holding twenty or thirty gallons. ⁷Jesus said to the servants, "Fill the jars with water." And they filled them up to the brim. ⁸He said to them, "Now draw some out, and take it to the chief steward." So they took it. ⁹When the steward tasted the water that had become wine, and did not know where it came from (though the servants who had drawn the water knew), the steward called the bridegroom ¹⁰and said to him, "Everyone serves the good wine first, and then the inferior wine after the guests have become drunk. But you have kept the good wine until now." ¹¹Jesus did this, the first of his signs, in Cana of Galilee, and revealed his glory; and the disciples believed in Jesus.

12 After this Jesus went down to Capernaum with his mother, his brothers, and the disciples; and they remained there a few days.

---

h Or Christ   i From the word for *rock* in Aramaic (*kepha*) and Greek (*petra*), respectively
j Both instances of the Greek word for *you* in this verse are plural

Jesus Protests in the Temple

13 The Passover was near, and Jesus went up to Jerusalem. ¹⁴In the temple he found people selling cattle, sheep, and doves, and the money changers seated at their tables. ¹⁵Making a whip of cords, Jesus drove all of them out of the temple, both the sheep and the cattle. He also poured out the coins of the money changers and overturned their tables. ¹⁶Jesus told those who were selling the doves, "Take these things out of here! Stop making the house of my Father-Mother into a marketplace!" ¹⁷The disciples remembered that it was written, "Zeal for your house will consume me." ¹⁸The religious authorities then said to Jesus, "What sign can you show us for doing this?" ¹⁹Jesus answered them, "Destroy this temple, and in three days I will raise it up." ²⁰The authorities then said, "This temple has been under construction for forty-six years, and will you raise it up in three days?" ²¹But Jesus was speaking of the temple of his body. ²²After Jesus was raised from the dead, the disciples remembered that Jesus had said this; and they believed the scripture and the word that Jesus had spoken.

23 When Jesus was in Jerusalem during the Passover festival, many believed in Jesus' name because they saw the signs that he was doing. ²⁴But Jesus on his part would not entrust himself to them, because he knew all people ²⁵and needed no one to testify about anyone; for Jesus knew what was in everyone.

Nicodemus Visits Jesus

3 Now there was a Pharisee named Nicodemus, a leader of the Jews. ²He came to Jesus by night and said, "Rabbi, we know that you are a teacher who has come from God; for no one can do these signs that you do apart from the presence of God." ³Jesus answered him, "Very truly, I tell you, no one can see the dominion of God without being born from above."ᵏ ⁴Nicodemus replied, "How can anyone be born after having grown old? Can one enter a second time into the mother's womb and be born?" ⁵Jesus answered, "Very truly, I tell you, no one can enter the dominion of God without being born of water and Spirit. ⁶What is born of the flesh is flesh, and what is born of the Spirit is spirit.ˡ ⁷Do not be astonished that I said to you, 'Youᵐ must be born from above.'ⁿ ⁸The windˡ blows where it chooses, and you hear the sound of it, but you do not know where it comes from or where it goes. So it is with everyone who is born of the Spirit." ⁹Nicodemus said to Jesus, "How can these things be?" ¹⁰Jesus answered, "Are you a teacher of Israel, and yet you do not understand these things?

11 "Very truly, I tell you, we speak of what we know and testify to what we have seen; yet youᵒ do not receive our testimony. ¹²If I have told you

k Or *born anew*   l The same Greek word means both *wind* and *spirit*
m The Greek word for *you* here is plural   n Or *anew*
o The Greek word for *you* here and in verse 12 is plural

about earthly things and you do not believe, how can you believe if I tell you about heavenly things? [13] No one has ascended into heaven except the one who descended from heaven, the Human One.[p] [14] And just as Moses lifted up the serpent in the wilderness, so must the Human One be lifted up, [15] that whoever believes in that one may have eternal life.[q]

16 "For God so loved the world that God gave God's only Child, so that everyone who believes in that Child may not perish but may have eternal life.

17 "Indeed, God did not send the Child into the world to condemn the world, but in order that through the Child the world might be saved. [18] Those who believe in the Child are not condemned; but those who do not believe are condemned already, because they have not believed in the name of the only Child of God. [19] And this is the judgment, that the light has come into the world, and people loved the night rather than the day because their deeds were evil. [20] For all who do evil hate the light and do not come to the light, so that their deeds may not be exposed. [21] But those who do what is true come to the light, so that it may be clearly seen that their deeds have been done in God."[q]

Jesus and John the Baptist

22 After this Jesus and the disciples went into the Judean countryside, and he spent some time there with them and baptized. [23] John also was baptizing at Aenon near Salim because water was abundant there; and people kept coming and were being baptized [24] —John, of course, had not yet been thrown into prison.

25 Now a discussion about purification arose between John's disciples and a Jew.[r] [26] They came to John and said to him, "Rabbi, the one who was with you across the Jordan, to whom you testified, is baptizing and attracting everyone." [27] John answered, "No one can receive anything except what has been given from heaven. [28] You yourselves are my witnesses that I said, 'I am not the Messiah,[s] but I have been sent ahead of the Messiah.' [29] The one who has the bride is the bridegroom. The friend of the bridegroom, who stands and listens, rejoices greatly at the bridegroom's voice. For this reason my joy has been fulfilled. [30] That one must increase, but I must decrease."[t]

The One Who Comes from Heaven

31 The one who comes from above is above all; the one who is of the earth belongs to the earth and speaks about earthly things. The one who comes from heaven is above all [32] and testifies to what has been seen and heard, yet no one accepts the testimony. [33] Whoever has accepted it has certified[u] this, that God is true. [34] The one whom God has sent speaks the words of God, for God gives

---

p Other ancient authorities add *who is in heaven*
q Some interpreters hold that the quotation concludes with verse 15
r Other ancient authorities read *the Jews*   s Or *the Christ*
t Some interpreters hold that the quotation continues through verse 36   u Gk *set a seal to*

the Spirit without measure. ³⁵The Father-Mother loves the Child and has placed all things in the Child's hands. ³⁶Whoever believes in the Child has eternal life; whoever disobeys the Child will not see life, but must endure God's wrath.

Jesus and the Woman of Samaria

4 Now when Jesus learned that the Pharisees had heard, "Jesus is making and baptizing more disciples than John" ²—although it was not actually Jesus but the disciples who baptized— ³he left Judea and started back to Galilee. ⁴But he had to go through Samaria. ⁵So he came to a Samaritan city called Sychar, near the plot of ground that Jacob had given to his son Joseph. ⁶Jacob's well was there, and Jesus, tired out by the journey, was sitting by the well. It was about noon.

7 A Samaritan woman came to draw water, and Jesus said to her, "Give me a drink." ⁸(The disciples had gone to the city to buy food.) ⁹The Samaritan woman said to Jesus, "How is it that you, a Jew, ask a drink of me, a woman of Samaria?" (Jews do not share things in common with Samaritans.)ᵛ ¹⁰Jesus answered her, "If you knew the gift of God, and who it is that is saying to you, 'Give me a drink,' you would have asked him, and he would have given you living water." ¹¹The woman said, "Sir, you have no bucket, and the well is deep. Where do you get that living water? ¹²Are you greater than our ancestor Jacob, who gave us the well, and with his children and his flocks drank from it?" ¹³Jesus said to her, "Everyone who drinks of this water will be thirsty again, ¹⁴but those who drink of the water that I will give them will never be thirsty. The water that I will give will become in them a spring of water gushing up to eternal life." ¹⁵The woman said to Jesus, "Sir, give me this water, so that I may never be thirsty or have to keep coming here to draw water."

16 Jesus said to her, "Go, call your husband, and come back." ¹⁷The woman answered, "I have no husband." Jesus said to her, "You are right in saying, 'I have no husband'; ¹⁸for you have had five husbands, and the one you have now is not your husband. What you have said is true!" ¹⁹The woman said to Jesus, "Sir, I see that you are a prophet. ²⁰Our ancestors worshiped on this mountain, but youʷ say that the place where people must worship is in Jerusalem." ²¹Jesus said to her, "Woman, believe me, the hour is coming when you will worship God neither on this mountain nor in Jerusalem. ²²You worship what you do not know; we worship what we know, for salvation is from the Jews. ²³But the hour is coming, and is now here, when the true worshipers will worship God in spirit and truth, for God seeks such as these as worshipers. ²⁴God is spirit, and those who worship God must worship in spirit and truth." ²⁵The woman said to Jesus, "I know that Messiah is coming" (who

---

v Other ancient authorities lack this sentence
w The Greek word for *you* here and in verses 21 and 22 is plural

is called Christ). "Having come, that one will proclaim all things to us." [26]Jesus said to her, "I[x] who speak to you am that very one."

27 Just then the disciples came. They were astonished that Jesus was speaking with a woman, but no one said, "What do you want?" or, "Why are you speaking with her?" [28]Then the woman left her water jar and went back to the city. She said to the people, [29]"Come and see someone who told me everything I have ever done! This cannot be the Messiah,[y] can it?" [30]They left the city and were on their way to Jesus.

31 Meanwhile the disciples were urging Jesus, "Rabbi, eat something." [32]But he said to them, "I have food to eat that you do not know about." [33]So the disciples said to one another, "Surely no one has brought him something to eat?" [34]Jesus said to them, "My food is to do the will of God who sent me and to complete God's work. [35]Do you not say, 'Four months more, then comes the harvest'? But I tell you, look around you, and see how the fields are ripe for harvesting. [36]The reaper is already receiving[z] wages and is gathering fruit for eternal life, so that sower and reaper may rejoice together. [37]For here the saying holds true, 'One sows and another reaps.' [38]I sent you to reap that for which you did not labor. Others have labored, and you have entered into their labor."

39 Many Samaritans from that city believed in Jesus because of the woman's testimony, "He told me everything I have ever done." [40]So when the Samaritans approached, they asked Jesus to stay with them; and he stayed there two days. [41]And many more believed because of Jesus' word. [42]They said to the woman, "It is no longer because of what you said that we believe, for we have heard for ourselves, and we know that this is truly the Savior of the world."

Jesus Returns to Galilee

43 When the two days were over, Jesus went from that place to Galilee [44](for Jesus himself had testified that a prophet has no honor in the prophet's own country). [45]When Jesus came to Galilee, the Galileans welcomed him, since they had seen all that he had done in Jerusalem at the festival; for they too had gone to the festival.

Jesus Heals an Official's Son

46 Then Jesus came again to Cana in Galilee where he had changed the water into wine. Now there was a royal official whose son lay ill in Capernaum. [47]When he heard that Jesus had come from Judea to Galilee, he went and begged Jesus to come down and heal his son, who was at the point of death. [48]Then Jesus said to the official, "Unless you[a] see signs and wonders you will not believe." [49]The official responded, "Sir, come down before my little boy

---

x Gk *I am*   y Or *the Christ*
z Or *35. . . the fields are already ripe for harvesting. 36The reaper is receiving*
a Both instances of the Greek word for *you* in this verse are plural

dies." ⁵⁰Jesus replied, "Go; your son will live." The man believed the word that
Jesus spoke to him and started on his way. ⁵¹As he was going down, those
enslaved to him met him and told him that his child was alive. ⁵²So he asked
them the hour when the child began to recover, and they replied, "Yesterday at
one in the afternoon the fever left him." ⁵³The father realized that this was the
hour when Jesus had said to him, "Your son will live." So he himself believed,
along with his whole household. ⁵⁴Now this was the second sign that Jesus did
after coming from Judea to Galilee.

Jesus Heals on the Sabbath

5 After this there was another Jewish festival, and Jesus went up to Jerusalem.

2 Now in Jerusalem by the Sheep Gate there is a pool, called in Hebrewᵇ
Beth-zatha,ᶜ which has five porticoes. ³In these lay many people who were
invalids—those who were blind, lame, and paralyzed.ᵈ ⁵One person was there
who had been ill for thirty-eight years. ⁶When Jesus saw this person lying
there for what he knew had been a long time, Jesus said, "Do you want to be
made well?" ⁷The sick person answered, "Sir, I have no one to put me into the
pool when the water is stirred up; and while I am making my way, someone
else steps down ahead of me." ⁸Jesus said, "Stand up, take your mat and walk."
⁹At once the person was made well, and took up the mat and began to
walk.

Now that day was a sabbath. ¹⁰So the religious authorities said to the one
who had been cured, "It is the sabbath; it is not lawful for you to carry your
mat." ¹¹But the person who had been healed answered them, "The one who
made me well said to me, 'Take up your mat and walk.'" ¹²They asked, "Who
said to you, 'Take it up and walk'?" ¹³Now the person who had been healed
did not know who it was, for Jesus had disappeared inᵉ the crowd that was
there. ¹⁴Later Jesus found the person in the temple and said, "See, you have
been made well! Do not sin any more, so that nothing worse happens to you."
¹⁵The one who had been healed went away and told the religious authorities
that Jesus was the healer. ¹⁶Therefore the authorities started persecuting Jesus
for doing such things on the sabbath. ¹⁷But Jesus answered them, "My
Father-Mother is still working, and I also am working." ¹⁸For this reason the
religious authorities were seeking all the more to kill Jesus, not only for
breaking the sabbath, but also for calling God his own Father-Mother, thereby
claiming equality with God.

---

b That is, *Aramaic*   c Other ancient authorities read *Bethesda*, others *Bethsaida*
d Other ancient authorities add, wholly or in part, *waiting for the stirring of the water; 4for an
angel of God went down at certain seasons into the pool, and stirred up the water; whoever
stepped in first after the stirring of the water was made well from whatever disease that person
had.*   e Or *had left because of*

The Authority of the Child

19 Jesus said to them, "Very truly, I tell you, the Child can do nothing alone, but only what the Child sees the Father-Mother doing; for whatever that one does, the Child does likewise. 20 The Father-Mother loves the Child and shows the Child all that the Father-Mother is doing; and the Father-Mother will show the Child greater works than these, so that you will be astonished. 21 Indeed, just as the Father-Mother raises the dead and gives them life, so also the Child gives life to whomever the Child wishes. 22 The Father-Mother judges no one but has given all judgment to the Child, 23 so that all may honor the Child just as they honor the Father-Mother. Anyone who does not honor the Child does not honor God who sent the Child. 24 Very truly, I tell you, anyone who hears my word and believes the one who sent me has eternal life, and does not come under judgment, but has passed from death to life.

25 "Very truly, I tell you, the hour is coming, and is now here, when the dead will hear the voice of the Child of God, and those who hear will live. 26 For just as God has life in Godself, so God has granted the same thing to the Child, 27 and has given the Child authority to execute judgment, because of being the Human One. 28 Do not be astonished at this; for the hour is coming when all who are in their graves will hear that one's voice 29 and will come out—those who have done good, to the resurrection of life, and those who have done evil, to the resurrection of condemnation.

Witnesses to Jesus

30 "I can do nothing on my own. As I hear, I judge; and my judgment is just, because I seek to do not my own will but the will of the one who sent me.

31 "If I testify about myself, my testimony is not true. 32 There is another who testifies on my behalf, and I know that the testimony which that one bears to me is true. 33 You sent messengers to John, and he testified to the truth. 34 Not that I accept such human testimony, but I say these things so that you may be saved. 35 John was a burning and shining lamp, and you were willing to rejoice for a while in his light. 36 But I have a testimony greater than John's. The works that God has given me to complete, the very works that I am doing, testify on my behalf that God has sent me. 37 And God who sent me has indeed testified on my behalf. You have never heard God's voice or seen God's form, 38 and you do not have God's word abiding in you, because you do not believe the one whom God has sent.

39 "You search the scriptures because you think that in them you have eternal life; and it is they that testify on my behalf. 40 Yet you refuse to come to me to have life. 41 I do not accept glory from human beings. 42 But I know that you do not have the love of God in^f you. 43 I have come in the name of my Father-Mother, and you do not accept me; if others come in their own

---

f Or *among*

name, you will accept them. [44]How can you believe when you accept glory from one another and do not seek the glory that comes from the one who alone is God? [45]Do not think that I will accuse you before God; your accuser is Moses, on whom you have set your hope. [46]If you believed Moses, you would believe me, for he wrote about me. [47]But if you do not believe what Moses wrote, how will you believe what I say?"

Feeding the Five Thousand

6 After this Jesus went to the other side of the Sea of Galilee, also called the Sea of Tiberias.[g] [2]A large crowd kept following him, because they saw the signs that he was doing for the sick. [3]Jesus went up the mountain and sat down there with the disciples. [4]Now the Passover was near. [5]Looking up and seeing a large crowd approaching, Jesus said to Philip, "Where are we to buy bread for these people to eat?" [6]Jesus said this to test Philip, for Jesus himself knew what he was going to do. [7]Philip answered, "Six months' wages would not buy enough bread for each of them to get a little." [8]One of the disciples, Andrew, Simon Peter's brother, said to Jesus, [9]"There is a boy here who has five barley loaves and two fish. But what are they among so many people?" [10]Jesus said, "Make the people sit down." Now there was a great deal of grass in the place; so they sat down, about five thousand in all. [11]Then Jesus took the loaves, and having given thanks, distributed them to those who were seated; so also the fish, as much as they wanted. [12]When they were satisfied, Jesus told the disciples, "Gather up the fragments left over, so that nothing may be lost." [13]So they gathered them up, and from the fragments of the five barley loaves, left by those who had eaten, they filled twelve baskets. [14]When the people saw the sign that Jesus had done, they began to say, "This is indeed the prophet who is to come into the world."

15 When Jesus realized that they were about to come and take him by force to make him king, he withdrew again to the mountain alone.

Jesus Walks on the Water

16 When evening came, the disciples went down to the sea, [17]got into a boat, and started across the sea to Capernaum. It was now night, and Jesus had not yet come to them. [18]The sea became rough because a strong wind was blowing. [19]When they had rowed about three or four miles, they saw Jesus walking on the sea and coming near the boat, and they were terrified. [20]But Jesus said to them, "It is I;[h] do not be afraid." [21]Then they wanted to take Jesus into the boat, and immediately the boat reached the land toward which they were going.

The Bread from Heaven

22 The next day the crowd that had stayed on the other side of the sea saw that there had been only one boat there. They also saw that Jesus had not got

g Gk *of Galilee of Tiberias*   h Gk *I am*

into the boat with the disciples, but that the disciples had gone away alone. [23]Then some boats from Tiberias came near the place where they had eaten the bread after the Lord had given thanks.[i] [24]So when the crowd saw that neither Jesus nor the disciples were there, they themselves got into the boats and went to Capernaum looking for Jesus.

[25] When they found Jesus on the other side of the sea, they said to him, "Rabbi, when did you come here?" [26]Jesus answered them, "Very truly, I tell you, you are looking for me, not because you saw signs, but because you ate your fill of the loaves. [27]Do not work for the food that perishes, but for the food that endures for eternal life, which the Human One will give you. For it is that one whom God the Father-Mother has confirmed." [28]Then they said to him, "What must we do to perform the works of God?" [29]Jesus answered them, "This is the work of God, that you believe in the one whom God has sent." [30]So they said to Jesus, "What sign are you going to give us then, so that we may see it and believe you? What work are you performing? [31]Our ancestors ate the manna in the wilderness; as it is written, 'God gave them bread from heaven to eat.'" [32]Then Jesus said to them, "Very truly, I tell you, it was not Moses who gave you the bread from heaven, but it is my Father-Mother who gives you the true bread from heaven. [33]For the bread of God is that which[j] comes down from heaven and gives life to the world." [34]They said to Jesus, "Sir, give us this bread always."

[35] Jesus said to them, "I am the bread of life. Whoever comes to me will never be hungry, and whoever believes in me will never be thirsty. [36]But I said to you that you have seen me and yet do not believe. [37]Everything that God gives me will come to me, and anyone who comes to me I will never drive away; [38]for I have come down from heaven, not to do my own will, but the will of the one who sent me. [39]And this is the will of the one who sent me, that I should lose nothing of all that God has given me, but raise it up on the last day. [40]This is indeed the will of my Father-Mother that all who see the Child and believe in the Child may have eternal life; and I will raise them up on the last day."

[41] Then the religious authorities began to complain about Jesus for saying, "I am the bread that came down from heaven." [42]They were saying, "Is not this Jesus, the son of Joseph, whose father and mother we know? How can he now say, 'I have come down from heaven'?" [43]Jesus answered them, "Do not complain among yourselves. [44]No one can come to me unless drawn by God who sent me; and I will raise that person up on the last day. [45]It is written in the prophets, 'And they shall all be taught by God.' Everyone who has heard and learned from God comes to me. [46]Not that anyone has seen God except the one who is from God; that one has seen God. [47]Very truly, I tell you, whoever believes has eternal life. [48]I am the bread of life. [49]Your ancestors ate the manna in the wilderness, and they died. [50]This is the bread that comes

---

i Other ancient authorities lack *after the Lord had given thanks*   j Or *the one who*

down from heaven, so that one may eat of it and not die. [51]I am the living bread that came down from heaven. Whoever eats of this bread will live forever; and the bread that I will give for the life of the world is my flesh."

52 The religious authorities then disputed among themselves, saying, "How can this man give us his flesh to eat?" [53]So Jesus said to them, "Very truly, I tell you, unless you eat the flesh and drink the blood of the Human One you have no life in you. [54]Those who eat my flesh and drink my blood have eternal life, and I will raise them up on the last day; [55]for my flesh is true food and my blood is true drink. [56]Those who eat my flesh and drink my blood abide in me, and I in them. [57]Just as the living God sent me, and I live because of God, so whoever eats me will live because of me. [58]This is the bread that came down from heaven, not like that which your ancestors ate, and they died. But the one who eats this bread will live forever." [59]Jesus said these things while he was teaching in the synagogue at Capernaum.

The Words of Eternal Life

60 When many of the disciples heard it, they said, "This teaching is difficult; who can accept it?" [61]But Jesus, being aware that the disciples were complaining about it, said to them, "Does this offend you? [62]Then what if you were to see the Human One ascending back to heaven? [63]It is the spirit that gives life; the flesh is useless. The words that I have spoken to you are spirit and life. [64]But among you there are some who do not believe." For Jesus knew from the first who were the ones that did not believe, and who was the one that would betray him. [65]And Jesus said, "For this reason I have told you that no one can come to me unless it is granted by God."

66 Because of this many of the disciples turned back and no longer went about with him. [67]So Jesus asked the twelve, "Do you also wish to go away?" [68]Simon Peter answered, "Lord, to whom can we go? You have the words of eternal life. [69]We have come to believe and know that you are the Holy One of God."[k] [70]Jesus answered them, "Did I not choose you, the twelve? Yet one of you is a devil." [71]Jesus was speaking of Judas son of Simon Iscariot,[l] for he, though one of the twelve, was going to betray Jesus.

The Unbelief of Jesus' Brothers

7 After this Jesus went about in Galilee. He did not wish[m] to go about in Judea because the religious authorities were looking for an opportunity to kill him. [2]Now the festival of Booths[n] was near. [3]So Jesus' brothers said to him, "Leave here and go to Judea so that your disciples also may see the works you are doing; [4]for no one who wants[o] to be widely known acts in secret. If

k Other ancient authorities read *the Christ, the Child of the living God*
l Other ancient authorities read *Judas Iscariot son of Simon;* others, *Judas son of Simon from Karyot* (Kerioth)   m Other ancient authorities read *was not at liberty*   n Or *Tabernacles*
o Other ancient authorities read *wants it*

you do these things, show yourself to the world." ⁵(For not even his brothers believed in him.) ⁶Jesus said to them, "My time has not yet come, but your time is always here. ⁷The world cannot hate you, but it hates me because I testify against it that its works are evil. ⁸Go to the festival yourselves. I am not^p going to this festival, for my time has not yet fully come." ⁹After saying this, Jesus remained in Galilee.

Jesus at the Festival of Booths

10 But after his brothers had gone to the festival, then he also went, not publicly but as it were^q in secret. ¹¹The religious authorities were looking for Jesus at the festival and saying, "Where is he?" ¹²And there was considerable complaining about him among the crowds. While some were saying, "He is a good man," others were saying, "No, he is deceiving the crowd." ¹³Yet no one would speak openly about him for fear of the religious authorities.

14 About the middle of the festival Jesus went up into the temple and began to teach. ¹⁵The religious authorities were astonished at it, saying, "How does this man have such learning,^r when he has never been taught?" ¹⁶Then Jesus answered them, "My teaching is not mine but belongs to the one who sent me. ¹⁷Anyone who resolves to do the will of God will know whether the teaching is from God or whether I am speaking on my own. ¹⁸Those who speak on their own seek their own glory; but the person who seeks the glory of the one who sent that person is true and has nothing false within.

19 "Did not Moses give you the law? Yet none of you keeps the law. Why are you looking for an opportunity to kill me?" ²⁰The crowd answered, "You have a demon! Who is trying to kill you?" ²¹Jesus answered them, "I performed one work, and all of you are astonished. ²²Moses gave you circumcision (it is, of course, not from Moses, but from our ancestors), and you circumcise a man on the sabbath. ²³If a man receives circumcision on the sabbath in order that the law of Moses may not be broken, are you angry with me because I healed a person's whole body on the sabbath? ²⁴Do not judge by appearances, but judge with right judgment."

Is This the Christ?

25 Now some of the people of Jerusalem were saying, "Is not this the one whom they are trying to kill? ²⁶And here he is, speaking openly, but they say nothing to him! Can it be that the authorities really know that this is the Messiah?^s ²⁷Yet we know where this man is from; but when the Messiah^s comes, no one will know where the Messiah^s is from." ²⁸Then Jesus cried out as he was teaching in the temple, "You know me, and you know where I am from. I have not come on my own. But the one who sent me is true, and you do not know who it is. ²⁹I know who it is, because it is from God that I have

---

p Other ancient authorities add *yet*   q Other ancient authorities lack *as it were*
r Or *this man know his letters*   s Or *the Christ*

come, and God sent me." ³⁰Then they tried to arrest Jesus, but no one laid hands on him, because his hour had not yet come. ³¹Yet many in the crowd believed in Jesus and were saying, "When the Messiah^t comes, will the Messiah^t do more signs than this person has done?"^u

Officers Are Sent to Arrest Jesus

32 The Pharisees heard the crowd muttering such things about Jesus, and the chief priests and Pharisees sent temple police to arrest him. ³³Jesus then said, "I will be with you a little while longer, and then I am going to the one who sent me. ³⁴You will search for me, but you will not find me; and where I am, you cannot come." ³⁵The religious authorities said to one another, "Where does this man intend to go that we will not find him? Does he intend to go to the Dispersion among the Greeks and teach the Greeks? ³⁶What does he mean by saying, 'You will search for me and you will not find me' and 'Where I am, you cannot come'?"

Rivers of Living Water

37 On the last day of the festival, the great day, while Jesus was standing there, he cried out, "Let anyone who is thirsty come to me, ³⁸and let the one who believes in me drink. As^v the scripture has said, 'Out of the believer's heart^w shall flow rivers of living water.' " ³⁹Now Jesus said this about the Spirit, which believers in Jesus were to receive; for as yet there was no Spirit,^x because Jesus was not yet glorified.

Division among the People

40 When they heard these words, some in the crowd said, "This is really the prophet." ⁴¹Others said, "This is the Messiah."^t But some said, "Surely the Messiah^t will not come from Galilee! ⁴²Has not the scripture said that the Messiah^t is descended from David and comes from Bethlehem, the village where David lived?" ⁴³So there was a division in the crowd because of Jesus. ⁴⁴Some of them wanted to arrest him, but no one laid hands on him.

The Unbelief of Those in Authority

45 Then the temple police went back to the chief priests and Pharisees, who asked them, "Why did you not arrest Jesus?" ⁴⁶The police answered, "Never has anyone spoken like this!" ⁴⁷Then the Pharisees replied, "Surely you have not been deceived too, have you? ⁴⁸Has any one of the authorities or of the Pharisees believed in Jesus? ⁴⁹But this crowd, which does not know the law—they are accursed." ⁵⁰Nicodemus, who had gone to Jesus before, and who

---

t Or *the Christ*   u Other ancient authorities read *is doing*
v Or *come to me and drink. 38The one who believes in me, as*
w Gk *out of the believer's belly*
x Other ancient authorities read *for as yet the Spirit* (others, *Holy Spirit*) *had not been given*

was one of them, asked, [51]"Our law does not judge people without first giving them a hearing to find out what they are doing, does it?" [52]They replied, "Surely you are not also from Galilee, are you? Search and you will see that no prophet is to arise from Galilee."

The Woman Caught in Adultery

8 ⟦[53]Then each of them went home, [1]while Jesus went to the Mount of Olives. [2]Early in the morning he came again to the temple. All the people came to him and he sat down and began to teach them. [3]The scribes and the Pharisees brought a woman who had been caught in adultery; and making her stand before all of them, [4]they said, "Teacher, this woman was caught in the very act of committing adultery. [5]In the law, Moses commanded us to stone such women. Now, what do you say?" [6]They said this to test him, so that they might have some charge to bring against him. Jesus bent down and wrote with his finger on the ground. [7]When they kept on questioning him, he straightened up and said to them, "Let anyone among you who is without sin be the first to throw a stone at her." [8]And once again he bent down and wrote on the ground.[y] [9]When they heard it, they went away, one by one, beginning with the elders; and Jesus was left alone with the woman standing before him. [10]Jesus straightened up and said to her, "Woman, where are they? Has no one condemned you?" [11]She said, "No one, sir."[z] And Jesus said, "Neither do I condemn you. Go your way, and from now on do not sin again."⟧[a]

Jesus the Light of the World

12 Again Jesus spoke to them, saying, "I am the light of the world. Whoever follows me will never walk in the night but will have the light of life." [13]Then the Pharisees said to him, "You are testifying on your own behalf; your testimony is not valid." [14]Jesus answered, "Even if I testify on my own behalf, my testimony is valid because I know where I have come from and where I am going, but you do not know where I come from or where I am going. [15]You judge by human standards;[b] I judge no one. [16]Yet even if I do judge, my judgment is valid; for it is not I alone who judge, but I and the Father-Mother who sent me. [17]In your law it is written that the testimony of two witnesses is valid. [18]I testify on my own behalf, and the Father-Mother who sent me testifies on my behalf." [19]Then they said to him, "Where is your Father-Mother?" Jesus answered, "You know neither me nor my Father-Mother. If you knew me, you would know my Father-Mother also." [20]Jesus spoke these words while teaching in the treasury of the temple, but no one made an arrest because Jesus' hour had not yet come.

---

y Other ancient authorities add *the sins of each of them*   z Or *Lord*
a The most ancient authorities lack 7.53—8.11; other authorities add the passage here or after 7.36 or after 21.25 or after Luke 21.38, with variations of text; some mark the passage as doubtful.   b Gk *according to the flesh*

Jesus Foretells His Death

21 Again Jesus said to them, "I am going away, and you will search for me, but you will die in your sin. Where I am going, you cannot come." 22 Then the religious authorities said, "Is he going to commit suicide? Is that what he means by saying, 'Where I am going, you cannot come'?" 23 Jesus said to them, "You are from below, I am from above; you are of this world, I am not of this world. 24 I told you that you would die in your sins, for you will die in your sins unless you believe that I am the one."c 25 They said to Jesus, "Who are you?" Jesus said to them, "Why do I speak to you at all?d 26 I have much to say about you and much to condemn; but the one who sent me is true, and I declare to the world what I have heard from that one." 27 They did not understand that he was speaking to them about God. 28 So Jesus said, "When you have lifted up the Human One, then you will realize that I am the one,c and that I do nothing on my own, but I speak these things as God instructed me. 29 And the one who sent me is with me, and has not left me alone, for I always do what is pleasing to that one." 30 As Jesus was saying these things, many believed in him.

True Disciples

31 Then Jesus said to the Jews who had believed in him, "If you continue in my word, you are truly my disciples; 32 and you will know the truth, and the truth will make you free." 33 They answered, "We are descendants of Abraham and Sarah and have never been enslaved to anyone. What do you mean by saying, 'You will be made free'?"

34 Jesus answered them, "Very truly, I tell you, everyone who commits sin is enslaved to sin. 35 One who is enslaved does not have a permanent place in the household; the heir has a place there forever. 36 So if the Child makes you free, you will be free indeed. 37 I know that you are descendants of Abraham and Sarah; yet you look for an opportunity to kill me, because there is no place in you for my word. 38 I declare what I have seen in God's presence; as for you, you should do what you have heard from God."e

Jesus and Abraham

39 They replied, "Abraham is our ancestor." Jesus said, "If you were Abraham's children, you would be doing what Abraham did, 40 but now you are trying to kill me, someone who has told you the truth that I heard from God. This is not what Abraham did. 41 You are indeed doing what your ancestor does." They said to Jesus, "We are not illegitimate children; we have one ancestor, God alone." 42 Jesus said to them, "If God were your Father-Mother, you would love me, for I came from God and now I am here. I did not come

---

c Gk *I am*   d Or *What I have told you from the beginning*
e Other ancient authorities read *you do what you have heard from your ancestor*

on my own, but God sent me. [43] Why do you not understand what I say? It is because you cannot accept my word. [44] You are descended from the devil, and you choose to do the devil's desires. The devil was a murderer from the beginning and does not stand in the truth, having no truth within. When the devil lies, it is only natural, for the devil is a liar and the source of lies. [45] But because I tell the truth, you do not believe me. [46] Which of you convicts me of sin? If I tell the truth, why do you not believe me? [47] Whoever is from God hears the words of God. The reason you do not hear them is that you are not from God."

48 The religious leaders answered Jesus, "Are we not right in saying that you are a Samaritan and have a demon?" [49] Jesus answered, "I do not have a demon; but I honor my Father-Mother, and you dishonor me. [50] Yet I do not seek my own glory; there is one who seeks it and that one is the judge. [51] Very truly, I tell you, whoever keeps my word will never see death." [52] The leaders said to him, "Now we know that you have a demon. Abraham and Sarah died, and so did the prophets; yet you say, 'Whoever keeps my word will never taste death.' [53] Are you greater than our ancestors Abraham and Sarah, who died? The prophets also died. Who do you claim to be?" [54] Jesus answered, "If I glorify myself, my glory is nothing. It is God, my Father-Mother, who glorifies me, the one of whom you say, 'This is our God,' [55] though you do not know God. But I know God; if I would say that I do not know God, I would be a liar like you. But I do know God and I keep God's word. [56] Your ancestors Abraham and Sarah rejoiced that they would see my day; they saw it and were glad." [57] Then the leaders said to him, "You are not yet fifty years old, and have you seen Abraham and Sarah?"[f] [58] Jesus said to them, "Very truly, I tell you, before Abraham and Sarah were, I am." [59] So they picked up stones to throw at him, but Jesus hid and went out of the temple.

A Person Born Blind Receives Sight

9 As Jesus walked along, he saw a man blind from birth. [2] The disciples asked him, "Rabbi, who sinned, this man or his parents, that he was born blind?" [3] Jesus answered, "Neither this man nor his parents sinned; he was born blind so that God's works might be revealed in him. [4] We[g] must work the works of the one who sent me[h] while it is day; night is coming when no one can work. [5] As long as I am in the world, I am the light of the world." [6] When Jesus had said this, he spat on the ground and made mud with the saliva and spread the mud on the man's eyes, [7] saying, "Go, wash in the pool of Siloam" (which means Sent). Then he went and washed and came back able to see. [8] The neighbors and those who had seen him before as a beggar began to ask, "Is this not the man who used to sit and beg?" [9] Some were saying, "It is." Others were saying, "No, but they look alike." The man kept saying, "I am the one." [10] But

---

f Other ancient authorities read *have Abraham and Sarah seen you?*

g Other ancient authorities read *I*   h Other ancient authorities read *us*

they kept asking, "Then how were your eyes opened?" [11] He answered, "The man called Jesus made mud, spread it on my eyes, and said to me, 'Go to Siloam and wash.' Then I went and washed and received my sight." [12] They said, "Where is he?" The man replied, "I do not know."

The Pharisees Investigate the Healing

13 They brought to the Pharisees the man who had formerly been blind. [14] Now it was a sabbath day when Jesus made the mud and opened his eyes. [15] Then the Pharisees also began to ask the man how he had received his sight. He said to them, "He put mud on my eyes. Then I washed, and now I see." [16] Some of the Pharisees said, "This one is not from God, for he does not observe the sabbath." But others said, "How can a person who is a sinner perform such signs?" And they were divided. [17] So they said again to the man, "What do you say about him? It was your eyes he opened." He said, "He is a prophet."

18 The religious leaders did not believe that he had been blind and had received sight until they called the parents of the man who had received sight [19] and asked them, "Is this your son, who you say was born blind? How then does he now see?" [20] The parents answered, "We know that this is our son, who was born blind; [21] but we do not know how it is that now he sees, nor do we know who opened his eyes. Ask him; he is of age and will speak for himself." [22] The parents said this because they were afraid of the religious authorities, who had already agreed that anyone who confessed Jesus to be the Messiah[i] would be put out of the synagogue. [23] Therefore the parents said, "He is of age; ask him."

24 So for the second time they called the man who had been blind, and they said, "Give glory to God! We know that this man is a sinner." [25] He answered, "I do not know whether he is a sinner. One thing I do know, that though I was blind, now I see." [26] They said, "What did he do to you? How did he open your eyes?" [27] He answered them, "I have told you already, and you would not listen. Why do you want to hear it again? Do you also want to become Jesus' disciples?" [28] Then they reviled him, saying, "You are his disciple, but we are disciples of Moses. [29] We know that God has spoken to Moses, but as for this man, we do not know where he comes from." [30] The man answered, "Here is an astonishing thing! You do not know where he comes from, and yet he opened my eyes. [31] We know that God does not listen to sinners, but does listen to one who worships God and obeys God's will. [32] Never since the world began has it been heard that anyone opened the eyes of a person born blind. [33] If this man were not from God, he could do nothing." [34] They answered, "You were born entirely in sin, and are you trying to teach us?" And they drove out the man who had been blind.

---

i Or *the Christ*

Spiritual Blindness

35 When Jesus found the person who he heard had been driven out, he said, "Do you believe in the Human One?"ʲ ³⁶The man born blind answered, "And who is that, sir?ᵏ Tell me, so that I may believe in that one." ³⁷Jesus said, "You have seen who it is, and it is the one speaking with you." ³⁸The man who had been blind said, "Lord,ᵏ I believe," and worshiped Jesus. ³⁹Jesus said, "I came into this world for judgment so that those who do not see may see, and those who do see may become blind." ⁴⁰Some of the Pharisees nearby heard this and said to Jesus, "Surely we are not blind, are we?" ⁴¹Jesus said to them, "If you were blind, you would not have sin. But now that you say, 'We see,' your sin remains.

Jesus the Good Shepherd

10 "Very truly, I tell you, anyone who does not enter the sheepfold by the gate but climbs in by another way is a thief and a bandit. ²The one who enters by the gate is the shepherd of the sheep. ³The gatekeeper opens the gate for the shepherd, and the sheep hear the voice of the shepherd who calls each of them by name and leads them out. ⁴After bringing all of them out, the shepherd goes ahead of them, and the sheep follow because they know the shepherd's voice. ⁵They will not follow a stranger, but they will run away because they do not know the voice of strangers." ⁶Jesus used this figure of speech with them, but they did not understand what he was saying to them.

7 So again Jesus said to them, "Very truly, I tell you, I am the gate for the sheep. ⁸All who came before me are thieves and bandits; but the sheep did not listen to them. ⁹I am the gate. Whoever enters by me will be saved, and will come in and go out and find pasture. ¹⁰The thief comes only to steal and kill and destroy. I came that they may have life, and have it abundantly.

11 "I am the good shepherd. The good shepherd is willing to die for the sheep. ¹²The hired hand, who is not the shepherd and does not own the sheep, sees the wolf coming and leaves the sheep and runs away—and the wolf snatches them and scatters them. ¹³The hired hand runs away because a hired hand does not care for the sheep. ¹⁴I am the good shepherd. I know my own and my own know me, ¹⁵just as God knows me and I know God. And I lay down my life for the sheep. ¹⁶I have other sheep that do not belong to this fold. I must bring them also, and they will listen to my voice. So there will be one flock, one shepherd. ¹⁷For this reason God loves me, because I lay down my life in order to take it up again. ¹⁸No one takesˡ it from me, but I lay it down of my own accord. I have power to lay it down, and I have power to take it up again. I have received this command from my Father-Mother."

19 Again the religious leaders were divided because of these words. ²⁰Many

---

j Other ancient authorities read *the Child of God*
k *Sir* and *Lord* translate the same Greek word   l Other ancient authorities read *has taken*

of them were saying, "He has a demon and is out of his mind. Why listen to him?" 21 Others were saying, "These are not the words of one who has a demon. Can a demon open the eyes of people who are blind?"

Jesus Is Rejected by the Religious Leaders

22 At that time the festival of the Dedication took place in Jerusalem. It was winter, 23 and Jesus was walking in the temple, in the portico of Solomon. 24 So the religious authorities gathered around Jesus and said, "How long will you keep us in suspense? If you are the Messiah,ᵐ tell us plainly." 25 Jesus answered, "I have told you, and you do not believe. The works that I do in the name of my Father-Mother testify to me; 26 but you do not believe, because you do not belong to my sheep. 27 My sheep hear my voice. I know them, and they follow me. 28 I give them eternal life, and they will never perish. No one will snatch them out of my hand. 29 What my Father-Mother has given me is greater than all else, and no one can snatch it out of God's hand.ⁿ 30 The Father-Mother and I are one."

31 The leaders took up stones again to stone him. 32 Jesus replied, "I have shown you many good works from God. For which of these are you going to stone me?" 33 The leaders answered, "It is not for a good work that we are going to stone you, but for blasphemy, because you, though only a human being, are making yourself God." 34 Jesus answered, "Is it not written in your law,ᵒ 'I said, you are gods'? 35 If those to whom the word of God came were called 'gods'—and the scripture cannot be annulled— 36 can you say that the one whom God has sanctified and sent into the world is blaspheming because I said, 'I am the Child of God'? 37 If I am not doing the works of my Father-Mother, then do not believe me. 38 But if I do them, even though you do not believe me, believe the works, so that you may know and understandᵖ that God is in me and I am in God." 39 Then they tried to arrest Jesus again, but he escaped from their hands.

40 Jesus went away again across the Jordan to the place where John had been baptizing earlier, and remained there. 41 Many came to him, and they were saying, "John performed no sign, but everything that John said about this person was true." 42 And many believed in Jesus there.

The Death of Lazarus

11 Now a certain man was ill, Lazarus of Bethany, the village of Mary and her sister Martha. 2 Mary was the one who anointed the Lord with perfume and wiped his feet with her hair; her brother Lazarus was ill. 3 So the sisters sent a message to Jesus, "Lord, Lazarus, whom you love, is ill." 4 But

---

m Or *the Christ*
n Other ancient authorities read *God who has given them to me is greater than all, and no one can snatch them out of God's hand*   o Other ancient authorities read *in the law*
p Other ancient authorities lack *and understand*; others read *and believe*

when Jesus heard it, he said, "This illness does not lead to death; rather it is for God's glory, so that the Child of God may be glorified through it." [5]Accordingly, though Jesus loved Martha and her sister and Lazarus, [6]after having heard that Lazarus was ill, Jesus stayed two days longer in the place where he was.

7 Then after this Jesus said to the disciples, "Let us go to Judea again." [8]The disciples protested, "Rabbi, the religious authorities were just now trying to stone you, and are you going there again?" [9]Jesus answered, "Are there not twelve hours of daylight? Those who walk during the day do not stumble, because they see the light of this world. [10]But those who walk at night stumble, because the light is not in them." [11]After saying this, he told them, "Our friend Lazarus has fallen asleep, but I am going there to awaken him." [12]The disciples replied, "Lord, if he has fallen asleep, he will be all right." [13]Jesus, however, had been speaking about his death, but they thought that he was referring merely to sleep. [14]Then Jesus told them plainly, "Lazarus is dead. [15]For your sake I am glad I was not there, so that you may believe. But let us go to him." [16]Thomas, who was called the Twin,[q] said to the other disciples, "Let us also go, that we may die with him."

Jesus the Resurrection and the Life

17 When Jesus arrived, he found that Lazarus had already been in the tomb four days. [18]Now Bethany was near Jerusalem, some two miles away, [19]and many of the Jews had come to Martha and Mary to console them about their brother. [20]When Martha heard that Jesus was coming, she went and met him, while Mary stayed at home. [21]Martha said to Jesus, "Lord, if you had been here, my brother would not have died. [22]But even now I know that God will give you whatever you ask." [23]Jesus said to her, "Your brother will rise again." [24]Martha said to him, "I know that he will rise again in the resurrection on the last day." [25]Jesus said to her, "I am the resurrection and the life.[r] Those who believe in me, even though they die, will live, [26]and everyone who lives and believes in me will never die. Do you believe this?" [27]She said to him, "Yes, Lord, I believe that you are the Messiah,[s] the Child of God, the one coming into the world."

Jesus Weeps

28 When Martha had said this, she went back and called her sister Mary, and told her privately, "The Teacher is here and is calling for you." [29]And when Mary heard it, she got up quickly and went to him. [30]Now Jesus had not yet come to the village, but was still at the place where Martha had met him. [31]The Jews who were with her in the house, consoling her, saw Mary get up quickly and go out. They followed her because they thought that she was going to the tomb to weep there. [32]When Mary came where Jesus was and saw him, she knelt at his feet and said, "Lord, if you had been here, my brother would not

---

q Gk *Didymus*   r Other ancient authorities lack *and the life*   s Or *the Christ*

have died." 33When Jesus saw her weeping, and the Jews who came with her also weeping, he was greatly disturbed in spirit and deeply moved. 34He said, "Where have you laid Lazarus?" They answered, "Lord, come and see." 35Jesus began to weep. 36So the Jews said, "See how Jesus loved him!" 37But some of them said, "Could not the one who opened the eyes of the man born blind have kept this man from dying?"

Jesus Raises Lazarus to Life

38 Then Jesus, again greatly disturbed, came to the tomb. It was a cave, and a stone was lying against it. 39Jesus said, "Take away the stone." Martha, the sister of the dead man, said to him, "Lord, already there is a stench because he has been dead four days." 40Jesus said to her, "Did I not tell you that if you believed, you would see the glory of God?" 41So they took away the stone. And Jesus looked upward and said, "God, I thank you for having heard me. 42I knew that you always hear me, but I have said this for the sake of the crowd standing here, so that they may believe that you sent me." 43When Jesus had said this, he cried with a loud voice, "Lazarus, come out!" 44The dead man came out, his hands and feet bound with strips of cloth, and his face wrapped in a cloth. Jesus said to them, "Unbind him, and let him go."

The Plot to Kill Jesus

45 Many of the Jews therefore, who had come with Mary and had seen what Jesus did, believed in him. 46But some of them went to the Pharisees and told them what Jesus had done. 47So the chief priests and the Pharisees called a meeting of the council, and said, "What are we to do? This man is performing many signs. 48If we let it continue like this, everyone will believe in him, and the Romans will come and destroy both our holy place† and our nation." 49But one of them, Caiaphas, who was high priest that year, said to them, "You know nothing at all! 50You do not understand that it is better for you to have one person die for the people than to have the whole nation destroyed." 51Caiaphas did not say this on his own, but being high priest that year he prophesied that Jesus was about to die for the nation, 52and not for the nation only, but to gather into one the dispersed children of God. 53So from that day on they planned to put Jesus to death.

54 Jesus therefore no longer walked about openly among his own people, but went from there to a town called Ephraim in the region near the wilderness, and remained there with the disciples.

55 Now the Passover was near, and many went up from the country to Jerusalem before the Passover to purify themselves. 56They were looking for Jesus and were asking one another as they stood in the temple, "What do you think? Surely he will not come to the festival, will he?" 57Now the chief priests

---

t Or *our temple*; Greek *our place*

and the Pharisees had given orders that anyone who knew where Jesus was should let them know, so that they might arrest Jesus.

Mary Anoints Jesus

12 Six days before the Passover Jesus came to Bethany, the home of Lazarus, whom he had raised from the dead. ²There they gave a dinner for him. Martha served, and Lazarus was one of those at the table with him. ³Mary took a pound of costly perfume made of pure nard, anointed Jesus' feet, and wiped them with her hair. The house was filled with the fragrance of the perfume. ⁴But Judas Iscariot, one of the disciples (the one who was about to betray Jesus), said, ⁵"Why was this perfume not sold for a year's wages and the money given to those who are poor?" ⁶(Judas said this not because he cared about those who are poor, but because he was a thief; he kept the common purse and used to steal what was put into it.) ⁷Jesus said, "Leave her alone. She bought itᵘ so that she might keep it for the day of my burial. ⁸You always have those who are poor with you, but you do not always have me."

The Plot to Kill Lazarus

9 When the great crowd of the Jews learned that Jesus was there, they came not only because of Jesus but also to see Lazarus, whom Jesus had raised from the dead. ¹⁰So the chief priests planned to put Lazarus to death as well, ¹¹since it was on account of him that many of the Jews were deserting and were believing in Jesus.

Jesus' Triumphal Entry into Jerusalem

12 The next day the great crowd that had come to the festival heard that Jesus was coming to Jerusalem. ¹³So they took branches of palm trees and went out to meet him, shouting,

> "Hosanna!
> Blessed is the one who comes in the name
>   of the Lord—
>   the King of Israel!"

¹⁴Jesus found a young donkey and sat on it; as it is written:

15
> "Do not be afraid, beloved city of Zion.
> Look, your king is coming,
>   sitting on the colt of a donkey!"

¹⁶The disciples did not understand these things at first; but when Jesus was glorified, then they remembered that these things had been written of Jesus and had been done to him. ¹⁷So the crowd that had been with Jesus when he called

---

u Gk lacks *She bought it*

Lazarus out of the tomb and raised him from the dead continued to testify.[v] [18]It was also because they heard that Jesus had performed this sign that the crowd went to meet him. [19]The Pharisees then said to one another, "You see, you can do nothing. Look, the world has gone after him!"

Some Greeks Wish to See Jesus

20 Now among those who went up to worship at the festival were some Greeks. [21]They came to Philip, who was from Bethsaida in Galilee, and said, "Sir, we wish to see Jesus." [22]Philip went and told Andrew; then Andrew and Philip went and told Jesus. [23]Jesus answered them, "The hour has come for the Human One to be glorified. [24]Very truly, I tell you, unless a grain of wheat falls into the earth and dies, it remains just a single grain; but if it dies, it bears much fruit. [25]Those who love their life lose it, and those who hate their life in this world will keep it for eternal life. [26]Whoever serves me must follow me, and where I am, there will my servant be also. Whoever serves me, God will honor.

Jesus Speaks about His Death

27 "Now my soul is troubled. And what should I say—'Father-Mother, save me from this hour'? No, it is for this reason that I have come to this hour. [28]Father-Mother, glorify your name." Then a voice came from heaven, "I have glorified it, and I will glorify it again." [29]The crowd standing there heard it and said that it was thunder. Others said, "An angel has spoken to him." [30]Jesus answered, "This voice has come for your sake, not for mine. [31]Now is the judgment of this world; now the ruler of this world will be driven out. [32]And I, when I am lifted up from the earth, will draw all people[w] to myself." [33]He said this to indicate the kind of death he was to die. [34]The crowd answered him, "We have heard from the law that the Messiah[x] remains forever. How can you say that the Human One must be lifted up? Who is this Human One?" [35]Jesus said to them, "The light is with you for a little longer. Walk while you have the light, so that the night may not overtake you. If you walk in the night, you do not know where you are going. [36]While you have the light, believe in the light, so that you may become children of light."

The Unbelief of the People

After Jesus had said this, he departed and hid from them. [37]Although he had performed so many signs in their presence, they did not believe in him. [38]This was to fulfill the word spoken by the prophet Isaiah:

> "O God, who has believed our message,
>   and to whom has the arm of God been revealed?"

---

v Other ancient authorities read *with Jesus began to testify that he had called ... from the dead*
w Other ancient authorities read *all things*   x Or *the Christ*

[39] And so they could not believe, because Isaiah also said,

[40]
> "God has closed their eyes
>> and hardened their heart,
>> so that they might not perceive with their eyes,
>> and understand with their heart and turn—
>> and I would heal them."

[41] Isaiah said this because[y] he saw the glory of the Messiah[z] and spoke about the Messiah.[z] [42] Nevertheless many, even of the authorities, believed in Jesus. But because of the Pharisees they did not confess it, for fear that they would be put out of the synagogue; [43] for they loved human glory more than the glory that comes from God.

Summary of Jesus' Teaching

[44] Then Jesus cried aloud: "Whoever believes in me believes not in me but in the one who sent me. [45] And whoever sees me sees the one who sent me. [46] I have come as light into the world, so that everyone who believes in me should not remain in the night. [47] I do not judge anyone who hears my words and does not keep them, for I came not to judge the world, but to save the world. [48] The one who rejects me and does not receive my word has a judge; on the last day the word that I have spoken will serve as judge, [49] for I have not spoken on my own, but God who sent me has indeed given me a commandment about what to say and what to speak. [50] And I know that God's commandment is eternal life. What I speak, therefore, I speak just as God has told me."

Jesus Washes the Disciples' Feet

13 Now before the festival of the Passover, Jesus knew that the hour had come to depart from this world and go to God. Having loved his own who were in the world, he loved them to the end. [2] The devil had already put it into the heart of Judas son of Simon Iscariot to betray Jesus. And during supper [3] Jesus, knowing that God had given all things into his hands, and that he had come from God and was going to God, [4] got up from the table,[a] took off his outer robe, and tied a towel around himself. [5] Then Jesus poured water into a basin and began to wash the disciples' feet and to wipe them with the towel that was tied around him. [6] He came to Simon Peter, who said to him, "Lord, are you going to wash my feet?" [7] Jesus answered, "You do not know now what I am doing, but later you will understand." [8] Peter said to him, "You will never wash my feet." Jesus answered, "Unless I wash you, you have no share with me." [9] Simon Peter said to him, "Lord, not my feet only but also my hands and my head!" [10] Jesus said to him, "One who has bathed does not need to wash, except for the feet,[b] but is entirely clean. And you[c] are clean, though

---

y Other ancient witnesses read *when*　　z Or *the Christ*　　a Gk *from supper*
b Other ancient authorities lack *except for the feet*　　c The Greek word for *you* here is plural

not all of you." [11]For he knew who was to betray him; for this reason he said, "Not all of you are clean."

12 After Jesus had washed their feet, had put on his robe, and had returned to the table, he said to them, "Do you know what I have done to you? [13]You call me Teacher and Lord—and you are right, for that is what I am. [14]So if I, your Lord and Teacher, have washed your feet, you also ought to wash one another's feet. [15]For I have set you an example, that you also should do as I have done to you. [16]Very truly, I tell you, those who are enslaved are not greater than those who enslave them, nor are messengers greater than the one who sent them. [17]If you know these things, you are blessed if you do them. [18]I am not speaking of all of you; I know whom I have chosen. But it is to fulfill the scripture, 'The one who ate my bread[d] has lifted his heel against me.' [19]I tell you this now, before it occurs, so that when it does occur, you may believe that I am the one.[e] [20]Very truly, I tell you, whoever receives one whom I send receives me; and whoever receives me receives the one who sent me."

Jesus Foretells His Betrayal

21 After saying this Jesus was troubled in spirit, and declared, "Very truly, I tell you, one of you will betray me." [22]The disciples looked at one another, uncertain of whom he was speaking. [23]One of the disciples—the one whom Jesus loved—was reclining next to him; [24]Simon Peter therefore motioned to that disciple to ask Jesus of whom he was speaking. [25]So while reclining next to Jesus, the one whom Jesus loved asked him, "Lord, who is it?" [26]Jesus answered, "It is the one to whom I give this piece of bread when I have dipped it in the dish."[f] So having dipped the piece of bread, he gave it to Judas son of Simon Iscariot.[g] [27]After Judas received the piece of bread,[h] Satan entered into him. Jesus said to him, "Do quickly what you are going to do." [28]Now no one at the table knew why Jesus said this to Judas. [29]Some thought that, because Judas had the common purse, Jesus was telling him, "Buy what we need for the festival"; or, that he should give something to those who are poor. [30]So, after receiving the piece of bread, Judas immediately went out. And it was night.

The New Commandment

31 When he had gone out, Jesus said, "Now the Human One has been glorified, and in that one God has been glorified. [32]If God has been glorified in the Human One,[i] God will also glorify that very one in Godself and will glorify that one at once. [33]Little children, I am with you only a little longer.

---

d Other ancient authorities read *ate bread with me*   e Gk *I am*   f Gk *dipped it*
g Other ancient authorities read *Judas Iscariot son of Simon*; others, *Judas son of Simon from Karyot* (Kerioth)   h Gk *After the piece of bread*
i Other ancient authorities lack *If God has been glorified in the Human One*

You will look for me; and as I said to the religious leaders so now I say to you, 'Where I am going, you cannot come.' 34 I give you a new commandment, that you love one another. Just as I have loved you, you also should love one another. 35 By this everyone will know that you are my disciples, if you have love for one another."

Jesus Foretells Peter's Denial

36 Simon Peter said to Jesus, "Lord, where are you going?" Jesus answered, "Where I am going, you cannot follow me now; but you will follow afterward." 37 Peter said, "Lord, why can I not follow you now? I will lay down my life for you." 38 Jesus answered, "Will you lay down your life for me? Very truly, I tell you, before the cock crows, you will have denied me three times.

Jesus the Way to the Father-Mother

14 "Do not let your hearts be troubled. Believe[j] in God, believe also in me. 2 In the house of my Father-Mother there are many dwelling places. If it were not so, would I have told you that I go to prepare a place for you?[k] 3 And if I go and prepare a place for you, I will come again and will take you to myself, so that where I am, there you may be also. 4 And you know the way to the place where I am going."[l] 5 Thomas said to Jesus, "Lord, we do not know where you are going. How can we know the way?" 6 Jesus said to him, "I am the way, and the truth, and the life. No one comes to God except through me. 7 If you know me, you will know[m] my Father-Mother also. From now on you do know God and have seen God."

8 Philip said to Jesus, "Lord, show us God, and we will be satisfied." 9 Jesus replied, "Have I been with you all this time, Philip, and you still do not know me? Whoever has seen me has seen God. How can you say, 'Show us God'? 10 Do you not believe that I am in God and God is in me? The words that I say to you I do not speak on my own; but God who dwells in me does God's works. 11 Believe me that I am in God and God is in me; but if you do not, then believe me because of the works themselves. 12 Very truly, I tell you, the one who believes in me will also do the works that I do and, in fact, will do greater works than these, because I am going to God. 13 I will do whatever you ask in my name, so that the Father-Mother may be glorified in the Child. 14 If in my name you ask me[n] for anything, I will do it.

---

j Or *You believe*
k Or *If it were not so, I would have told you; for I go to prepare a place for you*
l Other ancient authorities read *Where I am going you know, and the way you know*
m Other ancient authorities read *If you had known me, you would have known*
n Other ancient authorities lack *me*

The Promise of the Holy Spirit

15 "If you love me, you will keep[o] my commandments. 16 And I will ask God,
who will give you another Advocate,[p] to be with you forever. 17 This is the
Spirit of truth, whom the world cannot receive, because it neither sees nor
knows the Spirit. You know the Spirit, because the Spirit abides with you and
will be in[q] you.

18 "I will not leave you orphaned; I am coming to you. 19 In a little while
the world will no longer see me, but you will see me; because I live, you also
will live. 20 On that day you will know that I am in my Father-Mother, and
you in me, and I in you. 21 They who have my commandments and keep them
are those who love me; and those who love me will be loved by my
Father-Mother, and I will love them and reveal myself to them." 22 Judas (not
Iscariot) said to Jesus, "Lord, how is it that you will reveal yourself to us, and
not to the world?" 23 Jesus answered him, "Those who love me will keep my
word, and my Father-Mother will love them, and we will come to them and
make our home with them. 24 Whoever does not love me does not keep my
words; and the word that you hear is not mine, but is from God who sent me.

25 "I have said these things to you while I am still with you. 26 But the
Advocate,[p] the Holy Spirit, whom God will send in my name, will teach you
everything, and remind you of all that I have said to you. 27 Peace I leave with
you; my peace I give to you. I do not give to you as the world gives. Do not
let your hearts be troubled, and do not let them be afraid. 28 You heard me say
to you, 'I am going away, and I am coming to you.' If you loved me, you
would rejoice that I am going to God, because God is greater than I. 29 And
now I have told you this before it occurs, so that when it does occur, you may
believe. 30 I will no longer talk much with you, for the ruler of this world is
coming. That ruler has no power over me; 31 but I do as God has commanded
me, so that the world may know that I love God. Rise, let us be on our way.

Jesus the True Vine

15 "I am the true vine, and my Father-Mother is the vinegrower. 2 God
removes every branch in me that bears no fruit. Every branch that bears
fruit God prunes[r] to make it bear more fruit. 3 You have already been
cleansed[r] by the word that I have spoken to you. 4 Abide in me as I abide in
you. Just as the branch cannot bear fruit by itself unless it abides in the vine,
neither can you unless you abide in me. 5 I am the vine, you are the branches.
Those who abide in me and I in them bear much fruit, because apart from me
you can do nothing. 6 Whoever does not abide in me is thrown away like a
branch and withers; such branches are gathered, thrown into the fire, and
burned. 7 If you abide in me, and my words abide in you, ask for whatever you

---

o Other ancient authorities read *me, keep* p Or *Helper* q Or *among*
r The same Greek root refers to pruning and cleansing

wish, and it will be done for you. ⁸My Father-Mother is glorified by this, that you bear much fruit and become^s my disciples. ⁹As God has loved me, so I have loved you; abide in my love. ¹⁰If you keep my commandments, you will abide in my love, just as I have kept God's commandments and abide in God's love. ¹¹I have said these things to you so that my joy may be in you, and that your joy may be complete.

12 "This is my commandment, that you love one another as I have loved you. ¹³No one has greater love than this, to lay down one's life for one's friends. ¹⁴You are my friends if you do what I command you. ¹⁵I do not call you slaves any longer, because those who are enslaved do not know what the one who enslaves them is doing; but I have called you friends, because I have made known to you everything that I have heard from my Father-Mother. ¹⁶You did not choose me but I chose you. And I appointed you to go and bear fruit, fruit that will last, so that God will give you whatever you ask in my name. ¹⁷I am giving you these commands so that you may love one another.

The World's Hatred

18 "If the world hates you, be aware that it hated me before it hated you. ¹⁹If you belonged to the world,^t the world would love you as its own. Because you do not belong to the world, but I have chosen you out of the world—therefore the world hates you. ²⁰Remember the word that I said to you, 'Slaves are not greater than their master.' If they persecuted me, they will persecute you; if they kept my word, they will keep yours also. ²¹But they will do all these things to you on account of my name, because they do not know the one who sent me. ²²If I had not come and spoken to them, they would not have sin; but now they have no excuse for their sin. ²³Whoever hates me hates my Father-Mother also. ²⁴If I had not done among them the works that no one else did, they would not have sin. But now they have seen and hated both me and my Father-Mother. ²⁵It was to fulfill the word that is written in their law, 'They hated me without a cause.'

26 "When the Advocate^u comes, whom I will send to you from God, the Spirit of truth who comes from God, that one will testify on my behalf. ²⁷You also are to testify because you have been with me from the beginning.

16 "I have said these things to you to keep you from stumbling. ²They will put you out of the synagogues. Indeed, an hour is coming when those who kill you will think that by doing so they are offering worship to God. ³And they will do this because they have not known God or me. ⁴But I have said these things to you so that when their hour comes you may remember that I told you about them.

---

s Or *be*   t Gk *were of the world*   u Or *Helper*

The Work of the Spirit

"I did not say these things to you from the beginning, because I was with you. [5]But now I am going to the one who sent me; yet none of you asks me, 'Where are you going?' [6]But because I have said these things to you, sorrow has filled your hearts. [7]Nevertheless I tell you the truth: it is to your advantage that I go away, for if I do not go away, the Advocate[v] will not come to you; but if I go, I will send the Advocate to you, [8]who, having come, will prove the world wrong about[w] sin and righteousness and judgment: [9]about sin, because they do not believe in me; [10]about righteousness, because I am going to God and you will see me no longer; [11]about judgment, because the ruler of this world has been condemned.

[12] "I still have many things to say to you, but you cannot bear them now. [13]When the Spirit of truth comes, that Spirit will guide you into all the truth; for the Spirit will not speak independently, but will speak whatever the Spirit hears, and will declare to you the things that are to come. [14]The Spirit will glorify me by taking what is mine and declaring it to you. [15]All that God has is mine. For this reason I said that the Spirit will take what is mine and declare it to you.

Sorrow Will Turn into Joy

[16] "A little while, and you will no longer see me, and again a little while, and you will see me." [17]Then some of the disciples said to one another, "What does Jesus mean by saying to us, 'A little while, and you will no longer see me, and again a little while, and you will see me'; and 'Because I am going to God'?" [18]They said, "What does Jesus mean by this 'a little while'? We do not know what he is talking about." [19]Jesus, knowing that they wanted to ask, said to them, "Are you discussing among yourselves what I meant when I said, 'A little while, and you will no longer see me, and again a little while, and you will see me'? [20]Very truly, I tell you, you will weep and mourn, but the world will rejoice; you will have pain, but your pain will turn into joy. [21]When a woman is in labor, she has pain, because her hour has come. But when her child is born, she no longer remembers the anguish because of the joy of having brought a human being into the world. [22]So you have pain now; but I will see you again, and your hearts will rejoice, and no one will take your joy from you. [23]On that day you will ask nothing of me.[x] Very truly, I tell you, if you ask anything of God in my name, God will give it to you.[y] [24]Until now you have not asked for anything in my name. Ask and you will receive, so that your joy may be complete.

---

v Or *Helper*   w Or *convict the world of*   x Or *will ask me no question*
y Other ancient authorities read *God, God will give it to you in my name*

Peace for the Disciples

25 "I have said these things to you in figures of speech. The hour is coming when I will no longer speak to you in figures, but will tell you plainly of God. 26 On that day you will ask in my name. I do not say to you that I will ask God on your behalf; 27 for God indeed loves you, because you have loved me and have believed that I came from God. 28 I came from God and have come into the world; again, I am leaving the world and am going to God."

29 Jesus' disciples said, "Yes, now you are speaking plainly, not in any figure of speech! 30 Now we know that you know all things, and do not need to have anyone question you; by this we believe that you came from God." 31 Jesus answered them, "Do you now believe? 32 The hour is coming, indeed it has come, when you will be scattered, each to your own home, and you will leave me alone. Yet I am not alone because God is with me. 33 I have said this to you, so that in me you may have peace. In the world you face persecution. But take courage; I have conquered the world!"

Jesus Prays for His Disciples

17 Having spoken these words, Jesus looked up to heaven and said, "Father-Mother, the hour has come; glorify your Child so that the Child may glorify you, 2 since you have given that Child authority over all people,[z] to give eternal life to all whom you have given your Child. 3 And this is eternal life, that they may know you, the only true God, and Jesus Christ whom you have sent. 4 I glorified you on earth by finishing the work that you gave me to do. 5 So now, Father-Mother, glorify me in your own presence with the glory that I had in your presence before the world existed.

6 "I have made your name known to those whom you gave me from the world. They were yours, and you gave them to me, and they have kept your word. 7 Now they know that everything you have given me is from you; 8 for the words that you gave to me I have given to them, and they have received them and know in truth that I came from you; and they have believed that you sent me. 9 I am asking on their behalf; I am not asking on behalf of the world, but on behalf of those whom you gave me, because they are yours. 10 All mine are yours, and yours are mine; and I have been glorified in them. 11 And now I am no longer in the world, but they are in the world, and I am coming to you. Holy Father-Mother, protect them in your name that you have given me, so that they may be one, as we are one. 12 While I was with them, I protected them in your name that[a] you have given me. I guarded them, and not one of them was lost except the one destined to be lost, so that the scripture might be fulfilled. 13 But now I am coming to you, and I speak these things in the world so that they may have my joy made complete in themselves.[b] 14 I have given

---

z Gk *flesh*   a Other ancient authorities read *protected in your name those whom*
b Or *among themselves*

them your word, and the world has hated them because they do not belong to the world, just as I do not belong to the world. ¹⁵I am not asking you to take them out of the world, but I ask you to protect them from the evil one.ᶜ ¹⁶They do not belong to the world, just as I do not belong to the world. ¹⁷Sanctify them in the truth; your word is truth. ¹⁸As you have sent me into the world, so I have sent them into the world. ¹⁹And for their sakes I sanctify myself, so that they also may be sanctified in truth.

20 "I ask not only on behalf of these, but also on behalf of those who will believe in me through their word, ²¹that they may all be one. As you, Father-Mother, are in me and I am in you, may they also be in us,ᵈ so that the world may believe that you have sent me. ²²The glory that you have given me I have given them, so that they may be one, as we are one, ²³I in them and you in me, that they may become completely one, so that the world may know that you have sent me and have loved them even as you have loved me. ²⁴Father-Mother, I desire that those also, whom you have given me, may be with me where I am, to see my glory, which you have given me because you loved me before the foundation of the world.

25 "Righteous Father-Mother, the world does not know you, but I know you; and these know that you have sent me. ²⁶I made your name known to them, and I will make it known, so that the love with which you have loved me may be in them, and I in them."

The Betrayal and Arrest of Jesus

18 Having spoken these words, Jesus went out with the disciples across the Kidron valley to a place where there was a garden, which they entered. ²Now Judas, who betrayed him, also knew the place, because Jesus often met there with the disciples. ³So Judas brought a detachment of soldiers together with police from the chief priests and the Pharisees, and they came there with lanterns and torches and weapons. ⁴Then Jesus, knowing all that was to happen to him, came forward and asked them, "Whom are you looking for?" ⁵They answered, "Jesus of Nazareth."ᵉ Jesus replied, "I am the one."ᶠ Judas, who betrayed Jesus, was standing with them. ⁶When Jesus said to them, "I am the one,"ᶠ they stepped back and fell to the ground. ⁷Again Jesus asked them, "Whom are you looking for?" And they said, "Jesus of Nazareth."ᵉ ⁸Jesus answered, "I told you that I am the one.ᶠ So if you are looking for me, let these others go." ⁹This was to fulfill the word that he had spoken, "I did not lose a single one of those whom you gave me." ¹⁰Then Simon Peter, who had a sword, drew it, struck the high priest's servant, and cut off his right ear. The servant's name was Malchus. ¹¹Jesus said to Peter, "Put your sword back into its sheath. Am I not to drink the cup that God has given me?"

---

c Or *from evil*   d Other ancient authorities read *be one in us*   e Gk *the Nazorean*
f Gk *I am*

Jesus before the High Priest

12 So the soldiers, their officer, and the Jewish police arrested Jesus and bound him. 13 First they took him to Annas, who was the father-in-law of Caiaphas, the high priest that year. 14 Caiaphas was the one who had advised the religious leaders that it was better to have one person die for the people.

Peter Denies Jesus

15 Simon Peter and another disciple followed Jesus. That disciple, who was known to the high priest, went with Jesus into the courtyard of the high priest, 16 but Peter was standing outside at the gate. So the other disciple, who was known to the high priest, went out, spoke to the woman who guarded the gate, and brought Peter in. 17 The woman said to Peter, "You are not also one of this man's disciples, are you?" He said, "I am not." 18 Now the servants and the police had made a charcoal fire because it was cold, and they were standing around it and warming themselves. Peter also was standing with them and warming himself.

The High Priest Questions Jesus

19 Then the high priest questioned Jesus about his disciples and about his teaching. 20 Jesus answered, "I have spoken openly to the world; I have always taught in synagogues and in the temple, where all the Jews come together. I have said nothing in secret. 21 Why do you ask me? Ask those who heard what I said to them; they know what I said." 22 When he had said this, one of the police standing nearby struck Jesus on the face, saying, "Is that how you answer the high priest?" 23 Jesus answered, "If I have spoken wrongly, testify to the wrong. But if I have spoken rightly, why do you strike me?" 24 Then Annas sent him bound to Caiaphas the high priest.

Peter Denies Jesus Again

25 Now Simon Peter was standing and warming himself. They asked him, "You are not also one of his disciples, are you?" He denied it and said, "I am not." 26 One of the servants of the high priest, a relative of the man whose ear Peter had cut off, asked, "Did I not see you in the garden with him?" 27 Again Peter denied it, and at that moment the cock crowed.

Jesus before Pilate

28 Then they took Jesus from Caiaphas to Pilate's headquarters.g It was early in the morning. They themselves did not enter the headquarters,g so as to avoid ritual defilement and to be able to eat the Passover. 29 So Pilate went out to them and said, "What accusation do you bring against this man?" 30 They answered, "If this man were not a criminal, we would not have handed him

---

g Gk the praetorium

over to you." ³¹Pilate said to them, "Take him yourselves and judge him according to your law." The religious leaders replied, "We are not permitted to put anyone to death." ³²(This was to fulfill what Jesus had said when he indicated the kind of death he was to die.)

33 Then Pilate entered the headquarters^h again, summoned Jesus, and asked him, "Are you the King of the Jews?" ³⁴Jesus answered, "Do you ask this on your own, or did others tell you about me?" ³⁵Pilate replied, "I am not a Jew, am I? Your own nation and the chief priests have handed you over to me. What have you done?" ³⁶Jesus answered, "My dominion is not from this world. If my dominion were from this world, my followers would be fighting to keep me from being handed over to the religious authorities. But as it is, my dominion is not from here." ³⁷Pilate asked Jesus, "So you are a king?" Jesus answered, "You say that I am a king. For this I was born, and for this I came into the world, to testify to the truth. Everyone who belongs to the truth listens to my voice." ³⁸Pilate asked Jesus, "What is truth?"

Jesus Sentenced to Death

Having said this, Pilate went out to the crowd again and told them, "I find no case against him. ³⁹But you have a custom that I release someone for you at the Passover. Do you want me to release for you the King of the Jews?" ⁴⁰They shouted in reply, "Not this man, but Barabbas!" Now Barabbas was a bandit.

19 Then Pilate had Jesus flogged. ²And the soldiers wove a crown of thorns and put it on his head, and they dressed him in a purple robe. ³They kept coming up to Jesus, saying, "Hail, King of the Jews!" and striking him on the face. ⁴Pilate went out again and said to the crowd, "Look, I am bringing him out to you to let you know that I find no case against him." ⁵So Jesus came out, wearing the crown of thorns and the purple robe. Pilate said to them, "Here is the man!" ⁶When the chief priests and the police saw Jesus, they shouted, "Crucify! Crucify!" Pilate said to them, "Take him yourselves and crucify him; I find no case against him." ⁷The religious authorities answered Pilate, "We have a law, and according to that law he ought to die because he has claimed to be the Child of God."

8 Now when Pilate heard this, he was more afraid than ever. ⁹He entered his headquarters^h again and asked Jesus, "From where have you come?" But Jesus gave him no answer. ¹⁰Pilate therefore said to him, "Do you refuse to speak to me? Do you not know that I have power to release you, and power to crucify you?" ¹¹Jesus replied, "You would have no power over me unless it had been given you from above; therefore the one who handed me over to you is guilty of a greater sin." ¹²From then on Pilate tried to release Jesus, but the religious authorities cried out, "If you release this man, you are no friend of the emperor. Everyone who claims to be a king opposes the emperor."

13 When Pilate heard these words, he brought Jesus outside and satⁱ on

---

h Gk *the praetorium*   i Or *seated him*

the judge's bench at a place called The Stone Pavement, or in Hebrew[j] Gabbatha. [14]Now it was the day of Preparation for the Passover; and it was about noon. Pilate said to the crowd, "Here is your King!" [15]They cried out, "Away with him! Away with him! Crucify him!" Pilate asked them, "Shall I crucify your King?" The chief priests answered, "We have no king but the emperor." [16]Then Pilate handed him over to them to be crucified.

The Crucifixion of Jesus

So they took Jesus, [17]who went out carrying his own cross to what is called The Place of the Skull, which in Hebrew[j] is called Golgotha. [18]There they crucified him, and with him two others, one on either side, with Jesus between them. [19]Pilate also had an inscription written and put on the cross. It read, "Jesus of Nazareth,[k] the King of the Jews." [20]Many of the Jews read this inscription, because the place where Jesus was crucified was near the city; and it was written in Hebrew,[j] in Latin, and in Greek. [21]Then the chief priests of the Jews said to Pilate, "Do not write, 'The King of the Jews,' but, 'This man said, I am King of the Jews.' " [22]Pilate answered, "What I have written I have written." [23]When the soldiers had crucified Jesus, they took his clothes and divided them into four parts, one for each soldier. They also took his tunic; now the tunic was seamless, woven in one piece from the top. [24]So they said to one another, "Let us not tear it, but cast lots for it to see who will get it." This was to fulfill what the scripture says,

> "They divided my clothes among themselves,
>   and for my clothing they cast lots."

[25]And that is what the soldiers did.

Meanwhile, standing near the cross of Jesus were his mother, and his mother's sister, Mary the wife of Clopas, and Mary Magdalene. [26]When Jesus saw his mother and the disciple whom he loved standing beside her, he said to his mother, "Woman, here is your child." [27]Then he said to the disciple, "Here is your mother." And from that hour the disciple took her into the disciple's own home.

[28] After this, knowing that all was now finished, Jesus said (in order to fulfill the scripture), "I am thirsty." [29]A jar full of sour wine was standing there. So they put a sponge full of the wine on a branch of hyssop and held it to his mouth. [30]Having received the wine, Jesus said, "It is finished." Then Jesus bowed his head and gave up the spirit.

Jesus' Side Is Pierced

[31] Since it was the day of Preparation, the religious authorities did not want the bodies left on the cross during the sabbath, especially because that sabbath was a day of great solemnity. So they asked Pilate to have the legs of those

---

j That is, *Aramaic*   k Gk *the Nazorean*

who had been crucified broken and the bodies removed. [32] Then the soldiers came and broke the legs of the first and of the other who had been crucified with Jesus. [33] But when they came to Jesus and saw that he was already dead, they did not break his legs. [34] Instead, one of the soldiers pierced Jesus' side with a spear, and at once blood and water came out. [35] (The one who saw this has testified so that you also may believe. This testimony is true, and the witness knows[l] that it is the truth.) [36] These things occurred so that the scripture might be fulfilled, "None of his bones shall be broken." [37] And again another passage of scripture says, "They will look on the one whom they have pierced."

The Burial of Jesus

38 After these things, Joseph of Arimathea, who was a disciple of Jesus, though a secret one because of his fear of the religious authorities, asked Pilate for permission to take away the body of Jesus. Pilate granted it; so Joseph came and removed Jesus' body. [39] Nicodemus, who had at first come to Jesus by night, also came, bringing a mixture of myrrh and aloes, weighing about a hundred pounds. [40] They took the body of Jesus and wrapped it with the spices in linen cloths, according to the burial custom of the Jews. [41] Now there was a garden in the place where Jesus was crucified, and in the garden there was a new tomb in which no one had ever been laid. [42] And so, because it was the Jewish day of Preparation, and the tomb was nearby, they laid Jesus there.

The Resurrection of Jesus

20 Early on the first day of the week, while it was not yet light, Mary Magdalene came to the tomb and saw that the stone had been removed from the tomb. [2] So she ran and went to Simon Peter and the other disciple, the one whom Jesus loved, and said to them, "They have taken the Lord out of the tomb, and we do not know where they have laid him." [3] Then Peter and the other disciple set out and went toward the tomb. [4] The two were running together, but the other disciple outran Peter, reached the tomb first, [5] and bending down to look in, saw the linen wrappings lying there, but did not go in. [6] Then Simon Peter came, following after, and went into the tomb. Peter saw the linen wrappings lying there, [7] and the cloth that had been on Jesus' head, not lying with the linen wrappings but rolled up in a place by itself. [8] Then the other disciple, who reached the tomb first, also went in, and saw and believed; [9] for as yet they did not understand the scripture, that Jesus must rise from the dead. [10] Then the disciples returned to their homes.

Jesus Appears to Mary Magdalene

11 But Mary stood weeping outside the tomb. As she wept, she bent over to look[m] into the tomb; [12] and she saw two angels in white, sitting where the body

---

l Or *there is one who knows*   m Gk lacks *to look*

of Jesus had been lying, one at the head and the other at the feet. 13They said to her, "Woman, why are you weeping?" She said to them, "They have taken away my Lord, and I do not know where they have laid him." 14When she had said this, she turned around and saw Jesus standing there, but she did not know that it was Jesus. 15Jesus said to her, "Woman, why are you weeping? Whom are you looking for?" Supposing it to be the gardener, she replied, "Sir, if you have carried Jesus away, tell me where you have laid him, and I will take him away." 16Jesus said to her, "Mary!" She turned and exclaimed in Hebrew,n "Rabbouni!" (which means Teacher). 17Jesus said to her, "Do not hold on to me, because I have not yet ascended to God. But go to my sisters and brothers and say to them, 'I am ascending to my Father-Mother and your Father-Mother, to my God and your God.'" 18Mary Magdalene went and announced to the disciples, "I have seen the Lord"; and she told them that Jesus had said these things to her.

Jesus Appears to the Disciples

19 When it was evening on that day, the first day of the week, and the doors of the house where the disciples had met were locked for fear of the religious authorities, Jesus came and stood among them and said, "Peace be with you." 20Having said this, Jesus showed them Jesus' hands and side. Then the disciples rejoiced when they saw the Lord. 21Jesus said to them again, "Peace be with you. As God has sent me, so I send you." 22Having said this, Jesus breathed on them and said to them, "Receive the Holy Spirit. 23If you forgive the sins of any, they are forgiven them; if you retain the sins of any, they are retained."

Jesus and Thomas

24 But Thomas (who was called the Twino), one of the twelve, was not with them when Jesus came. 25So the other disciples told him, "We have seen the Lord." But Thomas said to them, "Unless I see the mark of the nails in Jesus' hands, and put my finger in the mark of the nails and my hand in Jesus' side, I will not believe."

26 A week later the disciples were again in the house, and Thomas was with them. Although the doors were shut, Jesus came and stood among them and said, "Peace be with you." 27Then Jesus said to Thomas, "Put your finger here and see my hands. Reach out your hand and put it in my side. Do not doubt but believe." 28Thomas answered, "My Lord and my God!" 29Jesus said to him, "Have you believed because you have seen me? Blessed are those who have not seen and yet have come to believe."

The Purpose of This Book

30 Now Jesus did many other signs in the presence of the disciples, which are not written in this book. 31But these are written so that you may come to

---

n That is, *Aramaic*   o Gk *Didymus*

believe[p] that Jesus is the Messiah,[q] the Child of God, and that through believing you may have life in Jesus' name.

Jesus Appears to Seven Disciples

21 After these things Jesus appeared again to the disciples by the Sea of Tiberias, appearing in this way. 2 Gathered there together were Simon Peter, Thomas called the Twin,[r] Nathanael of Cana in Galilee, the sons of Zebedee, and two other disciples. 3 Simon Peter said to them, "I am going fishing." They said to him, "We will go with you." They went out and got into the boat, but that night they caught nothing.

4 Just after daybreak, Jesus stood on the beach; but the disciples did not know that it was Jesus. 5 Jesus said to them, "Children, you have no fish, have you?" They answered, "No." 6 Jesus said to them, "Cast the net to the right side of the boat, and you will find some." So they cast it, and now they were not able to haul it in because there were so many fish. 7 That disciple whom Jesus loved said to Peter, "It is the Lord!" When Simon Peter heard that it was the Lord, he put on some clothes, for he was naked, and jumped into the sea. 8 But the other disciples came in the boat, dragging the net full of fish, for they were not far from the land, only about a hundred yards[s] off.

9 When they had gone ashore, they saw a charcoal fire there, with fish on it, and bread. 10 Jesus said to them, "Bring some of the fish that you have just caught." 11 So Simon Peter went aboard and hauled the net ashore, full of large fish, a hundred fifty-three of them; and though there were so many, the net was not torn. 12 Jesus said to them, "Come and have breakfast." Now none of the disciples dared to ask, "Who are you?" because they knew it was the Lord. 13 Jesus came and took the bread and gave it to them, and did the same with the fish. 14 This was now the third time that Jesus appeared to the disciples after being raised from the dead.

Jesus and Peter

15 When they had finished breakfast, Jesus said to Simon Peter, "Simon son of John, do you love me more than these?" Peter said, "Yes, Lord; you know that I love you." Jesus said to Peter, "Feed my lambs." 16 A second time Jesus said to him, "Simon son of John, do you love me?" Peter replied, "Yes, Lord; you know that I love you." Jesus said, "Tend my sheep." 17 Jesus said to Peter the third time, "Simon son of John, do you love me?" Peter felt hurt because Jesus said to him the third time, "Do you love me?" And Peter said to Jesus, "Lord, you know everything; you know that I love you." Jesus said, "Feed my sheep. 18 Very truly, I tell you, when you were younger, you used to fasten your own belt and to go wherever you wished. But when you grow old, you will stretch out your hands, and someone else will fasten a belt around you and take you

---

p Other ancient authorities read *may continue to believe*   q Or *the Christ*   r Gk *Didymus*
s Gk *two hundred cubits*

where you do not wish to go." ¹⁹(Jesus said this to indicate the kind of death by which Peter would glorify God.) After this Jesus said to Peter, "Follow me."

Jesus and the Beloved Disciple

20 Peter turned and saw the disciple whom Jesus loved following them—the one who had reclined next to Jesus at the supper and had said, "Lord, who is it that is going to betray you?" ²¹When Peter saw that disciple, he said to Jesus, "Lord, what about that one?" ²²Jesus said to him, "If it is my will that this disciple remain until I come, what is that to you? Follow me!" ²³So the rumor spread in the community that this disciple would not die. Yet Jesus did not say that this disciple would not die, but, "If it is my will that he remain until I come, what is that to you?"ᵗ

24 This is the disciple who is testifying to these things and has written them, and we know that the testimony of this disciple is true. ²⁵But there are also many other things that Jesus did; if every one of them were written down, I suppose that the world itself could not contain the books that would be written.

---

t Other ancient authorities lack *what is that to you*

The Acts of the Apostles

The Promise of the Holy Spirit

1 In the first book, Theophilus, I wrote about all that Jesus did and taught from the beginning ²until the day when Jesus was taken up to heaven, after giving instructions through the Holy Spirit to the apostles whom Jesus had chosen. ³After suffering, the living Jesus encountered the apostles by many convincing proofs, appearing to them during forty days and speaking about the dominion of God. ⁴While staying^a with them, Jesus ordered them not to leave Jerusalem, but to wait there for the promise of God. "This," Jesus said, "is what you have heard from me; ⁵for John baptized with water, but you will be baptized with^b the Holy Spirit not many days from now."

The Ascension of Jesus

6 So when they had come together, they asked Jesus, "Lord, is this the time when you will restore the dominion to Israel?" ⁷Jesus replied, "It is not for you to know the times or periods that have been set by the authority of the Father-Mother. ⁸But you will receive power when the Holy Spirit has come upon you; and you will be my witnesses in Jerusalem, in all Judea and Samaria, and to the ends of the earth." ⁹Having said this, as the apostles were watching, Jesus was lifted up, and carried on a cloud out of their sight. ¹⁰While Jesus was going and they were gazing up toward heaven, suddenly two figures in white robes stood by them. ¹¹They said, "People of Galilee, why do you stand looking up toward heaven? This Jesus, who has been taken up from you into heaven, will come in the same way as you saw Jesus go into heaven."

---

a Or *eating*   b Or *by*

Matthias Chosen to Replace Judas

12 Then the apostles returned to Jerusalem from the mount called Olivet, which is near Jerusalem, a sabbath day's journey away. 13 When they had entered the city, they went to the room upstairs where they were staying, Peter, and John, and James, and Andrew, Philip and Thomas, Bartholomew and Matthew, James son of Alphaeus, and Simon the Zealot, and Judas son ofᶜ James. 14 All of them were constantly devoting themselves to prayer, together with certain women, including Mary the mother of Jesus, as well as Jesus' brothers.

15 In those days Peter stood up among the believers (together the crowd numbered about one hundred twenty persons) and said, 16 "Friends, the scripture had to be fulfilled, which the Holy Spirit through David foretold concerning Judas, who became a guide for those who arrested Jesus— 17 for Judas was numbered among us and was allotted a share in this ministry." 18 (Now this man acquired a field with the reward of his wickedness; and falling headlong,ᵈ he burst open in the middle and all his bowels gushed out. 19 This became known to all the residents of Jerusalem, so that the field was called in their language Hakeldama, that is, Field of Blood.) 20 "For it is written in the book of Psalms,

'Let his homestead become desolate,
and let there be no one to live in it';

and

'Let another take his position of overseer.'

21 So one of those who have accompanied us during all the time that the Lord Jesus went in and out among us, 22 beginning from the baptism of John until the day when Jesus was taken up from us—one of these must become a witness with us to Jesus' resurrection." 23 So they proposed two, Joseph called Barsabbas, who was also known as Justus, and Matthias. 24 Then they prayed and said, "Lord, you know everyone's heart. Show us which one of these two you have chosen 25 to take the placeᵉ in this ministry and apostleship from which Judas turned aside to go to his own place." 26 And they cast lots for them, and the lot fell on Matthias, who was added to the eleven apostles.

The Coming of the Holy Spirit

2 When the day of Pentecost had come, they were all together in one place. 2 And suddenly from heaven there came a sound like the rush of a violent wind, and it filled the entire house where they were sitting. 3 Divided tongues, as of fire, appeared among them, and a tongue rested on each of them. 4 All of

---

c Or *the brother of*   d Or *swelling up*   e Other ancient authorities read *the share*

them were filled with the Holy Spirit and began to speak in other languages, as the Spirit gave them ability.

5 Now there were devout Jews from every nation under heaven living in Jerusalem. 6 And at this sound the crowd gathered and was bewildered, because each one heard them speaking in the native language of each. 7 Amazed and astonished, they asked, "Are not all these who are speaking Galileans? 8 And how is it that we hear, each of us, in our own native language? 9 Parthians, Medes, Elamites, and residents of Mesopotamia, Judea and Cappadocia, Pontus and Asia, 10 Phrygia and Pamphylia, Egypt and the parts of Libya belonging to Cyrene, and visitors from Rome, both Jews and proselytes, 11 Cretans and Arabs—in our own languages we hear them speaking about God's deeds of power." 12 All were amazed and perplexed, saying to one another, "What does this mean?" 13 But others sneered and said, "They are filled with new wine."

Peter Addresses the Crowd

14 But Peter, standing with the eleven, raised his voice and addressed them, "People of Judea and all who live in Jerusalem, let this be known to you, and listen to what I say. 15 Indeed, they are not drunk, as you suppose, for it is only nine o'clock in the morning. 16 No, this is what was spoken through the prophet Joel:

17   'In the last days it will be, God declares,
           that I will pour out my Spirit upon all flesh,
              and your sons and your daughters shall prophesy,
           and the young people shall see visions,
              and the old people shall dream dreams.

18   Even upon those enslaved to me, both men and women,
           in those days I will pour out my Spirit;
            and they shall prophesy.

19   And I will show portents in the heaven above
           and signs on the earth below,
              blood, and fire, and smoky mist.

20   The sun's light shall be extinguished
           and the moon shall be turned to blood,
              before the coming of the Lord's great and glorious day.

21   Then everyone who calls on the name of the Lord shall
           be saved.'

22 "You that are Israelites, listen to what I have to say: Jesus of Nazareth,[f] attested to you by God with deeds of power, wonders, and signs that God did through him among you, as you yourselves know— 23 this Jesus, handed over to you according to the definite plan and foreknowledge of God,

---

f Gk *the Nazorean*

you crucified and killed by the hands of those outside the law. ²⁴But God raised Jesus, whom God freed from death,⁹ because it was impossible for Jesus to be held in its power. ²⁵For David says concerning Jesus,

> 'I saw the Lord always before me,
>   at my side so that I will not be shaken;
> 26   therefore my heart was glad, and my tongue rejoiced;
>   moreover my flesh will live in hope.
> 27   For you will not abandon my soul to Hades,
>   or let your Holy One experience corruption.
> 28   You have made known to me the ways of life;
>   you will make me full of gladness with your
>   presence.'

29 "Brothers and sisters, I may say to you confidently that our ancestor David both died and was buried, and his tomb is with us to this day. ³⁰David was a prophet, and knew that God had sworn with an oath to put one of David's descendants on the throne. ³¹Foreseeing this, David spoke of the resurrection of the Messiah,ʰ saying,

> 'That one was not abandoned to Hades,
>   and did not experience corruption of the flesh.'

³²This Jesus God raised up, and of that all of us are witnesses. ³³Being therefore exalted atⁱ the mighty hand of God, and having received from God the promise of the Holy Spirit, Jesus has poured out this that you both see and hear. ³⁴For David did not ascend into the heavens, but he himself says,

> 'God said to my Lord,
>   "Sit at my side,
> 35   until I make your enemies your footstool." '

³⁶Therefore let the entire house of Israel know with certainty that God has made both Lord and Messiah,ʲ this Jesus whom you crucified."

The First Converts

37 Now when those who were gathered heard this, they were cut to the heart and said to Peter and to the other apostles, "Sisters and brothers, what should we do?" ³⁸Peter said to them, "Repent, and be baptized every one of you in the name of Jesus Christ so that your sins may be forgiven; and you will receive the gift of the Holy Spirit. ³⁹For the promise is for you, for your children, and for all who are far away, everyone whom the Sovereign our God calls." ⁴⁰And Peter testified with many other arguments and exhorted them, saying, "Save yourselves from this corrupt generation." ⁴¹So those who welcomed his message were baptized, and that day about three thousand people

---

g Gk *the pains of death*   h Or *the Christ*   i Or *by*   j Or *Christ*

were added. [42]They devoted themselves to the apostles' teaching and community life, to the breaking of bread and the prayers.

Life among the Believers

43 Awe came upon everyone, because many wonders and signs were being done by the apostles. [44]All who believed were together and had all things in common; [45]they would sell their possessions and goods and distribute the proceeds[k] to all, as any had need. [46]Day by day, as they spent much time together in the temple, they broke bread at home[l] and ate their food with glad and generous[m] hearts, [47]praising God and having the goodwill of all the people. And day by day God added to their number those who were being saved.

Peter Heals a Person Who Was Lame

3 One day Peter and John were going up to the temple at the hour of prayer, at three o'clock in the afternoon. [2]And a man lame from birth was being carried in. People would lay him daily at the gate of the temple called the Beautiful Gate so that he could ask for alms from those entering the temple. [3]Seeing Peter and John about to go into the temple, the person who was lame asked them for alms. [4]Peter looked intently at him, as did John, and said, "Look at us." [5]And he fixed his attention on them, expecting to receive something from them. [6]But Peter said, "I have no silver or gold, but what I have I give you; in the name of Jesus Christ of Nazareth,[n] stand up and walk." [7]And Peter took him by the hand and raised him up; and immediately his feet and ankles were made strong. [8]Jumping up, he stood and began to walk, and he entered the temple with them, walking and leaping and praising God. [9]All the people saw him walking and praising God, [10]and they recognized him as the one who used to sit and ask for alms at the Beautiful Gate of the temple; and they were filled with wonder and amazement at what had happened to him.

Peter Speaks in Solomon's Portico

11 While he clung to Peter and John, all the people ran together to them in the portico called Solomon's Portico, utterly astonished. [12]When Peter saw it, he addressed the people, "You Israelites, why do you wonder at this, or why do you stare at us, as though by our own power or piety we had made him walk? [13]The God of Abraham, the God of Isaac, and the God of Jacob, the God of our ancestors has glorified God's servant[o] Jesus, whom you handed over and rejected in the presence of Pilate, though he had decided to release Jesus. [14]But you rejected the Holy and Righteous One and asked to have a murderer given to you, [15]and you killed the Author of life, whom God raised from the dead. To this we are witnesses. [16]And by faith in Jesus' name, that name itself has made this person strong, whom you see and know; and the faith that is through Jesus has given him this perfect health in the presence of all of you.

---

k Gk *them*   l Or *from house to house*   m Or *sincere*   n Gk *the Nazorean*   o Or *child*

17 "And now, friends, I know that you acted in ignorance, as did also your rulers. [18]In this way God fulfilled what God foretold through all the prophets, that the Messiah[p] would suffer. [19]Repent therefore, and turn to God so that your sins may be wiped out, [20]so that times of refreshing may come from the presence of God, and that God may send the Messiah[q] appointed for you, that is, Jesus, [21]who must remain in heaven until the time of universal restoration that God announced long ago through the holy prophets. [22]Moses said, 'The Sovereign your God will raise up for you from your own people a prophet like me. You must listen to whatever that one tells you. [23]And it will be that everyone who does not listen to that prophet will be utterly rooted out of the people.' [24]And all the prophets, as many as have spoken, from Samuel and those after him, also predicted these days. [25]You are the descendants of the prophets and of the covenant that God gave to your ancestors, saying to Abraham, 'And in your descendants all the families of the earth shall be blessed.' [26]When God raised up the servant,[r] God sent that servant first to you, to bless you by turning each of you from your wicked ways."

Peter and John before the Council

4 While Peter and John were speaking to the people, the priests, the captain of the temple, and the Sadducees came to them, [2]much annoyed because they were teaching the people and proclaiming that in Jesus there is the resurrection of the dead. [3]So they arrested them and put them in custody until the next day, for it was already evening. [4]But many of those who heard the word believed; and they numbered about five thousand.

5 The next day their rulers, elders, and scribes assembled in Jerusalem, [6]with Annas the high priest, Caiaphas, John,[s] and Alexander, and all who were of the high-priestly family. [7]When they had made the prisoners stand in their midst, they inquired, "By what power or by what name did you do this?" [8]Then Peter, filled with the Holy Spirit, said to them, "Rulers of the people and elders, [9]if we are questioned today because of a good deed done to someone who was sick and are asked how this person has been healed, [10]let it be known to all of you, and to all the people of Israel, that this person is standing before you in good health by the name of Jesus Christ of Nazareth,[t] whom you crucified, whom God raised from the dead. [11]This Jesus[u] is

'the stone that was rejected by you, the builders;
    it has become the cornerstone.'[v]

[12]There is salvation in no one else, for there is no other name under heaven given among mortals by which we must be saved."

13 Now when they saw the boldness of Peter and John and realized that they were uneducated and ordinary men, they were amazed and recognized

---

p Or *God's Christ*   q Or *the Christ*   r Or *child*
s Other ancient authorities read *Jonathan*   t Gk *the Nazorean*   u Gk *This*   v Or *keystone*

them as companions of Jesus. [14]When they saw the one who had been cured standing beside them, they had nothing to say in opposition. [15]So they ordered them to leave the council while they discussed the matter with one another. [16]They said, "What will we do with them? For it is obvious to all who live in Jerusalem that a notable sign has been done through them; we cannot deny it. [17]But to keep it from spreading further among the people, let us warn them to speak no more to anyone in this name." [18]So they called them and ordered them not to speak or teach at all in the name of Jesus. [19]But Peter and John answered them, "Whether it is right in God's sight to listen to you rather than to God, you must judge; [20]for we cannot keep from speaking about what we have seen and heard." [21]After threatening them again, they let them go, finding no way to punish them because of the people, for all of them praised God for what had happened. [22]For the person on whom this sign of healing had been performed was more than forty years old.

The Believers Pray for Boldness

23 After they were released, they went to their friends[w] and reported what the chief priests and the elders had said to them. [24]When they heard it, they raised their voices together to God and said, "Sovereign God, who made the heaven and the earth, the sea, and everything in them, [25]it is you who said by the Holy Spirit through our ancestor David, your servant:[x]

> 'Why did the Gentiles rage,
>   and the peoples imagine vain things?
26   The kings of the earth took their stand,
>   and the rulers have gathered together
>   against God and against God's Messiah.'[y]

[27]For in this city, in fact, both Herod and Pontius Pilate, with the Gentiles and the peoples of Israel, gathered together against your holy servant[x] Jesus, whom you anointed, [28]to do whatever your hand and your plan had predestined to take place. [29]And now, God, look at their threats, and grant to your servants[z] to speak your word with all boldness, [30]while you stretch out your hand to heal, and signs and wonders are performed through the name of your holy servant[x] Jesus." [31]When they had prayed, the place in which they were gathered together was shaken; and they were all filled with the Holy Spirit and spoke the word of God with boldness.

The Believers Share Their Possessions

32 Now the whole group of those who believed were of one heart and soul, and no one claimed private ownership of any possessions, but everything they owned was held in common. [33]With great power the apostles gave their testimony to the resurrection of the Lord Jesus, and great grace was upon them

---

w Gk *their own*   x Or *child*   y Or *God's Christ*   z Gk *slaves*

all. [34]There was not a needy person among them, for as many as owned lands or houses sold them and brought the proceeds of what was sold. [35]They laid it at the apostles' feet, and it was distributed to each as any had need. [36]There was a Levite, a native of Cyprus, Joseph, to whom the apostles gave the name Barnabas (which means "son of encouragement"). [37]He sold a field that belonged to him, then brought the money, and laid it at the apostles' feet.

Ananias and Sapphira

5 But a man named Ananias, with the consent of his wife Sapphira, sold a piece of property; [2]with his wife's knowledge, he kept back some of the proceeds, and brought only a part and laid it at the apostles' feet. [3]"Ananias," Peter asked, "why has Satan filled your heart to lie to the Holy Spirit and to keep back part of the proceeds of the land? [4]While it remained unsold, did it not remain your own? And after it was sold, were not the proceeds at your disposal? How is it that you have contrived this deed in your heart? You did not lie to us but to God!" [5]Now when Ananias heard these words, he fell down and died. And great fear seized all who heard of it. [6]The young men came and wrapped up his body,[a] then carried him out and buried him.

[7] After an interval of about three hours his wife came in, not knowing what had happened. [8]Peter said to her, "Tell me whether you and your husband sold the land for such and such a price." And she said, "Yes, that was the price." [9]Then Peter said to her, "How is it that you have agreed together to put the Spirit of the Lord to the test? Look, the feet of those who have buried your husband are at the door, and they will carry you out." [10]Immediately she fell down at his feet and died. When the young men came in they found her dead, so they carried her out and buried her beside her husband. [11]And great fear seized the whole church and all who heard of these things.

The Apostles Heal Many

[12] Now many signs and wonders were done among the people through the apostles. And they were all together in Solomon's Portico. [13]None of the rest dared to join them, but the people held them in high esteem. [14]Yet more than ever believers were added to the Lord, great numbers of both men and women, [15]so that they even carried out the sick into the streets, and laid them on cots and mats, in order that Peter's shadow might fall on some of them as he came by. [16]A great number of people would also gather from the towns around Jerusalem, bringing the sick and those tormented by unclean spirits, and they were all cured.

The Apostles Are Persecuted

[17] Then the high priest took action; he and all who were with him (that is, the sect of the Sadducees), being filled with jealousy, [18]arrested the apostles and put

---

a Meaning of Gk uncertain

them in the public prison. ¹⁹But during the night an angel of God opened the prison doors, brought them out, and said, ²⁰"Go, stand in the temple and tell the people the whole message about this life." ²¹When they heard this, they entered the temple at daybreak and went on with their teaching.

When the high priest and those with him arrived, they called together the council and the whole body of the elders of Israel, and sent to the prison to have them brought. ²²But when the temple police went there, they did not find them in the prison; so they returned and reported, ²³"We found the prison securely locked and the guards standing at the doors, but when we opened them, we found no one inside." ²⁴Now when the captain of the temple and the chief priests heard these words, they were perplexed about them, wondering what might be going on. ²⁵Then someone arrived and announced, "Look, those whom you put in prison are standing in the temple and teaching the people!" ²⁶Then the captain went with the temple police and brought the apostles, but without violence, for they were afraid of being stoned by the people.

27 When they had brought the apostles, they had them stand before the council. The high priest questioned them, ²⁸saying, "We gave you strict orders not to teach in this name,ᵇ yet here you have filled Jerusalem with your teaching and you are determined to bring this person's blood on us." ²⁹But Peter and the apostles answered, "We must obey God rather than any human authority. ³⁰The God of our ancestors raised up Jesus, whom you had killed by hanging on a tree. ³¹God exalted this Jesus at God's side as Leader and Savior, to give repentance to Israel and forgiveness of sins. ³²And we are witnesses to these things, and so is the Holy Spirit whom God has given to those who obey God."

33 When the officials heard this, they were enraged and wanted to kill them. ³⁴But a Pharisee in the council named Gamaliel, a teacher of the law, respected by all the people, stood up and ordered the apostles to be put outside for a short time. ³⁵Then he said to them, "People of Israel, consider carefully what you propose to do to these people. ³⁶For some time ago Theudas rose up, claiming to be somebody, and a number of people, about four hundred, joined him; but he was killed, and all who followed him were dispersed and disappeared. ³⁷After him Judas the Galilean rose up at the time of the census and got people to follow him; he also perished, and all who followed him were scattered. ³⁸So in the present case, I tell you, keep away from these people and let them alone; because if this plan or this undertaking is of human origin, it will fail; ³⁹but if it is of God, you will not be able to overthrow them—in that case you may even be found fighting against God!"

They were convinced by Gamaliel, ⁴⁰and when they had called in the apostles, they had them flogged. Then they ordered them not to speak in the name of Jesus, and let them go. ⁴¹As the apostles left the council, they rejoiced that they were considered worthy to suffer dishonor for the sake of the name.

---

b Other ancient authorities read *Did we not give you strict orders not to teach in this name?*

⁴²And every day in the temple and at home^c they did not cease to teach and proclaim Jesus as the Messiah.^d

Seven Chosen to Serve

6 Now during those days, when the disciples were increasing in number, the Hellenists complained against the Hebrews because their widows were being neglected in the daily distribution of food. ²And the twelve called together the whole community of the disciples and said, "It is not right that we should neglect the word of God in order to wait on tables.^e ³Therefore, friends, select from among yourselves seven people of good standing, full of the Spirit and of wisdom, whom we may appoint to this task, ⁴while we, for our part, will devote ourselves to prayer and to serving the word." ⁵What they said pleased the whole community, and they chose Stephen, a man full of faith and the Holy Spirit, together with Philip, Prochorus, Nicanor, Timon, Parmenas, and Nicolaus, a proselyte of Antioch. ⁶They had these people stand before the apostles, who prayed and laid their hands on them.

7 The word of God continued to spread; the number of the disciples increased greatly in Jerusalem, and a great many of the priests became obedient to the faith.

The Arrest of Stephen

8 Stephen, full of grace and power, did great wonders and signs among the people. ⁹Then some of those who belonged to the synagogue of the Freed (as it was called), Cyrenians, Alexandrians, and others of those from Cilicia and Asia, stood up and argued with Stephen. ¹⁰But they could not withstand the wisdom and the Spirit^f with which he spoke. ¹¹Then they secretly instigated some people to say, "We have heard him speak blasphemous words against Moses and God." ¹²They stirred up the people as well as the elders and the scribes; then they suddenly confronted Stephen, seized him, and brought him before the council. ¹³They set up false witnesses who said, "This man never stops saying things against this holy place and the law; ¹⁴for we have heard him say that this Jesus of Nazareth^g will destroy this place and will change the customs that Moses handed on to us." ¹⁵And all who sat in the council looked intently at Stephen, and they saw that his face was like the face of an angel.

Stephen's Speech to the Council

7 Then the high priest asked him, "Are these things so?" ²And Stephen replied:

"Friends, listen to me. The God of glory appeared to our ancestor Abraham when he was in Mesopotamia, before he lived in Haran, ³and said to him, 'Leave your country and your relatives and go to the land that I will show

---

c Or *from house to house*   d Or *the Christ*   e Or *keep accounts*   f Or *spirit*
g Gk *the Nazorean*

you.' 4Then he left the country of the Chaldeans and settled in Haran. After his father died, God had him move from there to this country in which you are now living. 5God did not give him any of it as a heritage, not even a foot's length, but promised to give it to him as his possession and to his descendants after him, even though he had no child. 6And God spoke in these terms, that Abraham's descendants would be resident aliens in a country belonging to others, who would enslave them and mistreat them during four hundred years. 7'But I will judge the nation that they serve,' said God, 'and after that they shall come out and worship me in this place.' 8Then God gave Abraham the covenant of circumcision. And so Abraham became the father of Isaac and circumcised him on the eighth day; and Isaac became the father of Jacob, and Jacob of the twelve patriarchs.

9 "Jealous of Joseph, the patriarchs sold him into Egypt; but God was with him, 10and rescued him from all his afflictions, and enabled him to win favor and to show wisdom when he stood before Pharaoh, king of Egypt, who appointed him ruler over Egypt and over all his household. 11Now there came a famine throughout Egypt and Canaan, and great suffering, and our ancestors could find no food. 12But when Jacob heard that there was grain in Egypt, he sent our ancestors there on their first visit. 13On the second visit Joseph made himself known to his brothers, and Joseph's family became known to Pharaoh. 14Then Joseph sent and invited his father Jacob and all his relatives to come to him, seventy-five in all. 15So Jacob went down to Egypt and died there along with our ancestors, 16and their bodies were brought back to Shechem and laid in the tomb that Abraham had bought for a sum of silver from the Hamorites in Shechem.

17 "But as the time drew near for the fulfillment of the promise that God had made to Abraham, our people in Egypt increased and multiplied 18until another king who had not known Joseph ruled over Egypt. 19He dealt craftily with our race and forced our ancestors to abandon their infants so that they would die. 20At this time Moses was born, and he was beautiful before God. For three months he was brought up in his family's house; 21and when he was abandoned, Pharaoh's daughter adopted him and brought him up as her own son. 22So Moses was instructed in all the wisdom of the Egyptians and was powerful in his words and deeds.

23 "When Moses was forty years old, it came into his heart to visit his relatives, the Israelites. 24When he saw one of them being wronged, he retaliated and avenged the oppressed person by striking down the Egyptian. 25Moses supposed that his kinsfolk would understand that God through him was rescuing them, but they did not understand. 26The next day Moses came to some of them as they were quarreling and tried to reconcile them, saying to them, 'You are brothers and sisters; why do you wrong one another?' 27But the one who was wronging a neighbor pushed Moses aside, saying, 'Who made you a ruler and a judge over us? 28Do you want to kill me as you killed the

Egyptian yesterday?' [29]When he heard this, Moses fled and became a resident alien in the land of Midian. There he became the father of two sons.

30 "Now when forty years had passed, an angel appeared to him in the wilderness of Mount Sinai, in the flame of a burning bush. [31]When Moses saw it, he was amazed at the sight; and as he approached to look, there came the voice of God: [32]'I am the God of your ancestors, the God of Abraham, Isaac, and Jacob.' Moses began to tremble and did not dare to look. [33]Then God said to him, 'Take off the sandals from your feet, for the place where you are standing is holy ground. [34]I have surely seen the mistreatment of my people who are in Egypt and have heard their groaning, and I have come down to rescue them. Come now, I will send you to Egypt.'

35 "It was this Moses whom they rejected when they said, 'Who made you a ruler and a judge?' and whom God now sent as both ruler and liberator through the angel who appeared to him in the bush. [36]Moses led them out, having performed wonders and signs in Egypt, at the Red Sea, and in the wilderness for forty years. [37]This is the Moses who said to the Israelites, 'God will raise up a prophet for you from your own people as God raised me up.' [38]Moses is the one who was in the congregation in the wilderness with the angel who spoke to him at Mount Sinai, and with our ancestors; and Moses received living oracles to give to us. [39]Our ancestors were unwilling to obey him; instead, they pushed him aside, and in their hearts they turned back to Egypt, [40]saying to Aaron, 'Make gods for us who will lead the way for us; as for this Moses who led us out from the land of Egypt, we do not know what has happened to him.' [41]At that time they made a calf, offered a sacrifice to the idol, and reveled in the works of their hands. [42]But God turned away from them and handed them over to worship the host of heaven, as it is written in the book of the prophets:

'Did you offer to me slain victims and sacrifices
    forty years in the wilderness, O house of Israel?
[43] No; you took along the tent of Moloch,
    and the star of your god Rephan,
      the images that you made to worship;
so I will remove you beyond Babylon.'

44 "Our ancestors had the tent of testimony in the wilderness, as God directed while speaking to Moses, ordering him to make it according to the pattern he had seen. [45]Our ancestors in turn brought it in with Joshua when they dispossessed the nations that God drove out before our ancestors. And it was there until the time of David, [46]who found favor with God and asked that he might find a dwelling place for the house of Jacob.[h] [47]But it was Solomon who built a house for God. [48]Yet the Most High does not dwell in houses made with human hands;[i] as the prophet says,

---

h Other ancient authorities read *for the God of Jacob*   i Gk *with hands*

49   'Heaven is my throne,
             and the earth is my footstool.
          What kind of house will you build for me, God asks,
             or what is the place of my rest?
50   Did not my hand make all these things?'

51 "You stiff-necked people, uncircumcised in heart and ears, you are forever opposing the Holy Spirit, just as your ancestors used to do. 52 Which of the prophets did your ancestors not persecute? They killed those who foretold the coming of the Righteous One, and now you have become that one's betrayers and murderers. 53 You are those who received the law as ordained by angels, and yet you have not kept it."

The Stoning of Stephen

54 When they heard these things, they became enraged and ground their teeth at Stephen. 55 But filled with the Holy Spirit, Stephen gazed into heaven and saw the glory of God and Jesus standing alongside of God. 56 "Look," he said, "I see the heavens opened and the Human One standing alongside of God!" 57 But they covered their ears, and with a loud shout all rushed together against him. 58 Then they dragged him out of the city and began to stone him; and the witnesses laid their coats at the feet of a young man named Saul. 59 While they were stoning Stephen, he prayed, "Lord Jesus, receive my spirit." 60 Then he knelt down and cried out in a loud voice, "Lord, do not hold this sin against 8 them." When he had said this, he died.[j] 1 And Saul approved of their killing Stephen.

Saul Persecutes the Church

That day a severe persecution began against the church in Jerusalem, and all except the apostles were scattered throughout the countryside of Judea and Samaria. 2 Devout people buried Stephen and made loud lamentation over him. 3 But Saul was ravaging the church by entering house after house; dragging off both men and women, he committed them to prison.

Philip Preaches in Samaria

4 Now those who were scattered went from place to place, proclaiming the word. 5 Philip went down to the city[k] of Samaria and proclaimed the Messiah[l] to them. 6 The crowds with one accord listened eagerly to what was said by Philip, hearing and seeing the signs that he did, 7 for unclean spirits, crying with loud shrieks, came out of many who were possessed; and many others who were paralyzed or lame were cured. 8 So there was great joy in that city.

9 Now a certain man named Simon had previously practiced magic in the city and amazed the people of Samaria, saying that he was someone great. 10 All

---

j Gk *fell asleep*   k Other ancient authorities read *a city*   l Or *the Christ* of them, from the least to the greatest, listened to him eagerly, saying, "This man is the power of God that is called Great." [11] And they listened eagerly to him because for a long time Simon had amazed them with his magic. [12] But when they believed Philip, who was proclaiming the good news about the dominion of God and the name of Jesus Christ, they were baptized, both men and women. [13] Even Simon himself believed. After being baptized, he stayed constantly with Philip and was amazed when he saw the signs and great miracles that took place.

14 Now when the apostles at Jerusalem heard that Samaria had accepted the word of God, they sent Peter and John to them. [15] The two went down and prayed for them that they might receive the Holy Spirit [16] (for as yet the Spirit had not come[m] upon any of them; they had only been baptized in the name of the Lord Jesus). [17] Then Peter and John laid their hands on them, and they received the Holy Spirit. [18] Now when Simon saw that the Spirit was given through the laying on of the apostles' hands, he offered them money, [19] saying, "Give me also this power so that anyone on whom I lay my hands may receive the Holy Spirit." [20] But Peter said to him, "May your silver perish with you, because you thought you could obtain God's gift with money! [21] You have no part or share in this, for your heart is not right before God. [22] Repent therefore of this wickedness of yours, and pray to God that, if possible, the intent of your heart may be forgiven you. [23] For I see that you are in the gall of bitterness and the chains of wickedness." [24] Simon answered, "Pray for me to God, that nothing of what you[n] have said may happen to me."

25 Now after Peter and John had testified and spoken the word of God, they returned to Jerusalem, proclaiming the good news to many villages of the Samaritans.

Philip and the Ethiopian Eunuch

26 Then an angel of God said to Philip, "Get up and go toward the south[o] to the road that goes down from Jerusalem to Gaza." (This is a wilderness road.) [27] So he got up and went. Now an Ethiopian eunuch (a court official of the Candace, queen of the Ethiopians, who was in charge of her entire treasury) had come to Jerusalem to worship [28] and was returning home. Seated in his chariot, he was reading the prophet Isaiah. [29] Then the Spirit said to Philip, "Go over to this chariot and join it." [30] So Philip ran up to it and heard the Ethiopian reading the prophet Isaiah, and asked, "Do you understand what you are reading?" [31] He replied, "How can I, unless someone guides me?" And he invited Philip to get in and sit beside him. [32] Now the passage of the scripture that he was reading was this:

> "As a sheep led to the slaughter,
>   or a lamb before its shearer is silent,

---

m Gk *fallen*   n The Greek word for *you* and the verb *pray* are plural   o Or *go at noon*

so this one does not say a word.
33 In the humiliation of the silent one, justice was denied.
Who can describe the generation
of the one whose life is taken away from the
earth?"

34 The eunuch asked Philip, "About whom, may I ask you, does the prophet say
this, about himself or about someone else?" 35 Then Philip began to speak, and
starting with this scripture, proclaimed to the Ethiopian the good news about
Jesus. 36 As they were going along the road, they came to some water; and the
eunuch said, "Look, here is water! What is to prevent me from being
baptized?"[p] 38 He commanded the chariot to stop, and both of them, Philip and
the eunuch, went down into the water, and Philip baptized him. 39 When they
came up out of the water, the Spirit of the Lord snatched Philip away; the
eunuch saw him no more, and went on his way rejoicing. 40 But Philip found
himself at Azotus, and as he was passing through the region, he proclaimed the
good news to all the towns until he came to Caesarea.

The Conversion of Saul

9 Meanwhile Saul, still breathing threats and murder against the disciples of
Jesus Christ, went to the high priest 2 and asked for letters to the
synagogues at Damascus, so that if he found any who belonged to the Way,
men or women, he might bring them bound to Jerusalem. 3 Now as Saul was
going along and approaching Damascus, suddenly a light from heaven flashed
around him. 4 He fell to the ground and heard a voice saying to him, "Saul,
Saul, why do you persecute me?" 5 He asked, "Who are you, Lord?" The reply
came, "I am Jesus, whom you are persecuting. 6 But get up and enter the city,
and you will be told what you are to do." 7 The people who were traveling
with Saul stood speechless because they heard the voice but saw no one. 8 Saul
got up from the ground, and though his eyes were open, he could see nothing;
so they led him by the hand and brought him into Damascus. 9 For three days
he was without sight, and neither ate nor drank.

10 Now there was a disciple in Damascus named Ananias. The Lord said
to him in a vision, "Ananias." He answered, "Here I am, Lord." 11 The Lord
said to him, "Get up and go to the street called Straight, and at the house of
Judas look for a man of Tarsus named Saul. At this moment he is praying,
12 and he has seen in a vision[q] a man named Ananias come in and lay his hands
on him so that he might regain his sight." 13 But Ananias answered, "Lord, I
have heard from many about this man, how much evil he has done to your
saints in Jerusalem; 14 and here he has authority from the chief priests to bind

---

p Other ancient authorities add all or most of verse 37, *And Philip said, "If you believe with all your heart, you may." And he replied, "I believe that Jesus Christ is the Child of God."*

q Other ancient authorities lack *in a vision*

all who invoke your name." 15But the Lord said to Ananias, "Go, for Saul is an instrument whom I have chosen to bring my name before Gentiles and rulers and before the people of Israel; 16I myself will show him how much he must suffer for the sake of my name." 17So Ananias went and entered the house. He laid his hands on Saul and said, "Brother Saul, the Lord Jesus, who appeared to you on your way here, has sent me so that you may regain your sight and be filled with the Holy Spirit." 18And immediately something like scales fell from his eyes, and his sight was restored. Then he got up and was baptized, 19and after taking some food, he regained his strength.

Saul Preaches in Damascus

For several days Saul was with the disciples in Damascus, 20and immediately he began to proclaim Jesus in the synagogues, saying, "This one is the Child of God." 21All who heard him were amazed and said, "Is not this the man who made havoc in Jerusalem among those who invoked this name? And has he not come here for the purpose of bringing them bound before the chief priests?" 22Saul became increasingly more powerful and confounded the Jews who lived in Damascus by proving that Jesus was the Messiah.r

Saul Escapes from the Jews

23 After some time had passed, the Jews plotted to kill him, 24but their plot became known to Saul. They were watching the gates day and night so that they might kill him; 25but his disciples took him by night and let him down through an opening in the wall,s lowering him in a basket.

Saul in Jerusalem

26 When Saul had come to Jerusalem, he attempted to join the disciples; and they were all afraid of him, for they did not believe that he was a disciple. 27But Barnabas took him, brought him to the apostles, and described for them how on the road he had seen the Lord, who had spoken to him, and how in Damascus he had spoken boldly in the name of Jesus. 28So he went in and out among them in Jerusalem, speaking boldly in the name of the Lord. 29He spoke and argued with the Hellenists; but they were attempting to kill him. 30When the believers learned of it, they brought him down to Caesarea and sent him off to Tarsus.

31 Meanwhile the church throughout Judea, Galilee, and Samaria had peace and was built up. Living in reverence for the Lord and in the comfort of the Holy Spirit, it increased in numbers.

The Healing of Aeneas

32 Now as Peter went here and there among all the believers, he came down also to the saints living in Lydda. 33There he found a man named Aeneas, who

---

r Or *the Christ*   s Gk *through the wall*

had been bedridden for eight years, for he was paralyzed. ³⁴Peter said to him, "Aeneas, Jesus Christ heals you; get up and make your bed!" And immediately he got up. ³⁵And all the residents of Lydda and Sharon saw him and turned to the Lord.

Peter in Lydda and Joppa

36 Now in Joppa there was a disciple whose name was Tabitha, which in Greek is Dorcas.ᵗ She was devoted to good works and acts of charity. ³⁷At that time she became ill and died. When they had washed her, they laid her in a room upstairs. ³⁸Since Lydda was near Joppa, the disciples, who heard that Peter was there, sent two people to him with the request, "Please come to us without delay." ³⁹So Peter got up and went with them; and when he arrived, they took him to the room upstairs. All the widows stood beside him, weeping and showing tunics and other clothing that Dorcas had made while she was with them. ⁴⁰Peter put all of them outside, and then he knelt down and prayed. He turned to the body and said, "Tabitha, get up." Then she opened her eyes, and seeing Peter, she sat up. ⁴¹He gave her his hand and helped her up. Then calling the saints and widows, he showed her to be alive. ⁴²This became known throughout Joppa, and many believed in the Lord. ⁴³Meanwhile Peter stayed in Joppa for some time with a certain Simon, a tanner.

Peter and Cornelius

10 In Caesarea there was a man named Cornelius, a centurion of the Italian Cohort, as it was called. ²He was a devout man who feared God with all his household; he gave alms generously to the people and prayed constantly to God. ³One afternoon at about three o'clock he had a vision in which he clearly saw an angel of God coming in and saying to him, "Cornelius." ⁴He stared at the angel in terror and said, "What is it, Lord?" The answer came, "Your prayers and your alms have ascended as a memorial before God. ⁵Now send men to Joppa for a certain Simon who is called Peter; ⁶he is lodging with Simon, a tanner, whose house is by the seaside." ⁷When the angel who spoke to him had left, Cornelius called two of those enslaved to him and a devout soldier from the ranks of those who served him, ⁸and after telling them everything, he sent them to Joppa.

9 About noon the next day, as they were on their journey and approaching the city, Peter went up on the roof to pray. ¹⁰He became hungry and wanted something to eat; and while it was being prepared, he fell into a trance. ¹¹He saw the heaven opened and something like a large sheet coming down, being lowered to the ground by its four corners. ¹²In it were all kinds of four-footed creatures and reptiles and birds of the air. ¹³Then he heard a voice saying, "Get up, Peter; kill and eat." ¹⁴But Peter said, "By no means, Lord; for I have never eaten anything that is profane or unclean." ¹⁵The voice said to him again, a

---

t The name Tabitha in Aramaic and the name Dorcas in Greek mean *a gazelle*

second time, "What God has made clean, you must not call profane." 16This happened three times, and the thing was suddenly taken up to heaven.

17 Now while Peter was greatly puzzled about what to make of the vision that he had seen, suddenly the people sent by Cornelius appeared. They were asking for Simon's house and were standing by the gate. 18They called out to ask whether Simon, who was called Peter, was staying there. 19While Peter was still thinking about the vision, the Spirit said to him, "Look, three[u] people are searching for you. 20Now get up, go down, and go with them without hesitation; for I have sent them." 21So Peter went down to them and said, "I am the one you are looking for; what is the reason for your coming?" 22They answered, "Cornelius, a centurion, an upright and God-fearing man, who is well spoken of by the whole Jewish nation, was directed by a holy angel to send for you to come to his house and to hear what you have to say." 23So Peter invited them in and gave them lodging.

The next day he got up and went with them, and some of the believers from Joppa accompanied him. 24The following day they came to Caesarea. Cornelius was expecting them and had called together his relatives and close friends. 25On Peter's arrival Cornelius met him, and falling at his feet, worshiped him. 26But Peter made him get up, saying, "Stand up; I am only a mortal." 27And as Peter talked with Cornelius, he went in and found that many had assembled; 28and he said to them, "You yourselves know that it is unlawful for a Jew to associate with or to visit a Gentile; but God has shown me that I should not call anyone profane or unclean. 29So when I was sent for, I came without objection. Now may I ask why you sent for me?"

30 Cornelius replied, "Four days ago at this very hour, at three o'clock, I was praying in my house when suddenly a figure in dazzling clothes stood before me, 31and said, 'Cornelius, your prayer has been heard and your alms have been remembered before God. 32Send therefore to Joppa and ask for Simon, who is called Peter; he is staying in the home of Simon, a tanner, by the sea.' 33Therefore I sent for you immediately, and you have been kind enough to come. So now all of us are here in the presence of God to listen to all that the Lord has commanded you to say."

Gentiles Hear the Good News

34 Then Peter began to speak to them: "I truly understand that God shows no partiality, 35but in every nation anyone who fears God and does what is right is acceptable to God. 36You know the message God sent to the people of Israel, preaching peace by Jesus Christ, the one who is Lord of all. 37That message spread throughout Judea, beginning in Galilee after the baptism that John announced: 38how God anointed Jesus of Nazareth with the Holy Spirit and with power; how Jesus went about doing good and healing all who were oppressed by the devil, for God was with him. 39We are witnesses to all that he

---

u One ancient authority reads *two*; others lack the word

did both in Judea and in Jerusalem. They put Jesus to death by hanging him on a tree; 40but God raised Jesus on the third day and allowed Jesus to appear, 41not to all the people but to us who were chosen by God as witnesses, and who ate and drank with Jesus after the resurrection from the dead. 42Jesus commanded us to preach to the people and to testify that Jesus is the one ordained by God as judge of the living and the dead. 43About this one all the prophets testify that everyone who believes in Jesus Christ receives forgiveness of sins through Jesus' name."

Gentiles Receive the Holy Spirit

44 While Peter was still speaking, the Holy Spirit fell upon all who heard the word. 45The believers who were under the law and had come with Peter were astounded that the gift of the Holy Spirit had been poured out even on the Gentiles, 46for they heard them speaking in tongues and extolling God. Then Peter said, 47"Can anyone withhold the water for baptizing these people who have received the Holy Spirit just as we have?" 48So he ordered them to be baptized in the name of Jesus Christ. Then they invited Peter to stay for several days.

Peter's Report to the Church at Jerusalem

11 Now the apostles and the believers who were in Judea heard that the Gentiles had also accepted the word of God. 2So when Peter went up to Jerusalem, the believersᵛ who were under the law criticized him, 3saying, "Why did you go to those who were outside the law and eat with them?" 4Then Peter began to explain it to them, step by step, saying, 5"I was in the city of Joppa praying, and in a trance I saw a vision. There was something like a large sheet coming down from heaven, being lowered by its four corners; and it came close to me. 6As I looked at it closely I saw four-footed animals, beasts of prey, reptiles, and birds of the air. 7I also heard a voice saying to me, 'Get up, Peter; kill and eat.' 8But I replied, 'By no means, Lord; for nothing profane or unclean has ever entered my mouth.' 9But a second time the voice answered from heaven, 'What God has made clean, you must not call profane.' 10This happened three times; then everything was pulled up again to heaven. 11At that very moment three people, sent to me from Caesarea, arrived at the house where we were. 12The Spirit told me to go with them and not to make a distinction between them and us.ʷ These six friends also accompanied me, and we entered the man's house. 13He told us how he had seen the angel standing in his house and saying, 'Send to Joppa and bring Simon, who is called Peter; 14he will give you a message by which you and your entire household will be saved.' 15And as I began to speak, the Holy Spirit fell upon them just as it had upon us at the beginning. 16And I remembered the word of the Lord, who had said, 'John baptized with water,

---

v Gk lacks believers   w Or not to hesitate

but you will be baptized with the Holy Spirit.' [17]If then God gave to them the same gift as to us when we believed in the Lord Jesus Christ, who was I that I could hinder God?" [18]When they heard this, they were silenced. And they praised God, saying, "Then God has given even to the Gentiles the repentance that leads to life."

The Church in Antioch

19 Now those who were scattered because of the persecution that took place over Stephen traveled as far as Phoenicia, Cyprus, and Antioch, and they spoke the word to no one except Jews. [20]But among them were some people of Cyprus and Cyrene who, on coming to Antioch, spoke to the Hellenists[x] also, proclaiming the Lord Jesus. [21]The hand of the Lord was with them, and a great number became believers and turned to the Lord. [22]News of this came to the ears of the church in Jerusalem, and they sent Barnabas to Antioch. [23]When he came and saw the grace of God, he rejoiced, and he exhorted them all to remain faithful to the Lord with steadfast devotion; [24]for Barnabas was a good person, full of the Holy Spirit and of faith. And a great many people were brought to the Lord. [25]Then Barnabas went to Tarsus to look for Saul, [26]and when he had found him, he brought him to Antioch. So it was that for an entire year they met with[y] the church and taught a great many people, and it was in Antioch that the disciples were first called "Christians."

27 At that time prophets came down from Jerusalem to Antioch. [28]One of them named Agabus stood up and predicted by the Spirit that there would be a severe famine over all the world; and this took place during the reign of Claudius. [29]The disciples determined that according to their ability, each would send relief to the believers living in Judea; [30]this they did, sending it to the elders by Barnabas and Saul.

James Killed and Peter Imprisoned

12 About that time King Herod laid violent hands upon some who belonged to the church. [2]He had James, the brother of John, killed with the sword. [3]After Herod saw that it pleased the Jews, he proceeded to arrest Peter also. (This was during the festival of Unleavened Bread.) [4]When Herod had seized Peter, he put him in prison and handed him over to four squads of soldiers to guard him, intending to bring him out to the people after the Passover. [5]While Peter was kept in prison, the church prayed fervently to God for him.

Peter Delivered from Prison

6 The very night before Herod was going to bring him out, Peter, bound with two chains, was sleeping between two soldiers, while guards in front of the door were keeping watch over the prison. [7]Suddenly an angel of God appeared

---

x Other ancient authorities read *Greeks*   y Or *were guests of*

and a light shone in the cell. The angel tapped Peter on the side and woke him, saying, "Get up quickly." And the chains fell off his wrists. [8]The angel said to him, "Fasten your belt and put on your sandals." He did so. Then the angel said to him, "Wrap your cloak around you and follow me." [9]Peter went out and followed the angel; he did not realize that what was happening with the angel's help was real; he thought he was seeing a vision. [10]After they had passed the first and the second guard, they came before the iron gate leading into the city. It opened for them of its own accord, and they went outside and walked along a lane, when suddenly the angel left him. [11]Then Peter came to himself and said, "Now I am sure that God has sent this angel and rescued me from the hands of Herod and from all that the Jewish people were expecting."

12 As soon as Peter realized this, he went to the house of Mary, the mother of John whose other name was Mark, where many had gathered and were praying. [13]When he knocked at the outer gate, a womanservant named Rhoda came to answer. [14]On recognizing Peter's voice, she was so overjoyed that, instead of opening the gate, she ran in and announced that Peter was standing at the gate. [15]They said to her, "You are out of your mind!" But she insisted that it was so. They said, "It is Peter's angel." [16]Meanwhile Peter continued knocking; and when they opened the gate, they saw him and were amazed. [17]He motioned to them with his hand to be silent, and described for them how the Lord had brought him out of the prison. And he added, "Tell this to James and to the believers." Then he left and went to another place.

18 When morning came, there was no small commotion among the soldiers over what had become of Peter. [19]When Herod had searched for him and could not find him, he examined the guards and ordered them to be put to death. Then he went down from Judea to Caesarea and stayed there.

The Death of Herod

20 Now Herod was angry with the people of Tyre and Sidon. So they came to him in a body; and after winning over Blastus, the king's chamberlain, they asked for a reconciliation, because their country depended on the king's country for food. [21]On an appointed day Herod put on his royal robes, took his seat on the platform, and delivered a public address to them. [22]The people kept shouting, "The voice of a god, and not of a mortal!" [23]And immediately, because Herod had not given the glory to God, an angel of God struck him down, and he was eaten by worms and died.

24 But the word of God continued to advance and gain adherents. [25]Then after completing their mission Barnabas and Saul returned to[z] Jerusalem and brought with them John, whose other name was Mark.

---

z Other ancient authorities read *from*

Barnabas and Saul Commissioned

13 Now in the church at Antioch there were prophets and teachers: Barnabas, Simeon who was called Niger, Lucius of Cyrene, Manaen a member of the court of Herod the ruler,[a] and Saul. 2 While they were worshiping the Lord and fasting, the Holy Spirit said, "Set apart for me Barnabas and Saul for the work to which I have called them." 3 Then after fasting and praying they laid their hands on them and sent them off.

The Apostles Preach in Cyprus

4 So, being sent out by the Holy Spirit, they went down to Seleucia; and from there they sailed to Cyprus. 5 When they arrived at Salamis, they proclaimed the word of God in the synagogues of the Jews. And they had John also to assist them. 6 When they had gone through the whole island as far as Paphos, they met a certain magician, a Jewish false prophet, named Bar-Jesus. 7 He was with the proconsul, Sergius Paulus, an intelligent man, who summoned Barnabas and Saul and wanted to hear the word of God. 8 But the magician Elymas (for that is the translation of his name) opposed them and tried to turn the proconsul away from the faith. 9 But Saul, also known as Paul, filled with the Holy Spirit, looked intently at him 10 and said, "You son of the devil, you enemy of all righteousness, full of all deceit and villainy, will you not stop making crooked the straight paths of the Lord? 11 And now listen—the hand of the Lord is against you, and you will be blind for a while, unable to see the sun." Immediately mist and darkness came over him, and he went about groping for someone to lead him by the hand. 12 When the proconsul saw what had happened, he believed, for he was astonished at the teaching about the Lord.

Paul and Barnabas in Antioch of Pisidia

13 Then Paul and his companions set sail from Paphos and came to Perga in Pamphylia. John, however, left them and returned to Jerusalem; 14 but they went on from Perga and came to Antioch in Pisidia. And on the sabbath day they went into the synagogue and sat down. 15 After the reading of the law and the prophets, the officials of the synagogue sent them a message, saying, "Friends, if you have any word of exhortation for the people, give it." 16 So Paul stood up and with a gesture began to speak:

"You Israelites, and others who fear God, listen. 17 The God of this people Israel chose our ancestors and made the people great during their stay in the land of Egypt, and with uplifted arm God led them out of it. 18 For about forty years God put up with[b] them in the wilderness. 19 Having destroyed seven nations in the land of Canaan, God gave them their land as an inheritance 20 for about four hundred fifty years. After that God gave them judges until the time of the prophet Samuel. 21 Then they asked for a king; and God gave them Saul

---

a Gk *tetrarch*   b Other ancient authorities read *cared for*

son of Kish, a man of the tribe of Benjamin, who reigned for forty years. [22] When God had removed Saul, God made David their king. In testimony about him God said, 'I have found David, son of Jesse, to be a man after my heart, who will carry out all my wishes.' [23] From this man's posterity God has brought to Israel a Savior, Jesus, as God promised; [24] before his coming John had already proclaimed a baptism of repentance to all the people of Israel. [25] And as John was finishing his work, he said, 'What do you suppose that I am? I am not he. No, but one is coming after me; I am not worthy to untie the thong of the sandals[c] on his feet.'

[26] "My friends, you descendants of the family of Abraham and Sarah, and others who fear God, to us[d] the message of this salvation has been sent. [27] Because the residents of Jerusalem and their leaders did not recognize Jesus or understand the words of the prophets that are read every sabbath, they fulfilled those words by condemning him. [28] Even though they found no cause for a sentence of death, they asked Pilate to have him killed. [29] When they had carried out everything that was written about him, they took the body down from the tree and laid it in a tomb. [30] But God raised Jesus from the dead, [31] and for many days Jesus appeared to those who journeyed up with him from Galilee to Jerusalem, and they are now Jesus' witnesses to the people. [32] And we bring you the good news that what God promised to our ancestors [33] God has fulfilled for us, their children, by raising Jesus; as also it is written in the second psalm,

> 'You are my Child;
>   today I have begotten you.'

[34] As to God's raising Jesus from the dead, no more to return to corruption, God has spoken in this way,

> 'I will give you the holy promises made to David.'

[35] Therefore God has also said in another psalm,

> 'You will not let your Holy One experience corruption.'

[36] For David, after he had served the purpose of God in his own generation, died,[e] was laid beside his ancestors, and experienced corruption; [37] but the one whom God raised up experienced no corruption. [38] Let it be known to you therefore, my friends, that through this person forgiveness of sins is proclaimed to you; [39] by this Jesus[f] everyone who believes is set free from all those sins[g] from which you could not be freed by the law of Moses. [40] Beware, therefore, that what the prophets said does not happen to you:

[41]   'Look, you scoffers!
>   Be amazed and perish,

---

c Gk *untie the sandals*   d Other ancient authorities read *you*   e Gk *fell asleep*   f Gk *this*
g Gk *all*

> for in your days I am doing a work,
>> a work that you will never believe, even if someone
>> tells you.' "

42 As Paul and Barnabas were going out, the people urged them to speak about these things again the next sabbath. 43 When the meeting of the synagogue broke up, many Jews and devout converts to Judaism followed Paul and Barnabas, who spoke to them and urged them to continue in the grace of God.

44 The next sabbath almost the whole city gathered to hear the word of God. 45 But when the Jews saw the crowds, they were filled with jealousy; and blaspheming, they contradicted what was spoken by Paul. 46 Then both Paul and Barnabas spoke out boldly, saying, "It was necessary that the word of God should be spoken first to you. Since you reject it and judge yourselves to be unworthy of eternal life, we are now turning to the Gentiles. 47 For so God has commanded us, saying,

> 'I have set you to be a light for the Gentiles,
>> so that you may bring salvation to the ends of the
>> earth.' "

48 When the Gentiles heard this, they were glad and praised the word of God; and as many as had been destined for eternal life became believers. 49 Thus the word of God spread throughout the region. 50 But the Jews incited the devout women of high standing and the leading men of the city, and stirred up persecution against Paul and Barnabas, and drove them out of their region. 51 So they shook the dust off their feet in protest against them, and went to Iconium. 52 And the disciples were filled with joy and with the Holy Spirit.

Paul and Barnabas in Iconium

14 The same thing occurred in Iconium, where Paul and Barnabas went into the Jewish synagogue and spoke in such a way that a great number of both Jews and Greeks became believers. 2 But the Jews who did not believe stirred up the Gentiles and poisoned their minds against the believers. 3 So they remained for a long time, speaking boldly for the Lord, who testified to the word of grace by granting signs and wonders to be done through them. 4 But the residents of the city were divided; some sided with the Jews, and some with the apostles. 5 And when an attempt was made by both Gentiles and Jews, with their rulers, to mistreat them and to stone them, 6 the apostles learned of it and fled to Lystra and Derbe, cities of Lycaonia, and to the surrounding country; 7 and there they continued proclaiming the good news.

Paul and Barnabas in Lystra and Derbe

8 In Lystra there was a person sitting who could not use his feet and had never walked, for he had been lame from birth. 9 He listened to Paul speaking. And Paul, looking at him intently and seeing that he had faith to be healed,

10 said in a loud voice, "Stand upright on your feet." And the man sprang up and began to walk. 11 When the crowds saw what Paul had done, they shouted in the Lycaonian language, "The gods have come down to us in human form!" 12 Barnabas they called Zeus, and Paul they called Hermes, because he was the chief speaker. 13 The priest of Zeus, whose temple was just outside the city,ʰ brought oxen and garlands to the gates and, with the crowds, wanted to offer sacrifice. 14 When the apostles Barnabas and Paul heard of it, they tore their clothes and rushed out into the crowd, shouting, 15 "Friends, why are you doing this? We are mortals just like you, and we bring you good news, that you should turn from these worthless things to the living God, who made the heaven and the earth and the sea and all that is in them, 16 who in past generations allowed all the nations to follow their own ways; 17 yet God is not left without a witness in doing good—giving you rains from heaven and fruitful seasons, and filling you with food and your hearts with joy." 18 Even with these words, they scarcely restrained the crowds from offering sacrifice to them.

19 But Jews came there from Antioch and Iconium and won over the crowds. Then they stoned Paul and dragged him out of the city, supposing that he was dead. 20 But when the disciples surrounded him, he got up and went into the city. The next day Paul went on with Barnabas to Derbe.

The Return to Antioch in Syria

21 After they had proclaimed the good news to that city and had made many disciples, they returned to Lystra, then on to Iconium and Antioch. 22 There they strengthened the souls of the disciples and encouraged them to continue in the faith, saying, "It is through many persecutions that we must enter the dominion of God." 23 And after they had appointed elders for them in each church, with prayer and fasting they entrusted them to the Lord in whom they had come to believe.

24 Then they passed through Pisidia and came to Pamphylia. 25 When they had spoken the word in Perga, they went down to Attalia. 26 From there they sailed back to Antioch, where they had been commended to the grace of God for the workⁱ that they had completed. 27 When they arrived, they called the church together and related all that God had done with them, and how God had opened a door of faith for the Gentiles. 28 And they stayed there with the disciples for some time.

The Council at Jerusalem

15 Then certain individuals came down from Judea and were teaching the believers, "Unless you are circumcised according to the custom of Moses, you cannot be saved." 2 And after Paul and Barnabas had no small dissension and debate with them, Paul and Barnabas and some of the others were appointed to go up to Jerusalem to discuss this question with the apostles

---

h Or *The priest of Zeus-Outside-the-City*　　　i Or *committed in the grace of God to the work*

and the elders. ³So they were sent on their way by the church, and as they passed through both Phoenicia and Samaria, they reported the conversion of the Gentiles, and brought great joy to all the believers. ⁴When they came to Jerusalem, they were welcomed by the church and the apostles and the elders, and they reported all that God had done with them. ⁵But some believers who belonged to the sect of the Pharisees stood up and said, "It is necessary for them to be circumcised and ordered to keep the law of Moses."

6 The apostles and the elders met together to consider this matter. ⁷After there had been much debate, Peter stood up and said to them, "My friends, you know that in the early days God made a choice among you, that I should be the one through whom the Gentiles would hear the message of the good news and become believers. ⁸And God, who knows the human heart, testified to them by giving them the Holy Spirit, just as God did to us; ⁹and in cleansing their hearts by faith God has made no distinction between them and us. ¹⁰Now therefore why are you putting God to the test by placing on the neck of the disciples a yoke that neither our ancestors nor we have been able to bear? ¹¹On the contrary, we believe that we will be saved through the grace of the Lord Jesus, just as they will."

12 The whole assembly kept silent, and listened to Barnabas and Paul as they told of all the signs and wonders that God had done through them among the Gentiles. ¹³After they finished speaking, James replied, "My friends, listen to me. ¹⁴Simeon has related how God first looked favorably on the Gentiles, to take from among them a people for God's name. ¹⁵This agrees with the words of the prophets, as it is written,

16   'After this I will return,
        and I will rebuild the dwelling of David, which has
            fallen;
          from its ruins I will rebuild it,
            and I will set it up,
17   so that all other peoples may seek God—
          even all the Gentiles over whom my name has been
            called.
          Thus says God, who has been making these things
            ¹⁸known from long ago.'ʲ

¹⁹Therefore I have reached the decision that we should not trouble those Gentiles who are turning to God, ²⁰but we should write to them to abstain only from things polluted by idols and from fornication and from whatever has been strangledᵏ and from blood. ²¹For in every city, for generations past, Moses has had those who proclaim him, for he has been read aloud every sabbath in the synagogues."

---

j Other ancient authorities read *things. 18Known to God from of old are all his works.'*
k Other ancient authorities lack *and from whatever has been strangled*

The Council's Letter to Gentile Believers

22 Then the apostles and the elders, with the consent of the whole church, decided to choose delegates from among their members[l] and to send them to Antioch with Paul and Barnabas. They sent Judas called Barsabbas, and Silas, leaders among them, 23 with the following letter: "The believers, both the apostles and the elders, to the believers of Gentile origin in Antioch and Syria and Cilicia, greetings. 24 Since we have heard that certain persons who have gone out from us, though with no instructions from us, have said things to disturb you and have unsettled your minds,[m] 25 we have decided unanimously to choose representatives and send them to you, along with our beloved Barnabas and Paul, 26 who have risked their lives for the sake of our Lord Jesus Christ. 27 We have therefore sent Judas and Silas, who themselves will tell you the same things by word of mouth. 28 For it has seemed good to the Holy Spirit and to us to impose on you no further burden than these essentials: 29 that you abstain from what has been sacrificed to idols and from blood and from what is strangled[n] and from fornication. If you keep yourselves from these, you will do well. Farewell."

30 So they were sent off and went down to Antioch. When they gathered the congregation together, they delivered the letter. 31 When its members read it, they rejoiced at the exhortation. 32 Judas and Silas, who were themselves prophets, said much to encourage and strengthen the believers. 33 After they had been there for some time, they were sent off in peace by the believers to those who had sent them.[o] 35 But Paul and Barnabas remained in Antioch, and there, with many others, they taught and proclaimed the word of the Lord.

Paul and Barnabas Separate

36 After some days Paul said to Barnabas, "Come, let us return and visit the believers in every city where we proclaimed the word of the Lord and see how they are doing." 37 Barnabas wanted to take with them John called Mark. 38 But Paul decided not to take with them one who had deserted them in Pamphylia and had not accompanied them in the work. 39 The disagreement became so sharp that they parted company; Barnabas took Mark with him and sailed away to Cyprus. 40 But Paul chose Silas and set out, the believers commending him to the grace of the Lord. 41 He went through Syria and Cilicia, strengthening the churches.

---

l Gk *from among them*
m Other ancient authorities add *saying, 'You must be circumcised and keep the law,'*
n Other ancient authorities lack *and from what is strangled*
o Other ancient authorities add verse 34, *But it seemed good to Silas to remain there*

Timothy Joins Paul and Silas

16 Paul went on also to Derbe and to Lystra, where there was a disciple named Timothy, the son of a Jewish woman who was a believer; but his father was a Greek. ²He was well spoken of by the believers in Lystra and Iconium. ³Paul wanted Timothy to accompany him; and he took him and had him circumcised because of the Jews who were in those places, for they all knew that Timothy's father was a Greek. ⁴As they went from town to town, they delivered to them for observance the decisions that had been reached by the apostles and elders who were in Jerusalem. ⁵So the churches were strengthened in the faith and increased in numbers daily.

Paul's Vision of the Macedonian

6 They went through the region of Phrygia and Galatia, having been forbidden by the Holy Spirit to speak the word in Asia. ⁷When they had come opposite Mysia, they attempted to go into Bithynia, but the Spirit of Jesus did not allow them; ⁸so, passing by Mysia, they went down to Troas. ⁹During the night Paul had a vision: there stood a Macedonian pleading with him and saying, "Come over to Macedonia and help us." ¹⁰When he had seen the vision, we immediately tried to cross over to Macedonia, being convinced that God had called us to proclaim the good news to them.

The Conversion of Lydia

11 We set sail from Troas and took a straight course to Samothrace, the following day to Neapolis, ¹²and from there to Philippi, which is a leading city of the district^p of Macedonia and a Roman colony. We remained in this city for some days. ¹³On the sabbath day we went outside the gate by the river, where we supposed there was a place of prayer; and we sat down and spoke to the women who had gathered there. ¹⁴A certain woman named Lydia, a worshiper of God, was listening to us; she was from the city of Thyatira and a dealer in purple cloth. The Lord opened her heart to listen eagerly to what was said by Paul. ¹⁵When she and her household were baptized, she urged us, saying, "If you have judged me to be faithful to the Lord, come and stay at my home." And she prevailed upon us.

Paul and Silas in Prison

16 One day, as we were going to the place of prayer, we met a womanservant who had a spirit of divination and brought her owners a great deal of money by fortune-telling. ¹⁷While she followed Paul and us, she would cry out, "These people are enslaved to the Most High God, who proclaim to you^q a way of salvation." ¹⁸She kept doing this for many days. But Paul, very much annoyed,

---

p Other authorities read *a city of the first district*   q Other ancient authorities read *to us*

turned and said to the spirit, "I order you in the name of Jesus Christ to come out of her." And it came out that very hour.

19 But when her owners saw that their hope of making money was gone, they seized Paul and Silas and dragged them into the marketplace before the authorities. 20 When they had brought them before the magistrates, they said, "These men are disturbing our city; they are Jews 21 and are advocating customs that are not lawful for us as Romans to adopt or observe." 22 The crowd joined in attacking them, and the magistrates had them stripped of their clothing and ordered them to be beaten with rods. 23 After they had given them a severe flogging, they threw them into prison and ordered the jailer to keep them securely. 24 Following these instructions, he put them in the innermost cell and fastened their feet in the stocks.

25 About midnight Paul and Silas were praying and singing hymns to God, and the prisoners were listening to them. 26 Suddenly there was an earthquake, so violent that the foundations of the prison were shaken; and immediately all the doors were opened and everyone's chains were unfastened. 27 When the jailer woke up and saw the prison doors wide open, he drew his sword and was about to kill himself, since he supposed that the prisoners had escaped. 28 But Paul shouted in a loud voice, "Do not harm yourself, for we are all here." 29 The jailer called for lights, and rushing in, he fell down trembling before Paul and Silas. 30 Then he brought them outside and said, "Sirs, what must I do to be saved?" 31 They answered, "Believe on the Lord Jesus, and you will be saved, you and your household." 32 They spoke the word of the Lord^r to him and to all who were in his house. 33 At the same hour of the night the jailer took them and washed their wounds; then he and his entire family were baptized without delay. 34 Bringing them up into the house and setting food before them, the jailer and his entire household rejoiced that he had become a believer in God.

35 When morning came, the magistrates sent the police, saying, "Let those men go." 36 And the jailer reported the message to Paul, saying, "The magistrates sent word to let you go; therefore come out now and go in peace." 37 But Paul replied, "They have beaten us in public, uncondemned, men who are Roman citizens, and have thrown us into prison; and now are they going to discharge us in secret? Certainly not! Let them come and take us out themselves." 38 The police reported these words to the magistrates, and they were afraid when they heard that Paul and Silas were Roman citizens; 39 so they came and apologized to them. And they took them out and asked them to leave the city. 40 After leaving the prison they went to Lydia's home; and when they had seen and encouraged the brothers and sisters there, they departed.

---

r Other ancient authorities read *word of God*

The Uproar in Thessalonica

17 After Paul and Silas had passed through Amphipolis and Apollonia, they came to Thessalonica, where there was a synagogue of the Jews. ²And Paul went in, as was his custom, and on three sabbath days argued with them from the scriptures, ³explaining and proving that it was necessary for the Messiah[s] to suffer and to rise from the dead, and saying, "This is the Messiah,[s] Jesus whom I am proclaiming to you." ⁴Some of them were persuaded and joined Paul and Silas, as did a great many of the devout Greeks and not a few of the leading women. ⁵But the Jews became jealous, and with the help of some gangs in the marketplaces they formed a mob and set the city in an uproar. While they were searching for Paul and Silas to bring them out to the assembly, they attacked Jason's house. ⁶When they could not find them, they dragged Jason and some believers before the city authorities,[t] shouting, "These people who have been turning the world upside down have come here also, ⁷and Jason has entertained them as guests. They are all acting contrary to the decrees of the emperor, saying that there is another king named Jesus." ⁸The people and the city officials were disturbed when they heard this, ⁹and after they had taken bail from Jason and the others, they let them go.

Paul and Silas in Beroea

10 That very night the believers sent Paul and Silas off to Beroea; and when they arrived, they went to the Jewish synagogue. ¹¹These Jews were more receptive than those in Thessalonica, for they welcomed the message very eagerly and examined the scriptures every day to see whether these things were so. ¹²Many of them therefore believed, including not a few Greek women and men of high standing. ¹³But when the Jews of Thessalonica learned that the word of God had been proclaimed by Paul in Beroea as well, they came there too, to stir up and incite the crowds. ¹⁴Then the believers immediately sent Paul away to the coast, but Silas and Timothy remained behind. ¹⁵Those who conducted Paul brought him as far as Athens; and after receiving instructions to have Silas and Timothy join him as soon as possible, they left him.

Paul in Athens

16 While Paul was waiting for them in Athens, he was deeply distressed to see that the city was full of idols. ¹⁷So he argued in the synagogue with the Jews and the devout persons, and also in the marketplace[u] every day with those who happened to be there. ¹⁸Also some Epicurean and Stoic philosophers debated with him. Some said, "What does this babbler want to say?" Others said, "He seems to be a proclaimer of foreign divinities." (This was because he was telling the good news about Jesus and the resurrection.) ¹⁹So they took him and brought him to the Areopagus and asked him, "May we know what this new

---

s Or *the Christ*   t Gk *politarchs*   u Or *civic center*; Gk *agora*

teaching is that you are presenting? 20 It sounds rather strange to us, so we would like to know what it means." 21 Now all the Athenians and the foreigners living there would spend their time in nothing but telling or hearing something new.

22 Then Paul stood in front of the Areopagus and said, "Athenians, I see how extremely religious you are in every way. 23 For as I went through the city and looked carefully at the objects of your worship, I found among them an altar with the inscription, 'To an unknown god.' What therefore you worship as unknown, this I proclaim to you. 24 The God who made the world and everything in it, the one who is Sovereign of heaven and earth, does not live in shrines made by human hands, 25 and is not served by human hands, as though God needed anything, since God alone gives to all mortals life and breath and all things. 26 From one ancestor[v] God made all nations to inhabit the whole earth, having allotted the times of their existence and the boundaries of the places where they would live, 27 so that they would search for God[w] and perhaps grope for and find God—though indeed God is not far from each one of us. 28 For 'In this one we live and move and have our being'; as even some of your own poets have said,

> 'For we too are God's offspring.'

29 Since we are God's offspring, we ought not to think that the deity is like gold, or silver, or stone, an image formed by the art and imagination of mortals. 30 While God has overlooked the times of human ignorance, now God commands all people everywhere to repent, 31 because the day has been fixed on which God will have the world judged in righteousness by one whom God has appointed, and of this God has given assurance to all by raising that one from the dead."

32 When they heard of the resurrection of the dead, some scoffed; but others said, "We will hear you again about this." 33 At that point Paul left them. 34 But some of them joined him and became believers, including Dionysius the Areopagite and a woman named Damaris, and others with them.

Paul in Corinth

18 After this Paul left Athens and went to Corinth. 2 There he found a Jew named Aquila, a native of Pontus, who had recently come from Italy with his wife Priscilla, because Claudius had ordered all Jews to leave Rome. Paul went to see them, 3 and, because he was of the same trade, he stayed with them, and they worked together—by trade they were tentmakers. 4 Every sabbath he would argue in the synagogue and would try to convince Jews and Greeks.

5 When Silas and Timothy arrived from Macedonia, Paul was occupied

---

v Gk *From one*; other ancient authorities read *From one blood*
w Other ancient authorities read *the Lord*

with proclaiming the word,[x] testifying to the Jews that the Messiah[y] was Jesus. [6] When they opposed and reviled him, in protest he shook the dust from his clothes[z] and said to them, "Your blood be on your own heads! I am innocent. From now on I will go to the Gentiles." [7] Then he left the synagogue[a] and went to the house of a man named Titius[b] Justus, a worshiper of God; his house was next door to the synagogue. [8] Crispus, the official of the synagogue, became a believer in the Lord, together with all his household; and many of the Corinthians who heard Paul became believers and were baptized. [9] One night the Lord said to Paul in a vision, "Do not be afraid, but speak and do not be silent; [10] for I am with you, and no one will lay a hand on you to harm you, for there are many in this city who are my people." [11] He stayed there a year and six months, teaching the word of God among them.

12 But when Gallio was proconsul of Achaia, the Jews made a united attack on Paul and brought him before the tribunal. [13] They said, "This man is persuading people to worship God in ways that are contrary to the law." [14] Just as Paul was about to speak, Gallio said to the Jews, "If it were a matter of crime or serious villainy, I would be justified in accepting the complaint of you Jews; [15] but since it is a matter of questions about words and names and your own law, see to it yourselves; I do not wish to be a judge of these matters." [16] And he dismissed them from the tribunal. [17] Then all of them[c] seized Sosthenes, the official of the synagogue, and beat him in front of the tribunal. But Gallio paid no attention to any of these things.

Paul's Return to Antioch

18 After staying there for a considerable time, Paul said farewell to the believers and sailed for Syria, accompanied by Priscilla and Aquila. At Cenchreae he had his hair cut, for he was under a vow. [19] When they reached Ephesus, he left them there, but first he himself went into the synagogue and had a discussion with the Jews. [20] When they asked him to stay longer, he declined; [21] but on taking leave of them, he said, "I[d] will return to you, if God wills." Then Paul set sail from Ephesus.

22 After landing at Caesarea, Paul went up to Jerusalem[e] and greeted the church, and then went down to Antioch. [23] After spending some time there he departed and went from place to place through the region of Galatia[f] and Phrygia, strengthening all the disciples.

---

x Gk *with the word*   y Or *the Christ*   z Gk *reviled him, he shook out his clothes*
a Gk *left there*   b Other ancient authorities read *Titus*
c Other ancient authorities read *all the Greeks*
d Other ancient authorities read *I must at all costs keep the approaching festival in Jerusalem, but I*   e Gk *went up*   f Gk *the Galatian region*

Ministry of Apollos

24 Now there came to Ephesus a Jew named Apollos, a native of Alexandria. He was eloquent, and well-versed in the scriptures. 25 He had been instructed in the Way of the Lord; and he spoke with burning enthusiasm and taught accurately the things concerning Jesus, though he knew only the baptism of John. 26 He began to speak boldly in the synagogue; but when Priscilla and Aquila heard him, they took him aside and explained the Way of the Lord to him more accurately. 27 And when he wished to cross over to Achaia, the believers encouraged him and wrote to the disciples to welcome him. On his arrival he greatly helped those who through grace had become believers, 28 for he powerfully refuted the Jews in public, showing by the scriptures that the Messiah⁹ is Jesus.

Paul in Ephesus

19 While Apollos was in Corinth, Paul passed through the interior regions and came to Ephesus, where he found some disciples. 2 He said to them, "Did you receive the Holy Spirit when you became believers?" They replied, "No, we have not even heard that there is a Holy Spirit." 3 Then he said, "Into what then were you baptized?" They answered, "Into John's baptism." 4 Paul said, "John baptized with the baptism of repentance, telling the people to believe in the one who was to come after him, that is, in Jesus." 5 On hearing this, they were baptized in the name of the Lord Jesus. 6 When Paul had laid his hands on them, the Holy Spirit came upon them, and they spoke in tongues and prophesied— 7 altogether there were about twelve of them.

8 Paul entered the synagogue and for three months spoke out boldly, and argued persuasively about the dominion of God. 9 When some stubbornly refused to believe and spoke evil of the Way before the congregation, he left them, taking the disciples with him, and argued daily in the lecture hall of Tyrannus.ʰ 10 This continued for two years, so that all the residents of Asia, both Jews and Greeks, heard the word of the Lord.

The Sons of Sceva

11 God did extraordinary miracles through Paul, 12 so that when the handkerchiefs or aprons that had touched his skin were brought to the sick, their diseases left them, and the evil spirits came out of them. 13 Then some itinerant Jewish exorcists tried to use the name of the Lord Jesus over those who had evil spirits, saying, "I adjure you by the Jesus whom Paul proclaims." 14 Seven sons of a Jewish high priest named Sceva were doing this. 15 But the evil spirit said to them in reply, "Jesus I know, and Paul I know; but who are you?"

---

g Or *the Christ*
h Other ancient authorities read *of a certain Tyrannus, from eleven o'clock in the morning to four in the afternoon*

16 Then the person with the evil spirit leaped on them, and overpowered them all so completely that they fled out of the house naked and wounded. 17 When this became known to all residents of Ephesus, both Jews and Greeks, everyone was awestruck; and the name of the Lord Jesus was praised. 18 Also many of those who became believers confessed and disclosed their practices. 19 A number of those who practiced magic collected their books and burned them publicly; when the value of these books was calculated, it was found to come to fifty thousand silver coins. 20 So the word of the Lord grew mightily and prevailed.

The Riot in Ephesus

21 Now after these things had been accomplished, Paul resolved in the Spirit to go through Macedonia and Achaia, and then to go on to Jerusalem. He said, "After I have gone there, I must also see Rome." 22 So he sent two of his helpers, Timothy and Erastus, to Macedonia, while he himself stayed for some time longer in Asia.

23 About that time no little disturbance broke out concerning the Way. 24 A man named Demetrius, a silversmith who made silver shrines of Artemis, brought no little business to the artisans. 25 These he gathered together, with the workers of the same trade, and said to them, "You know that we get our wealth from this business. 26 You also see and hear that not only in Ephesus but in almost the whole of Asia this Paul has persuaded and drawn away a considerable number of people by saying that gods made with hands are not gods. 27 And there is danger not only that this trade of ours may come into disrepute but also that the temple of the great goddess Artemis will be scorned, and she will be deprived of her majesty that brought all Asia and the world to worship her."

28 When the workers heard this, they were enraged and shouted, "Great is Artemis of the Ephesians!" 29 The city was filled with the confusion; and people rushed together to the theater, dragging with them Gaius and Aristarchus, Macedonians who were Paul's travel companions. 30 Paul wished to go into the crowd, but the disciples would not let him; 31 even some officials of the province of Asia,[i] who were friendly to Paul, sent him a message urging him not to venture into the theater. 32 Meanwhile, some were shouting one thing, some another; for the assembly was in confusion, and most of them did not know why they had come together. 33 Some of the crowd gave instructions to Alexander, whom the Jews had pushed forward. And Alexander motioned for silence and tried to make a defense before the people. 34 But when they recognized that he was a Jew, for about two hours all of them shouted in unison, "Great is Artemis of the Ephesians!" 35 But when the town clerk had quieted the crowd, he said, "Citizens of Ephesus, who is there that does not know that the city of the Ephesians is the temple keeper of the great Artemis and of the statue that fell from heaven?[j] 36 Since these things cannot be denied,

---

i Gk *some of the Asiarchs*   j Meaning of Gk uncertain

you ought to be quiet and do nothing rash. 37You have brought these men here who are neither temple robbers nor blasphemers of our[k] goddess. 38If therefore Demetrius and the artisans with him have a complaint against anyone, the courts are open, and there are proconsuls; let them bring charges there against one another. 39If there is anything further[l] you want to know, it must be settled in the regular assembly. 40For we are in danger of being charged with rioting today, since there is no cause that we can give to justify this commotion." 41When the town clerk had said this, he dismissed the assembly.

Paul Goes to Macedonia and Greece

20 After the uproar had ceased, Paul sent for the disciples; and after encouraging them and saying farewell, he left for Macedonia. 2When he had gone through those regions and had given the believers much encouragement, he came to Greece, 3where he stayed for three months. He was about to set sail for Syria when a plot was made against him by the Jews, and so he decided to return through Macedonia. 4Paul was accompanied by Sopater son of Pyrrhus from Beroea, by Aristarchus and Secundus from Thessalonica, by Gaius from Derbe, and by Timothy, as well as by Tychicus and Trophimus from Asia. 5They went ahead and were waiting for us in Troas; 6but we sailed from Philippi after the days of Unleavened Bread, and in five days we joined them in Troas, where we stayed for seven days.

Paul's Farewell Visit to Troas

7 On the first day of the week, when we met to break bread, Paul was holding a discussion with them; since he intended to leave the next day, he continued speaking until midnight. 8There were many lamps in the room upstairs where we were meeting. 9A young man named Eutychus, who was sitting in the window, began to sink off into a deep sleep while Paul talked still longer. Overcome by sleep, he fell to the ground three floors below and was picked up dead. 10But Paul went down, and bending over him took him in his arms, and said, "Do not be alarmed, for his life is in him." 11Then Paul went upstairs, and after he had broken bread and eaten, he continued to converse with them until dawn; then he left. 12Meanwhile they had taken the boy away alive and were not a little comforted.

The Voyage from Troas to Miletus

13 We went ahead to the ship and set sail for Assos, intending to take Paul on board there; for he had made this arrangement, intending to go by land himself. 14When he met us in Assos, we took him on board and went to Mitylene. 15We sailed from there, and on the following day we arrived opposite Chios. The next day we touched at Samos, and[m] the day after that we came to Miletus.

---

k Other ancient authorities read *your*　　l Other ancient authorities read *about other matters*
m Other ancient authorities add *after remaining at Trogyllium*

16 For Paul had decided to sail past Ephesus, so that he might not have to spend time in Asia; he was eager to be in Jerusalem, if possible, on the day of Pentecost.

Paul Speaks to the Ephesian Elders

17 From Miletus Paul sent a message to Ephesus, asking the elders of the church to meet him. 18 When they came to him, he said to them:

"You yourselves know how I lived among you the entire time from the first day that I set foot in Asia, 19 serving the Lord with all humility and with tears, enduring the trials that came to me through the plots of the Jews. 20 I did not shrink from doing anything helpful, proclaiming the message to you and teaching you publicly and from house to house, 21 as I testified to both Jews and Greeks about repentance toward God and faith toward our Lord Jesus. 22 And now, as a captive to the Spirit,n I am on my way to Jerusalem, not knowing what will happen to me there, 23 except that the Holy Spirit testifies to me in every city that imprisonment and persecutions are waiting for me. 24 But I do not count my life of any value to myself, if only I may finish my course and the ministry that I received from the Lord Jesus, to testify to the good news of God's grace.

25 "And now I know that none of you, among whom I have gone about proclaiming the dominion of God, will ever see my face again. 26 Therefore I declare to you this day that I am not responsible for the blood of any of you, 27 for I did not shrink from declaring to you the whole purpose of God. 28 Keep watch over yourselves and over all the flock, of which the Holy Spirit has made you overseers, to shepherd the church of God,o obtained with the blood of God's own Child.p 29 I know that after I have gone, savage wolves will come in among you, not sparing the flock. 30 Some even from your own group will come distorting the truth in order to entice the disciples to follow them. 31 Therefore be alert, remembering that for three years I did not cease night or day to warn everyone with tears. 32 And now I commend you to God and to the message of God's grace, a message that is able to build you up and to give you the inheritance among all who are sanctified. 33 I coveted no one's silver or gold or clothing. 34 You know for yourselves that I worked with my own hands to support myself and my companions. 35 In all this I have given you an example that by such work we must support the weak, remembering the words of the Lord Jesus, the very one who said, 'It is more blessed to give than to receive.' "

36 When Paul had finished speaking, he knelt down with them all and prayed. 37 There was much weeping among them all; they embraced Paul and kissed him, 38 grieving especially because of what he had said, that they would not see him again. Then they brought him to the ship.

n Or *And now, bound in the spirit*   o Other ancient authorities read *of the Lord*
p Or *with God's own blood*; Gk *with the blood of God's Own*

Paul's Journey to Jerusalem

21 When we had parted from them and set sail, we came by a straight course to Cos, and the next day to Rhodes, and from there to Patara.q ²When we found a ship bound for Phoenicia, we went on board and set sail. ³We came in sight of Cyprus; and leaving it on our left, we sailed to Syria and landed at Tyre, because the ship was to unload its cargo there. ⁴We looked up the disciples and stayed there for seven days. Through the Spirit they told Paul not to go on to Jerusalem. ⁵When our days there were ended, we left and proceeded on our journey; and all of them, with wives and children, escorted us outside the city. There we knelt down on the beach and prayed ⁶and said farewell to one another. Then we went on board the ship, and they returned home.

7 When we had finishedr the voyage from Tyre, we arrived at Ptolemais; and we greeted the believers and stayed with them for one day. ⁸The next day we left and came to Caesarea; and we went into the house of Philip the evangelist, one of the seven, and stayed with him. ⁹Philip had four unmarried daughters who had the gift of prophecy. ¹⁰While we were staying there for several days, a prophet named Agabus came down from Judea. ¹¹He came to us and took Paul's belt, bound his own feet and hands with it, and said, "Thus says the Holy Spirit, 'This is the way the Jews in Jerusalem will bind the man who owns this belt and will hand him over to the Gentiles.' " ¹²When we heard this, we and the people there urged Paul not to go up to Jerusalem. ¹³Then Paul answered, "What are you doing, weeping and breaking my heart? For I am ready not only to be bound but even to die in Jerusalem for the name of the Lord Jesus." ¹⁴Since he would not be persuaded, we remained silent except to say, "The Lord's will be done."

15 After these days we got ready and started to go up to Jerusalem. ¹⁶Some of the disciples from Caesarea also came along and brought us to the house of Mnason of Cyprus, an early disciple, with whom we were to stay.

Paul Visits James at Jerusalem

17 When we arrived in Jerusalem, the believers welcomed us warmly. ¹⁸The next day Paul went with us to visit James; and all the elders were present. ¹⁹After greeting them, he related one by one the things that God had done among the Gentiles through his ministry. ²⁰When they heard it, they praised God. Then they said to Paul, "You see, brother, how many thousands of believers there are among the Jews, and they are all zealous for the law. ²¹They have been told about you that you teach all the Jews living among the Gentiles to forsake Moses, and that you tell them not to circumcise their children or observe the customs. ²²What then is to be done? They will certainly hear that you have come. ²³So do what we tell you. We have four people who are under

q Other ancient authorities add *and Myra*   r Or *continued*

a vow. 24Join them, go through the rite of purification with them, and pay for the shaving of their heads. Thus all will know that there is nothing in what they have been told about you, but that you yourself observe and guard the law. 25But as for the Gentiles who have become believers, we have sent a letter with our judgment that they should abstain from what has been sacrificed to idols and from blood and from what is strangled[s] and from fornication." 26Then Paul took them, and the next day, having purified himself, he entered the temple with them, making public the completion of the days of purification when the sacrifice would be made for each of them.

Paul Arrested in the Temple

27 When the seven days were almost completed, the Jews from Asia, who had seen Paul in the temple, stirred up the whole crowd. They seized him, 28shouting, "People of Israel, help! This is the man who is teaching everyone everywhere against our people, our law, and this place; more than that, he has actually brought Greeks into the temple and has defiled this holy place." 29For they had previously seen Trophimus the Ephesian with him in the city, and they supposed that Paul had brought him into the temple. 30Then all the city was aroused, and the people rushed together. They seized Paul and dragged him out of the temple, and immediately the doors were shut. 31While they were trying to kill him, word came to the tribune of the cohort that all Jerusalem was in an uproar. 32Immediately he took soldiers and centurions and ran down to them. When they saw the tribune and the soldiers, they stopped beating Paul. 33Then the tribune came, arrested him, and ordered him to be bound with two chains; he inquired who Paul was and what he had done. 34Some in the crowd shouted one thing, some another; and as the tribune could not learn the facts because of the uproar, he ordered Paul to be brought into the barracks. 35When Paul came to the steps, the violence of the mob was so great that he had to be carried by the soldiers. 36The crowd that followed kept shouting, "Away with him!"

Paul Defends Himself

37 Just as Paul was about to be brought into the barracks, he said to the tribune, "May I say something to you?" The tribune replied, "Do you know Greek? 38Then you are not the Egyptian who recently stirred up a revolt and led the four thousand assassins out into the wilderness?" 39Paul replied, "I am a Jew, from Tarsus in Cilicia, a citizen of an important city; I beg you, let me speak to the people." 40When the tribune had given him permission, Paul stood on the steps and motioned to the people for silence; and when there was a great hush, he addressed them in the Hebrew[t] language, saying:

---

s Other ancient authorities lack *and from what is strangled*   t That is, *Aramaic*

22 "Friends, listen to the defense that I now make before you."
2 When they heard him addressing them in Hebrew,ᵘ they became even more quiet. Then he said:

3 "I am a Jew, born in Tarsus in Cilicia, but brought up in this city at the feet of Gamaliel, educated strictly according to our ancestral law, being zealous for God, just as all of you are today. ⁴I persecuted this Way up to the point of death by binding both men and women and putting them in prison, ⁵as the high priest and the whole council of elders can testify about me. From them I also received letters to the believers in Damascus, and I went there in order to bind those who were there and to bring them back to Jerusalem for punishment.

Paul Tells of His Conversion

6 "While I was on my way and approaching Damascus, about noon a great light from heaven suddenly shone about me. ⁷I fell to the ground and heard a voice saying to me, 'Saul, Saul, why are you persecuting me?' ⁸I answered, 'Who are you, Lord?' Then I was answered, 'I am Jesus of Nazarethᵛ whom you are persecuting.' ⁹Now those who were with me saw the light but did not hear the voice of the one who was speaking to me. ¹⁰I asked, 'What am I to do, Lord?' The Lord said to me, 'Get up and go to Damascus; there you will be told everything that has been assigned to you to do.' ¹¹Since I could not see because of the brightness of that light, those who were with me took my hand and led me to Damascus.

12 "A certain Ananias, who was a devout man according to the law and well spoken of by all the Jews living there, ¹³came to me; and standing beside me, he said, 'Brother Saul, regain your sight!' In that very hour I regained my sight and saw him. ¹⁴Then Ananias said, 'The God of our ancestors has chosen you to know the divine will, to see the Righteous One and to hear that one's own voice; ¹⁵for to all the world you will be a witness to that one of what you have seen and heard. ¹⁶And now why do you delay? Get up, be baptized, and have your sins washed away, calling on the name of the Righteous One.'

Paul Sent to the Gentiles

17 "After I had returned to Jerusalem and while I was praying in the temple, Iʳ fell into a trance ¹⁸and saw Jesus saying to me, 'Hurry and get out of Jerusalem quickly, because they will not accept your testimony about me.' ¹⁹And I said, 'Lord, they themselves know that in every synagogue I imprisoned and beat those who believed in you. ²⁰And while the blood of your witness Stephen was shed, I myself was standing by, approving and keeping the coats of those who killed him.' ²¹Then Jesus said to me, 'Go, for I will send you far away to the Gentiles.' "

---

u That is, *Aramaic*   v Gk *the Nazorean*

Paul and the Roman Tribune

22 Up to this point they listened to him, but then they shouted, "Away with such a fellow from the earth! For he should not be allowed to live." 23 And while they were shouting, throwing off their cloaks, and tossing dust into the air, 24 the tribune directed that Paul was to be brought into the barracks, and ordered him to be examined by flogging, to find out the reason for this outcry against him. 25 But when they had tied him up with thongs,ʷ Paul said to the centurion who was standing by, "Is it legal for you to flog a Roman citizen who is uncondemned?" 26 When the centurion heard that, he went to the tribune and said to him, "What are you about to do? This person is a Roman citizen." 27 The tribune came and asked Paul, "Tell me, are you a Roman citizen?" And he said, "Yes." 28 The tribune answered, "It cost me a large sum of money to get my citizenship." Paul said, "But I was born a citizen." 29 Immediately those who were about to examine him drew back from him; and the tribune also was afraid, for he realized that Paul was a Roman citizen and that he had bound him.

Paul before the Council

30 Since the tribune wanted to find out what Paul was being accused of by the Jews, the next day he released him and ordered the chief priests and the entire council to meet. He brought Paul down and had him stand before them.

23 While Paul was looking intently at the council he said, "Friends, up to this day I have lived my life with a clear conscience before God." 2 Then the high priest Ananias ordered those standing near him to strike him on the mouth. 3 At this Paul said to him, "God will strike you, you whitewashed wall! Are you sitting there to judge me according to the law, and yet in violation of the law you order me to be struck?" 4 Those standing nearby said, "Do you dare to insult God's high priest?" 5 And Paul said, "I did not realize, friends, that he was high priest; for it is written, 'You shall not speak evil of a leader of your people.'"

6 When Paul noticed that some were Sadducees and others were Pharisees, he called out in the council, "Friends, I am a Pharisee, a son of Pharisees. I am on trial concerning the hope of the resurrectionˣ of the dead." 7 When he said this, a dissension began between the Pharisees and the Sadducees, and the assembly was divided. 8 (The Sadducees say that there is no resurrection, or angel, or spirit; but the Pharisees acknowledge all three.) 9 Then a great clamor arose, and certain scribes of the Pharisees' group stood up and contended, "We find nothing wrong with this man. What if a spirit or an angel has spoken to him?" 10 When the dissension became violent, the tribune, fearing that they would tear Paul to pieces, ordered the soldiers to go down, take him by force, and bring him into the barracks.

---

w Or *up for the lashes*   x Gk *concerning hope and resurrection*

11 That night the Lord stood near him and said, "Keep up your courage! For just as you have testified for me in Jerusalem, so you must bear witness also in Rome."

The Plot to Kill Paul

12 In the morning the Jews joined in a conspiracy and bound themselves by an oath neither to eat nor drink until they had killed Paul. 13 There were more than forty who joined in this conspiracy. 14 They went to the chief priests and elders and said, "We have strictly bound ourselves by an oath to taste no food until we have killed Paul. 15 Now then, you and the council must notify the tribune to bring him down to you, on the pretext that you want to make a more thorough examination of his case. And we are ready to do away with him before he arrives."

16 Now the son of Paul's sister heard about the ambush; so he went and gained entrance to the barracks and told Paul. 17 Paul called one of the centurions and said, "Take this young man to the tribune, for he has something to report to him." 18 So the centurion took Paul's nephew, brought him to the tribune, and said, "The prisoner Paul called me and asked me to bring this young man to you; he has something to tell you." 19 The tribune took him by the hand, drew him aside privately, and asked, "What is it that you have to report to me?" 20 He answered, "The Jews have agreed to ask you to bring Paul down to the council tomorrow, as though they were going to inquire more thoroughly into his case. 21 But do not be persuaded by them, for more than forty of their men are lying in ambush for him. They have bound themselves by an oath neither to eat nor drink until they kill him. They are ready now and are waiting for your consent." 22 So the tribune dismissed the young man, commanding him, "Tell no one that you have informed me of this."

Paul Sent to Felix the Governor

23 Then he summoned two of the centurions and said, "Get ready to leave by nine o'clock tonight for Caesarea with two hundred soldiers, seventy cavalry, and two hundred guards. 24 Also provide mounts for Paul to ride, and take him safely to Felix the governor." 25 He wrote a letter to this effect:

26 "Claudius Lysias to his Excellency the governor Felix, greetings. 27 This man was seized by the Jews and was about to be killed by them, but when I had learned that he was a Roman citizen, I came with the guard and rescued him. 28 Since I wanted to know the charge for which they accused him, I had him brought to their council. 29 I found that he was accused concerning questions of their law, but was charged with nothing deserving death or imprisonment. 30 When I was informed that there would be a plot against the man, I sent him to you at once, ordering his accusers also to state before you what they have against him.y"

---

y Other ancient authorities add *Farewell*

31 So the soldiers, according to their instructions, took Paul and brought him during the night to Antipatris. [32]The next day they let the cavalry go on with him, while they returned to the barracks. [33]When they came to Caesarea and delivered the letter to the governor, they presented Paul also before him. [34]On reading the letter, the governor asked what province Paul belonged to, and when he learned that he was from Cilicia, [35]he said, "I will give you a hearing when your accusers arrive." Then the governor ordered that Paul be kept under guard in Herod's headquarters.[z]

Paul before Felix at Caesarea

24 Five days later the high priest Ananias came down with some elders and an attorney, a certain Tertullus, and they reported their case against Paul to the governor. [2]When Paul had been summoned, Tertullus began to accuse him, saying:

"Your Excellency,[a] because of you we have long enjoyed peace, and reforms have been made for this people because of your foresight. [3]We welcome this in every way and everywhere with utmost gratitude. [4]But, to detain you no further, I beg you to hear us briefly with your customary graciousness. [5]We have, in fact, found this person to be dangerous, an agitator among all the Jews throughout the world, and a ringleader of the sect of the Nazarenes.[b] [6]He even tried to profane the temple, and so we seized him.[c] [8]By examining him yourself you will be able to learn from him concerning everything of which we accuse him."

9 The Jews also joined in the charge by asserting that all this was true.

Paul's Defense before Felix

10 When the governor motioned to him to speak, Paul replied:

"I cheerfully make my defense, knowing that for many years you have been a judge over this nation. [11]As you can find out, it is not more than twelve days since I went up to worship in Jerusalem. [12]They did not find me disputing with anyone in the temple or stirring up a crowd either in the synagogues or throughout the city. [13]Neither can they prove to you the charge that they now bring against me. [14]But this I admit to you, that according to the Way, which they call a sect, I worship the God of our ancestors, believing everything laid down according to the law or written in the prophets. [15]I have a hope in God—a hope that they themselves also accept—that there will be a resurrection of both[d] the righteous and the unrighteous. [16]Therefore I do my best always to have a clear conscience toward God and all people. [17]Now after some years I came to bring alms to my nation and to offer sacrifices. [18]While I was doing

---

z Gk *praetorium*   a Gk lacks *Your Excellency*   b Gk *Nazoreans*
c Other ancient authorities add *and we would have judged him according to our law. 7But the chief captain Lysias came and with great violence took him out of our hands, 8commanding his accusers to come before you.*   d Other ancient authorities read *of the dead, both of*

this, they found me in the temple, completing the rite of purification, without any crowd or disturbance. 19 But there were some Jews from Asia—they ought to be here before you to make an accusation, if they have anything against me. 20 Or let these people here tell what crime they had found when I stood before the council, 21 unless it was this one sentence that I called out while standing before them, 'It is about the resurrection of the dead that I am on trial before you today.' "

22 But Felix, who was rather well informed about the Way, adjourned the hearing with the comment, "When Lysias the tribune comes down, I will decide your case." 23 Then he ordered the centurion to keep Paul in custody, but to let him have some liberty and not to prevent any of his friends from taking care of his needs.

Paul Held in Custody

24 Some days later when Felix came with his wife Drusilla, who was Jewish, he sent for Paul and heard him speak concerning faith in Christ Jesus. 25 And as Paul discussed justice, self-control, and the coming judgment, Felix became frightened and said, "Go away for the present; when I have an opportunity, I will send for you." 26 At the same time he hoped that money would be given him by Paul, and for that reason he used to send for him very often and converse with him.

27 After two years had passed, Felix was succeeded by Porcius Festus; and since he wanted to grant the Jews a favor, Felix left Paul in prison.

Paul Appeals to the Emperor

25 Three days after Festus had arrived in the province, he went up from Caesarea to Jerusalem 2 where the chief priests and the leaders of the Jews gave him a report against Paul. They appealed to him 3 and requested, as a favor to them against Paul, to have him transferred to Jerusalem. They were, in fact, planning an ambush to kill him along the way. 4 Festus replied that Paul was being kept at Caesarea, and that he himself intended to go there shortly. 5 "So," he said, "let those of you who have the authority come down with me, and if there is anything wrong about the man, let them accuse him."

6 After Festus had stayed among them not more than eight or ten days, he went down to Caesarea; the next day he took his seat on the tribunal and ordered Paul to be brought. 7 When he arrived, the Jews who had gone down from Jerusalem surrounded him, bringing many serious charges against him, which they could not prove. 8 Paul said in his defense, "I have in no way committed an offense against the law of the Jews, or against the temple, or against the emperor." 9 But Festus, wishing to do the Jews a favor, asked Paul, "Do you wish to go up to Jerusalem and be tried there before me on these charges?" 10 Paul said, "I am appealing to the emperor's tribunal; this is where I should be tried. I have done no wrong to the Jews, as you very well know. 11 Now if I am in the wrong and have committed something for which I deserve

to die, I am not trying to escape death; but if there is nothing to their charges against me, no one can turn me over to them. I appeal to the emperor." 12 Then Festus, after he had conferred with the council, replied, "You have appealed to the emperor; to the emperor you will go."

Festus Consults King Agrippa

13 After several days had passed, King Agrippa and Bernice arrived at Caesarea to welcome Festus. 14 Since they were staying there several days, Festus laid Paul's case before the king, saying, "There is a man here who was left in prison by Felix. 15 When I was in Jerusalem, the chief priests and the elders of the Jews informed me about him and asked for a sentence against him. 16 I told them that it was not the custom of the Romans to hand over anyone before the accused had met the accusers face to face and had been given an opportunity to make a defense against the charge. 17 So when they met here, I lost no time, but on the next day took my seat on the tribunal and ordered the man to be brought. 18 When the accusers stood up, they did not charge him with any of the crimes^e that I was expecting. 19 Instead they had certain points of disagreement with him about their own religion and about a certain Jesus, who had died, but whom Paul asserted to be alive. 20 Since I was at a loss how to investigate these questions, I asked whether he wished to go to Jerusalem and be tried there on these charges.^f 21 But when Paul had appealed to be kept in custody for the decision of his Imperial Majesty, I ordered him to be held until I could send him to the emperor." 22 Agrippa said to Festus, "I would like to hear this person myself." "Tomorrow," he said, "you will hear him."

Paul Brought before Agrippa

23 So on the next day Agrippa and Bernice came with great pomp, and they entered the audience hall with the military tribunes and the prominent men of the city. Then Festus gave the order and Paul was brought in. 24 And Festus said, "King Agrippa and all here present with us, you see this one about whom the whole Jewish community petitioned me, both in Jerusalem and here, shouting that he ought not to live any longer. 25 But I found that he had done nothing deserving death; and when he appealed to his Imperial Majesty, I decided to send him. 26 But I have nothing definite to write to our sovereign about him. Therefore I have brought him before all of you, and especially before you, King Agrippa, so that, after we have examined him, I may have something to write— 27 for it seems to me unreasonable to send a prisoner without indicating the charges against him."

---

e Other ancient authorities read *with anything*   f Gk *on them*

Paul Defends Himself before Agrippa

26 Agrippa said to Paul, "You have permission to speak for yourself." Then Paul stretched out his hand and began to defend himself:

2 "I consider myself fortunate that it is before you, King Agrippa, I am to make my defense today against all the accusations of the Jews, 3 because you are especially familiar with all the customs and controversies of the Jews; therefore I beg of you to listen to me patiently.

4 "All the Jews know my way of life from my youth, a life spent from the beginning among my own people and in Jerusalem. 5 They have known for a long time, if they are willing to testify, that I have belonged to the strictest sect of our religion and lived as a Pharisee. 6 And now I stand here on trial on account of my hope in the promise made by God to our ancestors, 7 a promise that our twelve tribes hope to attain, as they earnestly worship day and night. It is for this hope, your Excellency, that I am accused by Jews! 8 Why is it thought incredible by any of you that God raises the dead?

9 "Indeed, I myself was convinced that I ought to do many things against the name of Jesus of Nazareth.9 10 And that is what I did in Jerusalem; with authority received from the chief priests, I not only locked up many of the saints in prison, but I also cast my vote against them when they were being condemned to death. 11 By punishing them often in all the synagogues I tried to force them to blaspheme; and since I was so furiously enraged at them, I pursued them even to foreign cities.

Paul Tells of His Conversion

12 "With this in mind, I was traveling to Damascus with the authority and commission of the chief priests, 13 when at midday along the road, your Excellency, I saw a light from heaven, brighter than the sun, shining around me and my companions. 14 When we had all fallen to the ground, I heard a voice saying to me in the Hebrew^h language, 'Saul, Saul, why are you persecuting me? It hurts you to kick against the goads.' 15 I asked, 'Who are you, Lord?' The Lord answered, 'I am Jesus whom you are persecuting. 16 But get up and stand on your feet; for I have appeared to you for this purpose, to appoint you to serve and testify to the things in which you have seen me^i and to those in which I will appear to you. 17 I will rescue you from your people and from the Gentiles—to whom I am sending you 18 to open their eyes so that they may turn from no light to light and from the power of Satan to God, so that they may receive forgiveness of sins and a place among those who are sanctified by faith in me.'

---

g Gk *the Nazorean*   h That is, *Aramaic*
i Other ancient authorities read *the things that you have seen*

Paul Tells of His Preaching

19 "After that, King Agrippa, I was not disobedient to the heavenly vision, 20 but declared first to those in Damascus, then in Jerusalem and throughout the countryside of Judea, and also to the Gentiles, that they should repent and turn to God and do deeds consistent with repentance. 21 For this reason the Jews seized me in the temple and tried to kill me. 22 To this day I have had help from God, and so I stand here, testifying to both small and great, saying nothing but what the prophets and Moses said would take place: 23 that the Messiah[j] must suffer, and by being the first to rise from the dead, would proclaim light both to our people and to the Gentiles."

Paul Appeals to Agrippa to Believe

24 While Paul was making this defense, Festus exclaimed, "You are out of your mind, Paul! Too much learning is driving you insane!" 25 But Paul said, "I am not out of my mind, most excellent Festus, but I am speaking the sober truth. 26 Indeed the king knows about these things, and to him I speak freely; for I am certain that none of these things has escaped his notice, for this was not done in a corner. 27 King Agrippa, do you believe the prophets? I know that you believe." 28 Agrippa said to Paul, "Are you so quickly persuading me to become a Christian?"[k] 29 Paul replied, "Whether quickly or not, I pray to God that not only you but also all who are listening to me today might become such as I am—except for these chains."

30 Then the king got up, and with him the governor and Bernice and those who had been seated with them; 31 and as they were leaving, they said to one another, "This man is doing nothing to deserve death or imprisonment." 32 Agrippa said to Festus, "This man could have been set free if he had not appealed to the emperor."

Paul Sails for Rome

27 When it was decided that we were to sail for Italy, Paul and some other prisoners were transferred to a centurion of the Augustan Cohort, named Julius. 2 Embarking on a ship of Adramyttium that was about to set sail to the ports along the coast of Asia, we put to sea, accompanied by Aristarchus, a Macedonian from Thessalonica. 3 The next day we put in at Sidon; and Julius treated Paul kindly, and allowed him to go to his friends to be cared for. 4 Putting out to sea from there, we sailed under the lee of Cyprus, because the winds were against us. 5 After we had sailed across the sea that is off Cilicia and Pamphylia, we came to Myra in Lycia. 6 There the centurion found an Alexandrian ship bound for Italy and put us on board. 7 We sailed slowly for a number of days and arrived with difficulty off Cnidus, and as the wind was

---

j Or the Christ   k Or Quickly you will persuade me to play the Christian

against us, we sailed under the lee of Crete off Salmone. [8] Sailing past it with difficulty, we came to a place called Fair Havens, near the city of Lasea.

9 Since much time had been lost and sailing was now dangerous, because even the Fast had already gone by, Paul advised them, [10] saying, "Sirs, I can see that the voyage will be with danger and much heavy loss, not only of the cargo and the ship, but also of our lives." [11] But the centurion paid more attention to the pilot and to the owner of the ship than to what Paul said. [12] Since the harbor was not suitable for spending the winter, the majority was in favor of putting to sea from there, on the chance that somehow they could reach Phoenix, where they could spend the winter. It was a harbor of Crete, facing southwest and northwest.

The Storm at Sea

13 When a moderate south wind began to blow, they thought they could achieve their purpose; so they weighed anchor and began to sail past Crete, close to the shore. [14] But soon a violent wind, called the northeaster, rushed down from Crete.[l] [15] Since the ship was caught and could not be turned head-on into the wind, we gave way to it and were driven. [16] By running under the lee of a small island called Cauda[m] we were scarcely able to get the ship's boat under control. [17] After hoisting it up they took measures[n] to undergird the ship; then, fearing that they would run on the Syrtis, they lowered the sea anchor and so were driven. [18] We were being pounded by the storm so violently that on the next day they began to throw the cargo overboard, [19] and on the third day with their own hands they threw the ship's tackle overboard. [20] When neither sun nor stars appeared for many days, and no small tempest raged, all hope of our being saved was at last abandoned.

21 Since they had been without food for a long time, Paul then stood up among them and said to them, "You should have listened to me and not have set sail from Crete and thereby avoided this damage and loss. [22] I urge you now to keep up your courage, for there will be no loss of life among you, but only of the ship. [23] For last night an angel of the God to whom I belong and whom I worship stood by me [24] and said, 'Do not be afraid, Paul; you must stand before the emperor; and indeed, God has granted safety to all those who are sailing with you.' [25] So keep up your courage, all of you, for I have faith in God that it will be exactly as I have been told. [26] But we will have to run aground on some island."

27 When the fourteenth night had come, as we were drifting across the sea of Adria, about midnight the sailors suspected that they were nearing land. [28] So they took soundings and found twenty fathoms; a little farther on they took soundings again and found fifteen fathoms. [29] Fearing that we might run on the rocks, they let down four anchors from the stern and prayed for day to come. [30] But when the sailors tried to escape from the ship and had lowered the boat

---

l Gk it   m Other ancient authorities read *Clauda*   n Gk *helps*

into the sea, on the pretext of putting out anchors from the bow, 31 Paul said to the centurion and the soldiers, "Unless these people stay in the ship, you cannot be saved." 32 Then the soldiers cut away the ropes of the boat and set it adrift.

33 Just before daybreak, Paul urged all of them to take some food, saying, "Today is the fourteenth day that you have been in suspense and remaining without food, having eaten nothing. 34 Therefore I urge you to take some food, for it will help you survive; for none of you will lose a hair from your heads." 35 Having said this, Paul took bread; and giving thanks to God in the presence of all, he broke it and began to eat. 36 Then all of them were encouraged and took food for themselves. 37 (We were in all two hundred seventy-six° persons in the ship.) 38 After they had satisfied their hunger, they lightened the ship by throwing the wheat into the sea.

The Shipwreck

39 In the morning they did not recognize the land, but they noticed a bay with a beach, on which they planned to run the ship ashore, if they could. 40 So they cast off the anchors and left them in the sea. At the same time they loosened the ropes that tied the steering-oars; then hoisting the foresail to the wind, they made for the beach. 41 But striking a reef,ᵖ they ran the ship aground; the bow stuck and remained immovable, but the stern was being broken up by the force of the waves. 42 The soldiers' plan was to kill the prisoners, so that none might swim away and escape; 43 but the centurion, wishing to save Paul, kept them from carrying out their plan. He ordered those who could swim to jump overboard first and make for the land, 44 and the rest to follow, some on planks and others on pieces of the ship. And so it was that all were brought safely to land.

Paul on the Island of Malta

28 After we had reached safety, we then learned that the island was called Malta. 2 The natives showed us unusual kindness. Since it had begun to rain and was cold, they kindled a fire and welcomed all of us around it. 3 Paul had gathered a bundle of brushwood and was putting it on the fire, when a snake, driven out by the heat, fastened itself on his hand. 4 When the natives saw the creature hanging from his hand, they said to one another, "This person must be a murderer; though he has escaped from the sea, justice has not allowed him to live." 5 He, however, shook off the creature into the fire and suffered no harm. 6 They were expecting him to swell up or drop dead, but after they had waited a long time and saw that nothing unusual had happened to him, they changed their minds and began to say that he was a god.

7 Now in the neighborhood of that place were lands belonging to the leading man of the island, named Publius, who received us and entertained us

---

o Other ancient authorities read *seventy-six*; others, *about seventy-six*   p Gk *place of two seas* hospitably for three days. [8]It so happened that the father of Publius lay sick in bed with fever and dysentery. Paul visited him and cured him by praying and putting his hands on him. [9]After this happened, the rest of the people on the island who had diseases also came and were cured. [10]They bestowed many honors on us, and when we were about to sail, they put on board all the provisions we needed.

Paul Arrives at Rome

11 Three months later we set sail on a ship that had wintered at the island, an Alexandrian ship with the Twin Brothers as its figurehead. [12]We put in at Syracuse and stayed there for three days; [13]then we weighed anchor and came to Rhegium. After one day there a south wind sprang up, and on the second day we came to Puteoli. [14]There we found believers and were invited to stay with them for seven days. And so we came to Rome. [15]The believers from there, when they heard of us, came as far as the Forum of Appius and Three Taverns to meet us. On seeing them, Paul thanked God and took courage.

16 When we came into Rome, Paul was allowed to live by himself, with the soldier who was guarding him.

Paul and Jewish Leaders in Rome

17 Three days later he called together the local leaders of the Jews. When they had assembled, he said to them, "Friends, though I had done nothing against our people or the customs of our ancestors, yet I was arrested in Jerusalem and handed over to the Romans. [18]When they had examined me, the Romans wanted to release me, because there was no reason for the death penalty in my case. [19]But when the Jews objected, I was compelled to appeal to the emperor—even though I had no charge to bring against my nation. [20]For this reason therefore I have asked to see you and speak with you,[q] since it is for the sake of the hope of Israel that I am bound with this chain." [21]They replied, "We have received no letters from Judea about you, and none of the believers coming here has reported or spoken anything evil about you. [22]But we would like to hear from you what you think, for with regard to this sect we know that everywhere it is spoken against."

Paul Preaches in Rome

23 After they had set a day to meet with him, they came to him at his lodgings in great numbers. From morning until evening he explained the matter to them, testifying to the dominion of God and trying to convince them about Jesus both from the law of Moses and from the prophets. [24]Some were convinced by what he had said, while others refused to believe. [25]So they disagreed with each other; and as they were leaving, Paul made one further

q Or *I have asked you to see me and speak with me*

statement: "The Holy Spirit was right in saying to your ancestors through the prophet Isaiah,

26   'Go to this people and say,
              You will indeed listen, but never understand,
                and you will indeed look, but never perceive.

27   For this people's heart has grown dull,
                and they have covered their ears,
                    and they have shut their eyes;
                      so that they might not look with their eyes,
                and listen with their ears,
          and understand with their heart and turn—
            and I would heal them.'

28 Let it be known to you then that this salvation of God has been sent to the Gentiles; they will listen."[r]

30 Paul lived there two whole years at his own expense[s] and welcomed all who came to him, 31 proclaiming the dominion of God and teaching about the Lord Jesus Christ with all boldness and without hindrance.

---

r Other ancient authorities add verse 29, *And when he had said these words, the Jews departed, arguing vigorously among themselves*   s Or *in his own hired dwelling*

The Letter of Paul to the Romans

Salutation

1 Paul, a servant of Jesus Christ, called to be an apostle, set apart for the gospel of God, ²which was promised by God beforehand through the prophets in the holy scriptures, ³the gospel concerning the Child of God, who was descended from David according to the flesh ⁴and was declared to be Child of God with power according to the spirit[a] of holiness by resurrection from the dead, Jesus Christ our Lord. ⁵Through Christ we have received grace and apostleship to bring about the obedience of faith among all the Gentiles for the sake of Christ's name, ⁶including yourselves who are called to belong to Jesus Christ,

7 To all God's beloved in Rome, who are called to be saints:

Grace to you and peace from God our Father-Mother and from the Lord Jesus Christ.

Prayer of Thanksgiving

8 First, I thank my God through Jesus Christ for all of you, because your faith is proclaimed throughout the world. ⁹For God, whom I serve with my spirit by announcing the gospel[b] of God's Child, is my witness that without ceasing I remember you always in my prayers, ¹⁰asking that by God's will I may somehow at last succeed in coming to you. ¹¹For I am longing to see you so that I may share with you some spiritual gift to strengthen you— ¹²or rather so that we may be mutually encouraged by each other's faith, both yours and mine. ¹³I want you to know, brothers and sisters, that I have often intended to come to you (but thus far have been prevented), in order that I may reap some harvest among you as I have among the rest of the Gentiles. ¹⁴I am a debtor

---

a Or *Spirit*   b Gk *my spirit in the gospel*

both to Greeks and to barbarians, both to the wise and to the foolish [15]—hence my eagerness to proclaim the gospel to you also who are in Rome.

The Power of the Gospel

16 For I am not ashamed of the gospel; it is the power of God for salvation to everyone who has faith, to the Jew first and also to the Greek. [17]For in it the righteousness of God is revealed through faith for faith; as it is written, "The one who is righteous will live by faith."[c]

The Guilt of Humankind

18 For the wrath of God is revealed from heaven against all ungodliness and wickedness of those who by their wickedness suppress the truth. [19]For what can be known about God is plain to them, because God has shown it to them. [20]Ever since the creation of the world God's eternal power and divine nature, invisible though they are, have been understood and seen through the things God has made. So they are without excuse; [21]for though they knew God, they did not honor God as God or give thanks to God, but they became futile in their thinking, and their senseless minds were further confused. [22]Claiming to be wise, they became fools; [23]and they exchanged the glory of the immortal God for images resembling a mortal human being or birds or four-footed animals or reptiles.

24 Therefore God gave them up in the lusts of their hearts to impurity, to the degrading of their bodies among themselves, [25]because they exchanged the truth about God for a lie and worshiped and served the creature rather than the Creator, who is blessed forever! Amen.

26 For this reason God gave them up to degrading passions. Their women exchanged natural intercourse for unnatural, [27]and in the same way also the men, giving up natural intercourse with women, were consumed with passion for one another. Men committed shameless acts with men and received in their own persons the due penalty for their error.

28 And since they did not see fit to acknowledge God, God gave them up to a debased mind and to things that should not be done. [29]They were filled with every kind of wickedness, evil, covetousness, malice. Full of envy, murder, strife, deceit, craftiness, they are gossips, [30]slanderers, God-haters,[d] insolent, haughty, boastful, inventors of evil, rebellious toward parents, [31]foolish, faithless, heartless, ruthless. [32]They know God's decree, that those who practice such things deserve to die—yet they not only do them but even applaud others who practice them.

---

c Or *The one who is righteous through faith will live*   d Or *God-hated*

The Righteous Judgment of God

2 Therefore you have no excuse, whoever you are, when you judge others; for in passing judgment on another you condemn yourself, because you, the judge, are doing the very same things. [2] You say,[e] "We know that God's judgment on those who do such things is in accordance with truth." [3] Do you imagine, whoever you are, that when you judge those who do such things and yet do them yourself, you will escape the judgment of God? [4] Or do you despise the riches of God's kindness and forbearance and patience? Do you not realize that God's kindness is meant to lead you to repentance? [5] But by your hard and impenitent heart you are storing up wrath for yourself on the day of wrath, when God's righteous judgment will be revealed. [6] For God will repay according to each one's deeds: [7] for those who by patiently doing good seek for glory and honor and immortality, there will be eternal life; [8] while for those who are self-seeking and who obey not the truth but wickedness, there will be wrath and fury. [9] There will be anguish and distress for everyone who does evil, the Jew first and also the Greek, [10] but glory and honor and peace for everyone who does good, the Jew first and also the Greek. [11] For God shows no partiality.

[12] All who have sinned apart from the law will also perish apart from the law, and all who have sinned under the law will be judged by the law. [13] For it is not the hearers of the law who are righteous in God's sight, but the doers of the law who will be justified. [14] When Gentiles, who do not possess the law, do instinctively what the law requires, these, though not having the law, are a law to themselves. [15] They show that what the law requires is written on their hearts, to which their own conscience also bears witness; and their conflicting thoughts will accuse or perhaps excuse them [16] on the day when, according to my gospel, God, through Jesus Christ, will judge the secret thoughts of all.

The Jews and the Law

[17] But if you call yourself a Jew and rely on the law and boast of your relation to God [18] and know God's will and determine what is best because you are instructed in the law, [19] and if you are sure that you are a guide to those who are blind, a light to those who need it, [20] a corrector of the foolish, a teacher of children, having in the law the embodiment of knowledge and truth, [21] you, then, that teach others, will you not teach yourself? While you preach against stealing, do you steal? [22] You that forbid adultery, do you commit adultery? You that abhor idols, do you rob temples? [23] You that boast in the law, do you dishonor God by breaking the law? [24] For, as it is written, "The name of God is blasphemed among the Gentiles because of you."

[25] Circumcision indeed is of value if you obey the law; but if you break the law, your circumcision has become uncircumcision. [26] So, if those who are

---

e Gk lacks *You say*

uncircumcised keep the requirements of the law, will not their uncircumcision be regarded as circumcision? [27] Then those who are physically uncircumcised but keep the law will condemn you that have the written code and circumcision but break the law. [28] For a person is not a Jew who is one outwardly, nor is true circumcision something external and physical. [29] Rather, a person is a Jew who is one inwardly, and real circumcision is a matter of the heart—it is spiritual and not literal. Such a person receives praise not from others but from God.

3 Then what advantage has the Jew? Or what is the value of circumcision? [2] Much, in every way. For in the first place the Jews were entrusted with the oracles of God. [3] What if some were unfaithful? Will their faithlessness nullify the faithfulness of God? [4] By no means! Although everyone is a liar, let God be proved true, as it is written,

> "So that you may be justified in your words,
>   and prevail in your judging."[f]

[5] But if our injustice serves to confirm the justice of God, what should we say? That God is unjust to inflict wrath on us? (I speak in a human way.) [6] By no means! For then how could God judge the world? [7] But if through my falsehood God's truthfulness abounds to God's glory, why am I still being condemned as a sinner? [8] And why not say (as some people slander us by saying that we say), "Let us do evil so that good may come"? Their condemnation is deserved!

None Is Righteous

[9] What then? Are we any better off?[g] No, not at all; for we have already charged that all, both Jews and Greeks, are under the power of sin, [10] as it is written:

> "There is no one who is righteous, not even one;
[11]   there is no one who has understanding,
>   there is no one who seeks God.
[12]   All have turned aside, together they have become
>   worthless;
>   there is no one who shows kindness,
>   there is not even one."
[13]   "Their throats are opened graves;
>   they use their tongues to deceive."
>   "The venom of vipers is under their lips."
[14]   "Their mouths are full of cursing and bitterness."
[15]   "Their feet are swift to shed blood;
[16]   ruin and misery are in their paths,

---

f Gk *when you are being judged*   g Or *at any disadvantage?*

17   and the way of peace they have not known."

18   "There is no awe of God before their eyes."

19 Now we know that whatever the law says, it speaks to those who are under the law, so that every mouth may be silenced, and the whole world may be held accountable to God. 20 For "no human being will be justified in God's sight" by deeds prescribed by the law, for through the law comes the knowledge of sin.

Righteousness through Faith

21 But now, apart from law, the righteousness of God has been disclosed, and is attested by the law and the prophets, 22 the righteousness of God through faith in Jesus Christ[h] for all who believe. For there is no distinction, 23 since all have sinned and fall short of the glory of God; 24 they are now justified by God's grace as a gift, through the redemption that is in Christ Jesus, 25 whom God put forward as a blood sacrifice of atonement,[i] effective through faith. This was to show God's righteousness, because in divine forbearance God had passed over the sins previously committed; 26 it was to prove at the present time that God is indeed righteous and justifies the one who has faith in Jesus.[j]

27 Then what becomes of boasting? It is excluded. By what law? By that of works? No, but by the law of faith. 28 For we hold that a person is justified by faith apart from works prescribed by the law. 29 Or is God the God of Jews only? Is God not the God of Gentiles also? Yes, of Gentiles also, 30 since God is one, and will justify those under law on the ground of faith and those not under the law through that same faith. 31 Do we then overthrow the law by this faith? By no means! On the contrary, we uphold the law.

The Example of Abraham

4 What then are we to say was gained by[k] Abraham, our ancestor according to the flesh? 2 For if Abraham was justified by works, he has something to boast about, but not before God. 3 For what does the scripture say? "Abraham believed God, and it was reckoned to him as righteousness." 4 Now to someone who works, wages are not reckoned as a gift but as something due. 5 But to someone who without works trusts the one who justifies the ungodly, such faith is reckoned as righteousness. 6 So also David speaks of the blessedness of those to whom God reckons righteousness apart from works:

7   "Blessed are those whose iniquities are forgiven,
         and whose sins are covered;

8   blessed is the one against whom God will not reckon
         sin."

---

h Or *through the faith of Jesus Christ*   i Or *a place of atonement*
j Or *who has the faith of Jesus*   k Other ancient authorities read *say about*

9 Is this blessedness, then, pronounced only on the circumcised, or also on the uncircumcised? We say, "Faith was reckoned to Abraham as righteousness." 10 How then was it reckoned to him? Was it before or after he had been circumcised? It was not after, but before. 11 Abraham received the sign of circumcision as a seal of the righteousness that he had by faith while he was still uncircumcised. The purpose was to make Abraham the ancestor of all who believe without being circumcised and who thus have righteousness reckoned to them, 12 and likewise the ancestor of the circumcised who are not only circumcised but who also follow the example of the faith that our ancestor Abraham had before circumcision.

God's Promise Realized through Faith

13 For the promise that they would inherit the world did not come to Abraham and Sarah or to their descendants through the law but through the righteousness of faith. 14 If it is the adherents of the law who are to be the heirs, faith is null and the promise is void. 15 For the law brings wrath; but where there is no law, neither is there violation.

16 For this reason it depends on faith, in order that the promise may rest on grace and be guaranteed to all their descendants, not only to the adherents of the law but also to those who share the faith of Abraham (who with Sarah is the ancestor of all of us, 17 as it is written, "I have made you the ancestor of many nations")—in the presence of the God in whom he believed, who gives life to the dead and calls into existence the things that do not exist. 18 Hoping against hope, Abraham believed that he would become "the ancestor of many nations," according to what was said, "So numerous shall your descendants be." 19 Abraham did not weaken in faith when he considered his own body, which was already[l] as good as dead (for he was about a hundred years old), or when he considered the infertility of Sarah's womb. 20 No distrust made him waver concerning the promise of God, but he grew strong in faith, giving glory to God, 21 being fully convinced that God was able to do what God had promised. 22 Therefore Abraham's faith "was reckoned to him as righteousness." 23 Now the words, "it was reckoned to him," were written not for Abraham's sake alone, 24 but for ours also. It will be reckoned to us who believe in the one who raised Jesus our Lord from the dead, 25 who was handed over to death for our trespasses and was raised for our justification.

Results of Justification

5 Therefore, since we are justified by faith, we[m] have peace with God through our Lord Jesus Christ, 2 through whom we have obtained access[n] to this grace in which we stand; and we[o] boast in our hope of sharing the glory of God. 3 And not only that, but we[o] also boast in our sufferings,

---

l Other ancient authorities lack *already*   m Other ancient authorities read *let us*
n Other ancient authorities add *by faith*   o Or *let us*

knowing that suffering produces endurance, 4 and endurance produces character,
and character produces hope, 5 and hope does not disappoint us, because God's
love has been poured into our hearts through the Holy Spirit that has been
given to us.
6 For while we were still weak, at the right time Christ died for the
ungodly. 7 Indeed, rarely will anyone die for a righteous person—though
perhaps for a good person someone might actually dare to die. 8 But God
proves God's love for us in that while we still were sinners Christ died for us.
9 Much more surely then, now that we have been justified by the blood of
Christ, will we be saved through Christ from the wrath of God.[p] 10 For if while
we were enemies, we were reconciled to God through the death of Christ,
much more surely, having been reconciled, will we be saved by Christ's life.
11 But more than that, we even boast in God through our Lord Jesus Christ,
through whom we have now received reconciliation.

Adam and Christ

12 Therefore, just as sin came into the world through one human being, and
death came through sin, and so death spread to all because all have sinned—
13 sin was indeed in the world before the law, but sin is not reckoned when
there is no law. 14 Yet death exercised dominion from Adam to Moses, even
over those whose sins were not like the transgression of Adam, who is a type
of the one who was to come.
15 But the free gift is not like the trespass. For if the many died through
the one person's trespass, much more surely have the grace of God and the free
gift in the grace of the one person, Jesus Christ, abounded for the many. 16 And
the free gift is not like the effect of the one person's sin. For the judgment
following one trespass brought condemnation, but the free gift following many
trespasses brings justification. 17 If, because of the one person's trespass, death
exercised dominion through that one, much more surely will those who receive
the abundance of grace and the free gift of righteousness exercise dominion in
life through the one person, Jesus Christ.
18 Therefore just as one person's trespass led to condemnation for all, so
one person's act of righteousness leads to justification and life for all. 19 For just
as by the one person's disobedience the many were made sinners, so by the one
person's obedience the many will be made righteous. 20 But law came in, with
the result that the trespass multiplied; but where sin increased, grace abounded
all the more, 21 so that, just as sin exercised dominion in death, so grace might
also exercise dominion through justification[q] leading to eternal life through
Jesus Christ our Lord.

---

p Gk *the wrath* q Or *righteousness*

Dying and Rising with Christ

6 What then are we to say? Should we continue in sin in order that grace may abound? [2]By no means! How can we who died to sin go on living in it? [3]Do you not know that all of us who have been baptized into Christ Jesus were baptized into Christ's death? [4]Therefore we have been buried with Christ by baptism into death, so that, just as Christ was raised from the dead by the glory of the Father-Mother, so we too might walk in newness of life.

5 For if we have been united with Christ in a death like that of Christ, we will certainly be united with Christ in a resurrection like that of Christ. [6]We know that our old self was crucified with Christ so that the body of sin might be destroyed, and we might no longer be enslaved to sin. [7]For whoever has died is freed from sin. [8]But if we have died with Christ, we believe that we will also live with Christ. [9]We know that Christ, being raised from the dead, will never die again; death no longer has dominion over Christ. [10]The death Christ died, Christ died to sin, once for all; but the life Christ lives, Christ lives to God. [11]So you also must consider yourselves dead to sin and alive to God in Christ Jesus.

12 Therefore, do not let sin exercise dominion in your mortal bodies, to make you obey their passions. [13]No longer present your members to sin as instruments[r] of wickedness, but present yourselves to God as those who have been brought from death to life, and present your members to God as instruments[r] of righteousness. [14]For sin will have no dominion over you, since you are not under law but under grace.

Enslaved to Righteousness

15 What then? Should we sin because we are not under law but under grace? By no means! [16]Do you not know that if you present yourselves to anyone as obedient slaves, you are enslaved to the one whom you obey, either of sin, which leads to death, or of obedience, which leads to righteousness? [17]But thanks be to God that you, having once been enslaved to sin, have become obedient from the heart to the form of teaching to which you were entrusted, [18]and that you, having been set free from sin, have become enslaved to righteousness. [19]I am speaking in human terms because of your natural limitations.[s] For just as you once presented your members as enslaved to impurity and to greater and greater iniquity, so now present your members as enslaved to righteousness for sanctification.

20 When you were enslaved to sin, you were free in regard to righteousness. [21]So what advantage did you then get from the things of which you now are ashamed? The end of those things is death. [22]But now that you have been freed from sin and enslaved to God, the advantage you get is sanctification. The

---

r Or *weapons*   s Gk *the weakness of your flesh*

end is eternal life. 23 For the wages of sin is death, but the free gift of God is eternal life in Christ Jesus our Lord.

An Analogy from Marriage

7 Do you not know, brothers and sisters—I am speaking to those who know the law—that the law is binding on a person only during that person's lifetime? 2 Thus a married woman is bound by the law to her husband as long as he lives; but if her husband dies, she is discharged from the law concerning the husband. 3 Accordingly, she will be called an adulterer if she lives with another man while her husband is alive. But if her husband dies, she is free from that law, and if she marries another man, she is not an adulterer.

4 In the same way, my friends, you have died to the law through the body of Christ, so that you may belong to another, to the one who has been raised from the dead in order that we may bear fruit for God. 5 While we were living in the flesh, our sinful passions, aroused by the law, were at work in our members to bear fruit for death. 6 But now we are discharged from the law, dead to that which held us captive, so that we are not enslaved under the old written code but in the new life of the Spirit.

The Law and Sin

7 What then should we say? That the law is sin? By no means! Yet, if it had not been for the law, I would not have known sin. I would not have known what it is to covet if the law had not said, "You shall not covet." 8 But sin, seizing an opportunity in the commandment, produced in me all kinds of covetousness. Apart from the law sin lies dead. 9 I was once alive apart from the law, but when the commandment came, sin revived 10 and I died, and the very commandment that promised life proved to be death to me. 11 For sin, seizing an opportunity in the commandment, deceived me and through it killed me. 12 So the law is holy, and the commandment is holy and just and good.

13 Did what is good, then, bring death to me? By no means! It was sin, working death in me through what is good, in order that sin might be shown to be sin, and through the commandment might become sinful beyond measure.

The Inner Conflict

14 For we know that the law is spiritual; but I am of the flesh, sold under sin. 15 I do not understand my own actions. For I do not do what I want, but I do the very thing I hate. 16 Now if I do what I do not want, I agree that the law is good. 17 But in fact it is no longer I that do it, but sin that dwells within me. 18 For I know that nothing good dwells within me, that is, in my flesh. I can will what is right, but I cannot do it. 19 For I do not do the good I want, but the evil I do not want is what I do. 20 Now if I do what I do not want, it is no longer I that do it, but sin that dwells within me.

21 So I find it to be a law that when I want to do what is good, evil lies close at hand. 22 For I delight in the law of God in my inmost self, 23 but I see

in my members another law at war with the law of my mind, making me captive to the law of sin that dwells in my members. 24How miserable I am! Who will rescue me from this body of death? 25Thanks be to God through Jesus Christ our Lord!

So then, with my mind I am enslaved to the law of God, but with my flesh I am enslaved to the law of sin.

Life in the Spirit

8 There is therefore now no condemnation for those who are in Christ Jesus. 2For the law of the Spirit[t] of life in Christ Jesus has set you[u] free from the law of sin and of death. 3For God has done what the law, weakened by the flesh, could not do: by sending God's own Child in the likeness of sinful flesh, and to deal with sin,[v] God condemned sin in the flesh, 4so that the just requirement of the law might be fulfilled in us, who walk not according to the flesh but according to the Spirit.[t] 5For those who live according to the flesh set their minds on the things of the flesh, but those who live according to the Spirit[t] set their minds on the things of the Spirit.[t] 6To set the mind on the flesh is death, but to set the mind on the Spirit[t] is life and peace. 7For this reason the mind that is set on the flesh is hostile to God; it does not submit to God's law—indeed it cannot, 8and those who are in the flesh cannot please God.

9 But you are not in the flesh; you are in the Spirit,[t] since the Spirit of God dwells in you. Anyone who does not have the Spirit of Christ does not belong to Christ. 10But if Christ is in you, though the body is dead because of sin, the Spirit[t] is life because of righteousness. 11If the Spirit of the one who raised Jesus from the dead dwells in you, the one who raised Christ[w] from the dead will give life to your mortal bodies also through[x] the same Spirit that dwells in you.

12 So then, sisters and brothers, we are debtors, not to the flesh, to live according to the flesh— 13for if you live according to the flesh, you will die; but if by the Spirit you put to death the deeds of the body, you will live. 14For all who are led by the Spirit of God are children of God. 15For you did not receive a spirit of slavery to fall back into fear, but you have received a spirit of adoption. When we cry, "Abba! Father-Mother!" 16it is that very Spirit bearing witness[y] with our spirit that we are children of God, 17and if children, then heirs, heirs of God and joint heirs with Christ—if, in fact, we suffer with Christ so that we may also be glorified with Christ.

---

t Or *spirit*
u Here the Greek word *you* is singular number; other ancient authorities read *me* or *us*
v Or *and as a sin offering*
w Other ancient authorities read *the Christ* or *Christ Jesus* or *Jesus Christ*
x Other ancient authorities read *on account of*
y Or *15a spirit of adoption, by which we cry, "Abba! Father-Mother!" 16The Spirit itself bears witness*

Future Glory

18 I consider that the sufferings of this present time are not worth comparing with the glory about to be revealed to us. [19]For the creation waits with eager longing for the revealing of the children of God; [20]for the creation was subjected to futility, not of its own will but by the will of the one who subjected it, in hope [21]that the creation itself will be set free from its bondage to decay and will obtain the freedom of the glory of the children of God. [22]We know that the whole creation has been groaning in labor pains until now; [23]and not only the creation, but we ourselves, who have the first fruits of the Spirit, groan inwardly while we wait for adoption, the redemption of our bodies. [24]For in[z] hope we were saved. Now hope that is seen is not hope. For who hopes[a] for what is seen? [25]But if we hope for what we do not see, we wait for it with patience.

26 Likewise the Spirit helps us in our weakness; for we do not know how to pray as we ought, but that very Spirit intercedes[b] with sighs too deep for words. [27]And God, who searches the heart, knows what is the mind of the Spirit, because the Spirit intercedes for the saints according to the will of God.[c]

28 We know that all things work together for good[d] for those who love God, who are called according to God's purpose. [29]For those whom God foreknew were also predestined to be conformed to the image of God's Child, in order that Christ might be the firstborn within a large family. [30]And those whom God predestined God also called; and those whom God called God also justified; and those whom God justified God also glorified.

God's Love in Christ Jesus

31 What then are we to say about these things? If God is for us, who is against us? [32]Will not God, who did not withhold God's own Child, but gave up that Child for all of us, also give us everything else? [33]Who will bring any charge against God's elect? It is God who justifies. [34]Who is to condemn? It is Christ Jesus, who died, yes, who was raised, who is alongside of God, who indeed intercedes for us.[e] [35]Who will separate us from the love of Christ? Will hardship, or distress, or persecution, or famine, or nakedness, or peril, or sword? [36]As it is written,

> "For your sake we are being killed all day long;
> we are accounted as sheep to be slaughtered."

[37]No, in all these things we are more than conquerors through the one who loved us. [38]For I am convinced that neither death, nor life, nor angels, nor

---

z Or *by*   a Other ancient authorities read *awaits*   b Other ancient authorities add *for us*
c Gk *according to God*
d Other ancient authorities read God *makes all things work together for good*, or *in all things God works for good*   e Or *Is it Christ Jesus ... for us?*

rulers, nor things present, nor things to come, nor powers, ³⁹nor height, nor depth, nor anything else in all creation, will be able to separate us from the love of God in Christ Jesus our Lord.

God's Election of Israel

9 I am speaking the truth in Christ—I am not lying; my conscience confirms it by the Holy Spirit— ²I have great sorrow and unceasing anguish in my heart. ³For I could wish that I myself were accursed and cut off from Christ for the sake of my own people, my kindred according to the flesh. ⁴They are Israelites, and to them belong the adoption, the glory, the covenants, the giving of the law, the worship, and the promises; ⁵to them belong the ancestors in faith, and from them, according to the flesh, comes the Messiah,^f who is over all, God blessed forever.^g Amen.

6 It is not as though the word of God had failed. For not all Israelites truly belong to Israel, ⁷and not all of the children of Abraham and Sarah are their true descendants; but "It is through Isaac that descendants shall be named for you." ⁸This means that it is not the children of the flesh who are the children of God, but the children of the promise are counted as descendants. ⁹For this is what the promise said, "About this time I will return and Sarah shall have a son." ¹⁰Nor is that all; something similar happened to Rebecca when she had conceived children by one husband, our ancestor Isaac. ¹¹Even before they had been born or had done anything good or bad (so that God's purpose of election might continue, ¹²not by works but by God's call) she was told, "The elder shall serve the younger." ¹³As it is written,

> "I have loved Jacob,
>   but I have hated Esau."

14 What then are we to say? Is there injustice on God's part? By no means! ¹⁵For God says to Moses,

> "I will have mercy on whom I have mercy,
>   and I will have compassion on whom I have
>   compassion."

¹⁶So it depends not on human will or exertion, but on God who shows mercy. ¹⁷For the scripture says to Pharaoh, "I have raised you up for the very purpose of showing my power in you, so that my name may be proclaimed in all the earth." ¹⁸So then God has mercy on whomever God chooses, and God hardens the heart of whomever God chooses.

---

f Or *the Christ*

g Or *Messiah, who is God over all, blessed forever*; or *Messiah. May the one who is God over all be blessed forever*

God's Wrath and Mercy

19 You will say to me then, "Why then does God still find fault? For who can resist God's will?" 20 But who indeed are you, a human being, to argue with God? Will what is molded say to the one who molds it, "Why have you made me like this?" 21 Has the potter no right over the clay, to make out of the same lump one object for special use and another for ordinary use? 22 What if God, desiring to show God's wrath and to make known God's power, has endured with much patience the objects of wrath that are made for destruction; 23 and what if God has done so in order to make known the riches of God's glory for the objects of mercy, prepared beforehand for glory— 24 including us whom God has called, not from the Jews only but also from the Gentiles? 25 As indeed God says in Hosea,

> "Those who were not my people I will call 'my people,'
>   and the one who was not beloved I will call
>   'beloved.' "
26   "And in the very place where it was said to them, 'You
>   are not my people,'
>   there they shall be called children of the living God."

27 And Isaiah cries out concerning Israel, "Though the number of the children of Israel were like the sand of the sea, only a remnant of them will be saved; 28 for God will pronounce judgment on the earth quickly and decisively."[h] 29 And as Isaiah predicted,

> "If the God of hosts had not left survivors[i] to us,
>   we would have fared like Sodom
>   and been made like Gomorrah."

Israel's Unbelief

30 What then are we to say? Gentiles, who did not strive for righteousness, have attained it, that is, righteousness through faith; 31 but Israel, who did strive for the righteousness that is based on the law, did not succeed in fulfilling that law. 32 Why not? Because they did not strive for it on the basis of faith, but as if it were based on works. They have stumbled over the stumbling stone, 33 as it is written,

> "See, I am laying in Zion a stone that will make people
>   stumble, a rock that will make them fall,
>   and whoever trusts in it will not be put to shame."

---

h Other ancient authorities read *for he will finish his work and cut it short in righteousness, because the Lord will make the sentence shortened on the earth*   i Or *descendants*; Gk *seed*

10 Brothers and sisters, my heart's desire and prayer to God for them is that they may be saved. ²I can testify that they have a zeal for God, but it is not enlightened. ³For, being ignorant of the righteousness that comes from God, and seeking to establish their own, they have not submitted to God's righteousness. ⁴For Christ is the end of the law so that there may be righteousness for everyone who believes.

Salvation Is for All

5 Moses writes concerning the righteousness that comes from the law, that "the person who does these things will live by them." ⁶But the righteousness that comes from faith says, "Do not say in your heart, 'Who will ascend into heaven?' " (that is, to bring Christ down) ⁷"or 'Who will descend into the abyss?' " (that is, to bring Christ up from the dead). ⁸But what does it say?

> "The word is near you,
>   on your lips and in your heart"

(that is, the word of faith that we proclaim); ⁹because[j] if you confess with your lips that Jesus is Lord and believe in your heart that God raised Jesus from the dead, you will be saved. ¹⁰For one believes with the heart and so is justified, and one confesses with the mouth and so is saved. ¹¹The scripture says, "No one who believes in the one who is coming will be put to shame." ¹²For there is no distinction between Jew and Greek; the same Lord is Lord of all and is generous to all who call on that Lord. ¹³For, "Everyone who calls on the name of the Lord shall be saved."

14 But how are they to call on one in whom they have not believed? And how are they to believe in one of whom they have never heard? And how are they to hear without someone to preach? ¹⁵And how are they to preach unless they are sent? As it is written, "How beautiful are the feet of those who bring good news!" ¹⁶But not all have obeyed the good news;[k] for Isaiah says, "O God, who has believed our message?" ¹⁷So faith comes from what is heard, and what is heard comes through the word of Christ.[l]

18 But I ask, have they not heard? Indeed they have; for

> "Their voice has gone out to all the earth,
>   and their words to the ends of the world."

¹⁹Again I ask, did Israel not understand? First Moses says,

> "I will make you jealous of those who are not a nation;
>   with a foolish nation I will make you angry."

²⁰Then Isaiah is so bold as to say,

> "I have been found by those who did not seek me;

---

j Or *namely, that*   k Or *gospel*   l Or *about Christ*; other ancient authorities read *of God*

I have shown myself to those who did not ask for
    me."

21 But of Israel it is said, "All day long I have held out my hands to a
disobedient and contrary people."

Israel's Rejection Is Not Final

11 I ask, then, has God rejected God's own people? By no means! I myself
am an Israelite, a descendant of Abraham and Sarah, a member of the
tribe of Benjamin. 2 God has not rejected the people whom God foreknew. Do
you not know what the scripture says of Elijah, how he pleads with God
against Israel? 3 "O God, they have killed your prophets, they have demolished
your altars; I alone am left, and they are seeking my life." 4 But what is the
divine reply to him? "I have kept for myself seven thousand who have not
bowed the knee to Baal." 5 So too at the present time there is a remnant, chosen
by grace. 6 But if it is by grace, it is no longer on the basis of works, otherwise
grace would no longer be grace.[m]

7 What then? Israel failed to obtain what it was seeking. The elect obtained
it, but the rest were hardened, 8 as it is written,

> "God gave them a sluggish spirit,
>   eyes that would not see
>   and ears that would not hear,
> down to this very day."

9 And David says,

> "Let their table become a snare and a trap,
>   a stumbling block and a retribution for them;
10   let their eyes be covered so that they cannot see,
>   and keep their backs forever bent."

The Salvation of the Gentiles

11 So I ask, have they stumbled so as to fall? By no means! But through their
stumbling[n] salvation has come to the Gentiles, so as to make Israel jealous.
12 Now if their stumbling[n] means riches for the world, and if their defeat means
riches for Gentiles, how much more will their full inclusion mean!

13 Now I am speaking to you Gentiles. Inasmuch then as I am an apostle
to the Gentiles, I glorify my ministry 14 in order to make my own people[o]
jealous, and thus save some of them. 15 For if their rejection is the reconciliation
of the world, what will their acceptance be but life from the dead! 16 If the part
of the dough offered as first fruits is holy, then the whole batch is holy; and if
the root is holy, then the branches also are holy.

---

m Other ancient authorities add *But if it is by works, it is no longer on the basis of grace,
otherwise work would no longer be work*   n Gk *transgression*   o Gk *my flesh*

17 But if some of the branches were broken off, and you, a wild olive shoot, were grafted in their place to share the rich root[p] of the olive tree, 18 do not boast over the branches. If you do boast, remember that it is not you that support the root, but the root that supports you. 19 You will say, "Branches were broken off so that I might be grafted in." 20 That is true. They were broken off because of their unbelief, but you stand only through faith. So do not become proud, but stand in awe. 21 For if God did not spare the natural branches, perhaps God will not spare you.[q] 22 Note then the kindness and the severity of God: severity toward those who have fallen, but God's kindness toward you, provided you continue in that kindness; otherwise you also will be cut off. 23 And even those of Israel,[r] if they do not persist in unbelief, will be grafted in, for God has the power to graft them in again. 24 For if you have been cut from what is by nature a wild olive tree and grafted, contrary to nature, into a cultivated olive tree, how much more will these natural branches be grafted back into their own olive tree.

All Israel Will Be Saved

25 So that you may not claim to be wiser than you are, sisters and brothers, I want you to understand this mystery: a hardening has come upon part of Israel, until the full number of the Gentiles has come in. 26 And so all Israel will be saved; as it is written,

> "Out of Zion will come the Deliverer,
>   who will banish ungodliness from Jacob."
27   "And this is my covenant with them,
>   when I take away their sins."

28 As regards the gospel they are enemies of God[s] for your sake; but as regards election they are beloved, for the sake of their ancestors; 29 for the gifts and the calling of God are irrevocable. 30 Just as you were once disobedient to God but have now received mercy because of their disobedience, 31 so they have now been disobedient in order that, by the mercy shown to you, they too may now[t] receive mercy. 32 For God has imprisoned all in disobedience in order to be merciful to all.

33 O the depth of the riches and wisdom and knowledge of God! How unsearchable are God's judgments and how inscrutable God's ways!

34   "For who has known the mind of God?
>   Or who has been God's counselor?"
35   "Or who has given a gift to God,
>   to receive a gift in return?"

---

p Other ancient authorities read *the richness*
q Other ancient authorities read *neither will God spare you*   r Gk lacks *of Israel*
s Gk lacks *of God*   t Other ancient authorities lack *now*

36 For from God and through God and to God are all things. To God be the glory forever. Amen.

The New Life in Christ

12 I appeal to you therefore, brothers and sisters, by the mercies of God, to present your bodies as a living sacrifice, holy and acceptable to God, which is your spiritual[u] worship. 2 Do not be conformed to this world,[v] but be transformed by the renewing of your minds, so that you may discern what is the will of God—what is good and acceptable and perfect.[w]

3 For by the grace given to me I say to everyone among you not to think of yourself more highly than you ought to think, but to think with sober judgment, each according to the measure of faith that God has assigned. 4 For as in one body we have many members, and not all the members have the same function, 5 so we, who are many, are one body in Christ, and individually we are members one of another. 6 We have gifts that differ according to the grace given to us: prophecy, in proportion to faith; 7 ministry, in ministering; the teacher, in teaching; 8 the exhorter, in exhortation; the giver, in generosity; the leader, in diligence; the compassionate, in cheerfulness.

Marks of the True Christian

9 Let love be genuine; hate what is evil, hold fast to what is good; 10 love one another with mutual affection; outdo one another in showing honor. 11 Do not lag in zeal, be ardent in spirit, serve the Lord.[x] 12 Rejoice in hope, be patient in suffering, persevere in prayer. 13 Contribute to the needs of the saints; extend hospitality to strangers.

14 Bless those who persecute you; bless and do not curse them. 15 Rejoice with those who rejoice, weep with those who weep. 16 Live in harmony with one another; do not be haughty, but associate with the lowly;[y] do not claim to be wiser than you are. 17 Do not repay anyone evil for evil, but take thought for what is noble in the sight of all. 18 If it is possible, so far as it depends on you, live peaceably with all. 19 Beloved, never avenge yourselves, but leave room for the wrath of God;[z] for it is written, "God says vengeance is mine, I will repay." 20 No, "if your enemies are hungry, feed them; if they are thirsty, give them something to drink; for by doing this you will heap burning coals on their heads." 21 Do not be overcome by evil, but overcome evil with good.

Being Subject to Authorities

13 Let every person be subject to the governing authorities; for there is no authority except from God, and those authorities that exist have been instituted by God. 2 Therefore whoever resists authority resists what God has

---

u Or *reasonable*   v Gk *age*   w Or *what is the good and acceptable and perfect will of God*
x Other ancient authorities read *serve the opportune time*
y Or *give yourselves to humble tasks*   z Gk *the wrath*

appointed, and those who resist will incur judgment. [3]For rulers are not a terror to good conduct, but to bad. Do you wish to have no fear of the authority? Then do what is good, and you will receive its approval; [4]for it is God's servant for your good. But if you do what is wrong, you should be afraid, for the authority does not bear the sword in vain! It is the servant of God to execute wrath on the wrongdoer. [5]Therefore one must be subject, not only because of wrath but also because of conscience. [6]For the same reason you also pay taxes, for the authorities are God's servants, busy with this very thing. [7]Pay to all what is due them—taxes to whom taxes are due, revenue to whom revenue is due, respect to whom respect is due, honor to whom honor is due.

Love for One Another

8 Owe no one anything, except to love one another; for the one who loves another has fulfilled the law. [9]The commandments, "You shall not commit adultery; You shall not murder; You shall not steal; You shall not covet"; and any other commandment, are summed up in this word, "Love your neighbor as yourself." [10]Love does no wrong to a neighbor; therefore, love is the fulfilling of the law.

An Urgent Appeal

11 Besides this, you know what time it is, how it is now the moment for you to wake from sleep. For salvation is nearer to us now than when we became believers; [12]the night is far gone, the day is near. Let us then lay aside the works of the night and put on the armor of the day; [13]let us live honorably as in the day, not in reveling and drunkenness, not in debauchery and licentiousness, not in quarreling and jealousy. [14]Instead, put on the Lord Jesus Christ, and make no provision for the flesh, to gratify its desires.

Do Not Judge Another

14 Welcome those who are weak in faith,[a] but not for the purpose of quarreling over opinions. [2]Some believe in eating anything, while the weak eat only vegetables. [3]Those who eat must not despise those who abstain, and those who abstain must not pass judgment on those who eat; for God has welcomed them. [4]Who are you to pass judgment on servants of another? It is before their own lord that they stand or fall. And they will be upheld, for the Lord[b] is able to make them stand.

5 Some judge one day to be better than another, while others judge all days to be alike. Let all be fully convinced in their own minds. [6]Those who observe the day, observe it in honor of the Lord. Also those who eat, eat in honor of the Lord, since they give thanks to God; while those who abstain, abstain in honor of the Lord and give thanks to God.

7 We do not live to ourselves, and we do not die to ourselves. [8]If we live,

a Or *conviction*   b Other ancient authorities read *for God* we live to the Lord, and if we die, we die to the Lord; so then, whether we live or whether we die, we are the Lord's. [9]For to this end Christ died and lived again, so as to be Lord of both the dead and the living.

10 Why do you pass judgment on your brother or sister? Or you, why do you despise your sister or brother? For we will all stand before the judgment seat of God.[c] [11]For it is written,

> "As I live, says God, every knee shall bow to me,
>   and every tongue shall give praise to[d] God."

[12]So then, each of us will be accountable to God.[e]

Do Not Make Another Stumble

13 Let us therefore no longer pass judgment on one another, but resolve instead never to put a stumbling block or hindrance in the way of another. [14]I know and am persuaded in the Lord Jesus that nothing is unclean in itself; but it is unclean for anyone who thinks it unclean. [15]If your sister or brother is being injured by what you eat, you are no longer walking in love. Do not let what you eat cause the ruin of one for whom Christ died. [16]So do not let your good be spoken of as evil. [17]For the dominion of God is not food and drink but righteousness and peace and joy in the Holy Spirit. [18]The one who thus serves Christ is acceptable to God and has human approval. [19]Let us then pursue what makes for peace and for mutual upbuilding. [20]Do not, for the sake of food, destroy the work of God. Everything is indeed clean, but it is wrong for you to make others fall by what you eat; [21]it is good not to eat meat or drink wine or do anything that makes your brother or sister stumble.[f] [22]The faith that you have, have as your own conviction before God. Blessed are those who have no reason to condemn themselves because of what they approve. [23]But those who have doubts are condemned if they eat, because they do not act from faith;[g] for whatever does not proceed from faith[g] is sin.[h]

Please Others, Not Yourselves

15 We who are strong ought to put up with the failings of the weak, and not to please ourselves. [2]Each of us must please our neighbor for the good purpose of building up the neighbor. [3]For Christ did not please Christ's self; but, as it is written, "The insults of those who insult you have fallen on me." [4]For whatever was written in former days was written for our instruction, so that by steadfastness and by the encouragement of the scriptures we might have hope. [5]May the God of steadfastness and encouragement grant you to live in harmony with one another, in accordance with Christ Jesus, [6]so that together

---

c Other ancient authorities read *of Christ*   d Or *confess*
e Other ancient authorities lack *to God*
f Other ancient authorities add *or be upset or be weakened*   g Or *conviction*
h Other authorities, some ancient, add here 16.25-27

you may with one voice glorify the God and Father-Mother of our Lord Jesus Christ.

The Gospel for Jews and Gentiles Alike

7 Welcome one another, therefore, just as Christ has welcomed you, for the glory of God. [8]For I tell you that Christ has become a servant of those under the law on behalf of the truth of God in order to confirm the promises given to their ancestors, [9]and in order that the Gentiles might glorify God for showing mercy. As it is written,

> "Therefore I will confess[i] you among the Gentiles,
>   and sing praises to your name";

[10]and again it is said,

> "Rejoice, O Gentiles, with the people of God";

[11]and again,

> "Praise God, all you Gentiles,
>   and let all the peoples praise God";

[12]and again Isaiah says,

> "The root of Jesse shall come,
>   the one who rises to rule the Gentiles,
> in whom the Gentiles shall hope."

[13]May the God of hope fill you with all joy and peace in believing, so that you may abound in hope by the power of the Holy Spirit.

Paul's Reason for Writing So Boldly

14 I myself feel confident about you, my sisters and brothers, that you yourselves are full of goodness, filled with all knowledge, and able to instruct one another. [15]Nevertheless on some points I have written to you rather boldly by way of reminder, because of the grace given me by God [16]to be a minister of Christ Jesus to the Gentiles in the priestly service of the gospel of God, so that the offering of the Gentiles may be acceptable, sanctified by the Holy Spirit. [17]In Christ Jesus, then, I have reason to boast of my work for God. [18]For I will not venture to speak of anything except what Christ has accomplished[j] through me to win obedience from the Gentiles, by word and deed, [19]by the power of signs and wonders, by the power of the Spirit of God,[k] so that from Jerusalem and as far around as Illyricum I have fully proclaimed the good news[l] of Christ. [20]Thus I make it my ambition to proclaim the good

---

i Or thank   j Gk speak of those things that Christ has not accomplished
k Other ancient authorities read of the Spirit or of the Holy Spirit   l Or gospel

news,^m not where Christ has already been named, so that I do not build on someone else's foundation, ²¹but as it is written,

> "Those who have never been told of the one who is
>   coming shall see,
>   and those who have never heard shall understand."

Paul's Plan to Visit Rome

22 This is the reason that I have so often been hindered from coming to you. ²³But now, with no further place for me in these regions, I desire, as I have for many years, to come to you ²⁴when I go to Spain. For I do hope to see you on my journey and to be sent on by you, once I have enjoyed your company for a little while. ²⁵At present, however, I am going to Jerusalem in a ministry to the saints; ²⁶for Macedonia and Achaia have been pleased to share their resources with the poor among the saints at Jerusalem. ²⁷They were pleased to do this, and indeed they owe it to them; for if the Gentiles have come to share in their spiritual blessings, they ought also to be of service to them in material things. ²⁸So, when I have completed this, and have delivered to them what has been collected,ⁿ I will set out by way of you to Spain; ²⁹and I know that when I come to you, I will come in the fullness of the blessing^o of Christ.

30 I appeal to you, brothers and sisters, by our Lord Jesus Christ and by the love of the Spirit, to join me in earnest prayer to God on my behalf, ³¹that I may be rescued from the unbelievers in Judea, and that my ministry^p to Jerusalem may be acceptable to the saints, ³²so that by God's will I may come to you with joy and be refreshed in your company. ³³The God of peace be with all of you.^q Amen.

Personal Greetings

16 I commend to you our sister Phoebe, a deacon^r of the church at Cenchreae, ²so that you may welcome her in the Lord as is fitting for the saints, and help her in whatever she may require from you, for she has been a benefactor of many and of myself as well.

3 Greet Prisca and Aquila, who work with me in Christ Jesus, ⁴and who risked their necks for my life, to whom not only I give thanks, but also all the churches of the Gentiles. ⁵Greet also the church in their house. Greet my beloved Epaenetus, who was the first convert^s in Asia for Christ. ⁶Greet Mary, who has worked very hard among you. ⁷Greet Andronicus and Junia,^t my relatives^u who were in prison with me; they are prominent among the apostles, and they were in Christ before I was. ⁸Greet Ampliatus, my beloved in the

---

m Or *gospel*   n Gk *have sealed to them this fruit*
o Other ancient authorities add *of the gospel*
p Other ancient authorities read *my bringing of a gift*
q One ancient authority adds 16.25-27 here   r Or *minister*   s Gk *firstfruits*
t Or *Junias*; other ancient authorities read *Julia*   u Or *compatriots*

Lord. [9]Greet Urbanus, our coworker in Christ, and my beloved Stachys. [10]Greet Apelles, who is approved in Christ. Greet those who belong to the family of Aristobulus. [11]Greet my relative[v] Herodion. Greet those in the Lord who belong to the family of Narcissus. [12]Greet those women who are workers in the Lord, Tryphaena and Tryphosa. Greet the beloved Persis—she has worked hard in the Lord. [13]Greet Rufus, chosen in the Lord; and greet his mother—a mother to me also. [14]Greet Asyncritus, Phlegon, Hermes, Patrobas, Hermas, and the sisters and brothers who are with them. [15]Greet Philologus, Julia, Nereus and his sister, and Olympas, and all the saints who are with them. [16]Greet one another with a holy kiss. All the churches of Christ greet you.

Final Instructions

17 I urge you, brothers and sisters, to keep an eye on those who cause dissensions and offenses, in opposition to the teaching that you have learned; avoid them. [18]For such people do not serve our Lord Christ, but their own appetites,[w] and by smooth talk and flattery they deceive the hearts of the simple-minded. [19]For while your obedience is known to all, so that I rejoice over you, I want you to be wise in what is good and guileless in what is evil. [20]The God of peace will shortly crush Satan under your feet. The grace of our Lord Jesus Christ be with you.[x]

21 Timothy, my coworker, greets you; so do Lucius and Jason and Sosipater, my relatives.[y]

22 I Tertius, the writer of this letter, greet you in the Lord.[z]

23 Gaius, who is host to me and to the whole church, greets you. Erastus, the city treasurer, and our brother Quartus, greet you.[a]

Final Doxology

25 Now to God[b] who is able to strengthen you according to my gospel and the proclamation of Jesus Christ, according to the revelation of the mystery that was kept secret for long ages [26]but is now disclosed, and through the prophetic writings is made known to all the Gentiles, according to the command of the eternal God, to bring about the obedience of faith— [27]to the only wise God, through Jesus Christ, to whom[c] be the glory forever! Amen.[d]

---

v Or *compatriot*   w Gk *their own belly*   x Other ancient authorities lack this sentence
y Or *compatriots*   z Or *I Tertius, writing this letter in the Lord, greet you*
a Other ancient authorities add verse 24, *The grace of our Lord Jesus Christ be with all of you. Amen.*   b Gk *the one*
c Other ancient authorities lack *to whom*. The verse then reads, *to the only wise God be the glory through Jesus Christ forever. Amen.*
d Other ancient authorities lack 16.25-27 or include it after 14.23 or 15.33; others put verse 24 after verse 27

The First Letter of Paul to the Corinthians

Salutation

1 Paul, called to be an apostle of Christ Jesus by the will of God, and our brother Sosthenes,

2 To the church of God that is in Corinth, to those who are sanctified in Christ Jesus, called to be saints, together with all those who in every place call on the name of our Lord Jesus Christ, both theirs and ours:

3 Grace to you and peace from God our Father-Mother and the Lord Jesus Christ.

4 I give thanks to my[a] God always for you because of the grace of God that has been given you in Christ Jesus, 5for in every way you have been enriched in Christ, in speech and knowledge of every kind— 6just as the testimony of[b] Christ has been strengthened among you— 7so that you are not lacking in any spiritual gift as you wait for the revealing of our Lord Jesus Christ, 8who will also strengthen you to the end, so that you may be blameless on the day of our Lord Jesus Christ. 9God is faithful and called you into the community of God's Child, Jesus Christ our Lord.

Divisions in the Church

10 Now I appeal to you, sisters and brothers, by the name of our Lord Jesus Christ, that all of you be in agreement and that there be no divisions among you, but that you be united in the same mind and the same purpose. 11For it has been reported to me by Chloe's people that there are quarrels among you, my brothers and sisters. 12What I mean is that each of you says, "I belong to Paul," or "I belong to Apollos," or "I belong to Cephas," or "I belong to Christ." 13Has Christ been divided? Was Paul crucified for you? Or were you

---

a Other ancient authorities lack *my*   b Or *to*

baptized in the name of Paul? ¹⁴I thank God^c that I baptized none of you except Crispus and Gaius, ¹⁵so that no one can say that you were baptized in my name. ¹⁶(I did baptize also the household of Stephanas; beyond that, I do not know whether I baptized anyone else.) ¹⁷For Christ did not send me to baptize but to proclaim the gospel, and not with eloquent wisdom, so that the cross of Christ might not be emptied of its power.

Christ the Power and Wisdom of God

18 For the message about the cross is foolishness to those who are perishing, but to us who are being saved it is the power of God. ¹⁹For it is written,

> "I will destroy the wisdom of the wise,
>   and the discernment of the discerning I will thwart."

²⁰Where is the one who is wise? Where is the scribe? Where is the debater of this age? Has not God made foolish the wisdom of the world? ²¹For since, in the wisdom of God, the world did not know God through wisdom, God decided, through the foolishness of our proclamation, to save those who believe. ²²For Jews demand signs and Greeks desire wisdom, ²³but we proclaim Christ crucified, a stumbling block to Jews and foolishness to Gentiles, ²⁴but to those who are the called, both Jews and Greeks, Christ the power of God and the wisdom of God. ²⁵For God's foolishness is wiser than human wisdom, and God's weakness is stronger than human strength.

26 Consider your own call, sisters and brothers: not many of you were wise by human standards,^d not many were powerful, not many were of noble birth. ²⁷But God chose what is foolish in the world to shame the wise; God chose what is weak in the world to shame the strong; ²⁸God chose what is low and despised in the world, things that are not, to reduce to nothing things that are, ²⁹so that no one might boast in the presence of God. ³⁰God is the source of your life in Christ Jesus, who became for us wisdom from God, and righteousness and sanctification and redemption, ³¹in order that, as it is written, "Let the one who boasts, boast in^e the Lord."

Proclaiming Christ Crucified

2 When I came to you, brothers and sisters, I did not come proclaiming the mystery^f of God to you in lofty words or wisdom. ²For I decided to know nothing among you except Jesus Christ— indeed, Christ crucified. ³And I came to you in weakness and in fear and in much trembling. ⁴My speech and my proclamation were not with plausible words of wisdom,^g but with a demonstration of the Spirit and of power, ⁵so that your faith might rest not on human wisdom but on the power of God.

---

c Other ancient authorities read *I am thankful*   d Gk *according to the flesh*   e Or *of*
f Other ancient authorities read *testimony*
g Other ancient authorities read *the persuasiveness of wisdom*

The True Wisdom of God

6 Yet among the mature we do speak wisdom, though it is not a wisdom of this age or of the rulers of this age, who are doomed to perish. [7]But we speak God's wisdom, secret and hidden, which God decreed before the ages for our glory. [8]None of the rulers of this age understood this; for if they had, they would not have crucified the Lord of glory. [9]But, as it is written,

> "What no eye has seen, nor ear heard,
>   nor the human heart conceived,
> what God has prepared for those who love God"—

[10]these things God has revealed to us through the Spirit; for the Spirit searches everything, even the depths of God. [11]For who among us knows what a person is except the spirit of a person that is within? So also no one comprehends what is truly God's except the Spirit of God. [12]Now we have received not the spirit of the world, but the Spirit that is from God, so that we may understand the gifts bestowed on us by God. [13]And we speak of these things in words not taught by human wisdom but taught by the Spirit, interpreting spiritual things to those who are spiritual.[h]

14 Those who are unspiritual[i] do not receive the gifts of God's Spirit, for they are foolishness to them, and they are unable to understand them because they are spiritually discerned. [15]Those who are spiritual discern all things, and they are themselves subject to no one else's scrutiny.

16   "For who has known the mind of God
         so as to instruct God?"

But we have the mind of Christ.

On Divisions in the Corinthian Church

3 And so, sisters and brothers, I could not speak to you as spiritual people, but rather as people of the flesh, as infants in Christ. [2]I fed you with milk, not solid food, for you were not ready for solid food. Even now you are still not ready, [3]for you are still of the flesh. For as long as there is jealousy and quarreling among you, are you not of the flesh, and behaving according to human inclinations? [4]For when one says, "I belong to Paul," and another, "I belong to Apollos," are you not merely human?

5 What then is Apollos? What is Paul? Servants through whom you came to believe, as the Lord assigned to each. [6]I planted, Apollos watered, but God gave the growth. [7]So neither the one who plants nor the one who waters is anything, but only God who gives the growth. [8]The one who plants and the one who waters have a common purpose, and each will receive wages according

---

h Or interpreting spiritual things in spiritual language, or comparing spiritual things with spiritual
i Or natural

to the labor of each. ⁹For we are God's servants, working together; you are God's field, God's building.

10 According to the grace of God given to me, like an exceptionally skilled builder I laid a foundation, and someone else is building on it. Each builder must choose with care how to build on it. ¹¹For no one can lay any foundation other than the one that has been laid; that foundation is Jesus Christ. ¹²Now if anyone builds on the foundation with gold, silver, precious stones, wood, hay, straw— ¹³the work of each builder will become visible, for the Day will disclose it, because it will be revealed with fire, and the fire will test what sort of work each has done. ¹⁴If what has been built on the foundation survives, the builder will receive a reward. ¹⁵If the work is burned up, the builder will suffer loss; the builder will be saved, but only as through fire.

16 Do you not know that you are God's temple and that God's Spirit dwells in you?ʲ ¹⁷If anyone destroys God's temple, God will destroy that person. For God's temple is holy, and you are that temple.

18 Do not deceive yourselves. If you think that you are wise in this age, you should become fools so that you may become wise. ¹⁹For the wisdom of this world is foolishness with God. For it is written,

> "God catches the wise in their craftiness,"

²⁰and again,

> "God knows the thoughts of the wise,
>   that they are futile."

²¹So let no one boast about human leaders. For all things are yours, ²²whether Paul or Apollos or Cephas or the world or life or death or the present or the future—all belong to you, ²³and you belong to Christ, and Christ belongs to God.

The Ministry of the Apostles

4 Think of us in this way, as servants of Christ and administrators of God's mysteries. ²Moreover, it is required of adminstrators that they be found trustworthy. ³But with me it is a very small thing that I should be judged by you or by any human court. I do not even judge myself. ⁴I am not aware of anything against myself, but I am not thereby acquitted. It is the Lord who judges me. ⁵Therefore do not pronounce judgment before the time, before the Lord comes, who will bring to light the things now hidden and will disclose the purposes of the heart. Then each one will receive commendation from God.

6 I have applied all this to Apollos and myself for your benefit, brothers and sisters, so that you may learn through us the meaning of the saying, "Nothing beyond what is written," so that none of you will be puffed up in

---

j In verses 16 and 17 the Greek word for *you* is plural

favor of one against another. ⁷For who sees anything different in you?ᵏ What do you have that you did not receive? And if you received it, why do you boast as if it were not a gift?

8 Already you have all you want! Already you have become rich! Quite apart from us you have become rulers! Indeed, I wish that you did rule, so that we might rule with you! ⁹For I think that God has exhibited us apostles as last of all, as though sentenced to death, because we have become a spectacle to the world, to angels and to mortals. ¹⁰We are fools for the sake of Christ, but you are wise in Christ. We are weak, but you are strong. You are held in honor, but we in disrepute. ¹¹To the present hour we are hungry and thirsty, we are poorly clothed and beaten and homeless, ¹²and we grow weary from the work of our own hands. When reviled, we bless; when persecuted, we endure; ¹³when slandered, we speak kindly. We have become like the rubbish of the world, the dregs of all things, to this very day.

Parental Admonition

14 I am not writing this to make you ashamed, but to admonish you as my beloved children. ¹⁵For though you might have ten thousand guardians in Christ, you do not have many spiritual parents. Indeed, in Christ Jesus I became your spiritual parent through the gospel. ¹⁶I appeal to you, then, be imitators of me. ¹⁷For this reason I sentˡ you Timothy, who is my beloved and faithful child in the Lord, to remind you of my ways in Christ Jesus, as I teach them everywhere in every church. ¹⁸But some of you, thinking that I am not coming to you, have become arrogant. ¹⁹But I will come to you soon, if God wills, and I will find out not the talk of these arrogant people but their power. ²⁰For the dominion of God depends not on talk but on power. ²¹What would you prefer? Am I to come to you with a stick, or with love in a spirit of gentleness?

Sexual Immorality Defiles the Church

5 It is actually reported that there is sexual immorality among you, and of a kind that is not found even among pagans; for a man is living with his father's wife. ²And you are arrogant! Should you not rather have mourned, so that the one who has done this would have been removed from among you?

3 For though absent in body, I am present in spirit; and as if present I have already pronounced judgment ⁴in the name of the Lord Jesus on the one who has done such a thing.ᵐ When you are assembled, and my spirit is present with the power of our Lord Jesus, ⁵you are to hand this man over to Satan for the destruction of the flesh, so that his spirit may be saved in the day of the Lord.ⁿ

---

k Or *Who makes you different from another?*   l Or *am sending*
m Or *on the one who has done such a thing in the name of the Lord Jesus*
n Other ancient authorities add *Jesus*

6 Your boasting is not a good thing. Do you not know that a little yeast leavens the whole batch of dough? 7Clean out the old yeast so that you may be a new batch, as you really are unleavened. For our paschal lamb, Christ, has been sacrificed. 8Therefore, let us celebrate the festival, not with the old yeast, the yeast of malice and evil, but with the unleavened bread of sincerity and truth.

Sexual Immorality Must Be Judged

9 I wrote to you in my letter not to associate with sexually immoral persons— 10not at all meaning the immoral of this world, or the greedy and robbers, or idolaters, since you would then need to go out of the world. 11But now I am writing to you not to associate with anyone who bears the name of sister or brother who is sexually immoral or greedy, or is an idolater, reviler, drunkard, or robber. Do not even eat with such a one. 12For what have I to do with judging those outside? Is it not those who are inside that you are to judge? 13God will judge those outside. "Drive out the wicked person from among you."

Lawsuits among Believers

6 When any of you has a grievance against another, do you dare to take it to court before the unrighteous, instead of taking it before the saints? 2Do you not know that the saints will judge the world? And if the world is to be judged by you, are you incompetent to try trivial cases? 3Do you not know that we are to judge angels—to say nothing of ordinary matters? 4If you have ordinary cases, then, do you appoint as judges those who have no standing in the church? 5I say this to your shame. Can it be that there is no one among you wise enough to decide between one believer and another, 6but a believer goes to court against a believer—and before unbelievers at that?

7 In fact, to have lawsuits at all with one another is already a defeat for you. Why not rather be wronged? Why not rather be defrauded? 8But you yourselves wrong and defraud—and believers at that.

9 Do you not know that wrongdoers will not inherit the dominion of God? Do not be deceived! People who are sexually immoral, idolaters, adulterers, male prostitutes, 10thieves, the greedy, drunkards, revilers, robbers—none of these will inherit the dominion of God. 11And this is what some of you used to be. But you were washed, you were sanctified, you were justified in the name of the Lord Jesus Christ and in the Spirit of our God.

Glorify God in Body and Spirit

12 "All things are lawful for me," but not all things are beneficial. "All things are lawful for me," but I will not be dominated by anything. 13"Food is meant for the stomach and the stomach for food,"o and God will destroy both one

---

o The quotation may extend to the word *other*

and the other. The body is meant not for sexual immorality but for Christ, and Christ for the body. [14] And God raised Christ and will also raise us by God's power. [15] Do you not know that your bodies are members of Christ? Should I therefore take those members of Christ and make them members of a person who is sexually promiscuous? Never! [16] Do you not know that whoever is united to someone who is sexually promiscous becomes united with that person's body? For it is said, "The two shall be one flesh." [17] But anyone united to Christ becomes one spirit with Christ. [18] Shun sexual immorality! Every sin that a person commits is outside the body; but the one who is sexually immoral sins against the body itself. [19] Or do you not know that your body is a temple[p] of the Holy Spirit within you, which you have from God, and that you are not your own? [20] For you were bought with a price; therefore glorify God in your body.

Directions concerning Marriage

7 Now concerning the matters about which you wrote: "It is well for a man not to touch a woman." [2] But because of cases of sexual immorality, each man should have his own wife and each woman her own husband. [3] The husband should give to his wife her conjugal rights, and likewise the wife to her husband. [4] For the wife does not have authority over her own body, but the husband does; likewise the husband does not have authority over his own body, but the wife does. [5] Do not deprive one another except perhaps by agreement for a set time, to devote yourselves to prayer, and then come together again, so that Satan may not tempt you because of your lack of self-control. [6] This I say by way of concession, not of command. [7] I wish that all were as I myself am. But each has a particular gift from God, one having one kind and another a different kind.

8 To the unmarried and the widows I say that it is well for them to remain unmarried as I am. [9] But if they are not practicing self-control, they should marry. For it is better to marry than to be aflame with passion.

10 To the married I give this command—not I but Christ—that the wife should not separate from her husband [11] (but if she does separate, let her remain unmarried or else be reconciled to her husband), and that the husband should not divorce his wife.

12 To the rest I say—I and not Christ—that if any believer has a wife who is an unbeliever, and she consents to live with him, he should not divorce her. [13] And if any woman has a husband who is an unbeliever, and he consents to live with her, she should not divorce him. [14] For the unbelieving husband is made holy through his wife, and the unbelieving wife is made holy through her husband. Otherwise, your children would be unclean, but as it is, they are holy. [15] But if the unbelieving partner separates, let it be so; in such a case the brother or sister is not bound. It is to peace that God has called you.[q] [16] Wife, for all

---

p Or *sanctuary*   q Other ancient authorities read *us*

you know, you might save your husband. Husband, for all you know, you might save your wife.

The Life That the Lord Has Assigned

17 However that may be, let each of you lead the life that the Lord has assigned, to which God called you. This is my rule in all the churches. 18 Was anyone at the time of his call already circumcised? Let him not seek to remove the marks of circumcision. Was anyone at the time of his call uncircumcised? Let him not seek circumcision. 19 Circumcision is nothing, and uncircumcision is nothing; but obeying the commandments of God is everything. 20 Let each of you remain in the condition in which you were called.

21 Were you enslaved to another person when you were called? Do not be concerned about it. Even if you can gain your freedom, make use of your present condition now more than ever.ʳ 22 For whoever was called in the Lord as an enslaved person is a freed person belonging to the Lord, just as whoever was free when called is enslaved to Christ. 23 You were bought with a price; do not become enslaved to human beings. 24 In whatever condition you were called, sisters and brothers, there remain with God.

The Unmarried and the Widows

25 Now concerning virgins, I have no command of Christ, but I give my opinion as one who by the mercy of Christ is trustworthy. 26 I think that, in view of the impendingˢ crisis, it is well for you to remain as you are. 27 Are you bound to a wife? Do not seek to be free. Are you free from a wife? Do not seek a wife. 28 But if you marry, you do not sin, and if a virgin marries, she does not sin. Yet those who marry will experience distress in this life,ᵗ and I would spare you that. 29 I mean, brothers and sisters, the appointed time has grown short; from now on, let even those who have wives be as though they had none, 30 and those who mourn as though they were not mourning, and those who rejoice as though they were not rejoicing, and those who buy as though they had no possessions, 31 and those who deal with the world as though they had no dealings with it. For the present form of this world is passing away.

32 I want you to be free from anxieties. The unmarried man is anxious about the affairs of the Lord, how to please the Lord; 33 but the married man is anxious about the affairs of the world, how to please his wife, 34 and his interests are divided. And the unmarried woman and the virgin are anxious about the affairs of the Lord, so that they may be holy in body and spirit; but the married woman is anxious about the affairs of the world, how to please her husband. 35 I say this for your own benefit, not to put any restraint upon you, but to promote good order and unhindered devotion to the Lord.

36 If anyone thinks that he is not behaving properly toward his fiancée, if

---

r Or *avail yourself of the opportunity*   s Or *present*   t Gk *in the flesh* his passions are strong, and so it has to be, let him marry as he wishes; it is no sin. Let them marry. 37But if someone stands firm in his resolve, being under no necessity but having his own desire under control, and has determined in his own mind to keep her as his fiancée, he will do well. 38So then, he who marries his fiancée does well; and he who refrains from marriage will do better.

39 A wife is bound as long as her husband lives. But if the husband dies,ᵘ she is free to marry anyone she wishes, only in the Lord. 40But in my judgment she is more blessed if she remains as she is. And I think that I too have the Spirit of God.

Food Offered to Idols

8 Now concerning food sacrificed to idols: we know that "all of us possess knowledge." Knowledge puffs up, but love builds up. 2Anyone who claims to know something does not yet have the necessary knowledge; 3but anyone who loves God is known by God.

4 Hence, as to the eating of food offered to idols, we know that "no idol in the world really exists," and that "there is no God but one." 5Indeed, even though there may be so-called gods in heaven or on earth—as in fact there are many gods and many lords— 6yet for us there is one God, the Father-Mother, from whom are all things and for whom we exist, and one Lord, Jesus Christ, through whom are all things and through whom we exist.

7 It is not everyone, however, who has this knowledge. Since some have become so accustomed to idols until now, they still think of the food they eat as food offered to an idol; and their conscience, being weak, is defiled. 8"Food will not bring us close to God."ᵛ We are no worse off if we do not eat, and no better off if we do. 9But take care that this liberty of yours does not somehow become a stumbling block to the weak. 10For if others see you, who possess knowledge, eating in the temple of an idol, might they not, since their conscience is weak, be encouraged to the point of eating food sacrificed to idols? 11So by your knowledge those weak believers for whom Christ died are destroyed. 12But when you thus sin against members of your family, and wound their conscience when it is weak, you sin against Christ. 13Therefore, if food is a cause of their falling, I will never eat meat, so that I may not cause one of them to fall.

The Rights of an Apostle

9 Am I not free? Am I not an apostle? Have I not seen Jesus our Lord? Are you not my work in the Lord? 2If I am not an apostle to others, at least I am to you; for you are the seal of my apostleship in the Lord.

3 This is my defense to those who would examine me. 4Do we not have

---

u Gk *falls asleep* v The quotation may extend to the end of the verse the right to our food and drink? 5 Do we not have the right to be accompanied by a believing spouse, as do the other apostles and the brothers of Jesus and Cephas? 6 Or is it only Barnabas and I who have no right to refrain from working for a living? 7 Who at any time pays the expenses for doing military service? Who plants a vineyard and does not eat any of its fruit? Or who tends a flock and does not get any of its milk?

8 Do I say this on human authority? Does not the law also say the same? 9 For it is written in the law of Moses, "You shall not muzzle an ox while it is treading out the grain." Is it for oxen that God is concerned? 10 Or does God not speak entirely for our sake? It was indeed written for our sake, for whoever plows should plow in hope and whoever threshes should thresh in hope of a share in the crop. 11 If we have sown spiritual good among you, is it too much if we reap your material benefits? 12 If others share this rightful claim on you, do not we still more?

Nevertheless, we have not made use of this right, but we endure everything rather than put an obstacle in the way of the gospel of Christ. 13 Do you not know that those who are employed in the temple service get their food from the temple, and those who serve at the altar share in what is sacrificed on the altar? 14 In the same way, the Lord commanded that those who proclaim the gospel should get their living by the gospel.

15 But I have made no use of any of these rights, nor am I writing this so that they may be applied in my case. Indeed, I would rather die than that—no one will deprive me of my ground for boasting! 16 If I proclaim the gospel, this gives me no ground for boasting, for an obligation is laid on me, and woe to me if I do not proclaim the gospel! 17 For if I do this of my own will, I have a reward; but if not of my own will, I am entrusted with a commission. 18 What then is my reward? Just this: that in my proclamation I may make the gospel free of charge, so as not to make full use of my rights in the gospel.

19 For though I am free with respect to all, I have enslaved myself to all, so that I might win more of them. 20 To the Jews I became as a Jew, in order to win Jews. To those under the law I became as one under the law (though I myself am not under the law) so that I might win those under the law. 21 To those outside the law I became as one outside the law (though I am not free from God's law but am under Christ's law) so that I might win those outside the law. 22 To the weak I became weak, so that I might win the weak. I have become all things to all people, that I might by all means save some. 23 I do it all for the sake of the gospel, so that I may share in its blessings.

24 Do you not know that in a race the runners all compete, but only one receives the prize? Run in such a way that you may win it. 25 Athletes exercise self-control in all things; they do it to receive a perishable wreath, but we an imperishable one. 26 So I do not run aimlessly, nor do I box as though beating the air; 27 but I punish my body and enslave it, so that after proclaiming to others I myself should not be disqualified.

Warnings from Israel's History

10 I do not want you to be unaware, sisters and brothers, that our ancestors were all under the cloud, and all passed through the sea, 2 and all were baptized into Moses in the cloud and in the sea, 3 and all ate the same spiritual food, 4 and all drank the same spiritual drink. For they drank from the spiritual rock that followed them, and the rock was Christ. 5 Nevertheless, God was not pleased with most of them, and they were struck down in the wilderness.

6 Now these things occurred as examples for us, so that we might not desire evil as they did. 7 Do not become idolaters as some of them did; as it is written, "The people sat down to eat and drink, and they rose up to play." 8 We must not indulge in irresponsible sexual behavior as some of them did, and twenty-three thousand fell in a single day. 9 We must not put Christ[w] to the test, as some of them did, and were destroyed by serpents. 10 And do not complain as some of them did, and were destroyed by the destroyer. 11 These things happened to them to serve as an example, and they were written down to instruct us, on whom the ends of the ages have come. 12 So if you think you are standing, watch out that you do not fall. 13 No testing has overtaken you that is not common to everyone. God is faithful and will not let you be tested beyond your strength, but with the testing God will also provide the way out so that you may be able to endure it.

14 Therefore, my dear friends, flee from the worship of idols. 15 I speak as to sensible people; judge for yourselves what I say. 16 The cup of blessing that we bless, is it not a sharing in the blood of Christ? The bread that we break, is it not a sharing in the body of Christ? 17 Because there is one bread, we who are many are one body, for we all partake of the one bread. 18 Consider the people of Israel; are not those who eat the sacrifices partners in the altar? 19 What do I imply then? That food sacrificed to idols is anything, or that an idol is anything? 20 No, I imply that what pagans sacrifice, they sacrifice to demons and not to God. I do not want you to be partners with demons. 21 You cannot drink the cup of the Lord and the cup of demons. You cannot partake of the table of the Lord and the table of demons. 22 Or are we provoking the Lord to jealousy? Are we stronger than the Lord?

Do All to the Glory of God

23 "All things are lawful," but not all things are beneficial. "All things are lawful," but not all things build up. 24 Do not seek your own advantage, but that of the other. 25 Eat whatever is sold in the meat market without raising any question on the ground of conscience, 26 for "the earth and its fullness are God's." 27 If an unbeliever invites you to a meal and you are disposed to go, eat whatever is set before you without raising any question on the ground of

---

w Other ancient authorities read *the Lord*

conscience. 28But if someone says to you, "This has been offered in sacrifice," then do not eat it, out of consideration for the one who informed you, and for the sake of conscience— 29I mean the other's conscience, not your own. For why should my liberty be subject to the judgment of someone else's conscience? 30If I partake with thankfulness, why should I be denounced because of that for which I give thanks?

31 So, whether you eat or drink, or whatever you do, do everything for the glory of God. 32Give no offense to Jews or to Greeks or to the church of God, 33just as I try to please everyone in everything I do, not seeking my own **11** advantage, but that of many, so that they may be saved. 1Be imitators of me, as I am of Christ.

Head Coverings

2 I commend you because you remember me in everything and maintain the traditions just as I handed them on to you. 3But I want you to understand that Christ is the head of every man, and the husband[x] is the head of his wife,[y] and God is the head of Christ. 4Any man who prays or prophesies with something on his head disgraces his head, 5but any woman who prays or prophesies with her head unveiled disgraces her head—it is one and the same thing as having her head shaved. 6For if a woman will not veil herself, then she should cut off her hair; but if it is disgraceful for a woman to have her hair cut off or to be shaved, she should wear a veil. 7For a man ought not to have his head veiled, since he is the image and reflection[z] of God; but woman is the reflection[z] of man. 8Indeed, man was not made from woman, but woman from man. 9Neither was man created for the sake of woman, but woman for the sake of man. 10For this reason a woman ought to have a symbol of[a] authority on her head,[b] because of the angels. 11Nevertheless, in the Lord woman is not independent of man or man independent of woman. 12For just as woman came from man, so man comes through woman; but all things come from God. 13Judge for yourselves: is it proper for a woman to pray to God with her head unveiled? 14Does not nature itself teach you that if a man wears his hair long, it is degrading to him, 15but if a woman wears her hair long, it is her glory? For her hair is given to her for a covering. 16But if anyone is disposed to be contentious—we have no such custom, nor do the churches of God.

Misuses of the Lord's Supper

17 Now in the following instructions I do not commend you, because when you come together it is not for the better but for the worse. 18For, to begin with, when you come together as a church, I hear that there are divisions among you; and to some extent I believe it. 19Indeed, there have to be factions among you, for only so will it become clear who among you are genuine.

---

x The same Greek word means *man* or *husband*   y Or *head of the woman*   z Or *glory*
a Gk lacks *a symbol of*   b Or *have freedom of choice regarding her head*

20 When you come together, it is not really to eat the Lord's supper. 21 For when the time comes to eat, each of you goes ahead with your own supper, and one goes hungry and another becomes drunk. 22 What! Do you not have homes to eat and drink in? Or do you show contempt for the church of God and humiliate those who have nothing? What should I say to you? Should I commend you? In this matter I do not commend you!

The Institution of the Lord's Supper

23 For I received from the Lord what I also handed on to you, that the Lord Jesus on the night of betrayal took a loaf of bread, 24 and having given thanks, broke it and said, "This is my body that is for^c you. Do this in remembrance of me." 25 In the same way Jesus took the cup also, after supper, saying, "This cup is the new covenant in my blood. Do this, as often as you drink it, in remembrance of me." 26 For as often as you eat this bread and drink the cup, you proclaim Christ's death until Christ comes.

Partaking of the Supper Unworthily

27 Whoever, therefore, eats the bread or drinks the cup of the Lord in an unworthy manner will be answerable for the body and blood of the Lord. 28 Examine yourselves, and only then eat of the bread and drink of the cup. 29 For all who eat and drink^d without discerning the body,^e eat and drink judgment against themselves. 30 For this reason many of you are weak and ill, and some have died.^f 31 But if we judged ourselves, we would not be judged. 32 But when we are judged by the Lord, we are disciplined^g so that we may not be condemned along with the world.

33 So then, my brothers and sisters, when you come together to eat, wait for one another. 34 If you are hungry, eat at home, so that when you come together, it will not be for your condemnation. About the other things I will give instructions when I come.

Spiritual Gifts

12 Now concerning spiritual gifts,^h sisters and brothers, I do not want you to be uninformed. 2 You know that when you were pagans, you were enticed and led astray to idols that could not speak. 3 Therefore I want you to understand that no one speaking by the Spirit of God ever says "Let Jesus be cursed!" and no one can say "Jesus is Lord" except by the Holy Spirit.

4 Now there are varieties of gifts, but the same Spirit; 5 and there are varieties of services, but the same Lord; 6 and there are varieties of activities, but it is the same God who activates all of them in everyone. 7 To each is given the

---

c Other ancient authorities read *is broken for*
d Other ancient authorities add *in an unworthy manner,*
e Other ancient authorities read *the Lord's body*   f Gk *fallen asleep*
g Or *When we are judged, we are being disciplined by the Lord*   h Or *spiritual persons*

manifestation of the Spirit for the common good. 8To one is given through the Spirit the utterance of wisdom, and to another the utterance of knowledge according to the same Spirit, 9to another faith by the same Spirit, to another gifts of healing by the one Spirit, 10to another the working of miracles, to another prophecy, to another the discernment of spirits, to another various kinds of tongues, to another the interpretation of tongues. 11All these are activated by one and the same Spirit, who allots to each one individually just as the Spirit chooses.

One Body with Many Members

12 For just as the body is one and has many members, and all the members of the body, though many, are one body, so it is with Christ. 13For in the one Spirit we were all baptized into one body—Jews or Greeks, enslaved or free—and we were all made to drink of one Spirit.

14 Indeed, the body does not consist of one member but of many. 15If the foot would say, "Because I am not a hand, I do not belong to the body," that would not make it any less a part of the body. 16And if the ear would say, "Because I am not an eye, I do not belong to the body," that would not make it any less a part of the body. 17If the whole body were an eye, where would the hearing be? If the whole body were hearing, where would the sense of smell be? 18But as it is, God arranged the members in the body, each one of them, as God chose. 19If all were a single member, where would the body be? 20As it is, there are many members, yet one body. 21The eye cannot say to the hand, "I have no need of you," nor again the head to the feet, "I have no need of you." 22On the contrary, the members of the body that seem to be weaker are indispensable, 23and those members of the body that we think less honorable we clothe with greater honor, and our less respectable members are treated with greater respect; 24whereas our more respectable members do not need this. But God has so arranged the body, giving the greater honor to the inferior member, 25that there may be no dissension within the body, but the members may have the same care for one another. 26If one member suffers, all suffer together with it; if one member is honored, all rejoice together with it.

27 Now you are the body of Christ and individually members of it. 28And God has appointed in the church first apostles, second prophets, third teachers; then deeds of power, then gifts of healing, forms of assistance, forms of leadership, various kinds of tongues. 29Are all apostles? Are all prophets? Are all teachers? Do all work miracles? 30Do all possess gifts of healing? Do all speak in tongues? Do all interpret? 31But strive for the greater gifts. And I will show you a still more excellent way.

The Gift of Love

13 If I speak in the tongues of mortals and of angels, but do not have love, I am a noisy gong or a clanging cymbal. 2And if I have prophetic powers, and understand all mysteries and all knowledge, and if I have all faith, so as to remove mountains, but do not have love, I am nothing. ³If I give away all my possessions, and if I hand over my body so that I may boast,ⁱ but do not have love, I gain nothing.

4 Love is patient; love is kind; love is not envious or boastful or arrogant ⁵or rude. It does not insist on its own way; it is not irritable or resentful; ⁶it does not rejoice in wrongdoing, but rejoices in the truth. ⁷It bears all things, believes all things, hopes all things, endures all things.

8 Love never ends. But as for prophecies, they will come to an end; as for tongues, they will cease; as for knowledge, it will come to an end. ⁹For we know only in part, and we prophesy only in part; ¹⁰but when the complete comes, the partial will come to an end. ¹¹When I was a child, I spoke like a child, I thought like a child, I reasoned like a child; when I became an adult, I put an end to childish ways. ¹²For now we see in a mirror, dimly,ʲ but then we will see face to face. Now I know only in part; then I will know fully, even as I have been fully known. ¹³And now faith, hope, and love abide, these three; and the greatest of these is love.

Gifts of Prophecy and Tongues

14 Pursue love and strive for the spiritual gifts, and especially that you may prophesy. ²For those who speak in a tongue do not speak to other people but to God; for nobody understands them, since they are speaking mysteries in the Spirit. ³On the other hand, those who prophesy speak to other people for their upbuilding and encouragement and consolation. ⁴Those who speak in a tongue build up themselves, but those who prophesy build up the church. ⁵Now I would like all of you to speak in tongues, but even more to prophesy. One who prophesies is greater than one who speaks in tongues, unless someone interprets, so that the church may be built up.

6 Now, brothers and sisters, if I come to you speaking in tongues, how will I benefit you unless I speak to you in some revelation or knowledge or prophecy or teaching? ⁷It is the same way with lifeless instruments that produce sound, such as the flute or the harp. If they do not give distinct notes, how will anyone know what is being played? ⁸And if the bugle gives an indistinct sound, who will get ready for battle? ⁹So with yourselves; if in a tongue you utter speech that is not intelligible, how will anyone know what is being said? For you will be speaking into the air. ¹⁰There are doubtless many different kinds of sounds in the world, and nothing is without sound. ¹¹If then I do not know the meaning of a sound, I will be a foreigner to the speaker and the speaker a foreigner to me. ¹²So with yourselves; since you are eager for spiritual gifts, strive to excel in them for building up the church.

13 Therefore, one who speaks in a tongue should pray for the power to interpret. ¹⁴For if I pray in a tongue, my spirit prays but my mind is unproductive. ¹⁵What should I do then? I will pray with the spirit, but I will

---

i Other ancient authorities read *body to be burned*   j Gk *in a riddle*

pray with the mind also; I will sing praise with the spirit, but I will sing praise with the mind also. ¹⁶Otherwise, if you say a blessing with the spirit, how can anyone in the position of an outsider say the "Amen" to your thanksgiving, since the outsider does not know what you are saying? ¹⁷For you may give thanks well enough, but the other person is not built up. ¹⁸I thank God that I speak in tongues more than all of you; ¹⁹nevertheless, in church I would rather speak five words with my mind, in order to instruct others also, than ten thousand words in a tongue.

20 Brothers and sisters, do not be children in your thinking; rather, be infants in evil, but in thinking be adults. ²¹In the law it is written,

> "By people of strange tongues
>   and by the lips of foreigners
> I will speak to this people;
>   yet even then they will not listen to me,"

says God. ²²Tongues, then, are a sign not for believers but for unbelievers, while prophecy is not for unbelievers but for believers. ²³If, therefore, the whole church comes together and all speak in tongues, and outsiders or unbelievers enter, will they not say that you are out of your mind? ²⁴But if all prophesy, an unbeliever or outsider who enters is reproved by all and called to account by all. ²⁵After the secrets of the unbeliever's heart are disclosed, that person will bow down and worship God, declaring, "God is really among you."

Orderly Worship

26 What should be done then, my friends? When you come together, each one has a hymn, a lesson, a revelation, a tongue, or an interpretation. Let all things be done for building up. ²⁷If anyone speaks in a tongue, let there be only two or at most three, and each in turn; and let one interpret. ²⁸But if there is no one to interpret, let them be silent in church and speak to themselves and to God. ²⁹Let two or three prophets speak, and let the others weigh what is said. ³⁰If a revelation is made to someone else sitting nearby, let the first person be silent. ³¹For you can all prophesy one by one, so that all may learn and all be encouraged. ³²And the spirits of prophets are subject to the prophets, ³³for God is a God not of disorder but of peace.

(As in all the churches of the saints, ³⁴women should be silent in the churches. For they are not permitted to speak, but should be subordinate, as the law also says. ³⁵If there is anything they desire to know, let them ask their husbands at home. For it is shameful for a woman to speak in church.ᵏ ³⁶Or did the word of God originate with you? Or are you the only ones it has reached?)

37 Anyone who claims to be a prophet, or to have spiritual powers, must acknowledge that what I am writing to you is a command of the Lord.

---

k Other ancient authorities put verses 34-35 after verse 40

³⁸Anyone who does not recognize this is not to be recognized. ³⁹So, my friends, be eager to prophesy, and do not forbid speaking in tongues; ⁴⁰but all things should be done decently and in order.

The Resurrection of Christ

15 Now I would remind you, sisters and brothers, of the good news[1] that I proclaimed to you, which you in turn received, in which also you stand, ²through which also you are being saved, if you hold firmly to the message that I proclaimed to you—unless you have come to believe in vain.

3 For I handed on to you as of first importance what I in turn had received: that Christ died for our sins in accordance with the scriptures, ⁴and was buried; and that Christ was raised on the third day in accordance with the scriptures, ⁵and appeared to Cephas, then to the twelve. ⁶Then Christ appeared to more than five hundred brothers and sisters at one time, most of whom are still alive, though some have died.[m] ⁷Then Christ appeared to James, then to all the apostles. ⁸Last of all, as to one untimely born, Christ appeared also to me. ⁹For I am the least of the apostles, unfit to be called an apostle, because I persecuted the church of God. ¹⁰But by the grace of God I am what I am, and God's grace toward me has not been in vain. On the contrary, I worked harder than any of them—though it was not I, but the grace of God that is with me. ¹¹Whether then it was I or they, so we proclaim and so you have come to believe.

The Resurrection of the Dead

12 Now if Christ is proclaimed as raised from the dead, how can some of you say there is no resurrection of the dead? ¹³If there is no resurrection of the dead, then Christ has not been raised; ¹⁴and if Christ has not been raised, then our proclamation has been in vain and your faith has been in vain. ¹⁵We are even found to be misrepresenting God, because we testified of God that God raised Christ—whom God did not raise if it is true that the dead are not raised. ¹⁶For if the dead are not raised, then Christ has not been raised. ¹⁷If Christ has not been raised, your faith is futile and you are still in your sins. ¹⁸Then those also who have died[m] in Christ have perished. ¹⁹If for this life only we have hoped in Christ, we are of all people most to be pitied.

20 But in fact Christ has been raised from the dead, the firstfruits of those who have died.[m] ²¹For since death came through a human being, the resurrection of the dead has also come through a human being; ²²for as all die in Adam, so all will be made alive in Christ. ²³But each in the proper order: Christ the firstfruits, then at Christ's coming those who belong to Christ. ²⁴Then comes the end,[n] when Christ delivers the sovereignty to God the Father-Mother, after destroying every ruler and every authority and power. ²⁵For Christ must reign until all enemies are put under Christ's feet. ²⁶The last

---

l Or *gospel*   m Gk *fallen asleep*   n Or *Then come the rest* enemy to be destroyed is death. 27For "God has put all things in subjection under Christ's feet." But when it says, "All things are put in subjection," it is plain that this does not include the one who put all things in subjection under Christ. 28When all things are subjected to Christ, then Christ will also be subjected to God who put all things under Christ, so that God may be all in all.

29 Otherwise, what will those people do who receive baptism on behalf of the dead? If the dead are not raised at all, why are people baptized on their behalf?

30 And why are we putting ourselves in danger every hour? 31I die every day! That is as certain, sisters and brothers, as my boasting of you—a boast that I make in Christ Jesus our Lord. 32If with merely human hopes I fought with wild animals at Ephesus, what would I have gained by it? If the dead are not raised,

> "Let us eat and drink,
>   for tomorrow we die."

33Do not be deceived:

> "Bad company ruins good morals."

34Come to a sober and right mind, and sin no more; for some people have no knowledge of God. I say this to your shame.

The Resurrection Body

35 But someone will ask, "How are the dead raised? With what kind of body do they come?" 36Fool! What you sow does not come to life unless it dies. 37And as for what you sow, you do not sow the body that is to be, but a bare seed, perhaps of wheat or of some other grain. 38But God gives it a body as God has chosen, and to each kind of seed its own body. 39Not all flesh is alike, but there is one flesh for human beings, another for animals, another for birds, and another for fish. 40There are both heavenly bodies and earthly bodies, but the glory of the heavenly is one thing, and that of the earthly is another. 41There is one glory of the sun, and another glory of the moon, and another glory of the stars; indeed, star differs from star in glory.

42 So it is with the resurrection of the dead. What is sown is perishable, what is raised is imperishable. 43It is sown in dishonor, it is raised in glory. It is sown in weakness, it is raised in power. 44It is sown a physical body, it is raised a spiritual body. If there is a physical body, there is also a spiritual body. 45Thus it is written, "The first human being, Adam, became a living being"; the last Adam became a life-giving spirit. 46But it is not the spiritual that is first, but the physical, and then the spiritual. 47The first was from the earth, made of dust; the second is° from heaven. 48As was the one made of dust, so are those

---

o Other ancient authorities add *the Lord*

who are of the dust; and as is the one of heaven, so are those who are of heaven. [49]Just as we have borne the image of the one of dust, we will[p] also bear the image of the one of heaven.

50 What I am saying, brothers and sisters, is this: flesh and blood cannot inherit the dominion of God, nor does the perishable inherit the imperishable. [51]Listen, I will tell you a mystery! We will not all die,[q] but we will all be changed, [52]in a moment, in the twinkling of an eye, at the last trumpet. For the trumpet will sound, and the dead will be raised imperishable, and we will be changed. [53]For this perishable body must put on imperishability, and this mortal body must put on immortality. [54]When this perishable body puts on imperishability, and this mortal body puts on immortality, then the saying that is written will be fulfilled:

> "Death has been swallowed up in victory."
55 "Where, O death, is your victory?
> Where, O death, is your sting?"

[56]The sting of death is sin, and the power of sin is the law. [57]But thanks be to God, who gives us the victory through our Lord Jesus Christ.

58 Therefore, my beloved, be steadfast, immovable, always excelling in the work of the Lord, because you know that in the Lord your labor is not in vain.

The Collection for the Saints

16 Now concerning the collection for the saints: you should follow the directions I gave to the churches of Galatia. [2]On the first day of every week, each of you is to put aside and save whatever extra you earn, so that collections need not be taken when I come. [3]And when I arrive, I will send any whom you approve with letters to take your gift to Jerusalem. [4]If it seems advisable that I should go also, they will accompany me.

Plans for Travel

5 I will visit you after passing through Macedonia—for I intend to pass through Macedonia— [6]and perhaps I will stay with you or even spend the winter, so that you may send me on my way, wherever I go. [7]I do not want to see you now just in passing, for I hope to spend some time with you, if the Lord permits. [8]But I will stay in Ephesus until Pentecost, [9]for a wide door for effective work has opened to me, and there are many adversaries.

10 If Timothy comes, see that he has nothing to fear among you, for he is doing the work of the Lord just as I am; [11]therefore let no one despise him. Send him on his way in peace, so that he may come to me; for I am expecting him along with the others.

12 Now concerning our brother Apollos, I strongly urged him to visit you

---

p Other ancient authorities read *let us*   q Gk *fall asleep* along with the others, but he was not at all willing[r] to come now. He will come when he has the opportunity.

Final Messages and Greetings

13 Keep alert, stand firm in your faith, be courageous, be strong. [14]Let all that you do be done in love.

15 Now, sisters and brothers, you know that members of the household of Stephanas were the first converts in Achaia, and they have devoted themselves to the service of the saints; [16]I urge you to put yourselves at the service of such people, and of everyone who works and toils with them. [17]I rejoice at the coming of Stephanas and Fortunatus and Achaicus, because they have made up for your absence; [18]for they refreshed my spirit as well as yours. So give recognition to such persons.

19 The churches of Asia send greetings. Aquila and Prisca, together with the church in their house, greet you warmly in the Lord. [20]All the brothers and sisters send greetings. Greet one another with a holy kiss.

21 I, Paul, write this greeting with my own hand. [22]Let anyone be accursed who has no love for the Lord. Our Lord, come![s] [23]The grace of the Lord Jesus be with you. [24]My love be with all of you in Christ Jesus.[t]

---

r Or it was not at all God's will for him
s Gk Marana tha. These Aramaic words can also be read Maran atha, meaning Our Lord has come   t Other ancient authorities add Amen

The Second Letter of Paul to the Corinthians

Salutation

1 Paul, an apostle of Christ Jesus by the will of God, and Timothy our brother,

To the church of God that is in Corinth, including all the saints throughout Achaia:

2 Grace to you and peace from God our Father-Mother and the Lord Jesus Christ.

Paul's Thanksgiving after Affliction

3 Blessed be the God and Father-Mother of our Lord Jesus Christ—the God of all mercies and of all consolation— ⁴who consoles us in all our affliction, so that we may be able to console those who are in any affliction with the consolation with which we ourselves are consoled by God. ⁵For just as the sufferings of Christ are abundant for us, so also our consolation is abundant through Christ. ⁶If we are being afflicted, it is for your consolation and salvation; if we are being consoled, it is for your consolation, which you experience when you patiently endure the same sufferings that we are also suffering. ⁷Our hope for you is unshaken; for we know that as you share in our sufferings, so also you share in our consolation.

8 We do not want you to be unaware, brothers and sisters, of the affliction we experienced in Asia; for we were so utterly, unbearably crushed that we despaired of life itself. ⁹Indeed, we felt that we had received the sentence of death so that we would rely not on ourselves but on God who raises the dead. ¹⁰The one who rescued us from so deadly a peril will continue to rescue us; on God we have set our hope that God will rescue us again, ¹¹as you also join in

helping us by your prayers, so that many will give thanks on our[a] behalf for the blessing granted us through the prayers of many.

The Postponement of Paul's Visit

12 Indeed, this is our boast, the testimony of our conscience: we have behaved in the world with frankness[b] and godly sincerity, not by earthly wisdom but by the grace of God—and all the more toward you. [13] For we write you nothing other than what you can read and also understand; I hope you will understand until the end— [14] as you have already understood us in part—that on the day of the Lord Jesus we are your boast even as you are our boast.

15 Since I was sure of this, I wanted to come to you first, so that you might have a double favor;[c] [16] I wanted to visit you on my way to Macedonia, and to come back to you from Macedonia and have you send me on to Judea. [17] Was I vacillating when I wanted to do this? Do I make my plans according to ordinary human standards,[d] ready to say "Yes, yes" and "No, no" at the same time? [18] As surely as God is faithful, our word to you has not been "Yes and No." [19] For the Child of God, Jesus Christ, whom we proclaimed among you, Silvanus and Timothy and I, was not "Yes and No"; but in Christ it is always "Yes." [20] For in Christ every one of God's promises is a "Yes." For this reason it is through Christ that we say the "Amen," to the glory of God. [21] But it is God who establishes us with you in Christ and has anointed us, [22] by putting the seal of Christ on us and giving us the Spirit in our hearts as a first installment.

23 But I call on God as witness against me: it was to spare you that I did not come again to Corinth. [24] I do not mean to imply that we lord it over your faith; rather, we are workers with you for your joy, because you stand firm in the faith. [2] [1] So I made up my mind not to make you another painful visit. [2] For if I cause you pain, who is there to make me glad but the one whom I have pained? [3] And I wrote as I did, so that when I came, I might not suffer pain from those who should have made me rejoice; for I am confident about all of you, that my joy would be the joy of all of you. [4] For I wrote you out of much distress and anguish of heart and with many tears, not to cause you pain, but to let you know the abundant love that I have for you.

Forgiveness for the Offender

5 But if anyone has caused pain, that person has caused it not to me, but to some extent—not to exaggerate it—to all of you. [6] This punishment by the majority is enough; [7] so now instead you should forgive and console anyone who has caused pain, so that such a person may not be overwhelmed by excessive sorrow. [8] So I urge you to reaffirm your love for that person. [9] I wrote for this reason: to test you and to know whether you are obedient in

---

a Other ancient authorities read *your*   b Other ancient authorities read *holiness*
c Other ancient authorities read *pleasure*   d Gk *according to the flesh*

everything. ¹⁰Anyone whom you forgive, I also forgive. What I have forgiven, if I have forgiven anything, has been for your sake in the presence of Christ. ¹¹And we do this so that we may not be outwitted by Satan; for we are not ignorant of Satan's designs.

Paul's Anxiety in Troas

12 When I came to Troas to proclaim the good news of Christ, a door was opened for me in the Lord; ¹³but my mind could not rest because I did not find my brother Titus there. So I said farewell to them and went on to Macedonia.

14 But thanks be to God, who in Christ always leads us in triumphal procession, and through us spreads in every place the fragrance that comes from knowing Christ. ¹⁵For we are the aroma of Christ to God among those who are being saved and among those who are perishing; ¹⁶to the one a fragrance from death to death, to the other a fragrance from life to life. Who is sufficient for these things? ¹⁷For we are not peddlers of God's word like so many;ᵉ but in Christ we speak as persons of sincerity, as persons sent from God and standing in God's presence.

Ministers of the New Covenant

3 Are we beginning to commend ourselves again? Surely we do not need, as some do, letters of recommendation to you or from you, do we? ²You yourselves are our letter, written on ourᶠ hearts, to be known and read by all; ³and you show that you are a letter of Christ, prepared by us, written not with ink but with the Spirit of the living God, not on tablets of stone but on tablets of human hearts.

4 Such is the confidence that we have through Christ toward God. ⁵Not that we are competent of ourselves to claim anything as coming from us; our competence is from God, ⁶who has made us competent to be ministers of a new covenant, not of letter but of spirit; for the letter kills, but the Spirit gives life.

7 Now if the ministry of death, chiseled in letters on stone tablets,ᵍ came in glory so that the people of Israel could not gaze at Moses' face because of the glory of his face, a glory now set aside, ⁸how much more will the ministry of the Spirit come in glory? ⁹For if there was glory in the ministry of condemnation, much more does the ministry of justification abound in glory! ¹⁰Indeed, what once had glory has lost its glory because of the greater glory; ¹¹for if what was set aside came through glory, much more has the permanent come in glory!

12 Since, then, we have such a hope, we act with great boldness, ¹³not like Moses, who put a veil over his face to keep the people of Israel from gazing at

---

e Other ancient authorities read *like the others*   f Other ancient authorities read *your*
g Gk *on stones*

the end of the glory that[h] was being set aside. [14] But their minds were hardened. Indeed, to this very day, when they hear the reading of the old covenant, that same veil is still there, since only in Christ is it set aside. [15] Indeed, to this very day whenever Moses is read, a veil lies over their minds; [16] but when one turns to the Lord, the veil is removed. [17] Now the Lord is the Spirit, and where the Spirit of the Lord is, there is freedom. [18] And all of us, with unveiled faces, seeing the glory of the Lord as though reflected in a mirror, are being transformed into the same image from one degree of glory to another; for this comes from the Lord, the Spirit.

Treasure in Clay Jars

4 Therefore, since it is by God's mercy that we are engaged in this ministry, we do not lose heart. [2] We have renounced the shameful things that one hides; we refuse to practice cunning or to falsify God's word; but by the open statement of the truth we commend ourselves to the conscience of everyone in the sight of God. [3] And even if our gospel is veiled, it is veiled to those who are perishing. [4] In their case the god of this world has blinded the minds of the unbelievers, to keep them from seeing the light of the gospel of the glory of Christ, who is the image of God. [5] For we do not proclaim ourselves; we proclaim Jesus Christ as Lord and ourselves as those enslaved to you for Jesus' sake. [6] For the God who said, "Let light shine out of the night" has shone in our hearts to give the light of the knowledge of the glory of God in the face of Jesus Christ.

7 But we have this treasure in clay jars, so that it may be made clear that this extraordinary power belongs to God and does not come from us. [8] We are afflicted in every way, but not crushed; perplexed, but not driven to despair; [9] persecuted, but not forsaken; struck down, but not destroyed; [10] always carrying in the body the death of Jesus, so that the life of Jesus may also be made visible in our bodies. [11] For while we live, we are always being given up to death for Jesus' sake, so that the life of Jesus may be made visible in our mortal flesh. [12] So death is at work in us, but life in you.

13 But just as we have the same spirit of faith that is in accordance with scripture—"I believed, and so I spoke"—we also believe, and so we speak, [14] because we know that the one who raised the Lord Jesus will raise us also with Jesus, and will present us together with you. [15] Yes, everything is for your sake, so that grace, as it extends to more and more people, may increase thanksgiving, to the glory of God.

Living by Faith

16 So we do not lose heart. Even though our outer nature is wasting away, our inner nature is being renewed day by day. [17] For this slight momentary affliction is preparing us for an eternal weight of glory beyond all measure, [18] because we

---

h Gk of what

look not at what can be seen but at what cannot be seen; for what can be seen is temporary, but what cannot be seen is eternal.

5 For we know that if the earthly tent we live in is destroyed, we have a building from God, a house not made with hands, eternal in the heavens. ²For in this tent we groan, longing to be clothed with our heavenly dwelling— ³if indeed, when we have taken it off[i] we will not be found naked. ⁴For while we are still in this tent, we groan under our burden, because we wish not to be unclothed but to be further clothed, so that what is mortal may be swallowed up by life. ⁵The one who has prepared us for this very thing is God, who has given us the Spirit as a guarantee.

6 So we are always confident; even though we know that while we are at home in the body we are away from Christ— ⁷for we walk by faith, not by sight. ⁸Yes, we do have confidence, and we would rather be away from the body and at home with Christ. ⁹So whether we are at home or away, we make it our aim to please Christ. ¹⁰For all of us must appear before the judgment seat of Christ, so that each may receive recompense for what has been done in the body, whether good or evil.

The Ministry of Reconciliation

11 Therefore, knowing the fear of the Lord, we try to persuade others; but we ourselves are well known to God, and I hope that we are also well known to your consciences. ¹²We are not commending ourselves to you again, but giving you an opportunity to boast about us, so that you may be able to answer those who boast in outward appearance and not in the heart. ¹³For if we are beside ourselves, it is for God; if we are in our right mind, it is for you. ¹⁴For the love of Christ urges us on, because we are convinced that one has died for all; therefore all have died. ¹⁵And Christ died for all, so that those who live might live no longer for themselves, but for the one who died and was raised for them.

16 From now on, therefore, we regard no one from a human point of view;[j] even though we once knew Christ from a human point of view,[j] we know Christ no longer in that way. ¹⁷So if anyone is in Christ, there is a new creation: everything old has passed away; see, everything has become new! ¹⁸All this is from God, with whom we have been reconciled through Christ, and by whom we have been given the ministry of reconciliation; ¹⁹that is, in Christ God was reconciling the world to Godself,[k] not counting the people's trespasses against them, and entrusting the message of reconciliation to us. ²⁰So we are ambassadors for Christ, since God is exhorting you through us; we entreat you on behalf of Christ, be reconciled to God. ²¹For our sake God made Christ to be sin who knew no sin, so that in Christ we might become the righteousness of God.

---

i Other ancient authorities read *put it on*   j Gk *according to the flesh*
k Or *God was in Christ reconciling the world to Godself*

6 As we work together with God,[1] we urge you also not to accept the grace of God in vain. [2]For God says,

> "At an acceptable time I have listened to you,
>   and on a day of salvation I have helped you."

See, now is the acceptable time; see, now is the day of salvation! [3]We are putting no obstacle in anyone's way, so that no fault may be found with our ministry, [4]but as servants of God we have commended ourselves in every way: through great endurance, in afflictions, hardships, calamities, [5]beatings, imprisonments, riots, labors, sleepless nights, hunger; [6]by purity, knowledge, patience, kindness, holiness of spirit, genuine love, [7]truthful speech, and the power of God; with the weapons of righteousness for the right hand and for the left; [8]in honor and dishonor, in ill repute and good repute. We are treated as impostors, and yet are true; [9]as unknown, and yet are well known; as dying, and see—we are alive; as punished, and yet not killed; [10]as sorrowful, yet always rejoicing; as poor, yet making many rich; as having nothing, and yet possessing everything.

11 We have spoken frankly to you Corinthians; our heart is wide open to you. [12]There is no restriction in our affections, but only in yours. [13]In return—I speak as to children—open wide your hearts also.

The Temple of the Living God

14 Do not be mismatched with unbelievers. For what partnership is there between righteousness and lawlessness? Or what do day and night have in common? [15]What agreement does Christ have with Beliar? Or what does a believer share with an unbeliever? [16]What agreement has the temple of God with idols? For we[m] are the temple of the living God; as God said,

> "I will live in them and walk among them,
>   and I will be their God,
>   and they shall be my people.
> 17 Therefore come out from them,
>   and be separate from them, says God,
>   and touch nothing unclean;
>   then I will welcome you,
> 18   and I will be your mother and father,
>   and you shall be my sons and daughters,
>   says God Almighty."

7 Since we have these promises, beloved, let us cleanse ourselves from every defilement of body and of spirit, making holiness perfect in the fear of God.

---

l Gk *As we work together*   m Other ancient authorities read *you*

Paul's Joy at the Church's Repentance

2 Make room in your hearts[n] for us; we have wronged no one, we have corrupted no one, we have taken advantage of no one. ³I do not say this to condemn you, for I said before that you are in our hearts, to die together and to live together. ⁴I often boast about you; I have great pride in you; I am filled with consolation; I am overjoyed in all our affliction.

5 For even when we came into Macedonia, our bodies had no rest, but we were afflicted in every way—disputes without and fears within. ⁶But God, who consoles the downcast, consoled us by the arrival of Titus, ⁷and not only by his coming, but also by the consolation with which Titus was consoled about you, as he told us of your longing, your mourning, your zeal for me, so that I rejoiced still more. ⁸For even if I made you sorry with my letter, I do not regret it (though I did regret it, for I see that I grieved you with that letter, though only briefly). ⁹Now I rejoice, not because you were grieved, but because your grief led to repentance; for you felt a godly grief, so that you were not harmed in any way by us. ¹⁰For godly grief produces a repentance that leads to salvation and brings no regret, but worldly grief produces death. ¹¹For see what earnestness this godly grief has produced in you, what eagerness to clear yourselves, what indignation, what alarm, what longing, what zeal, what punishment! At every point you have proved yourselves guiltless in the matter. ¹²So although I wrote to you, it was not on account of the one who did the wrong, nor on account of the one who was wronged, but in order that your zeal for us might be made known to you before God. ¹³In this we find comfort.

In addition to our own consolation, we rejoiced still more at the joy of Titus, because his mind has been set at rest by all of you. ¹⁴For if I have been somewhat boastful about you to him, I was not disgraced; but just as everything we said to you was true, so our boasting to Titus has proved true as well. ¹⁵And his heart goes out all the more to you, as he remembers the obedience of all of you, and how you welcomed him with fear and trembling. ¹⁶I rejoice, because I have complete confidence in you.

Encouragement to Be Generous

8 We want you to know, sisters and brothers, about the grace of God that has been granted to the churches of Macedonia; ²for during a severe ordeal of affliction, their abundant joy and their extreme poverty have overflowed in a wealth of generosity on their part. ³For, as I can testify, they voluntarily gave according to their means, and even beyond their means, ⁴begging us earnestly for the privilege[o] of sharing in this ministry to the saints— ⁵and this, not merely as we expected; they gave themselves first to Christ and, by the will of God, to us, ⁶so that we might urge Titus that, as he had already made a beginning, so he should also complete this generous undertaking[p] among you.

---

n Gk lacks *in your hearts*   o Gk *grace*   p Gk *this grace*

7 Now as you excel in everything—in faith, in speech, in knowledge, in utmost eagerness, and in our love for you[q]—so we want you to excel also in this generous undertaking.[r]

8 I do not say this as a command, but I am testing the genuineness of your love against the earnestness of others. 9 For you know the generous act[s] of our Lord Jesus Christ, who though rich, yet for your sakes became poor, so that by the poverty of Christ you might become rich. 10 And in this matter I am giving my advice: it is appropriate for you who began last year not only to do something but even to desire to do something— 11 now finish doing it, so that your eagerness may be matched by completing it according to your means. 12 For if the eagerness is there, the gift is acceptable according to what one has—not according to what one does not have. 13 I do not mean that there should be relief for others and pressure on you, but it is a question of a fair balance between 14 your present abundance and their need, so that their abundance may be for your need, in order that there may be a fair balance. 15 As it is written,

"The one who had much did not have too much,
    and the one who had little did not have too little."

Commendation of Titus

16 But thanks be to God who put in the heart of Titus the same eagerness for you that I myself have. 17 For he not only accepted our appeal, but since he is more eager than ever, he is going to you of his own accord. 18 With Titus we are sending the brother who is famous among all the churches for proclaiming the good news,[t] 19 and moreover has been appointed by the churches to travel with us while we are administering this generous undertaking[r] for the glory of the Lord and to show our goodwill. 20 We intend that no one should blame us about this generous gift that we are administering, 21 for we intend to do what is right not only in the Lord's sight but also in the sight of others. 22 And with them we are sending our brother whom we have often tested and found eager in many matters, but who is now more eager than ever because of having great confidence in you. 23 As for Titus, he is my partner and coworker in your service; as for the others, they are messengers[u] of the churches, the glory of Christ. 24 Therefore openly before the churches, show them the proof of your love and of our reason for boasting about you.

The Collection for Christians at Jerusalem

9 Now it is not necessary for me to write you about the ministry to the saints, 2 for I know your eagerness, which is the subject of my boasting about you to the people of Macedonia, saying that Achaia has been ready since

---

q Other ancient authorities read *your love for us*   r Gk *this grace*   s Gk *the grace*
t Or *the gospel*   u Gk *apostles*

last year; and your zeal has stirred up most of them. [3]But I am sending the others in order that our boasting about you may not prove to have been empty in this case, so that you may be ready, as I said you would be; [4]otherwise, if some Macedonians come with me and find that you are not ready, we would be humiliated—to say nothing of you—in this undertaking.[v] [5]So I thought it necessary to urge the others to go on ahead to you, and arrange in advance for this bountiful gift that you have promised, so that it may be ready as a voluntary gift and not as an extortion.

6 The point is this: the one who sows sparingly will also reap sparingly, and the one who sows bountifully will also reap bountifully. [7]Each of you must give as you have made up your mind, not reluctantly or under compulsion, for God loves a cheerful giver. [8]And God is able to provide you with every blessing in abundance, so that by always having enough of everything, you may share abundantly in every good work. [9]As it is written,

> "God scatters abroad and gives to those who are poor;
> God's righteousness[w] endures forever."

[10]The one who supplies seed to the sower and bread for food will supply and multiply your seed for sowing and increase the harvest of your righteousness.[w] [11]You will be enriched in every way for your great generosity, which will produce thanksgiving to God through us; [12]for the rendering of this ministry not only supplies the needs of the saints but also overflows with many thanksgivings to God. [13]Through the testing of this ministry you glorify God by your obedience to the confession of the gospel of Christ and by the generosity of your sharing with them and with all others, [14]while they long for you and pray for you because of the surpassing grace of God that has been given you. [15]Thanks be to God for God's indescribable gift!

Paul Defends His Ministry

10 I myself, Paul, appeal to you by the meekness and gentleness of Christ—I who am humble when face to face with you, but bold toward you when I am away!— [2]I ask that when I am present I need not show boldness by daring to oppose those who think we are acting according to human standards.[x] [3]Indeed, we live as human beings,[y] but we do not wage war according to human standards;[x] [4]for the weapons of our warfare are not merely human,[z] but they have divine power to destroy strongholds. We destroy arguments [5]and every proud obstacle raised up against the knowledge of God, and we take every thought captive to obey Christ. [6]We are ready to punish every disobedience when your obedience is complete.

7 Look at what is before your eyes. If you are confident that you belong to Christ, remind yourself of this, that just as you belong to Christ, so also do

---

v Other ancient authorities add *of boasting*   w Or *benevolence*   x Gk *according to the flesh*
y Gk *in the flesh*   z Gk *fleshly*

we. ⁸Now, even if I boast a little too much of our authority, which the Lord gave for building you up and not for tearing you down, I will not be ashamed of it. ⁹I do not want to seem as though I am trying to frighten you with my letters. ¹⁰For they say, "Paul's letters are weighty and strong, but his bodily presence is weak, and his speech contemptible." ¹¹Let such people understand that what we say by letter when absent, we will also do when present.

12 We do not dare to classify or compare ourselves with some of those who commend themselves. But when they measure themselves by one another, and compare themselves with one another, they do not show good sense. ¹³We, however, will not boast beyond limits, but will keep within the field that God has assigned to us, to reach out even as far as you. ¹⁴For we were not overstepping our limits when we reached you; we were the first to come all the way to you with the good news[a] of Christ. ¹⁵We do not boast beyond limits, that is, in the labors of others; but our hope is that, as your faith increases, our sphere of action among you may be greatly enlarged, ¹⁶so that we may proclaim the good news[a] in lands beyond you, without boasting of work already done in someone else's sphere of action. ¹⁷"Let the one who boasts, boast in the Lord." ¹⁸For it is not those who commend themselves that are approved, but those whom the Lord commends.

Paul and the False Apostles

11 I wish you would bear with me in a little foolishness. Do bear with me! ²I feel a divine jealousy for you, for I promised you in marriage to one spouse, to present you as a pure virgin to Christ. ³But I am afraid that as the serpent deceived Eve by its cunning, your thoughts will be led astray from a sincere and pure[b] devotion to Christ. ⁴For if someone comes and proclaims another Jesus than the one we proclaimed, or if you receive a different spirit from the one you received, or a different gospel from the one you accepted, you submit to it readily enough. ⁵I think that I am not in the least inferior to these super-apostles. ⁶I may be untrained in speech, but not in knowledge; certainly in every way and in all things we have made this evident to you.

7 Did I commit a sin by humbling myself so that you might be exalted, because I proclaimed God's good news[c] to you free of charge? ⁸I robbed other churches by accepting support from them in order to serve you. ⁹And when I was with you and was in need, I did not burden anyone, for my needs were supplied by the friends who came from Macedonia. So I refrained and will continue to refrain from burdening you in any way. ¹⁰As the truth of Christ is in me, this boast of mine will not be silenced in the regions of Achaia. ¹¹And why? Because I do not love you? God knows I do!

12 And what I do I will also continue to do, in order to deny an opportunity to those who want an opportunity to be recognized as our equals in what they boast about. ¹³For such boasters are false apostles, deceitful

---

a Or *the gospel*   b Other ancient authorities lack *and pure*   c Gk *the gospel of God*

workers, disguising themselves as apostles of Christ. ¹⁴And no wonder! Even
Satan adopts the disguise of an angel of light. ¹⁵So it is not strange if Satan's
ministers also disguise themselves as ministers of righteousness. Their end will
match their deeds.

Paul's Sufferings as an Apostle

16 I repeat, let no one think that I am a fool; but if you do, then accept me
as a fool, so that I too may boast a little. ¹⁷What I am saying in regard to this
boastful confidence, I am saying not with the Lord's authority, but as a fool;
¹⁸since many boast according to human standards,^d I will also boast. ¹⁹For you
gladly put up with fools, being wise yourselves! ²⁰For you put up with it when
someone enslaves you, or preys upon you, or takes advantage of you, or puts
on airs, or gives you a slap in the face. ²¹To my shame, I must say, we were
too weak for that!

But whatever anyone dares to boast of—I am speaking as a fool—I also
dare to boast of that. ²²Are they Hebrews? So am I. Are they Israelites? So am
I. Are they descendants of Abraham? So am I. ²³Are they ministers of Christ?
I am talking like a madman—I am a better one: with far greater labors, far
more imprisonments, with countless floggings, and often near death. ²⁴Five
times I have received from the Jews the forty lashes minus one. ²⁵Three times
I was beaten with rods. Once I received a stoning. Three times I was
shipwrecked; for a night and a day I was adrift at sea; ²⁶on frequent journeys,
in danger from rivers, danger from bandits, danger from my own people, danger
from Gentiles, danger in the city, danger in the wilderness, danger at sea,
danger from false brothers and sisters; ²⁷in toil and hardship, through many a
sleepless night, hungry and thirsty, often without food, cold and naked. ²⁸And,
besides other things, I am under daily pressure because of my anxiety for all
the churches. ²⁹Who is weak, and I am not weak? Who is made to stumble, and
I am not indignant?

30 If I must boast, I will boast of the things that show my weakness.
³¹The God and Father-Mother, of the Lord Jesus (blessed be God forever!)
knows that I do not lie. ³²In Damascus, the governor^e under King Aretas
guarded the city of Damascus in order to^f seize me, ³³but I was let down in a
basket through a window in the wall,^g and escaped from his hands.

Paul's Visions and Revelations

12 It is necessary to boast; nothing is to be gained by it, but I will go on
to visions and revelations of the Lord. ²I know a person in Christ who
fourteen years ago was caught up to the third heaven—whether in the body or
out of the body I do not know; God knows. ³And I know that such a
person—whether in the body or out of the body I do not know; God knows—

---

d Gk *according to the flesh*   e Gk *ethnarch*   f Other ancient authorities read *and wanted to*
g Gk *through the wall*

[4]was caught up into Paradise and heard things that are not to be told, that no mortal is permitted to repeat. [5]On behalf of such a one I will boast, but on my own behalf I will not boast, except of my weaknesses. [6]But if I wish to boast, I will not be a fool, for I will be speaking the truth. But I refrain from it, so that no one may think better of me than what is seen in me or heard from me, [7]even considering the exceptional character of the revelations. Therefore, to keep[h] me from being too elated, a thorn was given me in the flesh, a messenger of Satan to torment me, to keep me from being too elated.[i] [8]Three times I appealed to the Lord about this, that it would leave me, [9]but the Lord said to me, "My grace is sufficient for you, for power[j] is made perfect in weakness." So, I will boast all the more gladly of my weaknesses, so that the power of Christ may dwell in me. [10]Therefore I am content with weaknesses, insults, hardships, persecutions, and calamities for the sake of Christ; for whenever I am weak, then I am strong.

Paul's Concern for the Corinthian Church

11 I have been a fool! You forced me to it. Indeed you should have been the ones commending me, for I am not at all inferior to these super-apostles, even though I am nothing. [12]The signs of a true apostle were performed among you with utmost patience, signs and wonders and mighty works. [13]How have you been worse off than the other churches, except that I myself did not burden you? Forgive me this wrong!

14 Here I am, ready to come to you this third time. And I will not be a burden, because I do not want what is yours but you; for children ought not to put aside resources for their parents, but parents for their children. [15]I will most gladly spend and be spent for you. If I love you more, am I to be loved less? [16]Let it be assumed that I did not burden you. Nevertheless (you say) since I was crafty, I took you in by deceit. [17]Did I take advantage of you through any of those whom I sent to you? [18]I urged Titus to go, and sent the coworker with him. Titus did not take advantage of you, did he? Did we not conduct ourselves with the same spirit? Did we not take the same steps?

19 Have you been thinking all along that we have been defending ourselves before you? We are speaking in Christ before God. Everything we do, beloved, is for the sake of building you up. [20]For I fear that when I come, I may find you not as I wish, and that you may find me not as you wish; I fear that there may perhaps be quarreling, jealousy, anger, selfishness, slander, gossip, conceit, and disorder. [21]I fear that when I come again, my God may humble me before you, and that I may have to mourn over many who previously sinned and have not repented of the impurity, sexual immorality, and licentiousness that they have practiced.

---

h Other ancient authorities read *To keep*
i Other ancient authorities lack *to keep me from being too elated*
j Other ancient authorities read *my power*

Further Warning

13 This is the third time I am coming to you. "Any charge must be sustained by the evidence of two or three witnesses." 2I warned those who sinned previously and all the others, and I warn them now while absent, as I did when present on my second visit, that if I come again, I will not be lenient— 3since you desire proof that Christ is speaking in me. Christ is not weak in dealing with you, but is powerful in you. 4For Christ was crucified in weakness, but lives by the power of God. For we are weak in Christ,[k] but in dealing with you we will live with Christ by the power of God.

5 Examine yourselves to see whether you are living in the faith. Test yourselves. Do you not realize that Jesus Christ is in you?—unless, indeed, you fail to meet the test! 6I hope you will find out that we have not failed. 7But we pray to God that you may not do anything wrong—not that we may appear to have met the test, but that you may do what is right, though we may seem to have failed. 8For we cannot do anything against the truth, but only for the truth. 9For we rejoice when we are weak and you are strong. This is what we pray for, that you may become perfect. 10So I write these things while I am away from you, so that when I come, I may not have to be severe in using the authority that the Lord has given me for building up and not for tearing down.

Final Greetings and Benediction

11 Finally, sisters and brothers, farewell.[l] Put things in order, listen to my appeal,[m] agree with one another, live in peace; and the God of love and peace will be with you. 12Greet one another with a holy kiss. All the saints greet you.

13 The grace of the Lord Jesus Christ, the love of God, and the communion of[n] the Holy Spirit be with all of you.

---

k Other ancient authorities read *with Christ*   l Or *rejoice*   m Or *encourage one another*
n Or *and the sharing in*

The Letter of Paul to the Galatians

Salutation

1 Paul an apostle—sent neither by human commission nor from human authorities, but through Jesus Christ and God the Father-Mother, who raised Christ from the dead— ²and all the members of God's family who are with me,

To the churches of Galatia:

3 Grace to you and peace from God our Father-Mother and the Lord Jesus Christ, ⁴who gave up life for our sins to set us free from the present evil age, according to the will of our God and Father-Mother, ⁵to whom be the glory forever and ever. Amen.

There Is No Other Gospel

6 I am astonished that you are so quickly deserting the one who called you in the grace of Christ and are turning to a different gospel— ⁷not that there is another gospel, but there are some who are confusing you and want to pervert the gospel of Christ. ⁸But even if we or an angel[a] from heaven should proclaim to you a gospel contrary to what we proclaimed to you, let that one be accursed! ⁹As we have said before, so now I repeat, if anyone proclaims to you a gospel contrary to what you received, let that one be accursed!

10 Am I now seeking human approval, or God's approval? Or am I trying to please people? If I were still pleasing human beings, I would not be a servant of Christ.

Paul's Vindication of His Apostleship

11 For I want you to know, brothers and sisters, that the gospel that was proclaimed by me is not of human origin; ¹²for I did not receive it from a

---

a Or *a messenger*

human source, nor was I taught it, but I received it through a revelation of Jesus Christ.

13 You have heard, no doubt, of my earlier life in Judaism. I was violently persecuting the church of God and was trying to destroy it. ¹⁴I advanced in Judaism beyond many among my people of the same age, for I was far more zealous for the traditions of my ancestors. ¹⁵But when God, who had set me apart before I was born and called me through God's grace, was pleased ¹⁶to reveal God's Child to me,ᵇ so that I might proclaim that Child among the Gentiles, I did not confer with any human being, ¹⁷nor did I go up to Jerusalem to those who were already apostles before me, but I went away at once into Arabia, and afterwards I returned to Damascus.

18 Then after three years I did go up to Jerusalem to visit Cephas and stayed with him fifteen days; ¹⁹but I did not see any other apostle except James the brother of Jesus. ²⁰In what I am writing to you, before God, I do not lie! ²¹Then I went into the regions of Syria and Cilicia, ²²and I was still unknown by sight to the churches of Judea that are in Christ; ²³they only heard it said, "The one who formerly was persecuting us is now proclaiming the faith he once tried to destroy." ²⁴And they glorified God because of me.

Paul and the Other Apostles

2 Then after fourteen years I went up again to Jerusalem with Barnabas, taking Titus along with me. ²I went up in response to a revelation. Then I laid before them (though only in a private meeting with the acknowledged leaders) the gospel that I proclaim among the Gentiles, in order to make sure that I was not running, or had not run, in vain. ³But even Titus, who was with me, was not compelled to be circumcised, though he was a Greek. ⁴But because of false believers secretly brought in, who slipped in to spy on the freedom we have in Christ Jesus, so that they might enslave us— ⁵we did not submit to them even for a moment, so that the truth of the gospel might always remain with you. ⁶And from those who were supposed to be acknowledged leaders (what they actually were makes no difference to me; God shows no partiality) —those leaders contributed nothing to me. ⁷On the contrary, when they saw that I had been entrusted with the gospel for those outside the law, just as Peter had been entrusted with the gospel for those under the law ⁸(for the one who worked through Peter making him an apostle to those under the law also worked through me in sending me to the Gentiles), ⁹and when James and Cephas and John, who were acknowledged pillars, recognized the grace that had been given to me, they shook hands with Barnabas and me, agreeing that we should go to the Gentiles and they to those under the law. ¹⁰They asked only one thing, that we remember those who are poor, which was actually what I wasᶜ eager to do.

---

b Gk *in me*   c Or *had been*

Paul Rebukes Cephas at Antioch

11 But when Cephas came to Antioch, I opposed him to his face, because he stood self-condemned; 12 for until certain people came from James, he used to eat with the Gentiles. But after they came, he drew back and kept himself separate for fear of the faction advocating being under the law. 13 And the other Jews joined him in this hypocrisy, so that even Barnabas was led astray by their hypocrisy. 14 But when I saw that they were not acting consistently with the truth of the gospel, I said to Cephas before them all, "If you, though a Jew, live like a Gentile and not like a Jew, how can you compel the Gentiles to live like Jews?"d

Jews and Gentiles Are Saved by Faith

15 We ourselves are Jews by birth and not Gentile sinners; 16 yet we know that a person is justifiede not by the works of the law but through faith in Jesus Christ.f And we have come to believe in Christ Jesus, so that we might be justified by faith in Christ,g and not by doing the works of the law, because no one will be justified by the works of the law. 17 But if, in our effort to be justified in Christ, we ourselves have been found to be sinners, is Christ then a servant of sin? Certainly not! 18 But if I build up again the very things that I once tore down, then I demonstrate that I am a transgressor. 19 For through the law I died to the law, so that I might live to God. I have been crucified with Christ; 20 and it is no longer I who live, but it is Christ who lives in me. And the life I now live in the flesh I live by faith in the Child of God,h who loved me and gave up life for me. 21 I do not nullify the grace of God; for if justificationi comes through the law, then Christ died for nothing.

Law or Faith

3 You foolish Galatians! Who has put a spell on you? It was before your eyes that Jesus Christ was publicly exhibited as crucified! 2 The only thing I want to learn from you is this: Did you receive the Spirit by doing the works of the law or by believing what you heard? 3 Are you so foolish? Having started with the Spirit, are you now ending with the flesh? 4 Did you experience so much for nothing?—if it really was for nothing. 5 Well then, does God supply you with the Spirit and work miracles among you by your doing the works of the law, or by your believing what you heard?

6 Just as Abraham "believed God, and it was reckoned to him as righteousness," 7 so, you see, those who believe are the descendants of Abraham and Sarah. 8 And the scripture, foreseeing that God would justify the Gentiles by faith, declared the gospel beforehand to Abraham, saying, "All the Gentiles shall

---

d Some interpreters hold that the quotation extends into the following paragraph
e Or *reckoned as righteous;* and so elsewhere   f Or *the faith of Jesus Christ*
g Or *the faith of Christ*   h Or *by the faith of the Child of God*   i Or *righteousness*

be blessed in you." [9]For this reason, those who believe are blessed with Abraham who believed.

10 For all who rely on the works of the law are under a curse; for it is written, "Cursed is everyone who does not observe and obey all the things written in the book of the law." [11]Now it is evident that no one is justified before God by the law; for "The one who is righteous will live by faith."[j] [12]But the law does not rest on faith; on the contrary, "Whoever does the works of the law[k] will live by them." [13]Christ redeemed us from the curse of the law by becoming a curse for us—for it is written, "Cursed is everyone who hangs on a tree"— [14]in order that in Christ Jesus the blessing of Abraham might come to the Gentiles, so that we might receive the promise of the Spirit through faith.

The Promise to Abraham

15 Sisters and brothers, I give an example from daily life: once a person's will[l] has been ratified, no one adds to it or annuls it. [16]Now the promises were made to Abraham and to his offspring; it does not say, "And to offsprings," as of many; but it says, "And to your offspring," that is, to one person, who is Christ. [17]My point is this: the law, which came four hundred thirty years later, does not annul a covenant previously ratified by God, so as to nullify the promise. [18]For if the inheritance comes from the law, it no longer comes from the promise; but God granted it to Abraham through the promise.

The Purpose of the Law

19 Why then the law? It was added because of transgressions, until the offspring would come to whom the promise had been made; and it was ordained through angels by a mediator. [20]Now a mediator involves more than one party; but God is one.

21 Is the law then opposed to the promises of God? Certainly not! For if a law had been given that could make alive, then righteousness would indeed come through the law. [22]But the scripture has imprisoned all things under the power of sin, so that what was promised through faith in Jesus Christ[m] might be given to those who believe.

23 Now before faith came, we were imprisoned and guarded under the law until faith would be revealed. [24]Therefore the law was our guide until Christ came, so that we might be justified by faith. [25]But now that faith has come, we are no longer subject to a guide, [26]for in Christ Jesus you are all children of God through faith. [27]As many of you as were baptized into Christ have clothed yourselves with Christ. [28]There is no longer Jew or Greek, there is no longer enslaved or free, there is no longer male and female; for all of you are one in

---

j Or *The one who is righteous through faith will live*   k Gk *does them*
l Or *covenant* (as in verse 17)   m Or *through the faith of Jesus Christ*

Christ Jesus. [29] And if you belong to Christ, then you are Abraham's offspring, heirs according to the promise.

4 My point is this: heirs, as long as they are minors, are no better than those who are enslaved, though they are the owners of all the property; [2] but they remain under guardians and trustees until the date set by a parent. [3] So with us; while we were minors, we were enslaved to the elemental spirits[n] of the world. [4] But when the fullness of time had come, God sent God's Child, born of a woman, born under the law, [5] in order to redeem those who were under the law, so that we might receive adoption as children. [6] And because you are children, God has sent the Spirit of God's Child into our[o] hearts, crying, "Abba! Father-Mother!" [7] So you are no longer enslaved but rather you are a child, and if a child then also an heir, through God.[p]

Paul Reproves the Galatians

8 Formerly, when you did not know God, you were enslaved to beings that by nature are not gods. [9] Now, however, that you have come to know God, or rather to be known by God, how can you turn back again to the weak and beggarly elemental spirits?[q] How can you want to be enslaved to them again? [10] You are observing special days, and months, and seasons, and years. [11] I am afraid that my work for you may have been wasted.

12 Friends, I beg you, become as I am, for I also have become as you are. You have done me no wrong. [13] You know that it was because of a physical infirmity that I first announced the gospel to you; [14] though my condition put you to the test, you did not scorn or despise me, but welcomed me as a messenger of God, as Christ Jesus. [15] What has become of the goodwill you felt? For I testify that, had it been possible, you would have torn out your eyes and given them to me. [16] Have I now become your enemy by telling you the truth? [17] They make much of you, but for no good purpose; they want to exclude you, so that you may make much of them. [18] It is good to be made much of for a good purpose at all times, and not only when I am present with you. [19] My little children, for whom I am again in the pain of childbirth until Christ is formed in you, [20] I wish I were present with you now and could change my tone, for I am perplexed about you.

The Allegory of Hagar and Sarah

21 Tell me, you who desire to be subject to the law, will you not listen to the law? [22] For it is written that Abraham had two children, one with an enslaved woman and the other with a free woman. [23] One, the child of the enslaved woman, was born according to the flesh; the other, the child of the free woman, was born through the promise. [24] Now this is an allegory: these women are two covenants. One woman, in fact, is Hagar, from Mount Sinai, bearing children to

---

n Or *the rudiments*   o Other ancient authorities read *your*
p Other ancient authorities read *an heir of God through Christ*   q Or *beggarly rudiments*

be enslaved. 25 Now Hagar is Mount Sinai in Arabia[r] and corresponds to the present Jerusalem, for she is in slavery with her children. 26 But the other woman corresponds to the Jerusalem above; she is free, and she is our mother. 27 For it is written,

> "Rejoice, you childless one, you who bear no children,
>   burst into song and shout, you who endure no birth
>   pangs;
>   for the children of the desolate woman are more
>   numerous
>   than the children of the one who is married."

28 Now you,[s] my friends, are children of the promise, like Isaac. 29 But just as at that time the child who was born according to the flesh persecuted the child who was born according to the Spirit, so it is now also. 30 But what does the scripture say? "Drive out the enslaved woman and her child; for the child of the enslaved woman will not share the inheritance with the child of the free woman." 31 So then, friends, we are children, not of the enslaved woman but of the free woman. 1 For freedom Christ has set us free. Stand firm, therefore, and do not submit again to a yoke of slavery.

5

The Nature of Christian Freedom

2 Listen! I, Paul, am telling you that if you let yourselves be circumcised, Christ will be of no benefit to you. 3 Once again I testify to all who let themselves be circumcised that they are obliged to obey the entire law. 4 You who want to be justified by the law have cut yourselves off from Christ; you have fallen away from grace. 5 For through the Spirit, by faith, we eagerly wait for the hope of righteousness. 6 For in Christ Jesus neither being under the law nor being outside the law counts for anything; the only thing that counts is faith working[t] through love.

7 You were running well; who prevented you from obeying the truth? 8 Such persuasion does not come from the one who calls you. 9 A little yeast leavens the whole batch of dough. 10 I am confident about you in the Lord that you will not think otherwise. But whoever it is that is confusing you will pay the penalty. 11 But my friends, why am I still being persecuted if I am still preaching circumcision? In that case the offense of the cross has been removed. 12 I wish those who unsettle you would castrate themselves!

13 For you were called to freedom, brothers and sisters; only do not use your freedom as an opportunity for self-indulgence,[u] but through love serve one another. 14 For the whole law is summed up in a single commandment, "You shall love your neighbor as yourself." 15 If, however, you bite and devour one another, take care that you are not consumed by one another.

---

r Other ancient authorities read *For Sinai is a mountain in Arabia*
s Other ancient authorities read *we*   t Or *made effective*   u Gk *the flesh*

The Works of the Flesh

16 Live by the Spirit, I say, and do not gratify the desires of the flesh. [17]For what the flesh desires is opposed to the Spirit, and what the Spirit desires is opposed to the flesh; for these are opposed to each other, to prevent you from doing what you want. [18]But if you are led by the Spirit, you are not subject to the law. [19]Now the works of the flesh are obvious: fornication, impurity, licentiousness, [20]idolatry, sorcery, enmities, strife, jealousy, anger, quarrels, dissensions, factions, [21]envy,[v] drunkenness, carousing, and things like these. I am warning you, as I warned you before: those who do such things will not inherit the dominion of God.

The Fruit of the Spirit

22 By contrast, the fruit of the Spirit is love, joy, peace, patience, kindness, generosity, faithfulness, [23]gentleness, and self-control. There is no law against such things. [24]And those who belong to Christ Jesus have crucified the flesh with its passions and desires. [25]If we live by the Spirit, let us also be guided by the Spirit. [26]Let us not become conceited, competing against one another, envying one another.

Bear One Another's Burdens

6 My friends, if anyone is detected in a transgression, you who have received the Spirit should restore such a one in a spirit of gentleness. Take care that you yourselves are not tempted. [2]Bear one another's burdens, and in this way you will fulfill[w] the law of Christ. [3]For if those who are nothing think they are something, they deceive themselves. [4]All must test their own work; then that work, rather than their neighbor's work, will become a cause for pride. [5]For all must carry their own loads.

6 Those who are taught the word must share in all good things with their teacher.

7 Do not be deceived; God is not mocked, for you reap whatever you sow. [8]If you sow to your own flesh, you will reap corruption from the flesh; but if you sow to the Spirit, you will reap eternal life from the Spirit. [9]So let us not grow weary in doing what is right, for we will reap at harvest time, if we do not give up. [10]So then, whenever we have an opportunity, let us work for the good of all, and especially for those of the family of faith.

Final Admonitions and Benediction

11 See what large letters I make when I am writing in my own hand! [12]It is those who want to make a good showing in the flesh that try to compel you to be circumcised—only that they may not be persecuted for the cross of Christ. [13]Even the circumcised do not themselves obey the law, but they want you to

---

v Other ancient authorities add *murder*   w Other ancient authorities read *in this way fulfill*

be circumcised so that they may boast about your flesh. [14]May I never boast of anything except the cross of our Lord Jesus Christ, by which[x] the world has been crucified to me, and I to the world. [15]For[y] neither circumcision nor uncircumcision is anything; but a new creation is everything! [16]As for those who will follow this rule—peace be upon them, and mercy, and upon the Israel of God.

17 From now on, let no one make trouble for me; for I carry the marks of Jesus branded on my body.

18 May the grace of our Lord Jesus Christ be with your spirit, sisters and brothers. Amen.

---

x Or *through whom*   y Other ancient authorities add *in Christ Jesus*

The Letter of Paul to the Ephesians

Salutation

1 Paul, an apostle of Christ Jesus by the will of God,
To the saints who are in Ephesus and are faithful[a] in Christ Jesus:
2 Grace to you and peace from God our Father-Mother and the Lord Jesus Christ.

Spiritual Blessings in Christ

3 Blessed be the God and Father-Mother of our Lord Jesus Christ, who has blessed us in Christ with every spiritual blessing in the heavenly places, 4 just as God chose us in Christ before the foundation of the world to be holy and blameless before God in love, 5 God destined us for adoption as God's children through Jesus Christ, according to the good pleasure of God's will, 6 to the praise of God's glorious grace, freely bestowed on us in the Beloved, 7 through whose blood, we have redemption and the forgiveness of our trespasses, according to the riches of God's grace 8 lavished upon us. With all wisdom and insight 9 God has made known to us the mystery of God's will, according to God's good pleasure set forth in Christ, 10 as a plan for the fullness of time, to gather up all things in Christ, things in heaven and things on earth. 11 In Christ we have also obtained an inheritance,[b] having been destined according to the purpose of God who accomplishes all things according to God's counsel and will, 12 so that we, who were the first to set our hope on Christ, might live for the praise of God's glory. 13 In Christ you also, when you had heard the word of truth, the gospel of your salvation, and had believed in Christ, were marked with the seal of the promised Holy Spirit; 14 this[c] is the pledge of our

---

a Other ancient authorities lack *in Ephesus*, reading *saints who are also faithful*
b Or *been made a heritage*   c Other ancient authorities read *who*

inheritance toward redemption as God's own people, to the praise of the glory of God.

Paul's Prayer

15 I have heard of your faith in the Lord Jesus and your love[d] toward all the saints, and for this reason [16] I do not cease to give thanks for you as I remember you in my prayers. [17] I pray that the God of our Lord Jesus Christ, the God of glory, may give you a spirit of wisdom and revelation as you come to know him, [18] so that, with the eyes of your heart enlightened, you may know what is the hope to which you have been called, what are the riches of God's glorious inheritance among the saints, [19] and what is the immeasurable greatness of God's power for us who believe, according to the working of God's great power. [20] God put this power to work in Christ when God raised Christ from the dead and seated Christ at God's side in the heavenly places, [21] far above all rule and authority and power and dominion, and above every name that is named, not only in this age but also in the age to come. [22] And God has put all things under Christ's feet and has made Christ the head over all things for the church, [23] which is Christ's body, the fullness of the one who fills all in all.

From Death to Life

2 You were dead through the trespasses and sins [2] in which you once lived, following the course of this world, following the ruler of the power of the air, the spirit that is now at work among those who are disobedient. [3] All of us once lived among them in the passions of our flesh, following the desires of flesh and senses, and we were by nature children of wrath, like everyone else. [4] But God, who is rich in mercy, out of the great love with which God loved us [5] even when we were dead through our trespasses, made us alive together with Christ[e]—by grace you have been saved— [6] and raised us up with Christ and seated us with Christ in the heavenly places in Christ Jesus, [7] so that in the ages to come God might show the immeasurable riches of God's grace in kindness toward us in Christ Jesus. [8] For by grace you have been saved through faith, and this is not your own doing; it is the gift of God— [9] not the result of works, so that no one may boast. [10] For we are what God has made us, created in Christ Jesus for good works, which God prepared beforehand to be our way of life.

One in Christ

11 So then, remember that at one time you Gentiles by birth,[f] called "the uncircumcision" by those who are called "the circumcision"—a physical circumcision made in the flesh by human hands— [12] remember that you were at that time without Christ, being aliens from the commonwealth of Israel, and

---

d Other ancient authorities lack *and your love*   e Other ancient authorities read *in Christ*
f Gk *in the flesh*

strangers to the covenants of promise, having no hope and without God in the world. 13 But now in Christ Jesus you who once were far off have been brought near by the blood of Christ. 14 For Christ is our peace; who, in the flesh, has made both groups into one and has broken down the dividing wall, that is, the hostility between us. 15 Christ has abolished the law with its commandments and ordinances, in order to create in Christ's self one new humanity in place of the two, thus making peace, 16 and might reconcile both groups to God in one body⁹ through the cross, thus putting to death that hostility through it.ʰ 17 So Christ came and proclaimed peace to you who were far off and peace to those who were near; 18 for through Christ both of us have access in one Spirit to the Father-Mother. 19 So then you are no longer strangers and aliens, but you are citizens with the saints and also members of the household of God, 20 built upon the foundation of the apostles and prophets, with Christ Jesus as the cornerstone.ⁱ 21 In Christ the whole structure is joined together and grows into a holy temple in the Lord; 22 in whom you also are built together spirituallyʲ into a dwelling place for God.

Paul's Ministry to the Gentiles

3 This is the reason that I Paul am a prisoner forᵏ Christ Jesus for the sake of you Gentiles— 2 for surely you have already heard of the commission of God's grace that was given me for you, 3 and how the mystery was made known to me by revelation, as I wrote above in a few words, 4 a reading of which will enable you to perceive my understanding of the mystery of Christ. 5 In former generations this mystery was not made known to humankind, as it has now been revealed to Christ's holy apostles and prophets by the Spirit: 6 that is, the Gentiles have become joint heirs, members of the same body, and sharers in the promise in Christ Jesus through the gospel.

7 Of this gospel I have become a minister according to the gift of God's grace that was given me by the working of God's power. 8 Although I am the very least of all the saints, this grace was given to me to bring to the Gentiles the news of the boundless riches of Christ, 9 and to make everyone seeˡ what is the plan of the mystery hidden for ages inᵐ God who created all things; 10 so that through the church the wisdom of God in its rich variety might now be made known to the rulers and authorities in the heavenly places. 11 This was in accordance with the eternal purpose that God has carried out in Christ Jesus our Lord, 12 in whom we have access to God in boldness and confidence through faith in Christ.ⁿ 13 I pray therefore that youᵒ may not lose heart over my sufferings for you; they are your glory.

---

g Or *reconcile both of us in one body for God*   h Or *in Christ,* or *in Christ's self*
i Or *keystone*   j Gk *in the Spirit*   k Or *of*
l Other ancient authorities read *to bring to light*   m Or *by*   n Or *the faith of Christ*
o Or *I*

Prayer for the Readers

14 For this reason I bow my knees before the Father-Mother,[p] [15]from whom every family in heaven and on earth takes its name. [16]I pray that, according to the riches of God's glory, God may grant that you may be strengthened in your inner being with power through God's Spirit, [17]and that Christ may dwell in your hearts through faith, as you are being rooted and grounded in love. [18]I pray that you may have the power to comprehend, with all the saints, what is the breadth and length and height and depth, [19]and to know the love of Christ that surpasses knowledge, so that you may be filled with all the fullness of God.

20 Now to the one who by the power at work within us is able to accomplish abundantly far more than all we can ask or imagine, [21]to God be glory in the church and in Christ Jesus to all generations, forever and ever. Amen.

Unity in the Body of Christ

4 I therefore, the prisoner in the Lord, beg you to lead a life worthy of the calling to which you have been called, [2]with all humility and gentleness, with patience, bearing with one another in love, [3]making every effort to maintain the unity of the Spirit in the bond of peace. [4]There is one body and one Spirit, just as you were called to the one hope of your calling, [5]one Lord, one faith, one baptism, [6]one God and Father-Mother of all, who is above all and through all and in all.

7 But each of us was given grace according to the measure of Christ's gift. [8]Therefore it is said,

> "The one who ascended on high made captivity itself
>   a captive;
>   and gave gifts to the people."

[9](When it says, "The one who ascended," what does it mean but that the same one had also descended[q] into the lower parts of the earth? [10]The one who descended is the same one who ascended far above all the heavens, in order to fill all things.) [11]The gifts Christ gave were that some would be apostles, some prophets, some evangelists, some pastors and teachers, [12]to equip the saints for the work of ministry, for building up the body of Christ, [13]until all of us come to the unity of the faith and of the knowledge of the Child of God, to maturity, to the measure of the full stature of Christ. [14]We must no longer be children, tossed to and fro and blown about by every wind of doctrine, by people's trickery, by their craftiness in deceitful scheming. [15]But speaking the truth in love, we must grow up in every way into the one who is the head—into Christ— [16]from whom the whole body, joined and knit together by

---

p Other ancient authorities add *of our Lord Jesus Christ*   q Other ancient authorities add *first*

every ligament with which it is equipped, as each part is working properly, promotes the body's growth in building itself up in love.

The Old Life and the New

17 Now this I affirm and insist on in the Lord: you must no longer live as the Gentiles live, in the futility of their minds. 18 They are darkened in their understanding, alienated from the life of God because of their ignorance and hardness of heart. 19 They have lost all sensitivity and have abandoned themselves to licentiousness, greedy to practice every kind of impurity. 20 That is not the way you learned Christ! 21 For surely you have heard about Christ and were taught in Christ, as truth is in Jesus. 22 You were taught to put away your former way of life, your old self, corrupt and deluded by its lusts, 23 and to be renewed in the spirit of your minds, 24 and to clothe yourselves with the new self, created according to the likeness of God in true righteousness and holiness.

Rules for the New Life

25 So then, putting away falsehood, let all of us speak the truth to our neighbors, for we are members of one another. 26 Be angry but do not sin; do not let the sun go down on your anger, 27 and do not make room for the devil. 28 Thieves must give up stealing; rather let them labor and work honestly with their own hands, so as to have something to share with the needy. 29 Let no evil talk come out of your mouths, but only what is useful for building up,ʳ as there is need, so that your words may give grace to those who hear. 30 And do not grieve the Holy Spirit of God, with which you were marked with a seal for the day of redemption. 31 Put away from you all bitterness and wrath and anger and wrangling and slander, together with all malice, 32 and be kind to one another, tenderhearted, forgiving one another, as God in Christ has forgiven
5 you.ˢ 1 Therefore be imitators of God, as beloved children, 2 and live in love, as Christ loved usᵗ and gave up life for us, a fragrant offering and sacrifice to God.

Renounce Pagan Ways

3 But fornication and impurity of any kind, or greed, must not even be mentioned among you, as is proper among saints. 4 Entirely out of place is obscene, silly, and vulgar talk; but instead, let there be thanksgiving. 5 Be sure of this, that no person who is sexually immoral or otherwise impure, or one who is greedy (that is, an idolater), has any inheritance in the dominion of Christ and of God.

6 Let no one deceive you with empty words, for because of these things the wrath of God comes on those who are disobedient. 7 Therefore do not be associated with them. 8 For once you were like night, but now in Christ you are

---

r Other ancient authorities read *building up faith*   s Other ancient authorities read *us*
t Other ancient authorities read *you*

light. Live as children of light— [9]for the fruit of the light is found in all that is good and right and true. [10]Try to find out what is pleasing to the Lord. [11]Take no part in the unfruitful works of the night, but instead expose them. [12]For it is shameful even to mention what such people do secretly; [13]but everything exposed by the light becomes visible, [14]for everything that becomes visible is light. Therefore it says,

> "Sleeper, awake!
>   Rise from the dead,
>   and Christ will shine on you."

15 Be careful then how you live, not as unwise people but as wise, [16]making the most of the time, because the days are evil. [17]So do not be foolish, but understand what the will of God is. [18]Do not get drunk with wine, for that is debauchery; but be filled with the Spirit, [19]as you sing psalms and hymns and spiritual songs among yourselves, singing and making melody to God in your hearts, [20]giving thanks to God the Father-Mother at all times and for everything in the name of our Lord Jesus Christ.

The Christian Household

21 Be committed to one another out of reverence for Christ.

22 Wives, be committed to your husbands as you are to Christ. [23]For the husband is the head of the wife just as Christ is the head of the church, the body of which Christ is the Savior. [24]Just as the church is committed to Christ, so also wives ought to be committed to their husbands in everything.

25 Husbands, love your wives, just as Christ loved the church and gave up life for it, [26]in order to make it holy by cleansing it with the washing of water by the word, [27]so as to present the church to Christ in splendor, without a spot or wrinkle or anything of the kind—yes, so that the church may be holy and without blemish. [28]In the same way, husbands should love their wives as they do their own bodies. A husband who loves his wife loves himself. [29]For people never hate their own body, but nourish and tenderly care for it, just as Christ does for the church, [30]because we are members of Christ's body.[u] [31]"For this reason a man will leave his father and mother and be joined to his wife, and the two will become one flesh." [32]This is a great mystery, and I am applying it to Christ and the church. [33]Each of you, however, should love his wife as himself, and a wife should respect her husband.

Children and Parents

6 Children, heed your parents in Christ,[v] for this is right. [2]"Honor your father and mother"—this is the first commandment with a promise: [3]"so that it may be well with you and you may live long on the earth."

---

u Other ancient authorities add *of Christ's flesh and of Christ's bones*
v Other ancient authorities lack *in Christ*

4 And, parents, do not provoke your children to anger, but bring them up in the guidance and instruction of Christ.

Masters and the Enslaved

5 You who are enslaved, heed your earthly masters with fear and trembling, in singleness of heart, as you obey Christ; [6]not only while being watched, and in order to please them, but as those enslaved to Christ, doing the will of God from the heart. [7]Render service with enthusiasm, as to Christ and not to men and women, [8]knowing that whatever good we do, we will receive the same again from God, whether we are enslaved or free.

9 And, masters, do the same to them. Stop threatening them, for you know that both of you have the same God in heaven, and with God there is no partiality.

The Whole Armor of God

10 Finally, be strong in Christ and in the strength of Christ's power. [11]Put on the whole armor of God, so that you may be able to stand against the wiles of the devil. [12]For our[w] struggle is not against enemies made of blood and flesh, but against the rulers, against the authorities, against the cosmic powers of this present evil age, against the spiritual forces of evil in the heavenly places. [13]Therefore take up the whole armor of God, so that you may be able to withstand on that evil day, and having done everything, to stand firm. [14]Stand therefore, and fasten the belt of truth around your waist, and put on the breastplate of righteousness. [15]As shoes for your feet put on whatever will make you ready to proclaim the gospel of peace. [16]With all of these,[x] take the shield of faith, with which you will be able to quench all the flaming arrows of the evil one. [17]Take the helmet of salvation, and the sword of the Spirit, which is the word of God.

18 Pray in the Spirit at all times in every prayer and supplication. To that end keep alert and always persevere in supplication for all the saints. [19]Pray also for me, so that when I speak, a message may be given to me to make known with boldness the mystery of the gospel,[y] [20]for which I am an ambassador in chains. Pray that I may declare it boldly, as I must speak.

Personal Matters and Benediction

21 So that you also may know how I am and what I am doing, Tychicus will tell you everything. He is a dear brother and a faithful minister in Christ. [22]I

---

w Other ancient authorities read *your*　　x Or *In all circumstances*
y Other ancient authorities lack *of the gospel*

am sending him to you for this very purpose, to let you know how we are, and to encourage your hearts.

23 Peace be to the whole community, and love with faith, from God the Father-Mother and the Lord Jesus Christ. [24] Grace be with all who have an undying love for our Lord Jesus Christ.[z]

---

z Other ancient authorities add *Amen*

The Letter of Paul to the Philippians

Salutation

1 Paul and Timothy, servants of Christ Jesus,
To all the saints in Christ Jesus who are in Philippi, with the bishops[a] and deacons:[b]

2 Grace to you and peace from God our Father-Mother and the Lord Jesus Christ.

Paul's Prayer for the Philippians

3 I thank my God every time I remember you, [4]constantly praying with joy in every one of my prayers for all of you, [5]because of your sharing in the gospel from the first day until now. [6]I am confident of this, that the one who began a good work among you will bring it to completion by the day of Jesus Christ. [7]It is right for me to think this way about all of you, because you hold me in your heart,[c] for all of you share in God's grace[d] with me, both in my imprisonment and in the defense and confirmation of the gospel. [8]For God is my witness, how I long for all of you with the compassion of Christ Jesus. [9]And this is my prayer, that your love may overflow more and more with knowledge and full insight [10]to help you to determine what is best, so that in the day of Christ you may be pure and blameless, [11]having produced the harvest of righteousness that comes through Jesus Christ for the glory and praise of God.

Paul's Present Circumstances

12 I want you to know, beloved, that what has happened to me has actually helped to spread the gospel, [13]so that it has become known throughout the

---

a Or *overseers*   b Or *overseers and helpers*   c Or *because I hold you in my heart*
d Gk *in grace*

whole imperial guard[e] and to everyone else that my imprisonment is for Christ; [14]and most of the brothers and sisters, having been made confident in Christ by my imprisonment, dare to speak the word[f] with greater boldness and without fear.

15 Some proclaim Christ from envy and rivalry, but others from goodwill. [16]These proclaim Christ out of love, knowing that I have been put here for the defense of the gospel; [17]the others proclaim Christ out of selfish ambition, not sincerely but intending to increase my suffering in my imprisonment. [18]What does it matter? Just this, that Christ is proclaimed in every way, whether out of false motives or true; and in that I rejoice.

Yes, and I will continue to rejoice, [19]for I know that through your prayers and the help of the Spirit of Jesus Christ this will turn out for my deliverance. [20]It is my eager expectation and hope that I will not be put to shame in any way, but that by my speaking with all boldness, Christ will be exalted now as always in my body, whether by life or by death. [21]For to me, living is Christ and dying is gain. [22]If I am to live in the flesh, that means fruitful labor for me; and I do not know which I prefer. [23]I am hard pressed between the two: my desire is to depart and be with Christ, for that is far better; [24]but to remain in the flesh is more necessary for you. [25]Since I am convinced of this, I know that I will remain and continue with all of you for your progress and joy in faith, [26]so that I may share abundantly in your boasting in Christ Jesus when I come to you again.

27 Only, live your life in a manner worthy of the gospel of Christ, so that, whether I come and see you or am absent and hear about you, I will know that you are standing firm in one spirit, striving side by side with one mind for the faith of the gospel, [28]and are in no way intimidated by your opponents. For them this is evidence of their destruction, but of your salvation. And this is God's doing. [29]For you have been graciously granted the privilege not only of believing in Christ, but of suffering for Christ as well— [30]since you are having the same struggle that you saw I had and now hear that I still have.

Imitating Christ's Humility

2 If then there is any encouragement in Christ, any consolation from love, any sharing in the Spirit, any compassion and sympathy, [2]make my joy complete: be of the same mind, having the same love, being in full accord and of one mind. [3]Do nothing from selfish ambition or conceit, but in humility regard others as better than yourselves. [4]Let each of you look not to your own interests, but to the interests of others. [5]Let the same mind be in you that was[g] in Christ Jesus,

[6]   who, though being in the form of God,
          did not regard equality with God

---

e Gk *whole praetorium*   f Other ancient authorities read *word of God*   g Or *that you have*

as something to be exploited,
7   but emptied Christ's self,
      taking the form of a servant,
      being born in human likeness.
    And being found in human form,
8   Christ humbled Christ's self,
      and was obedient to the point of death—
      even death on a cross.

9   Therefore God also highly exalted Jesus
      and gave Jesus the name
      that is above every name,
10   so that at the name of Jesus
      every knee should bend,
      in heaven and on earth and under the earth,
11   and every tongue should confess
      that Jesus Christ is Lord,
      to the glory of God the Father-Mother.

Shining as Lights in the World

12 Therefore, my beloved, just as you have always obeyed me, not only in my presence, but much more now in my absence, work out your own salvation with fear and trembling; 13 for it is God who is at work in you, enabling you both to will and to work for God's good pleasure.

14 Do all things without murmuring and arguing, 15 so that you may be blameless and innocent, children of God without blemish in the midst of a crooked and perverse generation, in which you shine like stars in the world. 16 It is by your holding fast to the word of life that I can boast on the day of Christ that I did not run in vain or labor in vain. 17 But even if I am being poured out as a libation over the sacrifice and the offering of your faith, I am glad and rejoice with all of you— 18 and in the same way you also must be glad and rejoice with me.

Timothy and Epaphroditus

19 I hope in the Lord Jesus to send Timothy to you soon, so that I may be cheered by news of you. 20 I have no one like him who will be genuinely concerned for your welfare. 21 All of them are seeking their own interests, not those of Jesus Christ. 22 But Timothy's worth you know, how like a son with a father he has served with me in the work of the gospel. 23 I hope therefore to send him as soon as I see how things go with me; 24 and I trust in the Lord that I will also come soon.

25 Still, I think it necessary to send to you Epaphroditus—my brother,

coworker, and companion in the struggle, your messenger[h] and minister to my need; 26for he has been longing for[i] all of you, and has been distressed because you heard that he was ill. 27He was indeed so ill that he nearly died. But God had mercy on him, and not only on him but on me also, so that I would not have one sorrow after another. 28I am the more eager to send him, therefore, in order that you may rejoice at seeing him again, and that I may be less anxious. 29Welcome him then in Christ with all joy, and honor such people, 30because he came close to death for the work of Christ,[j] risking his life to make up for those services that you could not give me.

3 Finally, my sisters and brothers, rejoice[k] in the Lord.

Breaking with the Past

To write the same things to you is not troublesome to me, and for you it is a safeguard.

2 Beware of the dogs, beware of the evil workers, beware of those who mutilate the flesh![l] 3For it is we who are the people of the circumcision, who worship in the Spirit of God[m] and boast in Christ Jesus and have no confidence in the flesh— 4even though I, too, have reason for confidence in the flesh.

If anyone else has reason to be confident in the flesh, I have more: 5circumcised on the eighth day, a member of the people of Israel, of the tribe of Benjamin, a Hebrew born of Hebrews; as to the law, a Pharisee; 6as to zeal, a persecutor of the church; as to righteousness under the law, blameless.

7 Yet whatever gains I had, these I have come to regard as loss because of Christ. 8More than that, I regard everything as loss because of the surpassing value of knowing Christ Jesus my Lord, for whose sake I have suffered the loss of all things, and I regard them as rubbish, in order that I may gain Christ 9and be found in Christ, not having a righteousness of my own that comes from the law, but one that comes through faith in Christ,[n] the righteousness from God based on faith. 10I want to know Christ and the power of Christ's resurrection and the sharing of Christ's sufferings, taking the same form that Christ took in death, 11if somehow I may attain the resurrection from the dead.

Pressing toward the Goal

12 Not that I have already obtained this or have already reached the goal;[o] but I press on to make it my own, because I have been claimed by Christ Jesus. 13Beloved, I do not consider that I have made it my own;[p] but this one thing I do: forgetting what lies behind and straining forward to what lies ahead, 14I

---

h Gk apostle   i Other ancient authorities read longing to see
j Other ancient authorities read of the Lord   k Or farewell   l Gk the mutilation
m Other ancient authorities read worship God in spirit   n Or through the faith of Christ
o Or have already been made perfect   p Other ancient authorities read my own yet

press on toward the goal for the prize of the heavenly[q] call of God in Christ Jesus. [15]Let those of us then who are mature be of the same mind; and if you think differently about anything, this too God will reveal to you. [16]Only let us hold fast to what we have attained.

17 Brothers and sisters, join in imitating me, and observe those who live according to the example you have in us. [18]For many live as enemies of the cross of Christ; I have often told you of them, and now I tell you even with tears. [19]Their end is destruction; their god is the belly; and their glory is in their shame; their minds are set on earthly things. [20]But our citizenship[r] is in heaven, and it is from there that we are expecting a Savior, the Lord Jesus Christ, [21]who will transform the body of our humiliation[s] that it may be conformed to the body of Christ's glory,[t] by that power in which all things have also been made subject to Christ by Christ. [1]Therefore, my sisters and brothers, whom I love and long for, my joy and crown, stand firm in Christ in this way, my beloved.

Exhortations

2 I urge Euodia and I urge Syntyche to be of the same mind in Christ. [3]Yes, and I ask you also, my loyal companion,[u] help these women, for they have struggled beside me in the work of the gospel, together with Clement and the rest of my coworkers, whose names are in the book of life.

4 Rejoice[v] in the Lord always; again I will say, Rejoice.[v] [5]Let your gentleness be known to everyone. Christ is near. [6]Do not worry about anything, but in everything by prayer and supplication with thanksgiving let your requests be made known to God. [7]And the peace of God, which surpasses all understanding, will guard your hearts and your minds in Christ Jesus.

8 Finally, beloved, whatever is true, whatever is honorable, whatever is just, whatever is pure, whatever is pleasing, whatever is commendable, if there is any excellence and if there is anything worthy of praise, think about[w] these things. [9]Keep on doing the things that you have learned and received and heard and seen in me, and the God of peace will be with you.

Acknowledgment of the Philippians' Gift

10 I rejoice[x] in the Lord greatly that now at last you have revived your concern for me; indeed, you were concerned for me, but had no opportunity to show it.[y] [11]Not that I am referring to being in need; for I have learned to be content with whatever I have. [12]I know what it is to have little, and I know what it is to have plenty. In any and all circumstances I have learned the secret of being well-fed and of going hungry, of having plenty and of being in need.

---

q Gk *upward*   r Or *commonwealth*   s Or *our humble bodies*   t Or *Christ's glorious body*
u Or *loyal Syzygus*   v Or *Farewell*   w Gk *take account of*   x Gk *I rejoiced*
y Gk lacks *to show it*

¹³I can do all things through the one who strengthens me. ¹⁴In any case, it was kind of you to share my distress.

15 You Philippians indeed know that in the early days of the gospel, when I left Macedonia, no church shared with me in the matter of giving and receiving, except you alone. ¹⁶For even when I was in Thessalonica, you sent me help for my needs more than once. ¹⁷Not that I seek the gift, but I seek the profit that accumulates to your account. ¹⁸I have been paid in full and have more than enough; I am fully satisfied, now that I have received from Epaphroditus the gifts you sent, a fragrant offering, a sacrifice acceptable and pleasing to God. ¹⁹And my God will fully satisfy every need of yours according to God's riches in glory in Christ Jesus. ²⁰To our God and Father-Mother be glory forever and ever. Amen.

Final Greetings and Benediction

21 Greet every saint in Christ Jesus. The friends who are with me greet you. ²²All the saints greet you, especially those of the emperor's household.

23 The grace of the Lord Jesus Christ be with your spirit.[z]

---

z Other ancient authorities add *Amen*

The Letter of Paul to the Colossians

Salutation

1 Paul, an apostle of Christ Jesus by the will of God, and Timothy our brother,

2 To the saints and faithful brothers and sisters in Christ in Colossae: Grace to you and peace from God our Father-Mother.

Paul Thanks God for the Colossians

3 In our prayers for you we always thank God, the Father-Mother of our Lord Jesus Christ, ⁴for we have heard of your faith in Christ Jesus and of the love that you have for all the saints, ⁵because of the hope laid up for you in heaven. You have heard of this hope before in the word of the truth, the gospel ⁶that has come to you. Just as it is bearing fruit and growing in the whole world, so it has been bearing fruit among yourselves from the day you heard it and truly comprehended the grace of God. ⁷This you learned from Epaphras, a beloved servant with us. He is a faithful minister of Christ on your[a] behalf, ⁸and he has made known to us your love in the Spirit.

9 For this reason, since the day we heard it, we have not ceased praying for you and asking that you may be filled with the knowledge of God's will in all spiritual wisdom and understanding, ¹⁰so that you may lead lives worthy of the Lord, fully pleasing to the Lord in everything, as you bear fruit in every good work and as you grow in the knowledge of God. ¹¹May you be made strong with all the strength that comes from God's glorious power, and may you be prepared to endure everything with patience, while joyfully ¹²giving thanks to the Father-Mother, who has enabled[b] you[c] to share in the inheritance of the saints in the light. ¹³God has rescued us from the power of evil

---

a Other ancient authorities read *our*   b Other ancient authorities read *called*
c Other ancient authorities read *us*

and transferred us into the dominion of God's beloved Child, [14]in whom we have redemption, the forgiveness of sins.[d]

The Supremacy of Christ

15 Christ is the image of the invisible God, the firstborn of all creation; [16]for in[e] Christ all things in heaven and on earth were created, things visible and invisible, whether thrones or dominions or rulers or powers—all things have been created through Christ and for Christ. [17]Christ is before all things, and in[e] Christ all things hold together. [18]Christ is the head of the body, the church, and is the beginning, the firstborn from the dead, so that Christ might come to have first place in everything. [19]For in Christ all the fullness of God was pleased to dwell, [20]and through Christ God was pleased to reconcile to Godself all things, whether on earth or in heaven, by making peace through the blood of the cross.

21 And you who were once estranged and hostile in mind, doing evil deeds, [22]Christ has now reconciled[f] in Christ's fleshly body[g] through death, so as to present you holy and blameless and irreproachable before God— [23]provided that you continue securely established and steadfast in the faith, without shifting from the hope promised by the gospel that you heard, which has been proclaimed to every creature under heaven. I, Paul, became a minister of this gospel.

Paul's Interest in the Colossians

24 I am now rejoicing in my sufferings for your sake, and in my flesh I am completing what is lacking in Christ's afflictions for the sake of Christ's body, that is, the church. [25]I became its minister according to God's commission that was given to me for you, to make the word of God fully known, [26]the mystery that has been hidden throughout the ages and generations but has now been revealed to the saints. [27]To them God chose to make known how great among the Gentiles are the riches of the glory of this mystery, which is Christ in you, the hope of glory. [28]It is Christ whom we proclaim, warning everyone and teaching everyone in all wisdom, so that we may present everyone mature in Christ. [29]For this I toil and struggle with all the energy that God powerfully inspires within me.

2 For I want you to know how much I am struggling for you, and for those in Laodicea, and for all who have not seen me face to face. [2]I want their hearts to be encouraged and united in love, so that they may have all the riches of assured understanding and have the knowledge of God's mystery, that is, Christ,[h] [3]in whom are hidden all the treasures of wisdom and knowledge. [4]I

---

d Other ancient authorities add *through Christ's blood*   e Or *by*

f Other ancient authorities read *you have now been reconciled*

g Gk *in the body of Christ's flesh*

h Other ancient authorities read *of the mystery of God, both of the Father-Mother and of Christ*

am saying this so that no one may deceive you with plausible arguments. [5] For though I am absent in body, yet I am with you in spirit, and I rejoice to see your morale and the firmness of your faith in Christ.

Fullness of Life in Christ

6 As you therefore have received Christ Jesus the Lord, continue to live your lives[i] in Christ, [7] rooted and built up in Christ and established in the faith, just as you were taught, abounding in thanksgiving.

8 See to it that no one takes you captive through philosophy and empty deceit, according to human tradition, according to the elemental spirits of the universe,[j] and not according to Christ. [9] For in Christ the whole fullness of deity dwells bodily, [10] and you have come to fullness in Christ, who is the head of every ruler and authority. [11] In Christ also you were circumcised with a spiritual circumcision,[k] by putting off the body of the flesh in the circumcision of Christ; [12] when you were buried with Christ in baptism, you were also raised with Christ through faith in the power of God, who raised Christ from the dead. [13] And when you were dead in trespasses and the uncircumcision of your flesh, God made you[l] alive together with Christ having forgiven us all our trespasses, [14] erasing the record that stood against us with its legal demands. God set this aside, nailing it to the cross, [15] disarming the rulers and authorities and making a public example of them, triumphing over them in it.

16 Therefore do not let anyone condemn you in matters of food and drink or of observing festivals, new moons, or sabbaths. [17] These are only a shadow of what is to come, but the substance belongs to Christ. [18] Do not let anyone disqualify you, insisting on self-abasement and worship of angels, dwelling[m] on visions,[n] puffed up without cause by a human way of thinking,[o] [19] and not holding fast to the head, from whom the whole body, nourished and held together by its ligaments and sinews, grows with a growth that is from God.

Warnings against False Teachers

20 If with Christ you died to the elemental spirits of the universe,[j] why do you live as if you still belonged to the world? Why do you submit to regulations, [21] "Do not handle, Do not taste, Do not touch"? [22] All these regulations refer to things that perish with use; they are simply human commands and teachings. [23] These have indeed an appearance of wisdom in promoting self-imposed piety, humility, and severe treatment of the body, but they are of no value in checking self-indulgence.[p]

---

i Gk *to walk*   j Or *the rudiments of the world*   k Gk *a circumcision made without hands*
l Other ancient authorities read *made us*; others, *made*
m Other ancient authorities read *not dwelling*   n Meaning of Gk uncertain
o Gk *by the mind of one's flesh*   p Or *are of no value, serving only to indulge the flesh*

The New Life in Christ

3 So if you have been raised with Christ, seek the things that are above, where Christ is, seated at the mighty hand of God. ²Set your minds on things that are above, not on things that are on earth, ³for you have died, and your life is hidden with Christ in God. ⁴When Christ who is your^q life is revealed, then you also will be revealed with Christ in glory.

5 Put to death, therefore, whatever in you is earthly: fornication, impurity, passion, evil desire, and greed (which is idolatry). ⁶On account of these the wrath of God is coming on those who are disobedient.^r ⁷These are the ways you also once followed, when you were living that life.^s ⁸But now you must get rid of all such things—anger, wrath, malice, slander, and abusive^t language from your mouth. ⁹Do not lie to one another, seeing that you have stripped off the old self with its practices ¹⁰and have clothed yourselves with the new self, which is being renewed in knowledge according to the image of its creator. ¹¹In that renewal^u there is no longer Greek and Jew, circumcised and uncircumcised, barbarian, Scythian, enslaved and free; but Christ is all and in all!

12 As God's chosen ones, holy and beloved, clothe yourselves with compassion, kindness, humility, meekness, and patience. ¹³Bear with one another and, if anyone has a complaint against another, forgive each other; just as the Lord^v has forgiven you, so you also must forgive. ¹⁴Above all, clothe yourselves with love, which binds everything together in perfect harmony. ¹⁵And let the peace of Christ rule in your hearts, to which indeed you were called in the one body. And be thankful. ¹⁶Let the word of Christ^w dwell in you richly; teach and admonish one another in all wisdom; and with gratitude in your hearts sing psalms, hymns, and spiritual songs to God.^x ¹⁷And whatever you do, in word or deed, do everything in the name of the Lord Jesus, giving thanks to God the Father-Mother through Jesus Christ.

Rules for Christian Households

18 Wives, be committed to your husbands, as is fitting in Christ. ¹⁹Husbands, love your wives and never treat them harshly.

20 Children, heed your parents in everything, for this is your acceptable duty in Christ. ²¹Parents, do not provoke your children, or they may lose heart. ²²You who are enslaved, heed your earthly masters^y in everything, not only while being watched and in order to please them, but wholeheartedly, revering the Lord.^y ²³Whatever your task, put yourselves into it, as done for the Lord

---

q Other authorities read *our*
r Other ancient authorities lack *on those who are disobedient* (Gk *the children of disobedience*)
s Or *living among such people*   t Or *filthy*   u Gk *its creator,* 11*where*
v Other ancient authorities read *just as Christ*
w Other ancient authorities read *of God,* or *of the Lord*
x Other ancient authorities read *to the Lord*
y In Greek the same word is used for *master* or *lord* or *Lord*

and not for human beings, [24] since you know that from the Lord you will receive the inheritance as your reward; you serve[z] the Lord Christ. [25] For the wrongdoer will be paid back for whatever wrong has been done, and there is

4 no partiality. [1] Masters, treat those enslaved to you justly and fairly, for you know that you also have one Lord in heaven whom you must obey.

Further Instructions

2 Devote yourselves to prayer, keeping alert in it with thanksgiving. [3] At the same time pray for us as well that God will open to us a door for the word, that we may declare the mystery of Christ, for which I am in prison, [4] so that I may reveal it clearly, as I should.

5 Conduct yourselves wisely toward outsiders, making the most of the time.[a] [6] Let your speech always be gracious, seasoned with salt, so that you may know how you ought to answer everyone.

Final Greetings and Benediction

7 Tychicus will tell you all the news about me; he is a beloved brother, a faithful minister, and a servant with us in Christ. [8] I have sent him to you for this very purpose, so that you may know how we are[b] and that he may encourage your hearts. [9] Tychicus is coming with Onesimus, the faithful and beloved brother, who is one of you. They will tell you about everything here.

10 Aristarchus, a prisoner with me, greets you, as does Mark the cousin of Barnabas, concerning whom you have received instructions—if he comes to you, welcome him. [11] And Jesus who is called Justus greets you. These are the only ones of the circumcision among my coworkers for the dominion of God, and they have been a comfort to me. [12] Epaphras, who is one of you, a servant of Christ Jesus, greets you. He is always wrestling in his prayers on your behalf, so that you may stand mature and fully assured in everything that God wills. [13] For I testify for Epaphras that he has worked hard for you and for those in Laodicea and in Hierapolis. [14] Luke, the beloved physician, and Demas greet you. [15] Give my greetings to the brothers and sisters in Laodicea, and to Nympha and the church in her house. [16] And when this letter has been read among you, have it read also in the church of the Laodiceans; and see that you read also the letter from Laodicea. [17] And say to Archippus, "See that you complete the task that you have received in Christ."

18 I, Paul, write this greeting with my own hand. Remember my chains. Grace be with you.[c]

---

z Or *you are enslaved to*, or *be enslaved to*   a Or *opportunity*
b Other authorities read *that I may know how you are*   c Other ancient authorities add *Amen*

The First Letter of Paul to the Thessalonians

Salutation

1 Paul, Silvanus, and Timothy,

To the church of the Thessalonians in God the Father-Mother and the Lord Jesus Christ:

Grace to you and peace.

The Thessalonians' Faith and Example

2 We always give thanks to God for all of you and mention you in our prayers, constantly ³remembering before our God and Father-Mother your work of faith and labor of love and steadfastness of hope in our Lord Jesus Christ. ⁴For we know, brothers and sisters beloved by God, that God has chosen you, ⁵because our message of the gospel came to you not in word only, but also in power and in the Holy Spirit and with full conviction; just as you know what kind of persons we proved to be among you for your sake. ⁶And you became imitators of us and of Christ, for in spite of persecution you received the word with joy inspired by the Holy Spirit, ⁷so that you became an example to all the believers in Macedonia and in Achaia. ⁸For the word of the Lord has sounded forth from you not only in Macedonia and Achaia, but in every place your faith in God has become known, so that we have no need to speak about it. ⁹For the people of those regions report about us what kind of welcome we had among you, and how you turned to God from idols, to serve a living and true God, ¹⁰and to wait for God's Child from heaven, whom God raised from the dead—Jesus, who rescues us from the wrath that is coming.

Paul's Ministry in Thessalonica

2 You yourselves know, sisters and brothers, that our coming to you was not in vain, ²but though we had already suffered and been shamefully mistreated at Philippi, as you know, we had courage in our God to declare to you the gospel of God in spite of great opposition. [3]For our appeal does not spring from deceit or impure motives or trickery, [4]but just as we have been approved by God to be entrusted with the message of the gospel, even so we speak, not to please mortals, but to please God who tests our hearts. [5]As you know and as God is our witness, we never came with words of flattery or with a pretext for greed; [6]nor did we seek praise from mortals, whether from you or from others, [7]though we might have made demands as apostles of Christ. But we were gentle[a] among you, like a nurse tenderly caring for her own children. [8]So deeply do we care for you that we are determined to share with you not only the gospel of God but also our own selves, because you have become very dear to us.

9 You remember our labor and toil, brothers and sisters; we worked night and day, so that we might not burden any of you while we proclaimed to you the gospel of God. [10]You are witnesses, and God also, how pure, upright, and blameless our conduct was toward you believers. [11]As you know, we dealt with each one of you like a parent with a child, [12]urging and encouraging you and pleading that you lead a life worthy of God, who calls you into God's own dominion and glory.

13 We also constantly give thanks to God for this, that when you received the word of God that you heard from us, you accepted it not as a human word but as what it really is, God's word, which is also at work in you believers. [14]For you, sisters and brothers, became imitators of the churches of God in Christ Jesus that are in Judea, for you suffered the same things from your own compatriots as they did from those [15]who killed both the Lord Jesus and the prophets,[b] and drove us out; they displease God and oppose everyone [16]by hindering us from speaking to the Gentiles so that they may be saved. Thus they have constantly been filling up the measure of their sins; but God's wrath has overtaken them at last.[c]

Paul's Desire to Visit the Thessalonians Again

17 As for us, brothers and sisters, when, for a short time, we were made orphans by being separated from you—in person, not in heart—we longed with great eagerness to see you face to face. [18]For we wanted to come to you— certainly I, Paul, wanted to again and again—but Satan blocked our way. [19]For what is our hope or joy or crown of boasting before our Lord Jesus when Jesus comes? Is it not you? [20]Yes, you are our glory and joy!

3 Therefore when we could bear it no longer, we decided to be left alone in Athens; [2]and we sent Timothy, our brother and coworker for God in proclaiming[d] the gospel of Christ, to strengthen and encourage you for the sake of your faith, [3]so that no one would be shaken by these persecutions. Indeed, you yourselves know that this is what we are destined for. [4]In fact, when we

---

a Other ancient authorities read *infants*   b Other ancient authorities read *their own prophets*
c Or *completely* or *forever*   d Gk lacks *proclaiming*

were with you, we told you beforehand that we were to suffer persecution; so it turned out, as you know. 5For this reason, when I could bear it no longer, I sent to find out about your faith; I was afraid that somehow the tempter had tempted you and that our labor had been in vain.

Timothy's Encouraging Report

6 But Timothy has just now come to us from you, and has brought us the good news of your faith and love. He has told us also that you always remember us kindly and long to see us—just as we long to see you. 7For this reason, sisters and brothers, during all our distress and persecution we have been encouraged about you through your faith. 8For we now live, if you continue to stand firm in Christ. 9How can we thank God enough for you in return for all the joy that we feel before our God because of you? 10Night and day we pray most earnestly that we may see you face to face and restore whatever is lacking in your faith.

11 Now may our God and Father-Mother and our Lord Jesus direct our way to you. 12And may the Lord make you increase and abound in love for one another and for all, just as we abound in love for you, 13in order to strengthen your hearts in holiness that you may be blameless before our God and Father-Mother at the coming of our Lord Jesus with all the saints.

A Life Pleasing to God

4 Finally, brothers and sisters, we ask and urge you in the Lord Jesus that, as you learned from us how you ought to live and to please God (as, in fact, you are doing), you should do so more and more. 2For you know what instructions we gave you through the Lord Jesus. 3For this is the will of God, your sanctification: that you abstain from fornication; 4that each one of you know how to control your own body in holiness and honor, 5not with lustful passion, like the Gentiles who do not know God; 6that no one wrong or exploit a sister or brother in this matter, because the Lord is an avenger in all these things, just as we have already told you beforehand and solemnly warned you. 7For God did not call us to impurity but in holiness. 8Therefore whoever rejects this rejects not human authority but God, who also gives the Holy Spirit to you.

9 Now concerning love of the brothers and sisters, you do not need to have anyone write to you, for you yourselves have been taught by God to love one another; 10and indeed you do love all the sisters and brothers throughout Macedonia. But we urge you, beloved, to do so more and more, 11to aspire to live quietly, to mind your own affairs, and to work with your hands, as we directed you, 12so that you may behave properly toward outsiders and be dependent on no one.

The Coming of Christ

13 But we do not want you to be uninformed, brothers and sisters, about those who have died,[e] so that you may not grieve as others do who have no hope. [14]For since we believe that Jesus died and rose again, even so, through Jesus, God will bring with Jesus those who have died.[e] [15]For this we declare to you by the word of Christ, that we who are alive, who are left until the coming of Christ, will by no means precede those who have died.[e] [16]For Christ indeed, with a cry of command, with the archangel's call and with the sound of God's trumpet, will descend from heaven, and the dead in Christ will rise first. [17]Then we who are alive, who are left, will be caught up in the clouds together with them to meet Christ in the air; and so we will be with Christ forever. [18]Therefore encourage one another with these words.

5 Now concerning the times and the seasons, sisters and brothers, you do not need to have anything written to you. [2]For you yourselves know very well that the day of the Lord will come like a thief in the night. [3]When they say, "There is peace and security," then sudden destruction will come upon them, as labor pains come upon a pregnant woman, and there will be no escape! [4]But you, beloved, are not in the night, for that day to surprise you like a thief; [5]for you are all children of light and children of the day; we are not of the night or without light. [6]So then let us not fall asleep as others do, but let us keep awake and be sober; [7]for those who sleep sleep at night, and those who are drunk get drunk at night. [8]But since we belong to the day, let us be sober, and put on the breastplate of faith and love, and for a helmet the hope of salvation. [9]For God has destined us not for wrath but for obtaining salvation through our Lord Jesus Christ, [10]who died for us, so that whether we are awake or asleep we may live with Christ. [11]Therefore encourage one another and build up each one, as indeed you are doing.

Final Exhortations, Greetings, and Benediction

12 But we appeal to you, brothers and sisters, to respect those who labor among you, and have charge of you in Christ and admonish you; [13]esteem them very highly in love because of their work. Be at peace among yourselves. [14]And we urge you, beloved, to admonish the idlers, encourage the faint hearted, help the weak, be patient with all of them. [15]See that none of you repays evil for evil, but always seek to do good to one another and to all. [16]Rejoice always, [17]pray without ceasing, [18]give thanks in all circumstances; for this is the will of God in Christ Jesus for you. [19]Do not quench the Spirit. [20]Do not despise the words of prophets,[f] [21]but test everything; hold fast to what is good; [22]abstain from every form of evil.

23 May the God of peace sanctify you entirely; and may your spirit and

---

e Gk *fallen asleep*   f Gk *despise prophecies*

soul and body be kept sound[g] and blameless at the coming of our Lord Jesus Christ. [24]The one who calls you is faithful, and will do this.

25 Beloved, pray for us.

26 Greet all the sisters and brothers with a holy kiss. [27]I solemnly command you by Christ that this letter be read to all of them.

28 The grace of our Lord Jesus Christ be with you.[h]

---

g Or *complete*   h Other ancient authorities add *Amen*

The Second Letter of Paul to the Thessalonians

Salutation

1 Paul, Silvanus, and Timothy,
To the church of the Thessalonians in God our Father-Mother and the Lord Jesus Christ:

2 Grace to you and peace from God our[a] Father-Mother and the Lord Jesus Christ.

Thanksgiving

3 We must always give thanks to God for you, brothers and sisters, as is right, because your faith is growing abundantly, and the love of everyone of you for one another is increasing. 4Therefore we ourselves boast of you among the churches of God for your steadfastness and faith during all your persecutions and the afflictions that you are enduring.

The Judgment at Christ's Coming

5 This is evidence of the righteous judgment of God, and is intended to make you worthy of the dominion of God, for which you are also suffering. 6For it is indeed just of God to repay with affliction those who afflict you, 7and to give relief to the afflicted as well as to us, when the Lord Jesus is revealed from heaven with the mighty angels 8in flaming fire, inflicting vengeance on those who do not know God and on those who do not obey the gospel of our Lord Jesus. 9These will suffer the punishment of eternal destruction, separated from the presence of Christ and from the glory of Christ's might, 10when Christ comes to be glorified by the saints and to be marveled at on that day among all who have believed, because our testimony to you was believed. 11To this end we always pray for you, asking that our God will make you worthy of God's

---

a Other ancient authorities read *the*

call and will fulfill with God's power every good resolve and work of faith, [12]so that the name of our Lord Jesus may be glorified in you, and you in it, according to the grace of our God and the Lord Jesus Christ.

The Lawless One

2 As to the coming of our Lord Jesus Christ and our being gathered together to Christ, we beg you, sisters and brothers, [2]not to be quickly shaken in mind or alarmed, either by spirit or by word or by letter, as though from us, to the effect that the day of the Lord is already here. [3]Let no one deceive you in any way; for that day will not come unless the rebellion comes first and the lawless one[b] is revealed, the one destined for destruction. [4]The lawless one opposes and claims greater glory than every so-called god or object of worship, in order to take a seat in the temple of God, and claim to be God. [5]Do you not remember that I told you these things when I was still with you? [6]And you know what is now the restraining power, so that the lawless one may be revealed when the time comes. [7]For the mystery of lawlessness is already at work, but only until the one who now restrains it is removed. [8]And then the lawless one will be revealed, and will be destroyed[c] by the breath of the mouth of the Lord Jesus,[d] and will be annihilated by the manifestation of Jesus' coming. [9]The coming of the lawless one is apparent in the working of Satan, who uses all power, signs, lying wonders, [10]and every kind of wicked deception for those who are perishing, because they refused to love the truth and so be saved. [11]For this reason God sends them a powerful delusion, leading them to believe what is false, [12]so that all who have not believed the truth but took pleasure in unrighteousness will be condemned.

Chosen for Salvation

13 But we must always give thanks to God for you, brothers and sisters beloved by the Lord, because God chose you as the firstfruits[e] for salvation through sanctification by the Spirit and through belief in the truth. [14]For this purpose God called you through our proclamation of the good news,[f] so that you may obtain the glory of our Lord Jesus Christ. [15]So then, sisters and brothers, stand firm and hold fast to the traditions that you were taught by us, either by word of mouth or by our letter.

16 Now may our Lord Jesus Christ and God our Father-Mother, who loved us and through grace gave us eternal comfort and good hope, [17]comfort your hearts and strengthen them in every good work and word.

---

b Other ancient authorities read *the sinful one*   c Other ancient authorities read *consumed*
d Other ancient authorities lack *Jesus*   e Other ancient authorities read *from the beginning*
f Or *through our gospel*

Request for Prayer

3 Finally, brothers and sisters, pray for us, so that the word of Christ may spread rapidly and be glorified everywhere, just as it is among you, 2and that we may be rescued from wicked and evil people; for not all have faith. 3But Christ is faithful and will strengthen you and guard you from the evil one.9 4And we have confidence in Christ concerning you, that you are doing and will go on doing the things that we command. 5May Christ direct your hearts to the love of God and to the steadfastness of Christ.

Warning against Idleness

6 Now we command you, beloved, in the name of our Lord Jesus Christ, to keep away from believers who are living in idleness and not according to the tradition that theyh received from us. 7For you yourselves know how you ought to imitate us; we were not idle when we were with you, 8and we did not eat anyone's bread without paying for it; but with toil and labor we worked night and day, so that we might not burden any of you. 9This was not because we do not have that right, but in order to give you an example to imitate. 10For even when we were with you, we gave you this command: Anyone unwilling to work should not eat. 11For we hear that some of you are living in idleness, mere busybodies, not doing any work. 12Now such persons we command and exhort in the Lord Jesus Christ to do their work quietly and to earn their own living. 13Sisters and brothers, do not be weary in doing what is right.

14 Take note of those who do not obey what we say in this letter; have nothing to do with them, so that they may be ashamed. 15Do not regard them as enemies, but warn them as believers.

Final Greetings and Benediction

16 Now may the Lord of peace give you peace at all times in all ways. The Lord be with all of you.

17 I, Paul, write this greeting with my own hand. This is the mark in every letter of mine; it is the way I write. 18The grace of our Lord Jesus Christ be with all of you.i

---

g Or *from evil*   h Other ancient authorities read *you*   i Other ancient authorities add *Amen*

The First Letter of Paul to Timothy

Salutation

1 Paul, an apostle of Christ Jesus by the command of God our Savior and of Christ Jesus our hope,

2 To Timothy, my loyal child in the faith:

Grace, mercy, and peace from God the Father-Mother and Christ Jesus our Lord.

Warning against False Teachers

3 I urge you, as I did when I was on my way to Macedonia, to remain in Ephesus so that you may instruct certain people not to teach any different doctrine, ⁴and not to occupy themselves with myths and endless genealogies that promote speculations rather than the divine training[a] that is known by faith. ⁵But the aim of such instruction is love that comes from a pure heart, a good conscience, and sincere faith. ⁶Some people have deviated from these and turned to meaningless talk, ⁷desiring to be teachers of the law, without understanding either what they are saying or the things about which they make assertions.

8 Now we know that the law is good, if one uses it legitimately. ⁹This means understanding that the law is laid down not for the innocent but for the lawless and disobedient, for the godless and sinful, for the unholy and profane, for those who kill their father or mother, for murderers, ¹⁰for those who are sexually immoral, for male prostitutes, slave traders, liars, perjurers, and whatever else is contrary to the sound teaching ¹¹that conforms to the glorious gospel of the blessed God, which God entrusted to me.

---

a Or *plan*

Gratitude for Mercy

12 I am grateful to Christ Jesus our Lord, who has strengthened me, having judged me faithful and appointed me to serve, [13] even though I was formerly a blasphemer, a persecutor, and a person of violence. But I received mercy because I had acted ignorantly in unbelief, [14] and the grace of God overflowed for me with the faith and love that are in Christ Jesus. [15] The saying is sure and worthy of full acceptance, that Christ Jesus came into the world to save sinners—of whom I am the foremost. [16] But for that very reason I received mercy, so that in me, as the foremost, Jesus Christ might display the utmost patience, making me an example to those who would come to believe in Christ for eternal life. [17] To the Ruler of the ages, immortal, invisible, the only God, be honor and glory forever and ever.[b] Amen.

18 I am giving you these instructions, Timothy, my child, in accordance with the prophecies made earlier about you, so that by following them you may fight the good fight, [19] having faith and a good conscience. By rejecting conscience, certain persons have suffered shipwreck in the faith; [20] among them are Hymenaeus and Alexander, whom I have turned over to Satan, so that they may learn not to blaspheme.

Instructions concerning Prayer

2 First of all, then, I urge that supplications, prayers, intercessions, and thanksgivings be made for everyone, [2] for rulers and all who are in high positions, so that we may lead a quiet and peaceable life in all godliness and dignity. [3] This is right and is acceptable in the sight of God our Savior, [4] who desires everyone to be saved and to come to the knowledge of the truth. [5] For

> there is one God;
>> there is also one mediator between God and
>>> humankind,
>> Christ Jesus, a human being,
>>> who gave life itself as a ransom for all

6

—this was attested at the right time. [7] For this I was appointed a herald and an apostle (I am telling the truth,[c] I am not lying), a teacher of the Gentiles in faith and truth.

8 I desire, then, that in every place the men should pray, lifting up holy hands without anger or argument; [9] also that the women should dress themselves modestly and decently in suitable clothing, not with their hair braided, or with gold, pearls, or expensive clothes, [10] but with good works, as is proper for women who profess reverence for God. [11] Let a woman[d] learn in silence with full obedience. [12] I permit no woman[d] to teach or to have authority over a

---

b Gk *to the ages of the ages*   c Other ancient authorities add *in Christ*   d Or *wife*

322

man;[e] she is to keep silent. [13]For Adam was formed first, then Eve; [14]and Adam was not deceived, but the woman was deceived and became a transgressor. [15]Yet she will be saved through childbearing, provided they continue in faith and love and holiness, with modesty.

Qualifications of Bishops

3 The saying is sure:[f] whoever aspires to the office of bishop[g] desires a noble task. [2]Now a bishop[h] must be above reproach, married only once, temperate, sensible, respectable, hospitable, an apt teacher, [3]not a drunkard, not violent but gentle, not quarrelsome, and not a lover of money. [4]Bishops must manage their households well, keeping their children obedient and respectful in every way— [5]for if they do not know how to manage their households, how can they take care of God's church? [6]A bishop must not be a recent convert in order not to be puffed up with conceit and fall into the condemnation of the devil. [7]Moreover, a bishop must be well thought of by outsiders, in order not to fall into disgrace and the snare of the devil.

Qualifications of Deacons

8 Deacons likewise must be serious, not double-tongued, not indulging in much wine, not greedy for money; [9]they must hold fast to the mystery of the faith with a clear conscience. [10]And let them first be tested; then, if they prove themselves blameless, let them serve as deacons. [11]Women[i] likewise must be serious, not slanderers, but temperate, faithful in all things. [12]Let deacons be married only once, and let them manage their children and their households well; [13]for those who serve well as deacons gain a good standing for themselves and great boldness in the faith that is in Christ Jesus.

The Mystery of Our Religion

14 I hope to come to you soon, but I am writing these instructions to you so that, [15]if I am delayed, you may know how one ought to behave in the household of God, which is the church of the living God, the pillar and bulwark of the truth. [16]Without any doubt, the mystery of our religion is great:

> Who[j] was revealed in flesh,
>   vindicated[k] in spirit,[l]
>   seen by angels,
>   proclaimed among Gentiles,
>   believed in throughout the world,
>   taken up in glory.

---

e Or *her husband*
f Some interpreters place these words at the end of the previous paragraph. Other ancient authorities read *The saying is commonly accepted*   g Or *overseer*   h Or *an overseer*
i Or *Their wives*, or *Women deacons*   j Or Other ancient authorities read *God*; others, *Which*
k Or *justified*   l Or *by the Spirit*

False Asceticism

4 Now the Spirit expressly says that in later[m] times some will renounce the faith by paying attention to deceitful spirits and teachings of demons, 2through the hypocrisy of liars whose consciences are seared with a hot iron. 3They forbid marriage and demand abstinence from foods, which God created to be received with thanksgiving by those who believe and know the truth. 4For everything created by God is good, and nothing is to be rejected, provided it is received with thanksgiving; 5for it is sanctified by God's word and by prayer.

A Good Minister of Jesus Christ

6 If you put these instructions before the sisters and brothers, you will be a good servant[n] of Christ Jesus, nourished on the words of the faith and of the sound teaching that you have followed. 7Have nothing to do with profane myths and superstitions. Train yourself in godliness, 8for, while physical training is of some value, godliness is valuable in every way, holding promise for both the present life and the life to come. 9The saying is sure and worthy of full acceptance. 10For to this end we toil and struggle,[o] because we have our hope set on the living God, who is the Savior of all people, especially of those who believe.

11 These are the things you must insist on and teach. 12Let no one despise your youth, but set the believers an example in speech and conduct, in love, in faith, in purity. 13Until I arrive, give attention to the public reading of scripture,[p] to exhorting, to teaching. 14Do not neglect the gift that is in you, which was given to you through prophecy with the laying on of hands by the council of elders.[q] 15Put these things into practice, devote yourself to them, so that all may see your progress. 16Pay close attention to yourself and to your teaching; continue in these things, for in doing this you will save both yourself and your hearers.

Duties toward Believers

5 Do not speak harshly to an older man,[r] but speak to him as to a father, to younger men as brothers, 2to older women as mothers, to younger women as sisters—with absolute purity.

3 Honor widows who are really widows. 4If a widow has children or grandchildren, they should first learn their religious duty to their own family and make some repayment to their parents; for this is pleasing in God's sight. 5The real widow, left alone, has set her hope on God and continues in supplications and prayers night and day; 6but the widow who lives for pleasure

---

m Or *the last*   n Or *deacon*   o Other ancient authorities read *suffer reproach*
p Gk *to the reading*   q Gk *by the presbytery*   r Or *an elder,* or *a presbyter*

is dead even while she lives. ⁷Give these commands as well, so that they may be above reproach. ⁸And whoever does not provide for relatives, and especially for family members, has denied the faith and is worse than an unbeliever.

9 Let a widow be put on the list if she is not less than sixty years old and has been married only once;ˢ ¹⁰she must be well attested for her good works, as one who has brought up children, shown hospitality, washed the saints' feet, helped the afflicted, and devoted herself to doing good in every way. ¹¹But refuse to put younger widows on the list; for when their sensual desires alienate them from Christ, they want to marry, ¹²and so they incur condemnation for having violated their first pledge. ¹³Besides that, they learn to be idle, gadding about from house to house; and they are not merely idle, but also gossips and busybodies, saying what they should not say. ¹⁴So I would have younger widows marry, bear children, and manage their households, so as to give the adversary no occasion to revile us. ¹⁵For some have already turned away to follow Satan. ¹⁶If any believing womanᵗ has relatives who are really widows, let her assist them; let the church not be burdened, so that it can assist those who are real widows.

17 Let the elders who rule well be considered worthy of double honor,ᵘ especially those who labor in preaching and teaching; ¹⁸for the scripture says, "You shall not muzzle an ox while it is treading out the grain," and, "The laborer deserves to be paid." ¹⁹Never accept any accusation against an elder except on the evidence of two or three witnesses. ²⁰As for those who persist in sin, rebuke them in the presence of all, so that the rest also may stand in fear. ²¹In the presence of God and of Christ Jesus and of the elect angels, I warn you to keep these instructions without prejudice, doing nothing on the basis of partiality. ²²Do not ordainᵛ anyone hastily, and do not participate in the sins of others; keep yourself pure.

23 No longer drink only water, but take a little wine for the sake of your stomach and your frequent ailments.

24 The sins of some people are conspicuous and precede them to judgment, while the sins of others follow them there. ²⁵So also good works are conspicuous; and even when they are not, they cannot remain hidden.

6 Let all who are enslaved regard those who enslave them as worthy of all honor, so that the name of God and the teaching may not be blasphemed. ²Those who are enslaved by believers must not be disrespectful to them on the ground that they are members of the church; rather they must serve them all the more, since those who benefit by their service are believers and beloved.ʷ

---

s Gk *the wife of one husband*
t Other ancient authorities read *believing man or woman*; others, *believing man*
u Or *compensation*   v Gk *Do not lay hands on*
w Or *since they are believers and beloved, who devote themselves to good deeds*

False Teaching and True Riches

Teach and urge these duties. [3] Whoever teaches otherwise and does not agree with the sound words of our Lord Jesus Christ and the teaching that is in accordance with godliness, [4] is conceited, understanding nothing, and has a morbid craving for controversy and for disputes about words. From these come envy, dissension, slander, base suspicions, [5] and wrangling among those who are depraved in mind and bereft of the truth, imagining that godliness is a means of gain.[x] [6] Of course, there is great gain in godliness combined with contentment; [7] for we brought nothing into the world, so that[y] we can take nothing out of it; [8] but if we have food and clothing, we will be content with these. [9] But those who want to be rich fall into temptation and are trapped by many senseless and harmful desires that plunge people into ruin and destruction. [10] For the love of money is a root of all kinds of evil, and in their eagerness to be rich some have wandered away from the faith and pierced themselves with many pains.

The Good Fight of Faith

11 Since you are a person of God, shun all this; pursue righteousness, godliness, faith, love, endurance, gentleness. [12] Fight the good fight of the faith; take hold of the eternal life, to which you were called and for which you made[z] the good confession in the presence of many witnesses. [13] In the presence of God, who gives life to all things, and of Christ Jesus, who in testifying before Pontius Pilate made the good confession, I charge you [14] to keep the commandment without spot or blame until the manifestation of our Lord Jesus Christ, [15] which will be brought about at the right time—by the one who is the blessed and only powerful one, Rulers of rulers and Sovereign of sovereigns. [16] It is that one alone who has immortality and dwells in unapproachable light, whom no one has ever seen or can see, to whom be honor and eternal dominion. Amen.

17 As for those who in the present age are rich, command them not to be haughty, or to set their hopes on the uncertainty of riches, but rather on God who richly provides us with everything for our enjoyment. [18] They are to do good, to be rich in good works, generous, and ready to share, [19] thus storing up for themselves the treasure of a good foundation for the future, so that they may take hold of the life that really is life.

---

x Other ancient authorities add *Withdraw yourself from such people*
y Other ancient authorities read *world—it is certain that*   z Gk *confessed*

Personal Instructions and Benediction

20 Timothy, guard what has been entrusted to you. Avoid the profane chatter and contradictions of what is falsely called knowledge; 21 by professing it some have missed the mark as regards the faith.

Grace be with you.[a]

---

a The Greek word for *you* here is plural; in other ancient authorities it is singular. Other ancient authorities add *Amen*

The Second Letter of Paul to Timothy

1 Paul, an apostle of Christ Jesus by the will of God, for the sake of the promise of life that is in Christ Jesus,

2 To Timothy, my beloved child:

Grace, mercy, and peace from God the Father-Mother and Christ Jesus our Lord.

Thanksgiving and Encouragement

3 I am grateful to God—whom I worship with a clear conscience, as my ancestors did—when I remember you constantly in my prayers night and day. ⁴Recalling your tears, I long to see you so that I may be filled with joy. ⁵I am reminded of your sincere faith, a faith that lived first in your grandmother Lois and your mother Eunice and now, I am sure, lives in you. ⁶For this reason I remind you to rekindle the gift of God that is within you through the laying on of my hands; ⁷for God did not give us a spirit of cowardice, but rather a spirit of power and of love and of self-discipline.

8 Do not be ashamed, then, of the testimony about Christ or of me the prisoner of Christ, but join with me in suffering for the gospel, relying on the power of God, ⁹who saved us and called us with a holy calling, not according to our works but according to God's own purpose and grace. This grace was given to us in Christ Jesus before the ages began, ¹⁰but it has now been revealed through the appearing of our Savior Christ Jesus, who abolished death and brought life and immortality to light through the gospel. ¹¹For this gospel I was appointed a herald and an apostle and a teacher,ᵃ ¹²and for this reason I suffer as I do. But I am not ashamed, for I know the one in whom I have put my trust, and I am sure that God is able to guard until that day what has been

---

a Other ancient authorities add *of the Gentiles*

entrusted to me.[b] [13]Hold to the standard of sound teaching that you have heard from me, in the faith and love that are in Christ Jesus. [14]Guard the good treasure entrusted to you, with the help of the Holy Spirit living in us.

[15] You are aware that all who are in Asia have turned away from me, including Phygelus and Hermogenes. [16]May the Lord grant mercy to the household of Onesiphorus, because he often refreshed me and was not ashamed of my chain; [17]when he arrived in Rome, he eagerly[c] searched for me and found me [18]—may the Lord grant that Onesiphorus will find mercy from the Lord on that day! And you know very well how much service he rendered in Ephesus.

A Good Soldier of Christ Jesus

2 You then, my child, be strong in the grace that is in Christ Jesus; [2]and what you have heard from me through many witnesses entrust to faithful people who will be able to teach others as well. [3]Share in suffering like a good soldier of Christ Jesus. [4]No one serving in the army gets entangled in everyday affairs; the soldier's aim is to please the enlisting officer. [5]And in the case of an athlete, no one is crowned without competing according to the rules. [6]It is the farmer who does the work who ought to have the first share of the crops. [7]Think over what I say, for the Lord will give you understanding in all things.

[8] Remember Jesus Christ, raised from the dead, a descendant of David—that is my gospel, [9]for which I suffer hardship, even to the point of being chained like a criminal. But the word of God is not chained. [10]Therefore I endure everything for the sake of the elect, so that they may also obtain the salvation that is in Christ Jesus, with eternal glory. [11]The saying is sure:

> If we have died with Christ, we will also live with
> Christ;
[12]   if we endure, we will also reign with Christ;
> if we deny Christ, Christ will also deny us;
[13]   if we are faithless, Christ remains faithful—
> for Christ cannot deny Christ's self.

A Worker Approved by God

[14] Remind them of this, and warn them before God[d] that they are to avoid wrangling over words, which does no good but only ruins those who are listening. [15]Do your best to present yourself to God as one who has been approved, a worker who has no need to be ashamed, rightly explaining the word of truth. [16]Avoid profane chatter, for it will lead people into more and more impiety, [17]and their talk will spread like gangrene. Among them are Hymenaeus and Philetus, [18]who have swerved from the truth by claiming that

b Or *what I have entrusted to God*   c Or *promptly*
d Other ancient authorities read *the Lord*

the resurrection has already taken place. They are upsetting the faith of some.
19 But God's firm foundation stands, bearing this inscription: "Christ knows
those who belong to Christ," and, "Let everyone who calls on the name of
Christ turn away from wickedness."

20 In a large house there are utensils not only of gold and silver but also
of wood and clay, some for special use, some for ordinary. 21 All who cleanse
themselves of the things I have mentioned[e] will become special utensils,
dedicated and useful to the owner of the house, ready for every good work.
22 Shun youthful passions and pursue righteousness, faith, love, and peace, along
with those who call on the Lord from a pure heart. 23 Have nothing to do with
stupid and senseless controversies; you know that they breed quarrels. 24 And
the Lord's servant must not be quarrelsome but kindly to everyone, an apt
teacher, patient, 25 correcting opponents with gentleness. God may perhaps grant
that they will repent and come to know the truth, 26 and that they may escape
from the snare of the devil, having been held captive by the devil to do the
devil's will.[f]

Godlessness in the Last Days

3 You must understand this, that in the last days distressing times will come.
2 For people will be lovers of themselves, lovers of money, boasters,
arrogant, abusive, disobedient to their parents, ungrateful, unholy, 3 inhuman,
implacable, slanderers, profligates, brutes, haters of good, 4 treacherous, reckless,
swollen with conceit, lovers of pleasure rather than lovers of God, 5 holding to
the outward form of godliness but denying its power. Avoid them! 6 For among
them are those who make their way into households and captivate the unwary,
overwhelmed by their sins and swayed by all kinds of desires, 7 who are always
being instructed and can never arrive at a knowledge of the truth. 8 As Jannes
and Jambres opposed Moses, so these people, of corrupt mind and counterfeit
faith, also oppose the truth. 9 But they will not make much progress, because, as
in the case of those two, their folly will become plain to everyone.

Paul's Charge to Timothy

10 Now you have observed my teaching, my conduct, my aim in life, my faith,
my patience, my love, my steadfastness, 11 my persecutions and suffering the
things that happened to me in Antioch, Iconium, and Lystra. What persecutions
I endured! Yet the Lord rescued me from all of them. 12 Indeed, all who want
to live a godly life in Christ Jesus will be persecuted. 13 But wicked people and
impostors will go from bad to worse, deceiving others and being deceived.
14 But as for you, continue in what you have learned and firmly believed,
knowing from whom you learned it, 15 and how from childhood you have
known the sacred writings that are able to instruct you for salvation through

---

e Gk *of these things*   f Or *by God, to do God's will*

faith in Christ Jesus. 16 All scripture is inspired by God and is^g useful for teaching, for reproof, for correction, and for training in righteousness, 17 so that everyone who belongs to God may be proficient, equipped for every good work.

4 In the presence of God and of Christ Jesus, who is to judge the living and the dead, and in view of the appearing and dominion of Christ, I solemnly urge you: 2 proclaim the message; be persistent whether the time is favorable or unfavorable; convince, rebuke, and encourage, with the utmost patience in teaching. 3 For the time is coming when people will not put up with sound doctrine, but having itching ears, they will accumulate for themselves teachers to suit their own desires, 4 and will turn away from listening to the truth and wander away to myths. 5 As for you, always be sober, endure suffering, do the work of an evangelist, carry out your ministry fully.

6 As for me, I am already being poured out as a libation, and the time of my departure has come. 7 I have fought the good fight, I have finished the race, I have kept the faith. 8 From now on there is reserved for me the crown of righteousness, which Christ, the righteous judge, will give me on that day, and not only to me but also to all who have longed for Christ's appearing.

Personal Instructions

9 Do your best to come to me soon, 10 for Demas, in love with this present world, has deserted me and gone to Thessalonica; Crescens has gone to Galatia,^h Titus to Dalmatia. 11 Only Luke is with me. Get Mark and bring him with you, for he is useful in my ministry. 12 I have sent Tychicus to Ephesus. 13 When you come, bring the cloak that I left with Carpus at Troas, also the books, and above all the parchments. 14 Alexander the coppersmith did me great harm; the Lord will pay him back for his deeds. 15 You also must beware of him, for he strongly opposed our message.

16 At my first defense no one came to my support, but all deserted me. May it not be counted against them! 17 But Christ stood by me and gave me strength, so that through me the message might be fully proclaimed and all the Gentiles might hear it. So I was rescued from the lion's mouth. 18 The Lord will rescue me from every evil attack and save me for the heavenly realm. To that one be the glory forever and ever. Amen.

Final Greetings and Benediction

19 Greet Prisca and Aquila, and the household of Onesiphorus. 20 Erastus remained in Corinth; Trophimus I left ill in Miletus. 21 Do your best to come before winter. Eubulus sends greetings to you, as do Pudens and Linus and Claudia and all the brothers and sisters.

22 Christ be with your spirit. Grace be with you.ⁱ

---

g Or *Every scripture inspired by God is also*   h Other ancient authorities read *Gaul*
i The Greek word for *you* here is plural. Other ancient authorities add *Amen*

The Letter of Paul to Titus

Salutation

1 Paul, a servant of God and an apostle of Jesus Christ, for the sake of the faith of God's elect and the knowledge of the truth that is in accordance with godliness, 2in the hope of eternal life that God, who never lies, promised before the ages began— 3in due time God revealed God's word through the proclamation with which I have been entrusted by the command of God our Savior,

4 To Titus, my loyal child in the faith we share:

Grace[a] and peace from God the Father-Mother and Christ Jesus our Savior.

Titus in Crete

5 I left you behind in Crete for this reason, so that you should put in order what remained to be done, and should appoint elders in every town, as I directed you: 6someone who is blameless, married only once, whose children are believers, not accused of debauchery and not rebellious. 7For a bishop,[b] as manager on God's behalf, must be blameless, not be arrogant or quick-tempered or addicted to wine or violent or greedy for gain, 8but rather must be hospitable, a lover of goodness, prudent, upright, devout, and self-controlled. 9A bishop must have a firm grasp of the word that is trustworthy in accordance with the teaching, in order to be able both to preach with sound doctrine and to refute those who contradict it.

10 There are also many rebellious people, idle talkers and deceivers, especially those of the circumcision; 11they must be silenced, since they are

---

a Other ancient authorities read *Grace, mercy,*   b Or *an overseer*

upsetting whole families by teaching for sordid gain what it is not right to teach. [12] It was one of them, their very own prophet, who said,

"Cretans are always liars, vicious brutes, lazy gluttons."

[13] That testimony is true. For this reason rebuke them sharply, so that they may become sound in the faith, [14] not paying attention to Jewish myths or to commandments of those who reject the truth. [15] To the pure all things are pure, but to the corrupt and unbelieving nothing is pure. Their very minds and consciences are corrupted. [16] They profess to know God, but they deny God by their actions. They are detestable, disobedient, unfit for any good work.

Teach Sound Doctrine

2 But as for you, teach what is consistent with sound doctrine. [2] Tell the older men to be temperate, serious, prudent, and sound in faith, in love, and in endurance.

[3] Likewise, tell the older women to be reverent in behavior, not to be slanderous or addicted to drink; they are to teach what is good, [4] so that they may encourage the young women to love their husbands, to love their children, [5] to be self-controlled, chaste, good managers of the household, kind, being committed to their husbands, so that the word of God may not be discredited.

[6] Likewise, urge the younger men to be self-controlled. [7] Show yourself in all respects a model of good works, and in your teaching show integrity, gravity, [8] and sound speech that cannot be censured; then any opponent will be put to shame, having nothing evil to say of us.

[9] Tell those who are enslaved to accept the authority of those who enslave them and to give satisfaction in every respect; they are not to talk back, [10] not to pilfer, but to show complete and perfect fidelity, so that in everything they may be an ornament to the doctrine of God our Savior.

[11] For the grace of God has appeared, bringing salvation to all,[c] [12] training us to renounce impiety and worldly passions, and in the present age to live lives that are self-controlled, upright, and godly, [13] while we wait for the blessed hope and the manifestation of the glory of our great God and Savior,[d] Jesus Christ [14] who gave Christ's own life for us in order to redeem us from all iniquity and purify a people for Christ's own possession who are zealous for good deeds.

[15] Declare these things; exhort and reprove with all authority.[e] Let no one look down on you.

---

c Or *has appeared to all, bringing salvation*   d Or *of the great God and our Savior*
e Gk *commandment*

Maintain Good Deeds

3 Remind them to be subject to rulers and authorities, to be obedient, to be ready for every good work, ²to speak evil of no one, to avoid quarreling, to be gentle, and to show every courtesy to everyone. ³For we ourselves were once foolish, disobedient, led astray, slaves to various passions and pleasures, passing our days in malice and envy, despicable, hating one another. ⁴But when the goodness and loving kindness of God our Savior appeared, ⁵we were saved, not because of any works of righteousness that we had done, but according to God's mercy, through the water^f of rebirth and renewal by the Holy Spirit, ⁶which God poured out richly upon us through Jesus Christ our Savior, ⁷so that, having been justified by God's grace, we might become heirs according to the hope of eternal life. ⁸The saying is sure.

I desire that you insist on these things, so that those who have come to believe in God may be careful to devote themselves to good works; these things are excellent and profitable to everyone. ⁹But avoid stupid controversies, genealogies, dissensions, and quarrels about the law, for they are unprofitable and worthless. ¹⁰After a first and second admonition, have nothing more to do with anyone who causes divisions, ¹¹since you know that such a person is perverted and sinful, being self-condemned.

Final Messages and Benediction

12 When I send Artemas to you, or Tychicus, do your best to come to me at Nicopolis, for I have decided to spend the winter there. ¹³Make every effort to send Zenas the lawyer and Apollos on their way, and see that they lack nothing. ¹⁴And let people learn to devote themselves to good works in order to meet urgent needs, so that they may not be unproductive.

15 All who are with me send greetings to you. Greet those who love us in the faith.

Grace be with all of you.^g

---

f Gk *washing*   g Other ancient authorities add *Amen*

The Letter of Paul to Philemon

Salutation

1 Paul, a prisoner of Christ Jesus, and Timothy our brother,

To Philemon our dear friend and coworker, ²to Apphia our sister, to Archippus our companion in struggle, and to the church in your house:

3 Grace to you and peace from God our Father-Mother and the Lord Jesus Christ.

Philemon's Love and Faith

4 When I remember you[a] in my prayers, I always thank my God ⁵because I hear of your love for all the saints and your faith toward the Lord Jesus. ⁶I pray that the sharing of your faith may become effective when you perceive all the good that we[b] may do for Christ. ⁷I have indeed received much joy and encouragement from your love, because the hearts of the saints have been refreshed through you, my brother.

Paul's Plea for Onesimus

8 For this reason, though I am bold enough in Christ to command you to do your duty, ⁹yet I would rather appeal to you on the basis of love—and I, Paul, do this as an old man, and now also as a prisoner of Christ Jesus.[c] ¹⁰I am appealing to you for my child, Onesimus, whose father I have become during my imprisonment. ¹¹Formerly he was useless to you, but now he is indeed useful[d] both to you and to me. ¹²I am sending Onesimus, that is, my own heart, back to you. ¹³I wanted to keep him with me, so that he might be of service to me in your place during my imprisonment for the gospel; ¹⁴but I

---

a From verse 4 through verse 21, *you* is singular   b Other ancient authorities read *you* (plural)
c Or *as an ambassador of Christ Jesus, and now also Christ's prisoner*
d The name Onesimus means *useful* or (compare verse 20) *beneficial*

preferred to do nothing without your consent, in order that your good deed might be voluntary and not something forced. [15]Perhaps this is the reason he was separated from you for a while, so that you might have him back forever, [16]no longer as one enslaved but more than that, a beloved brother—especially to me but how much more to you, both in the flesh and in Christ.

17 So if you consider me your partner, welcome Onesimus as you would welcome me. [18]If he has wronged you in any way, or owes you anything, charge that to my account. [19]I, Paul, am writing this with my own hand: I will repay it. I say nothing about your owing me even your own self. [20]Yes, brother, let me have this benefit from you in Christ! Refresh my heart in Christ. [21]Confident of your obedience, I am writing to you, knowing that you will do even more than I say.

22 One thing more—prepare a guest room for me, for I am hoping through your prayers to be restored to you.

Final Greetings and Benediction

23 Epaphras, a prisoner with me in Christ Jesus, sends greetings to you,[e] [24]and so do Mark, Aristarchus, Demas, and Luke, my coworkers.

25 The grace of the Lord Jesus Christ be with your spirit.[f]

---

e Here *you* is singular   f Other ancient authorities add *Amen*

The Letter to the Hebrews

God Has Spoken by God's Child

1 Long ago God spoke to our ancestors in many and various ways by the prophets, 2but in these last days God has spoken to us by a Child,[a] whom God appointed heir of all things, through whom God also created the worlds, 3and who is the reflection of God's glory and the exact imprint of God's very being, and sustains[b] all things by a powerful word. Having made purification for sins, the heir of God sat down beside the Majesty on high, 4having become as much superior to angels as the name the heir has inherited is more excellent than theirs.

The Child Is Superior to Angels

5 For to which of the angels did God ever say,

> "You are my Child;
>> today I have begotten you"?

Or again,

> "I will be a parent to the Child,
>> and the Child will be my very own"?

6And again, bringing the firstborn into the world, God says,

> "Let all God's angels worship this Child."

7Of the angels it is said,

> "God makes the angels into winds,
>> and the servants of God into flames of fire."

---

a Or *the Child* b Or *bears along*

8 But of the Child it is said,

> "Your throne, O God,c is forever and ever,
>   and the righteous scepter is the scepter of yourd
>   dominion.
> 9   You have loved righteousness and hated wickedness;
>   therefore God, your God, has anointed you
>   with the oil of gladness beyond your companions."

10 And,

> "In the beginning, God, you founded the earth,
>   and the heavens are the work of your hands;
> 11   they will perish, but you remain;
>   they will all wear out like clothing;
> 12   like a cloak you will roll them up,
>   and like clothinge they will be changed.
> But you are the same,
>   and your years will never end."

13 But to which of the angels has God ever said,

> "Sit beside me
>   until I make your enemies a footstool for your feet"?

14 Are not all angels spirits in the divine service, sent to serve for the sake of those who are to inherit salvation?

Warning to Pay Attention

2 Therefore we must pay greater attention to what we have heard, so that we do not drift away from it. 2 For if the message declared through angels was valid, and every transgression or disobedience received a just penalty, 3 how can we escape if we neglect so great a salvation? It was declared at first through the Lord, and it was attested to us by those who heard the Lord, 4 while God added testimony by signs and wonders and various miracles, and by gifts of the Holy Spirit, distributed according to God's will.

Exaltation through Abasement

5 Now God did not subject the coming world, about which we are speaking, to angels. 6 But someone has testified somewhere,

> "What are human beings that you are mindful of them,
>   or mortals, that you care for them?

---

c Or *God is your throne*   d Other ancient authorities read *the Child's*
e Other ancient authorities lack *like clothing*

7   You have made them for a little while lower[f] than the
            angels;
         you have crowned them with glory and honor,[g]
8   subjecting all things under their feet."

Now in subjecting all things to them, God left nothing outside their control. As it is, we do not yet see everything in subjection to them, [9]but we do see Jesus, who for a little while was made lower[h] than the angels, now crowned with glory and honor because of the suffering of death, so that by the grace of God[i] Jesus might taste death for everyone.

10 It was fitting that God, for whom and through whom all things exist, in bringing many children to glory, should make the pioneer of their salvation perfect through sufferings. [11]For the one who sanctifies and those who are sanctified all have a Father-Mother in common. For this reason Jesus is not ashamed to call them brothers and sisters, [12]saying,

      "I will proclaim your name to my sisters and brothers,
        in the midst of the congregation I will praise you."

[13]And again,

      "I will put my trust in God."

And again,

      "Here am I and the children whom God has given me."

14 Since, therefore, the children share flesh and blood, Jesus likewise shared the same things, in order to destroy through death the one who has the power of death, that is, the devil, [15]and free those who all their lives were held in slavery by the fear of death. [16]For it is clear that Jesus did not come to help angels, but the descendants of Abraham and Sarah. [17]Therefore Jesus had to become like human beings in every respect, so as to be a merciful and faithful high priest in the service of God, to make a sacrifice of atonement for the sins of the people. [18]Because of having been tested by suffering, Jesus is able to help those who are being tested.

Moses a Servant, Christ a Child

3 Therefore, brothers and sisters, holy partners in a heavenly calling, consider that Jesus, the apostle and high priest of our confession, [2]was faithful to the one who appointed him, just as Moses also "was faithful in all[j] God's house." [3]Yet Jesus is worthy of more glory than Moses, just as the builder of a house has more honor than the house itself. [4](For every house is built by

---

f Or *them only a little lower*
g Other ancient authorities add *and set them over the works of your hands*
h Or *who was made a little lower*   i Other ancient authorities read *apart from God*
j Other ancient authorities lack *all*

someone, but the builder of all things is God.) ⁵Now Moses was faithful in all God's house as a servant, to testify to the things that would be spoken later. ⁶Christ, however, was faithful over God's house as an heir, and we are God's house if we hold firmᵏ the confidence and the pride that belong to hope.

Warning against Unbelief

7 Therefore, as the Holy Spirit says,

> "Today, if you hear God's voice,
> 8 do not harden your hearts as in the rebellion,
>   as on the day of testing in the wilderness,
> 9 where your ancestors put me to the test,
>   though they had seen my works ¹⁰for forty years.
> Therefore I was angry with that generation,
> and I said, 'They always go astray in their hearts,
>   and they have not known my ways.'
> 11 As in my anger I swore,
>   'They will not enter my rest.' "

¹²Take care, sisters and brothers, that none of you may have an evil, unbelieving heart that turns away from the living God. ¹³But exhort one another every day, as long as it is called "today," so that none of you may be hardened by the deceitfulness of sin. ¹⁴For we have become partners of Christ, if only we hold our first confidence firm to the end. ¹⁵As it is said,

> "Today, if you hear God's voice,
> do not harden your hearts as in the rebellion."

¹⁶Now who were they who heard and yet were rebellious? Was it not all those who left Egypt under the leadership of Moses? ¹⁷But with whom was God angry forty years? Was it not those who sinned, whose bodies fell in the wilderness? ¹⁸And to whom did God swear that they would not enter God's rest, if not to those who were disobedient? ¹⁹So we see that they were unable to enter because of unbelief.

The Rest That God Promised

4 Therefore, while the promise of entering God's rest is still open, let us take care that none of you should seem to have failed to reach it. ²For indeed the good news came to us just as to them; but the message they heard did not benefit them, because they were not united by faith with those who listened.ˡ ³For we who have believed enter that rest, just as God has said,

---

k Other ancient authorities add *to the end*
l Other ancient authorities read *it did not meet with faith in those who listened*

> "As in my anger I swore,
> 'They shall not enter my rest,' "

though God's works were finished at the foundation of the world. ⁴For in one place it speaks about the seventh day as follows, "And God rested on the seventh day from all God's works." ⁵And again in this place it says, "They shall not enter my rest." ⁶Since therefore it remains open for some to enter it, and those who formerly received the good news failed to enter because of disobedience, ⁷again God sets a certain day—"today"—saying through David much later, in the words already quoted,

> "Today, if you hear God's voice,
> do not harden your hearts."

⁸For if Joshua had given them rest, God would not speak later about another day. ⁹So then, a sabbath rest still remains for the people of God; ¹⁰for those who enter God's rest cease from their labors as God also did. ¹¹Let us therefore make every effort to enter that rest, so that no one may fall through such disobedience as theirs.

12 Indeed, the word of God is living and active, sharper than any two-edged sword, piercing until it divides soul from spirit, joints from marrow; it is able to judge the thoughts and intentions of the heart. ¹³And before God no creature is hidden, but all are naked and laid bare to the eyes of the one to whom we must render an account.

Jesus the Great High Priest

14 Since, then, we have a great high priest who has passed through the heavens, Jesus, the Child of God, let us hold fast to our confession. ¹⁵For we do not have a high priest who is unable to sympathize with our weaknesses, but we have one who in every respect has been tested[m] as we are, yet without sin. ¹⁶Let us therefore approach the throne of grace with boldness, so that we may receive mercy and find grace to help in time of need.

5 Every high priest chosen from among mortals is put in charge of things pertaining to God on their behalf, to offer gifts and sacrifices for sins. ²High priests are able to deal gently with the ignorant and wayward, since they themselves are subject to weakness; ³and because of this they must offer sacrifice for their own sins as well as for those of the people. ⁴And they do not presume to take this honor, but take it only when called by God, just as Aaron was.

5 So also Christ did not claim the exalted offer of a high priest, but was appointed by the one who said,

> "You are my Child,
> today I have begotten you";

---

m Or *tempted*

[6]and who says also in another place,

> "You are a priest forever,
>   according to the order of Melchizedek."

7 While in the flesh, Jesus offered up prayers and supplications, with loud cries and tears, to the one who was able to save him from death, and was heard because of his reverence. [8]Although a Child, Jesus learned obedience through suffering; [9]and having been made perfect, became the source of eternal salvation for all who obey Jesus, [10]having been designated by God a high priest according to the order of Melchizedek.

Warning against Falling Away

11 About this[n] we have much to say that is hard to explain, since you have become dull in understanding. [12]For though by this time you ought to be teachers, you need someone to teach you again the basic elements of the oracles of God. You need milk, not solid food; [13]for everyone who lives on milk, being still an infant, is unskilled in the word of righteousness. [14]But solid food is for the mature, for those whose faculties have been trained by practice to distinguish good from evil.

The Peril of Falling Away

6 Therefore let us go on toward perfection,[o] leaving behind the basic teaching about Christ, and not laying again the foundation: repentance from dead works and faith toward God, [2]instruction about baptisms, laying on of hands, resurrection of the dead, and eternal judgment. [3]And we will do[p] this, if God permits. [4]For it is impossible to restore again to repentance those who have once been enlightened, and have tasted the heavenly gift, and have shared in the Holy Spirit, [5]and have tasted the goodness of the word of God and the powers of the age to come, [6]and then have fallen away, since on their own they are crucifying again the Child of God and are holding that Child up to contempt. [7]Ground that drinks up the rain falling on it repeatedly, and that produces a crop useful to those for whom it is cultivated, receives a blessing from God. [8]But if it produces thorns and thistles, it is worthless and on the verge of being cursed; its end is to be burned over.

9 Even though we speak in this way, beloved, we are confident of better things in your case, things that belong to salvation. [10]For God is not so unjust as to overlook your work and the love that you showed for God's sake[q] in serving the saints, as you still do. [11]And we want each one of you to show the same diligence so as to realize the full assurance of hope to the very end, [12]so that you may not become sluggish, but imitators of those who through faith and patience inherit the promises.

---

n Or *Jesus*   o Or *toward maturity*   p Other ancient authorities read *let us do*
q Gk *for God's name*

The Certainty of God's Promise

13 When God made a promise to Abraham, because God had no one greater by whom to swear, God swore by Godself, 14saying, "I will surely bless you and multiply you." 15And thus Abraham, having patiently endured, obtained the promise. 16Human beings, of course, swear by someone greater than themselves, and an oath given as confirmation puts an end to all dispute. 17In the same way, when God desired to show even more clearly to the heirs of the promise the unchangeable character of God's purpose, God guaranteed it by an oath, 18so that through two unchangeable things, in which it is impossible that God would prove false, we who have taken refuge might be strongly encouraged to seize the hope set before us. 19We have this hope, a sure and steadfast anchor of the soul, a hope that enters the inner shrine behind the curtain, 20where Jesus, a forerunner on our behalf, has entered, having become a high priest forever according to the order of Melchizedek.

The Priestly Order of Melchizedek

7 This "King Melchizedek of Salem, priest of the Most High God, met Abraham as he was returning from defeating the kings and blessed him"; 2and to him Abraham apportioned "one-tenth of everything." His name, in the first place, means "king of righteousness"; next he is also king of Salem, that is, "king of peace." 3Without father, without mother, without genealogy, having neither beginning of days nor end of life, but resembling the Child of God, Melchizedek remains a priest forever.

4 See how great Melchizedek is! Even[r] Abraham the patriarch gave him a tenth of the spoils. 5And those descendants of Levi who receive the priestly office have a commandment in the law to collect tithes[s] from the people, that is, from their relatives, though these also are descended from Abraham. 6But this man, who does not belong to their ancestry, collected tithes[s] from Abraham and blessed Abraham who had received the promises. 7It is beyond dispute that the inferior is blessed by the superior. 8In the one case, tithes are received by those who are mortal; in the other, by one of whom it is testified that Melchizedek lives. 9One might even say that Levi himself, who receives tithes, paid tithes through Abraham, 10for Levi was still in the loins of his ancestor when Melchizedek met him.

Another Priest, Like Melchizedek

11 Now if perfection had been attainable through the levitical priesthood—for the people received the law under this priesthood—what further need would there have been to speak of another priest arising according to the order of Melchizedek, rather than one according to the order of Aaron? 12For when there is a change in the priesthood, there is necessarily a change in the law as

---

r Other ancient authorities lack *Even*   s Or *a tenth*

343

well. ¹³Now the one of whom these things are spoken belonged to another tribe, from which no one has ever served at the altar. ¹⁴For it is evident that Jesus was descended from Judah, and in connection with that tribe Moses said nothing about priests.

15 It is even more obvious when another priest arises, resembling Melchizedek, ¹⁶one who has become a priest, not through a legal requirement concerning physical descent, but through the power of an indestructible life. ¹⁷For it is attested of him,

> "You are a priest forever,
>   according to the order of Melchizedek."

¹⁸There is, on the one hand, the abrogation of an earlier commandment because it was weak and ineffectual ¹⁹(for the law made nothing perfect); there is, on the other hand, the introduction of a better hope, through which we approach God.

20 This was confirmed with an oath; for others who became priests took their office without an oath, ²¹but this one became a priest with an oath, because of the one who said to him,

> "God has sworn
>   and will not regret it,
>   'You are a priest forever' "—

²²accordingly Jesus has also become the guarantee of a better covenant.

23 Furthermore, the former priests were many in number, because they were prevented by death from continuing in office; ²⁴but Jesus, who continues forever, holds the priesthood premanently ²⁵and so is able for all time to save[t] those who approach God through Jesus, who always lives to make intercession for them.

26 For it was fitting that we should have such a high priest, holy, blameless, undefiled, separated from sinners, and exalted above the heavens. ²⁷Unlike the other[u] high priests, who offered sacrifices day after day, first for their own sins, and then for those of the people, Jesus did this once for all by offering Jesus' own life. ²⁸For the law appoints as high priests those who are subject to weakness, but the word of the oath, which came later than the law, appoints a Child who has been made perfect forever.

Mediator of a Better Covenant

8 Now the main point in what we are saying is this: we have such a high priest, one who is seated beside the throne of the Majesty in the heavens, ²a minister in the sanctuary and the true tent[v] that God, and not any mortal, has set up. ³For every high priest is appointed to offer gifts and sacrifices; hence it is necessary for this priest also to have something to offer. ⁴Now if

---

t Or *able to save completely*   u Gk lacks *other*   v Or *tabernacle*

Christ were on earth, Christ would not be a priest at all, since there are priests who offer gifts according to the law. [5] They offer worship in a sanctuary that is a sketch and shadow of the heavenly one; for Moses, when he was about to erect the tent,[w] was warned, "See that you make everything according to the pattern that was shown you on the mountain." [6] But Jesus has now obtained a more excellent ministry, and to that degree is the mediator of a better covenant, which has been enacted through better promises. [7] For if that first covenant had been faultless, there would have been no need to look for a second one.

8 God finds fault with them, saying:

> "The days are surely coming, says God,
> when I will establish a new covenant with the house
> of Israel
> and with the house of Judah;
>
> [9] not like the covenant that I made with their ancestors,
> on the day when I took them by the hand to lead
> them out of the land of Egypt;
> for they did not continue in my covenant,
> and so I had no concern for them, says God.
>
> [10] This is the covenant that I will make with the house
> of Israel
> after those days, says God:
> I will put my laws in their minds,
> and write them on their hearts,
> and I will be their God,
> and they shall be my people.
>
> [11] And they shall not teach one another
> or say to each other, 'Know God,'
> for they shall all know me,
> from the least of them to the greatest.
>
> [12] For I will be merciful toward their iniquities,
> and I will remember their sins no more."

[13] In speaking of "a new covenant," God has made the first one obsolete. And what is obsolete and growing old will soon disappear.

The Earthly and the Heavenly Sanctuaries

9 Now even the first covenant had regulations for worship and an earthly sanctuary. [2] For a tent[w] was constructed, the first one, in which were the lampstand, the table, and the bread of the Presence;[x] this is called the Holy Place. [3] Behind the second curtain was a tent[w] called the Holy of Holies. [4] In it stood the golden altar of incense and the ark of the covenant overlaid on all sides with gold, in which there were a golden urn holding the manna, and

---

w Or *tabernacle*   x Gk *the presentation of the loaves*

Aaron's rod that budded, and the tablets of the covenant; [5]above it were the cherubim of glory overshadowing the mercy seat.[y] Of these things we cannot speak now in detail.

6 Such preparations having been made, the priests go continually into the first tent[z] to carry out their ritual duties; [7]but only the high priest goes into the second, and he but once a year, and not without taking the blood that he offers for himself and for the sins committed unintentionally by the people. [8]By this the Holy Spirit indicates that the way into the sanctuary has not yet been disclosed as long as the first tent[z] is still standing. [9]This is a symbol[a] of the present time, during which gifts and sacrifices are offered that cannot perfect the conscience of the worshiper, [10]but deal only with food and drink and various baptisms, regulations for the body imposed until the time comes to set things right.

11 But when Christ came as a high priest of the good things that have come,[b] then through the greater and perfect[c] tent[z] (not made with hands, that is, not of this creation), [12]Christ entered once for all into the Holy Place, not with the blood of goats and calves, but with Christ's own blood, thus obtaining eternal redemption. [13]For if the blood of goats and bulls, with the sprinkling of the ashes of a heifer, sanctifies those who have been defiled so that their flesh is purified, [14]how much more will the blood of Christ, who through the eternal Spirit[d] offered Christ's self without blemish to God, purify our[e] conscience from dead works to worship the living God!

15 For this reason Christ is the mediator of a new covenant, so that those who are called may receive the promised eternal inheritance, because a death has occurred that redeems them from the transgressions under the first covenant.[f] [16]Where a will[f] is involved, the death of the one who made it must be established. [17]For a will[f] takes effect only at death, since it is not in force as long as the one who made it is alive. [18]Hence not even the first covenant was inaugurated without blood. [19]For when every commandment had been told to all the people by Moses in accordance with the law, Moses took the blood of calves and goats,[g] with water and scarlet wool and hyssop, and sprinkled both the scroll itself and all the people, [20]saying, "This is the blood of the covenant that God has ordained for you." [21]And in the same way Moses sprinkled with the blood both the tent[z] and all the vessels used in worship. [22]Indeed, under the law almost everything is purified with blood, and without the shedding of blood there is no forgiveness of sins.

---

y Or *the place of atonement*   z Or *tabernacle*   a Gk *parable*
b Other ancient authorities read *good things to come*   c Gk *more perfect*
d Other ancient authorities read *Holy Spirit*   e Other ancient authorities read *your*
f The Greek word used here means both *covenant* and *will*
g Other ancient authorities lack *and goats*

Christ's Sacrifice Takes Away Sin

23 Thus it was necessary for the sketches of the heavenly things to be purified with these rites, but the heavenly things themselves need better sacrifices than these. 24 For Christ did not enter a sanctuary made by human hands, a mere copy of the true one, but entered into heaven itself, now to appear in the presence of God on our behalf. 25 Nor was it to offer Christ's self again and again, as the high priest enters the Holy Place year after year with blood that is not the high priest's own; 26 for then Christ would have had to suffer again and again since the foundation of the world. But as it is, Christ has appeared once for all at the end of the age to remove sin through Christ's sacrifice. 27 And just as it is appointed for mortals to die once, and after that the judgment, 28 so Christ, having been offered once to bear the sins of many, will appear a second time, not to deal with sin, but to save those who are eagerly waiting for Christ.

Christ's Sacrifice Once for All

10 Since the law has only a shadow of the good things to come and not the true form of these realities, it[h] can never, by the same sacrifices that are continually offered year after year, make perfect those who approach. 2 Otherwise, would they not have ceased being offered, since the worshipers, cleansed once for all, would no longer have any consciousness of sin? 3 But in these sacrifices there is a reminder of sin year after year. 4 For it is impossible for the blood of bulls and goats to take away sins. 5 Consequently, having come into the world, Christ said,

> "Sacrifices and offerings you have not desired,
>   but a body you have prepared for me;
> 6 in burnt offerings and sin offerings
>   you have taken no pleasure.
> 7 Then I said, 'See, God, I have come to do your will, O
>   God'
>   (in the scroll of the book[i] it is written of me)."

8 When Christ said above, "You have neither desired nor taken pleasure in sacrifices and offerings and burnt offerings and sin offerings" (these are offered according to the law), 9 then Christ added, "See, I have come to do your will." Christ abolishes the first in order to establish the second. 10 And it is by God's will that we have been sanctified through the offering of the body of Jesus Christ once for all.

11 And every priest stands ministering day after day, offering again and again the same sacrifices that can never take away sins. 12 But Christ, having offered for all time a single sacrifice for sins, "sat down beside God," 13 and

---

h Other ancient authorities read *they*   i Meaning of Gk uncertain

since then has been waiting "until all enemies would be made a footstool for Christ's feet." [14] For by a single offering Christ has perfected for all time those who are sanctified. [15] And the Holy Spirit also testifies to us, for after saying,

[16]
>   "This is the covenant that I will make with them
>   after those days, says God:
>   I will put my laws in their hearts,
>   and I will write them on their minds,"

[17] it is added,

>   "I will remember[j] their sins and their lawless deeds no
>   more."

[18] Where there is forgiveness of these, there is no longer any offering for sin.

A Call to Persevere

19 Therefore, my friends, since we have confidence to enter the sanctuary by the blood of Jesus, [20] by the new and living way that Jesus opened for us through the curtain (that is, through Jesus' flesh), [21] and since we have a great priest over the house of God, [22] let us approach with a true heart in full assurance of faith, with our hearts sprinkled clean from an evil conscience and our bodies washed with pure water. [23] Let us hold fast to the confession of our hope without wavering, for the one who has promised is faithful. [24] And let us consider how to provoke one another to love and good deeds, [25] not neglecting to meet together, as is the habit of some, but encouraging one another, and all the more as you see the Day approaching.

26 For if we willfully persist in sin after having received the knowledge of the truth, there no longer remains a sacrifice for sins, [27] but a fearful prospect of judgment, and a fury of fire that will consume the adversaries. [28] Anyone who has violated the law of Moses dies without mercy "on the testimony of two or three witnesses." [29] How much worse punishment do you think will be deserved by those who have spurned the Child of God, profaned the blood of the covenant by which they were sanctified, and outraged the Spirit of grace? [30] For we know the one who said, "Vengeance is mine, I will repay." And again, "God will judge God's people." [31] It is a fearful thing to fall into the hands of the living God.

32 But recall those earlier days when, after you had been enlightened, you endured a hard struggle with sufferings, [33] sometimes being publicly exposed to abuse and persecution, and sometimes being partners with those so treated. [34] For you had compassion for those who were in prison, and you cheerfully accepted the plundering of your possessions, knowing that you yourselves possessed something better and more lasting. [35] Do not, therefore, abandon that confidence of yours; it brings a great reward. [36] For you need endurance, so that

---

j Gk *on their minds and I will remember*

when you have done the will of God, you may receive what was promised.

37   For yet "in a very little while,
           the one who is coming will come and will not delay;
38   but my righteous one will live by faith.
           My soul takes no pleasure in anyone who shrinks
           back."

39 But we are not among those who shrink back and so are lost, but among those who have faith and so are saved.

The Meaning of Faith

11 Now faith is the assurance of things hoped for, the conviction of things not seen. 2 Indeed, by faith our ancestors received approval. 3 By faith we understand that the worlds were prepared by the word of God, so that what is seen was made from things that are not visible.[k]

The Examples of Abel, Enoch, and Noah

4 By faith Abel offered to God a more acceptable[l] sacrifice than Cain's, through which Abel received approval as righteous, God indeed giving approval to his gifts; Abel died, but through his faith he still speaks. 5 By faith Enoch was taken so that he did not experience death; and "he was not found, because God had taken him." For it was attested before Enoch was taken away that "he had pleased God." 6 And without faith it is impossible to please God, for whoever would approach God must believe that God exists and rewards those who seek God. 7 By faith Noah, warned by God about events as yet unseen, respected the warning and built an ark to save his household; by this Noah condemned the world and became an heir to the righteousness that is in accordance with faith.

The Faith of Abraham

8 By faith Abraham obeyed when he was called to set out for a place that he was to receive as an inheritance; and he set out, not knowing where he was going. 9 By faith Abraham stayed for a time in the land he had been promised, as in a foreign land, living in tents, as did Isaac and Jacob, who were heirs with him of the same promise. 10 For Abraham looked forward to the city that has foundations, whose architect and builder is God. 11 By faith Abraham received power of procreation, even though he was too old—and Sarah herself was childless—because Abraham considered God faithful who had made the promise.[m] 12 Therefore from one person, and this one as good as dead, descendants

---

k Or was not made out of visible things   l Gk greater
m Or By faith Sarah herself, though childless, received power to conceive, even when she was too old, because she considered God faithful who had promised.

were born, "as many as the stars of heaven and as the innumerable grains of sand by the seashore."

13 All of these died in faith without having received the promises, but from a distance they saw and greeted them. They confessed that they were strangers and foreigners on the earth, 14for people who speak in this way make it clear that they are seeking a homeland. 15If they had been thinking of the land that they had left behind, they would have had opportunity to return. 16But as it is, they desire a better country, that is, a heavenly one. Therefore God is not ashamed to be called their God; indeed, God has prepared a city for them.

17 By faith Abraham, when put to the test, offered up Isaac. He who had received the promises was ready to offer up his only son, 18of whom he had been told, "It is through Isaac that descendants shall be named for you." 19Abraham considered the fact that God is able even to raise someone from the dead—and figuratively speaking, Abraham did receive Isaac back. 20By faith Isaac invoked blessings for the future on Jacob and Esau. 21By faith Jacob, when dying, blessed each of the sons of Joseph, "bowing in worship over the top of his staff." 22By faith Joseph, at the end of his life, made mention of the exodus of the Israelites and gave instructions about his burial.ⁿ

The Faith of Moses

23 By faith Moses was hidden by his parents for three months after his birth, because they saw that the child was beautiful; and they were not afraid of the king's edict.ᵒ 24By faith Moses, when he was grown up, refused to be called a son of Pharaoh's daughter, 25choosing rather to share ill-treatment with the people of God than to enjoy the fleeting pleasures of sin. 26Moses considered dishonor like that suffered by Christᵖ to be greater wealth than the treasures of Egypt, for he was looking ahead to the reward. 27By faith Moses left Egypt, unafraid of the king's anger; for he persevered as thoughq he saw the one who is invisible. 28By faith he kept the Passover and the sprinkling of blood, so that the destroyer of the firstborn would not touch the firstborn of Israel.ʳ

The Faith of Other Israelite Heroes

29 By faith the people passed through the Red Sea as if it were dry land, but when the Egyptians attempted to do so they were drowned. 30By faith the walls of Jericho fell after they had been encircled for seven days. 31By faith Rahab the prostitute did not perish with those who were disobedient,ˢ because she had received the spies in peace.

32 And what more should I say? For time would fail me to tell of Gideon,

n Gk *his bones*
o Other ancient authorities add *By faith Moses, when he was grown up, killed the Egyptian, because he observed the humiliation of his people*   p Or *the Messiah*   q Or *because*
r Gk *would not touch them*   s Or *unbelieving*

Barak, Samson, Jephthah, of David and Samuel and the prophets— [33]who through faith conquered kingdoms, administered justice, obtained promises, shut the mouths of lions, [34]quenched raging fire, escaped the edge of the sword, won strength out of weakness, became mighty in war, put foreign armies to flight. [35]Women received their dead by resurrection. Others were tortured, refusing to accept release, in order to obtain a better resurrection. [36]Others suffered mocking and flogging, and even chains and imprisonment. [37]They were stoned to death, they were sawn in two,[t] they were killed by the sword; they went about in skins of sheep and goats, destitute, persecuted, tormented— [38]of whom the world was not worthy. They wandered in deserts and mountains, and in caves and holes in the ground.

39 Yet all these, though they were commended for their faith, did not receive what was promised, [40]since God had provided something better so that they would not, apart from us, be made perfect.

The Example of Jesus

12 Therefore, since we are surrounded by so great a cloud of witnesses, let us also lay aside every weight and the sin that clings so closely,[u] and let us run with perseverance the race that is set before us, [2]looking to Jesus the pioneer and perfecter of our faith, who for the sake of[v] the joy that lay ahead endured the cross, disregarding its shame, and sat down beside the throne of God.

3 Consider the one who endured such hostility from sinners,[w] so that you may not grow weary or lose heart. [4]In your struggle against sin you have not yet resisted to the point of shedding your blood. [5]And you have forgotten the exhortation that addresses you as children—

> "My child, do not regard lightly God's guidance,
>   or lose heart when you are punished by God;
> [6]   for God guides those whom God loves,
>   and chastises every child whom God accepts."

[7]Endure trials for the sake of guidance. God is treating you as children; for what child is there whom a parent does not guide? [8]If you do not have that guidance in which all children share, then you are illegitimate and not God's true children. [9]Moreover, we had human parents to guide us, and we respected them. Should we not be even more willing to be subject to the God of spirits and live? [10]For our parents guided us for a short time as seemed best to them, but God guides us for our good, in order that we may share God's holiness. [11]Now, guidance always seems painful rather than pleasant at the time, but later yields the peaceful fruit of righteousness to those who have lived by it.

---

t Other ancient authorities add *they were tempted*
u Other ancient authorities read *sin that easily distracts*   v Or *who instead of*
w Other ancient authorities read *such hostility from sinners*

12 Therefore lift your drooping hands and strengthen your weak knees,
13 and make straight paths for your feet, so that what is lame may not be put
out of joint, but rather be healed.

Warnings against Rejecting God's Grace

14 Pursue peace with everyone, and the holiness without which no one will see
the Lord. 15 See to it that no one fails to obtain the grace of God; that no root
of bitterness springs up and causes trouble, and through it many become
defiled. 16 See to it that no one becomes like Esau, an immoral and godless
person, who sold his birthright for a single meal. 17 You know that later, when
Esau wanted to inherit the blessing, he was rejected, for he found no chance to
repent,[x] even though he sought the blessing with tears.

18 You have not come to something[y] that can be touched, a blazing fire,
and darkness, and gloom, and a tempest, 19 and the sound of a trumpet, and a
voice whose words made the hearers beg that not another word be spoken to
them. 20 (For they could not endure the order that was given, "If even an animal
touches the mountain, it shall be stoned to death." 21 Indeed, so terrifying was
the sight that Moses said, "I tremble with fear.") 22 But you have come to
Mount Zion and to the city of the living God, the heavenly Jerusalem, and
to innumerable angels in festal gathering, 23 and to the assembly[z] of the firstborn who are enrolled in heaven, and to God the judge of all, and to the
spirits of the righteous made perfect, 24 and to Jesus, the mediator of a new
covenant, and to the sprinkled blood that speaks a better word than the blood
of Abel.

25 See that you do not refuse the one who is speaking; for if they did not
escape when they refused the one who warned them on earth, how much less
will we escape if we reject the one who warns from heaven, 26 whose voice
shook the earth at that time, but now has promised, "Yet once more I will
shake not only the earth but also the heaven." 27 This phrase, "Yet once more,"
indicates the removal of what is shaken—that is, created things—so that what
cannot be shaken may remain. 28 Therefore, since we are receiving a dominion
that cannot be shaken, let us give thanks, by which we offer to God an
acceptable worship with reverence and awe; 29 for indeed our God is a consum-
ing fire.

Service Well-Pleasing to God

13 Let mutual love continue. 2 Do not neglect to show hospitality to
strangers, for by doing that some have entertained angels without
knowing it. 3 Remember those who are in prison, as though you were in prison
with them; those who are being tortured, as though you yourselves were being

---

x Or *no chance to change his father's mind*   y Other ancient authorities read *a mountain*
z Or *angels, and to the festal gathering* 23 *and assembly*

tortured.[a] [4] Let marriage be held in honor by all, and let the marriage bed be kept undefiled; for God will judge people who are sexually immoral and those who are unfaithful to their spouses. [5] Keep your lives free from the love of money, and be content with what you have; for God has said, "I will never leave you or forsake you." [6] So we can say with confidence,

> "God is my helper;
> I will not be afraid.
> What can anyone do to me?"

[7] Remember your leaders, those who spoke the word of God to you; consider the outcome of their way of life, and imitate their faith. [8] Jesus Christ is the same yesterday and today and forever. [9] Do not be carried away by all kinds of strange teachings; for it is well for the heart to be strengthened by grace, not by regulations about food,[b] which have not benefited those who observe them. [10] We have an altar from which those who officiate in the tent[c] have no right to eat. [11] For the bodies of those animals whose blood is brought into the sanctuary by the high priest as a sacrifice for sin are burned outside the camp. [12] Therefore Jesus also suffered outside the city gate in order to sanctify the people by Jesus' own blood. [13] Let us then go to Jesus outside the camp and bear the abuse Jesus endured. [14] For here we have no lasting city, but we are looking for the city that is to come. [15] Through Jesus, then, let us continually offer a sacrifice of praise to God, that is, the fruit of lips that confess Jesus' name. [16] Do not neglect to do good and to share what you have, for such sacrifices are pleasing to God.

[17] Obey your leaders and submit to them, for they are keeping watch over your souls and will give an account. Let them do this with joy and not with sighing—for that would be harmful to you.

[18] Pray for us; we are sure that we have a clear conscience, desiring to act honorably in all things. [19] I urge you all the more to do this, so that I may be restored to you very soon.

Benediction

[20] Now may the God of peace, who brought back from the dead our Lord Jesus, the great shepherd of the sheep, by the blood of the eternal covenant, [21] make you complete in everything good so that you may do God's will, working among us[d] that which is pleasing in God's sight, through Jesus Christ, to whom be the glory forever and ever. Amen.

---

a Gk *were in the body*   b Gk *not by foods*   c Or *tabernacle*
d Other ancient authorities read *you*

Final Exhortation and Greetings

22 I appeal to you, sisters and brothers, bear with my word of exhortation, for I have written to you briefly. 23 I want you to know that our brother Timothy has been set free; and if he comes in time, he will be with me when I see you. 24 Greet all your leaders and all the saints. Those from Italy send you greetings. 25 Grace be with all of you.[e]

e Other ancient authorities add *Amen*

The Letter of James

Salutation

1 James, a servant of God and of the Lord Jesus Christ,
   To the twelve tribes in the Dispersion:
   Greetings.

Faith and Wisdom

2 My brothers and sisters, whenever you face trials of any kind, consider it nothing but joy, 3because you know that the testing of your faith produces endurance; 4and let endurance have its full effect, so that you may be mature and complete, lacking in nothing.

5 If any of you is lacking in wisdom, ask God, who gives to all generously and ungrudgingly, and it will be given you. 6But ask in faith, never doubting, for the one who doubts is like a wave of the sea, driven and tossed by the wind; 7, 8for the doubter, being double-minded and unstable in every way, must not expect to receive anything from God.

Poverty and Riches

9 Let the believer who is lowly boast in being raised up, 10and the rich in being brought low, because the rich will disappear like a flower in the field. 11For the sun rises with its scorching heat and withers the field; its flower falls, and its beauty perishes. It is the same way with the rich; in the midst of a busy life, they will wither away.

Trial and Temptation

12 Blessed is anyone who endures temptation. Such a one has stood the test and will receive the crown of life that was promised to those who love the

Lord.[a] 13No one, when tempted, should say, "I am being tempted by God"; for God cannot be tempted by evil and God tempts no one. 14But one is tempted by one's own desire, being lured and enticed by it; 15then, when that desire has conceived, it gives birth to sin, and that sin, when it is fully grown, gives birth to death. 16Do not be deceived, my beloved.

17 Every generous act of giving, with every perfect gift, is from above, coming down from the God of lights, with whom there is no variation or shadow due to change.[b] 18In fulfillment of God's own purpose we were given birth by the word of truth, so that we would become a kind of firstfruits of God's creatures.

Hearing and Doing the Word

19 You must understand this, my beloved: let everyone be quick to listen, slow to speak, slow to anger; 20for your anger does not produce God's righteousness. 21Therefore rid yourselves of all sordidness and rank growth of wickedness, and welcome with meekness the implanted word that has the power to save your souls.

22 But be doers of the word, and not merely hearers who deceive themselves. 23For if any are hearers of the word and not doers, they are like those who look at themselves[c] in a mirror; 24for they look at themselves and, on going away, immediately forget what they were like. 25But those who look into the perfect law, the law of liberty, and persevere, being not hearers who forget but doers who act—they will be blessed in their doing.

26 If any think they are religious, and do not bridle their tongues but deceive their hearts, their religion is worthless. 27Religion that is pure and undefiled before God, the Father-Mother, is this: to care for orphans and widows in their distress, and to keep oneself unstained by the world.

Warning against Partiality

2 My sisters and brothers, do you with your acts of favoritism really believe in our glorious Lord Jesus Christ?[d] 2For if a person with gold rings and in fine clothes comes into your assembly, and if a poor person in dirty clothes also comes in, 3and if you take notice of the one wearing the fine clothes and say, "Have a seat here, please," while to the one who is poor you say, "Stand there," or, "Sit at my feet,"[e] 4have you not made distinctions among your-selves, and become judges with evil thoughts? 5Listen, my beloved brothers and sisters. Has not God chosen those who are poor in the world to be rich in faith and to be heirs of the dominion that God has promised to those who love

a Other ancient authorities read *God*
b Other ancient authorities read *variation due to a shadow of turning*
c Gk *at the face of their birth*
d Or *hold the faith of our glorious Lord Jesus Christ without acts of favoritism*
e Gk *Sit under my footstool*

God? 6But you have dishonored those who are poor. Is it not the rich who oppress you? Is it not they who drag you into court? 7Is it not they who blaspheme the excellent name that was invoked over you?

8 You do well if you really fulfill the royal law according to the scripture, "You shall love your neighbor as yourself." 9But if you show partiality, you commit sin and are convicted by the law as transgressors. 10For whoever keeps the whole law but fails in one point has become accountable for all of it. 11For the one who said, "You shall not commit adultery," also said, "You shall not murder." Now if you do not commit adultery but if you murder, you have become a transgressor of the law. 12So speak and so act as those who are to be judged by the law of liberty. 13For judgment will be without mercy to anyone who has shown no mercy; mercy triumphs over judgment.

Faith without Works Is Dead

14 What good is it, my sisters and brothers, if you say you have faith but do not have works? Can faith save you? 15If a brother or sister is naked and lacks daily food, 16and one of you says to them, "Go in peace; keep warm and eat your fill," and yet you do not supply their bodily needs, what is the good of that? 17So faith by itself, if it has no works, is dead.

18 But someone will say, "You have faith and I have works." Show me your faith apart from your works, and I by my works will show you my faith. 19You believe that God is one; you do well. Even the demons believe—and shudder. 20Do you want to be shown, you fool, that faith apart from works is useless? 21Was not our ancestor Abraham justified by works when he offered his son Isaac on the altar? 22You see that faith was active along with the works, and faith was brought to completion by the works. 23Thus the scripture was fulfilled that says, "Abraham believed God, and it was reckoned to him as righteousness," and he was called the friend of God. 24You see that a person is justified by works and not by faith alone. 25Likewise, was not Rahab the prostitute also justified by works when she welcomed the messengers and sent them out by another road? 26For just as the body without the spirit is dead, so faith without works is also dead.

Taming the Tongue

3 Not many of you should become teachers, my sisters and brothers, for you know that we who teach will be judged with greater strictness. 2For all of us make many mistakes. Anyone who makes no mistakes in speaking is perfect, able to keep the whole body in check with a bridle. 3If we put bits into the mouths of horses to make them obey us, we guide their whole bodies. 4Or look at ships: though they are so large that it takes strong winds to drive them, yet they are guided by a very small rudder wherever the will of the pilot directs. 5So also the tongue is a small member, yet it boasts of great exploits.

How great a forest is set ablaze by a small fire! 6And the tongue is a fire. The tongue is placed among our members as a world of iniquity; it stains the whole body, sets on fire the cycle of nature,[f] and is itself set on fire by hell.[g] [7]For every species of beast and bird, of reptile and sea creature, can be tamed and has been tamed by the human species, [8]but no one can tame the tongue—a restless evil, full of deadly poison. [9]With it we bless God, the Father-Mother, and with it we curse those who are made in the likeness of God. [10]From the same mouth come blessing and cursing. My brothers and sisters, this ought not to be so. [11]Does a spring pour forth from the same opening both fresh and brackish water? [12]Can a fig tree, my sisters and brothers, yield olives, or a grapevine figs? No more can salt water yield fresh.

Two Kinds of Wisdom

[13] Who is wise and understanding among you? Show by your good life that your works are done with gentleness born of wisdom. [14]But if you have bitter envy and selfish ambition in your hearts, do not be boastful and false to the truth. [15]Such wisdom does not come down from above, but is earthly, unspiritual, devilish. [16]For where there is envy and selfish ambition, there will also be disorder and wickedness of every kind. [17]But the wisdom from above is first pure, then peaceable, gentle, willing to yield, full of mercy and good fruits, without a trace of partiality or hypocrisy. [18]And a harvest of righteousness is sown in peace for[h] those who make peace.

Friendship with the World

4 Those conflicts and disputes among you, where do they come from? Do they not come from your cravings that are at war within you? [2]You want something and do not have it; so you commit murder. And you covet[i] something and cannot obtain it; so you engage in disputes and conflicts. You do not have, because you do not ask. [3]You ask and do not receive, because you ask wrongly, in order to spend what you get on your pleasures. [4]Adulterers! Do you not know that friendship with the world is enmity with God? Therefore whoever wishes to be a friend of the world becomes an enemy of God. [5]Or do you suppose that it is for nothing that the scripture says, "God yearns jealously for the spirit that God has been made to dwell in us"? [6]But God gives all the more grace; therefore it says,

> "God opposes the proud,
>   but gives grace to the humble."

[7]Submit yourselves therefore to God. Resist the devil, and the devil will flee from you. [8]Draw near to God, and God will draw near to you. Cleanse your hands, you sinners, and purify your hearts, you double-minded. [9]Lament and mourn and weep. Let your laughter be turned into mourning and your joy into dejection. [10]Humble yourselves before God who will exalt you.

---

f Or *wheel of birth*   g Gk *Gehenna*   h Or *by*   i Or *you murder and you covet*

Warning against Judging Another

11 Do not speak evil against one another, brothers and sisters. Whoever speaks evil against another or judges another, speaks evil against the law and judges the law; but if you judge the law, you are not a doer of the law but a judge. 12 There is one lawgiver and judge who is able to save and to destroy. So who, then, are you to judge your neighbor?

Boasting about Tomorrow

13 Come now, you who say, "Today or tomorrow we will go to such and such a town and spend a year there, doing business and making money." 14 Yet you do not even know what tomorrow will bring. What is your life? For you are a mist that appears for a little while and then vanishes. 15 Instead you ought to say, "If God wishes, we will live and do this or that." 16 As it is, you boast in your arrogance; all such boasting is evil. 17 Anyone, then, who knows the right thing to do and fails to do it, commits sin.

Warning to Rich Oppressors

5 Come now, you rich people, weep and wail for the miseries that are coming to you. 2 Your riches have rotted, and your clothes are moth-eaten. 3 Your gold and silver have rusted, and their rust will be evidence against you, and it will eat your flesh like fire. You have laid up treasure[j] for the last days. 4 Listen! The wages of the laborers who mowed your fields, which you kept back by fraud, cry out, and the cries of the harvesters have reached the ears of the God of hosts. 5 You have lived on the earth in luxury and in pleasure; you have fattened your hearts in a day of slaughter. 6 You have condemned and murdered the righteous one, who does not resist you.

Patience in Suffering

7 Be patient, therefore, friends, until the coming of Christ. The farmer waits for the precious crop from the earth, being patient with it until it receives the early and the late rains. 8 You also must be patient. Strengthen your hearts, for the coming of Christ is near.[k] 9 Friends, do not grumble against one another, so that you may not be judged. See, the Judge is standing at the doors! 10 As an example of suffering and patience, friends, take the prophets who spoke in the name of God. 11 Indeed we call blessed those who showed endurance. You have heard of the endurance of Job, and you have seen the purpose of God, how God is compassionate and merciful.

12 Above all, my friends, do not swear, either by heaven or by earth or by any other oath, but let your "Yes" be yes and your "No" be no, so that you may not fall under condemnation.

---

j Or *will eat your flesh, since you have stored up fire*   k Or *is at hand*

The Prayer of Faith

13 Are any among you suffering? They should pray. Are any cheerful? They should sing songs of praise. [14]Are any among you sick? They should call for the elders of the church and have them pray over them, anointing them with oil in the name of Jesus. [15]The prayer of faith will save the sick, and Jesus will raise them up; and anyone who has committed sins will be forgiven. [16]Therefore confess your sins to one another, and pray for one another, so that you may be healed. The prayer of the righteous is powerful and effective. [17]Elijah was a human being like us, and he prayed fervently that it might not rain, and for three years and six months it did not rain on the earth. [18]Then Elijah prayed again, and the heaven gave rain and the earth yielded its harvest.

19 My sisters and brothers, if anyone among you wanders from the truth and is brought back by another, [20]you should know that whoever brings back a sinner from wandering will save the sinner's soul from death and will cover a multitude of sins.

The First Letter of Peter

Salutation

1 Peter, an apostle of Jesus Christ,

To the exiles of the Dispersion in Pontus, Galatia, Cappadocia, Asia, and Bithynia, 2 who have been chosen and destined by God the Father-Mother and sanctified by the Spirit to be obedient to Jesus Christ and to be sprinkled with the blood of Christ:

May grace and peace be yours in abundance.

A Living Hope

3 Blessed be the God and Father-Mother of our Lord Jesus Christ, who by great mercy has given us a new birth into a living hope through the resurrection of Jesus Christ from the dead, 4 and into an inheritance that is imperishable, undefiled, and unfading, kept in heaven for you, 5 who are being protected by the power of God through faith for a salvation ready to be revealed in the last time. 6 In this you rejoice,[a] even if now for a little while you have had to suffer various trials, 7 so that the genuineness of your faith—being more precious than gold that, though perishable, is tested by fire—may be found to result in praise and glory and honor when Jesus Christ is revealed. 8 Although you have not seen[b] Christ, you love Christ; and even though you do not see Christ now, you believe in Christ and rejoice with an indescribable and glorious joy, 9 for you are receiving the outcome of your faith, the salvation of your souls.

10 Concerning this salvation, the prophets who prophesied of the grace that was to be yours made careful search and inquiry, 11 inquiring about the person or time that the Spirit of Christ within them indicated when it testified in advance to the sufferings destined for Christ and the subsequent glory. 12 It was revealed to them that they were serving not themselves but you, in regard

---

a Or *Rejoice in this*   b Other ancient authorities read *known*

to the things that have now been announced to you through those who brought you good news by the Holy Spirit sent from heaven—things into which angels long to look!

A Call to Holy Living

13 Therefore prepare your minds for action;[c] discipline yourselves; hope entirely in the grace that will come to you at the revelation of Jesus Christ. [14]Like obedient children, do not be conformed to the desires that you formerly had in ignorance. [15]Instead, as God who called you is holy, be holy yourselves in all your conduct; [16]for it is written, "You shall be holy, for I am holy."

17 If you invoke as Father-Mother the one who judges all people impartially according to their deeds, live in reverent fear during the time of your exile. [18]You know that you were ransomed from the futile ways inherited from your ancestors, not with perishable things like silver or gold, [19]but with the precious blood of Christ, like that of a lamb without defect or blemish. [20]Christ was destined before the foundation of the world, but was revealed at the end of the ages for your sake. [21]Through Christ you have come to trust in God, who raised Christ from the dead and gave Christ glory, so that your faith and hope are set on God.

22 Now that you have purified your souls by your obedience to the truth[d] so that you have genuine mutual love, love one another deeply[e] from the heart.[f] [23]You have been born anew, not of perishable but of imperishable seed, through the living and enduring word of God.[g] [24]For

> "All flesh is like grass
>   and all its glory like the flower of grass.
> The grass withers,
>   and the flower falls,
25   but the word of the Lord endures forever."

That word is the good news that was announced to you.

The Living Stone and a Chosen People

2 Rid yourselves, therefore, of all malice, and all guile, insincerity, envy, and all slander. [2]Like newborn infants, long for the pure, spiritual milk, so that by it you may grow into salvation— [3]if indeed you have tasted that God is good.

4 Come to Christ, a living stone, though rejected by mortals yet chosen and precious in God's sight, and [5]like living stones, let yourselves be built[h] into a spiritual house, to be a holy priesthood, to offer spiritual sacrifices acceptable to God through Jesus Christ. [6]For it stands in scripture:

---

c Gk *gird up the loins of your mind*   d Other ancient authorities add *through the Spirit*
e Or *constantly*   f Other ancient authorities read *a pure heart*
g Or *through the word of the living and enduring God*   h Or *you yourselves are being built*

> "See, I am laying in Zion a stone,
>   a cornerstone chosen and precious;
> and whoever believes in that one[i] will not be put to
>   shame."

7 To you then who believe, that one is precious; but for those who do not believe,

> "The stone that the builders rejected
>   has become the very head of the corner,"

8 and

> "A stone that makes them stumble,
>   and a rock that makes them fall."

They stumble because they disobey the word, as they were destined to do.

9 But you are a chosen race, a royal priesthood, a holy nation, God's own people,[j] in order that you may proclaim the mighty acts of the one who called you out of night into God's marvelous light.

10
>   Once you were not a people,
>   but now you are God's people;
>   once you had not received mercy,
>   but now you have received mercy.

Live as Servants of God

11 Beloved, I urge you as aliens and exiles to abstain from the desires of the flesh that wage war against the soul. 12 Conduct yourselves honorably among the Gentiles, so that, though they malign you as evildoers, they may see your honorable deeds and glorify God when God comes to judge.[k]

13 For the sake of God accept the authority of every human institution,[l] whether of the emperor as supreme, 14 or of governors, sent by the emperor to punish those who do wrong and to praise those who do right. 15 For it is God's will that by doing right you should silence the ignorance of the foolish. 16 As servants of God, live as free people, yet do not use your freedom as a pretext for evil. 17 Honor everyone. Love the family of believers. Fear God. Honor the emperor.

The Example of Christ's Suffering

18 You who are enslaved, accept the authority of those who enslave you with all deference, not only those who are kind and gentle but also those who are harsh. 19 For it is a credit to you if, being aware of God, you endure pain while suffering unjustly. 20 If you endure when you are beaten for doing wrong, what

---

i Or *it*   j Gk *a people for God's possession*   k Gk *God on the day of visitation*
l Or *every institution ordained for human beings*

credit is that? But if you endure when you do right and suffer for it, you have God's approval. [21]For to this you have been called, because Christ also suffered for you, leaving you an example, so that you should follow in the steps of Christ,

[22]   "who committed no sin,
            and spoke without deceit,"

[23]who when abused, did not return abuse, and when suffering did not threaten, but trusted in the one who judges justly. [24]Christ bore our sins in Christ's body on the cross,[m] so that, free from sins, we might live for righteousness; by Christ's wounds[n] you have been healed. [25]For you were going astray like sheep, but now you have returned to the shepherd and guardian of your souls.

Wives and Husbands

3 Wives, in the same way, be committed to your husbands, so that, even if some of them do not obey the word, they may be won over without a word by their wives' conduct, [2]when they see the purity and reverence of your lives. [3]Do not adorn yourselves outwardly by braiding your hair, and by wearing gold ornaments or fine clothing; [4]rather, let your adornment be the inner self with the lasting beauty of a gentle and quiet spirit, which is very precious in God's sight. [5]It was in this way long ago that the holy women who hoped in God used to adorn themselves by committing themselves to their husbands. [6]Thus Sarah listened to Abraham and gave him her allegiance. You have become her daughters as long as you do what is good and never let fears alarm you.

[7] Husbands, in the same way, show consideration for your wives in your life together, paying honor to the woman in her vulnerabilities, since they too are also heirs of the gracious gift of life—so that nothing may hinder your prayers.

Suffering for Doing Right

[8] Finally, all of you, have unity of spirit, sympathy, love for one another, a tender heart, and a humble mind. [9]Do not repay evil for evil or abuse for abuse; but, on the contrary, repay with a blessing. It is for this that you were called—that you might inherit a blessing. [10]For

"Those who desire life
    and desire to see good days,
let them keep their tongues from evil
    and their lips from speaking deceit;
[11]   let them turn away from evil and do good;
        let them seek peace and pursue it.

---

m Or *carried up our sins in Christ's body to the tree*   n Gk *bruise*

12   For the eyes of God are on the righteous,
         and the ears of God are open to their prayer.
       But the face of God is against those who do evil."

13 Now who will harm you if you are eager to do what is good? 14But even if you do suffer for doing what is right, you are blessed. Do not fear what they fear,[o] and do not be intimidated, 15but in your hearts sanctify Christ as Lord. Always be ready to make your defense to anyone who demands from you an accounting for the hope that is in you; 16yet do it with gentleness and reverence.[p] Keep your conscience clear, so that, when you are maligned, those who abuse you for your good conduct in Christ may be put to shame. 17For it is better to suffer for doing good, if suffering should be God's will, than to suffer for doing evil. 18For Christ also suffered[q] for sins once for all, the righteous for the unrighteous, in order to bring you[r] to God. Christ, being put to death in the flesh, was alive in the spirit, 19in which also Christ went and made a proclamation to the spirits in prison, 20who in former times did not obey, when God waited patiently in the days of Noah, during the building of the ark, in which a few, that is, eight people, were saved through water. 21And baptism, which this prefigured, now saves you—not as a removal of dirt from the body, but as an appeal to God for[s] a good conscience, through the resurrection of Jesus Christ, 22who has gone into heaven and is at God's side, to rule over angels, authorities, and powers.

Good Stewards of God's Grace

4 Since therefore Christ suffered in the flesh,[t] arm yourselves also with the same intention (for whoever has suffered in the flesh has finished with sin), 2so as to live for the rest of your earthly life[u] no longer by human desires but by the will of God. 3You have already spent enough time in doing what the Gentiles like to do, living in licentiousness, passions, drunkenness, revels, carousing, and lawless idolatry. 4They are surprised that you no longer join them in the same excesses of dissipation, and so they blaspheme.[v] 5But they will have to give an accounting to the one who stands ready to judge the living and the dead. 6For this is the reason the gospel was proclaimed even to the dead, so that, though they had been judged in the flesh as everyone is judged, they might live in the spirit as God does.

7 The end of all things is near;[w] therefore be serious and discipline yourselves for the sake of your prayers. 8Above all, maintain constant love for one another, for love covers a multitude of sins. 9Be hospitable to one another without complaining. 10Like good stewards of the manifold grace of God, serve one another with whatever gift each of you has received. 11Whoever speaks

---

o Gk *their fear*   p Or *respect*   q Other ancient authorities read *died*
r Other ancient authorities read *us*   s Or *a pledge to God from*
t Other ancient authorities add *for us*; others, *for you*   u Gk *rest of the time in the flesh*
v Or *they malign you*   w Or *is at hand*

must do so as one speaking the very words of God; whoever serves must do so with the strength that God supplies, so that God may be glorified in all things through Jesus Christ, to whom belongs the glory and the power forever and ever. Amen.

Suffering as a Christian

12 Beloved, do not be surprised at the fiery ordeal that is taking place among you to test you, as though something strange were happening to you. [13]But rejoice insofar as you are sharing Christ's sufferings, so that you may also be glad and shout for joy when Christ's glory is revealed. [14]If you are reviled for the name of Christ, you are blessed, because the spirit of glory,[x] which is the Spirit of God, is resting on you.[y] [15]But let none of you suffer as a murderer, a thief, a criminal, or even as a mischief maker. [16]Yet if any of you suffers as a Christian, do not consider it a disgrace, but glorify God because you bear this name. [17]For the time has come for judgment to begin with the household of God; if it begins with us, what will be the end for those who do not obey the gospel of God? [18]And

> "If it is hard for the righteous to be saved,
>   what will become of the ungodly and the sinners?"

[19]Therefore, let those suffering in accordance with God's will entrust themselves to a faithful Creator, while continuing to do good.

Tending the Flock of God

5 Now as an elder myself and a witness of the sufferings of Christ, as well as one who shares in the glory to be revealed, I exhort the elders among you [2]to tend the flock of God that is in your charge, exercising the oversight,[z] not under compulsion but willingly, as God would have you do it[a]—not for sordid gain but eagerly. [3]Do not intimidate those in your charge, but be examples to the flock. [4]And when the chief shepherd appears, you will win the crown of glory that never fades away. [5]In the same way, you who are younger must accept the authority of the elders.[b] And all of you must clothe yourselves with humility in your dealings with one another, for

> "God opposes the proud,
>   but gives grace to the humble."

6 Humble yourselves therefore under the mighty hand of God, so that God may exalt you in due time. [7]Cast all your anxiety on God, because God

---

x Other ancient authorities add *and of power*
y Other ancient authorities add *On their part Christ is blasphemed, but on your part Christ is glorified*   z Other ancient authorities lack *exercising the oversight*
a Other ancient authorities lack *as God would have you do it*   b Or *of those who are older*

cares for you. 8Discipline yourselves, keep alert.c Like a roaring lion your adversary the devil prowls around, looking for someone to devour. 9Resist the devil, steadfast in your faith, for you know that your brothers and sisters in all the world are undergoing the same kinds of suffering. 10And after you have suffered for a little while, the God of all grace, who has called you to eternal glory in Christ, will himself restore, support, strengthen, and establish you. 11To God be the power forever and ever. Amen.

Final Greetings and Benediction

12 Through Silvanus, whom I consider a faithful brother, I have written this short letter to encourage you and to testify that this is the true grace of God. Stand fast in it. 13Your church in Babylon, chosen together with you, sends you greetings; and so does my son Mark. 14Greet one another with a kiss of love.

Peace to all of you who are in Christ.d

---

c Or *be vigilant*   d Other ancient authorities add *Amen*

The Second Letter of Peter

Salutation

1 Simeon[a] Peter, a servant and apostle of Jesus Christ,

To those who have received a faith as precious as ours through the righteousness of our God and Savior Jesus Christ:[b]

2 May grace and peace be yours in abundance in the knowledge of God and of Jesus our Lord.

The Christian's Call and Election

3 God's divine power has given us everything needed for life and godliness, through the knowledge of God who called us by[c] God's own glory and goodness. [4]Thus God has given us, through these things, precious and very great promises, so that through them you may escape from the corruption that is in the world because of lust, and may become participants of the divine nature. [5]For this very reason, you must make every effort to support your faith with goodness, and goodness with knowledge, [6]and knowledge with self-control, and self-control with endurance, and endurance with godliness, [7]and godliness with mutual affection, and mutual affection with love. [8]For if these things are yours and are increasing among you, they keep you from being ineffective and unfruitful in the knowledge of our Lord Jesus Christ. [9]For anyone who lacks these things does not understand, and is forgetful of the cleansing of past sins. [10]Therefore, brothers and sisters, be all the more eager to confirm your call and election, for if you do this, you will never stumble. [11]For in this way, entry into the eternal realm of our Lord and Savior Jesus Christ will be richly provided for you.

12 Therefore I intend to keep on reminding you of these things, though

---

a Other ancient authorities read *Simon*   b Or *of our God and the Savior Jesus Christ*
c Other ancient authorities read *through*

you know them already and are established in the truth that has come to you. [13]I think it right, as long as I am in this body,[d] to refresh your memory, [14]since I know that my death[e] will come soon, as indeed our Lord Jesus Christ has made clear to me. [15]And I will make every effort so that after my departure you may be able at any time to recall these things.

Eyewitnesses of Christ's Glory

16 For we did not follow cleverly devised myths when we made known to you the power and coming of our Lord Jesus Christ, but we had been eyewitnesses of the majesty of Christ, [17]who received honor and glory from God the Father-Mother when the voice of the Majestic Glory was heard, saying to Christ, "This is my Child, my Beloved,[f] with whom I am well pleased." [18]We ourselves heard this voice come from heaven, while we were with Christ on the holy mountain.

19 So we have the prophetic message more fully confirmed. You will do well to be attentive to this as to a lamp shining in a dark place, until the day dawns and the morning star rises in your hearts. [20]First of all you must understand this, that no prophecy of scripture is a matter of one's own interpretation, [21]because no prophecy ever came by human will, but men and women moved by the Holy Spirit spoke from God.[g]

False Prophets and Their Punishment

2 But false prophets also arose among the people, just as there will be false teachers among you, who will secretly bring in destructive opinions. They will even deny the Sovereign God who bought them—bringing swift destruction on themselves. [2]Even so, many will follow their licentious ways, and because of these teachers the way of truth will be maligned. [3]And in their greed they will exploit you with deceptive words. Their condemnation, pronounced against them long ago, has not been idle, and their destruction is not asleep.

4 For if God did not spare the angels when they sinned, but cast them into hell[h] and imprisoned them in the deepest part of the night to be kept until the judgment; [5]and if God did not spare the ancient world, even though God saved Noah, a herald of righteousness, with seven others, by bringing a flood on a world of the ungodly; [6]and if by turning the cities of Sodom and Gomorrah to ashes God condemned them to extinction[i] and made them an example of what is coming to the ungodly;[j] [7]and if God rescued Lot, a righteous man greatly distressed by the licentiousness of the lawless [8](for that righteous man, Lot, living among them day after day, was tormented in his

---

d Gk *tent*   e Gk *the putting off of my tent*
f Other ancient authorities read *my beloved Child*
g Other ancient authorities read *but moved by the Holy Spirit saints of God spoke*
h Gk *Tartaros*   i Other ancient authorities lack *to extinction*
j Other ancient authorities read *an example to those who were to be ungodly*

righteous soul by their lawless deeds that he saw and heard), 9 then God knows how to rescue the godly from trial, and to keep the unrighteous under punishment until the day of judgment 10 —especially those who indulge their flesh in corrupt desires, and who despise authority.

Bold and willful, they are not afraid to slander the glorious ones,[k] 11 whereas angels, though greater in might and power, do not bring against them a slanderous judgment from God.[l] 12 These people, however, are like irrational animals, mere creatures of instinct, born to be caught and killed. They slander what they do not understand, and when those creatures are destroyed,[m] they also will be destroyed, 13 suffering[n] the penalty for doing wrong. They count it a pleasure to revel in the daytime. They are blots and blemishes, reveling in their dissipation[o] while they feast with you. 14 They have eyes full of adultery, insatiable for sin. They entice unsteady people. They have hearts trained in greed. Accursed children! 15 They have left the straight road and have gone astray, following the road of Balaam son of Bosor,[p] who loved the wages of doing wrong, 16 but was rebuked for his own transgression; a speechless donkey spoke with a human voice and restrained the prophet's madness.

17 These are waterless springs and mists driven by a storm; for them the deepest part of the night has been reserved. 18 For they speak bombastic nonsense, and with licentious desires of the flesh they entice people who have just[q] escaped from those who live in error. 19 They promise them freedom, but they themselves are enslaved to corruption; for people are enslaved to whatever rules them. 20 For if, after they have escaped the defilements of the world through the knowledge of our Lord and Savior Jesus Christ, they are again entangled in them and overpowered, the last state has become worse for them than the first. 21 For it would have been better for them never to have known the way of righteousness than, after knowing it, to turn back from the holy commandment that was passed on to them. 22 It has happened to them according to the true proverb,

> "The dog turns back to its own vomit,"

and,

> "The sow is washed only to wallow in the mud."

The Promise of Christ's Coming

3 This is now, beloved, the second letter I am writing to you; in them I am trying to arouse your sincere intention by reminding you 2 that you should remember the words spoken in the past by the holy prophets, and the commandment of the Lord and Savior spoken through your apostles. 3 First of

---

k Or angels; Gk glories   l Other ancient authorities read before God; others lack the phrase
m Gk in their destruction   n Other ancient authorities read receiving
o Other ancient authorities read love feasts   p Other ancient authorities read Beor
q Other ancient authorities read actually

all you must understand this, that in the last days scoffers will come, scoffing and indulging their own lusts ⁴and saying, "Where is the promise of Christ's coming? For ever since our ancestors died,ʳ all things continue as they were from the beginning of creation!" ⁵They deliberately ignore this fact, that by the word of God heavens existed long ago and an earth was formed out of water and by means of water, ⁶through which the world of that time was deluged with water and perished. ⁷But by the same word the present heavens and earth have been reserved for fire, being kept until the day of judgment and destruction of the godless.

8 But do not ignore this one fact, beloved, that with God one day is like a thousand years, and a thousand years are like one day. ⁹God of the promise does not delay, as some think of slowness, but is patient with you,ˢ not wanting any to perish, but all to come to repentance. ¹⁰But the day of the Lord will come like a thief, and then the heavens will pass away with a loud noise, and the elements will be dissolved with fire, and the earth and everything that is done on it will be disclosed.ᵗ

11 Since all these things are to be dissolved in this way, what sort of persons ought you to be in leading lives of holiness and godliness, ¹²waiting for and hasteningᵘ the coming of the day of the Lord, because of which the heavens will be set ablaze and dissolved, and the elements will melt with fire? ¹³But, in accordance with God's promise, we wait for new heavens and a new earth, where righteousness is at home.

Final Exhortation and Doxology

14 Therefore, beloved, while you are waiting for these things, strive to be found by God at peace, without spot or blemish; ¹⁵and regard the patience of our God as salvation. So also our beloved brother Paul wrote to you according to the wisdom given him, ¹⁶speaking of this as he does in all his letters. There are some things in them hard to understand, which the ignorant and unstable twist to their own destruction, as they do the other scriptures. ¹⁷You therefore, beloved, since you are forewarned, beware that you are not carried away with the error of the lawless and lose your own stability. ¹⁸But grow in the grace and knowledge of our Lord and Savior Jesus Christ, to whom be the glory both now and to the day of eternity. Amen.ᵛ

r Gk *our ancestors fell asleep*   s Other ancient authorities read *on your account*
t Other ancient authorities read *will be burned up*   u Or *earnestly desiring*
v Other ancient authorities lack *Amen*

The First Letter of John

The Word of Life

1 We declare to you what was from the beginning, what we have heard, what we have seen with our eyes, what we have looked at and touched with our hands, concerning the word of life— ²this life was revealed, and we have seen it and testify to it, and declare to you the eternal life that was with the Father-Mother and was revealed to us— ³we declare to you what we have seen and heard so that you also may be partners with us; and truly our partnership is with the Father-Mother and with God's Child Jesus Christ. ⁴We are writing these things so that our[a] joy may be complete.

God Is Light

5 This is the message we have heard from Jesus Christ and proclaim to you, that God is light and in God light is never absent. ⁶If we say that we are partners with God while we are walking without light, we lie and do not do what is true; ⁷but if we walk in the light as God is in the light, we are partners with one another, and the blood of Jesus, Child of God, cleanses us from all sin. ⁸If we say that we have no sin, we deceive ourselves, and the truth is not in us. ⁹If we confess our sins, God who is faithful and just will forgive us our sins and cleanse us from all unrighteousness. ¹⁰If we say that we have not sinned, we make God a liar, and God's word is not in us.

Christ Our Advocate

2 My little children, I am writing these things to you so that you may not sin. But if anyone does sin, we have an advocate with God—Jesus Christ the righteous ²who is the atoning sacrifice for our sins, and not for ours only but also for the sins of the whole world.

---

a Other ancient authorities read *your*

3 Now by this we may be sure that we know Christ, if we obey the commandments of Christ. ⁴Whoever says, "I have come to know Christ," but does not obey the commandments, is a liar, and in such a person the truth does not exist; ⁵but whoever obeys the word of Christ, truly in this person the love of God has reached perfection. By this we may be sure that we are in Christ: ⁶whoever says, "I abide in Christ," ought to walk just as Christ walked.

A New Commandment

7 Beloved, I am writing you no new commandment, but an old commandment that you have had from the beginning; the old commandment is the word that you have heard. ⁸Yet I am writing you a new commandment that is true in Christ and in you, becauseᵇ the night is passing away and the true light is already shining. ⁹Whoever says, "I am in the light," while hating a brother or sister, is still in the night. ¹⁰Whoever loves a sister or brother lives in the light, and in such a personᶜ there is no cause for stumbling. ¹¹But whoever hates another believer is in the night, walks in the night, and does not know the way to go, because of losing the way.

12   I am writing to you, little children,
           because your sins are forgiven on account of the name
               of Jesus Christ.

13   I am writing to you, parents,
           because you know the one who is from the beginning.
        I am writing to you, young people,
           because you have conquered the evil one.

14   I write to you, children,
           because you know the Father-Mother.
        I write to you, parents,
           because you know the one who is from the beginning.
        I write to you, young people,
           because you are strong
           and the word of God abides in you,
              and you have overcome the evil one.

15 Do not love the world or the things in the world. The love of God is not in those who love the world; ¹⁶for all that is in the world—the desire of the flesh, the desire of the eyes, the pride in riches—comes not from God but from the world. ¹⁷And the world and its desireᵈ are passing away, but those who do the will of God live forever.

Warning against Antichrists

18 Children, it is the last hour! As you have heard that antichrist is coming, so now many antichrists have come. From this we know that it is the last hour.

---

b Or *that*   c Or *in it*   d Or *the desire for it*

¹⁹They went out from us, but they did not belong to us; for if they had belonged to us, they would have remained with us. But by going out they made it plain that none of them belongs to us. ²⁰But you have been anointed by the Holy One, and all of you have knowledge.ᵉ ²¹I write to you, not because you do not know the truth, but because you know it, and you know that no lie comes from the truth. ²²Who is the liar but the one who denies that Jesus is the Christ?ᶠ This is the antichrist, the one who denies the Father-Mother and the Child. ²³No one who denies the Child has the Father-Mother; everyone who confesses the Child has the Father-Mother also. ²⁴Let what you heard from the beginning abide in you. If what you heard from the beginning abides in you, then you will abide in the Child and in the Father-Mother. ²⁵And this is what has been promised to us,ᵍ eternal life.

26 I write these things to you concerning those who would deceive you. ²⁷As for you, the anointing that you received from Christ abides in you, and so you do not need anyone to teach you. But as this anointing teaches you about all things, and is true and is not a lie, and just as it has taught you, abide in Christ.ʰ

28 And now, little children, abide in Christ, so that when Christ is revealed we may have confidence and not be put to shame before Christ when Christ comes.

Children of God

29 If you know that Christ is righteous, you may be sure that everyone who does right has been born of Christ Jesus. ¹See what love the Father-Mother has given us, that we should be called children of God; and that is what we are. The reason the world does not know us is that it did not know Christ. ²Beloved, we are God's children now; what we will be has not yet been revealed. What we do know is this: when Jesus Christʰ is revealed, we will be like Christ, for we will see Christ as Christ is. ³And all who have this hope in Christ purify themselves, just as Christ is pure.

4 Everyone who commits sin is guilty of lawlessness; sin is lawlessness. ⁵You know that Christ was revealed to take away sins, and in Christ there is no sin. ⁶No one who abides in Christ sins; no one who sins has either seen or known Christ. ⁷Little children, let no one deceive you. Everyone who does what is right is righteous, just as Jesus Christ is righteous. ⁸Everyone who commits sin is a child of the devil; for the devil has been sinning from the beginning. The Child of God was revealed for this purpose, to destroy the works of the devil. ⁹Those who have been born of God do not sin, because God's seed abides in them;ⁱ they cannot sin, because they have been born of God. ¹⁰The children of God and the children of the devil are revealed in this

---

e Other ancient authorities read *you know all things*　　f Or *the Messiah*
g Other ancient authorities read *you*　　h Or *it*
i Or *because the children of God abide in God*

way: all who do not do what is right are not from God, nor are those who do not love their brothers and sisters.

Love One Another

11 For this is the message you have heard from the beginning, that we should love one another. 12 We must not be like Cain who was from the evil one and murdered his brother. And why did Cain murder his brother Abel? Because his own deeds were evil and his brother's righteous. 13 Do not be astonished, sisters and brothers, that the world hates you. 14 We know that we have passed from death to life because we love one another. Whoever does not love abides in death. 15 All who hate a brother or sister are murderers, and you know that murderers do not have eternal life abiding in them. 16 We know love by this, that Christ laid down even life for us—and we ought to lay down even our lives for one another. 17 How does God's love abide in anyone who has the world's goods and sees a brother or sister in need and yet refuses help?

18 Little children, let us love, not in word or speech, but in truth and action. 19 And by this we will know that we are from the truth and will reassure our hearts before God 20 whenever our hearts condemn us; for God is greater than our hearts, and knows everything. 21 Beloved, if our hearts do not condemn us, we have boldness before God; 22 and we receive from God whatever we ask, because we obey the commandments and do what pleases God.

23 And this is God's commandment, that we should believe in the name of God's Child Jesus Christ and love one another, just as God has commanded us. 24 All who obey the commandments abide in God, and God abides in them. And by this we know that God abides in us, by the Spirit that God has given us.

Testing the Spirits

4 Beloved, do not believe every spirit, but test the spirits to see whether they are from God; for many false prophets have gone out into the world. 2 By this you know the Spirit of God: every spirit that confesses that Jesus Christ has come in the flesh is from God, 3 and every spirit that does not confess Jesus[j] is not from God. And this is the spirit of the antichrist, of which you have heard that it is coming; and now it is already in the world. 4 Little children, you are from God, and have conquered them; for the one who is in you is greater than the one who is in the world. 5 They are from the world; therefore what they say is from the world, and the world listens to them. 6 We are from God. Whoever knows God listens to us, and whoever is not from God does not listen to us. From this we know the spirit of truth and the spirit of error.

---

j Other ancient authorities read *does away with Jesus* (Gk *dissolves Jesus*)

God Is Love

7 Beloved, let us love one another, because love is from God; everyone who loves is born of God and knows God. 8 Whoever does not love does not know God, for God is love. 9 God's love was revealed among us in this way: God sent God's only Child into the world so that we might live through that Child. 10 In this is love, not that we loved God but that God loved us and sent God's own Child to be the atoning sacrifice for our sins. 11 Beloved, since God loved us so much, we also ought to love one another. 12 No one has ever seen God; if we love one another, God lives in us, and God's love is perfected in us.

13 By this we know that we abide in God and God in us, because God has given us of the Spirit. 14 And we have seen and do testify that the Father-Mother has sent the Child as the Savior of the world. 15 God abides in those who confess that Jesus is the Child of God, and they abide in God. 16 So we have known and believe the love that God has for us.

God is love, and those who abide in love abide in God, and God abides in them. 17 Love has been perfected among us in this: that we may have boldness on the day of judgment, because as God is, so are we in this world. 18 There is no fear in love, but perfect love casts out fear; for fear has to do with punishment, and whoever fears has not reached perfection in love. 19 We love[k] because God first loved us. 20 Those who say, "I love God," and hate their sisters or brothers, are liars; for those who do not love a brother or sister whom they have seen, cannot love God whom they have not seen. 21 The commandment we have from God is this: those who love God must love their sisters and brothers also.

Faith Conquers the World

5 Everyone who believes that Jesus is the Christ[l] has been born of God, and everyone who loves the parent loves the child. 2 By this we know that we love the children of God, when we love God and obey God's commandments. 3 For the love of God is this, that we obey God's commandments. And these commandments are not burdensome, 4 for whatever is born of God conquers the world. And this is the victory that conquers the world, our faith. 5 Who is it that conquers the world but the one who believes that Jesus is the Child of God?

Testimony concerning the Child of God

6 This is the one who came by water and blood, Jesus Christ, not with the water only but with the water and the blood. And the Spirit is the one that

---

k Other ancient authorities add *God*   l Or *the Messiah* testifies, for the Spirit is the truth. [7] There are three that testify:[m] [8] the Spirit and the water and the blood, and these three agree. [9] If we receive human testimony, the testimony of God is greater; for this is the testimony of God that God has testified to God's own Child. [10] Those who believe in the Child of God have the testimony in their hearts. Those who do not believe in God[n] have made God a liar by not believing in the testimony that God has given concerning God's own Child. [11] And this is the testimony: God gave us eternal life, and this life is in God's Child. [12] Whoever has the Child has life; whoever does not have the Child of God does not have life.

Epilogue

13 I write these things to you who believe in the name of the Child of God, so that you may know that you have eternal life.

14 And this is the boldness we have in Christ, that if we ask anything according to God's will, God hears us. [15] And if we know that God hears us in whatever we ask, we know that we have obtained the requests made of God. [16] If you see your brother or sister committing what is not a mortal sin, you will ask, and God will give life to such a one—to those whose sin is not mortal. There is sin that is mortal; I do not say that you should pray about that. [17] All wrongdoing is sin, but there is sin that is not mortal.

18 We know that those who are born of God do not sin, but the one who was born of God protects them, and the evil one does not touch them. [19] We know that we are God's children, and that the whole world lies under the power of the evil one. [20] And we know that the Child of God has come and has given us understanding so that we may know the one who is true;[o] and we are in the one who is true, in God's Child, Jesus Christ. This one is the true God and eternal life.

21 Little children, keep yourselves from idols.[p]

---

m A few other authorities read (with variations) *7There are three that testify in heaven, the Father-Mother, the Word, and the Holy Spirit, and these three are one. 8And there are three that testify on earth:*   n Other ancient authorities read *in the Child*
o Other ancient authorities read *know the true God*   p Other ancient authorities add *Amen*

The Second Letter of John

Salutation

1 The elder to the elect lady and her children, whom I love in the truth, and not only I but also all who know the truth, 2 because of the truth that abides in us and will be with us forever:

3 Grace, mercy, and peace will be with us from God the Father-Mother and from[a] Jesus Christ, Child of the Father-Mother, in truth and love.

Truth and Love

4 I was overjoyed to find some of your children walking in the truth, just as we have been commanded by God. 5 But now, dear sister, I ask you, not as though I were writing you a new commandment, but one we have had from the beginning, let us love one another. 6 And this is love, that we walk according to God's commandments; this is the commandment just as you have heard it from the beginning—you must walk in it.

7 Many deceivers have gone out into the world, those who do not confess that Jesus Christ has come in the flesh; any such person is the deceiver and the antichrist! 8 Be on your guard, so that you do not lose what we[b] have worked for, but may receive a full reward. 9 Everyone who does not abide in the teaching of Christ, but goes beyond it, does not have God; whoever abides in the teaching has both the Father-Mother and the Child. 10 Do not receive into the house or welcome anyone who comes to you and does not bring this teaching; 11 for to welcome is to participate in the evil deeds of such a person.

---

a Other ancient authorities add *the Lord*   b Other ancient authorities read *you*

Final Greetings

12 Although I have much to write to you, I would rather not use paper and ink; instead I hope to come to you and talk with you face to face, so that our joy may be complete.

13 The children of your elect sister send you their greetings.[c]

---

c Other ancient authorities add *Amen*

The Third Letter of John

Salutation

1 The elder to the beloved Gaius, whom I love in truth.

Gaius Commended for His Hospitality

2 Beloved, I pray that all may go well with you and that you may be in good health, just as it is well with your soul. ³I was overjoyed when some of the friends arrived and testified to your faithfulness to the truth, namely how you walk in the truth. ⁴I have no greater joy than this, to hear that my children are walking in the truth.

5 Beloved, you do faithfully whatever you do for the friends, even though they are strangers to you; ⁶they have testified to your love before the church. You will do well to send them on in a manner worthy of God; ⁷for they began their journey for the sake of Christ,ᵃ accepting no support from nonbelievers.ᵇ ⁸Therefore we ought to support such people, so that we may become coworkers with the truth.

Diotrephes and Demetrius

9 I have written something to the church; but Diotrephes, who likes to put himself first, does not acknowledge our authority. ¹⁰So if I come, I will call attention to what he is doing in spreading false charges against us. And not content with those charges, Diotrephes refuses to welcome the friends, and even prevents those who want to do so and expels them from the church.

11 Beloved, do not imitate what is evil but imitate what is good. Whoever does good is from God; whoever does evil has not seen God. ¹²Everyone has testified favorably about Demetrius, and so has the truth itself. We also testify for him,ᶜ and you know that our testimony is true.

---

a Gk *for the sake of the name*   b Gk *the Gentiles*   c Gk lacks *for him*

Final Greetings

13 I have much to write to you, but I would rather not write with pen and ink; 14 instead I hope to see you soon, and we will talk together face to face.

15 Peace to you. The friends send you their greetings. Greet the friends there, each by name.

The Letter of Jude

Salutation

1 Jude,[a] a servant of Jesus Christ and brother of James,

To those who are called, who are beloved[b] in[c] God the Father-Mother and kept safe for[c] Jesus Christ:

2 May mercy, peace, and love be yours in abundance.

Occasion of the Letter

3 Beloved, while eagerly preparing to write to you about the salvation we share, I find it necessary to write and appeal to you to contend for the faith that was once for all entrusted to the saints. [4]For certain intruders have stolen in among you, people who long ago were designated for this condemnation as ungodly, who pervert the grace of our God into licentiousness and deny our only Sovereign God and Lord, Jesus Christ.[d]

Judgment on False Teachers

5 Now I desire to remind you, though you are fully informed, that God, who once for all saved[e] a people out of the land of Egypt, afterward destroyed those who did not believe. [6]And the angels who did not keep their own position, but left their proper dwelling, God has kept in chains in the deepest part of the night for the judgment of the great Day. [7]Likewise, Sodom and Gomorrah and the surrounding cities, which, in the same manner as they, committed immoral acts and attempted rape,[f] serve as an example by undergoing a punishment of eternal fire.

---

a Gk *Judas*   b Other ancient authorities read *sanctified*   c Or *by*
d Or *the only Sovereign God and our Lord Jesus Christ*
e Other ancient authorities read *though you were once for all fully informed, that Jesus* (or *Joshua*) *who saved*   f Gk *went after other flesh*

8 Yet in the same way these dreamers also defile the flesh, reject authority, and slander the glorious ones.g 9But when the archangel Michael contended with the devil and disputed about the body of Moses, Michael did not dare to bring a condemnation of slanderh against the devil, but said, "God rebuke you!" 10But these people slander whatever they do not understand, and they are destroyed by those things that, like irrational animals, they know by instinct. 11Woe to them! For they go the way of Cain, and abandon themselves to Balaam's error for the sake of gain, and perish in Korah's rebellion. 12These are blemishesi on your love-feasts, while they feast with you without fear, feeding themselves.j They are waterless clouds carried along by the winds; autumn trees without fruit, twice dead, uprooted; 13wild waves of the sea, casting up the foam of their own shame; wandering stars, for whom the deepest part of the night has been reserved forever.

14 It was also about these that Enoch, in the seventh generation from Adam, prophesied, saying, "See, the Lord is comingk with ten thousands of the holy ones, 15to execute judgment on all, and to convict everyone of all the deeds of ungodliness that they have committed in such an ungodly way, and of all the harsh things that ungodly sinners have spoken against the Lord." 16These are grumblers and malcontents; they indulge their own lusts; they are bombastic in speech, flattering people to their own advantage.

Warnings and Exhortations

17 But you, beloved, must remember the predictions of the apostles of our Lord Jesus Christ; 18for they said to you, "In the last time there will be scoffers, indulging their own ungodly lusts." 19It is these worldly people, devoid of the Spirit, who are causing divisions. 20But you, beloved, build yourselves up on your most holy faith; pray in the Holy Spirit; 21keep yourselves in the love of God; look forward to the mercy of our Lord Jesus Christ that leads tol eternal life. 22And have mercy on some who are wavering; 23save others by snatching them out of the fire; and have mercy on still others with fear, hating even the tunic defiled by their bodies.m

Benediction

24 Now to the one who is able to keep you from falling, and to make you stand without blemish in the presence of God's glory with rejoicing, 25to the only God our Savior, through Jesus Christ our Lord, be glory, majesty, power, and authority, before all time and now and forever. Amen.

---

g Or angels; Gk glories   h Or condemnation for blasphemy   i Or reefs
j Or without fear. They are shepherds who care only for themselves   k Gk came
l Gk Christ to
m Gk by the flesh. The Greek text of verses 22-23 is uncertain at several points

The Revelation to John

Introduction and Salutation

1 The revelation of Jesus Christ, which God gave Christ to show the servants of God what must soon take place; Christ made it known by sending an angel to the servant of Christ, John, ²who testified to the word of God and to the testimony of Jesus Christ, even to all that he saw.

3 Blessed is the one who reads aloud the words of the prophecy, and blessed are those who hear and who keep what is written in it; for the time is near.

4 John to the seven churches that are in Asia:

Grace to you and peace from the one who is and who was and who is to come, and from the seven spirits who are before God's throne, ⁵and from Jesus Christ, the faithful witness, the firstborn of the dead, and the ruler of the monarchs of the earth.

To the one who loves us and freed[a] us from our sins by a blood sacrifice, ⁶and made us to be a nation, priests serving[b] the God of Jesus Christ, the Father-Mother, to whom be glory and dominion forever and ever. Amen.

7   Look! There is one coming with the clouds,
        whom every eye will see,
     even those who pierced that one,
        on whose account all the tribes of the earth will wail.

So it is to be. Amen.

8 "I am the Alpha and the Omega," says the Sovereign God, who is and who was and who is to come, the Almighty.

---

a Other ancient authorities read *washed*   b Gk *priests to*

A Vision of Christ

9 I, John, your brother who share with you in Jesus the persecution and the dominion and the patient endurance, was on the island called Patmos because of the word of God and the testimony of Jesus.[c] 10 I was in the spirit[d] on the Lord's day, and I heard behind me a loud voice like a trumpet 11 saying, "Write in a book what you see and send it to the seven churches, to Ephesus, to Smyrna, to Pergamum, to Thyatira, to Sardis, to Philadelphia, and to Laodicea."

12 Then I turned to see whose voice it was that spoke to me, and on turning I saw seven golden lampstands, 13 and in the midst of the lampstands I saw one like the Human One, clothed with a long robe and with a golden sash from shoulder to waist. 14 The head and the hair of that one were white as white wool, white as snow; the eyes were like a flame of fire, 15 and the feet were like burnished bronze, refined as in a furnace, and the voice was like the sound of many waters. 16 The right hand held seven stars, and from the mouth came a sharp, two-edged sword, and the face was like the sun shining with full force.

17 When I saw one like the Human One, I fell down as though dead. But placing the right hand on me, that one said, "Do not be afraid; I am the first and the last, 18 and the living one. I was dead, and see, I am alive forever and ever; and I have the keys of Death and of Hades. 19 Now write what you have seen, what is, and what is to take place after this. 20 As for the mystery of the seven stars that you saw in my right hand, and the seven golden lampstands: the seven stars are the angels of the seven churches, and the seven lampstands are the seven churches.

The Message to Ephesus

2 "To the angel of the church in Ephesus write: These are the words of the one whose right hand holds the seven stars, who walks among the seven golden lampstands:

2 "I know your works, your toil and your patient endurance. I know that you cannot tolerate evildoers; you have tested those who claim to be apostles but are not, and have found them to be false. 3 I also know that you are enduring patiently and bearing up for the sake of my name, and that you have not grown weary. 4 But I have this against you, that you have abandoned the love you had at first. 5 Remember then from what you have fallen; repent, and do the works you did at first. If not, I will come to you and remove your lampstand from its place, unless you repent. 6 Yet this is to your credit: you hate the works of the Nicolaitans, which I also hate. 7 Let everyone pay attention to what the Spirit is saying to the churches. To everyone who conquers, I will give permission to eat from the tree of life that is in the paradise of God.

---

c Or *testimony to Jesus*   d Or *in the Spirit*

The Message to Smyrna

8 "And to the angel of the church in Smyrna write: These are the words of the first and the last, who was dead and came to life:

9 "I know your affliction and your poverty, even though you are rich. I know the slander on the part of those who say that they are Jews and are not, but are a synagogue of Satan. 10Do not fear what you are about to suffer. Beware, the devil is about to throw some of you into prison so that you may be tested, and for ten days you will have affliction. Be faithful until death, and I will give you the crown of life. 11Let everyone pay attention to what the Spirit is saying to the churches. Whoever conquers will not be harmed by the second death.

The Message to Pergamum

12 "And to the angel of the church in Pergamum write: These are the words of the one who has the sharp two-edged sword:

13 "I know where you are living, where Satan's throne is. Yet you are holding fast to my name, and you did not deny your faith in me[e] even in the days of Antipas my witness, my faithful one, who was killed among you, where Satan lives. 14But I have a few things against you: you have some there who hold to the teaching of Balaam, who taught Balak to put a stumbling block before the people of Israel, so that they would eat food sacrificed to idols and practice sexual immorality. 15So you also have some who hold to the teaching of the Nicolaitans. 16Repent then. If not, I will come to you soon and make war against them with the sword of my mouth. 17Let everyone pay attention to what the Spirit is saying to the churches. To everyone who conquers I will give some of the hidden manna, and I will give a white stone, and on the white stone is written a new name that no one knows except the one who receives it.

The Message to Thyatira

18 "And to the angel of the church in Thyatira write: These are the words of the Human One, who has eyes like a flame of fire, and whose feet are like burnished bronze:

19 "I know your works—your love, faith, service, and patient endurance. I know that your last works are greater than the first. 20But I have this against you: you tolerate that woman Jezebel, who calls herself a prophet and is teaching and beguiling my servants to practice sexual immorality and to eat food sacrificed to idols. 21I gave her time to repent, but she refuses to repent of her sexual immorality. 22Beware, I am throwing her on a bed, and those who commit adultery with her I am throwing into great distress, unless they repent of her doings; 23and I will strike her children dead. And all the churches will know that I am the one who searches minds and hearts, and I will give to each

---

e Or *deny my faith*

of you as your works deserve. 24But to the rest of you in Thyatira, who do not hold this teaching, who have not learned what some call 'the deep things of Satan,' to you I say, I do not lay on you any other burden; 25only hold fast to what you have until I come. 26To everyone who conquers and continues to do my works to the end,

> I will give authority over the nations;
27 > to rule[f] them with an iron rod,
>> as when clay pots are shattered—

28even as I also received authority from my Father-Mother. To the one who conquers I will also give the morning star. 29Let everyone pay attention to what the Spirit is saying to the churches.

The Message to Sardis

3 "And to the angel of the church in Sardis write: These are the words of the one who has the seven spirits of God and the seven stars:

"I know your works; you have a name of being alive, but you are dead. 2Wake up, and strengthen what remains and is on the point of death, for I have not found your works perfect in the sight of my God. 3Remember then what you received and heard; obey it, and repent. If you do not wake up, I will come like a thief, and you will not know at what hour I will come to you. 4Yet you have still a few persons in Sardis who have not soiled their clothes; they will walk with me, dressed in white, for they are worthy. 5If you conquer, you will be clothed like them in white robes, and I will not blot your name out of the book of life; I will confess your name before my Father-Mother, and before God's angels. 6Let everyone pay attention to what the Spirit is saying to the churches.

The Message to Philadelphia

7 "And to the angel of the church in Philadelphia write:

> These are the words of the holy one, the true one,
>> who has the key of David,
>> who opens and no one will shut,
>>> who shuts and no one opens:

8 "I know your works. Look, I have set before you an open door, which no one is able to shut. I know that you have but little power, and yet you have kept my word and have not denied my name. 9I will make those of the synagogue of Satan who say that they are Jews and are not, but are lying—I will make them come and bow down before your feet, and they will learn that I have loved you. 10Because you have kept my word of patient endurance, I will keep you from the hour of trial that is coming on the whole world to test

---

f Or to shepherd

the inhabitants of the earth. [11] I am coming soon; hold fast to what you have, so that no one may seize your crown. [12] If you conquer, I will make you a pillar in the temple of my God; you will never go out of it. I will write on you the name of my God, and the name of the city of my God, the new Jerusalem that comes down from my God out of heaven, and my own new name. [13] Let everyone pay attention to what the Spirit is saying to the churches.

The Message to Laodicea

14 "And to the angel of the church in Laodicea write: The words of the Amen, the faithful and true witness, the origin[g] of God's creation:

15 "I know your works; you are neither cold nor hot. I wish that you were either cold or hot. [16] So, because you are lukewarm, and neither cold nor hot, I am about to spit you out of my mouth. [17] For you say, 'I am rich, I have prospered, and I need nothing.' You do not realize that you are wretched, pitiable, poor, blind, and naked. [18] Therefore I counsel you to buy from me gold refined by fire so that you may be rich; and white robes to clothe you and to keep the shame of your nakedness from being seen; and salve to anoint your eyes so that you may see. [19] I reprove and discipline those whom I love. Be earnest, therefore, and repent. [20] Listen! I am standing at the door, knocking; if you hear my voice and open the door, I will come in to you and eat with you, and you with me. [21] To the one who conquers I will give a place with me on my throne, just as I myself conquered and sat down with my Father-Mother on God's throne. [22] Let everyone pay attention to what the Spirit is saying to the churches."

The Heavenly Worship

4 After this I looked, and there in heaven a door stood open! And the first voice, which I had heard speaking to me like a trumpet, said, "Come up here, and I will show you what must take place after this." [2] At once I was in the spirit,[h] and there in heaven stood a throne, with one seated on the throne! [3] And the one seated there looks like jasper and carnelian, and around the throne is a rainbow that looks like an emerald. [4] Around the throne are twenty-four thrones, and seated on the thrones are twenty-four elders, dressed in white robes, with golden crowns on their heads. [5] Coming from the throne are flashes of lightning, and rumblings and peals of thunder, and in front of the throne burn seven flaming torches, which are the seven spirits of God; [6] and in front of the throne there is something like a sea of glass, like crystal.

Around the throne, and on each side of the throne, are four living creatures, full of eyes in front and behind: [7] the first living creature like a lion, the second living creature like an ox, the third living creature with a face like a human face, and the fourth living creature like a flying eagle. [8] And the four

---

g Or *beginning*   h Or *in the Spirit*

living creatures, each of them with six wings, are full of eyes all around and inside. Day and night without ceasing they sing,

"Holy, holy, holy,
the Sovereign God the Almighty,
who was and is and is to come."

9 And whenever the living creatures give glory and honor and thanks to the one who is seated on the throne, who lives forever and ever, 10 the twenty-four elders fall before the one who is seated on the throne and worship the one who lives forever and ever; they cast their crowns before the throne, singing,

11   "You are worthy, our Sovereign and God,
to receive glory and honor and power,
for you created all things,
and by your will they existed and were created."

The Scroll and the Lamb

5 Then I saw in the hand of the one seated on the throne a scroll written on the inside and on the back, sealed[i] with seven seals; 2 and I saw a mighty angel proclaiming with a loud voice, "Who is worthy to open the scroll and break its seals?" 3 And no one in heaven or on earth or under the earth was able to open the scroll or to look into it. 4 And I began to weep bitterly because no one was found worthy to open the scroll or to look into it. 5 Then one of the elders said to me, "Do not weep. See, the Lion of the tribe of Judah, the Root of David, has conquered, and therefore that one can open the scroll and its seven seals."

6 Then I saw between the throne and the four living creatures and among the elders a Lamb standing as if it had been slaughtered, having seven horns and seven eyes, which are the seven spirits of God sent out into all the earth. 7 The Lamb went and took the scroll from the hand of the one who was seated on the throne. 8 When the Lamb had taken the scroll, the four living creatures and the twenty-four elders fell before the Lamb, each holding a harp and golden bowls full of incense, which are the prayers of the saints. 9 They sing a new song:

"You are worthy to take the scroll
and to open its seals,
for you were slaughtered and by your blood you
ransomed for God
saints from[j] every tribe and language and people
and nation;

---

i Or *written on the inside, and sealed on the back*   j Gk *ransomed for God from*

10   you have made them to be a nation and priests serving[k]
                 our God,
              and they will reign on earth."

11 Then I looked, and I heard the voice of many angels surrounding the throne and the living creatures and the elders; they numbered myriads of myriads and thousands of thousands, 12 singing with full voice,

> "Worthy is the Lamb that was slaughtered
> to receive power and wealth and wisdom and might
> and honor and glory and blessing!"

13 Then I heard every creature in heaven and on earth and under the earth and in the sea, and all that is in them, singing,

> "To the one seated on the throne and to the Lamb
> be blessing and honor and glory and might
> forever and ever!"

14 And the four living creatures said, "Amen!" And the elders fell down and worshiped.

The Seven Seals

6 Then I saw the Lamb open one of the seven seals, and I heard one of the four living creatures call out, as with a voice of thunder, "Come!"[l] 2 I looked, and there was a white horse! Its rider had a bow; a crown was given to the rider, who came out conquering and to conquer.

3 When the Lamb opened the second seal, I heard the second living creature call out, "Come!"[l] 4 And out came[m] another horse, bright red; its rider was permitted to take peace from the earth, so that people would slaughter one another; and this rider was given a great sword.

5 When the Lamb opened the third seal, I heard the third living creature call out, "Come!"[l] I looked, and there was a black horse! Its rider held aloft a pair of scales, 6 and I heard what seemed to be a voice in the midst of the four living creatures saying, "A quart of wheat for a day's pay,[n] and three quarts of barley for a day's pay,[n] but do not damage the olive oil and the wine!"

7 When the Lamb opened the fourth seal, I heard the voice of the fourth living creature call out, "Come!"[l] 8 I looked and there was a pale green horse! Its rider's name was Death, and Hades followed along; they were given authority over a fourth of the earth, to kill with sword, famine, and pestilence, and by the wild animals of the earth.

9 When the Lamb opened the fifth seal, I saw under the altar the souls of those who had been slaughtered for the word of God and for the testimony they had given; 10 they cried out with a loud voice, "Sovereign God, holy and

---

k Gk *priests to*   l Or *"Go!"*   m Or *went*   n Gk *a denarius*

true, how long will it be before you judge and avenge our blood on the inhabitants of the earth?" [11] They were each given a white robe and told to rest a little longer, until the number would be complete both of the other servants and of their brothers and sisters, who were soon to be killed as they themselves had been killed.

12 When the Lamb opened the sixth seal, I looked, and there came a great earthquake; the sun became black as sackcloth, the full moon became like blood, [13] and the stars of the sky fell to the earth as the fig tree drops its winter fruit when shaken by a gale. [14] The sky vanished like a scroll rolling itself up, and every mountain and island was removed from its place. [15] Then the rulers of the earth and the magnates and the generals and the rich and the powerful, and everyone, enslaved and free, hid in the caves and among the rocks of the mountains, [16] calling to the mountains and rocks, "Fall on us and hide us from the face of the one seated on the throne and from the wrath of the Lamb; [17] for the great day of their wrath has come, and who is able to stand?"

The 144,000 of Israel Sealed

7 After this I saw four angels standing at the four corners of the earth, holding back the four winds of the earth so that no wind could blow on earth or sea or against any tree. [2] I saw another angel ascending from the rising of the sun, having the seal of the living God, and the angel called with a loud voice to the four angels who had been given power to damage earth and sea, [3] saying, "Do not damage the earth or the sea or the trees, until we have marked the servants of our God with a seal on their foreheads."

4 And I heard the number of those who were sealed, one hundred forty-four thousand, sealed out of every tribe of the people of Israel:

5 From the tribe of Judah twelve thousand sealed,
   from the tribe of Reuben twelve thousand,
   from the tribe of Gad twelve thousand,
6 from the tribe of Asher twelve thousand,
   from the tribe of Naphtali twelve thousand,
   from the tribe of Manasseh twelve thousand,
7 from the tribe of Simeon twelve thousand,
   from the tribe of Levi twelve thousand,
   from the tribe of Issachar twelve thousand,
8 from the tribe of Zebulun twelve thousand,
   from the tribe of Joseph twelve thousand,
   from the tribe of Benjamin twelve thousand sealed.

The Multitude from Every Nation

9 After this I looked, and there was a great multitude that no one could count, from every nation, from all tribes and peoples and languages, standing before the throne and before the Lamb, robed in white, with palm branches in their hands. [10] They cried out in a loud voice, saying,

> "Salvation belongs to our God who is seated on the
> throne, and to the Lamb!"

11 And all the angels stood around the throne and around the elders and the
four living creatures, and they fell on their faces before the throne and
worshiped God, 12 singing,

> "Amen! Blessing and glory and wisdom
> and thanksgiving and honor
> and power and might
> be to our God forever and ever! Amen."

13 Then one of the elders addressed me, saying, "Who are these, robed in
white, and where have they come from?" 14 I said to the elder, "You are the
one that knows." Then the elder said to me, "These are they who have come
out of the great ordeal; they have washed their robes and made them white in
the blood of the Lamb.

15   For this reason they are before the throne of God,
>   and worship God day and night within the temple,
>   and the one who is seated on the throne will shelter
>   them.
16   They will hunger no more, and thirst no more;
>   the sun will not strike them,
>   nor any scorching heat;
17   for the Lamb at the center of the throne will be their
>   shepherd,
>   and the Lamb will guide them to springs of the water
>   of life,
> and God will wipe away every tear from their eyes."

The Seventh Seal and the Golden Censer

8 When the Lamb opened the seventh seal, there was silence in heaven for
about half an hour. 2 And I saw the seven angels who stand before God,
and seven trumpets were given to them.

3 Another angel with a golden censer came and stood at the altar; this
angel was given a great quantity of incense to offer with the prayers of all the
saints on the golden altar that is before the throne. 4 And the smoke of the
incense, with the prayers of the saints, rose before God from the hand of
the angel. 5 Then the angel took the censer and filled it with fire from the altar
and threw it on the earth; and there were peals of thunder, rumblings, flashes of
lightning, and an earthquake.

The Seven Trumpets

6 Now the seven angels who had the seven trumpets made ready to blow them.
7 The first angel sounded the trumpet, and there came hail and fire, mixed

with blood, and they were hurled to the earth; and a third of the earth was
burned up, and a third of the trees were burned up, and all green grass was
burned up.
8 The second angel sounded the trumpet, and something like a great
mountain, burning with fire, was thrown into the sea. 9A third of the sea
became blood, a third of the living creatures in the sea died, and a third of the
ships were destroyed.
10 The third angel sounded the trumpet, and a great star fell from heaven,
blazing like a torch, and it fell on a third of the rivers and on the springs of
water. 11The name of the star is Wormwood. A third of the waters became
wormwood, and many died from the water, because it was made bitter.
12 The fourth angel sounded the trumpet, and a third of the sun was
struck, and a third of the moon, and a third of the stars, so that a third of their
light was extinguished; a third of the day was kept from shining, and likewise
the night.
13 Then I looked, and I heard an eagle crying with a loud voice as it flew
in midheaven, "Woe, woe, woe to the inhabitants of the earth, at the blasts of
the other trumpets that the three angels are about to blow!"
9 And the fifth angel sounded the trumpet, and I saw a star that had fallen
from heaven to earth, and this one, given the key to the shaft of the
bottomless pit, 2opened it, and from the shaft rose smoke like the smoke of a
great furnace, and the sun and the air were darkened with the smoke from the
shaft. 3Then from the smoke came locusts on the earth, and they were given
authority like the authority of scorpions of the earth. 4They were told not to
damage the grass of the earth or any green growth or any tree, but only those
people who do not have the seal of God on their foreheads. 5They were
allowed to torture them for five months, but not to kill them, and their torture
was like the torture of a scorpion when it stings someone. 6And in those days
people will seek death but will not find it; they will long to die, but death will
flee from them.
7 In appearance the locusts were like horses equipped for battle. On their
heads were what looked like crowns of gold; their faces were like human faces,
8their hair like women's hair, and their teeth like lions' teeth; 9they had scales
like iron breastplates, and the noise of their wings was like the noise of many
chariots with horses rushing into battle. 10They have tails like scorpions, with
stingers, and in their tails is their power to harm people for five months.
11They have as ruler over them the angel of the bottomless pit, whose name in
Hebrew is Abaddon,[o] and in Greek is Apollyon.[p]
12 The first woe has passed. There are still two woes to come.
13 Then the sixth angel sounded the trumpet, and I heard a voice from the
four[q] horns of the golden altar before God, 14saying to the sixth angel who
had the trumpet, "Release the four angels who are bound at the great river

o That is, *Destruction* p That is, *Destroyer* q Other ancient authorities lack *four*

Euphrates." ¹⁵So the four angels were released, who had been held ready for the hour, the day, the month, and the year, to kill a third of humankind. ¹⁶The number of the troops of cavalry was two hundred million; I heard their number. ¹⁷And this was how I saw the horses in my vision: the riders wore breastplates the color of fire and of sapphire^r and of sulfur; the heads of the horses were like lions' heads, and fire and smoke and sulfur came out of their mouths. ¹⁸By these three plagues a third of humankind was killed, by the fire and smoke and sulfur coming out of their mouths. ¹⁹For the power of the horses is in their mouths and in their tails; their tails are like serpents, having heads; and with them they inflict harm.

20 The rest of humankind, who were not killed by these plagues, did not repent of the works of their hands or give up worshiping demons and idols of gold and silver and bronze and stone and wood, which cannot see or hear or walk. ²¹And they did not repent of their murders or their sorceries or their sexual immorality or their thefts.

The Angel with the Little Scroll

10 And I saw another mighty angel coming down from heaven, wrapped in a cloud, with a rainbow overhead, whose face was like the sun, and whose legs were like pillars of fire. ²This angel held a little scroll open. Setting one foot on the sea and the other foot on the land, ³the angel gave a great shout, like a lion roaring. And when the angel shouted, the seven thunders sounded. ⁴And when the seven thunders had sounded, I was about to write, but I heard a voice from heaven saying, "Seal up what the seven thunders have said, and do not write it down." ⁵Then the angel whom I saw standing on the sea and the land

> raised a hand to heaven
> 6   and swore by that one who lives forever and ever,

who created heaven and what is in it, the earth and what is in it, and the sea and what is in it: "There will be no more delay, ⁷but in the days when the seventh angel is to sound the trumpet, the mystery of God will be fulfilled, as God announced to God's servants the prophets."

8 Then the voice that I had heard from heaven spoke to me again, saying, "Go, take the scroll that is open in the hand of the angel who is standing on the sea and on the land." ⁹So I went to the angel whom I told to give me the little scroll; and the angel said to me, "Take it, and eat; it will be bitter to your stomach, but sweet as honey in your mouth." ¹⁰So I took the little scroll from the hand of the angel and ate it; it was sweet as honey in my mouth, but when I had eaten it, my stomach was made bitter.

11 Then they said to me, "You must prophesy again about many peoples and nations and languages and rulers."

---

r Gk *hyacinth*

The Two Witnesses

11 Then I was given a measuring rod like a staff, and I was told, "Come and measure the temple of God and the altar and those who worship there, ²but do not measure the court outside the temple; leave that out, for it is given over to the nations, and they will trample over the holy city for forty-two months. ³And I will grant my two witnesses authority to prophesy for one thousand two hundred sixty days, wearing sackcloth."

4 These are the two olive trees and the two lampstands that stand before the Sovereign of the earth. ⁵And if anyone wants to harm them, fire pours from their mouth and consumes their foes; anyone who wants to harm them must be killed in this manner. ⁶They have authority to shut the sky, so that no rain may fall during the days of their prophesying, and they have authority over the waters to turn them into blood, and to strike the earth with every kind of plague, as often as they desire.

7 When they have finished their testimony, the beast that comes up from the bottomless pit will make war on them and conquer them and kill them, ⁸and their dead bodies will lie in the street of the great city that is prophetically[s] called Sodom and Egypt, where also their Lord was crucified. ⁹For three and a half days members of the peoples and tribes and languages and nations will gaze at their dead bodies and refuse to let them be placed in a tomb; ¹⁰and the inhabitants of the earth will gloat over them and celebrate and exchange presents, because these two prophets had been a torment to the inhabitants of the earth.

11 But after the three and a half days, the breath[t] of life from God entered them, and they stood on their feet, and those who saw them were terrified. ¹²Then they[u] heard a loud voice from heaven saying to them, "Come up here!" And they went up to heaven in a cloud while their enemies watched them. ¹³At that moment there was a great earthquake, and a tenth of the city fell; seven thousand people were killed in the earthquake, and the rest were terrified and gave glory to the God of heaven.

14 The second woe has passed. The third woe is coming very soon.

The Seventh Trumpet

15 Then the seventh angel sounded the trumpet, and there were loud voices in heaven, saying,

> "The dominion of the world has become the dominion
>   of our God
>   and of God's Messiah,[v]
> and this one will reign forever and ever."

---

s Or *allegorically*; Gk *spiritually*   t Or *the spirit*   u Other ancient authorities read *I*
v Gk *Christ*

16 Then the twenty-four elders who sit on their thrones before God fell on their faces and worshiped God, 17 singing,

> "We give you thanks, Sovereign God the Almighty,
>   who are and who were,
> for you have taken your great power
>   and begun to reign.
> 18 The nations raged,
>   but your wrath has come,
>   and the time for judging the dead,
> for rewarding your servants, the prophets
>   and saints and all who fear your name,
>   both small and great,
> and for destroying those who destroy the earth."

19 Then God's temple in heaven was opened, and the ark of the covenant was seen within God's temple; and there were flashes of lightning, rumblings, peals of thunder, an earthquake, and heavy hail.

The Woman and the Dragon

12 A great portent appeared in heaven: a woman clothed with the sun, with the moon under her feet, and on her head a crown of twelve stars. 2 She was pregnant and was crying out in birth pangs, in the agony of giving birth. 3 Then another portent appeared in heaven: a great red dragon, with seven heads and ten horns, and a diadem on each head. 4 The dragon's tail swept down a third of the stars of heaven and threw them to the earth. Then the dragon stood before the woman who was about to bear a child, in order to devour her child as soon as it was born. 5 And she gave birth to a son, a male child, who is to rule^w all the nations with a rod of iron. But her child was snatched away and taken to God and to God's throne; 6 and the woman fled into the wilderness, where she has a place prepared by God, so that there she can be nourished for one thousand two hundred sixty days.

Michael Defeats the Dragon

7 And war broke out in heaven; Michael and Michael's angels fought against the dragon. The dragon and the dragon's angels fought back, 8 but they were defeated, and there was no longer any place for them in heaven. 9 The great dragon was thrown down, that ancient serpent, who is called the Devil and Satan, the deceiver of the whole world—the dragon was thrown down to the earth, along with the angels of the dragon.

10 Then I heard a loud voice in heaven, proclaiming,

> "Now have come the salvation and the power

---

w Or *to shepherd*

11

12

and the dominion of our God
and the authority of God's Messiah,[x]
for the accuser of our comrades has been thrown down,
who accuses them day and night before our God.
But they have conquered the accuser by the blood of
the Lamb
and by the word of their testimony,
for they did not cling to life even in the face of death.
Rejoice then, you heavens
and those who dwell in them!
But woe to the earth and the sea,
for the devil has come down to you
with great wrath,
knowing that the time is short!"

The Dragon Fights Again on Earth

13 So the dragon, seeing that it had been thrown down to the earth, pursued[y] the woman who had given birth to the male child. [14]But the woman was given the two wings of the great eagle, so that she could fly from the serpent into the wilderness, to her place where she is nourished for a time, and times, and half a time. [15]Then from the serpent's mouth poured water like a river after the woman, to sweep her away with the flood. [16]But the earth came to the help of the woman; it opened its mouth and swallowed the river that the dragon's mouth had poured forth. [17]Then the dragon was angry with the woman, and went off to make war on the rest of her children, those who keep the commandments of God and hold the testimony of Jesus.

The First Beast

13 18 Then the dragon[z] stood on the sand of the seashore. [1]And I saw a beast rising out of the sea, having ten horns and seven heads; and on its horns were ten diadems, and on its heads were blasphemous names. [2]And the beast that I saw was like a leopard, its feet were like a bear's, and its mouth was like a lion's mouth. And the dragon gave to the beast its own power and throne and great authority. [3]One of its heads seemed to have received a death-blow, but its mortal wound[a] had been healed. In amazement the whole earth followed the beast. [4]They worshiped the dragon, who had given authority to the beast, and they worshiped the beast, saying, "Who is like the beast, and who can fight against it?"

5 The beast was given a mouth uttering haughty and blasphemous words, and it was allowed to exercise authority for forty-two months. [6]It opened its mouth to utter blasphemies against God, blaspheming God's name and God's

---

x Gk *Christ*   y Or *persecuted*   z Gk *Then he*; other ancient authorities read *Then I stood*
a Gk *the plague of its death*

dwelling, that is, those who dwell in heaven. [7] Also it was allowed to make war on the saints and to conquer them.[b] It was given authority over every tribe and people and language and nation, [8] and all the inhabitants of the earth will worship it, everyone whose name has not been written from the foundation of the world in the book of life of the Lamb that was slaughtered.[c]

9 Let everyone pay attention to this:

10

> If you are to be taken captive,
>   into captivity you go;
> if you kill with the sword,
>   with the sword you must be killed.

Here is a call for the endurance and faith of the saints.

The Second Beast

11 Then I saw another beast that rose out of the earth; it had two horns like a lamb and it spoke like a dragon. [12] It exercises all the authority of the first beast on its behalf, and it makes the earth and its inhabitants worship the first beast, whose mortal wound[d] had been healed. [13] It performs great signs, even making fire come down from heaven to earth in the sight of all; [14] and by the signs that it is allowed to perform on behalf of the beast, it deceives the inhabitants of earth, telling them to make an image for the beast that had been wounded by the sword[e] and yet lived; [15] and it was allowed to give breath[f] to the image of the beast so that the image of the beast could even speak and cause those who would not worship the image of the beast to be killed. [16] Also it causes all, both small and great, both rich and poor, both free and slave, to be marked on the hand or the forehead, [17] so that no one can buy or sell who does not have the mark, that is, the name of the beast or the number of its name. [18] This calls for wisdom: let anyone with understanding calculate the number of the beast, for it is the number of a person. Its number is six hundred sixty-six.[g]

The Lamb and the 144,000

14 Then I looked, and there was the Lamb, standing on Mount Zion! And with the Lamb were one hundred forty-four thousand who had the name of the Lamb and the name of God written on their foreheads. [2] And I heard a voice from heaven like the sound of many waters and like the sound of loud thunder; the voice I heard was like the sound of harpists playing on their harps, [3] and they sing a new song before the throne and before the four living creatures and before the elders. No one could learn that song except the one

---

b Other ancient authorities lack this sentence
c Or *written in the book of life of the Lamb that was slaughtered from the foundation of the world*   d Gk *whose plague of its death*   e Or *that had received the plague of the sword*
f Or *spirit*   g Other ancient authorities read *six hundred sixteen*

hundred forty-four thousand who have been redeemed from the earth. [4]It is these who have not defiled themselves by having sexual relations, for they are virgins; these follow the Lamb wherever the Lamb goes. They have been redeemed from humankind as firstfruits for God and the Lamb, [5]and in their mouth no lie was found; they are blameless.

The Messages of the Three Angels

6 Then I saw another angel flying in midheaven, with an eternal gospel to proclaim to those who live[h] on the earth—to every nation and tribe and language and people. [7]The angel said in a loud voice, "Fear God and give God glory, for the hour of God's judgment has come; and worship the one who made heaven and earth, the sea and the springs of water."

8 Then another angel, a second, followed, saying, "Fallen, fallen is Babylon the great! Babylon has made all nations drink of the wine of the wrath of the city's sexual immorality."

9 Then another angel, a third, followed them, crying with a loud voice, "Those who worship the beast and its image, and receive a mark on their foreheads or on their hands, [10]they will also drink the wine of God's wrath, poured unmixed into the cup of God's anger, and they will be tormented with fire and sulfur in the presence of the holy angels and in the presence of the Lamb. [11]And the smoke of their torment goes up forever and ever. There is no rest day or night for those who worship the beast and its image and for anyone who receives the mark of its name."

12 Here is a call for the endurance of the saints, those who keep the commandments of God and hold fast to the faith of[i] Jesus.

13 And I heard a voice from heaven saying, "Write this: Blessed are the dead who from now on die in the Lord." "Yes," says the Spirit, "they will rest from their labors, for their deeds follow them."

Reaping the Earth's Harvest

14 Then I looked, and there was a white cloud, and seated on the cloud was one like the Human One, crowned with a golden crown and holding a sharp sickle. [15]Another angel came out of the temple, calling with a loud voice to the one who sat on the cloud, "Use your sickle and reap, for the hour to reap has come, because the harvest of the earth is fully ripe." [16]So the one who sat on the cloud swung the sickle over the earth, and the earth was reaped.

17 Then another angel came out of the temple in heaven, and this one too had a sharp sickle. [18]Then another angel came out from the altar, the angel who has authority over fire, and this angel called with a loud voice to the one who had the sharp sickle, "Use your sharp sickle and gather the clusters of the vine of the earth, for its grapes are ripe." [19]So the angel swung the sickle over the earth and gathered the vintage of the earth, and threw it into the great wine-

---

h Gk *sit*   i Or *to their faith in*

press of the wrath of God. [20] And the winepress was trodden outside the city, and blood flowed from the winepress, as high as a horse's bridle, for a distance of about two hundred miles.[j]

The Angels with the Seven Last Plagues

15 Then I saw another portent in heaven, great and amazing: seven angels with seven plagues, which are the last, for with them the wrath of God is ended.

2 And I saw what appeared to be a sea of glass mixed with fire, and those who had conquered the beast and its image and the number of its name, standing beside the sea of glass with harps of God in their hands. [3] And they sing the song of Moses, the servant of God, and the song of the Lamb:

> "Great and amazing are your deeds,
>   Sovereign God the Almighty!
> Just and true are your ways,
>   Ruler of the nations![k]
> 4   God, who will not fear
>   and glorify your name?
> For you alone are holy.
>   All nations will come
>   and worship before you,
> for your judgments have been revealed."

5 After this I looked, and the temple of the tent[l] of witness in heaven was opened, [6] and out of the temple came the seven angels with the seven plagues, robed in pure bright linen,[m] with golden sashes across their chests. [7] Then one of the four living creatures gave the seven angels seven golden bowls full of the wrath of God, who lives forever and ever; [8] and the temple was filled with smoke from the glory of God and from God's power, and no one could enter the temple until the seven plagues of the seven angels were ended.

The Bowls of God's Wrath

16 Then I heard a loud voice from the temple telling the seven angels, "Go and empty on the earth the seven bowls of the wrath of God."

2 So the first angel went and emptied a bowl on the earth, and a foul and painful sore came on those who had the mark of the beast and who worshiped its image.

3 The second angel emptied a bowl into the sea, and it became like the blood of a corpse, and every living thing in the sea died.

---

j Gk *one thousand six hundred stadia*   k Other ancient authorities read *the ages*
l Or *tabernacle*   m Other ancient authorities read *stone*

4 The third angel emptied a bowl into the rivers and the springs of water, and they became blood. 5 And I heard the angel of the waters say,

> "You are just, O Holy One, who are and were,
>   for you have judged these things;
> 6   because they shed the blood of saints and prophets,
>   you have given them blood to drink.
> It is what they deserve!"

7 And I heard the altar respond,

> "Yes, O Sovereign God, the Almighty,
>   your judgments are true and just!"

8 The fourth angel emptied a bowl on the sun, and it was allowed to scorch them with fire; 9 they were scorched by the fierce heat, but they cursed the name of God, who had authority over these plagues, and they did not repent and give God glory.

10 The fifth angel emptied a bowl on the throne of the beast, and its dominion was plunged into the outer regions; people gnawed their tongues in agony, 11 and cursed the God of heaven because of their pains and sores, and they did not repent of their deeds.

12 The sixth angel emptied a bowl on the great river Euphrates, and its water was dried up in order to prepare the way for the rulers from the east. 13 And I saw three foul spirits like frogs coming from the mouth of the dragon, from the mouth of the beast, and from the mouth of the false prophet. 14 These are demonic spirits, performing signs, who go abroad to the rulers of the whole world, to assemble them for battle on the great day of God the Almighty. 15 ("See, I am coming like a thief! Blessed is the one who stays awake and is clothed,[n] not going about naked and exposed to shame.") 16 And they assembled them at the place that in Hebrew is called Harmagedon.

17 The seventh angel emptied a bowl into the air, and a loud voice came out of the temple, from the throne, saying, "It is done!" 18 And there came flashes of lightning, rumblings, peals of thunder, and a violent earthquake, such as had not occurred since people were upon the earth, so violent was that earthquake. 19 The great city was split into three parts, and the cities of the nations fell. God remembered great Babylon and gave it the wine-cup of the fury of God's wrath. 20 And every island fled away, and no mountains were to be found; 21 and huge hailstones, each weighing about a hundred pounds,[o] dropped from heaven on people, until they cursed God for the plague of the hail, so fearful was that plague.

---

n Gk *and keeps one's robes*   o Gk *weighing about a talent*

The Great Prostitute and the Beast

17 Then one of the seven angels who had the seven bowls came and said to me, "Come, I will show you the judgment of the great prostitute who is seated on many waters, [2] with whom the rulers of the earth have committed sexual immorality, and with the wine of whose sexual immorality the inhabitants of the earth have become drunk." [3] So the angel carried me away in the spirit[p] into a wilderness, and I saw a person sitting on a scarlet beast that was full of blasphemous names, and it had seven heads and ten horns. [4] The person was clothed in purple and scarlet, and adorned with gold and jewels and pearls, holding a golden cup full of abominations and the impurities of this one's sexual immorality; [5] and on the person's forehead was written a name, a mystery: "Babylon the great, the city that produces prostitutes and abominations of the earth." [6] And I saw that this one was drunk with the blood of the saints and the blood of the witnesses to Jesus.

When I saw this, I was greatly amazed. [7] But the angel said to me, "Why are you so amazed? I will tell you the mystery of this person, and of the beast with seven heads and ten horns that carries this person. [8] The beast that you saw was, and is not, and is about to ascend from the bottomless pit and go to destruction. And the inhabitants of the earth, whose names have not been written in the book of life from the foundation of the world, will be amazed when they see the beast, because it was and is not and is to come.

[9] "This calls for a mind that has wisdom: the seven heads are seven mountains on which this one is seated; also, they are seven rulers, [10] of whom five have fallen, one is living, and the other has not yet come; and when the other one comes, that one must remain only a little while. [11] As for the beast that was and is not, it is an eighth but it belongs to the seven, and it goes to destruction. [12] And the ten horns that you saw are ten rulers who have not yet received a dominion, but they are to receive authority as rulers for one hour, together with the beast. [13] These are united in yielding their power and authority to the beast; [14] they will make war on the Lamb, and the Lamb will conquer them, for the Lamb is Sovereign of sovereigns and Ruler of rulers, and those with the Lamb are called and chosen and faithful."

[15] And the angel said to me, "The waters that you saw, where the prostitute is seated, are peoples and multitudes and nations and languages. [16] And the ten horns that you saw, they and the beast will hate the prostitute; they will make the prostitute desolate and naked; they will devour the flesh and burn up the body with fire. [17] For God has put it into their hearts to carry out God's purpose by agreeing to give their dominion to the beast, until the words of God will be fulfilled. [18] The prostitute you saw is the great city that rules over the rulers of the earth."

---

p Or *in the Spirit*

The Fall of Babylon

18 After this I saw another angel coming down from heaven, having great authority; and the earth was made bright with the splendor of this angel. ²This one called out with a mighty voice,

> "Fallen, fallen is Babylon the great!
>> It has become a dwelling place of demons,
>> a haunt of every foul spirit,
>> a haunt of every foul bird,
>> a haunt of every foul and hateful beast.[q]
>> For all the nations have drunk[r]
>> of the wine of the wrath of the city's fornication,
>> and the rulers of the earth have committed sexual
>>> immorality with Babylon,
>> and the merchants of the earth have grown rich from
>>> the power[s] of its luxury."

4 Then I heard another voice from heaven saying,

> "Come out of Babylon, my people,
>> so that you do not take part in its sins,
>> and so that you do not share in its plagues;
>> for the sins of Babylon are heaped high as heaven,
>> and God has remembered its iniquities.
>> Render to Babylon as Babylon itself has rendered,
>> and repay it double for its deeds;
>> mix a double draught for it in the cup it mixed.
>> As Babylon glorified itself and lived luxuriously,
>> so give it a like measure of torment and grief.
>> Since in its heart Babylon says,
>> 'I rule as a monarch;
>> I am not bereaved,
>> and I will never see grief,'
>> therefore its plagues will come in a single day—
>> pestilence and mourning and famine—
>> and the city will be burned with fire;
>> for mighty is the Sovereign God who judges
>>> Babylon."

9 And the rulers of the earth, who committed sexual immorality and lived

---

q Other ancient authorities lack the words *a haunt of every foul beast* and attach the words *and hateful* to the previous line so as to read *a haunt of every foul and hateful bird*
r Other ancient authorities read *it has made all nations drink*   s Or *resources*

in luxury with Babylon, will weep and wail over it when they see the smoke of its burning; 10 they will stand far off, in fear of its torment, and say,

> "Alas, alas, the great city,
>   Babylon, the mighty city!
> For in one hour your judgment has come."

11 And the merchants of the earth weep and mourn for the city, since no one buys their cargo anymore, 12 cargo of gold, silver, jewels and pearls, fine linen, purple, silk and scarlet, all kinds of scented wood, all articles of ivory, all articles of costly wood, bronze, iron, and marble, 13 cinnamon, spice, incense, myrrh, frankincense, wine, olive oil, choice flour and wheat, cattle and sheep, horses and chariots, servants—and human lives.[t]

14
> "The fruit for which your soul longed
>   has gone from you,
> and all your dainties and your splendor
>   are lost to you,
>   never to be found again!"

15 The merchants of these wares, who gained wealth from Babylon, will stand far off, in fear of its torment, weeping and mourning aloud,

16
> "Alas, alas, the great city,
>   clothed in fine linen,
>   in purple and scarlet,
>   adorned with gold,
>   with jewels, and with pearls!

17
> For in one hour all this wealth has been laid waste!"

And all shipmasters and seafarers, sailors and all whose trade is on the sea, stood far off 18 and cried out as they saw the smoke of Babylon burning,

> "What city was like the great city?"

19 And they threw dust on their heads, as they wept and mourned, crying out,

> "Alas, alas, the great city,
>   where all who had ships at sea
>   grew rich by its wealth!
> For in one hour the city has been laid waste."

20 Rejoice over Babylon, O heaven, you saints and apostles and prophets! For God has given judgment for you against Babylon.

21 Then a mighty angel took up a stone like a great millstone and threw it into the sea, saying,

---

t Or chariots, and human bodies and souls

"With such violence Babylon the great city
    will be thrown down,
    and will be found no more;

22 and the sound of harpists and minstrels and of flutists
        and trumpeters
    will be heard in you no more;
and an artisan of any trade
    will be found in you no more;
and the sound of the millstone
    will be heard in you no more;

23 and the light of a lamp
    will shine in you no more;
and the voice of bridegroom and bride
    will be heard in you no more;
for your merchants were the magnates of the earth,
    and all nations were deceived by your sorcery.

24 And in you[u] was found the blood of prophets and of
        saints,
    and of all who have been slaughtered on earth."

The Rejoicing in Heaven

19 After this I heard what seemed to be the loud voice of a great multitude in heaven, saying,

"Hallelujah!
Salvation and glory and power to our God,
    for God's judgments are true and just;

2 God has judged the great prostitute
    who corrupted the earth with sexual immorality,
and God has avenged on Babylon the blood of God's
    servants."

3 Once more they said,

"Hallelujah!
The smoke goes up from Babylon forever and ever."

4 And the twenty-four elders and the four living creatures fell down and worshiped God who is seated on the throne, saying,

"Amen. Hallelujah!"

5 And from the throne came a voice saying,

"Praise our God,

---

u Gk *it*

> all you God's servants,
> and all who fear God,
>   small and great."

6 Then I heard what seemed to be the voice of a great multitude, like the sound of many waters and like the sound of mighty thunderpeals, crying out,

> "Hallelujah!
> For the Sovereign our God
>   the Almighty reigns.
> 7 Let us rejoice and exult
>   and give God the glory,
> for the marriage of the Lamb has come,
>   and the betrothed of the Lamb is ready;
> 8 to that one it has been granted to be clothed
>   with fine linen, bright and pure"—

for the fine linen is the righteous deeds of the saints.

9 And the angel said to me, "Write this: Blessed are those who are invited to the marriage supper of the Lamb." And the angel said to me, "These are true words of God." 10 Then I fell down and worshiped at the angel's feet, but the angel said to me, "You must not do that! I am a servant along with you and your comrades who hold the testimony of Jesus.ᵛ Worship God! For the testimony of Jesusᵛ is the spirit of prophecy."

The Rider on the White Horse

11 Then I saw heaven opened, and there was a white horse! Its rider, who judges in righteousness and makes war, is called Faithful and True. 12 The eyes of the rider are like a flame of fire, and on the rider's head are many diadems; and the rider has a name inscribed that no one else knows. 13 The rider, whose name is called The Word of God, is clothed in a robe dipped inʷ blood. 14 And the armies of heaven, wearing fine linen, spotless and pure, were following along on white horses. 15 From the rider's mouth comes a sharp sword with which to strike down the nations. The rider will ruleˣ them with a rod of iron and will tread the winepress of the fury of the wrath of God the Almighty. 16 On the robe and thigh of the rider a name is inscribed, "Ruler of rulers and Sovereign of sovereigns."

The Beast and Its Armies Defeated

17 Then I saw an angel standing in the sun, and with a loud voice the angel called to all the birds that fly in midheaven, "Come, gather for the great supper of God, 18 to eat the flesh of rulers, the flesh of generals, the flesh of the mighty, the flesh of horses and their riders—flesh of all, both free and enslaved,

---

v Or *to Jesus*   w Other ancient authorities read *sprinkled with*   x Or *will shepherd*

both small and great." ¹⁹Then I saw the beast and the rulers of the earth with their armies gathered to make war against the rider on the horse and against the rider's army. ²⁰And the beast was captured, and with it the false prophet who had performed in its presence the signs by which that false prophet deceived those who had received the mark of the beast and those who worshiped its image. These two were thrown alive into the lake of fire that burns with sulfur. ²¹And the rest were killed by the sword of the rider on the horse, the sword that came from the rider's mouth; and all the birds were gorged with their flesh.

The Thousand Years

20 Then I saw an angel coming down from heaven, holding the key to the bottomless pit and a great chain. ²The angel seized the dragon, that ancient serpent, who is the Devil and Satan, and bound the dragon for a thousand years, ³and threw it into the pit, and locked and sealed the pit over it, so as to prevent any more deception of the nations, until the thousand years were ended. After that the dragon must be let out for a little while.

4 Then I saw thrones, and those seated on them were given authority to judge. I also saw the souls of those who had been beheaded for their testimony to Jesus[y] and for the word of God. They had not worshiped the beast or its image and had not received its mark on their foreheads or their hands. They came to life and reigned with Christ a thousand years. ⁵(The rest of the dead did not come to life until the thousand years were ended.) This is the first resurrection. ⁶Blessed and holy are those who share in the first resurrection. Over these the second death has no power, but they will be priests of God and of Christ, and they will reign with that one a thousand years.

Satan's Doom

7 When the thousand years are ended, Satan will be released from prison ⁸and will come out to deceive the nations at the four corners of the earth, Gog and Magog, in order to gather them for battle; they are as numerous as the sands of the sea. ⁹They marched up over the breadth of the earth and surrounded the camp of the saints and the beloved city. And fire came down from heaven[z] and consumed them. ¹⁰And the devil who had deceived them was thrown into the lake of fire and sulfur, where the beast and the false prophet were, and they will be tormented day and night forever and ever.

The Dead Are Judged

11 Then I saw a great white throne and the one who sat on it; the earth and the heaven fled from God's presence, and no place was found for them. ¹²And I saw the dead, great and small, standing before the throne, and books were

---

y Or *for the testimony of Jesus*
z Other ancient authorities read *from God, out of heaven,* or *out of heaven from God*

opened. Also another book was opened, the book of life. And the dead were judged according to their works, as recorded in the books. ¹³ And the sea gave up the dead that were in it, Death and Hades gave up the dead that were in them, and all were judged according to what they had done. ¹⁴ Then Death and Hades were thrown into the lake of fire. This is the second death, the lake of fire; ¹⁵ and anyone whose name was not found written in the book of life was thrown into the lake of fire.

The New Heaven and the New Earth

21 Then I saw a new heaven and a new earth; for the first heaven and the first earth had passed away, and the sea was no more. ² And I saw the holy city, the new Jerusalem, coming down out of heaven from God, prepared as a bride and bridegroom adorned for each other. ³ And I heard a loud voice from the throne saying,

> "See, the home[a] of God is among mortals.
> God will dwell[b] with them;
> they will be God's peoples,[c]
> and God will indeed will be with them;[d]
>
> 4 God will wipe every tear from their eyes.
> Death will be no more;
> mourning and crying and pain will be no more,
> for the first things have passed away."

5 And the one who was seated on the throne said, "See, I am making all things new." And this one also said, "Write this, for these words are trustworthy and true." ⁶ Then the same one said to me, "It is done! I am the Alpha and the Omega, the beginning and the end. To the thirsty I will give water as a gift from the spring of the water of life. ⁷ Those who conquer will inherit these things, and I will be their God and they will be my children. ⁸ But as for the cowardly, the faithless,[e] the polluted, the murderers, the sexually immoral, the sorcerers, the idolaters, and all liars, their place will be in the lake that burns with fire and sulfur, which is the second death."

Vision of the New Jerusalem

9 Then one of the seven angels who had the seven bowls full of the seven last plagues came and said to me, "Come, I will show you the betrothed, the one wed to the Lamb." ¹⁰ And in the spirit[f] the angel carried me away to a great, high mountain and showed me the holy city Jerusalem coming down out of heaven from God. ¹¹ It has the glory of God and a radiance like a very rare jewel, like jasper, clear as crystal. ¹² It has a great, high wall with twelve gates, and at the gates twelve angels, and on the gates are inscribed the names of the

---

a Gk *tabernacle*   b Gk *will tabernacle*   c Other ancient authorities read *people*
d Other ancient authorities add *and be their God*   e Or *the unbelieving*   f Or *in the Spirit*

twelve tribes of the Israelites; [13] on the east three gates, on the north three gates, on the south three gates, and on the west three gates. [14] And the wall of the city has twelve foundations, and on them are the twelve names of the twelve apostles of the Lamb.

15 The angel who talked to me had a measuring rod of gold to measure the city and its gates and walls. [16] The city lies foursquare, its length the same as its width; and the angel measured the city with a rod, fifteen hundred miles;[g] its length and width and height are equal. [17] The angel also measured its wall, almost seventy-five yards[h] by human measurement, which the angel was using. [18] The wall is built of jasper, while the city is pure gold, clear as glass. [19] The foundations of the wall of the city are adorned with every jewel; the first was jasper, the second sapphire, the third agate, the fourth emerald, [20] the fifth onyx, the sixth carnelian, the seventh chrysolite, the eighth beryl, the ninth topaz, the tenth chrysoprase, the eleventh jacinth, the twelfth amethyst. [21] And the twelve gates are twelve pearls, each of the gates is a single pearl, and the street of the city is pure gold, transparent as glass.

22 I saw no temple in the city, for its temple is the Sovereign God the Almighty and the Lamb. [23] And the city has no need of sun or moon to shine on it, for the glory of God is its light, and its lamp is the Lamb. [24] The nations will walk by its light, and the rulers of the earth will bring their glory into it. [25] Its gates will never be shut by day—and there will be no night there. [26] People will bring into it the glory and the honor of the nations. [27] But nothing unclean will enter it, nor anyone who practices abomination or falsehood, but only those who are written in the Lamb's book of life.

The River of Life

22 Then the angel showed me the river of the water of life, bright as crystal, flowing from the throne of God and of the Lamb [2] through the middle of the street of the city. On either side of the river is the tree of life[i] with its twelve kinds of fruit, producing its fruit each month; and the leaves of the tree are for the healing of the nations. [3] Nothing accursed will be found there any more. But the throne of God and of the Lamb will be in it, and God's servants will worship God; [4] they will see God's face, and God's name will be on their foreheads. [5] And there will be no more night; they need no light of lamp or sun, for the Sovereign God will be their light, and they will reign forever and ever.

6 And the angel said to me, "These words are trustworthy and true, for the Lord, the God of the spirits of the prophets, has sent an angel to show God's servants what must soon take place."

---

g Gk *twelve thousand stadia*   h That is, one hundred forty-four cubits
i Or *the Lamb. 2In the middle of the street of the city, and on either side of the river, is the tree of life*

7 "See, I am coming soon! Blessed is the one who keeps the words of the prophecy of this book."

Epilogue and Benediction

8 I, John, am the one who heard and saw these things. And when I heard and saw them, I fell down to worship at the feet of the angel who showed them to me; 9 but the angel said to me, "You must not do that! I am a servant along with you and your comrades the prophets, and with those who keep the words of this book. Worship God!"

10 And the angel said to me, "Do not seal up the words of the prophecy of this book, for the time is near. 11 Let the evildoer still do evil, and the filthy still be filthy, and the righteous still do right, and the holy still be holy."

12 "See, I am coming soon; my reward is with me, to repay according to everyone's work. 13 I am the Alpha and the Omega, the first and the last, the beginning and the end."

14 Blessed are those who wash their robes,ʲ so that they will have the right to the tree of life and may enter the city by the gates. 15 Outside are the dogs and sorcerers, the sexually immoral and murderers and idolaters, and everyone who loves and practices falsehood.

16 "It is I, Jesus, who sent my angel to you with this testimony for the churches. I am the root and the descendant of David, the bright morning star."

17   The Spirit and the one betrothed say, "Come."
         And let everyone who hears say, "Come."
         And let everyone who is thirsty come.
         Let anyone who wishes take the water of life as a gift.

18 I warn everyone who hears the words of the prophecy of this book: if anyone adds to them, God will add to that person the plagues described in this book; 19 if anyone takes away from the words of the book of this prophecy, God will take away that person's share in the tree of life and in the holy city, which are described in this book.

20 The one who testifies to these things says, "Surely I am coming soon." Amen. Come, Lord Jesus!

21 The grace of the Lord Jesus be with all the saints. Amen.ᵏ

---

j Other ancient authorities read *do the commandments*
k Other ancient authorities lack *all*; others lack *the saints*; others lack *Amen*

The Psalms

The Psalms

BOOK I

Psalm 1

The Two Ways

1 Blessed are those
who do not follow the advice of
the wicked,
or take the path that sinners tread,
or sit in the seat of scoffers;
2 but their delight is in the law of
GOD,
and on that law they meditate
day and night.
3 They are like trees
planted by streams of water,
which yield their fruit in its season,
and their leaves do not wither.
In all that they do, they prosper.

4 The wicked are not so,
but are like chaff that the wind
drives away.
5 Therefore the wicked will not stand
in the judgment,
nor sinners in the congregation
of the righteous;
6 for GOD watches over the way of
the righteous,

but the way of the wicked will
perish.

Psalm 2

God's Promise to God's Anointed

1 Why do the nations conspire,
and the peoples plot in vain?
2 The kings of the earth set
themselves,
and the rulers take counsel
together,
against GOD and God's anointed,
saying,
3 "Let us burst their bonds asunder,
and cast their cords from us."

4 God who sits in the heavens
laughs,
and has them in derision.
5 Then God will speak to them in
anger,
and terrify them in fury, saying,
6 "I have set my king on Zion, my
holy hill."

7 I will tell of the decree of GOD,

who said to me, "You are my
 child;
 today I have begotten
 you.
8 Ask of me, and I will make the
 nations your heritage,
 and the ends of the earth your
 possession.
9 You shall break them with a rod
 of iron,
 and dash them in pieces like a
 potter's vessel."

10 Now therefore, O kings, be wise;
 be warned, O rulers of the earth.
11 Serve GOD with awe,
 with trembling 12 kiss God's feet,[a]
 or God will be angry, and you will
 perish in the way;
 for God's wrath is quickly
 kindled.

Blessed are all who take refuge
 in God.

Psalm 3
Trust in God under Adversity

*A Psalm of David, when he fled from
his son Absalom.*

1 O GOD, how many are my foes!
 Many are rising against me;
2 many are saying to me,
 "There is no help for you[b] in
 God."   *Selah*

3 But you, O GOD, are a shield
 around me,
 my glory, and the one who lifts
 up my head.
4 I cry aloud to GOD,
 who answers me from God's
 holy hill.   *Selah*

5 I lie down and sleep;
 I wake again, for GOD sustains
 me.

6 I am not afraid of ten thousands of
 people
 who have set themselves against
 me all around.

7 Rise up, O GOD!
 Deliver me, O my God!
For you strike all my enemies on
 the cheek;
 you break the teeth of the
 wicked.

8 Deliverance belongs to GOD;
 may your blessing be on your
 people!   *Selah*

Psalm 4
Confident Plea for Deliverance
from Enemies

*To the leader: with stringed instruments.
A Psalm of David.*

1 Answer me when I call, O God of
 my right!
 You gave me room when I was
 in distress.
 Be gracious to me, and hear my
 prayer.

2 How long, you people, shall my
 honor suffer shame?
 How long will you love vain
 words, and seek after lies?
    Selah

3 But know that GOD has set apart
 the faithful as God's own.
 GOD hears when I call.

4 When you are disturbed,[c] do not
 sin;

---

a Cn: Meaning of Heb of verses 11b and 12a
is uncertain b Syr: Heb *him* c Or *are
angry*

ponder it on your beds, and be
    silent.   *Selah*
5 Offer right sacrifices,
    and put your trust in GOD.

6 There are many who say, "O that
    we might see some good!
    Let the light of your face shine
    on us, O GOD!"
7 You have put gladness in my heart
    more than when their grain and
    wine abound.

8 I will both lie down and sleep in
    peace;
    for you alone, O GOD, make me
    lie down in safety.

Psalm 5

Trust in God for Deliverance from Enemies

To the leader: for the flutes. A Psalm of David.

1 Give ear to my words, O GOD;
    give heed to my sighing.
2 Listen to the sound of my cry,
    my Sovereign and my God,
    for to you I pray.
3 O GOD, in the morning you hear
    my voice;
    in the morning I plead my case
    to you, and watch.

4 For you are not a God who
    delights in wickedness;
    evil will not sojourn with you.
5 The boastful will not stand before
    your eyes;
    you hate all evildoers.
6 You destroy those who speak lies;
    GOD abhors the bloodthirsty and
    deceitful.

7 But I, through the abundance of
    your steadfast love,

will enter your house,
I will bow down toward your holy
    temple
    in awe of you.
8 Lead me, O GOD, in your
    righteousness
    because of my enemies;
    make your way straight
    before me.

9 For there is no truth in their
    mouths;
    their hearts are destruction;
their throats are open graves;
    they flatter with their tongues.
10 Make them bear their guilt,
    O God;
    let them fall by their own
    counsels;
because of their many transgressions
    cast them out,
    for they have rebelled against
    you.

11 But let all who take refuge in you
    rejoice;
    let them ever sing for joy.
Spread your protection over them,
    so that those who love your
    name may exult in you.
12 For you bless the righteous,
    O GOD;
    you cover them with favor as
    with a shield.

Psalm 6

Prayer for Recovery from Grave Illness

To the leader: with stringed instruments; according to The Sheminith. A Psalm of David.

1 O GOD, do not rebuke me in your
    anger,

or discipline me in your wrath.

2 Be gracious to me, O GOD, for I
am languishing;
O GOD, heal me, for my bones
are shaking with terror.
3 My soul also is struck with terror,
while you, O GOD—how long?

4 Turn, O GOD, save my life;
deliver me for the sake of your
steadfast love.
5 For in death there is no
remembrance of you;
in Sheol who can give you
praise?

6 I am weary with my moaning;
every night I flood my bed with
tears;
I drench my couch with my
weeping.
7 My eyes waste away because of
grief;
they grow weak because of all
my foes.

8 Depart from me, all you workers
of evil,
for GOD has heard the sound of
my weeping.
9 GOD has heard my supplication;
GOD accepts my prayer.
10 All my enemies shall be ashamed
and struck with terror;
they shall turn back, and in a
moment be put to shame.

Psalm 7

Plea for Help against Persecutors

*A Shiggaion of David, which he sang to
GOD concerning Cush, a Benjaminite.*

1 O GOD my God, in you I take
refuge;

save me from all my pursuers
and deliver me,
2 or like a lion they will tear me
apart;
they will drag me away, with no
one to rescue.

3 O GOD my God, if I have done
this,
if there is wrong in my hands,
4 if I have repaid my ally with harm
or plundered my foe without
cause,
5 then let the enemy pursue and
overtake me,
trample my life to the ground,
and lay my soul in the dust.
Selah

6 Rise up, O GOD, in your anger;
lift yourself up against the fury
of my enemies;
awake, O my God;[d] you have
appointed a judgment.
7 Let the assembly of the peoples be
gathered around you,
and over it take your seat[e] on
high.
8 GOD judges the peoples;
judge me, O GOD, according to
my righteousness
and according to the integrity
that is in me.

9 O let the evil of the wicked come
to an end,
but establish the righteous,
you who test the minds and hearts,
O righteous God.
10 God is my shield,
who saves the upright in heart.

---

d Or *awake for me*   e Cn: Heb *return*

11 God is a righteous judge,
    and a God who has indignation
    every day.

12 If one does not repent, God will
    sharpen a sword;
    God has bent and strung the
    bow,

13 and has prepared the weapons of
    death,
    making arrows into fiery shafts.

14 See how they conceive evil,
    and are pregnant with mischief,
    and bring forth lies.

15 They make a pit, digging it out,
    and fall into the hole that they
    have made.

16 Their mischief returns upon their
    own heads,
    and on their own heads their
    violence descends.

17 I will give to GOD the thanks due
    to God's righteousness,
    and sing praise to the name of
    GOD, the Most High.

Psalm 8

Divine Majesty and Human Dignity

To the leader: according to The Gittith.
A Psalm of David.

1 O GOD, our Sovereign,
    how majestic is your name in all
    the earth!

You have set your glory above the
    heavens.
2   Out of the mouths of babes and
    infants
you have founded a bulwark
    because of your foes,
    to silence the enemy and the
    avenger.

3 When I look at your heavens, the
    work of your fingers,
    the moon and the stars that you
    have established;

4 what are human beings that you
    are mindful of them,
    mortals that you care for them?

5 Yet you have made them a little
    lower than God,[f]
    and crowned them with glory
    and honor.

6 You have given them dominion
    over the works of your hands;
    you have put all things under
    their feet,

7 all sheep and oxen,
    and also the beasts of the field,

8 the birds of the air, and the fish of
    the sea,
    whatever passes along the paths
    of the seas.

9 O GOD, our Sovereign,
    how majestic is your name in all
    the earth!

Psalm 9

God's Power and Justice

To the leader: according to Muth-labben.
A Psalm of David.

1 I will give thanks to GOD with my
    whole heart;
    I will tell of all your wonderful
    deeds.

2 I will be glad and exult in you;
    I will sing praise to your name,
    O Most High.

---

f Or *than the divine beings* or *angels*: Heb
elohim

3 When my enemies turned back,
    they stumbled and perished
        before you.
4 For you have maintained my just
        cause;
    you have sat on the throne
        giving righteous judgment.

5 You have rebuked the nations, you
        have destroyed the wicked;
    you have blotted out their name
        forever and ever.
6 The enemies have vanished in
        everlasting ruins;
    their cities you have rooted out;
    the very memory of them has
        perished.

7 But GOD sits enthroned forever,
    God's throne is established for
        judgment.
8 God judges the world with
        righteousness,
    and judges the peoples with
        equity.

9 GOD is a stronghold for the
        oppressed,
    a stronghold in times of trouble.
10 And those who know your name
        put their trust in you,
    for you, O GOD, have not
        forsaken those who seek you.

11 Sing praises to GOD, who dwells in
        Zion.
    Declare among the peoples the
        deeds of God.
12 For the one who avenges blood is
        mindful of them,
    and does not forget the cry of
        the afflicted.

13 Be gracious to me, O GOD.
    See what I suffer from those
        who hate me;
    you are the one who lifts me up

from the gates of death,
14 so that I may recount all your
        praises,
    and, in the gates of the beloved
        city of Zion,
    rejoice in your deliverance.

15 The nations have sunk in the pit
        that they made;
    in the net that they hid has their
        own foot been caught.
16 GOD has made Godself known,
        and has executed judgment;
    the wicked are snared in the
        work of their own hands.
                        Higgaion. Selah

17 The wicked shall depart to Sheol,
    all the nations that forget God.

18 For the needy shall not always be
        forgotten,
    nor the hope of the poor perish
        forever.

19 Rise up, O GOD! Do not let
        mortals prevail;
    let the nations be judged before
        you.
20 Put them in awe, O GOD;
    let the nations know that they
        are only human.   *Selah*

Psalm 10

Prayer for Deliverance from
Enemies

1 Why, O GOD, do you stand far
        off?
    Why do you hide yourself in
        times of trouble?
2 In arrogance the wicked persecute
        the poor—
    let them be caught in the
        schemes they have devised.

3 For the wicked boast of the desires
  of their heart,
    those greedy for gain curse and
    renounce GOD.
4 In the pride of their countenance
  the wicked say, "God will not
  seek it out";
    all their thoughts are, "There is
    no God."

5 Their ways prosper at all times;
    your judgments are on high, out
    of their sight;
    as for their foes, they scoff at
    them.
6 They think in their heart, "We
  shall not be moved;
    throughout all generations we
    shall not meet adversity."

7 Their mouths are filled with cursing
  and deceit and oppression;
    under their tongues are mischief
    and iniquity.
8 They sit in ambush in the villages;
    in hiding places they murder the
    innocent.

  Their eyes stealthily watch for the
  helpless;
9   they lurk in secret like a lion in
    its covert;
  they lurk that they may seize the
  poor;
    they seize the poor and drag
    them off in their net.

10 They stoop, they crouch,
    and the helpless fall by their
    might.
11 They think in their heart, "God has
  forgotten,
    and has hidden God's face, and
    will never see it."

12 Rise up, O GOD; O God, lift up
  your hand;
    do not forget the oppressed.
13 Why do the wicked renounce God,
    and say in their hearts, "You will
    not call us to account"?

14 But you do see! Indeed you note
  trouble and grief,
    that you may take it into your
    hands;
  the helpless commit themselves
  to you;
    you have been the helper of the
    orphan.

15 Break the arm of the wicked and
  evildoers;
    seek out their wickedness until
    you find none.
16 GOD rules forever and ever;
    the nations shall perish from
    God's land.

17 O GOD, you will hear the desire of
  the meek;
    you will strengthen their heart,
    you will incline your ear
18 to do justice for the orphan and
  the oppressed,
    so that those from earth may
    strike terror no more.[g]

Psalm 11

Song of Trust in God

To the leader. Of David.

1 In GOD I take refuge; how can you
  say to me,
    "Flee like a bird to the
    mountains;[h]
2 for look, the wicked bend the bow,

---

g Meaning of Heb uncertain   h Gk Syr
Jerome Tg: Heb *flee to your mountain,*
O bird

they have fitted their arrow to
　　the string,
to shoot in the dark at the
　　upright in heart.
3 If the foundations are destroyed,
　　what can the righteous do?"

4 GOD is in God's holy temple;
　　GOD's throne is in heaven.
　God's eyes behold, the gaze of
　　God examines humankind.
5 GOD tests the righteous and the
　　wicked,
　and God's soul hates the lover of
　　violence.
6 On the wicked God will rain coals
　　of fire and sulfur;
　a scorching wind shall be the
　　portion of their cup.
7 For GOD is righteous,
　and loves righteous deeds;
　　the upright shall behold the face
　　of God.

Psalm 12

Plea for Help in Evil Times

*To the leader: according to The Sheminith.
A Psalm of David.*

1 Help, O GOD, for there is no
　　longer anyone who is godly;
　the faithful have disappeared from
　　humankind.
2 They utter lies to each other;
　with flattering lips and a double
　　heart they speak.

3 May GOD cut off all flattering lips,
　the tongue that makes great
　　boasts,
4 those who say, "With our tongues
　　we will prevail;
　our lips are our own—who is
　　over us?"

5 "Because the poor are despoiled,

because the needy groan,
　I will now rise up," GOD says;
　"I will place them in the safety
　　for which they long."
6 The promises of GOD are promises
　　that are pure,
　silver refined in a furnace on the
　　ground,
　purified seven times.

7 You, O GOD, will protect us;
　you will guard us from this
　　generation forever.
8 On every side the wicked prowl,
　as vileness is exalted among
　　humankind.

Psalm 13

Prayer for Deliverance from Enemies

To the leader.　A Psalm of David.

1 How long, O GOD? Will you
　　forget me forever?
　How long will you hide your
　　face from me?
2 How long must I bear pain[i] in
　　my soul,
　and have sorrow in my heart all
　　day long?
　How long shall my enemy be
　　exalted over me?

3 Consider and answer me, O GOD
　　my God!
　Give light to my eyes, or I will
　　sleep the sleep of death,
4 and my enemy will say, "I have
　　prevailed";
　my foes will rejoice because I am
　　shaken.

5 But I trusted in your steadfast love;

---

i Syr: Heb *hold counsels*

my heart shall rejoice in your
   salvation.
6 I will sing to GOD,
   because God has dealt bountifully
      with me.

Psalm 14

Denunciation of Godlessness

To the leader. Of David.

1 Fools say in their hearts, "There is
      no God."
   They are corrupt, they do
      abominable deeds;
   there is no one who does good.

2 GOD looks down from heaven on
      humankind
   to see if there are any who are
      wise,
   who seek after God.

3 They have all gone astray, they are
      all alike perverse;
   there is no one who does good,
      no, not one.

4 Have they no knowledge, all the
      evildoers
   who eat up my people as they
      eat bread,
   and do not call upon GOD?

5 There they shall be in great terror,
      for God is with the company of
      the righteous.
6 You would confound the plans of
      the poor,
   but GOD is their refuge.

7 O that deliverance for Israel would
      come from Zion!
   When GOD restores the fortunes
      of God's people,
   Jacob will rejoice; Israel will be
      glad.

Psalm 15

Who Shall Abide in God's Sanctuary?

A Psalm of David.

1 O GOD, who may abide in your
      tent?
   Who may dwell on your holy
      hill?

2 Those who walk blamelessly, and
      do what is right,
   and speak the truth from their
      heart;
3 who do not slander with their
      tongue,
   and do no evil to their friends,
      nor take up a reproach against
      their neighbors;
4 in whose eyes the wicked are
      despised,
   but who honor those who revere
      GOD;
   who stand by their oath even to
      their hurt;
5 who do not lend money at interest,
      and do not take a bribe against
      the innocent.

Those who do these things shall
   never be moved.

Psalm 16

Song of Trust and Security in God

A Miktam of David.

1 Protect me, O God, for in you I
      take refuge.
2 I say to GOD, "You are my
      Sovereign;
   I have no good apart from
      you."ʲ

---

j Jerome Tg: Meaning of Heb uncertain

3 As for the holy ones in the land,
   they are the noble,
      in whom is all my delight.

4 Those who choose another god
   multiply their sorrows;[k]
      their drink offerings of blood I
      will not pour out
      or take their names upon my
      lips.

5 GOD is my chosen portion and my
   cup;
      you hold my lot.
6 The boundary lines have fallen for
   me in pleasant places;
      I have a goodly heritage.

7 I bless GOD who gives me counsel;
   in the night also my heart
   instructs me.
8 I keep GOD always before me;
   because God is at my side, I
   shall not be moved.

9 Therefore my heart is glad, and my
   soul rejoices;
      my body also rests secure.
10 For you do not give me up to
   Sheol,
      or let your faithful one see the
      Pit.

11 You show me the path of life.
   In your presence there is fullness
   of joy;
      in your mighty hand are
      pleasures forevermore.

Psalm 17

Prayer for Deliverance from Persecutors

A Prayer of David.

1 Hear a just cause, O GOD; attend
   to my cry;

give ear to my prayer from lips
free of deceit.
2 From you let my vindication come;
   let your eyes see the right.

3 If you try my heart, if you visit
   me by night,
      if you test me, you will find no
      wickedness in me;
      my mouth does not transgress.
4 As for what others do, by the
   word of your lips
      I have avoided the ways of the
      violent.
5 My steps have held fast to your
   paths;
      my feet have not slipped.

6 I call upon you, for you will
   answer me, O God;
      incline your ear to me, hear my
      words.
7 Wondrously show your steadfast
   love,
      O savior of those who seek
      refuge
      from their adversaries at your
      side.

8 Guard me as the apple of the eye;
   hide me in the shadow of your
   wings,
9 from the wicked who despoil me,
   my deadly enemies who
   surround me.
10 They close their hearts to pity;
   with their mouths they speak
   arrogantly.
11 They track me down;[l] now they
   surround me;
      they set their eyes to cast me to
      the ground.

---

k Cn: Meaning of Heb uncertain   l One
Ms Compare Syr: MT *Our steps*

12 They are like a lion eager to tear,
like a young lion lurking in
ambush.

13 Rise up, O GOD, confront them,
overthrow them!
By your sword deliver my life
from the wicked,
14 from mortals—by your hand,
O GOD—
from mortals whose portion in
life is in this world.
May their bellies be filled with
what you have stored up for
them;
may their children have more
than enough;
may they leave something over to
their little ones.

15 As for me, I shall behold your face
in righteousness;
when I awake I shall be satisfied,
beholding your likeness.

Psalm 18
Royal Thanksgiving for Victory

*To the leader. A Psalm of David, the
servant of GOD, who addressed the words
of this song to GOD on the day when GOD
delivered David from the hand of all his
enemies, and from the hand of Saul.
David said:*

1 I love you, O GOD, my strength.
2 GOD is my rock, my fortress, and
my deliverer,
my God, my rock in whom I
take refuge,
my shield, and the horn of my
salvation, my stronghold.
3 I call upon GOD, who is worthy to
be praised,
so I shall be saved from my
enemies.

4 The cords of death encompassed
me;
the torrents of perdition
assailed me;
5 the cords of Sheol entangled me;
the snares of death confronted
me.

6 In my distress I called upon GOD;
to my God I cried for help.
From the temple God heard my
voice,
and my cry reached God's ears.

7 Then the earth reeled and rocked;
the foundations also of the
mountains trembled
and quaked, because God was
angry.
8 Smoke went up from God's
nostrils,
and devouring fire from God's
mouth;
glowing coals flamed forth from
God.
9 God bowed the heavens, and came
down;
thick darkness was under God's
feet.
10 God rode on a cherub, and flew,
coming swiftly upon the wings of
the wind.
11 God made darkness a covering all
around,
and thick clouds dark with water
a canopy.
12 Out of the brightness before God,
hailstones and coals of fire
broke through God's clouds.
13 GOD also thundered in the heavens,
and the voice of the Most High
broke forth.ᵐ

m Gk See 2 Sam 22.14: Heb adds *hailstones
and coals of fire*

14 And God sent out arrows, and
  scattered them;
  God flashed forth lightnings, and
  routed them.
15 Then the channels of the sea were
  seen,
  and the foundations of the world
  were laid bare
  at your rebuke, O GOD,
  at the blast of the breath of your
  nostrils.
16 God reached down from on high,
  and took me;
  God drew me out of mighty
  waters.
17 God delivered me from my strong
  enemy,
  and from those who hated me;
  for they were too mighty for me.
18 They confronted me in the day of
  my calamity;
  but GOD was my support.
19 God brought me out into a broad
  place;
  and delivered me, because God
  delighted in me.

20 GOD rewarded me according to my
  righteousness;
  according to the cleanness of my
  hands God recompensed me.
21 For I have kept the ways of GOD,
  and have not wickedly departed
  from my God.
22 For all God's ordinances were
  before me,
  and God's statutes I did not put
  away from me.
23 I was blameless before God,
  and I kept myself from guilt.
24 Therefore GOD has recompensed me
  according to my righteousness,
  according to the cleanness of my
  hands in God's sight.

25 With the loyal you show yourself
  loyal;
  with the blameless you show
  yourself blameless;
26 with the pure you show yourself
  pure;
  and with the crooked you show
  yourself perverse.
27 For you deliver a humble people,
  but the haughty eyes you bring
  down.
28 It is you who light my lamp;
  GOD, my God, lights up my
  darkness.
29 By you I can crush an army,
  and by my God I can leap over
  a wall.
30 The way of this God is perfect;
  the promise of GOD proves true;
  God is a shield for all who take
  refuge there.

31 For who is God except our GOD?
  And who is a rock besides our
  God?—
32 God who girded me with strength,
  and made my way safe.
33 God made my feet like the feet of
  a deer,
  and set me secure on the heights.
34 God trains my hands for war,
  so that my arms can bend a bow
  of bronze.
35 You have given me the shield of
  your salvation,
  and your right hand has
  supported me;
  your help[n] has made me great.
36 You gave me a wide place for my
  steps under me,
  and my feet did not slip.

_____

n Or *gentleness*

37 I pursued my enemies and overtook
them;
and did not turn back until they
were consumed.
38 I struck them down, so that they
were not able to rise;
they fell under my feet.
39 For you girded me with strength
for the battle;
you made my assailants sink
under me.
40 You made my enemies turn their
backs to me,
and those who hated me I
destroyed.
41 They cried for help, but there was
no one to save them;
they cried to GOD, who did not
answer them.
42 I beat them fine, like dust before
the wind;
I cast them out like the mire of
the streets.

43 You delivered me from strife with
the peoples;o
you made me head of the
nations;
people whom I had not known
served me.
44 As soon as they heard of me they
obeyed me;
foreigners came cringing to me.
45 Foreigners lost heart,
and came trembling out of their
strongholds.

46 GOD lives! Blessed be my rock,
and exalted be the God of my
salvation,
47 the God who gave me vengeance
and subdued peoples under me;
48 who delivered me from my
enemies;

indeed, you exalted me above my
adversaries;
you delivered me from the
violent.

49 For this I will extol you, O GOD,
among the nations,
and sing praises to your name.
50 Great triumphs God gives to the
king,
and shows steadfast love to
God's anointed,
to David and his descendants
forever.

Psalm 19
God's Glory in Creation and the Law

To the leader. A Psalm of David.

1 The heavens are telling the glory of
God;
and the firmamentp proclaims
God's handiwork.
2 Day to day pours forth speech,
and night to night declares
knowledge.
3 There is no speech, nor are there
words;
their voice is not heard;
4 yet their voiceq goes out through
all the earth,
and their words to the end of
the world.

In the heavens God has set a tent
for the sun,
5 which comes out like a bridegroom
from his wedding canopy,
and like an athlete runs the
course with joy.

---

o Gk Tg: Heb *people*   p Or *dome*
q Gk Jerome Compare Syr: Heb *line*

6 Its rising is from the end of the
    heavens,
  and its circuit to the end of
    them;
  and nothing is hid from its heat.

7 The law of GOD is perfect,
    reviving the soul;
  the decrees of GOD are sure,
    making wise the simple;
8 the precepts of GOD are right,
    rejoicing the heart;
  the commandment of GOD is clear,
    enlightening the eyes;
9 the reverence of GOD is pure,
    enduring forever;
  the ordinances of GOD are true
    and righteous altogether.
10 More to be desired are they than
    gold,
      even much fine gold;
  sweeter also than honey,
    and drippings of the honeycomb.

11 Moreover by them is your servant
    warned;
  in keeping them there is great
    reward.
12 But who can detect their errors?
  Clear me from hidden faults.
13 Keep back your servant also from
    the insolent;[r]
  do not let them have dominion
    over me.
  Then I shall be blameless,
    and innocent of great
    transgression.

14 Let the words of my mouth and
    the meditation of my heart
  be acceptable to you,
    O GOD, my rock and my
    redeemer.

Psalm 20

Prayer for Victory

To the leader. A Psalm of David.

1 May GOD answer you in the day
    of trouble!
  The name of the God of Jacob
    protect you!
2 May God send you help from the
    sanctuary,
  and give you support from Zion.
3 May God remember all your
    offerings,
  and regard with favor your burnt
    sacrifices.   *Selah*

4 May God grant you your heart's
    desire,
  and fulfill all your plans.
5 May we shout for joy over your
    victory,
  and in the name of our God set
    up our banners.
  May GOD fulfill all your petitions.

6 Now I know that GOD will help
    God's anointed;
  and will answer God's anointed
    one from God's holy heaven
  with mighty victories by God's
    strong hand.
7 Some take pride in chariots, and
    some in horses,
  but our pride is in the name of
    our God, the Most High.
8 They will collapse and fall,
  but we shall rise and stand
    upright.

9 Give victory to the ruler, O GOD;
  answer us when we call.[s]

---

r Or *from proud thoughts*   s Gk: Heb *give
victory, O GOD; let the Ruler answer us when
we call*

Psalm 21

Thanksgiving for Victory

To the leader. A Psalm of David.

1 In your strength the ruler rejoices,
   O God,
   and greatly exults in your help!
2 You have satisfied the desire of the
      ruler's heart,
   and have not withheld the
      request of the ruler's lips. *Selah*
3 For with rich blessings you meet
      the ruler,
   upon whose head you set a
      crown of fine gold.
4 The ruler asked you for life; you
      gave it—
   length of days forever and ever.
5 Through your help, great is the
      glory of the ruler,
   upon whose head you bestow
      splendor and majesty.
6 You bestow on the ruler blessings
      forever,
   and gladness with the joy of
      your presence.
7 For the ruler trusts in God,
   and through the steadfast love of
      the Most High, the ruler shall
      not be moved.

8 Your hand will find out all your
      enemies;
   your mighty hand will find out
      those who hate you.
9 You will make them like a fiery
      furnace
   when you appear.
   God will swallow them up in
      anger,
   and fire will consume them.
10 You will destroy their offspring
      from the earth,
   and their children from among
      humankind.
11 If they plan evil against you,
   if they devise mischief, they will
      not succeed.
12 For you will put them to flight;
   you will aim at their faces with
      your bows.

13 Be exalted, O God, in your
      strength!
   We will sing and praise your
      power.

Psalm 22

Plea for Deliverance from Suffering and Hostility

To the leader: according to The Deer of the Dawn. A Psalm of David.

1 My God, my God, why have you
      forsaken me?
   Why are you so far from helping
      me, from the words of my
      groaning?
2 O my God, I cry by day, but you
      do not answer;
   and by night, but find no rest.

3 Yet you are holy,
   enthroned on the praises of
      Israel.
4 In you our ancestors trusted;
   they trusted, and you delivered
      them.
5 To you they cried, and were saved;
   in you they trusted, and were
      not put to shame.

6 But I am a worm, and not human;
   scorned by others, and despised
      by the people.
7 All who see me mock at me;
   they make mouths at me, they
      shake their heads;

8 "Commit your cause to GOD; let
    God deliver—
    let God rescue the one in whom
    God delights!"

9 Yet it was you who took me from
    the womb;
    you kept me safe on my
    mother's breast.

10 On you I was cast from my birth,
    and since my mother bore me
    you have been my God.

11 Do not be far from me,
    for trouble is near
    and there is no one to help.

12 Many bulls encircle me,
    strong bulls of Bashan surround
    me;

13 they open wide their mouths at me,
    like a ravening and roaring lion.

14 I am poured out like water,
    and all my bones are out of
    joint;
    my heart is like wax;
    it is melted within my breast;

15 my mouth[t] is dried up like a
    potsherd,
    and my tongue sticks to my
    jaws;
    you lay me in the dust of death.

16 For dogs are all around me;
    a company of evildoers
    encircles me.
    My hands and feet have shriveled;[u]

17 I can count all my bones.
    They stare and gloat over me;

18 they divide my clothes among
    themselves,
    and for my clothing they cast
    lots.

19 But you, O GOD, do not be far
    away!
    O my help, come quickly to
    my aid!

20 Deliver my soul from the sword,
    my life[v] from the power of the
    dog!

21 Save me from the mouth of the
    lion!

    From the horns of the wild oxen
    you have rescued[w] me.

22 I will tell of your name to my
    brothers and sisters;
    in the midst of the congregation
    I will praise you:

23 You who revere GOD, give praise!
    All you offspring of Jacob,
    Rachel and Leah, glorify God;
    stand in awe of God, all you
    offspring of Israel!

24 For God did not despise or abhor
    the affliction of the afflicted,
    and did not hide God's face from
    me,
    but heard me when I cried to
    God.

25 From you comes my praise in the
    great congregation;
    my vows I will pay before those
    who revere God.

26 The poor[x] shall eat and be
    satisfied;
    those who seek God shall give
    praise.
    May your hearts live forever!

27 All the ends of the earth shall
    remember
    and turn to GOD;
    and all the families of the nations
    shall worship before God.[y]

---

t Cn: Heb *strength*   u Meaning of Heb
uncertain   v Heb *my only one*
w Heb *answered*   x Or *afflicted*
y Gk Syr Jerome: Heb *you*

28 For dominion belongs to GOD,
     who rules over the nations.

29 To God,[z] indeed, shall all who
     sleep in[a] the earth bow down;
     before God shall bow all who go
     down to the dust,
     and I shall live for God.[b]
30 Posterity will serve God;
     future generations will be told
     about God,
31 and[c] proclaim God's deliverance to
     a people yet unborn,
     saying that God has done it.

Psalm 23

The Divine Shepherd

A Psalm of David.

1 GOD is my shepherd, I shall not
     want.
2   God makes me lie down in green
     pastures,
  and leads me beside still waters;[d]
3   God restores my soul.[e]
  God leads me in paths of
     righteousness[f]
  for the sake of God's name.

4 Even though I walk through the
     valley of the shadow of death,
     I fear no evil;
  for you are with me;
     your rod and your staff—
     they comfort me.

5 You prepare a table before me
     in the presence of my enemies;
  you anoint my head with oil;
     my cup overflows.
6 Surely[g] goodness and mercy[h] shall
     follow me
     all the days of my life,
  and I shall dwell in the house of
     GOD
     my whole life long.[i]

Psalm 24

Entrance into the Temple

Of David. A Psalm.

1 The earth is GOD's and all that is
     in it,
     the world, and those who live in
     it;
2 for God has founded it on the
     seas,
     and established it on the rivers.

3 Who shall ascend the hill of GOD?
     And who shall stand in God's
     holy place?
4 Those who have clean hands and
     pure hearts,
     who do not lift up their souls to
     what is false,
     and do not swear deceitfully.
5 They will receive blessing from
     GOD,
     and vindication from the God of
     their salvation.
6 Such is the company of those who
     seek God,
     who seek the face of the God of
     Jacob.[j]   *Selah*

7 Lift up your heads, O gates!
     and be lifted up, O ancient
     doors!
     that the Ruler of glory may
     come in.

---

z Cn: Heb *They have eaten and*
a Cn: Heb *all the fat ones*   b Compare
Gk Syr Vg: Heb *and any who cannot keep
themselves alive*   c Compare Gk: Heb *it
will be told about God to the generation,
31they will come and*   d Heb *waters of rest*
e Or *life*   f Or *right paths*   g Or *Only*
h Or *kindness*   i Heb *for length of days*
j Gk Syr: Heb *your face, O Jacob*

8 Who is the Ruler of glory?
   GOD, strong and mighty,
   GOD, mighty in battle.
9 Lift up your heads, O gates!
   and be lifted up, O ancient
      doors!
   that the Ruler of glory may
      come in.
10 Who is this Ruler of glory?
   The GOD of hosts,
   God is the Ruler of glory. *Selah*

Psalm 25

Prayer for Guidance and for Deliverance

Of David.

1 To you, O GOD, I lift up my soul.
2 O my God, in you I trust;
   do not let me be put to shame;
   do not let my enemies exult
      over me.
3 Do not let those who wait for you
      be put to shame;
   let them be ashamed who are
      wantonly treacherous.

4 Make me to know your ways,
   O GOD;
   teach me your paths.
5 Lead me in your truth, and teach
      me,
   for you are the God of my
      salvation;
   for you I wait all day long.

6 Be mindful of your mercy, O GOD,
   and of your steadfast love,
   for they have been from of old.
7 Do not remember the sins of my
      youth or my transgressions;
   according to your steadfast love
   remember me,
   for your goodness' sake, O GOD!

8 Good and upright is GOD;
   therefore God instructs sinners in
      the way.
9 God leads the humble in what is
      right,
   and teaches the humble God's
      way.
10 All the paths of GOD are steadfast
      love and faithfulness,
   for those who keep God's
      covenant and decrees.

11 For your name's sake, O GOD,
   pardon my guilt, for it is great.
12 Who are they that revere GOD?
   God will teach them the way
      that they should choose.

13 They will abide in prosperity,
   and their children shall possess
      the land.
14 The friendship of GOD is for those
      who revere God,
   who makes the covenant known
      to them.
15 My eyes are ever toward GOD,
   who will pluck my feet out of
      the net.

16 Turn to me and be gracious to me,
   for I am lonely and afflicted.
17 Relieve the troubles of my heart,
   and bring me[k] out of my
      distress.
18 Consider my affliction and my
      trouble,
   and forgive all my sins.

19 Consider how many are my foes,
   and with what violent hatred
      they hate me.
20 O guard my life, and deliver me;

---

k Or *The troubles of my heart are enlarged;*
bring me

do not let me be put to shame,
for I take refuge in you.
21 May integrity and uprightness
preserve me,
for I wait for you.

22 Redeem Israel, O God,
out of all its troubles.

Psalm 26

Plea for Justice and Declaration of Righteousness

Of David.

1 Vindicate me, O GOD,
for I have walked in my
integrity,
and I have trusted in GOD
without wavering.
2 Prove me, O GOD, and try me;
test my heart and mind.
3 For your steadfast love is before
my eyes,
and I walk in faithfulness to
you.¹

4 I do not sit with the worthless,
nor do I consort with hypocrites;
5 I hate the company of evildoers,
and will not sit with the wicked.

6 I wash my hands in innocence,
and go around your altar,
O GOD,
7 singing aloud a song of
thanksgiving,
and telling all your wondrous
deeds.

8 O GOD, I love the house in which
you dwell,
and the place where your glory
abides.
9 Do not sweep me away with
sinners,
nor my life with the bloodthirsty,

10 those in whose hands are evil
devices,
and whose strong hands are full
of bribes.

11 But as for me, I walk in my
integrity;
redeem me, and be gracious
to me.
12 My foot stands on level ground;
in the great congregation I will
bless my GOD.

Psalm 27

Triumphant Song of Confidence

Of David.

1 GOD is my light and my salvation;
whom shall I fear?
GOD is the strongholdᵐ of my life;
of whom shall I be afraid?

2 When evildoers assail me
to devour my flesh—
my adversaries and foes—
they shall stumble and fall.

3 Though an army encamp against
me,
my heart shall not fear;
though war rise up against me,
yet I will be confident.

4 One thing I asked of GOD,
that will I seek after:
to live in GOD's house
all the days of my life,
to behold GOD's beauty,
and to inquire in God's temple.

5 For God will shelter me
in the day of trouble,
and will conceal me under the
cover of God's tent;

---

l Or *in your faithfulness*   m Or *refuge*

God will set me high on a rock.

6 Now my head is lifted up
    above my enemies all around me,
and I will offer in God's tent
    sacrifices with shouts of joy;
I will sing and make melody to
    God.

7 Hear, O God, when I cry aloud,
    be gracious to me and answer
    me!
8 "Come," my heart says, "seek
    God's face!"
Your face, God, do I seek.
9   Do not hide your face from me.

Do not turn your servant away in
    anger,
    you who have been my help.
Do not cast me off, do not
    forsake me,
    O God of my salvation!
10 If my father and mother forsake
    me,
    God will take me up.

11 Teach me your way, O God,
    and lead me on a level path
    because of my enemies.
12 Do not give me up to the will of
    my adversaries,
    for false witnesses have risen
    against me,
    and they are breathing out
    violence.

13 I believe that I shall see the
    goodness of God
    in the land of the living.
14 Wait for God;
    be strong, and let your heart take
    courage;
    wait for God!

Psalm 28
Prayer for Help and
Thanksgiving for It

Of David.

1 To you, O God, I call;
    my rock, do not refuse to
    hear me,
for if you are silent to me,
    I shall be like those who go
    down to the Pit.
2 Hear the voice of my supplication,
    as I cry to you for help,
as I lift up my hands
    toward your most holy
    sanctuary.[n]

3 Do not drag me away with the
    wicked,
    with those who are workers
    of evil,
who speak peace with their
    neighbors,
    while mischief is in their hearts.
4 Repay them according to their
    work,
    and according to the evil of their
    deeds;
repay them according to the work
    of their hands;
    render them their due reward.
5 Because they do not regard the
    works of God,
    or the work of God's hands,
God will break them down and
    build them up no more.

6 Blessed be God,
    who has heard the sound of my
    pleadings.
7 God is my strength and my shield,

---

n Heb *your innermost sanctuary*

the one in whom my heart
trusts;
so I am helped, and my heart
exults,
and with my song I give thanks
to God.

8 GOD is the strength of God's
people,
the saving refuge of God's
anointed.
9 O save your people, and bless your
heritage;
be their shepherd, and carry them
forever.

Psalm 29

The Voice of God in a Great Storm

A Psalm of David.

1 Ascribe to the LORD,[o] O heavenly
beings,
ascribe to the LORD glory and
strength.
2 Ascribe to the LORD the glory of
that name;
worship the LORD in holy
splendor.

3 The voice of GOD is over the
waters;
the God of glory thunders,
GOD, over mighty waters.
4 The voice of GOD is powerful;
the voice of GOD is full of
majesty.

5 The voice of GOD breaks the
cedars;
GOD breaks the cedars of
Lebanon,
6 making Lebanon skip like a calf,
and Sirion like a young wild ox.
7 The voice of GOD flashes forth
flames of fire.
8 The voice of GOD shakes the
wilderness;
GOD shakes the wilderness of
Kadesh.

9 The voice of GOD causes the oaks
to whirl,[p]
and strips the forest bare;
and in the temple of God all say,
"Glory!"

10 The LORD sits enthroned over the
flood;
the LORD sits enthroned as ruler
forever.
11 May the LORD give strength to the
people!
May the LORD bless the people
with peace!

Psalm 30

Thanksgiving for Recovery from Grave Illness

A Psalm. A Song at the dedication of the temple. Of David.

1 I will extol you, O GOD, for you
have drawn me up,
and did not let my foes rejoice
over me.
2 O GOD my God, I cried to you
for help,
and you have healed me.
3 O GOD, you brought up my soul
from Sheol,
restored me to life from among
those gone down to the Pit.[q]

---

o *LORD* has been retained in vs 1, 2, 10, 11 to preserve the parallel with a Canaanite hymn to Baal. p Or *causes the deer to calve* q Or *that I should not go down to the Pit*

4 Sing praises to GOD, O you faithful
    ones,
  and give thanks to God's holy
    name.
5 For God's anger is but for a
    moment;
  God's favor is for a lifetime.
  Weeping may linger for the night,
    but joy comes with the morning.

6 As for me, I said in my prosperity,
    "I shall never be moved."
7 By your favor, O GOD,
    you had established me as a
      strong mountain;
  you hid your face;
    I was dismayed.

8 To you, O GOD, I cried,
    and to GOD I made supplication:
9 "What profit is there in my death,
    if I go down to the Pit?
  Will the dust praise you?
    Will it tell of your faithfulness?
10 Hear, O GOD, and be gracious to
    me!
  O GOD, be my helper!"

11 You have turned my mourning into
    dancing;
  you have taken off my sackcloth
    and clothed me with joy,
12 so that my soul[r] may praise you
    and not be silent.
  O GOD my God, I will give
    thanks to you forever.

Psalm 31

Prayer and Praise for Deliverance from Enemies

To the leader. A Psalm of David.

1 In you, O GOD, I seek refuge;
    do not let me ever be put to
      shame;
  in your righteousness deliver me.
2 Incline your ear to me;
    rescue me speedily.
  Be a rock of refuge for me,
    a strong fortress to save me.

3 You are indeed my rock and my
    fortress;
  for your name's sake lead me
    and guide me,
4 take me out of the net that is
    hidden for me,
  for you are my refuge.
5 Into your hand I commit my spirit;
    you have redeemed me, O GOD,
      faithful God.

6 You hate[s] those who pay regard to
    worthless idols,
  but I trust in GOD.
7 I will exult and rejoice in your
    steadfast love,
  because you have seen my
    affliction;
  you have taken heed of my
    adversities,
8 and have not delivered me into the
    hand of the enemy;
  you have set my feet in a broad
    place.

9 Be gracious to me, O GOD, for I
    am in distress;
  my eye wastes away from grief,
    my soul and body also.
10 For my life is spent with sorrow,
    and my years with sighing;
  my strength fails because of my
    misery,[t]
    and my bones waste away.

---

r Heb *that glory*   s One Heb Ms Gk Syr
Jerome: MT *I hate*   t Gk Syr: Heb *my*
iniquity

11 I am the scorn of all my
    adversaries,
    a horror[u] to my neighbors,
an object of dread to my
    acquaintances;
    those who see me in the street
    flee from me.
12 I have passed out of mind like one
    who is dead;
    I have become like a broken
    vessel.
13 For I hear the whispering of
    many—
    terror all around!—
as they scheme together against me,
    as they plot to take my life.
14 But I trust in you, O GOD;
    I say, "You are my God."
15 My times are in your hand;
    deliver me from the hand of my
    enemies and persecutors.
16 Let your face shine upon your
    servant;
    save me in your steadfast love.
17 Do not let me be put to shame,
    O GOD,
    for I call on you;
let the wicked be put to shame;
    let them go dumbfounded to
    Sheol.
18 Let the lying lips be stilled
    that speak insolently against the
    righteous
    with pride and contempt.

19 O how abundant is your goodness
    that you have laid up for those
    who are in awe of you,
and accomplished for those who
    take refuge in you,
    in the sight of everyone!
20 In the shelter of your presence you
    hide them
    from human plots;

you hold them safe under your
    shelter
    from contentious tongues.

21 Blessed be GOD,
    who has wondrously shown
    steadfast love to me
    when I was beset as a city under
    siege.
22 I had said in my alarm,
    "I am driven far[v] from your
    sight."
But you heard my supplications
    when I cried out to you for
    help.

23 Love GOD, all you saints of God.
    GOD preserves the faithful,
    but abundantly repays the one
    who acts haughtily.
24 Be strong, and let your heart take
    courage,
    all you who wait for GOD.

Psalm 32
The Joy of Forgiveness
Of David. A Maskil.

1 Blessed are those whose
    transgression is forgiven,
    whose sin is covered.
2 Blessed are those to whom GOD
    imputes no iniquity,
    and in whose spirit there is no
    deceit.

3 While I kept silence, my body
    wasted away
    through my groaning all day
    long.
4 For day and night your hand was
    heavy upon me;

---

u Cn: Heb *exceedingly*   v Another reading
is *cut off*

my strength was dried up[w] as by
  the heat of summer.   *Selah*

5 Then I acknowledged my sin to
    you,
  and I did not hide my iniquity;
  I said, "I will confess my
    transgressions to GOD,"
  and you forgave the guilt of
    my sin.   *Selah*

6 Therefore let all who are faithful
    offer prayer to you;
  at a time of distress,[x] the rush of
    mighty waters
  shall not reach them.
7 You are a hiding place for me;
  you preserve me from trouble;
  you surround me with glad cries
    of deliverance.   *Selah*

8 I will instruct you and teach you
    the way you should go;
  I will counsel you with my eye
    upon you.
9 Do not be like a horse or a mule,
    without understanding,
  whose temper must be curbed
    with bit and bridle,
  else it will not stay near you.

10 Many are the torments of the
    wicked,
  but steadfast love surrounds those
    who trust in GOD.
11 Be glad in GOD and rejoice,
    O righteous,
  and shout for joy, all you
    upright in heart.

Psalm 33

The Greatness and Goodness of
God

1 Rejoice in GOD, O you righteous.
  Praise befits the upright.

2 Praise GOD with the lyre;
  make melody with the harp of
    ten strings.
3 Sing to God a new song;
  play skillfully on the strings, with
    loud shouts.

4 For the word of GOD is upright,
  and all God's work is done in
    faithfulness.
5 God loves righteousness and justice;
  the earth is full of the steadfast
    love of GOD.

6 By the word of GOD the heavens
    were made,
  and all their host by the breath
    of God's mouth.
7 God gathered the waters of the sea
    as in a bottle,
  and put the deeps in storehouses.

8 Let all the earth revere GOD;
  let all the inhabitants of the
    world stand in awe.
9 For God spoke, and it came to be;
  God commanded, and it stood
    firm.

10 GOD brings the counsel of the
    nations to nothing,
  and frustrates the plans of the
    peoples.
11 The counsel of GOD stands forever,
  the thoughts of God's heart to
    all generations.
12 Blessed is the nation whose God is
    the Most High,
  the people whom God has
    chosen as a heritage.

13 GOD looks down from heaven,
  and sees all humankind.

---

w Meaning of Heb uncertain   x Cn: Heb
at a time of finding only

14 From where God sits enthroned
  God watches
  all the inhabitants of the earth—
15 God who fashions the hearts of
  them all,
  and observes all their deeds.
16 A ruler is not saved by a great
  army;
  a warrior is not delivered by
  great strength.
17 The war horse is a vain hope for
  victory,
  and by its great might it cannot
  save.

18 Truly the eye of GOD is on those
  who revere God,
  on those who hope in God's
  steadfast love,
19 to deliver their soul from death,
  and to keep them alive in famine.

20 Our soul waits for GOD,
  who is our help and shield.
21 Our heart is glad in God,
  because we trust in God's holy
  name.
22 Let your steadfast love, O GOD, be
  upon us,
  even as we hope in you.

Psalm 34

Praise for Deliverance from Trouble

*Of David, when he feigned madness before
Abimelech, so that he drove him out, and
he went away.*

1 I will bless GOD at all times;
  God's praise shall continually be
  in my mouth.
2 My soul makes its boast in GOD;
  let the humble hear and be glad.
3 O magnify GOD with me,
  and let us exalt God's name
  together.

4 I sought GOD, who answered me,
  and delivered me from all my
  fears.
5 Look to God, and be radiant;
  so your[y] faces shall never be
  ashamed.
6 This poor soul cried, and was
  heard by GOD,
  and was saved from every
  trouble.
7 The angel of GOD encamps
  around those who revere God,
  and delivers them.
8 O taste and see that GOD is good;
  happy are those who take refuge
  in God.
9 Be in awe of the Most High, you
  holy ones of God,
  for those who revere God have
  no want.
10 The young lions suffer want and
  hunger,
  but those who seek GOD lack no
  good thing.
11 Come, O children, listen to me;
  I will teach you to revere GOD.
12 Which of you desires life,
  and covets many days to enjoy
  good?
13 Keep your tongue from evil,
  and your lips from speaking
  deceit.
14 Depart from evil, and do good;
  seek peace, and pursue it.

15 The eyes of GOD are on the
  righteous,
  and God's ears are open to their
  cry.

---

y Gk Syr Jerome: Heb *their*

16 The face of GOD is against
      evildoers,
    to cut off the remembrance of
      them from the earth.
17 When the righteous cry for help,
      GOD hears,
    and rescues them from all their
      troubles.
18 GOD is near to the brokenhearted,
    and saves the crushed in spirit.

19 Many are the afflictions of the
      righteous,
    but GOD rescues them from them
      all.
20 God keeps all their bones;
    not one of them will be broken.
21 Evil brings death to the wicked,
    and those who hate the righteous
      will be condemned.
22 GOD redeems the life of God's
      servants;
    none of those who take refuge in
      God will be condemned.

Psalm 35

Prayer for Deliverance from
Enemies

Of David.

1 Contend, O GOD, with those who
      contend with me;
    fight against those who fight
      against me!
2 Take hold of shield and buckler,
    and rise up to help me!
3 Draw the spear and javelin
      against my pursuers;
    say to my soul,
      "I am your salvation."

4 Let them be put to shame and
      dishonor
    who seek after my life.

Let them be turned back and
  confounded
who devise evil against me.
5 Let them be like chaff before the
    wind,
  with the angel of GOD driving
    them on.
6 Let their way be dark and slippery,
    with the angel of GOD pursuing
      them.

7 For without cause they hid their
      net[z] for me;
    without cause they dug a pit[a]
      for my life.
8 Let ruin come on them unawares.
  And let the net that they hid
      ensnare them;
    let them fall in it—to their ruin.

9 Then my soul shall rejoice in the
      LORD,
    exulting in God's deliverance.
10 All my bones shall say,
      "O LORD, who is like you?
  You deliver the weak
      from those too strong for them,
    the weak and needy from those
      who despoil them."

11 Malicious witnesses rise up;
    they ask me about things I do
      not know.
12 They repay me evil for good;
    my soul is forlorn.
13 But as for me, when they were
      sick,
    I wore sackcloth;
    I afflicted myself with fasting.
  I prayed with head bowed[b] on my
      bosom,

---

z Heb *a pit, their net*   a The word *pit* is
transposed from the preceding line
b Or *My prayer turned back*

438

14 as though I grieved for a friend
or a brother;
I went about as one who laments
for a mother,
bowed down and in mourning.

15 But at my stumbling they gathered
in glee,
they gathered together against me;
ruffians whom I did not know
tore at me without ceasing;
16 they impiously mocked more and
more,[c]
gnashing at me with their teeth.

17 How long, O GOD, will you look
on?
Rescue me from their ravages,
my life from the lions!
18 Then I will thank you in the great
congregation;
in the mighty throng I will
praise you.

19 Do not let my treacherous enemies
rejoice over me,
or those who hate me without
cause wink the eye.
20 For they do not speak peace,
but they conceive deceitful words
against those who are quiet in
the land.
21 They open wide their mouths
against me;
they say, "Aha, Aha,
our eyes have seen it."

22 You have seen, O GOD; do not be
silent!
O God, do not be far from me!
23 Wake up! Bestir yourself for my
defense,
for my cause, my God and my
Sovereign!
24 Vindicate me, O GOD, my God,
according to your righteousness,

and do not let them rejoice
over me.
25 Do not let them say to themselves,
"Aha, we have our heart's
desire."
Do not let them say, "We have
swallowed you[d] up."

26 Let all those who rejoice at my
calamity
be put to shame and confusion;
let those who exalt themselves
against me
be clothed with shame and
dishonor.

27 Let those who desire my
vindication
shout for joy and be glad,
and say evermore,
"Great is GOD,
who delights in the welfare of
God's servant."
28 Then my tongue shall tell of your
righteousness
and of your praise all day long.

Psalm 36

Human Wickedness and Divine Goodness

To the leader. Of David, the servant of GOD.

1 Transgression speaks to the wicked
deep in their hearts;
there is no reverence for God
before their eyes.
2 For they flatter themselves in their
own eyes
that their iniquity cannot be
found out and hated.

---

c Cn Compare Gk: Heb *like the profanest of mockers of a cake*   d Heb *that one*

3 The words of their mouths are
    mischief and deceit;
   they have ceased to act wisely
    and do good.
4 They plot mischief while on their
    beds;
   they are set on a way that is
    not good;
   they do not reject evil.

5 Your steadfast love, O GOD,
    extends to the heavens,
   your faithfulness to the clouds.
6 Your righteousness is like the
    mighty mountains,
   your judgments are like the great
    deep;
   you save humans and animals
    alike, O GOD.

7 How precious is your steadfast
    love, O God!
   All people may take refuge in
    the shadow of your wings.
8 They feast on the abundance of
    your house,
   and you give them drink from
    the river of your delights.
9 For with you is the fountain of
    life;
   in your light we see light.

10 O continue your steadfast love to
    those who know you,
   and your salvation to the upright
    of heart!
11 Do not let the foot of the arrogant
    tread on me,
   or the hand of the wicked drive
    me away.
12 There the evildoers lie prostrate;
   they are thrust down, unable
    to rise.

Psalm 37

Exhortation to Patience and Trust

Of David.

1 Do not fret because of the wicked;
   do not be envious of wrongdoers,
2 for they will soon fade like the
    grass,
   and wither like the green herb.

3 Trust in GOD, and do good;
   so you will live in the land, and
    enjoy security.
4 Take delight in GOD;
   God will give you the desires of
    your heart.

5 Commit your way to GOD;
   trust in God, and God will act.
6 God will make your vindication
    shine like the light,
   and the justice of your cause like
    the noonday.

7 Be still before GOD, and wait
    patiently for God;
   do not fret over those who
    prosper in their way,
   over those who carry out evil
    devices.

8 Refrain from anger, and forsake
    wrath.
   Do not fret—it leads only to
    evil.
9 For the wicked shall be cut off,
   but those who wait for GOD
    shall inherit the land.

10 Yet a little while, and the wicked
    will be no more;
   though you look diligently for
    their place, they will not
    be there.
11 But the meek shall inherit the land,

and delight themselves in
abundant prosperity.

12 The wicked plot against the
righteous,
and gnash their teeth at them;
13 but GOD laughs at the wicked,
and sees that their day is coming.

14 The wicked draw the sword and
bend their bows
to bring down the poor and
needy,
to kill those who walk uprightly;
15 their sword shall enter their own
heart,
and their bows shall be broken.

16 Better is a little that the righteous
person has
than the abundance of many
wicked.
17 For the arms of the wicked shall
be broken,
but GOD upholds the righteous.

18 GOD knows the days of the
blameless,
and their heritage will abide
forever;
19 they are not put to shame in evil
times,
in the days of famine they have
abundance.

20 But the wicked perish,
and the enemies of GOD are like
the glory of the pastures;
they vanish—like smoke they
vanish away.

21 The wicked borrow, and do not
pay back,
but the righteous are generous
and keep giving;
22 for those blessed by GOD shall
inherit the land,

but those cursed by God shall be
cut off.

23 Our steps[e] are made firm by GOD,
when God delights in our[f] way;
24 though we stumble,[g] we[h] shall not
fall headlong,
for GOD holds us[i] by the hand.

25 I have been young, and now am
old,
yet I have not seen the righteous
forsaken
or their children begging bread.
26 They are ever giving liberally and
lending,
and their children become a
blessing.

27 Depart from evil, and do good;
so you shall abide forever.
28 For GOD loves justice,
and will not forsake God's
faithful ones.

The righteous shall be kept safe
forever,
but the children of the wicked
shall be cut off.
29 The righteous shall inherit the land,
and live in it forever.

30 The mouths of the righteous utter
wisdom,
and their tongues speak justice.
31 The law of their God is in their
hearts;
their steps do not slip.

32 The wicked watch for the
righteous,
and seek to kill them.

---

e Heb *People's steps*   f Heb *their*
g Heb *they stumble*   h Heb *they*
i Heb *them*

33 GOD will not abandon them to
their power,
or let them be condemned when
they are brought to trial.

34 Wait for GOD, and keep to God's
way,
and God will exalt you to inherit
the land;
you will look on the destruction
of the wicked.

35 I have seen the wicked oppressing,
and towering like a cedar of
Lebanon.ʲ
36 Again Iᵏ passed by, and they were
no more;
though I sought them, they could
not be found.

37 Mark the blameless, and behold the
upright,
for there is posterity for the
peaceable.
38 But transgressors shall be altogether
destroyed;
the posterity of the wicked shall
be cut off.

39 The salvation of the righteous is
from GOD;
God is their refuge in the time
of trouble.
40 GOD helps them and rescues them;
God rescues them from the
wicked, and saves them,
because they take refuge in God.

Psalm 38

A Penitent Sufferer's Plea for Healing

A Psalm of David, for the memorial offering.

1 O GOD, do not rebuke me in your
anger,

or discipline me in your wrath.
2 For your arrows have sunk into
me,
and your hand has come down
on me.

3 There is no soundness in my flesh
because of your indignation;
there is no health in my bones
because of my sin.
4 For my iniquities have gone over
my head;
they weigh like a burden too
heavy for me.

5 My wounds grow foul and fester
because of my foolishness;
6 I am utterly bowed down and
prostrate;
all day long I go around
mourning.
7 For my loins are filled with
burning,
and there is no soundness in my
flesh.
8 I am utterly spent and crushed;
I groan because of the tumult of
my heart.

9 O God, all my longing is known
to you;
my sighing is not hidden from
you.
10 My heart throbs, my strength
fails me;
as for the light of my eyes—it
also has gone from me.
11 My friends and companions stand
aloof from my affliction,
and my neighbors stand far off.

---

j Gk: Meaning of Heb uncertain   k Gk Syr
Jerome: Heb *that one*

12 Those who seek my life lay their
     snares;
   those who seek to hurt me speak
     of ruin,
   and meditate treachery all day
     long.

13 But I am like those who are deaf,
     I do not hear;
   like those who are mute, who
     cannot speak.
14 Truly, I am like one who does not
     hear,
   and in whose mouth is no retort.

15 But it is for you, O GOD, that I
     wait;
   it is you, O God my God, who
     will answer.
16 For I pray, "Only do not let them
     rejoice over me,
   those who boast against me when
     my foot slips."

17 For I am ready to fall,
   and my pain is ever with me.
18 I confess my iniquity;
   I am sorry for my sin.
19 Those who are my foes without
     cause[1] are mighty,
   and many are those who hate me
     wrongfully.
20 Those who render me evil for
     good
   are my adversaries because I
     follow after good.

21 Do not forsake me, O GOD;
   O my God, do not be far from
     me;
22 make haste to help me,
   O God, my salvation.

Psalm 39
Prayer for Wisdom and Forgiveness

To the leader: to Jeduthun. A Psalm of David.

1 I said, "I will guard my ways
     that I may not sin with my
       tongue;
   I will keep a muzzle on my mouth
     as long as the wicked are in my
       presence."
2 I was silent and still;
   I held my peace to no avail;
 my distress grew worse,
3   my heart became hot within me.
 While I mused, the fire burned;
   then I spoke with my tongue:

4 "O GOD, let me know my end,
     and what is the measure of my
       days;
   let me know how fleeting my
     life is.
5 You have made my days a few
     handbreadths,
   and my lifetime is as nothing in
     your sight.
 Surely everyone stands as a mere
     breath.   *Selah*
6   Surely everyone goes about like a
     shadow.
 Surely for nothing they are in
     turmoil;
   they heap up, and do not know
     who will gather.

7 "And now, O God, what do I wait
     for?
   My hope is in you.
8 Deliver me from all my
     transgressions.

---

1 Q Ms: MT *my living foes*

Do not make me the scorn of
    the fool.
9 I am silent; I do not open my
    mouth,
    for it is you who have done it.
10 Remove your stroke from me;
    I am worn down by the blows[m]
    of your hand.

11 "You chastise mortals
    in punishment for sin,
    consuming like a moth what is dear
    to them;
    surely everyone is a mere breath.
                  Selah

12 "Hear my prayer, O GOD,
    and give ear to my cry;
    do not hold your peace at my
    tears.
    For I am your passing guest,
    an alien, like all my forebears.
13 Turn your gaze away from me,
    that I may smile again,
    before I depart and am no
    more."

Psalm 40

Thanksgiving for Deliverance and Prayer for Help

To the leader. Of David. A Psalm.

1 I waited patiently for GOD;
    God inclined to me and heard
    my cry.
2 God drew me up from the desolate
    pit,[n]
    out of the miry bog,
    and set my feet upon a rock,
    making my steps secure.
3 God put a new song in my mouth,
    a song of praise to our God.
    Many will see and be in awe,
    and put their trust in GOD.

4 Blessed are those who put
    their trust in GOD,
    who do not turn to the proud,
    to those who go astray after false
    gods.
5 You have multiplied, O GOD my
    God,
    your wondrous deeds and your
    thoughts toward us;
    none can compare with you.
    Were I to proclaim and tell of
    them,
    they would be more than can be
    counted.

6 Sacrifice and offering you do not
    desire,
    but you have given me an open
    ear.[o]
    Burnt offering and sin offering
    you have not required.
7 Then I said, "Here I am;
    in the scroll of the book it is
    written of me.[p]
8 I delight to do your will, O my
    God;
    your law is within my heart."

9 I have told the glad news of
    deliverance
    in the great congregation;
    see, I have not restrained my lips,
    as you know, O GOD.
10 I have not hidden your saving help
    within my heart,
    I have spoken of your
    faithfulness and your salvation;
    I have not concealed your steadfast
    love and your faithfulness
    from the great congregation.

---

m Heb *hostility*   n Cn: Heb *pit of tumult*
o Heb *ears you have dug for me*
p Meaning of Heb uncertain

11 Do not, O GOD, withhold
your mercy from me;
let your steadfast love and your
faithfulness
keep me safe forever.
12 For evils have encompassed me
without number;
my iniquities have overtaken me,
until I cannot see;
they are more than the hairs of my
head,
and my heart fails me.

13 Be pleased, O GOD, to deliver me;
O GOD, make haste to help me.
14 Let all those be put to shame and
confusion
who seek to snatch away my life;
let those be turned back and
brought to dishonor
who desire my hurt.
15 Let those be appalled because of
their shame
who say to me, "Aha, Aha!"

16 But may all who seek you
rejoice and be glad in you;
may those who love your salvation
say continually, "GOD is great!"
17 As for me, I am poor and needy,
but the Lord takes thought for
me.
You are my help and my deliverer;
do not delay, O my God.

Psalm 41

Assurance of God's Help and a Plea for Healing

To the leader. A Psalm of David.

1 Blessed are those who consider the
poor;[q]
the LORD delivers them in the
day of trouble.
2 GOD protects them and keeps them
alive;
they are called happy in the land.
You do not give them up to the
will of their enemies.
3 GOD sustains them on their sickbed;
in their illness you heal all their
infirmities.[r]

4 As for me, I said, "O GOD, be
gracious to me;
heal me, for I have sinned against
you."
5 My enemies wonder in malice
when I will die, and my name
perish.
6 And when they come to see me,
they utter empty words,
while their hearts gather mischief;
when they go out, they tell it
abroad.
7 All who hate me whisper together
about me;
they imagine the worst for me.

8 They think that a deadly thing has
fastened on me,
that I will not rise again from
where I lie.
9 Even my good friend in whom I
trusted,
who ate of my bread, has lifted
the heel against me.
10 But you, O GOD, be gracious
to me,
and raise me up, that I may
repay them.

11 By this I know that you are
pleased with me;
because my enemy has not
triumphed over me.

---

q Or *weak* r Heb *you change all the bed*

12 But you have upheld me because of
    my integrity,
      and set me in your presence
        forever.

13 Blessed be the Most High, the God
    of Israel,
      from everlasting to everlasting.
        Amen and Amen.

BOOK II ☙ ☙ ☙ ☙ ☙

Psalm 42

Longing for God and God's Help in Distress

To the leader. A Maskil of the Korahites.

1 As a deer longs for flowing
    streams,
      so my soul longs for you,
        O God.
2 My soul thirsts for God,
    for the living God.
    When shall I come and behold
      the face of God?
3 My tears have been my food
    day and night,
    while people say to me continually,
      "Where is your God?"

4 These things I remember,
    as I pour out my soul:
    how I went with the throng,ˢ
      and led them in procession to
        the house of God,
    with glad shouts and songs of
      thanksgiving,
    a multitude keeping festival.
5 Why are you cast down, O my
    soul,
    and why are you disquieted
      within me?
Hope in God; for I shall again
    praise the one who is

my help 6and my God.

My soul is cast down within me;
    therefore I remember you
from the land of Jordan and of
    Hermon,
    from Mount Mizar.
7 Deep calls to deep
    at the thunder of your cataracts;
all your waves and your billows
    have gone over me.
8 By day GOD commands God's
    steadfast love,
    and at night God's song is with
      me,
    a prayer to the God of my life.
9 I say to God, my rock,
    "Why have you forgotten me?
Why must I walk about mournfully
    because the enemy oppresses
      me?"
10 As with a deadly wound in my
    body,
    my adversaries taunt me,
while they say to me continually,
    "Where is your God?"

11 Why are you cast down, O my
    soul,
    and why are you disquieted
      within me?
Hope in God; for I shall again
    praise the one
    who is my help and my God.

Psalm 43

Prayer to God in Time of Trouble

1 Vindicate me, O God, and defend
    my cause
    against an ungodly people;

ˢ Meaning of Heb uncertain

from those who are deceitful and
   unjust
   deliver me!
2 For you are the God in whom I
   take refuge;
   why have you cast me off?
Why must I walk about mournfully
   because of the oppression of the
   enemy?

3 O send out your light and your
   truth;
   let them lead me;
let them bring me to your holy hill
   and to your dwelling.
4 Then I will go to the altar of God,
   to God my exceeding joy;
and I will praise you with the
   harp,
   O God, my God.

5 Why are you cast down, O my
   soul,
   and why are you disquieted
   within me?
Hope in God; for I shall again
   praise the one
   who is my help and my God.

Psalm 44

National Lament and Prayer for Help

To the leader. Of the Korahites. A Maskil.

1 We have heard with our ears,
   O God,
   our ancestors have told us,
what deeds you performed in their
   days,
   in the days of old:
2 you with your own hand drove out
   the nations,
   but them you planted;
you afflicted the peoples,

but them you set free;
3 for not by their own sword did
   they win the land,
   nor did their own arm give them
   victory;
but your mighty hand, and your
   arm,
   and the light of your
   countenance,
   for you delighted in them.

4 You are my Sovereign and my
   God;
   you command[t] victories for
   Jacob.
5 Through you we push down our
   foes;
   through your name we tread
   down our assailants.
6 For not in my bow do I trust,
   nor can my sword save me.
7 But you have saved us from our
   foes,
   and have put to confusion those
   who hate us.
8 In God we have boasted
   continually,
   and we will give thanks to your
   name forever.   *Selah*

9 Yet you have rejected us and
   abased us,
   and have not gone out with our
   armies.
10 You made us turn back from
   the foe,
   and our enemies have gotten
   spoil.
11 You have made us like sheep for
   slaughter,
   and have scattered us among
   the nations.

---

t Gk Syr: Heb *You are my Sovereign, O God; command*

12 You have sold your people for a
         trifle,
     demanding no high price for
         them.

13 You have made us the taunt of our
         neighbors,
     the derision and scorn of those
         around us.

14 You have made us a byword
         among the nations,
     a laughingstock[u] among the
         peoples.

15 All day long my disgrace is before
         me,
     and shame has covered my face

16 at the words of the taunters and
         revilers,
     at the sight of the enemy and
         the avenger.

17 All this has come upon us,
     yet we have not forgotten you,
     or been false to your covenant.

18 Our heart has not turned back,
     nor have our steps departed from
         your way,

19 yet you have broken us in the
         haunt of jackals,
     and covered us with deep
         darkness.

20 If we had forgotten the name of
         our God,
     or spread out our hands to a
         strange god,

21 would not God discover this?
     For God knows the secrets of
         the heart.

22 Because of you we are being killed
         all day long,
     and accounted as sheep for the
         slaughter.

23 Rouse yourself! Why do you sleep,
         O God?

     Awake, do not cast us off
         forever!

24 Why do you hide your face?
     Why do you forget our affliction
         and oppression?

25 For we sink down to the dust;
     our bodies cling to the ground.

26 Rise up, come to our help.
     Redeem us for the sake of your
         steadfast love.

Psalm 45

Ode for a Royal Wedding

*To the leader: according to Lilies. Of the
Korahites. A Maskil. A love song.*

1 My heart overflows with a goodly
         theme;
     I address my verses to the king;[v]
     my tongue is like the pen of a
         ready scribe.

2 You are the most handsome of
         men;
     grace is poured upon your lips;
     therefore God has blessed you
         forever.

3 Gird your sword on your thigh,
         O mighty one,
     in your glory and majesty.

4 In your majesty ride on
         victoriously
     for the cause of truth and to
         defend[w] the right;
     let your mighty hand teach you
         dread deeds.

5 Your arrows are sharp

---

u Heb *a shaking of the head*   v Because
this particular psalm is an ode to a royal
wedding, the words *king, queen, prince* and
other terms for members of the royal
household have been retained.   w Cn: Heb
and the meekness of

in the heart of the king's
    enemies;
  the peoples fall under you.

6 Your throne, O God,[x] endures
    forever and ever.
  Your royal scepter is a scepter of
    equity;
7   you love righteousness and hate
    wickedness.
  Therefore God, your God, has
    anointed you
  with the oil of gladness beyond
    your companions;
8   your robes are all fragrant with
    myrrh and aloes and cassia.
  From ivory palaces stringed
    instruments make you glad;
9   princesses are among your ladies
    of honor;
  at your side stands the queen in
    gold of Ophir.

10 Hear, O daughter, consider and
    incline your ear;
  forget your people and your
    parents' house,
11   and the king will desire your
    beauty.
  Since he is your sovereign, bow to
    him;
12   the people of Tyre will seek
    your favor with gifts,
  the richest of the people [13]with
    all kinds of wealth.

In her chamber, the princess is
    clothed with gold-woven
    robes;[y]
14   in many-colored robes she is led
    to the king;
  behind her the virgins, her
    companions, follow.
15 With joy and gladness they are
    led along

as they enter the palace of the
    king.
16 In the place of ancestors you,
    O king,[z] shall have
    descendants;
  you will make them princes in
    all the earth.
17 I will cause your name to be
    celebrated in all generations;
  therefore the peoples will praise
    you forever and ever.

Psalm 46

God's Defense of God's City and People

To the leader. Of the Korahites.
According to Alamoth. A Song.

1 God is our refuge and strength,
  a very present[a] help in trouble.
2 Therefore we will not fear, though
    the earth should change,
  though the mountains shake in
    the heart of the sea;
3 though its waters roar and foam,
  though the mountains tremble
    with its tumult.   *Selah*

4 There is a river whose streams
    make glad the city of God,
  the holy habitation of the
    Most High.
5 God is in the midst of the city; it
    shall not be moved;
  God will help it when the
    morning dawns.
6 The nations are in an uproar, the
    empires totter;
  God thunders, the earth melts.
7 The GOD of hosts is with us;

---

x Or *Your throne is a throne of God, it*
y Or *people.* 13*All glorious is the princess*
within, gold embroidery is her clothing
z Heb lacks *O king*   a Or *well proved*

the God of Jacob is our refuge.[b]

Selah

8 Come, behold the works of GOD;
    see what desolations God has
        brought on the earth.
9 God makes wars cease to the end
        of the earth;
    God breaks the bow, and shatters
        the spear;
    God burns the shields with fire.
10 "Be still, and know that I am God!
    I am exalted among the nations,
    I am exalted in the earth."
11 The GOD of hosts is with us;
    the God of Jacob is our refuge.[b]

Selah

Psalm 47

God's Rule over the Nations

To the leader. Of the Korahites. A Psalm.

1 Clap your hands, all you peoples;
    shout to God with loud songs
        of joy.
2 For GOD, the Most High, is
        awesome,
    a great sovereign over all the
        earth.
3 God subdued peoples under us,
    and nations under our feet.
4 God chose our heritage for us,
    the pride of Jacob whom God
        loves.   *Selah*

5 God has gone up with a shout,
    GOD with the sound of a
        trumpet.
6 Sing praises to God, sing praises;
    sing praises to our Sovereign,
        sing praises.
7 For God is the sovereign of all the
        earth;
    sing praises with a psalm.[c]

8 God is sovereign over the nations;
    God sits on God's holy throne.
9 The nobles of the peoples gather
    as the people of the God of
        Abraham.
For the shields of the earth belong
        to God;
    God is highly exalted.

Psalm 48

The Glory and Strength of Zion

A Song. A Psalm of the Korahites.

1 Great is GOD and greatly to be
        praised
    in the city of our God.
God's holy mountain, 2beautiful in
        elevation,
    is the joy of all the earth,
Mount Zion, in the far north,
    the city of the great Sovereign.
3 Within its citadels God
    has proved to be a sure defense.

4 Then the rulers assembled,
    they came on together.
5 As soon as they saw it, they were
        astounded;
    they were in panic, they took to
        flight;
6 trembling took hold of them there,
    pains as of a woman in labor,
7 as when an east wind shatters
    the ships of Tarshish.
8 As we have heard, so have we seen
    in the city of the GOD of hosts,
in the city of our God,
    which God establishes forever.

Selah

9 We ponder your steadfast love,
    O God,
    in the midst of your temple.

---

b Or *fortress*   c Heb *Maskil*

10 Your name, O God, like your
        praise,
    reaches to the ends of the earth.
    Your mighty hand is filled with
        victory.
11   Let Mount Zion be glad,
    let the towns of Judah rejoice
        because of your judgments.

12 Walk about Zion, go all around it,
    count its towers,
13 consider well its ramparts;
    go through its citadels,
    that you may tell the next
        generation
14   that this is God,
    our God forever and ever.
    God will be our guide forever.

Psalm 49

The Folly of Trust in Riches

To the leader. Of the Korahites. A Psalm.

1 Hear this, all you peoples;
    give ear, all inhabitants of the
        world,
2 both low and high,
    rich and poor together.
3 My mouth shall speak wisdom;
    the meditation of my heart shall
        be understanding.
4 I will incline my ear to a proverb;
    I will solve my riddle to the
        music of the harp.

5 Why should I fear in times of
        trouble,
    when the iniquity of my
        persecutors surrounds me,
6 those who trust in their wealth
    and boast of the abundance of
        their riches?
7 Truly, no ransom avails for one's
    life,[d]

there is no price one can give to
    God for it.
8 For the ransom of life is costly,
    and can never suffice
9 that one should live on forever
    and never see the grave.[e]

10 When we look at the wise, they
        die;
    fool and dolt perish together
    and leave their wealth to others.
11 Their graves[f] are their homes
        forever,
    their dwelling places to all
        generations,
    though they named lands their
        own.
12 Mortals cannot abide in their pomp;
    they are like the animals that
        perish.

13 Such is the fate of the foolhardy,
    the end of those[g] who are
        pleased with their lot.   *Selah*
14 Like sheep they are appointed for
        Sheol;
    Death shall be their shepherd;
    straight to the grave they descend,[h]
    and their form shall waste away;
    Sheol shall be their home.[i]
15 But God will ransom my soul from
        the power of Sheol,
    for God will receive me.   *Selah*

16 Do not be afraid when some
        become rich,
    when the wealth of their houses
        increases.

---

d Another reading is *no one can ransom
another*   e Heb *the pit*   f Gk Syr
Compare Tg: Heb *their inward* (thought)
g Tg: Heb *after them*   h Cn: Heb *the
upright shall have dominion over them in the
morning*   i Meaning of Heb uncertain

17 For when they die they will carry
     nothing away;
   their wealth will not go down
     after them.
18 Though in their lifetime they count
     themselves happy
   —for you are praised when you
     do well for yourself—
19 they^j will go to the company of
     their ancestors,
   who will never again see the
     light.
20 Mortals cannot abide in their pomp;
   they are like the animals that
     perish.

Psalm 50

The Acceptable Sacrifice

A Psalm of Asaph.

1 The mighty one, God the Most
     High,
   speaks and summons the earth
   from the rising of the sun to its
     setting.
2 Out of Zion, the perfection of
     beauty,
   God shines forth.

3 Our God comes and does not keep
     silence,
   before God is a devouring fire,
   all around God a mighty tempest.
4 God calls to the heavens above
   and to the earth, in order to
     judge God's people:
5 "Gather to me my faithful ones,
   who made a covenant with me
     by sacrifice!"
6 The heavens declare God's
     righteousness,
   for it is God who judges.   *Selah*

7 "Hear, O my people, and I will
     speak,

O Israel, I will testify against
     you.
   I am God, your God.
8 Not for your sacrifices do I rebuke
     you;
   your burnt offerings are
     continually before me.
9 I will not accept a bull from your
     house,
   or goats from your folds.
10 For every wild animal of the forest
     is mine,
   the cattle on a thousand hills.
11 I know all the birds of the air,^k
   and all that moves in the field is
     mine.
12 "If I were hungry, I would not tell
     you,
   for the world and all that is in it
     is mine.
13 Do I eat the flesh of bulls,
   or drink the blood of goats?
14 Offer to God a sacrifice of
     thanksgiving,^l
   and pay your vows to the
     Most High.
15 Call on me in the day of trouble;
   I will deliver you, and you shall
     glorify me."

16 But to the wicked God says:
   "What right have you to recite
     my statutes,
   or take my covenant on your
     lips?
17 For you hate discipline,
   and you cast my words behind
     you.
18 You make friends with a thief
   when you see one,

---

j Cn: Heb *you*   k Gk Syr Tg: Heb
mountains   l Or *make thanksgiving your
sacrifice to God*

and you keep company with
adulterers.

19 "You give your mouth free rein
for evil,
and your tongue frames deceit.
20 You sit and speak against your kin;
you slander your own mother's
child.
21 These things you have done and I
have been silent;
you thought that I was one just
like yourself.
But now I rebuke you, and lay the
charge before you.

22 "Mark this, then, you who forget
God,
or I will tear you apart, and
there will be no one to deliver.
23 Those who bring thanksgiving as
their sacrifice honor me;
to those who go the right way^m
I will show the salvation of
God."

Psalm 51

Prayer for Cleansing and Pardon

*To the leader. A Psalm of David, when
the prophet Nathan came to him, after he
had gone in to Bathsheba.*

1 Have mercy on me, O God,
according to your steadfast love;
according to your abundant mercy
blot out my transgressions.
2 Wash me thoroughly from my
iniquity,
and cleanse me from my sin.

3 For I know my transgressions,
and my sin is ever before me.
4 Against you, you alone, have I
sinned,
and done what is evil in your
sight,

so that you are justified in your
sentence
and blameless when you pass
judgment.
5 Indeed, I was born guilty,
a sinner when my mother
conceived me.

6 You desire truth in the inward
being;^n
therefore teach me wisdom in my
secret heart.
7 Purge me with hyssop, and I shall
be clean;
wash me, and I shall be purer
than snow.
8 Let me hear joy and gladness;
let the bones that you have
crushed rejoice.
9 Hide your face from my sins,
and blot out all my iniquities.

10 Create in me a clean heart, O God,
and put a new and right^o spirit
within me.
11 Do not cast me away from your
presence,
and do not take your holy spirit
from me.
12 Restore to me the joy of your
salvation,
and sustain in me a willing^p
spirit.

13 Then I will teach transgressors your
ways,
and sinners will return to you.
14 Deliver me from bloodshed,
O God,
O God of my salvation,
and my tongue will sing aloud of
your deliverance.

---

m Heb *who set a way*   n Meaning of Heb
uncertain   o Or *steadfast*   p Or *generous*

15 O God, open my lips,
   and my mouth will declare your
      praise.
16 For you have no delight in
      sacrifice;
   if I were to give a burnt
      offering, you would not be
      pleased.
17 The sacrifice acceptable to God*q* is
      a broken spirit;
   a broken and contrite heart,
      O God, you will not despise.

18 Do good to Zion in your good
      pleasure;
   rebuild the walls of Jerusalem,
19 then you will delight in right
      sacrifices,
   in burnt offerings and whole
      burnt offerings;
   then bulls will be offered on
      your altar.

Psalm 52

Judgment on the Deceitful

*To the leader. A Maskil of David, when
Doeg the Edomite came to Saul and said to
him, "David has come to the house of
Ahimelech."*

1 Why do you boast, O mighty one,
   of mischief done against the
      godly?*r*
   All day long ²you are plotting
      destruction.
   Your tongue is like a sharp razor,
      you worker of treachery.
3 You love evil more than good,
   and lying more than speaking the
      truth.   *Selah*
4 You love all words that devour,
   O deceitful tongue.

5 But God will break you down
      forever;

God will snatch and tear you
   from your tent;
God will uproot you from the
   land of the living.   *Selah*
6 The righteous will see and be in
      awe,
   and will laugh at the evildoer,
      saying,
7 "See the one who would not take
      refuge in God,
   but trusted in abundant riches,
   and sought refuge in wealth!"*s*

8 But I am like a green olive tree
   in the house of God.
I trust in the steadfast love of God
   forever and ever.
9 I will thank you forever,
   because of what you have done.
In the presence of the faithful
   I will proclaim*t* your name, for
      it is good.

Psalm 53

Denunciation of Godlessness

*To the leader: according to Mahalath. A
Maskil of David.*

1 Fools say in their hearts, "There is
      no God."
   They are corrupt, they commit
      abominable acts;
   there is no one who does good.

2 God looks down from heaven on
      humankind
   to see if there are any who are
      wise,
   who seek after God.

---

q Or *My sacrifice, O God,*   r Cn Compare
Syr: Heb *the kindness of God*   s Syr Tg:
Heb *in the evildoer's destruction*
t Cn: Heb *wait for*

3 They have all fallen away, they are
all alike perverse;
there is no one who does good,
no, not one.

4 Have they no knowledge, those
evildoers,
who eat up my people as they
eat bread,
and do not call upon God?

5 There they shall be in great terror,
in terror such as has not been.
For God will scatter the bones of
the ungodly;[u]
they will be put to shame,[v] for
God has rejected them.

6 O that deliverance for Israel would
come from Zion!
When God restores the fortunes
of God's people,
Jacob will rejoice; Israel will be
glad.

Psalm 54
Prayer for Vindication

*To the leader: with stringed instruments. A
Maskil of David, when the Ziphites went
and told Saul, "David is in hiding among
us."*

1 Save me, O God, by your name,
and vindicate me by your might.
2 Hear my prayer, O God;
give ear to the words of my
mouth.

3 For the insolent have risen
against me,
the ruthless seek my life;
they do not set God before
them.   *Selah*

4 But surely, God is my helper
and is the upholder of[w] my life.

5 God will repay my enemies for
their evil.
In your faithfulness, put an end
to them.

6 With a freewill offering I will
sacrifice to you;
I will give thanks to your name,
O Most High, for it is good.
7 For God has delivered me from
every trouble,
and my eye has looked in
triumph on my enemies.

Psalm 55
Complaint about a Friend's Treachery

*To the leader: with stringed instruments. A
Maskil of David.*

1 Give ear to my prayer, O God;
do not hide yourself from my
supplication.
2 Attend to me, and answer me;
I am troubled in my complaint.
I am distraught ³by the noise of
the enemy,
because of the clamor of the
wicked.
For they bring[x] trouble upon me,
and in anger they cherish enmity
against me.

4 My heart is in anguish within me,
the terrors of death have fallen
upon me.
5 Fear and trembling come upon me,
and horror overwhelms me.

---

u Cn Compare Gk Syr: Heb *the one who
encamps against you*   v Gk: Heb *you have
put them to shame*   w Gk Syr Jerome: Heb
is of those who uphold or *is with those who
uphold*   x Cn Compare Gk: Heb *they cause
to totter*

6 And I say, "O that I had wings
    like a dove!
  I would fly away and be at rest;
7 truly, I would flee far away;
  I would lodge in the wilderness;
                                    Selah
8 I would hurry to find a shelter for
    myself
  from the raging wind and
    tempest."

9 Confuse, O God, confound their
    speech;
  for I see violence and strife in
    the city.
10 Day and night they go around it
    on its walls,
  and iniquity and trouble are
    within it;
11   ruin is in its midst;
  oppression and fraud
    do not depart from its
    marketplace.

12 It is not enemies who taunt me—
    I could bear that;
  it is not adversaries who deal
    insolently with me—
    I could hide from them.
13 But it is you, my equal,
    my companion, my familiar
    friend,
14 with whom I kept pleasant
    company;
  we walked in the house of God
    with the throng.
15 Let death come upon them;
  let them go down alive to Sheol;
  for evil is in their homes and in
    their hearts.

16 But I call upon God,
  and GOD will save me.
17 Evening and morning and at noon
  I utter my complaint and moan,

and God will hear my voice.
18 God will redeem me unharmed
    from the battle that I wage,
  for many are arrayed against me.
19 God, who is enthroned from of
    old,   *Selah*
  will hear, and will humble
    them—
  because they do not change,
    and do not revere God.

20 My companion laid hands on a
    friend
  and violated a covenant with me[y]
21 with speech smoother than butter,
    but with a heart set on war;
  with words that were softer than
    oil,
    but in fact were drawn swords.

22 Cast your burden[z] on GOD,
    who will sustain you,
  and will never permit
    the righteous to be moved.

23 But you, O God, will cast them
    down
    into the lowest pit;
  the bloodthirsty and treacherous
    shall not live out half their days.
  But I will trust in you.

Psalm 56

Trust in God under Persecution

*To the leader: according to The Dove on
Far-off Terebinths. Of David. A Miktam,
when the Philistines seized him in Gath.*

1 Be gracious to me, O God, for
    people trample on me;
  all day long foes oppress me;

---

y Heb lacks *with me*   z Or *Cast what* GOD
has given you

2 my enemies trample on me all day
  long,
  for many fight against me.
O Most High, ³when I am afraid,
  I put my trust in you.
4 In God, whose word I praise,
  in God I trust; I am not afraid;
  what can flesh do to me?

5 All day long they seek to injure
  my cause;
  all their thoughts are against me
  for evil.
6 They stir up strife, they lurk,
  they watch my steps.
As they hoped to have my life,
7   so repay[a] them for their crime;
  in wrath cast down the peoples,
  O God!

8 You have kept count of my
  tossings;
  put my tears in your bottle.
  Are they not in your record?
9 Then my enemies will retreat
  in the day when I call.
  This I know, that[b] God is for
  me.
10 In God, whose word I praise,
  in the Most High, whose word I
  praise,
11 in God I trust; I am not afraid.
  What can a mere mortal do to
  me?

12 My vows to you I must perform,
  O God;
  I will render thank offerings
  to you.
13 For you have delivered my soul
  from death,
  and my feet from falling,
  so that I may walk before God
  in the light of life.

Psalm 57

Praise and Assurance under Persecution

To the leader: Do Not Destroy.
Of David. A Miktam, when he fled from
Saul, in the cave.

1 Be merciful to me, O God, be
  merciful to me,
  for in you my soul takes refuge;
in the shadow of your wings I will
  take refuge,
  until the destroying storms
  pass by.
2 I cry to God Most High,
  to God who fulfills God's
  purpose for me.
3 God will send from heaven and
  save me,
  putting to shame those who
  trample on me.   *Selah*
God will send forth God's steadfast
  love and faithfulness.

4 I lie down among lions
  that greedily devour[c] human
  prey;
their teeth are spears and arrows,
  their tongues sharp swords.

5 Be exalted, O God, above the
  heavens.
  Let your glory be over all the
  earth.

6 They set a net for my steps;
  my soul was bowed down.
They dug a pit in my path,
  but they have fallen into it
  themselves.   *Selah*
7 My heart is steadfast, O God,
  my heart is steadfast.

---

a Cn: Heb *rescue*   b Or *because*
c Cn: Heb *are aflame for*

I will sing and make melody.
8   Awake, my soul!
Awake, O harp and lyre!
I will awake the dawn.
9 I will give thanks to you, O God,
among the peoples;
I will sing praises to you among
the nations.
10 For your steadfast love is as high
as the heavens;
your faithfulness extends to the
clouds.

11 Be exalted, O God, above the
heavens.
Let your glory be over all the
earth.

Psalm 58

Prayer for Vengeance

To the leader: Do Not Destroy.
Of David. A Miktam.

1 Do you indeed decree what is
right, you gods?
Do you judge people fairly?
2 No, in your hearts you devise
wrongs;
your hands deal out violence on
earth.

3 The wicked go astray from the
womb;
they err from their birth,
speaking lies.
4 They have venom like the venom
of a serpent,
like the deaf adder that stops
its ear,
5 so that it does not hear the voice
of charmers
or of the cunning enchanter.

6 O God, break the teeth in their
mouths;

tear out the fangs of the young
lions, O Most High!
7 Let them vanish like water that
runs away;
like grass let them be trodden
down[d] and wither.
8 Let them be like the snail that
dissolves into slime;
like the untimely birth that never
sees the sun.
9 Sooner than your pots can feel the
heat of thorns,
whether green or ablaze, may
God sweep them away!

10 The righteous will rejoice when
they see vengeance done;
they will bathe their feet in the
blood of the wicked.
11 People will say, "Surely there is a
reward for the righteous;
surely there is a God who judges
on earth."

Psalm 59

Prayer for Deliverance from
Enemies

To the leader: Do Not Destroy.
Of David. A Miktam, when Saul ordered
his house to be watched in order to kill
him.

1 Deliver me from my enemies,
O my God;
protect me from those who rise
up against me.
2 Deliver me from those who work
evil;
from the bloodthirsty save me.

3 Even now they lie in wait for my
life;

---

d Cn: Meaning of Heb uncertain

the mighty stir up strife against
me.
For no transgression or sin of
mine, O GOD,
4 for no fault of mine, they run
and make ready.

Rouse yourself, come to my help
and see!
5 You, O Most High God of
hosts, are God of Israel.
Awake to punish all the nations;
spare none of those who
treacherously plot evil.   *Selah*

6 Each evening they come back,
howling like dogs
and prowling about the city.
7 There they are, bellowing with their
mouths,
with sharp words[e] on their
lips—
for "Who," they think,[f] "will
hear us?"

8 But you laugh at them, O GOD;
you hold all the nations in
derision.
9 O my strength, I will watch for
you;
for you, O God, are my fortress.
10 My God will meet me in steadfast
love;
my God will let me look in
triumph on my enemies.

11 Do not kill them, or my people
may forget;
make them totter by your power,
and bring them down,
O God, our shield.
12 For the sin of their mouths, the
words of their lips,
let them be trapped in their
pride.

For the cursing and lies that they
utter,
13 consume them in wrath;
consume them until they are no
more.
Then it will be known to the ends
of the earth
that God rules over Jacob.   *Selah*

14 Each evening they come back,
howling like dogs
and prowling about the city.
15 They roam about for food,
and growl if they do not get
their fill.

16 But I will sing of your might;
I will sing aloud of your
steadfast love in the morning.
For you have been a fortress for
me
and a refuge in the day of my
distress.
17 O my strength, I will sing praises
to you,
for you, O God, are my fortress,
the God who shows me steadfast
love.

Psalm 60

Prayer for National Victory after Defeat

*To the leader: according to The Lily of the
Covenant. A Miktam of David; for
instruction; when he struggled with
Aram-naharaim and with Aram-zobah, and
when Joab on his return killed twelve
thousand Edomites in the Valley of Salt.*

1 O God, you have rejected us,
broken our defenses;
you have been angry; now
restore us!

---

e Heb *with swords*   f Heb lacks *they think*

2 You have caused the land to quake;
    you have torn it open;
  repair the cracks in it, for it is
    tottering.
3 You have made your people suffer
    hard things;
  you have given us wine to drink
    that made us reel.

4 You have set up a banner for those
    who are in awe of you,
  to rally to it out of bowshot.[g]
                 Selah
5 Give victory with your mighty
    hand, and answer us,[h]
  so that those whom you love
    may be rescued.

6 In the sanctuary[i] God has
    promised:
  "With exultation I will divide up
    Shechem,
  and portion out the Vale of
    Succoth.
7 Gilead is mine, and Manasseh is
    mine;
  Ephraim is my helmet;
  Judah is my scepter.
8 Moab is my washbasin;
  on Edom I hurl my shoe;
  over Philistia I shout in
    triumph."

9 Who will bring me to the fortified
    city?
  Who will lead me to Edom?
10 Have you not rejected us, O
    God?
  You do not go out, O God,
    with our armies.
11 O grant us help against the foe,
    for human help is worthless.
12 With God we shall do valiantly;

it is God who will tread down
    our foes.

Psalm 61

Assurance of God's Protection

To the leader: with stringed instruments.
Of David.

1 Hear my cry, O God;
    listen to my prayer.
2 From the end of the earth I call
    to you,
  when my heart is faint.

Lead me to the rock
    that is higher than I;
3 for you are my refuge,
    a strong tower against the enemy.

4 Let me abide in your tent forever,
    find refuge under the shelter of
    your wings.   *Selah*
5 For you, O God, have heard my
    vows;
  you have given me the heritage
    of those who revere your
    name.

6 Prolong the life of the ruler;
    may the ruler's years endure to
    all generations!
7 May the ruler be enthroned forever
    before God;
  appoint steadfast love and
    faithfulness for the
    ruler's protection!

8 So I will always sing praises to
    your name,
  as I pay my vows day after day.

---

g Gk Syr Jerome: Heb *because of the truth*
h Another reading is *me*   i Or *by God's*
holiness

Psalm 62

Song of Trust in God Alone

To the leader: according to Jeduthun.
A Psalm of David.

1 For God alone my soul waits in
     silence;
       from God comes my salvation.
2 God alone is my rock and my
     salvation,
       my fortress; I shall never be
       shaken.

3 How long will you assail a person,
     will you batter your victim, all
       of you,
     as you would a leaning wall, a
       tottering fence?
4 Their only plan is to bring down a
     person of prominence.
     They take pleasure in falsehood;
   they bless with their mouths,
     but inwardly they curse.   *Selah*

5 For God alone my soul waits in
     silence,
       for my hope is from God,
6 who alone is my rock and my
     salvation,
       my fortress; I shall not be
       shaken.
7 On God rests my deliverance and
     my honor;
       my mighty rock, my refuge is in
       God.

8 Trust in God at all times,
     O people;
     pour out your heart before God,
       who is a refuge for us.   *Selah*

9 Those of low estate are but a
     breath,
       those of high estate are a
       delusion;
   in the balances they go up;

they are together lighter than a
     breath.
10 Put no confidence in extortion,
     and set no vain hopes on
       robbery;
     if riches increase, do not set your
       heart on them.

11 Once God has spoken;
     twice have I heard this:
   that power belongs to God,
12   and steadfast love belongs to you,
       O God.
   For you repay to all
     according to their work.

Psalm 63

Comfort and Assurance in God's Presence

A Psalm of David, when he was in the
Wilderness of Judah.

1 O God, you are my God, I seek
     you,
       my soul thirsts for you;
   my flesh faints for you,
     as in a dry and weary land
     where there is no water.
2 So I have looked upon you in the
     sanctuary,
       beholding your power and glory.
3 Because your steadfast love is better
     than life,
       my lips will praise you.
4 So I will bless you as long as I
     live;
       I will lift up my hands and call
       on your name.

5 My soul is satisfied as with a rich
     feast,ʲ
       and my mouth praises you with
       joyful lips

---

j Heb *with fat and fatness*

6 when I think of you on my bed,
    and meditate on you in the
      watches of the night;
7 for you have been my help,
    and in the shadow of your wings
      I sing for joy.
8 My soul clings to you;
    your strong hand upholds me.

9 But those who seek to destroy
      my life
    shall go down into the depths of
      the earth;
10 they shall be given over to the
      power of the sword,
    they shall be prey for jackals.
11 But the ruler shall rejoice in God;
    all who swear by the ruler shall
      exult,
    for the mouths of liars will be
      stopped.

Psalm 64

Prayer for Protection from
Enemies

To the leader. A Psalm of David.

1 Hear my voice, O God, in my
      complaint;
    preserve my life from the dread
      enemy.
2 Hide me from the secret plots of
      the wicked,
    from the scheming of evildoers,
3 who sharpen their tongues like
      swords,
    who aim bitter words like
      arrows,
4 shooting from ambush at the
      blameless;
    they shoot suddenly and without
      fear.
5 They hold fast to their evil
      purpose;

they talk of laying snares
      secretly,
thinking, "Who can see us?[k]
6   Who can search out our crimes?[l]
We have thought out a cunningly
      conceived plot."
For the human heart and mind
    are deep.

7 But God will shoot at them with
      arrows;
    they will be wounded suddenly.
8 Because of their tongue God will
      bring them to ruin;[m]
    all who see them will shake with
      horror.
9 Then everyone will be in awe;
    they will tell what God has
      brought about,
    and ponder what God has done.

10 Let the righteous rejoice in GOD
    and take refuge in God.
Let all the upright in heart glory.

Psalm 65

Thanksgiving for Earth's Bounty

*To the leader. A Psalm of David.
A Song.*

1 Praise is due to you,
    O God, in Zion;
and to you shall vows be
      performed,
2   O you who answer prayer!
To you all flesh shall come.
3 When deeds of iniquity overwhelm
      us,
    you forgive our transgressions.
4 Blessed are those whom you choose
    and bring near

---

k Syr: Heb *them*   l Cn: Heb *They search
out crimes*   m Cn: Heb *They will bring
God to ruin, their tongue being against them*

to live in your courts.
We shall be satisfied with the
   goodness of your house,
   your holy temple.

5 By awesome deeds you answer us
   with deliverance,
   O God of our salvation;
you are the hope of all the ends of
   the earth
   and of the farthest seas.
6 By your[n] strength you established
   the mountains;
   you are girded with might.
7 You silence the roaring of the seas,
   the roaring of their waves,
   the tumult of the peoples.
8 Those who live at earth's farthest
   bounds are awed by your
   signs;
you make the gateways of the
   morning and the evening shout
   for joy.

9 You visit the earth and water it,
   you greatly enrich it;
the river of God is full of water;
   you provide the people with
   grain,
   for so you have prepared it.
10 You water its furrows abundantly,
   settling its ridges,
softening it with showers,
   and blessing its growth.
11 You crown the year with your
   bounty;
   your wagon tracks overflow with
   richness.
12 The pastures of the wilderness
   overflow,
   the hills gird themselves with joy,
13 the meadows clothe themselves with
   flocks,
   the valleys deck themselves with
   grain,

they shout and sing together for
   joy.

Psalm 66

Praise for God's Goodness to Israel

To the leader. A Song. A Psalm.

1 Make a joyful noise to God, all the
   earth;
2   sing the glory of God's name;
   give to God glorious praise.
3 Say to God, "How awesome are
   your deeds!
   Because of your great power,
   your enemies cringe
   before you.
4 All the earth worships you;
   they sing praises to you,
   sing praises to your name." *Selah*

5 Come and see what God has done:
   God does awesome deeds among
   mortals.
6 God turned the sea into dry land;
   they passed through the river
   on foot.
There we rejoiced in God,
7   who rules by might forever,
whose eyes keep watch on the
   nations—
   let the rebellious not exalt
   themselves.   *Selah*

8 Bless our God, O peoples,
   let the sound of God's praise be
   heard,
9 who has kept us among the living,
   and has not let our feet slip.
10 For you, O God, have tested us;
   you have tried us as silver is
   tried.
11 You brought us into the net;

---

n Gk Jerome: Heb *God's*

you laid burdens on our backs;

12 you let people ride over our heads;
we went through fire and
through water;
yet you have brought us out to a
spacious place.°

13 I will come into your house with
burnt offerings;
I will pay you my vows,

14 those that my lips uttered
and my mouth promised when I
was in trouble.

15 I will offer to you burnt offerings
of fatlings,
with the smoke of the sacrifice
of rams;
I will make an offering of bulls
and goats.   *Selah*

16 Come and hear, all you who revere
God,
and I will tell what God has
done for me.

17 I cried aloud to God,
and praised God with my tongue.

18 If I had cherished iniquity in my
heart,
God would not have listened.

19 But truly God has listened,
who has given heed to the words
of my prayer.

20 Blessed be God,
who has not rejected my prayer
or removed God's steadfast love
from me.

Psalm 67

The Nations Called to Praise God

To the leader: with stringed instruments.
A Psalm. A Song.

1 May God be gracious to us and
bless us

and make God's face to shine
upon us,   *Selah*

2 that your way may be known upon
earth,
your saving power among all
nations.

3 Let the peoples praise you, O God;
let all the peoples praise you.

4 Let the nations be glad and sing
for joy,
for you judge the peoples with
equity
and guide the nations upon earth.
                    Selah

5 Let the peoples praise you, O God;
let all the peoples praise you.

6 The earth has yielded its increase;
God, our God, has blessed us.

7 May God continue to bless us;
let all the ends of the earth
revere God.

Psalm 68

Praise and Thanksgiving

To the leader. Of David. A Psalm.
A Song.

1 Let God rise up, let God's enemies
be scattered;
let those who hate God flee
away.

2 As smoke is driven away, so drive
them away;
as wax melts before the fire,
let the wicked perish before God.

3 But let the righteous be joyful;
let them exult before God;
let them be jubilant with joy.

4 Sing to God, sing praises to God's
name;

---

o Cn Compare Gk Syr Jerome Tg: Heb *to a*
saturation

lift up a song to God who rides
upon the clouds,[p]
whose name is the Most High,
be exultant before God.

5 Guardian of orphans and protector
of widows
is God in God's holy habitation.
6 God gives the desolate a home to
live in,
and leads out the prisoners to
prosperity,
but the rebellious live in a
parched land.

7 O God, when you went out before
your people,
when you marched through the
wilderness, *Selah*
8 the earth quaked, the heavens
poured down rain
at the presence of God, the God
of Sinai,
at the presence of God, the God
of Israel.
9 Rain in abundance, O God, you
showered abroad;
you restored your heritage when
it languished;
10 your flock found a dwelling in it;
in your goodness, O God, you
provided for those who are
needy.

11 God gives the command;
great is the company of those[q]
who bore the tidings:
12 "The rulers of the armies, they
flee, they flee!"
The women at home divide the
spoil,
13 though they stay among the
sheepfolds—
the wings of a dove covered with
silver,
its pinions with green gold.
14 When the Almighty[r] scattered
rulers there,
snow fell on Zalmon.

15 O mighty mountain, mountain of
Bashan;
O many-peaked mountain,
mountain of Bashan!
16 Why do you look with envy,
O many-peaked mountain,
at the mount where God desired
to dwell,
where GOD will reside forever?

17 With mighty chariotry, twice ten
thousand,
thousands upon thousands,
God came from Sinai into the
holy place.[s]
18 You ascended the high mount,
leading captives in your train
and receiving gifts from people,
even from those who rebel against
the one who is abiding there,
God the Most High.
19 Blessed be God,
who daily bears us up;
God is our salvation. *Selah*
20 Our God is a God of salvation,
and to GOD, the Most High,
belongs escape from death.

21 But God will shatter the heads of
God's enemies,
the hairy crown of those who
walk in their guilty ways.
22 God said,
"I will bring them back from
Bashan,

---

p Or *cast up a highway for the one who rides through the deserts* q Or *company of the women* r Traditional rendering of Heb *Shaddai* s Cn: Heb *God among them Sinai in the holy* (place)

I will bring them back from the
    depths of the sea,
23 so that you may bathe[t] your feet
    in blood,
    so that the tongues of your dogs
    may have their share from the
    foe."

24 Your solemn processions are seen,[u]
    O God,
    the processions of my God, my
    Ruler, into the sanctuary—
25 the singers in front, the musicians
    last,
    between them girls playing
    tambourines:
26 "Bless God in the great
    congregation,
    bless GOD, O you who are of
    Israel's fountain!"
27 There is Benjamin, the least of
    them, in the lead,
    the princes of Judah in a body,
    the princes of Zebulun, the
    princes of Naphtali.

28 Summon your might, O God;
    show your strength, O God, as
    you have done for us before.
29 Because of your temple at
    Jerusalem
    rulers bear gifts to you.
30 Rebuke the wild animals that live
    among the reeds,
    the herd of bulls with the calves
    of the peoples.
    Trample[v] under foot those who
    lust after tribute;
    scatter the peoples who delight in
    war.[w]
31 Let bronze be brought from Egypt;
    let Ethiopia[x] hasten to stretch
    out its hands to God.

32 Sing to God, O nations of the
    earth;
    sing praises to God,   *Selah*
33 O rider in the heavens, the ancient
    heavens;
    listen, God thunders—it is the
    mighty voice of God.
34 Ascribe power to God,
    whose majesty is over Israel;
    and whose power is in the skies.
35 Awesome is God in the holy[y]
    sanctuary;
    the God of Israel
    gives power and strength to
    God's people.

Blessed be God!

Psalm 69
Prayer for Deliverance from Persecution

To the leader: according to Lilies.
Of David.

1 Save me, O God,
    for the waters have come up to
    my neck.
2 I sink in deep mire,
    where there is no foothold;
    I have come into deep waters,
    and the flood sweeps over me.
3 I am weary with my crying;
    my throat is parched.
    My eyes grow dim
    with waiting for my God.

4 More in number than the hairs of
    my head
    are those who hate me without
    cause;

---

t Gk Syr Tg: Heb *shatter*   u Or *have been
seen*   v Cn: Heb *Trampling*   w Meaning
of Heb of verse 30 is uncertain
x Or *Nubia*; Heb *Cush*   y Gk: Heb *from
your*

many are those who would destroy
me,
my enemies who accuse me
falsely.
What I did not steal
must I now restore?
5 O God, you know my folly;
the wrongs I have done are not
hidden from you.

6 Do not let those who hope in you
be put to shame because of
me,
O Sovereign GOD of hosts;
do not let those who seek you be
dishonored because of me,
O God of Israel.
7 It is for your sake that I have
borne reproach,
that shame has covered my face.
8 I have become a stranger to my
kindred,
an alien to my mother's children.

9 It is zeal for your house that has
consumed me;
the insults of those who insult
you have fallen on me.
10 When I humbled my soul with
fasting,^z
they insulted me for doing so.
11 When I made sackcloth my
clothing,
I became a byword to them.
12 I am the subject of gossip for
those who sit in the gate,
and the drunkards make songs
about me.

13 But as for me, my prayer is to
you, O GOD.
At an acceptable time, O God,
in the abundance of your
steadfast love, answer me.
With your faithful help 14rescue me

from sinking in the mire;
let me be delivered from my
enemies
and from the deep waters.
15 Do not let the flood sweep over
me,
or the deep swallow me up,
or the Pit close its mouth
over me.

16 Answer me, O GOD, for your
steadfast love is good;
according to your abundant
mercy, turn to me.
17 Do not hide your face from your
servant,
for I am in distress—make haste
to answer me.
18 Draw near to me, redeem me,
set me free because of my
enemies.

19 You know the insults I receive,
and my shame and dishonor;
my foes are all known to you.
20 Insults have broken my heart,
so that I am in despair.
I looked for pity, but there was
none;
and for comforters, but I found
none.
21 They gave me poison for food,
and for my thirst they gave me
vinegar to drink.

22 Let their table be a trap for them,
a snare for their allies.
23 Let their eyes be darkened so that
they cannot see,
and make their loins tremble
continually.

_____

z Gk Syr: Heb *I wept, with fasting my soul,*
or *I made my soul mourn with fasting*

24 Pour out your indignation upon
　　them,
　　and let your burning anger
　　　overtake them.
25 May their camp be a desolation;
　　let no one live in their tents.
26 For they persecute those whom
　　you have struck down,
　　and those whom you have
　　　wounded, they attack still
　　　more.[a]
27 Add guilt to their guilt;
　　may they have no acquittal from
　　　you.
28 Let them be blotted out of the
　　book of the living;
　　let them not be enrolled among
　　　the righteous.
29 But I am lowly and in pain;
　　let your salvation, O God,
　　　protect me.

30 I will praise the name of God with
　　a song;
　　I will magnify God with
　　　thanksgiving.
31 This will please GOD more than an
　　ox
　　or a bull with horns and hoofs.
32 Let the oppressed see it and be
　　glad;
　　you who seek God, let your
　　　hearts revive.
33 For GOD hears those who are
　　needy,
　　and does not despise God's own
　　　that are in bonds.

34 Let heaven and earth praise God,
　　the seas and everything that
　　　moves in them.
35 For God will save Zion
　　and rebuild the cities of Judah;
　　and God's servants shall live[b] there
　　　and possess it;

36 the children of God's servants
　　shall inherit it,
　　and those who love God's name
　　　shall live in it.

Psalm 70

Prayer for Deliverance from Enemies

To the leader. Of David, for the memorial offering.

1 Be pleased, O God, to deliver me.
　　O LORD, make haste to help me!
2 Let those be put to shame and
　　confusion
　　who seek my life.
　　Let those be turned back and
　　　brought to dishonor
　　who desire to hurt me.
3 Let those who say, "Aha, Aha!"
　　turn back because of their shame.

4 Let all who seek you
　　rejoice and be glad in you.
　　Let those who love your salvation
　　say evermore, "God is great!"
5 But I am poor and needy;
　　hasten to me, O Lord!
　　You are my help and my deliverer;
　　O GOD, do not delay!

Psalm 71

Prayer for Lifelong Protection and Help

1 In you, O GOD, I take refuge;
　　let me never be put to shame.
2 In your righteousness deliver me
　　and rescue me;
　　incline your ear to me and
　　　save me.
3 Be to me a rock of refuge,

---

a Gk Syr: Heb *recount the pain of*
b Syr: Heb *and they shall live*

a strong fortress,[c] to save me,
for you are my rock and my
fortress.

4 Rescue me, O my God, from the
hand of the wicked,
from the grasp of the unjust and
cruel.
5 For you, O God, are my hope,
my trust, O GOD, from my
youth.
6 Upon you I have leaned from my
birth;
it was you who took me from
my mother's womb.
My praise is continually of you.

7 I have been like a portent to many,
but you are my strong refuge.
8 My mouth is filled with your
praise,
and with your glory all day long.
9 Do not cast me off in the time of
old age;
do not forsake me when my
strength is spent.
10 For my enemies speak concerning
me,
and those who watch for my life
consult together.
11 They say, "Pursue and seize that
person
whom God has forsaken,
for there is no one to deliver."

12 O God, do not be far from me;
O my God, make haste to
help me!
13 Let my accusers be put to shame
and consumed;
let those who seek to hurt me
be covered with scorn and
disgrace.
14 But I will hope continually,

and will praise you yet more and
more.
15 My mouth will tell of your
righteous acts,
of your deeds of salvation all day
long,
though their number is past my
knowledge.
16 I will come praising the mighty
deeds of the Sovereign GOD,
I will praise your righteousness,
yours alone.

17 O God, from my youth you have
taught me,
and I still proclaim your
wondrous deeds.
18 So even to old age and gray hairs,
O God, do not forsake me,
until I proclaim your might
to all the generations to come.[d]
Your power 19and your
righteousness, O God,
reach the high heavens.

You who have done great things,
O God, who is like you?
20 You who have made me see many
troubles and calamities
will revive me again;
from the depths of the earth
you will bring me up again.
21 You will increase my honor,
and comfort me once again.

22 I will also praise you with the harp
for your faithfulness, O my God;
I will sing praises to you with the
lyre,
O Holy One of Israel.
23 My lips will shout for joy

---

c Gk Compare 31.3: Heb *to come continually
you have commanded*   d Gk Compare Syr:
Heb *to a generation, to all that come*

when I sing praises to you;
  my soul also, which you have
    rescued.
24 All day long my tongue will talk
  of your righteous help,
for those who tried to do me harm
  have been put to shame, and
    disgraced.

Psalm 72

Prayer for Guidance and Support
for the Ruler

Of Solomon.

1 Give the ruler your justice, O God,
  and your righteousness to a royal
    heir.
2 May the ruler judge your people
  with righteousness,
  and your poor with justice.
3 May the mountains yield prosperity
  for the people,
  and the hills, in righteousness.
4 May the ruler defend the cause of
  the poor of the people,
  give deliverance to those who are
    needy,
  and crush the oppressor.

5 May the ruler live[e] while the sun
  endures,
  and as long as the moon,
    throughout all generations.
6 May the ruler be like rain that falls
  on the mown grass,
  like showers that water the earth.
7 In those days may righteousness
  flourish
  and peace abound, until the
    moon is no more.

8 May the ruler have dominion from
  sea to sea,
  and from the River to the ends
    of the earth.

9 May the foes[f] of the ruler bow
  down,
  and the enemies lick the dust.
10 May the kings of Tarshish and of
  the isles
  render tribute,
  may the kings of Sheba and Seba
  bring gifts.
11 May all kings bow down,
  all nations serve the ruler.

12 For the ruler delivers those who
  are needy when they call,
  those who are poor and those
    who have no helper,
13 and has pity on the weak and the
  needy,
  and saves the lives of the needy.
14 The ruler redeems their life from
  oppression and violence;
  and views their life as precious.

15 Long may the ruler live!
  May gold of Sheba be given to
    the ruler.
  May prayer be offered continually,
  and blessings invoked for the
    ruler all day long.
16 May there be abundance of grain in
  the land;
  may it wave on the tops of the
    mountains;
  may its fruit be like Lebanon;
  and may people blossom in the
    cities
  like the grass of the field.
17 May the ruler's name endure
  forever;
  may it continue as long as the
    sun.

---

e Gk: Heb *may they revere you*
f Cn: Heb *those who live in the wilderness*

May all nations receive a royal
blessing;^g
may they pronounce the ruler
happy.

18 Blessed be the Most High, the God
of Israel,
who alone does wondrous things.
19 Blessed be God's glorious name
forever;
may God's glory fill the whole
earth.
Amen and Amen.

20 The prayers of David son of Jesse
are ended.

BOOK III ᕉ ᕉ ᕉ ᕉ ᕉ

Psalm 73

Plea for Relief from Oppressors

A Psalm of Asaph.

1 Truly God is good to the upright,^h
to those who are pure in heart.
2 But as for me, my feet had almost
stumbled;
my steps had nearly slipped.
3 For I was envious of the arrogant;
I saw the prosperity of the
wicked.

4 For they have no pain;
their bodies are sound and sleek.
5 They are not in trouble as others
are;
they are not plagued like other
people.
6 Therefore pride is their necklace;
violence covers them like a
garment.
7 Their eyes swell out with fatness;
their hearts overflow with follies.
8 They scoff and speak with malice;
loftily they threaten oppression.

9 They set their mouths against
heaven,
and their tongues range over the
earth.
10 Therefore the people turn and
praise them,ⁱ
and find no fault in them.^j
11 And they say, "How can God
know?
Is there knowledge in the
Most High?"
12 Such are the wicked;
always at ease, they increase in
riches.
13 All in vain I have kept my heart
clean
and washed my hands in
innocence.
14 For all day long I have been
plagued,
and am punished every morning.
15 If I had said, "I will talk on in
this way,"
I would have been untrue to the
circle of your children.
16 But when I thought how to
understand this,
it seemed to me a wearisome
task,
17 until I went into the sanctuary
of God;
then I perceived their end.
18 Truly you set them in slippery
places;
you make them fall to ruin.
19 How they are destroyed in a
moment,
swept away utterly by terrors!

g Or *bless themselves by the ruler*
h Or *good to Israel*   i Cn: Heb *God's*
people return here   j Cn: Heb *abundant*
waters are drained by them

20 They are[k] like a dream when one
    awakes;
    on awaking you despise their
    phantoms.

21 When my soul was embittered,
    when I was pricked in heart,
22 I was stupid and ignorant;
    I was like a brute beast toward
    you.
23 Nevertheless I am continually
    with you;
    you hold my hand.
24 You guide me with your counsel,
    and afterward you will receive
    me with honor.[l]
25 Whom have I in heaven but you?
    And there is nothing on earth
    that I desire other than you.
26 My flesh and my heart may fail,
    but God is the strength[m] of my
    heart and my portion forever.

27 Indeed, those who are far from you
    will perish;
    you put an end to those who are
    false to you.
28 But for me it is good to be near
    God;
    I have made the Sovereign GOD
    my refuge,
    to tell of all your works.

Psalm 74

Plea for Help in Time of
National Humiliation

A Maskil of Asaph.

1 O God, why do you cast us off
    forever?
    Why does your anger smoke
    against the sheep of your
    pasture?

2 Remember your congregation,
    which you acquired long ago,
    which you redeemed to be the
    tribe of your heritage.
    Remember Mount Zion, where
    you came to dwell.
3 Direct your steps to the perpetual
    ruins;
    the enemy has destroyed
    everything in the sanctuary.

4 Your foes have roared within your
    holy place;
    they set up their emblems there.
5 At the upper entrance they hacked
    the wooden trellis with axes.[n]
6 And then, with hatchets and
    hammers,
    they smashed all its carved work.
7 They set your sanctuary on fire;
    they desecrated the dwelling place
    of your name,
    bringing it to the ground.
8 They said to themselves, "We will
    utterly subdue them";
    they burned all the meeting
    places of God in the land.

9 We do not see our emblems;
    there is no longer any prophet,
    and there is no one among us
    who knows how long.
10 How long, O God, is the foe to
    scoff?
    Is the enemy to revile your name
    forever?
11 Why do you hold back your hand;
    why do you keep your hand in[o]
    your bosom?

---

k Cn: Heb *God is*   l Or *to glory*
m Heb *rock*   n Cn Compare Gk Syr:
Meaning of Heb uncertain   o Cn: Heb *do*
you consume your hand from

12 Yet God my Sovereign is from of
old,
   working salvation in the earth.
13 You divided the sea by your might;
   you broke the heads of the
   dragons in the waters.
14 You crushed the heads of
Leviathan;
   you gave him as food[p] for the
   creatures of the wilderness.
15 You cut openings for springs and
torrents;
   you dried up everflowing streams.
16 Yours is the day, yours also the
night;
   you established the luminaries[q]
   and the sun.
17 You have fixed all the bounds of
the earth;
   you made summer and winter.

18 Remember this, O GOD, how the
enemy scoffs,
   and an impious people reviles
   your name.
19 Do not deliver the soul of your
dove to the wild animals;
   do not forget the life of your
   poor forever.
20 Have regard for your[r] covenant,
   for the hidden places of the land
   are full of the haunts of
   violence.
21 Do not let the downtrodden be put
to shame;
   let the poor and needy praise
   your name.
22 Rise up, O God, plead your cause;
   remember how the impious scoff
   at you all day long.
23 Do not forget the clamor of your
foes,
   the uproar of your adversaries
   that goes up continually.

Psalm 75

Thanksgiving for God's Wondrous Deeds

*To the leader: Do Not Destroy. A Psalm
of Asaph. A Song.*

1 We give thanks to you, O God;
   we give thanks; your name is
   near.
People tell of your wondrous
   deeds.

2 At the set time that I appoint
   I will judge with equity.
3 When the earth totters, with all its
   inhabitants,
   it is I who keep its pillars
   steady.   *Selah*
4 I say to the boastful, "Do not
   boast,"
   and to the wicked, "Do not lift
   up your horn;
5 do not lift up your horn on high,
   or speak with insolent neck."

6 For not from the east or from
   the west
   and not from the wilderness
   comes lifting up;
7 but it is God who executes
   judgment,
   putting down one and lifting up
   another.
8 For in the hand of GOD there is a
   cup
   with foaming wine, well mixed;
God will pour a draught from it,
   and all the wicked of the earth
   shall drain it down to the dregs.
9 But I will rejoice[s] forever;

---

p Heb *food for the people*   q Or *moon*;
Heb *light*   r Gk Syr: Heb *the*
s Gk: Heb *declare*

I will sing praises to the God of
Jacob.

10 All the horns of the wicked I will
cut off,
but the horns of the righteous
shall be exalted.

Psalm 76
Israel's God—Judge of All the Earth

To the leader: with stringed instruments.
A Psalm of Asaph. A Song.

1 In Judah God is known,
God's name is great in Israel.
2 God's abode has been established in
Salem,
God's dwelling place in Zion.
3 There God broke the flashing
arrows,
the shield, the sword, and the
weapons of war.   *Selah*

4 Glorious are you, more majestic
than the everlasting mountains.[t]
5 The stouthearted were stripped of
their spoil;
they sank into sleep;
none of the troops
was able to lift a hand.
6 At your rebuke, O God of Jacob,
both rider and horse lay stunned.

7 But you indeed are awesome!
Who can stand before you
when once your anger is roused?
8 From the heavens you uttered
judgment;
the earth feared and was still
9 when God rose up to establish
judgment,
to save all the oppressed of the
earth.   *Selah*

10 Human wrath serves only to
praise you,
when you bind the last bit of
your[u] wrath around you.
11 Make vows to the Most High your
God, and perform them;
let all who are around God bring
gifts
to the one who is awesome,
12 who crushes the spirit of royalty,
who inspires fear in the rulers of
the earth.

Psalm 77
God's Mighty Deeds Recalled

To the leader: according to Jeduthun.
Of Asaph. A Psalm.

1 I cry aloud to God,
aloud to God, that God may
hear me.
2 In the day of my trouble I
seek God;
in the night my hand is stretched
out without wearying;
my soul refuses to be comforted.
3 I think of God, and I moan;
I meditate, and my spirit faints.
                            Selah

4 You keep my eyelids from closing;
I am so troubled that I cannot
speak.
5 I consider the days of old,
and remember the years of long
ago.
6 I commune[v] with my heart in the
night;
I meditate and search my spirit:[w]
7 "Will God spurn forever,

---

t Gk: Heb *the mountains of prey*
u Heb lacks *your*   v Gk Syr: Heb *My*
music   w Syr Jerome: Heb *my spirit*
searches

and never again be favorable?
8 Has God's steadfast love ceased
forever?
Are God's promises at an end
for all time?
9 Has God forgotten to be gracious?
Has God in anger shut up all
compassion?"   *Selah*
10 And I say, "It is my grief
that the mighty hand of the
Most High has changed."

11 I will call to mind the deeds of
GOD;
I will remember your wonders
of old.
12 I will meditate on all your work,
and muse on your mighty deeds.
13 Your way, O God, is holy.
What god is so great as our
God?
14 You are the God who works
wonders;
you have displayed your might
among the peoples.
15 With your strong arm you
redeemed your people,
the descendants of Jacob and
Joseph.   *Selah*

16 When the waters saw you, O God,
when the waters saw you, they
were afraid;
the very deep trembled.
17 The clouds poured out water;
the skies thundered;
your arrows flashed on every
side.
18 The crash of your thunder was in
the whirlwind;
your lightnings lit up the world;
the earth trembled and shook.
19 Your way was through the sea,
your path, through the mighty
waters;

yet your footprints were unseen.
20 You led your people like a flock
by the hand of Moses, Miriam,
and Aaron.

Psalm 78

God's Goodness and Israel's Ingratitude

A Maskil of Asaph.

1 Give ear, O my people, to my
teaching;
incline your ears to the words of
my mouth.
2 I will open my mouth in a parable;
I will utter obscure sayings from
of old,
3 things that we have heard and
known,
that our ancestors have told us.
4 We will not hide them from their
children;
we will tell to the coming
generation
the glorious deeds and might of
GOD,
and the wonders that God has
done.

5 God established a decree in Jacob,
and appointed a law in Israel,
which God commanded our
ancestors
to teach to their children;
6 that the next generation might
know them,
the children yet unborn,
and rise up and tell them to their
children,
7 so that they should set their
hope in God,
and not forget the works of God,
but keep God's commandments;

8 and that they should not be like
  their ancestors,
   a stubborn and rebellious
     generation,
   a generation whose heart was not
     steadfast,
   whose spirit was not faithful
     to God.

9 The Ephraimites, armed with* the
   bow,
   turned back on the day of battle.
10 They did not keep God's covenant,
   but refused to walk according to
     God's law.
11 They forgot what God had done,
   and the miracles that God had
     shown them.
12 In the sight of their ancestors God
   worked marvels
   in the land of Egypt, in the
     fields of Zoan.
13 God divided the sea and let them
   pass through it,
   and made the waters stand like
     a heap.
14 In the daytime God led them with
   a cloud,
   and all night long with a fiery
     light.
15 God split rocks open in the
   wilderness,
   and gave them drink abundantly
     as from the deep.
16 God made streams come out of the
   rock,
   and caused waters to flow down
     like rivers.

17 Yet they sinned still more against
   God,
   rebelling against the Most High
     in the desert.
18 They tested God in their heart

by demanding the food they
  craved.
19 They spoke against God, saying,
   "Can God spread a table in the
     wilderness?
20 Even though God struck the rock
   so that water gushed out
   and torrents overflowed,
   can God also give bread,
   or provide meat for God's
     people?"

21 Therefore, hearing this, GOD was
   full of rage;
   a fire was kindled against Jacob,
   God's anger mounted against
     Israel,
22 because they had no faith in God,
   and did not trust God's saving
     power.
23 Yet God commanded the skies
   above,
   and opened the doors of heaven;
24 God rained down on them manna
   to eat,
   and gave them the grain of
     heaven.
25 Mortals ate of the bread of angels;
   food was sent them in
     abundance.
26 God caused the east wind to blow
   in the heavens,
   and with power God led out the
     south wind;
27 God rained flesh upon them like
   dust,
   winged birds like the sand of the
     seas;
28 God let them fall within their
   camp,
   all around the dwellings.
29 And they ate and were well filled,

---

x Heb *armed with shooting*

for God gave them what they
craved.

30 But before they had satisfied their
craving,
while the food was still in their
mouths,

31 the anger of God rose against them
and God killed the strongest of
them,
and laid low the flower of Israel.

32 In spite of all this they still sinned;
they did not believe in God's
wonders.

33 So God made their days vanish like
a breath,
and their years in terror.

34 When God killed them, they sought
for God;
they repented and sought God
earnestly.

35 They remembered that God was
their rock,
the Most High God their
redeemer.

36 But they flattered God with their
mouths;
they lied to God with their
tongues.

37 Their heart was not steadfast
toward God;
they were not true to God's
covenant.

38 Yet being compassionate,
God forgave their iniquity,
and did not destroy them;
often God restrained God's anger,
and did not stir up all God's
wrath.

39 God remembered that they were
but flesh,
a wind that passes and does not
come again.

40 How often they rebelled against
God in the wilderness
and grieved God in the desert!

41 They tested God again and again,
and provoked the Holy One of
Israel.

42 They did not keep in mind God's
power,
or the day when God redeemed
them from the foe—

43 when God displayed the signs in
Egypt,
and the miracles in the fields of
Zoan.

44 God turned their rivers to blood,
so that they could not drink of
their streams.

45 God sent among them swarms of
flies, which devoured them,
and frogs, which destroyed them.

46 God gave their crops to the
caterpillar,
and the fruit of their labor to
the locust.

47 God destroyed their vines with hail,
and their sycamores with frost.

48 God gave over their cattle to the
hail,
and their flocks to thunderbolts.

49 God let loose on them God's fierce
anger,
wrath, indignation, and distress,
a company of destroying angels.

50 God made a path for God's anger;
and did not spare them from
death,
but gave their lives over to the
plague.

51 God struck all the firstborn in
Egypt,
the first issue of their strength in
the tents of Ham.

52 Then God led out the people like
sheep,

and guided them in the
wilderness like a flock.
53 God led them in safety, so that
they were not afraid;
but the sea overwhelmed their
enemies.
54 And God brought them to God's
holy hill,
to the mountain that God's
mighty hand had won.
55 God drove out nations before them;
God apportioned them for a
possession
and settled the tribes of Israel in
their tents.

56 Yet they tested the Most High
God,
and rebelled against the Most
High.
They did not observe God's
decrees,
57 but turned away and were faithless
like their ancestors;
they twisted like a treacherous
bow.
58 For they provoked the Most High
God to anger with their high
places;
they moved God to jealousy with
their idols.
59 When God heard, God was full of
wrath
and utterly rejected Israel.
60 God abandoned God's dwelling at
Shiloh,
the tent where God dwelt among
mortals,
61 and delivered power to captivity,
God's glory to the hand of the
foe.
62 God gave the people to the sword,
and vented God's wrath on
God's heritage.

63 Fire devoured their young men,
and their young women had no
marriage song.
64 Their priests fell by the sword,
and their widows made no
lamentation.
65 Then God awoke as from sleep,
like a warrior shouting because
of wine.
66 God put God's adversaries to rout;
and put them to everlasting
disgrace.

67 God rejected the tent of Joseph,
and did not choose the tribe of
Ephraim;
68 but God chose the tribe of Judah,
Mount Zion, which God loves.
69 God built a sanctuary like the high
heavens,
like the earth, which God has
founded forever.
70 God chose God's servant David,
and took him from the
sheepfolds;
71 from tending the nursing ewes God
brought David
to be the shepherd of the people
Jacob,
of Israel, God's inheritance.
72 With upright heart David tended
them,
and guided them with skillful
hand.

Psalm 79
Plea for Mercy for Jerusalem
A Psalm of Asaph.

1 O God, the nations have come into
your inheritance;
they have defiled your holy
temple;
they have laid Jerusalem in ruins.

2 They have given the bodies of your
  servants
    to the birds of the air for food,
    the flesh of your faithful to the
      wild animals of the earth.
3 They have poured out their blood
  like water
    all around Jerusalem,
    and there was no one to bury
      them.
4 We have become a taunt to our
  neighbors,
    mocked and derided by those
      around us.

5 How long, O GOD? Will you be
  angry forever?
    Will your jealous wrath burn like
      fire?
6 Pour out your anger on the nations
    that do not know you,
  and on the peoples
    that do not call on your name.
7 For they have devoured Jacob
    and laid waste the habitation of
      Israel.

8 Do not remember against us the
    iniquities of our ancestors;
  let your compassion come
    speedily to meet us,
  for we are brought very low.
9 Help us, O God of our salvation,
    for the glory of your name;
  deliver us, and forgive our sins,
    for your name's sake.
10 Why should the nations say,
    "Where is their God?"
  Let the avenging of the outpoured
    blood of your servants
  be known among the nations
    before our eyes.

11 Let the groans of the prisoners
    come before you;

according to your great power
    preserve those doomed to die.
12 Return sevenfold into the bosom of
    our neighbors
  the taunts with which they
    taunted you, O God!
13 Then we your people, the flock of
    your pasture,
  will give thanks to you forever;
  from generation to generation we
    will recount your praise.

Psalm 80
Prayer for Israel's Restoration

To the leader: on Lilies, a Covenant.
Of Asaph. A Psalm.

1 Give ear, O Shepherd of Israel,
    you who lead Joseph like a
      flock!
  You who are enthroned upon the
    cherubim, shine forth
2   before Ephraim and Benjamin
      and Manasseh.
  Stir up your might,
    and come to save us!

3 Restore us, O God;
    let your face shine, that we may
      be saved.

4 O Most High God of hosts,
    how long will you be angry with
      your people's prayers?
5 You have fed them with the bread
    of tears,
  and given them tears to drink in
    full measure.
6 You make us the scorn[y] of our
    neighbors;
  our enemies laugh among
    themselves.

7 Restore us, O God of hosts;

---

y Syr: Heb *strife*

let your face shine, that we may
be saved.

8 You brought a vine out of Egypt;
you drove out the nations and
planted it.
9 You cleared the ground for it;
it took deep root and filled the
land.
10 The mountains were covered with
its shade,
the mighty cedars with its
branches;
11 it sent out its branches to the sea,
and its shoots to the River.
12 Why then have you broken down
its walls,
so that all who pass along the
way pluck its fruit?
13 The boar from the forest ravages it,
and all that move in the field
feed on it.

14 Turn again, O God of hosts;
look down from heaven, and see;
have regard for this vine,
15   the stock that your strong hand
planted.[z]
16 They have burned it with fire, they
have cut it down;[a]
may they perish at the rebuke of
your countenance.
17 But let your hand be upon the one
at your side,
the one whom you made strong
for yourself.
18 Then we will never turn back from
you;
give us life, and we will call on
your name.

19 Restore us, O Most High God of
hosts;
let your face shine, that we may
be saved.

Psalm 81
God's Appeal to Stubborn Israel

*To the leader: according to The Gittith.
Of Asaph.*

1 Sing aloud to God our strength;
shout for joy to the God of
Jacob.
2 Raise a song, sound the
tambourine,
the sweet lyre with the harp.
3 Blow the trumpet at the new
moon,
at the full moon, on our
festal day.
4 For it is a statute for Israel,
an ordinance of the God of
Jacob.
5 God made it a decree in Joseph,
when God went out against the
land of Egypt.

I hear a voice I had not known:
6 "I relieved your[b] shoulder of the
burden;
your[b] hands were freed from the
basket.
7 In distress you called, and I
rescued you;
I answered you in the secret
place of thunder;
I tested you at the waters of
Meribah.   *Selah*
8 Hear, O my people, while I
admonish you;
O Israel, if you would but listen
to me!
9 There shall be no strange god
among you;

---

z Heb adds from verse 17 *and upon the one
whom you made strong for yourself*
a Cn: Heb *it is cut down*   b Heb *Joseph's*

480

you shall not bow down to a
foreign god.

10 I am the Most High your God,
who brought you up out of the
land of Egypt.
Open your mouth wide and I
will fill it.

11 "But my people did not listen to
my voice;
Israel would not submit to me.

12 So I gave them over to their
stubborn hearts,
to follow their own counsels.

13 O that my people would listen
to me,
that Israel would walk in my
ways!

14 Then I would quickly subdue their
enemies,
and turn my hand against their
foes.

15 Those who hate me would cringe
before me,
and their doom would last
forever.

16 I would feed you with the finest of
the wheat,
and with honey from the rock I
would satisfy you."

Psalm 82
A Plea for Justice
A Psalm of Asaph.

1 God sits in the divine council;
in the midst of the gods God
holds judgment:

2 "How long will you judge unjustly
and show partiality to the
wicked?   *Selah*

3 Give justice to the weak and the
orphan;

maintain the right of the lowly
and the destitute.

4 Rescue the weak and the needy;
deliver them from the hand of
the wicked."

5 They have neither knowledge nor
understanding,
they walk around in the gloom
of night;
all the foundations of the earth
are shaken.

6 I say, "You are gods,
children of the Most High, all
of you;

7 nevertheless, you shall die like
mortals,
and fall like any ruler."c

8 Rise up, O God, judge the earth;
for all the nations belong to you!

Psalm 83
Prayer for Judgment on Israel's Foes

A Song. A Psalm of Asaph.

1 O God, do not keep silence;
do not hold your peace or be
still, O God!

2 Even now your enemies are in
tumult;
those who hate you have raised
their heads.

3 They lay crafty plans against your
people;
they consult together against
those you protect.

4 They say, "Come, let us wipe them
out as a nation;
let the name of Israel be
remembered no more."

---

c Or *fall as one person, O rulers*

5 They conspire with one accord;
    against you they make a
        covenant—
6 the tents of Edom and the
        Ishmaelites,
    Moab and the Hagrites,
7 Gebal and Ammon and Amalek,
    Philistia with the inhabitants of
        Tyre;
8 Assyria also has joined them;
    they are the strong arm of the
        children of Lot.   *Selah*

9 Do to them as you did to Midian,
    as to Sisera and Jabin at the
        Wadi Kishon,
10 who were destroyed at En-dor,
    who became dung for the
        ground.
11 Make their nobles like Oreb and
        Zeeb,
    all their princes like Zebah and
        Zalmunna,
12 who said, "Let us take the pastures
        of God
    for our own possession."

13 O my God, make them like
        whirling dust,[d]
    like chaff before the wind.
14 As fire consumes the forest,
    as the flame sets the mountains
        ablaze,
15 so pursue them with your tempest
    and terrify them with your
        hurricane.
16 Fill their faces with shame,
    so that they may seek your
        name, O Most High.
17 Let them be put to shame and
        dismayed forever;
    let them perish in disgrace.
18 Let them know that you alone,
    whose name is GOD,

are the Most High over all the
    earth.

Psalm 84
The Joy of Worship in the Temple

To the leader: according to The Gittith.
Of the Korahites. A Psalm.

1 How lovely is your dwelling place,
    O GOD of hosts!
2 My soul longs, indeed it faints
    for the courts of GOD;
    my heart and my flesh sing for joy
    to the living God.

3 Even the sparrow finds a home,
    and the swallow a nest for
        herself,
    where she may lay her young,
    at your altars, O GOD of hosts,
    my Ruler and my God.
4 Blessed are those who live in your
        house,
    ever singing your praise.   *Selah*

5 Blessed are those whose strength is
        in you,
    in whose heart are the highways
        to Zion.[e]
6 As they go through the valley of
        Baca
    they make it a place of springs;
    the early rain also covers it with
        pools.
7 They go from strength to strength;
    the God of gods will be seen
        in Zion.

8 O Most High God of hosts, hear
        my prayer;
    give ear, O God of Jacob!   *Selah*
9 Behold our shield, O God;

—————————

d Or *a tumbleweed*   e Heb lacks *to Zion*

482

look on the face of your
anointed.

10 For a day in your courts is better
than a thousand elsewhere.
I would rather be a doorkeeper in
the house of my God
than live in the tents of
wickedness.
11 For God the Most High is a sun
and shield,
who bestows favor and honor.
No good thing does GOD withhold
from those who walk uprightly.
12 O GOD of hosts,
blessed is everyone who trusts
in you.

Psalm 85

Prayer for the Restoration of God's Favor

To the leader. Of the Korahites. A Psalm.

1 O GOD, you were favorable to
your land;
you restored the fortunes of
Jacob.
2 You forgave the iniquity of your
people;
you pardoned all their sin. *Selah*
3 You withdrew all your wrath;
you turned from your hot anger.

4 Restore us again, O God of our
salvation,
and put away your indignation
toward us.
5 Will you be angry with us forever?
Will you prolong your anger to
all generations?
6 Will you not revive us again,
so that your people may rejoice
in you?
7 Show us your steadfast love,
O GOD,

and grant us your salvation.

8 Let me hear what God the Most
High will speak,
for God will speak peace to
God's people,
to those who are faithful, to
those who turn to God in
their hearts.[f]
9 Surely salvation is at hand for
those who revere God,
that the glory of God may dwell
in our land.

10 Steadfast love and faithfulness
will meet;
righteousness and peace will kiss
each other.
11 Faithfulness will spring up from the
ground,
and righteousness will look down
from the sky.
12 GOD will give what is good,
and our land will yield its
increase.
13 Righteousness will go before God,
and will make a path for God's
steps.

Psalm 86

Supplication for Help against Enemies

A Prayer of David.

1 Incline your ear, O LORD, and
answer me,
for I am poor and needy.
2 Preserve my life, for I am devoted
to you;
save your servant who trusts
in you.

---

f Gk: Heb *but let them not turn back to folly*

483

You are my God; 3be gracious to
 me, O God,
   for to you do I cry all day long.
4 Gladden the soul of your servant,
   for to you, O God, I lift up my
      soul.
5 For you, O God, are good and
      forgiving,
   abounding in steadfast love to all
      who call on you.
6 Give ear, O GOD, to my prayer;
   listen to my cry of supplication.
7 In the day of my trouble I call
      on you,
   for you will answer me.

8 There is none like you among the
      gods, O God,
   nor are there any works like
      yours.
9 All the nations you have made
      shall come
   and bow down before you,
      O God,
   and shall glorify your name.
10 For you are great and do
      wondrous things;
   you alone are God.
11 Teach me your way, O GOD,
   that I may walk in your truth;
   give me an undivided heart to
      revere your name.
12 I give thanks to you, O God my
      God, with my whole heart,
   and I will glorify your name
      forever.
13 For great is your steadfast love
      toward me;
   you have delivered my soul from
      the depths of Sheol.

14 O God, the insolent rise up against
      me;
   a band of ruffians seeks my life,

and they do not set you before
      them.
15 But you, O God, are a god
      merciful and gracious,
   slow to anger and abounding in
      steadfast love and faithfulness.
16 Turn to me and be gracious to me;
   give your strength to your
      servant;
   save the child of your
      womanservant.
17 Show me a sign of your favor,
   so that those who hate me may
      see it and be put to shame,
   because you, LORD, have helped
      me and comforted me.

Psalm 87
The Joy of Living in Zion
Of the Korahites. A Psalm. A Song.

1 On the holy mount stands the city
      founded by GOD
2   who loves the gates of Zion
   more than all the dwellings of
      Jacob.
3 Glorious things are spoken of you,
   O city of God.   *Selah*

4 Among those who know me I
      mention Rahab and Babylon;
   Philistia too, and Tyre, with
      Ethiopia[g]—
   "This one was born there," they
      say.

5 And of Zion it shall be said,
   "This one and that one were
      born in it";
   for the Most High will establish
      it!
6 GOD records, registering the
      peoples,

___

g Or *Nubia*; Heb *Cush*

484

"This one was born there." *Selah*

7 Singers and dancers alike say,
"All my springs are in you."

Psalm 88
Prayer for Help in Despondency

A Song. A Psalm of the Korahites. To the leader: according to Mahalath Leannoth. A Maskil of Heman the Ezrahite.

1 O Most High, God of my
salvation,
when, at night, I cry out in your
presence,
2 let my prayer come before you;
incline your ear to my cry.

3 For my soul is full of troubles,
and my life draws near to Sheol.
4 I am counted among those who go
down to the Pit;
I am like those who have no
help,
5 like those forsaken among the dead,
like the slain that lie in the
grave,
like those whom you remember
no more,
for they are cut off from your
hand.
6 You have put me in the depths of
the Pit,
in the regions mysterious and
deep.
7 Your wrath lies heavy upon me,
and you overwhelm me with all
your waves. *Selah*

8 You have caused my companions to
shun me;
you have made me a thing of
horror to them.
I am shut in so that I cannot
escape;

9 my eye grows dim through
sorrow.
Every day I call on you, O GOD;
I spread out my hands to you.
10 Do you work wonders for the
dead?
Do the shades rise up to praise
you? *Selah*
11 Is your steadfast love declared in
the grave,
or your faithfulness in Abaddon?
12 Are your wonders known in the
night,
or your saving help in the land
of forgetfulness?

13 But I, O GOD, cry out to you;
in the morning my prayer comes
before you.
14 O GOD, why do you cast me off?
Why do you hide your face from
me?
15 Wretched and close to death from
my youth up,
I suffer your terrors; I am
desperate.[h]
16 Your wrath has swept over me;
your dread assaults destroy me.
17 They surround me like a flood all
day long;
from all sides they close in on
me.
18 You have caused friend and
neighbor to shun me;
my companions have disappeared.

Psalm 89
God's Covenant with David

A Maskil of Ethan the Ezrahite.

1 I will sing of your steadfast love,
O GOD,[i] forever;

---

h Meaning of Heb uncertain   i Gk: Heb
the steadfast love of GOD

with my mouth I will proclaim
  your faithfulness to all
  generations.
2 I declare that your steadfast love is
    established forever;
  your faithfulness is as firm as the
    heavens.

3 You said, "I have made a covenant
    with my chosen one,
  I have sworn to my servant
    David:
4 'I will establish your descendants
    forever,
  and build your throne for all
    generations.' "   *Selah*

5 Let the heavens praise your
    wonders, O GOD,
  your faithfulness in the assembly
    of the holy ones.
6 For who in the skies can be
    compared to GOD?
  Who among the heavenly beings
    is like GOD,
7 a god feared in the council of the
    holy ones,
  great and awesome[j] above all
    that are around God?
8 O Most High God of hosts,
  who is as mighty as you,
    O GOD?
  Your faithfulness surrounds you.
9 You rule the raging of the sea;
  when its waves rise, you still
    them.
10 You crushed Rahab like a carcass;
  you scattered your enemies with
    your mighty arm.
11 The heavens are yours, the earth
    also is yours;
  the world and all that is in it—
    you have founded them.
12 The north and the south[k]—you
    created them;

Tabor and Hermon joyously
    praise your name.
13 You have a mighty arm;
  strong is your hand, your
    powerful hand lifted high.
14 Righteousness and justice are the
    foundation of your throne;
  steadfast love and faithfulness go
    before you.
15 Blessed are the people who know
    the festal shout,
  who walk, O GOD, in the light
    of your countenance;
16 they exult in your name all day
    long,
  and extol[l] your righteousness.
17 For you are the glory of their
    strength;
  by your favor our horn is
    exalted.
18 For our shield belongs to GOD,
  our king to the Holy One of
    Israel.

19 Then you spoke in a vision to
    your faithful one, and said:
  "I have set the crown[m] on one
    who is mighty,
  I have exalted one chosen from
    the people.
20 I have found my servant David;
  with my holy oil I have anointed
    him;
21 my hand shall always remain with
    him;
  my arm also shall strengthen him.
22 The enemy shall not outwit him,
  the wicked shall not humble him.
23 I will crush David's foes before
    him

---

j Gk Syr: Heb *greatly awesome*
k Or *Zaphon and Yamin*   l Cn: Heb *are
exalted in*   m Cn: Heb *help*

and strike down those who hate
  him.

24 My faithfulness and steadfast love
    shall be with him;
  and in my name his horn shall
    be exalted.

25 I will set David's hand on the sea
    and his mighty hand on the
    rivers.

26 David shall cry to me, 'You are
    my Protector,
  my God, and the Rock of my
    salvation!'

27 I will make David the firstborn,
    the highest of the rulers of the
    earth.

28 Forever I will keep my steadfast
    love for David,
  and my covenant with him will
    stand firm.

29 I will establish David's line forever,
    and his throne as long as the
    heavens endure.

30 If his children forsake my law
    and do not walk according to
    my ordinances,

31 if they violate my statutes
    and do not keep my
    commandments,

32 then I will punish their
    transgression with the rod
  and their iniquity with scourges;

33 but I will not remove from David
    my steadfast love,
  or be false to my faithfulness.

34 I will not violate my covenant,
    or alter the word that went forth
    from my lips.

35 Once and for all I have sworn by
    my holiness;
  I will not lie to David.

36 His line shall continue forever,
    and his throne endure before me
    like the sun.

37 It shall be established forever like
    the moon,
  an enduring witness in the skies."
                                    Selah

38 But now you have spurned and
    rejected David;
  you are full of wrath against
    your anointed.

39 You have renounced the covenant
    with your servant;
  you have defiled his crown in
    the dust.

40 You have broken through all
    his walls;
  you have laid his strongholds
    in ruins.

41 All who pass by plunder him;
  he has become the scorn of his
    neighbors.

42 You have exalted the mighty hand
    of his foes;
  you have made all his enemies
    rejoice.

43 Moreover, you have turned back
    the edge of David's sword,
  and you have not supported
    David in battle.

44 You have removed the scepter from
    his hand,[n]
  and hurled his throne to the
    ground.

45 You have cut short the days of his
    youth;
  you have covered David with
    shame.   *Selah*

46 How long, O GOD? Will you hide
    yourself forever?
  How long will your wrath burn
    like fire?

---

n Cn: Heb *removed his cleanness*

47 Remember how short my time
is—[o]
for what vanity you have created
all mortals!
48 Who can live and never see death?
Who can escape the power of
Sheol? *Selah*

49 God, where is your steadfast love
of old,
which by your faithfulness you
swore to David?
50 Remember, O God, how your
servant is taunted;
how I bear in my bosom the
insults of the peoples,[p]
51 with which your enemies taunt,
O GOD,
with which they taunted the
footsteps of your anointed.

52 Blessed be GOD forever.
Amen and Amen.

BOOK IV

Psalm 90

God's Eternity and Human Frailty

A Prayer of Moses, the man of God.

1 God, you have been our dwelling
place[q]
in all generations.
2 Before the mountains were brought
forth,
or ever you had formed the earth
and the world,
from everlasting to everlasting
you are God.

3 You turn us[r] back to dust,
and say, "Turn back, you
mortals."
4 For a thousand years in your sight
are like yesterday when it is past,
or like a watch in the night.

5 You sweep them away; they are
like a dream,
like grass that is renewed in the
morning;
6 in the morning it flourishes and is
renewed;
in the evening it fades and
withers.

7 For we are consumed by your
anger;
by your wrath we are
overwhelmed.
8 You have set our iniquities
before you,
our secret sins in the light of
your countenance.

9 For all our days pass away under
your wrath;
our years come to an end[s] like
a sigh.
10 The days of our life are seventy
years,
or perhaps eighty, if we are
strong;
even then their span[t] is only toil
and trouble;
they are soon gone, and we fly
away.

11 Who considers the power of your
anger?
Your wrath is as great as the
awe that is due you.
12 So teach us to count our days
that we may gain a wise heart.

---

o Meaning of Heb uncertain p Cn: Heb *bosom all of many peoples* q Another reading is *our refuge* r Heb *humankind*
s Syr: Heb *we bring our years to an end*
t Cn Compare Gk Syr Jerome Tg: Heb *pride*

13 Turn, O God! How long?
    Have compassion on your
        servants!
14 Satisfy us in the morning with
        your steadfast love,
    so that we may rejoice and be
        glad all our days.
15 Make us glad as many days as you
        have afflicted us,
    and as many years as we have
        seen evil.
16 Let your work be manifest to your
        servants,
    and your glorious power to their
        children.
17 Let the favor of God, our God, be
        upon us,
    and prosper for us the work of
        our hands—
    O prosper the work of our
        hands!

Psalm 91

Assurance of God's Protection

1 You who live in the shelter of the
        Most High,
    who abide in the shadow of the
        Almighty,ᵘ
2 will say to God, "My refuge and
        my fortress;
    my God, in whom I trust."
3 For God will deliver you from the
        snare of the fowler
    and from the deadly pestilence;
4 God will cover you with God's
        pinions,
    and under God's wings you will
        find refuge;
    God's faithfulness is a shield and
        buckler.
5 You will not fear the terror of the
        night,
    or the arrow that flies by day,

6 or the pestilence that stalks at
        midnight,
    or the destruction that wastes at
        noonday.
7 A thousand may fall at your side,
    ten thousand at your mighty
        hand,
    but it will not come near you.
8 You will only look with your eyes
    and see the punishment of the
        wicked.
9 Because you have made God your
        refuge,ᵛ
    the Most High your dwelling
        place,
10 no evil shall befall you,
    no scourge come near your tent.
11 For God will command the angels
        concerning you
    to guard you in all your ways.
12 On their hands they will bear
        you up,
    so that you will not dash your
        foot against a stone.
13 You will tread on the lion and the
        adder,
    the young lion and the serpent
        you will trample under foot.

14 Those who love me, I will deliver;
    I will protect those who know
        my name.
15 When they call to me, I will
        answer them;
    I will be with them in trouble,
    I will rescue them and honor
        them.
16 With long life I will satisfy them,
    and show them my salvation.

u Traditional rendering of Heb *Shaddai*
v Cn: Heb *Because you, God, are my refuge;*
you have made

Psalm 92

Thanksgiving for Vindication

A Psalm. A Song for the Sabbath Day.

1 It is good to give thanks to GOD,
  to sing praises to your name,
  O Most High;
2 to declare your steadfast love in the
  morning,
  and your faithfulness by night,
3 to the music of the lute and the
  harp,
  to the melody of the lyre.
4 For you, O GOD, have made me
  glad by your work;
  at the works of your hands I
  sing for joy.

5 How great are your works,
  O GOD!
  Your thoughts are very deep!
6 The dullard cannot know,
  the stupid cannot understand
  this:
7 though the wicked sprout like
  grass
  and all evildoers flourish,
  they are doomed to destruction
  forever,
8   but you, O GOD, are on high
  forever.
9 For your enemies, O GOD,
  for your enemies shall perish;
  all evildoers shall be scattered.

10 But you have exalted my horn like
  that of the wild ox;
  you have poured over me^w
  fresh oil.
11 My eyes have seen the downfall of
  my enemies;
  my ears have heard the doom of
  my evil assailants.

12 The righteous flourish like the palm
  tree,
  and grow like a cedar in
  Lebanon.
13 They are planted in the house of
  GOD;
  they flourish in the courts of our
  God.
14 In old age they still produce fruit;
  they are always green and full
  of sap,
15 showing that GOD is upright.
  God is my rock, and in God
  there is no unrighteousness.

Psalm 93

The Majesty of God's Rule

1 GOD is sovereign and robed in
  majesty;
  GOD is robed and girded with
  strength.
  God has established the world; it
  shall never be moved;
2   your throne is established from
  of old;
  you are from everlasting.

3 The floods have lifted up, O GOD,
  the floods have lifted up their
  voice;
  the floods lift up their roaring.
4 More majestic than the thunders of
  mighty waters,
  more majestic than the waves^x of
  the sea,
  majestic on high is GOD!

5 Your decrees are very sure;
  holiness befits your house,
  O GOD, forevermore.

---

w Syr: Meaning of Heb uncertain
x Cn: Heb *majestic are the waves*

Psalm 94

God the Avenger of the Righteous

1 O GOD, you God of vengeance,
   you God of vengeance, shine
      forth!
2 Rise up, O judge of the earth;
   give to the proud what they
      deserve!
3 O GOD, how long shall the wicked,
   how long shall the wicked exult?

4 They pour out their arrogant
      words;
   all the evildoers boast.
5 They crush your people, O GOD,
   and afflict your heritage.
6 They kill the widow and the
      stranger,
   they murder the orphan,
7 and they say, "GOD does not see;
   the God of Jacob does not
      perceive."

8 Understand, O dullest of the
      people;
   fools, when will you be wise?
9 Does the one who planted the ear
      not hear?
   Does the one who formed the eye
      not see?
10 The one who disciplines the
      nations,
   and who teaches knowledge to
      humankind,
   does that one not chastise?
11 GOD knows our thoughts,ʸ
   that they are but an empty
      breath.

12 Blessed are those whom you
      discipline, O GOD,
   and whom you teach out of
      your law,

13 giving them respite from days of
      trouble,
   until a pit is dug for the wicked.
14 For GOD will not forsake God's
      people,
   and will not abandon God's
      heritage;
15 for justice will return to the
      righteous,
   and all the upright in heart will
      follow it.

16 Who rises up for me against the
      wicked?
   Who stands up for me against
      evildoers?
17 If GOD had not been my help,
   my soul would soon have lived
      in the land of silence.
18 When I thought, "My foot is
      slipping,"
   your steadfast love, O GOD, held
      me up.
19 When the cares of my heart are
      many,
   your consolations cheer my soul.
20 Can wicked rulers be allied
      with you,
   those who contrive mischief by
      statute?
21 They band together against the life
      of the righteous,
   and condemn the innocent to
      death.
22 But GOD has become my
      stronghold,
   and my God the rock of my
      refuge.
23 God will repay them for their
      iniquity
   and wipe them out for their
      wickedness;

---

y Heb *the thoughts of humankind*

God the Most High will wipe
them out.

Psalm 95

A Call to Worship and Obedience

1 O come, let us sing to GOD;
   let us make a joyful noise to the
      rock of our salvation!
2 Let us come into God's presence
      with thanksgiving;
   let us make a joyful noise to
      God with songs of praise!
3 For GOD is a great god,
   and a great Ruler above all gods.
4 In God's hand are the depths of
      the earth;
   the heights of the mountains are
      God's also.
5 The sea belongs to God, for God
      made it,
   and God's hands have formed the
      dry land.

6 O come, let us worship and bow
      down,
   let us kneel before GOD,
      our Maker!
7 For this is our God,
   and we are the people of God's
      pasture,
   and the sheep of God's hand.

   O that today you would listen to
      God's voice!
8   Do not harden your hearts, as at
      Meribah,
   as on the day at Massah in the
      wilderness,
9 when your ancestors tested me,
   and put me to the proof, though
      they had seen my work.
10 For forty years I loathed that
      generation

and said, "They are a people
   whose hearts go astray,
   and they do not regard my
      ways."
11 Therefore in my anger I swore,
   "They shall not enter my rest."

Psalm 96

Praise to God Who Comes in Judgment

1 O sing to GOD a new song;
   sing to GOD, all the earth.
2 Sing to GOD, bless that holy name;
   tell of God's salvation from day
      to day.
3 Declare God's glory among the
      nations,
   God's marvelous works among all
      the peoples.
4 For great is the Most High, and
      greatly to be praised;
   indeed, to be revered above
      all gods.
5 For all the gods of the peoples are
      idols,
   but the Most High made the
      heavens.
6 Honor and majesty are before God;
   strength and beauty are in God's
      sanctuary.

7 Ascribe to GOD, O families of the
      peoples,
   ascribe to GOD glory and
      strength.
8 Ascribe to GOD the glory due that
      holy name;
   bring an offering, and come into
      God's courts.
9 Worship GOD in holy splendor;
   tremble before God, all the earth.

10 Say among the nations, "GOD is
      sovereign!

The world is firmly established; it
shall never be moved.
God will judge the peoples with
equity."
11 Let the heavens be glad, and let the
earth rejoice;
let the sea roar, and all that
fills it;
12 let the field exult, and everything
in it.
Then shall all the trees of the
forest sing for joy
13 before GOD, who is coming to
judge the earth,
and who will judge the world with
righteousness,
and the peoples with truth.

Psalm 97
The Glory of God's Reign

1 GOD reigns! Let the earth rejoice;
let the many coastlands be glad!
2 Clouds and thick darkness are all
around God;
righteousness and justice are the
foundation of God's throne.
3 Fire goes before God,
and consumes God's adversaries
on every side.
4 God's lightnings light up the world;
the earth sees and trembles.
5 The mountains melt like wax before
GOD,
before the God of all the earth.

6 The heavens proclaim God's
righteousness;
and all the peoples behold God's
glory.
7 All worshipers of images are put
to shame,
those who make their boast in
worthless idols;
all gods bow down before God.

8 Zion hears and is glad,
and the towns of Judah rejoice,
because of your judgments,
O God.
9 For you, O GOD, are most high
over all the earth;
you are exalted far above
all gods.

10 GOD loves those who hate[z] evil,
and guards the lives of the
faithful,
and rescues them from the hand
of the wicked.
11 Light dawns[a] for the righteous,
and joy for the upright in heart.
12 Rejoice in GOD, O you righteous,
and give thanks to God's holy
name!

Psalm 98
Praise the Judge of the World
A Psalm.

1 O sing a new song to GOD,
who has done marvelous things,
whose strong hand and holy arm
have gotten victory.
2 GOD has made known the victory
and has revealed God's
vindication in the sight of the
nations.
3 God has remembered God's
steadfast love and faithfulness
to the house of Israel.
All the ends of the earth have seen
the victory of our God.

4 Make a joyful noise to GOD, all the
earth;
break forth into joyous song and
sing praises.

---

z Cn: Heb *You who love* GOD *hate*
a Gk Syr Jerome: Heb *is sown*

5 Sing praises to GOD with the lyre,
  with the lyre and the sound of
    melody.
6 With trumpets and the sound of
    the horn
  make a joyful noise before God,
    the Most High.

7 Let the sea roar, and all that
    fills it;
  the world and those who live
    in it.
8 Let the floods clap their hands;
  let the hills sing together for joy
9 at the presence of GOD who is
    coming
  to judge the earth,
to judge the world with
    righteousness,
  and the peoples with equity.

Psalm 99
Praise to God for God's
Holiness

1 GOD is sovereign; let the peoples
    tremble!
  God sits enthroned upon the
    cherubim; let the earth quake!
2 GOD is great in Zion,
  and is exalted over all the
    peoples.
3 Let them praise your great and
    awesome name.
  Holy is our God!
4 Mighty Sovereign,[b] lover of justice,
  you have established equity;
you have executed justice
  and righteousness in Jacob.
5 Extol the Most High our God;
  worship at God's footstool.
  Holy is our God!

6 Moses and Aaron were among
    God's priests,

Samuel also was among those
    who called on God's name.
  They cried to GOD who answered
    them,
7 and spoke to them in the pillar of
    cloud;
  they kept God's decrees,
  and the statutes that God gave
    them.

8 O GOD our God, you answered
    them;
  you were a forgiving god to
    them,
  but an avenger of their
    wrongdoings.
9 Extol the Most High our God,
  and worship at God's holy
    mountain;
  for the Most High our God is
    holy.

Psalm 100
All Lands Summoned to Praise
God

A Psalm of thanksgiving.

1 Make a joyful noise to GOD, all the
    earth.
2   Worship GOD with gladness;
  come into God's presence with
    singing.

3 Know that the Most High is God.
  It is God who made us, and to
    God we belong;[c]
  we are God's people, and the
    sheep of God's pasture.

4 Enter God's gates with
    thanksgiving,
  and God's courts with praise.

---

b Cn: Heb *And a ruler's strength*
c Another reading is *and not we ourselves*

Give thanks to God, bless God's
name.

5 For GOD is good;
  God's steadfast love endures
    forever,
  and God's faithfulness to all
    generations.

Psalm 101

A Sovereign's Pledge of Integrity and Justice

Of David. A Psalm.

1 I will sing of loyalty and of justice;
  to you, O GOD, I will sing.
2 I will study the way that is
    blameless.
  When shall I attain it?

  I will walk with integrity of heart
    within my house;
3 I will not set before my eyes
  anything that is base.

  I hate the work of those who
    fall away;
  it shall not cling to me.
4 Perverseness of heart shall be far
    from me;
  I will know nothing of evil.

5 One who secretly slanders a
    neighbor
  I will destroy.
  A haughty look and an arrogant
    heart
  I will not tolerate.

6 I will look with favor on the
    faithful in the land,
  so that they may live with me;
  whoever walks in the way that is
    blameless
  shall minister to me.

7 No one who practices deceit
    shall remain in my house;
  no one who utters lies
    shall continue in my presence.

8 Morning by morning I will destroy
    all the wicked in the land,
  cutting off all evildoers
    from the city of GOD.

Psalm 102

Prayer to the Eternal Ruler for Help

A prayer of one afflicted, when faint and pleading before GOD.

1 Hear my prayer, O GOD;
  let my cry come to you.
2 Do not hide your face from me
  in the day of my distress.
  Incline your ear to me;
    answer me speedily in the day
      when I call.

3 For my days pass away like smoke,
  and my bones burn like a
    furnace.
4 My heart is stricken and withered
    like grass;
  I am too wasted to eat my
    bread.
5 Because of my loud groaning
  my bones cling to my skin.
6 I am like an owl of the wilderness,
  like a little owl of the waste
    places.
7 I lie awake;
  I am like a lonely bird on the
    housetop.
8 All day long my enemies taunt
    me;
  those who deride me use my
    name for a curse.
9 For I eat ashes like bread,
  and mingle tears with my drink,

10 because of your indignation and
          anger;
      for you have lifted me up and
          thrown me aside.
11 My days are like an evening
          shadow;
      I wither away like grass.

12 But you, O GOD, are enthroned
          forever;
      your name endures to all
          generations.
13 You will rise up and have
          compassion on Zion,
      for it is time to favor it;
      the appointed time has come.
14 For your servants hold its stones
          dear,
      and have pity on its dust.
15 The nations will revere the name of
          the Most High,
      and all the rulers of the earth
          your glory.
16 For GOD will build up Zion
      and will appear in glory.
17 God will regard the prayer of the
          destitute,
      and will not despise their prayer.

18 Let this be recorded for a
          generation to come,
      so that a people yet unborn may
          praise GOD:
19 that God looked down from the
          holy height,
      and from heaven looked at the
          earth,
20 to hear the groans of the prisoners,
      to set free those who were
          doomed to die;
21 so that the name of the Most High
          may be declared in Zion
      and be praised in Jerusalem,

22 when peoples gather together,
      and nations, to worship GOD.
23 God has broken my strength in
          midcourse
      and has shortened my days.
24 "O my God," I say, "do not take
          me away
      at the mid-point of my life,
   you whose years endure
      throughout all generations."

25 Long ago you laid the foundation
          of the earth,
      and the heavens are the work of
          your hands.
26 They will perish, but you endure;
      they will all wear out like a
          garment.
   You change them like clothing, and
          they pass away;
27   but you are the same, and your
          years have no end.
28 The children of your servants shall
          live secure;
      their offspring shall be established
          in your presence.

Psalm 103

Thanksgiving for God's Goodness
Of David.

1 Bless GOD, O my soul,
      and all that is within me,
      bless God's holy name.
2 Bless GOD, O my soul,
      and do not forget all God's
          benefits—
3 who forgives all your iniquity,
      who heals all your diseases,
4 who redeems your life from the
          Pit,
      who crowns you with steadfast
          love and mercy,

5 who satisfies you with good as
    long as you live^d
  so that your youth is renewed
    like the eagle's.

6 GOD works vindication
    and justice for all who are
      oppressed.

7 God made known God's ways to
    Moses,
  God's acts to the people of
    Israel.

8 GOD is merciful and gracious,
    slow to anger and abounding in
      steadfast love.

9 God will not always accuse,
    and will not be angry forever.

10 God does not deal with us
    according to our sins,
  nor repay us according to our
    iniquities.

11 For as the heavens are high above
    the earth,
  so great is God's steadfast love
    toward those who revere God;

12 as far as the east is from the west,
    so far God removes our
      transgressions from us.

13 As parents have compassion for
    their children,
  so GOD has compassion for those
    who revere God.

14 For God knows how we were
    made,
  and remembers that we are dust.

15 As for mortals, their days are like
    grass;
  they flourish like a flower of the
    field;

16 for the wind passes over it, and it
    is gone,
  and its place knows it no more.

17 But the steadfast love of GOD is
    from everlasting to everlasting

on those who revere God,
  and God's righteousness to
    children's children,

18 to those who keep the covenant
    and remember to do God's
      commandments.

19 GOD has established a throne in the
    heavens,
  and God's dominion rules over
    all.

20 Bless GOD, O you angels,
    you mighty ones who do God's
      bidding,
  obedient to God's spoken word.

21 Bless GOD, all you hosts,
    you ministers who do God's will.

22 Bless GOD, all God's works,
    in all places of God's dominion.
  Bless GOD, O my soul.

Psalm 104

God the Creator and Provider

1 Bless GOD, O my soul.
    O GOD my God, you are very
      great.
  You are clothed with honor and
    majesty,

2   wrapped in light as with a
      garment.
  You stretch out the heavens like
    a tent,

3   you set the beams of your^e
      chambers on the waters,
  you make the clouds your^e chariot,
    you ride on the wings of the
      wind,

4 you make the winds your^e
    messengers,
  fire and flame your^e ministers.

---

d Meaning of Heb uncertain   e Heb God's

497

5 You set the earth on its
    foundations,
  so that it shall never be shaken.
6 You cover it with the deep as with
    a garment;
  the waters stood above the
    mountains.
7 At your rebuke they flee;
  at the sound of your thunder
    they take to flight.
8 They rose up to the mountains, ran
    down to the valleys
  to the place that you appointed
    for them.
9 You set a boundary that they may
    not pass,
  so that they might not again
    cover the earth.

10 You make springs gush forth in the
    valleys;
  they flow between the hills,
11 giving drink to every wild animal;
  the wild donkeys quench their
    thirst.
12 By the streams the birds of the air
    have their habitation;
  they sing among the branches.
13 From your lofty abode you water
    the mountains;
  the earth is satisfied with the
    fruit of your work.

14 You cause the grass to grow for
    the cattle,
  and plants for people to use,ᶠ
  to bring forth food from the earth,
15   and wine to gladden the human
      heart,
  oil to make the face shine,
    and bread to strengthen the
      human heart.
16 The trees of GOD are watered
    abundantly,

the cedars of Lebanon that God
    planted.
17 In them the birds build their nests;
  the stork has its home in the fir
    trees.
18 The high mountains are for the
    wild goats;
  the rocks are a refuge for the
    rabbits.
19 You have made the moon to mark
    the seasons;
  the sun knows its time for
    setting.
20 You make darkness, and it is night,
  when all the animals of the forest
    come creeping out.
21 The young lions roar for their
    prey,
  seeking their food from God.
22 When the sun rises, they withdraw
  and lie down in their dens.
23 People go out to their work
  and to their labor until the
    evening.

24 O GOD, how manifold are your
    works!
  In wisdom you have made
    them all;
  the earth is full of your
    creatures.
25 Yonder is the sea, great and wide,
  it is teeming with countless
    creatures,
  living things both small and
    great.
26 There go the ships,
  and Leviathan that you formed
    to sport in it.

27 These all look to you
  to give them their food in due
    season;

_____

f Or to cultivate

498

28 when you give to them, they gather
     it up;
   when you open your hand, they
     are filled with good things.
29 When you hide your face, they are
     dismayed;
   when you take away their breath,
     they die
   and return to their dust.
30 When you send forth your spirit,[g]
     they are created;
   and you renew the face of the
     ground.

31 May the glory of GOD endure
     forever;
   may GOD rejoice in the works of
     God—
32 who looks on the earth and it
     trembles,
   who touches the mountains and
     they smoke.
33 I will sing to GOD as long as
     I live;
   I will sing praise to my God
     while I have being.
34 May my meditation be pleasing
     to God,
   in whom I rejoice.
35 Let sinners be consumed from the
     earth,
   and let the wicked be no more.
   Bless GOD, O my soul.
   Hallelujah!

Psalm 105
God's Faithfulness to Israel

1 O give thanks to GOD, call on
     God's name,
   make known God's deeds among
     the peoples.
2 Sing to God, sing praises to God;
   tell of all God's wonderful
     works.

3 Glory in God's holy name;
   let the hearts of those who seek
     GOD rejoice.
4 Seek GOD and God's strength;
   seek God's presence continually.
5 Remember the wonderful works
     God has done,
   the miracles, and the judgments
     God uttered,
6 O offspring of Abraham and Sarah,
     God's servants,
   children of Jacob, Rachel, and
     Leah, God's chosen ones.

7 This is GOD our God,
   whose judgments are in all the
     earth.
8 God is mindful of the covenant
     forever,
   of the word commanded, for a
     thousand generations,
9 the covenant made with Abraham,
   God's sworn promise to Isaac,
10 and confirmed to Jacob as a statute,
   to Israel as an everlasting
     covenant,
11 saying, "To you I will give the
     land of Canaan
   as your portion for an
     inheritance."

12 When they were few in number,
   of little account, and strangers
     in it,
13 wandering from nation to nation,
   from one dominion to another
     people,
14 God allowed no one to oppress
     them;
   God rebuked rulers on their
     account,
15 saying, "Do not touch my anointed
     ones;

---

g Or your breath

do my prophets no harm."

16 When God summoned famine
against the land,
and broke every staff of bread,
17 God had sent a man ahead of
them,
Joseph, who was sold as a slave.
18 His feet were hurt with fetters,
his neck was put in a collar of
iron;
19 until what he had said came to
pass,
the word of GOD kept testing
Joseph.
20 The king sent and released him;
the ruler of the peoples set
Joseph free.
21 The king made Joseph lord of the
king's house,
and ruler of all his possessions,
22 to instruct[h] the officials at the
king's pleasure,
and to teach the elders wisdom.

23 Then Israel came to Egypt;
Jacob lived as an alien in the
land of Ham.
24 And GOD made Israel very fruitful,
and made them stronger than
their foes,
25 whose hearts God then turned to
hate Israel,
to deal craftily with God's
servants.

26 God sent God's servant Moses,
and Aaron whom God had
chosen.
27 They performed God's signs among
them,
and miracles in the land of Ham.
28 God sent the night, and took away
light from the land;

they rebelled[i] against God's
words.
29 God turned their waters into blood,
and caused their fish to die.
30 Their land swarmed with frogs,
even in the chambers of their
rulers.
31 God spoke, and there came swarms
of flies,
and gnats throughout their
country.
32 God gave them hail for rain,
and lightning that flashed through
their land.
33 God struck their vines and fig
trees,
and shattered the trees of their
country.
34 God spoke, and the locusts came,
and young locusts without
number;
35 they devoured all the vegetation in
their land,
and ate up the fruit of their
ground.
36 God struck down all the firstborn
in their land,
the first issue of all their
strength.

37 Then God brought Israel out with
silver and gold,
and there was no one among
their tribes who stumbled.
38 Egypt was glad when they
departed,
for dread of them had fallen
upon it.
39 God spread a cloud for a covering,
and fire to give light by night.

---

h Gk Syr Jerome: Heb *to bind*
i Cn Compare Gk Syr: Heb *they did not
rebel*

40 They asked, and God brought
   quails,
   and gave them food from heaven
   in abundance.
41 God opened the rock, and water
   gushed out;
   it flowed through the desert like
   a river.
42 For God remembered God's holy
   promise,
   and Abraham, God's servant.

43 So God brought God's people out
   with joy,
   the chosen ones with singing.
44 God gave them the lands of the
   nations,
   and they took possession of the
   wealth of the peoples,
45 that they might keep God's statutes
   and observe God's laws.
   Hallelujah!

Psalm 106

A Confession of Israel's Sins

1 Praise GOD!
   O give thanks to GOD, for God
   is good;
   for God's steadfast love endures
   forever.
2 Who can utter the mighty doings
   of GOD,
   or declare all God's praise?
3 Blessed are those who observe
   justice,
   who do righteousness at all times.

4 Remember me, O GOD, when you
   show favor to your people;
   help me when you deliver them;
5 that I may see the prosperity of
   your chosen ones,
   that I may rejoice in the gladness
   of your nation,

that I may glory in your
   heritage.

6 Both we and our ancestors have
   sinned;
   we have committed iniquity, have
   done wickedly.
7 Our ancestors, when they were in
   Egypt,
   did not consider your wonderful
   works;
   they did not remember the
   abundance of your steadfast
   love,
   but rebelled against the Most
   High^j at the Sea of Reeds,
8 and yet were saved for the sake of
   God's name's,
   in order to make known God's
   mighty power.
9 God rebuked the Sea of Reeds, and
   it became dry;
   God led them through the deep
   as through a desert.
10 So God saved them from the hand
   of the foe,
   and delivered them from the
   hand of the enemy.
11 The waters covered their
   adversaries;
   not one of them was left.
12 Then they believed God's words;
   they sang God's praise.

13 But they soon forgot God's works;
   they did not wait for God's
   counsel.
14 But they had a wanton craving in
   the wilderness,
   and put God to the test in the
   desert;
15 God gave them what they asked,

---

j Cn Compare 78.17, 56: Heb *rebelled at the
sea*

but sent a wasting disease among
them.

16 They were jealous of Moses in
the camp,
and of Aaron, the holy one of
GOD.

17 The earth opened and swallowed
up Dathan,
and covered the company of
Abiram.

18 Fire also broke out in their
company;
the flame burned up the wicked.

19 They made a calf at Horeb
and worshiped a cast image.

20 They exchanged the glory of God[k]
for the image of an ox that eats
grass.

21 They forgot God, their Savior,
who had done great things in
Egypt,

22 wondrous works in the land of
Ham,
and awesome deeds by the Sea of
Reeds.

23 Therefore God vowed to destroy
them—
had not Moses, God's chosen
one,
stood in the breach before God,
to turn away God's wrath from
destroying them.

24 Then they despised the pleasant
land,
having no faith in God's promise.

25 They grumbled in their tents,
and did not obey the voice of
GOD.

26 Therefore God raised a hand and
made an oath
to overthrow them in the
wilderness,

27 and to disperse[l] their descendants
among the nations,
scattering them over the lands.

28 Then they attached themselves to
the Baal of Peor,
and ate sacrifices offered to
the dead;

29 they provoked GOD to anger with
their deeds,
and a plague broke out among
them.

30 Then Phinehas stood up and
interceded,
and the plague was stopped.

31 And that has been reckoned to
Phinehas as righteousness
from generation to generation
forever.

32 They angered GOD at the waters of
Meribah,
and it went ill with Moses on
their account;

33 for they made Moses' spirit bitter,
and he spoke words that were
rash.

34 They did not destroy the peoples,
as GOD commanded them,

35 but they mingled with the nations
and learned to do as they did.

36 They served their idols,
which became a snare to them.

37 They sacrificed their sons
and their daughters to the
demons;

38 they poured out innocent blood,
the blood of their sons and
daughters,

k Compare Gk Mss: Heb *exchanged their
glory*   l Syr Compare Ezek 20.23: Heb *cause
to fall*

whom they sacrificed to the idols
    of Canaan;
  and the land was polluted with
    blood.

39 Thus they became unclean by their
    acts,
  and degraded themselves in their
    doings.

40 Then the anger of GOD was kindled
    against the people,
  and God abhorred the heritage;

41 God gave them into the hand of
    the nations,
  so that those who hated them
    ruled over them.

42 Their enemies oppressed them,
  and they were brought into
    subjection under their power.

43 Many times God delivered them,
  but they were rebellious in their
    purposes,
  and were brought low through
    their iniquity.

44 Nevertheless God regarded their
    distress
  when God heard their cry.

45 For their sake God remembered the
    covenant,
  and showed compassion according
    to the abundance of God's
    steadfast love.

46 God caused them to be pitied
  by all who held them captive.

47 Save us, O GOD our God,
  and gather us from among the
    nations,
  that we may give thanks to your
    holy name
  and glory in your praise.

48 Blessed be the Most High, the God
    of Israel,
  from everlasting to everlasting.

And let all the people say,
  "Amen."
Hallelujah!

BOOK V   ৶   ৶   ৶   ৶   ৶

Psalm 107

Thanksgiving for Deliverance from Many Troubles

1 O give thanks to the LORD, who is
    good,
  whose steadfast love endures
    forever.

2 Let the redeemed of GOD say so,
  those redeemed from trouble

3 and gathered in from the lands,
  from the east and from the west,
  from the north and from the
    south.ᵐ

4 Some wandered in desert wastes,
  finding no way to an inhabited
    town;

5 hungry and thirsty,
  their soul fainted within them.

6 Then they cried to GOD in their
    trouble,
  and God delivered them from
    their distress;

7 God led them by a straight way,
  until they reached an inhabited
    town.

8 Let them thank GOD for God's
    steadfast love,
  for the wonderful works to
    humankind.

9 For God satisfies the thirsty,
  and fills the hungry with good
    things.

10 Some sat in captivity and in gloom,
  prisoners in misery and in irons,

---

m Cn: Heb *sea*

11 for they had rebelled against the
      words of God,
   and spurned the counsel of the
      Most High.
12 Their hearts were bowed down
      with hard labor;
   they fell down, with no one
      to help.
13 Then they cried to GOD in their
      trouble,
   and God saved them from their
      distress;
14 God brought them out of captivity
      and gloom,
   and broke their bonds asunder.
15 Let them thank GOD for steadfast
      love,
   for God's wonderful works to
      humankind.
16 For God shatters the doors of
      bronze,
   and cuts in two the bars of iron.

17 Some were sick[n] through their
      sinful ways,
   and because of their iniquities
      endured affliction;
18 they loathed any kind of food,
   and they drew near to the gates
      of death.
19 Then they cried to GOD in their
      trouble,
   and were saved from their
      distress;
20 God sent out God's word and
      healed them,
   and delivered them from
      destruction.
21 Let them thank GOD for steadfast
      love,
   for God's wonderful works to
      humankind.
22 And let them offer thanksgiving
      sacrifices,

and tell of God's deeds with
      songs of joy.
23 Some went down to the sea
      in ships,
   doing business on the mighty
      waters;
24 they saw the deeds of GOD,
   the wondrous works in the deep.
25 For God commanded and raised
      the stormy wind,
   which lifted up the waves of
      the sea.
26 They mounted up to heaven, they
      went down to the depths;
   their courage melted away in
      their calamity;
27 they reeled and staggered like
      drunkards,
   and were at their wits' end.
28 Then they cried to GOD in their
      trouble,
   and were brought from their
      distress;
29 God made the storm be still,
   and the waves of the sea were
      hushed.
30 Then they were glad because they
      had quiet,
   and God brought them to their
      desired haven.
31 Let them thank GOD for steadfast
      love,
   for God's wonderful works to
      humankind.
32 Let them extol God in the
      congregation of the people,
   and praise God in the assembly
      of the elders.

33 God turns rivers into a desert,
      springs of water into thirsty
      ground,

---

n Cn: Heb *fools*

34 a fruitful land into a salty waste,
because of the wickedness of its inhabitants.
35 God turns a desert into pools of water,
a parched land into springs of water,
36 and there lets the hungry live,
and they establish a town to live in;
37 they sow fields, and plant vineyards,
and get a fruitful yield.
38 They multiply greatly by the blessing of God,
who does not let their cattle decrease.

39 When they are diminished and brought low
through oppression, trouble, and sorrow,
40 God pours contempt on nobles
and makes them wander in trackless wastes,
41 but raises up the needy out of distress,
and makes their families like flocks.
42 The upright see it and are glad;
and all wickedness stops its mouth.
43 Let those who are wise give heed to these things,
and consider the steadfast love of GOD.

Psalm 108

Praise and Prayer for Victory

A Song. A Psalm of David.

1 My heart is steadfast, O God, my heart is steadfast;[o]
I will sing and make melody.
Awake, my soul![p]
2 Awake, O harp and lyre!
I will awake the dawn.
3 I will give thanks to you, O GOD, among the peoples,
and I will sing praises to you among the nations.
4 For your steadfast love is higher than the heavens,
and your faithfulness reaches to the clouds.

5 Be exalted, O God, above the heavens,
and let your glory be over all the earth.
6 Give victory with your mighty hand, and answer me,
so that those whom you love may be rescued.

7 God has promised in God's sanctuary:[q]
"With exultation I will divide up Shechem,
and portion out the Vale of Succoth.
8 Gilead is mine; Manasseh is mine;
Ephraim is my helmet;
Judah is my scepter.
9 Moab is my washbasin;
on Edom I hurl my shoe;
over Philistia I shout in triumph."

10 Who will bring me to the fortified city?
Who will lead me to Edom?
11 Have you not rejected us, O God?
You do not go out, O God, with our armies.

---

o Heb Mss Gk Syr: MT lacks *my heart is steadfast* p Compare 57.8: Heb *also my soul* q Or *by God's holiness*

12 O grant us help against the foe,
   for human help is worthless.
13 With God we shall do valiantly;
   it is God who will tread down
   our foes.

Psalm 109

Prayer for Vindication and
Vengeance

To the leader. Of David. A Psalm.

1 Do not be silent, O God of my
   praise.
2 For wicked and deceitful mouths
   are opened against me,
   speaking against me with lying
   tongues.
3 They beset me with words
   of hate,
   and attack me without cause.
4 In return for my love they
   accuse me,
   even while I make prayer for
   them.
5 So they reward me evil for good,
   and hatred for my love.

6 They say,[r] "Appoint a wicked man
   against him;
   let an accuser stand beside him.
7 When he is tried, let him be found
   guilty;
   let his prayer be counted as sin.
8 May his days be few;
   may another seize his position.
9 May his children be orphans,
   and his wife a widow.
10 May his children wander about
   and beg;
   may they be driven out of[s] the
   ruins they inhabit.
11 May the creditor seize all that
   he has;

may strangers plunder the fruits
   of his toil.
12 May there be no one to do him a
   kindness,
   nor anyone to pity his orphaned
   children.
13 May his posterity be cut off;
   may his name be blotted out in
   the second generation.
14 May the iniquity of his father[t] be
   remembered before GOD,
   and do not let the sin of his
   mother be blotted out.
15 Let them be before GOD
   continually,
   and may his[u] memory be cut off
   from the earth.
16 For he did not remember to show
   kindness,
   but pursued the poor and needy
   and the brokenhearted to their
   death.
17 He loved to curse; let curses come
   on him.
   He did not like blessing; may it
   be far from him.
18 He clothed himself with cursing as
   his coat,
   may it soak into his body like
   water,
   like oil into his bones.
19 May it be like a garment that he
   wraps around himself,
   like a belt that he wears every
   day."

20 May that be the reward of my
   accusers from GOD,
   of those who speak evil against
   my life.

---

r Heb lacks *They say*   s Gk: Heb *and seek*
t Cn: Heb *fathers*   u Gk: Heb *their*

21 But you, O GOD my Sovereign,
     act on my behalf for your
       name's sake;
   because your steadfast love is
     good, deliver me.
22 For I am poor and needy,
     and my heart is pierced
       within me.
23 I am gone like a shadow at
     evening;
   I am shaken off like a locust.
24 My knees are weak through
     fasting;
   my body has become gaunt.
25 I am an object of scorn to my
     accusers;
   when they see me, they shake
     their heads.

26 Help me, O GOD my God!
   Save me according to your
     steadfast love.
27 Let them know that this is your
     hand;
   you, O GOD, have done it.
28 Let them curse, but you will
     bless.
   Let my assailants be put to
     shame;ᵛ may your servant be
     glad.
29 May my accusers be clothed with
     dishonor;
   may they be wrapped in their
     own shame as in a mantle.
30 With my mouth I will give great
     thanks to the LORD;
   I will praise God in the midst of
     the throng.
31 For God stands alongside of those
     who are needy,
   to save them from those who
     would condemn them to death.

Psalm 110

Assurance of Victory for God's Priest-Ruler

Of David. A Psalm.

1 GOD says to my sovereign,
     "Sit at my side
   until I make your enemies your
     footstool."

2 GOD sends out from Zion
     your mighty scepter.
   Rule in the midst of your foes.
3 Your people will offer themselves
     willingly
     on the day you lead your forces
     on the holy mountains.ʷ
   From the womb of the morning,
     like dew, your youthˣ will come
     to you.
4 GOD has sworn and will not
     reconsider,
   "You are a priest forever
     according to the order of
     Melchizedek."ʸ

5 God is at your side,
     and will shatter rulers on the day
     of God's wrath.
6 God will execute judgment among
     the nations,
     filling them with corpses;
   God will shatter heads
     over the wide earth.
7 The sovereign will drink from the
     stream by the path;
   therefore the sovereign will lift
     up his head.

---

v Gk: Heb *They have risen up and have
been put to shame*   w Another reading is
in holy splendor   x Cn: Heb *the dew of
your youth*   y Or *forever, a rightful ruler
by my edict*

Psalm 111

Praise for God's Wonderful Works

1 Hallelujah!
   I will give thanks to GOD with my
      whole heart,
         in the company of the upright, in
         the congregation.
2 Great are the works of GOD,
      studied by all who delight
      in them.
3 Full of honor and majesty is
      God's work,
      and God's righteousness endures
      forever.
4 God has gained renown by God's
      wonderful deeds;
   GOD is gracious and merciful.
5 God provides food for those who
      revere God;
   God is ever mindful of the
      covenant.
6 God has shown the people the
      power of the works,
      in giving them the heritage of the
      nations.
7 The works of God's hands are
      faithful and just;
      all God's precepts are
      trustworthy.
8 They are established forever and
      ever,
         to be performed with faithfulness
         and uprightness.
9 God sent redemption to the
      people,
      and has commanded the covenant
      forever.
      Holy and awesome is God's
      name.
10 Reverence for GOD is the beginning
      of wisdom;

all those who practice it[z] have a
   good understanding.
God's praise endures forever.

Psalm 112

Blessings of the Righteous

1 Hallelujah!
      Blessed are those who are in awe
      of GOD,
      who greatly delight in God's
      commandments.
2 Their descendants will be mighty in
      the land;
      the generation of the upright will
      be blessed.
3 Wealth and riches are in their
      houses,
      and their righteousness endures
      forever.
4 They rise in the nighttime as a
      light for the upright;
      they are gracious, merciful, and
      righteous.
5 It is well with those who deal
      generously and lend,
      who conduct their affairs with
      justice.
6 For the righteous will never
      be moved;
      they will be remembered forever.
7 They are not afraid of evil tidings;
      their hearts are firm, secure in
      GOD.
8 Their hearts are steady, they will
      not be afraid;
      in the end they will look in
      triumph on their foes.
9 They have distributed freely, they
      have given to those who are
      poor;

---

z Gk Syr: Heb *them*

their righteousness endures
forever;
their horn is exalted in honor.
10 The wicked see it and are angry;
they gnash their teeth and melt
away;
the desire of the wicked comes
to nothing.

Psalm 113

God the Helper of the Needy

1 Hallelujah!
Praise, O servants of GOD;
praise the name of the Most
High.

2 Blessed be the name of the Most
High
from this time on and
forevermore.
3 From the rising of the sun to its
setting
the name of the Most High is to
be praised.
4 GOD is high above all nations,
and God's glory above the
heavens.

5 Who is like GOD our God,
who is seated on high,
6 who looks far down
on the heavens and the earth?
7 God raises those who are poor
from the dust,
and lifts those who are needy
from the ash heap,
8 to make them sit with royalty,
with the nobles of the people.
9 God gives the childless woman a
home,
making her the joyous mother of
children.
Hallelujah!

Psalm 114

God's Wonders at the Exodus

1 When Israel went out from Egypt,
the house of Jacob from a people
of strange language,
2 Judah became God's sanctuary,
Israel God's dominion.

3 The sea looked and fled;
Jordan turned back.
4 The mountains skipped like rams,
the hills like lambs.

5 Why is it, O sea, that you flee?
O Jordan, that you turn back?
6 O mountains, that you skip like
rams?
O hills, like lambs?

7 Tremble, O earth, at the presence
of GOD,
at the presence of the God of
Jacob,
8 who turns the rock into a pool of
water,
the flint into a spring of water.

Psalm 115

The Impotence of Idols and the Greatness of God

1 Not to us, O GOD, not to us, but
to your name give glory,
for the sake of your steadfast
love and your faithfulness.
2 Why should the nations say,
"Where is their God?"

3 Our God is in the heavens
and does whatever God pleases.
4 Their idols are silver and gold,
the work of human hands.
5 They have mouths, but do not
speak;
eyes, but do not see.

6 They have ears, but do not hear;
   noses, but do not smell.
7 They have hands, but do not feel;
   feet, but do not walk;
   they make no sound in their
     throats.
8 Those who make them are like
   them;
   so are all who trust in them.

9 O Israel, trust in GOD,
   who is their help and their
     shield!
10 O house of Aaron, trust in GOD,
   who is their help and their
     shield!
11 You who revere GOD, trust in
   GOD,
   who is their help and their
     shield!

12 GOD has been mindful of us and
   will bless us;
   God will bless the house of
     Israel;
   God will bless the house of
     Aaron;
13 God will bless those who revere
   GOD,
   both small and great.

14 May GOD give you increase,
   both you and your children.
15 May you be blessed by GOD,
   who made heaven and earth.

16 The heavens are GOD's heavens,
   but the earth God has given to
     human beings.
17 The dead do not praise GOD,
   nor do any that go down into
     silence.
18 But we will bless GOD
   from this time on and
     forevermore.
   Hallelujah!

Psalm 116

Thanksgiving for Recovery from Illness

1 I love GOD, because God has heard
   my voice and my supplications.
2 Because God listened to me,
   therefore I will call on God as
     long as I live.
3 The snares of death encompassed
   me;
   the pangs of Sheol laid hold
     on me;
   I suffered distress and anguish.
4 Then I called on the name of
     GOD:
   "O GOD, I pray, save my life!"

5 GOD is gracious and righteous;
   our God is merciful.
6 GOD protects the simple;
   when I was brought low, God
     saved me.
7 Return, O my soul, to your rest,
   for GOD has dealt bountifully
     with you.

8 For you have delivered my soul
     from death,
   my eyes from tears,
   my feet from stumbling.
9 I walk before GOD
   in the land of the living.
10 I kept my faith, even when I said,
   "I am greatly afflicted";
11 I said in my consternation,
   "Everyone is a liar."

12 What shall I return to GOD
   for all God's bounty to me?
13 I will lift up the cup of salvation
   and call on the name of the
     Most High,
14 I will pay my vows to GOD

in the presence of all God's
      people.
15 Precious in the sight of GOD
      is the death of the faithful ones.
16 O GOD, I am your servant;
      I am your servant, the child of
      your womanservant.
      You have loosed my bonds.
17 I will offer to you a thanksgiving
      sacrifice
      and call on the name of the
      Most High.
18 I will pay my vows to GOD
      in the presence of all God's
      people,
19 in the courts of the house of
      GOD,
      in your midst, O Jerusalem.
   Hallelujah!

Psalm 117
Universal Call to Worship

1 Praise GOD, all you nations!
      Extol God, all you peoples!
2 For great is God's steadfast love
      toward us,
      and the faithfulness of GOD
      endures forever.
   Hallelujah!

Psalm 118
A Song of Victory

1 O give thanks to GOD, for God is
      good;
      God's steadfast love endures
      forever!

2 Let Israel say,
      "God's steadfast love endures
      forever."
3 Let the house of Aaron say,
      "God's steadfast love endures
      forever."

4 Let those who are in awe of GOD
      say,
      "God's steadfast love endures
      forever."

5 Out of my distress I called on
      GOD;
      GOD answered me and set me in
      a broad place.
6 With GOD on my side I do
      not fear.
      What can mortals do to me?
7 GOD is on my side to help me;
      I shall look in triumph on those
      who hate me.
8 It is better to take refuge in GOD
      than to put confidence in
      mortals.
9 It is better to take refuge in GOD
      than to put confidence in royalty.

10 All nations surrounded me;
      in the name of the Most High I
      cut them off!
11 They surrounded me, surrounded
      me on every side;
      in the name of the Most High I
      cut them off!
12 They surrounded me like bees;
      they blazed[a] like a fire of
      thorns;
      in the name of the Most High I
      cut them off!
13 I was pushed hard,[b] so that I was
      falling,
      but GOD helped me.
14 GOD is my strength and my might
      and has become my salvation.

15 There are glad songs of victory in
      the tents of the righteous:

---

a Gk: Heb *were extinguished*   b Gk Syr
Jerome: Heb *You pushed me hard*

"The mighty hand of God does
valiantly;
16 the mighty hand of God is
exalted;
the mighty hand of God does
valiantly."
17 I shall not die, but I shall live,
and recount the deeds of God.
18 God punished me severely,
but did not give me over to
death.

19 Open to me the gates of
righteousness,
that I may enter through them
and give thanks to God.

20 This is the gate of God;
the righteous shall enter
through it.

21 I thank you that you have
answered me
and have become my salvation.
22 The stone that the builders rejected
has become the chief cornerstone.
23 This is God's doing;
it is marvelous in our eyes.
24 This is the day that God has made;
let us rejoice and be glad in it.ᶜ
25 Save us, we beseech you, O God!
O God, we beseech you, give us
success!

26 Blessed is the one who comes in
the name of the Most High.ᵈ
We bless you from the house of
God.
27 The Most High is God
and has given us light.
Bind the festal procession with
branches,
up to the horns of the altar.ᵉ

28 You are my God, and I will give
thanks to you;

you are my God, I will extol
you.

29 O give thanks to God, who is
good,
whose steadfast love endures
forever.

Psalm 119
The Glories of God's Law

1 Blessed are those whose way is
blameless,
who walk in the law of God.
2 Blessed are those who keep God's
decrees,
who seek God with their whole
heart,
3 who also do no wrong,
but walk in God's ways.
4 You have commanded your
precepts
to be kept diligently.
5 O that my ways may be steadfast
in keeping your statutes!
6 Then I shall not be put to shame,
having my eyes fixed on all your
commandments.
7 I will praise you with an upright
heart,
when I learn your righteous
ordinances.
8 I will observe your statutes;
do not utterly forsake me.

9 How can young people keep their
way pure?
By guarding it according to your
word.
10 With my whole heart I seek you;
do not let me stray from your
commandments.

------

c Or *in God*   d Or *Blessed in the name of
the Most High is the one who comes*
e Meaning of Heb uncertain

11 I treasure your word in my heart,
    so that I may not sin against
    you.
12 Blessed are you, O GOD;
    teach me your statutes.
13 With my lips I declare
    all the ordinances of your mouth.
14 I delight in the way of your
    decrees
    as much as in all riches.
15 I will meditate on your precepts,
    and fix my eyes on your ways.
16 I will delight in your statutes;
    I will not forget your word.

17 Deal bountifully with your servant,
    so that I may live and observe
    your word.
18 Open my eyes, so that I may
    behold
    wondrous things out of your law.
19 I live as an alien in the land;
    do not hide your commandments
    from me.
20 My soul is consumed with longing
    for your ordinances at all times.
21 You rebuke the insolent, accursed
    ones,
    who wander from your
    commandments;
22 take away from me their scorn and
    contempt,
    for I have kept your decrees.
23 Even though nobles sit plotting
    against me,
    your servant will meditate on
    your statutes.
24 Your decrees are my delight,
    they are my counselors.

25 My soul clings to the dust;
    revive me according to your
    word.
26 When I told of my ways, you
    answered me;

    teach me your statutes.
27 Make me understand the way of
    your precepts,
    and I will meditate on your
    wondrous works.
28 My soul melts away for sorrow;
    strengthen me according to your
    word.
29 Put false ways far from me;
    and graciously teach me
    your law.
30 I have chosen the way of
    faithfulness;
    I set your ordinances before me.
31 I cling to your decrees, O GOD;
    let me not be put to shame.
32 I run the way of your
    commandments,
    for you enlarge my
    understanding.

33 Teach me, O GOD, the way of
    your statutes,
    and I will observe it to the end.
34 Give me understanding, that I may
    keep your law
    and observe it with my whole
    heart.
35 Lead me in the path of your
    commandments,
    for I delight in it.
36 Turn my heart to your decrees,
    and not to selfish gain.
37 Turn my eyes from looking at
    vanities;
    give me life in your ways.
38 Confirm to your servant your
    promise,
    which is for those who hold you
    in awe.
39 Turn away the disgrace that I
    dread,
    for your ordinances are good.

40 See, I have longed for your
 precepts;
 in your righteousness give
 me life.

41 Let your steadfast love come to
 me, O God,
 your salvation according to your
 promise.
42 Then I shall have an answer for
 those who taunt me,
 for I trust in your word.
43 Do not take the word of truth
 utterly out of my mouth,
 for my hope is in your
 ordinances.
44 I will keep your law continually,
 forever and ever.
45 I shall walk at liberty,
 for I have sought your precepts.
46 I will also speak of your decrees
 before rulers,
 and shall not be put to shame;
47 I find my delight in your
 commandments,
 because I love them.
48 I revere your commandments,
 which I love,
 and I will meditate on your
 statutes.

49 Remember your word to your
 servant,
 in which you have made
 me hope.
50 This is my comfort in my distress,
 that your promise gives me life.
51 The arrogant utterly deride me,
 but I do not turn away from
 your law.
52 When I think of your ordinances
 from of old,
 I take comfort, O God.
53 Hot indignation seizes me because
 of the wicked,

those who forsake your law.
54 Your statutes have been my songs
 wherever I make my home.
55 I remember your name in the
 night, O Most High,
 and keep your law.
56 This blessing has fallen to me,
 for I have kept your precepts.

57 God is my portion;
 I promise to keep your words.
58 I implore your favor with all my
 heart;
 be gracious to me according to
 your promise.
59 When I think of your ways,
 I turn my feet to your decrees;
60 I hurry and do not delay
 to keep your commandments.
61 Though the cords of the wicked
 ensnare me,
 I do not forget your law.
62 At midnight I rise to praise you,
 because of your righteous
 ordinances.
63 I am a companion of all who
 revere you,
 of those who keep your precepts.
64 The earth, O God, is full of your
 steadfast love;
 teach me your statutes.

65 You have dealt well with your
 servant,
 O God, according to your word.
66 Teach me good judgment and
 knowledge,
 for I believe in your
 commandments.
67 Before I was humbled I went
 astray,
 but now I keep your word.
68 You are good and do good;
 teach me your statutes.
69 The arrogant smear me with lies,

but with my whole heart I keep
  your precepts.
70 Their hearts are fat and gross,
  but I delight in your law.
71 It is good for me that I was
    humbled,
  so that I might learn your
    statutes.
72 The law of your mouth is better
    to me
  than thousands of gold and silver
    pieces.

73 Your hands have made and
    fashioned me;
  give me understanding that I may
    learn your commandments.
74 Those who revere you shall see me
    and rejoice,
  because I have hoped in your
    word.
75 I know, O GOD, that your
    judgments are right,
  and that in faithfulness you have
    humbled me.
76 Let your steadfast love become my
    comfort
  according to your promise to
    your servant.
77 Let your mercy come to me, that I
    may live;
  for your law is my delight.
78 Let the arrogant be put to shame,
  because they have subverted me
    with guile;
  as for me, I will meditate on
    your precepts.
79 Let those who revere you turn to
    me,
  so that they may know your
    decrees.
80 May my heart be blameless in your
    statutes,

so that I may not be put to
  shame.

81 My soul languishes for your
    salvation;
  I hope in your word.
82 My eyes fail with watching for
    your promise;
  I ask, "When will you comfort
    me?"
83 For I have become like a wineskin
    in the smoke,
  yet I have not forgotten your
    statutes.
84 How long must your servant
    endure?
  When will you judge those who
    persecute me?
85 The arrogant have dug pitfalls
    for me;
  they flout your law.
86 All your commandments are
    enduring;
  I am persecuted without cause;
    help me!
87 They have almost made an end of
    me on earth;
  but I have not forsaken your
    precepts.
88 In your steadfast love spare my
    life,
  so that I may keep the decrees
    of your mouth.

89 GOD exists forever;
  your word is firmly fixed in
    heaven.
90 Your faithfulness endures to all
    generations;
  you have established the earth,
    and it stands fast.
91 By your appointment they stand
    today,
  for all things are your servants.

92 If your law had not been my
        delight,
     I would have perished in my
        misery.
93 I will never forget your precepts,
     for by them you have given
        me life.
94 I am yours; save me,
     for I have sought your precepts.
95 The wicked lie in wait to
        destroy me,
     but I consider your decrees.
96 I have seen a limit to all perfection,
     but your commandment is
        exceedingly broad.

97 Oh, how I love your law!
     It is my meditation all day long.
98 Your commandment makes me
        wiser than my enemies,
     for it is always with me.
99 I have more understanding than all
        my teachers,
     for your decrees are my
        meditation.
100 I understand more than the aged,
     for I keep your precepts.
101 I hold back my feet from every
        evil way,
     in order to keep your word.
102 I do not turn away from your
        ordinances,
     for you have taught me.
103 How sweet are your words to my
        taste,
     sweeter than honey to my
        mouth!
104 Through your precepts I get
        understanding;
     therefore I hate every false way.

105 Your word is a lamp to my feet
     and a light to my path.
106 I have sworn an oath and
        confirmed it,

to observe your righteous
        ordinances.
107 I am severely afflicted;
     give me life, O GOD, according
        to your word.
108 Accept my offerings of praise,
        O GOD,
     and teach me your ordinances.
109 I hold my life in my hand
        continually,
     but I do not forget your law.
110 The wicked have laid a snare
        for me,
     but I do not stray from your
        precepts.
111 Your decrees are my heritage
        forever;
     they are the joy of my heart.
112 I incline my heart to perform your
        statutes
     forever, to the end.

113 I hate the double-minded,
     but I love your law.
114 You are my hiding place and my
        shield;
     I hope in your word.
115 Go away from me, you evildoers,
     that I may keep the
        commandments of my God.
116 Uphold me according to your
        promise, that I may live,
     and let me not be put to shame
        in my hope.
117 Hold me up, that I may be safe
     and have regard for your statutes
        continually.
118 You spurn all who go astray from
        your statutes;
     for their cunning is in vain.
119 All the wicked of the earth you
        count as dross;
     therefore I love your decrees.
120 My flesh trembles in awe of you,

and I am afraid of your
  judgments.

121 I have done what is just and right;
  do not leave me to my
  oppressors.
122 Guarantee your servant's
  well-being;
  do not let the godless oppress
  me.
123 My eyes fail from watching for
  your salvation,
  and for the fulfillment of your
  righteous promise.
124 Deal with your servant according
  to your steadfast love,
  and teach me your statutes.
125 I am your servant; give me
  understanding,
  so that I may know your
  decrees.
126 It is time for GOD to act,
  for your law has been broken.
127 Truly I love your commandments
  more than gold, more than
  fine gold.
128 Truly I direct my steps by all
  your precepts;f
  I hate every false way.

129 Your decrees are wonderful;
  therefore my soul keeps them.
130 The unfolding of your words gives
  light;
  it imparts understanding to the
  simple.
131 With open mouth I pant,
  because I long for your
  commandments.
132 Turn to me and be gracious to
  me,
  as is your custom toward those
  who love your name.
133 Keep my steps steady according to
  your promise,

and never let iniquity have
  dominion over me.
134 Redeem me from human
  oppression,
  that I may keep your precepts.
135 Make your face shine upon your
  servant,
  and teach me your statutes.
136 My eyes shed streams of tears
  because your law is not kept.

137 You are righteous, O GOD,
  and your judgments are right.
138 You have appointed your decrees
  in righteousness
  and in all faithfulness.
139 My zeal consumes me
  because my foes forget your
  words.
140 Your promise is well tried,
  and your servant loves it.
141 I am small and despised,
  yet I do not forget your
  precepts.
142 Your righteousness is an everlasting
  righteousness,
  and your law is the truth.
143 Trouble and anguish have come
  upon me,
  but your commandments are my
  delight.
144 Your decrees are righteous forever;
  give me understanding that I
  may live.

145 With my whole heart I cry;
  answer me, O GOD.
  I will keep your statutes.
146 I cry to you; save me,
  that I may observe your decrees.
147 I rise before dawn and cry
  for help;
  I put my hope in your words.

---

f Gk Jerome: Meaning of Heb uncertain

148 My eyes are awake before each
  watch of the night,
  that I may meditate on your
   promise.
149 In your steadfast love hear my
  voice;
  O God, in your justice preserve
   my life.
150 Those who persecute me with evil
  purpose draw near;
  they are far from your law.
151 Yet you are near, O God,
  and all your commandments
   are true.
152 Long ago I learned from your
  decrees
  that you have established them
   forever.

153 Look on my misery and rescue
  me,
  for I do not forget your law.
154 Plead my cause and redeem me;
  give me life according to your
   promise.
155 Salvation is far from the wicked,
  for they do not seek your
   statutes.
156 Great is your mercy, O God;
  give me life according to your
   justice.
157 Many are my persecutors and my
  adversaries,
  yet I do not swerve from your
   decrees.
158 I look at the faithless with disgust,
  because they do not keep your
   commands.
159 Consider how I love your
  precepts;
  preserve my life according to
   your steadfast love.
160 The sum of your word is truth;

and every one of your righteous
  ordinances endures forever.
161 Nobles persecute me without
  cause,
  but my heart stands in awe of
   your words.
162 I rejoice at your word
  like one who finds great spoil.
163 I hate and abhor falsehood,
  but I love your law.
164 Seven times a day I praise you
  for your righteous ordinances.
165 Great peace have those who love
  your law;
  nothing can make them stumble.
166 I hope for your salvation, O God,
  and I fulfill your
   commandments.
167 My soul keeps your decrees;
  I love them exceedingly.
168 I keep your precepts and decrees,
  for all my ways are before you.
169 Let my cry come before you,
  O God;
  give me understanding according
   to your word.
170 Let my supplication come before
  you;
  deliver me according to your
   promise.
171 My lips will pour forth praise,
  because you teach me your
   statutes.
172 My tongue will sing of your
  promise,
  for all your commandments are
   right.
173 Let your hand be ready to help
  me,
  for I have chosen your precepts.
174 I long for your salvation, O God,
  and your law is my delight.
175 Let me live that I may praise you,

and let your ordinances help me.
176 I have gone astray like a lost
      sheep; seek out your servant,
   for I do not forget your
      commandments.

Psalm 120

Prayer for Deliverance from Slanderers

A Song of Ascents.

1 In my distress I cry to GOD,
   that God may answer me:
2 "Deliver me, O GOD,
   from lying lips,
   from a deceitful tongue."

3 What shall be given to you?
   And what more shall be done
      to you,
   you deceitful tongue?
4 A warrior's sharp arrows,
   with glowing coals of the broom
      tree!

5 Woe is me, that I am an alien in
      Meshech,
   that I must live among the tents
      of Kedar.
6 Too long have I had my dwelling
   among those who hate peace.
7 I am for peace;
   but when I speak,
   they are for war.

Psalm 121

Assurance of God's Protection

A Song of Ascents.

1 I lift up my eyes to the hills—
   from where will my help come?
2 My help comes from GOD,
   who made heaven and earth.

3 God will not let your foot be
      moved;

the one who keeps you will not
   slumber.
4 The one who keeps Israel
   will neither slumber nor sleep.

5 GOD is your keeper;
   GOD is your shade at your side.
6 The sun shall not strike you
      by day,
   nor the moon by night.

7 GOD will keep you from all evil,
   and will keep your life.
8 GOD will keep
   your going out and your
      coming in
   from this time on and
      forevermore.

Psalm 122

Song of Praise and Prayer for Jerusalem

A Song of Ascents. Of David.

1 I was glad when they said to me,
   "Let us go to the house of
      GOD!"
2 Our feet are standing
   within your gates, O Jerusalem.

3 Jerusalem—built as a city
   that is bound firmly together.
4 To it the tribes go up,
   the tribes of GOD,
   as was decreed for Israel,
   to give thanks to the name of
      the Most High.
5 For there the thrones for judgment
      were set up,
   the thrones of the house of
      David.

6 Pray for the peace of Jerusalem:
   "May they prosper who love
      you.
7 Peace be within your walls,

and security within your towers."

8 For the sake of my relatives and
    friends
    I will say, "Peace be within
      you."
9 For the sake of the house of the
    Most High our God,
    I will seek your good.

Psalm 123

Supplication for Mercy

A Song of Ascents.

1 To you I lift up my eyes,
    O you who are enthroned in the
      heavens!
2 As the eyes of manservants
    look to the hand of the man for
      whom they work,
  as the eyes of womanservants
    to the hand of the woman for
      whom they work,
  so our eyes look to the Most High
    our God,
    until God has mercy upon us.

3 Have mercy upon us, O GOD, have
    mercy upon us,
    for we have had more than
      enough of contempt.
4 Our soul has had more than its fill
    of the scorn of those who are
      at ease,
    of the contempt of the proud.

Psalm 124

Thanksgiving for Israel's
Deliverance

A Song of Ascents. Of David.

1 If it had not been GOD who was
    on our side
    —let Israel now say—
2 if it had not been GOD who was
    on our side,

when our enemies attacked us,
3 then they would have swallowed us
    up alive,
    when their anger was kindled
      against us;
4 then the flood would have swept
    us away,
    the torrent would have gone
      over us;
5 then over us would have gone
    the raging waters.

6 Blessed be GOD,
    who has not given us
    as prey to their teeth.
7 We have escaped like a bird
    from the snare of the fowlers;
  the snare is broken,
    and we have escaped.

8 Our help is in the name of
    the Most High,
    who made heaven and earth.

Psalm 125

The Security of God's People

A Song of Ascents.

1 Those who trust in GOD are like
    Mount Zion,
    which cannot be moved, but
      abides forever.
2 As the mountains surround
    Jerusalem,
    so GOD surrounds God's people,
    from this time on and
      forevermore.
3 For the scepter of wickedness shall
    not rest
    on the land allotted to the
      righteous,
  so that the righteous might not
    stretch out
    their hands to do wrong.

4 Do good, O GOD, to those who
    are good,
    and to those who are upright in
        their hearts.
5 But those who turn aside to their
    own crooked ways
    GOD will lead away with
        evildoers.
    Peace be upon Israel!

Psalm 126
A Harvest of Joy

A Song of Ascents.

1 When GOD restored the fortunes of
    Zion,[g]
    we were like those who dream.
2 Then our mouth was filled with
        laughter,
    and our tongue with shouts
        of joy;
    then it was said among the nations,
    "GOD has done great things for
        them."
3 GOD has done great things for us,
    and we rejoiced.

4 Restore our fortunes, O GOD,
    like the watercourses in the
        Negeb.
5 May those who sow in tears
    reap with shouts of joy.
6 Those who go out weeping,
    bearing the seed for sowing,
    shall come home with shouts of
        joy,
    carrying their sheaves.

Psalm 127
God's Blessings in the Home

A Song of Ascents. Of Solomon.

1 Unless GOD builds the house,
    those who build it labor in vain.
    Unless GOD guards the city,

the guard keeps watch in vain.
2 It is in vain that you rise up early
    and go late to rest,
    eating the bread of anxious toil;
    for God gives sleep to God's
        beloved.[h]

3 Children are indeed a heritage from
        GOD,
    the fruit of the womb a reward.
4 Like arrows in the hand of a
        warrior
    are the children of one's youth.
5 Blessed is the one whose quiver is
    full of them,
    who shall not be put to shame
    when speaking with enemies in
        the gate.

Psalm 128
The Happy Home of the Faithful

A Song of Ascents.

1 Blessed is everyone who reveres
        GOD,
    who walks in God's ways.
2 You shall eat the fruit of the labor
    of your hands;
    you shall be happy, and it shall
    go well with you.

3 Your beloved will be like a fruitful
        vine
    within your house;
    your children will be like olive
        shoots
    around your table.
4 Thus shall the one be blessed
    who reveres GOD.

5 GOD bless you from Zion.

---

g Or *brought back those who returned to
Zion*   h Or *for God provides for God's
beloved during sleep*

May you see the prosperity of
　　Jerusalem
all the days of your life.
6 May you see your children's
　　children.
　　Peace be upon Israel!

Psalm 129

Prayer for the Downfall of
Israel's Enemies

A Song of Ascents.

1 "Often have they attacked me from
　　my youth"
　　—let Israel now say—
2 "often have they attacked me from
　　my youth,
　　yet they have not prevailed
　　　against me.
3 The plowers plowed on my
　　back;
　　they made their furrows
　　　long."
4 GOD is righteous
　　and has cut the cords of the
　　　wicked.
5 May all who hate Zion
　　be put to shame and turned
　　　backward.
6 Let them be like the grass on the
　　housetops
　　that withers before it grows
　　　up,
7 with which reapers do not fill their
　　hands
　　or binders of sheaves their
　　　arms,
8 while those who pass by do not
　　say,
　　"The blessing of GOD be upon
　　　you!
　　We bless you in the name of the
　　　Most High!"

Psalm 130

Waiting for Divine Redemption

A Song of Ascents.

1 Out of the depths I cry to you,
　　O GOD.
2　　God, hear my voice!
　　Let your ears be attentive
　　to the voice of my supplications!

3 If you, O GOD, should mark
　　iniquities,
　　who could stand?
4 But there is forgiveness with you,
　　so that you may be revered.

5 I wait for GOD, my soul waits,
　　and in God's word I hope;
6 my soul waits for God
　　more than those who watch for
　　　the morning,
　　more than those who watch for
　　　the morning.

7 O Israel, hope in GOD!
　　For with GOD there is steadfast
　　　love,
　　and with God is great power to
　　　redeem.
8 And God will redeem Israel
　　from all its iniquities.

Psalm 131

Song of Quiet Trust

A Song of Ascents. Of David.

1 O GOD, my heart is not lifted up,
　　my eyes are not raised too high;
　　I do not occupy myself with things
　　too great and too marvelous
　　　for me.
2 But I have calmed and quieted
　　my soul,
　　like a weaned child with its
　　mother;

my soul is like the weaned child
that is with me.[i]

3 O Israel, hope in GOD
from this time on and
forevermore.

Psalm 132

The Eternal Dwelling of God in Zion

A Song of Ascents.

1 O GOD, remember in David's favor
all the hardships he endured;
2 how David swore to GOD
and vowed to the Mighty One of
Jacob,
3 "I will not enter my house
or get into my bed;
4 I will not give sleep to my eyes
or slumber to my eyelids,
5 until I find a place for GOD,
a dwelling place for the Mighty
One of Jacob."

6 We heard of it in Ephrathah;
we found it in the fields of Jaar.
7 "Let us go to God's dwelling place;
let us worship at God's
footstool."

8 Rise up, O GOD, and go to your
resting place,
you and the ark of your might.
9 Let your priests be clothed with
righteousness,
and let your faithful shout
for joy.
10 For your servant David's sake
do not turn away the face of
your anointed one.

11 GOD swore to David a sure oath
and will not turn back on it:
"One of the offspring of your
body

I will set on your throne.
12 If your offspring keep my covenant
and my decrees that I shall teach
them,
their offspring also, forevermore,
shall sit on your throne."

13 For GOD has chosen Zion;
God has desired it for a
habitation:
14 "This is my resting place forever;
here I will reside, for I have
desired it.
15 I will abundantly bless its
provisions;
I will satisfy its poor with bread.
16 Its priests I will clothe with
salvation,
and its faithful will shout for joy.
17 There I will cause a horn to sprout
up for David;
I have prepared a lamp for my
anointed one.
18 The enemies of David I will clothe
with disgrace,
but on David, a crown will
gleam."

Psalm 133

The Blessedness of Unity

A Song of Ascents.

1 How very good and pleasant it is
when kindred live together in
unity!
2 It is like the precious oil on the
head,
running down upon the beard,
on the beard of Aaron,
running down over the collar of
his robes.
3 It is like the dew of Hermon,

---

i Or *my soul within me is like a weaned
child*

523

which falls on the mountains of
　　Zion.
For there GOD ordained a blessing,
　　life forevermore.

Psalm 134

Praise in the Night

A Song of Ascents.

1 Come, bless GOD, all you servants
　　of GOD,
　　who stand by night in the house
　　　of GOD!
2 Lift up your hands to the holy
　　place,
　　and bless GOD.

3 May GOD, maker of heaven and
　　earth,
　　bless you from Zion.

Psalm 135

Praise for God's Goodness and Might

1 Hallelujah!
　　Praise the name of the Most
　　　High;
　　give praise, O servants of GOD,
2 you that stand in the house of
　　　GOD,
　　in the courts of the house of
　　　our God.
3 Praise GOD, for GOD is good;
　　sing to God's name, for God is
　　　gracious.
4 For GOD has chosen Jacob as
　　God's own,
　　Israel as God's own possession.

5 For I know that GOD is great;
　　our God is above all gods.
6 Whatever GOD pleases God does,
　　in heaven and on earth,
　　in the seas and all deeps.

7 God it is who makes the clouds
　　rise at the end of the earth;
　　God makes lightnings for the
　　　rain
　　and brings out the wind from
　　　the storehouses.

8 God it was who struck down the
　　firstborn of Egypt,
　　both human beings and animals;
9 God sent signs and wonders
　　into your midst, O Egypt,
　　against Pharaoh and all his
　　　servants.
10 God struck down many nations
　　and killed mighty kings—
11 Sihon, king of the Amorites,
　　and Og, king of Bashan,
　　and all the kingdoms of
　　　Canaan—
12 and gave their land as a heritage,
　　a heritage to God's people Israel.

13 Your name, O GOD, endures
　　forever,
　　your renown, O GOD, throughout
　　　all ages.
14 For GOD will vindicate the people,
　　and have compassion on the
　　　servants.

15 The idols of the nations are silver
　　and gold,
　　the work of human hands.
16 They have mouths, but they do not
　　speak;
　　they have eyes, but they do
　　　not see;
17 they have ears, but they do not
　　hear,
　　and there is no breath in their
　　　mouths.
18 Those who make them
　　and all who trust them
　　shall become like them.

19 O house of Israel, bless GOD!
   O house of Aaron, bless GOD!
20 O house of Levi, bless GOD!
   You that revere GOD, bless
   GOD!
21 Blessed be GOD from Zion,
   the one who resides in Jerusalem.
Hallelujah!

Psalm 136

God's Work in Creation and in History

1 O give thanks to GOD, for God is
   good,
   for God's steadfast love endures
   forever.
2 O give thanks to the God of gods,
   whose steadfast love endures
   forever.
3 O give thanks to the Sovereign of
   sovereigns,
   whose steadfast love endures
   forever;

4 who alone does great wonders,
   for God's steadfast love endures
   forever;
5 who by understanding made the
   heavens,
   for God's steadfast love endures
   forever;
6 who spread out the earth on the
   waters,
   for God's steadfast love endures
   forever;
7 who made the great lights,
   for God's steadfast love endures
   forever;
8 the sun to rule over the day,
   for God's steadfast love endures
   forever;
9 the moon and stars to rule over
   the night,

for God's steadfast love endures
   forever;
10 who struck Egypt through their
   firstborn,
   for God's steadfast love endures
   forever;
11 and brought Israel out from among
   them,
   for God's steadfast love endures
   forever;
12 with a strong hand and an
   outstretched arm,
   for God's steadfast love endures
   forever;
13 who divided the Sea of Reeds in
   two,
   for God's steadfast love endures
   forever;
14 and made Israel pass through the
   midst of it,
   for God's steadfast love endures
   forever;
15 but overthrew Pharaoh and his
   army in the Sea of Reeds,
   for God's steadfast love endures
   forever;
16 who led the people through the
   wilderness,
   for God's steadfast love endures
   forever;
17 who struck down great kings,
   for God's steadfast love endures
   forever;
18 and killed famous kings,
   for God's steadfast love endures
   forever;
19 Sihon, king of the Amorites,
   for God's steadfast love endures
   forever;
20 and Og, king of Bashan,
   for God's steadfast love endures
   forever;
21 and gave their land as a heritage,

for God's steadfast love endures
    forever;
22 a heritage to God's servant Israel,
    for God's steadfast love endures
    forever.

23 It is God who remembered us in
    our low estate,
    for God's steadfast love endures
    forever;
24 and rescued us from our foes,
    for God's steadfast love endures
    forever;
25 who gives food to all flesh,
    for God's steadfast love endures
    forever.

26 O give thanks to the God of heaven,
    for God's steadfast love endures
    forever.

Psalm 137

Lament over the Destruction of Jerusalem

1 By the rivers of Babylon—
    there we sat down and there
    we wept
    when we remembered Zion.
2 On the willows[j] there
    we hung up our harps.
3 For there our captors
    asked us for songs,
    and our tormentors asked for
    mirth, saying,
    "Sing us one of the songs of
    Zion!"

4 How could we sing GOD's song
    in a foreign land?
5 If I forget you, O Jerusalem,
    let my mighty hand wither!
6 Let my tongue cling to the roof of
    my mouth,
    if I do not remember you,

if I do not set Jerusalem
    above my highest joy.

7 Remember, O GOD, against the
    Edomites
    the day of Jerusalem's fall,
    how they said, "Tear it down! Tear
    it down!
    Down to its foundations!"
8 O people of Babylon, you
    devastators![k]
    Blessed shall they be who pay
    you back
    what you have done to us!
9 Blessed shall they be who take
    your little ones
    and dash them against the rock!

Psalm 138

Thanksgiving and Praise

Of David.

1 I give you thanks, O GOD, with
    my whole heart;
    before the gods I sing your
    praise;
2 I bow down toward your holy
    temple
    and give thanks to your name
    for your steadfast love and
    your faithfulness;
    for you have exalted your name
    and your word
    above everything.[l]
3 On the day I called, you answered
    me,
    you increased my strength of
    soul.[m]

---

j Or *poplars*　　k Or *you who are devastated*
l Cn: Heb *you have exalted your word above
all your name*　　m Syr Compare Gk Tg:
Heb *you made me arrogant in my soul with
strength*

4 All the rulers of the earth shall
     praise you, O GOD,
  for they have heard the words of
     your mouth.
5 They shall sing of the ways of
     GOD,
  for great is the glory of GOD.
6 For though GOD is high, God
     regards the lowly;
  but the haughty God perceives
     from far away.

7 Though I walk in the midst of
     trouble,
  you preserve me against the
     wrath of my enemies;
  you stretch out your hand,
     and your mighty hand delivers
     me.
8 GOD will fulfill God's purpose
     for me;
  your steadfast love, O GOD,
     endures forever.
  Do not forsake the work of your
     hands.

Psalm 139

The Inescapable God

To the leader. Of David. A Psalm.

1 O GOD, you have searched me and
     known me.
2 You know when I sit down and
     when I rise up;
  you discern my thoughts from
     far away.
3 You search out my path and my
     lying down,
  and are acquainted with all
     my ways.
4 Even before a word is on my
     tongue,
  O GOD, you know it completely.
5 You hem me in, behind and before,

and lay your hand upon me.
6 Such knowledge is too wonderful
     for me;
  it is so high that I cannot
     attain it.

7 Where can I go from your spirit?
  Or where can I flee from your
     presence?
8 If I ascend to heaven, you are
     there;
  if I make my bed in Sheol, you
     are there.
9 If I take the wings of the morning
  and settle at the farthest limits of
     the sea,
10 even there your hand shall lead me,
  and your strong hand shall hold
     me fast.
11 If I say, "Surely the night shall
     cover me,
  and the light around me become
     night,"
12 even the night is not without light
     to you;
  the night is as bright as the day,
     for night is as light to you.

13 For it was you who formed my
     inward parts;
  you knit me together in my
     mother's womb.
14 I praise you, for I am fearfully and
     wonderfully made.
  Wonderful are your works;
  that I know very well.
15   My frame was not hidden from
     you,
  when I was being made in secret,
     intricately woven in the depths of
     the earth.
16 Your eyes beheld my unformed
     substance.
  In your book were written

all the days that were formed
    for me,
when none of them as yet
    existed.
17 How weighty to me are your
    thoughts, O God!
    How vast is the sum of them!
18 I try to count them—they are
    more than the sand;
    I come to the end[n]—I am still
    with you.

19 O that you would kill the wicked,
    O God,
    and that the bloodthirsty would
    depart from me—
20 those who speak of you
    maliciously,
    and lift themselves up against
    you for evil![o]
21 Do I not hate those who hate you,
    O GOD?
    And do I not loathe those who
    rise up against you?
22 I hate them with perfect hatred;
    I count them my enemies.
23 Search me, O God, and know my
    heart;
    test me and know my thoughts.
24 See if there is any wicked[p] way
    in me,
    and lead me in the way
    everlasting.[q]

Psalm 140

Prayer for Deliverance from Enemies

To the leader. A Psalm of David.

1 Deliver me, O GOD, from evildoers;
    protect me from those who are
    violent,
2 who plan evil things in their minds

and stir up wars continually.
3 They make their tongue sharp as a
    snake's,
    and under their lips is the venom
    of vipers.   *Selah*

4 Guard me, O GOD, from the hands
    of the wicked;
    protect me from the violent
    who have planned my downfall.
5 The arrogant have hidden a trap
    for me,
    and with cords they have spread
    a net,[r]
    along the road they have set
    snares for me.   *Selah*

6 I say to GOD, "You are my God;
    give ear, O GOD, to the voice
    of my supplications."
7 O GOD, my God, my strong
    deliverer,
    you have covered my head in
    the day of battle.
8 Do not grant, O GOD, the desires
    of the wicked;
    do not further their evil plot.[s]
          Selah

9 Those who surround me lift up
    their heads;[t]
    let the mischief of their lips
    overwhelm them!
10 Let burning coals fall on them!
    Let them be flung into pits, no
    more to rise!

---

n Or *I awake*   o Cn: Meaning of Heb
uncertain   p Heb *hurtful*   q Or *the
ancient way.* Compare Jer 6.16   r Or *they
have spread cords as a net*   s Heb adds
they are exalted   t Cn Compare Gk: Heb
those who surround me are uplifted in head;
Heb divides verses 8 and 9 differently

11 Do not let the slanderer be
       established in the land;
   let evil speedily hunt down the
       violent!

12 I know that the LORD maintains the
       cause of the needy,
   and executes justice for the poor.
13 Surely the righteous shall give
       thanks to your name;
   the upright shall live in your
       presence.

Psalm 141

Prayer for Preservation from Evil

A Psalm of David.

1 I call upon you, O GOD; come
       quickly to me;
   give ear to my voice when I call
       to you.
2 Let my prayer be counted as
       incense before you,
   and the lifting up of my hands
       as an evening sacrifice.

3 Set a guard over my mouth,
       O GOD;
   keep watch over the door of
       my lips.
4 Do not turn my heart to any evil,
   to busy myself with wicked
       deeds
   in company with those who work
       iniquity;
   do not let me eat of their
       delicacies.

5 Let the righteous strike me;
       let the faithful correct me.
   Never let the oil of the wicked
       anoint my head,[u]

for my prayer is continually[v]
       against their wicked deeds.
6 When they are given over to those
       who shall condemn them,
   then they shall learn that my
       words were pleasant.
7 Like a rock that one breaks apart
       and shatters on the land,
   so shall their bones be strewn at
       the mouth of Sheol.[w]

8 But my eyes are turned toward
       you, O GOD, my God;
   in you I seek refuge; do not
       leave me defenseless.
9 Keep me from the trap that they
       have laid for me,
   and from the snares of evildoers.
10 Let the wicked fall into their
       own nets,
   while I alone escape.

Psalm 142

Prayer for Deliverance from Persecutors

A Maskil of David. When he was in the cave. A Prayer.

1 With my voice I cry to GOD;
   with my voice I make
       supplication to GOD.
2 I pour out my complaint before
       God;
   I tell my trouble before God.
3 When my spirit is faint,
   you know my way.

   In the path where I walk
       they have hidden a trap for me.
4 Look around me and see—

---

u Gk: Meaning of Heb uncertain
v Cn: Heb *for continually and my prayer*
w Meaning of Heb of verses 5-7 is uncertain

there is no one who takes notice
    of me;
no refuge remains to me;
    no one cares for me.

5 I cry to you, O GOD;
    I say, "You are my refuge,
    my portion in the land of the
       living."
6 Give heed to my cry,
    for I am brought very low.

Save me from my persecutors,
    for they are too strong for me.
7 Bring me out of prison,
    so that I may give thanks to
       your name.
The righteous will surround me,
    for you will deal bountifully
       with me.

Psalm 143

Prayer for Deliverance from Enemies

A Psalm of David.

1 Hear my prayer, O GOD;
    give ear to my supplications in
       your faithfulness;
    answer me in your righteousness.
2 Do not enter into judgment with
       your servant,
    for no one living is righteous
       before you.

3 For the enemy has pursued me,
    crushing my life to the ground,
    making me sit in deep shadows
       like those long dead.
4 Therefore my spirit faints
       within me;
    my heart within me is appalled.

5 I remember the days of old,
    I think about all your deeds,

I meditate on the works of your
    hands.
6 I stretch out my hands to you;
    my soul thirsts for you like a
       parched land.   *Selah*

7 Answer me quickly, O GOD;
    my spirit fails.
Do not hide your face from me,
    or I shall be like those who go
       down to the Pit.
8 Let me hear of your steadfast love
       in the morning,
    for in you I put my trust.
Teach me the way I should go,
    for to you I lift up my soul.

9 Save me, O GOD, from my
       enemies;
    I have fled to you for refuge.ˣ
10 Teach me to do your will,
    for you are my God.
Let your good spirit lead me
    on a level path.

11 For your name's sake, O GOD,
    preserve my life.
In your righteousness bring me
    out of trouble.
12 In your steadfast love cut off my
       enemies,
    and destroy all my adversaries,
    for I am your servant.

Psalm 144

Prayer for National Deliverance and Security

Of David.

1 Blessed be GOD, my rock,
    who trains my hands for war,
    and my fingers for battle;

---

x One Heb Ms Gk: MT *to you I have
hidden*

2 my rock[y] and my fortress,
   my stronghold and my deliverer,
 my shield, in whom I take refuge,
   who subdues the peoples[z]
   under me.

3 O GOD, what are human beings
   that you regard them,
   or mortals that you think of
   them?
4 They are like a breath;
   their days are like a passing
   shadow.

5 Bow your heavens, O GOD, and
   come down;
   touch the mountains so that they
   smoke.
6 Make the lightning flash and scatter
   them;
   send out your arrows and rout
   them.
7 Stretch out your hand from on
   high;
   set me free and rescue me from
   the mighty waters,
   from the hand of aliens,
8 whose mouths speak lies,
   and whose hands are false.

9 I will sing a new song to you,
   O God;
   upon a ten-stringed harp I will
   play to you,
10 the one who gives victory to rulers,
   who rescues David, God's
   servant.
11 Rescue me from the cruel sword,
   and deliver me from the hand of
   aliens,
   whose mouths speak lies,
   and whose hands are false.

12 May our sons in their youth
   be like plants full grown,

our daughters like corner pillars,
   cut for the building of a palace.
13 May our barns be filled,
   with produce of every kind;
 may our sheep increase by
   thousands,
   by tens of thousands in our fields,
14   and may our cattle be heavy
   with young.
 May there be no breach in the
   walls,[a] no exile,
   and no cry of distress in our
   streets.

15 Blessed are the people to whom
   such blessings fall;
   blessed are the people whose
   God is the Most High.

Psalm 145

The Greatness and the Goodness of God

Praise. Of David.

1 I will extol you, my God and
   Sovereign,
   and bless your name forever
   and ever.
2 Every day I will bless you,
   and praise your name forever
   and ever.
3 Great is GOD, and greatly to be
   praised;
   the greatness of God is
   unsearchable.

4 One generation shall laud your
   works to another,
   and shall declare your mighty
   acts.

---

y With 18.2 and 2 Sam 22.2: Heb *my steadfast
love*   z Heb Mss Syr Aquila Jerome: MT *my
people*   a Heb lacks *in the walls*

5 On the glorious splendor of your
majesty,
and on your wondrous works, I
will meditate.
6 The might of your awesome deeds
shall be proclaimed,
and I will declare your greatness.
7 They shall celebrate the fame of
your abundant goodness,
and shall sing aloud of your
righteousness.

8 GOD is gracious and merciful,
slow to anger and abounding in
steadfast love.
9 GOD is good to all
and has compassion over all that
God has made.

10 All your works shall give thanks to
you, O GOD,
and all your faithful shall
bless you.
11 They shall speak of the glory of
your dominion,
and tell of your power,
12 to make known to all people your[b]
mighty deeds,
and the glorious splendor of
your[c] dominion.
13 Your realm is everlasting,
and your dominion endures
throughout all generations.

GOD is faithful in every word,
and gracious in every deed.[d]
14 GOD upholds all who are falling,
and raises up all who are bowed
down.
15 The eyes of all look to you,
and you give them their food in
due season.
16 You open your hand,

satisfying the desire of every
living thing.
17 GOD is just in every way,
and kind in every deed.
18 GOD is near to all who call,
to all who call on God in truth.
19 God fulfills the desire of all who
are in awe of God;
God also hears their cry, and
saves them.
20 GOD watches over all who
love God,
but will destroy all the wicked.

21 My mouth will speak the praise of
GOD,
and all flesh will bless God's
holy name forever and ever.

Psalm 146

Praise for God's Help

1 Hallelujah!
Praise GOD, O my soul!
2 I will praise GOD as long as I live;
I will sing praises to my God all
my life long.

3 Do not put your trust in royalty,
in mortals, in whom there is no
help.
4 When their breath departs, they
return to the earth;
on that very day their plans
perish.

5 Blessed are those whose help is the
God of Jacob,
whose hope is in the Most High
their God,
6 who made heaven and earth,

---

b Gk Jerome Syr: Heb *God's*   c Heb *God's*
d These two lines supplied by Q Ms Gk Syr

the sea, and all that is in them;
who keeps faith forever;
7   who executes justice for the
    oppressed;
who gives food to the hungry;
who sets the prisoners free.

8   GOD opens the eyes of the those
    who cannot see,
lifts up those who are bowed
  down,
and loves the righteous.
9 GOD watches over the stranger
and upholds the orphan and the
  widow,
but brings the way of the wicked
  to ruin.

10 GOD will reign forever,
  your God, O Zion, for all
    generations.
Hallelujah!

Psalm 147

Praise for God's Care for Jerusalem

1 Hallelujah!
How good it is to sing praises to
  our God,
  who is gracious; and a song of
    praise is fitting.
2 GOD builds up Jerusalem
  and gathers the outcasts of Israel.
3 God heals the brokenhearted,
  and binds up their wounds.
4 God determines the number of
  the stars,
  and gives to all of them their
    names.
5 Great is our God, and abundant
  in power,
  with understanding beyond
    measure.

6 The LORD lifts up the
  downtrodden,
  and casts the wicked to the
    ground.

7 Sing to GOD with thanksgiving;
  make melody to our God on
    the lyre.
8 God covers the heavens with
  clouds,
  prepares rain for the earth,
  makes grass grow on the hills.
9 God gives to the animals their
  food,
  and to the young ravens when
    they cry.
10 God takes no delight in the
  strength of the horse,
  nor pleasure in the speed of
    a runner,[e]
11 but GOD takes pleasure in those
  who are in awe of God,
  and in those who hope in God's
    steadfast love.

12 Praise GOD, O Jerusalem!
  Praise your God, O Zion!
13 For God strengthens the bars of
  your gates
  and blesses your children within
    you.
14 God grants peace[f] within your
  borders
  and fills you with the finest of
    wheat.
15 God sends out a command to the
  earth;
  God's word runs swiftly.
16 God gives snow like wool
  and scatters frost like ashes.
17 God hurls down hail like crumbs—
  who can stand before such cold?

_____

e Heb *legs of a person*   f Or *prosperity*

18 God sends out a word, and melts
  them,
  making the wind blow, and the
   waters flow.
19 God declares a word to Jacob,
  statutes and ordinances to Israel.
20 God has not dealt thus with any
   other nation;
  they do not know God's
   ordinances.
  Hallelujah!

Psalm 148

Praise for God's Universal Glory

1 Hallelujah!
 Praise GOD from the heavens;
  praise God in the heights!
2 Praise God, all you angels;
  praise God, all you multitudes in
   heaven!

3 Praise God, sun and moon;
  praise God, all you shining stars!
4 Praise God, you highest heavens,
  and you waters above the
   heavens!

5 Let them praise the name of
  the Most High,
  for God commanded and they
   were created.
6 God established them forever
  and ever;
  God fixed their bounds, which
   cannot be passed.g

7 Praise GOD from the earth,
  you sea monsters and all deeps,
8 fire and hail, snow and frost,
  stormy wind fulfilling God's
   command!

9 Mountains and all hills,
  fruit trees and all cedars!
10 Wild animals and all cattle,
  creeping things and flying birds!

11 Sovereigns of the earth and all
   peoples,
  royalty and all rulers of the
   earth!
12 Young men and women alike,
  old and young together!

13 Let them praise the name of GOD,
  for God's name alone is exalted;
  God's glory is above earth and
   heaven.
14 God has raised up a horn for
  God's people,
  praise for all the faithful,
  for the people of Israel who are
   close to God.
  Hallelujah!

Psalm 149

Praise for God's Goodness to
Israel

1 Hallelujah!
 Sing to GOD a new song,
  God's praise in the assembly of
   the faithful.
2 Let Israel be glad in its Maker;
  let the children of Zion rejoice in
   their Sovereign.
3 Let them praise God's name with
   dancing,
  making melody to God with
   tambourine and lyre.
4 For GOD takes pleasure in
  the people
  and adorns the humble with
   victory.

---

g Or *God set a law that cannot pass away*

5 Let the faithful exult in glory;
    let them sing for joy on their
    couches.
6 Let the high praises of God be in
    their throats
    and two-edged swords in their
    hands,
7 to execute vengeance on the nations
    and punishment on the peoples,
8 to bind their rulers with fetters
    and their nobles with chains
    of iron,
9 to execute on them the judgment
    decreed.
    This is glory for all God's
    faithful ones.
Hallelujah!

Psalm 150

Praise for God's Surpassing
Greatness

1 Hallelujah!
    Praise God in the sanctuary;
    praise God in the mighty
    firmament![h]
2 Praise God for God's mighty
    deeds;
    praise God according to God's
    surpassing greatness!
3 Praise God with trumpet sound;
    praise God with lute and
    harp!
4 Praise God with tambourine and
    dance;
    praise God with strings and
    pipe!
5 Praise God with clanging cymbals;
    praise God with loud clashing
    cymbals!
6 Let everything that breathes praise
    GOD!
Hallelujah!

---

h Or *dome*